WOMEN and GENDER
in the AMERICAN WEST

WOMEN and
GENDER
in the
AMERICAN WEST

Jensen–Miller Prize Essays from the
Coalition for Western Women's History

edited by
Mary Ann Irwin | James F. Brooks

University of New Mexico Press
Albuquerque

© 2004 by the University of New Mexico Press

All rights reserved. Published 2004

Library of Congress Cataloging-in-Publication Data

Women and gender in the West / [edited by] Mary Ann Irwin and James F. Brooks.— 1st ed.

p. cm.

ISBN 0-8263-3599-3 (pbk. : alk. paper)

1. Women—West (U.S.)—History. 2. Women—Canada, Western—History.

3. Indian women—West (U.S.)—History. 4. Indian women—Canada, Western—History.

5. Marriage—West (U.S.)—History. 6. Marriage—Canada, Western—History.

I. Irwin, Mary Ann, 1955– II. Brooks, James, 1955–

HQ1438.W45W66 2004

305.4'0978—dc22

2004010400

09   08   07   06   05   04   1   2   3   4   5

Printed and bound in the USA by Thomson Shore, Inc.

Typeset in Bembo family 11/14

Display type set in Mona Lisa Solid and Mona Lisa Recut

Design and composition: Robyn Mundy

Foreword

The essays presented here appear through the generosity of their authors and the journals in which they originally appeared. Each of the journals granted permission to reprint without fees, as did the authors. We thank them for their financial as well as their intellectual contributions to the growing field of western women's history. All proceeds from sale of this volume go to the Coalition for Western Women's History and will be used for future awards of the Jensen-Miller Best Article Prize and the Irene Ledesma Prize for graduate study.

—Mary Ann Irwin and James F. Brooks

Contents

Contents

About the Authors

Joan M. Jensen is retired from teaching now and is completing a book, *Calling This Place Home: Women on the Wisconsin Frontier, 1850–1925*. Her previous titles include *Loosening the Bonds* (1988) and *One Foot on the Rockies: Women and Creativity in the Modern American West* (1995). When not writing, she is usually making things out of fiber, bird watching, or flying kites.

Darlis A. Miller is Professor Emerita of History at New Mexico State University. She is the author of *Mary Hallock Foote: Author-Illustrator of the American West* (2002), and is currently working on a biography of Matilda Coxe Stevenson, the first woman anthropologist to work in the Southwest.

Carol Cornwall Madsen is an Associate Professor of History and Senior Research Historian in the Joseph Fielding Smith Institute for Church History at Brigham Young University. Among other works, she is the author of *A Bluestocking in Zion: The Literary Life of Emmeline B. Wells* (1983) and *Journey to Zion: Voices from the Mormon Trail* (1997), and the editor of *Battle for the Ballot: Essays on Woman Suffrage in Utah, 1870–1896* (1997).

Peggy Pascoe holds the Beekman Chair of Northwest and Pacific History at the University of Oregon, where she teaches courses on the history of race, gender, and sexuality and on the history of the U.S. West. A former co-president of the Coordinating Council for Women in History, she is the author of *Relations of Rescue: The Search for Female Moral Authority in the American West, 1874–1939* (1990), and is currently completing a book on the history of miscegenation law in the United States.

Antonia I. Castañeda is Associate Professor and O'Conner Chair in Borderlands History at St. Mary's University in San Antonio, Texas. In 2001, she secured National Endowment for the Humanities funding for study of "Gender and the Borderlands" at St. Mary's. Her numerous publications include "Gender, Race, and Culture: Spanish Mexican Women in the Historiography of Frontier California," "Engendering the History of Alta California, 1760–1848: Gender, Sexuality, and the Family," and "Language and Other Lethal Weapons: Cultural Politics and the Rites of Children as Translators of Culture."

Susan Lee Johnson is an Associate Professor of History and Chicana/o Studies at the University of Wisconsin-Madison. Johnson is the author of *Roaring Camp: The Social World of the California Gold Rush* (2000), the grandparent of five young westerners, and a summer resident of Santa Fe, New Mexico.

Amy Kaminsky is Professor of Women's Studies and Global Studies at the University of Minnesota. Her most recent book is *After Exile: Writing the Latin American Diaspora* (1999). With the help of an American Council of Learned Societies grant, she is currently working on a book-length project whose working title is "Argentina: International Imagination and National Identity."

Irene Ledesma was an Assistant Professor of History at the University of Texas-Pan American. She won the Jensen-Miller Prize in 1995; her death two years later deprived us of an important voice in Chicana history. In her honor, the Coalition for Western Women's History awards an annual Irene Ledesma Prize, which provides funding for graduate student research in western women's history.

James F. Brooks is a member of the research faculty and Director of SAR Press at the School of American Research in Santa Fe, New Mexico. His recent book, *Captives & Cousins: Slavery, Kinship, and Community in the Southwest Borderlands* (2002) garnered seven major prizes in 2003, including the Bancroft Prize, the Frederick Jackson Turner Award, the Francis Parkman Prize, the W. Turrentine Jackson Award, the Erminie Wheeler-Voegelin Prize, and it shared the Frederick Douglass Prize from Yale University's Gilder Lehrman Center for Studies in Slavery, Resistance, and Abolition.

Catherine A. Cavanaugh teaches history and women's studies at Athabasca University. Her recent work includes an exploration of the "Persons" case and the ways in which women remember this landmark decision in Canadian constitutional law. She is currently working on a biography of Irene Parlby, Member of the United Farmers Government of Alberta and the second woman minister in the British empire.

Jean Barman teaches in the Department of Educational Studies at the University of British Columbia and writes about Pacific Northwest history. Her most recent book, *Sojourning Sisters: The Lives and Letters of Jessie and Annie McQueen* (2003), won the Lieutenant Governor's Medal awarded by the British Columbia Historical Federation and the Clio Prize awarded by the Canadian Historical Association, both for best book on British Columbia history. She is a Fellow of the Royal Society of Canada.

Mary Ann Irwin is an independent scholar who writes and teaches history in the San Francisco Bay Area. She is currently working on a history of San Francisco's Emanu-El Sisterhood for Personal Service. In 2003, she was awarded one of six fellowships offered by the Jewish Women's Archives for its program honoring 350 years of "Jewish Women Building Community" in America.

Lynn M. Hudson is an Associate Professor in History at California Polytechnic State University, San Luis Obispo. She is the author of *The Making of "Mammy Pleasant": A Black Entrepreneur in Nineteenth-Century San Francisco* (2003), winner of the Barbara Penny Kanner Award from the Western Association of Women Historians. Her next project is tentatively titled "West of Jim Crow: The History and Memory of California's Color Line."

Laura Jane Moore is currently a Franklin Post-Doctoral Teaching Fellow at the University of Georgia in Athens. Laura Moore's interest in exploring gender and race in twentieth-century U.S. history has led her to focus especially on connections between women's history and Native American history in the U.S. Southwest. "Elle Meets the President" is drawn from her current book manuscript, tentatively titled " 'By Her Weaving': Gender, Art, Work, Modernity and the Navajo Rug Trade, 1870s–1930s."

Margaret D. Jacobs is an Associate Professor of History at the University of Nebraska at Lincoln. She is currently working on a project entitled "White Mother to a Dark Race: White Women and the Removal of Indigenous Children in the United States and Australia, 1880–1940." Her first book, *Engendered Encounters: Feminism and Pueblo Cultures, 1879–1934* (1999), won two major awards, including the Sierra Prize from the Western Association for Women Historians.

Introduction

Joan M. Jensen and Darlis A. Miller

THE thirteen articles in this book mark the development of the field of western women's history between 1980 and 2002. In 1980, the *Pacific Historical Review* published our article "The Gentle Tamers Revisited: New Approaches to the History of Women in the American West." As the authors, we were pleased that the essay won an award for the best article published on the history of the West in 1980. But what followed the publication was even more important to us.

The publication of this article, and its award, marked a growing concern among historians about how they would acknowledge and explain the role of women in that part of the country called the American West. Western history as taught in the academy had its own long lineage of excluding women; women's history was a new field demanding a place for those who had been excluded.

Three years after publication of the article, in 1983, a group of western historians formed the Coalition for Western Women's History (CWWH). In 1990, the CWWH established the Jensen-Miller Prize to encourage publishing historical research in this field. It is awarded annually for the "outstanding article on the history of women in the North American West," and includes Mexico, Canada, Alaska, and Hawai'i. To encourage a widening stream of research the CWWH in 2002 also established the Irene Ledesma Prize in memory of Irene Ledesma, winner of the 1995 Jensen-Miller Prize, whose article is included here and who died two years later. That prize is for graduate student research in western women's history. At the annual meetings of the Western History Association, the CWWH hosts afternoon workshops and early-bird breakfasts where scholars share current research on western women. The CWWH also publishes newsletters for scholars in the field.

The thirteen Jensen-Miller prize essays in this book were chosen by prize committees of almost a hundred scholars who read and discussed each year the articles published on the history of western women. The articles are exemplary, but form only a part of the work which has resulted from the increasing interest in western women's history since 1980. Between 1983 and 2002, six conferences brought together scholars to share current research on western women. These conferences have taken place at Sun Valley, Idaho; Tucson, Arizona; Park City, Utah; San Francisco, California; Lincoln, Nebraska; Pullman, Washington; and Calgary, Alberta, Canada. The conferences have inspired a number of important anthologies, including two edited by Susan Armitage and Elizabeth Jameson, *The Women's West* (1987) and *Writing the Range* (1997); and one collaboration by Lillian Schlissel, Vicki Ruiz, and Janice Monk, *Western Women: Their Land, Their Lives* (1988).

We invite readers to use the essays published here as an introduction to the emerging historical world of the women's West. Through them, one can glimpse the agency, the variety, the vitality of the women we now see peopling the West. They introduce a group of thoughtful, creative, and disciplined authors who have committed themselves to telling the stories of these western women.

These articles are part of an ongoing discussion about how to write the history of western women and what methodologies and theories to employ in that project. That discussion had already begun when we wrote our critical survey of the literature about western women in "The Gentle Tamers Revisited" over twenty-five years ago. At that time, the work was fragmentary and disconnected and failed to evoke a sense of the overall complexity, diversity, and importance of the lives of western women. There were many articles, but no framework from which to consider women's western history as a whole. Most earlier literature had described women from an Anglo-American perspective, assuming

Anglo-American women shared a common culture while using derogatory language in discussing women of other cultures or omitting them entirely. Dee Brown's book, *The Gentle Tamers*, originally published in 1958, was still being reprinted and used as an introduction to women of the American West.

We organized published works that touched on women's experiences in the West, and began a search for more inclusive modes of studying them. We suggested a few ways to look at women that might allow historians to work cross-culturally and to incorporate some of the insights from the new field of women's history, most of which was still confined to women in the eastern part of the United States. Our practical motivation in writing "The Gentle Tamers Revisited" was the frustration we experienced when confronted by "old" interpretations in books and articles that preempted the way in which western women should be discussed. This "older" work sometimes excluded women entirely, making the West an open plane for the actions of men, or included women only to patronize, denigrate, or dismiss them as unimportant. Much of the literature implicitly warned other historians away from examining women's history seriously, or from including it in any larger view of western history. Even the most benign work distracted historians from exploring new approaches to the history of western women, and yet cluttered the historical literature with the remnants of a time past when women had little voice in determining how history was to be written. As historians we were taught to look at and build upon past work, or to challenge it. We thought our collection of these sources and our comments might allow us and other historians to get down to the business of writing a new history without researching the fragmentary literature from scratch.

As the essays here show, representations of women's experiences in the West are immensely more varied, more complex, and more intriguing than they were twenty-five years ago. The authors not only write of the past, but also present a contemporary world of thought where the past is evaluated from new viewpoints. Through their studies, the past is refracted to illuminate the present as well, and the ways in which contemporary scholars are attempting to understand relations among women and between women and men, relations that range from the most intimate personal relations to global relations among empires. Empires were and still are mostly controlled by men–but we should not forget that it was a woman whose fortunes launched Spain's voyages that first brought large numbers of European men to this continent. The essays remind us that women are always a crucial part of these relations.

We like the specificity of these essays. After reading them we remember individual women: Malinche, her son hanged, her daughter disinherited; Mary Ellen Pleasant, wealthy enough to influence the outcome of a famous trial; Elle of Ganado (Asdzaa Lichii' in Diné or Navajo), whose finely woven blanket stood for a whole range of market relations between Native women and Anglo-American tourists. And groups of women who worked together: the Chicanas who unionized and went on strike to fight for their rights as employed workers; the United Farm Women of Alberta who fought for "Equal Custody and Equal Property Rights."

In her essay, Susan Lee Johnson refers to the "small mountain of scholarship on women in the West" researchers now need to be familiar with and understand. Scholars have been busy creating this small mountain. Small, and yet it is immense in the way it fills the western landscape. Two articles tackle the mountain itself, offering reviews and syntheses of a large body of literature devoted to race and gender. Antonia Castañeda analyzes the literature relating to race. Johnson reviews the issues of gender, or genders as she says. Both discuss underlying assumptions that guide research agendas, and influence scholarship in profound ways. Castañeda focuses on how race and gender are constructed. She analyses the content of the writing of the history of western women of color before 1990, and how those writings have raised new issues about how we look at the women's West. Johnson's essay reminds us how the concept of gender has functioned over time within the context of the western history in which it took form.

The overviews and arguments by Castañeda and Johnson have raised theoretical and political issues being addressed by many other scholars. Castañeda and Johnson explore how gender and racial dimensions have influenced not only historical women, but scholars' work as well. Historians now work with a consciousness of how theories of gender and race make their own assumptions a part of the discussion. That these issues of race and gender affect individual research can be seen clearly in all of these articles. The essays, reprinted here in the order of their publication, will introduce readers to a wide range of historical issues as they discuss specific aspects of women's lives in the West.

A number of these essays focus on the context of the language of colonization and the workplace. They examine the differing processes by which women were divided into separate groups and defined in gendered and racialized ways in different times and places. They argue that many of these attitudes continue into the present.

Carol Madsen analyzes the legal protection of plural wives in Utah. Early in Utah's history, Madsen points out, the Mormon-dominated legislature adopted domestic relation laws that protected plural wives and their children, crafting the statutes in such a way as to deflect scrutiny of the U. S. Supreme Court. When the federal government outlawed plural marriages, it failed to provide similar protection to former plural wives. Significantly, although non-Mormons viewed polygamy as a system of female bondage, Utah had liberal divorce laws, a direct result of the Mormon belief that to live in disharmony was sinful.

Studies of interracial marriages, Peggy Pascoe believes, can help solve some of the problems inherent in writing intercultural history, by seeing race and gender as social constructions and by developing a workable concept of culture. She urges scholars to view interracial marriage as both an issue of race relations and of gender relations. Pascoe suggests historians of the West who wish to develop a multicultural approach, examine carefully accepted definitions of culture and the paradigms that have developed around them. Historians must keep a firm eye on the tension between the power of the dominant groups and the agency of the oppressed, then recover both perspectives.

In "Gender, Race, *Raza*," Amy Kaminsky examines the formation of gendered racial concepts in overlapping historical periods, from 1492 to the twentieth century. Moving from the language used in Spain, to Spanish America, to the United States, she argues that if some scholars have been brought up to accept language uncritically, others have been conscious of it for a long time. She quotes Antonio de Nebrija, for example, in the 1492 dedication of his Spanish grammar to Queen

Isabella: "Language has always been the companion of empire." Kaminsky argues that although the dimensions of empire have changed, language has continued to construct race in ways that are unstable and changing. "When the meanings of racial categories change and when racial attribution disengages from identity," Kaminsky concludes, "race enters a state of flux that best serves liberatory ends if it refuses stability."

Irene Ledesma, in "Texas Newspapers and Chicana Workers' Activism, 1919–1974," uses a twentieth century case to discuss how language continued to distort the history of Chicana workers in twentieth century Texas. She explains how all the presses that covered the activities of Chicana workers—Spanish and English language, owner and labor—made it difficult for them to emerge as the women workers they were. Even Spanish-language presses, stressing positive images of them as Mexicanas, emphasized "proper behavior" and patronized women strikers.

James Brooks examines the trade in captives during the Spanish and Mexican occupations of New Mexico to discuss the experiences of women, who accounted for two-thirds of all captives. Although victims of a harsh practice, these women—Indian and non-Indian alike—found ways to gain more secure futures for themselves and their children. Captive women, Brooks points out, often became important in Spanish-Indian diplomacy, serving as interpreters and envoys. Working within "structures of constraints," these women gained special negotiating skills and served as bridges across cultures.

Moving north, Catharine A. Cavanaugh examines the use of language in "'No Place for a Woman': Engendering Western Canadian Settlement." She shows how settlement discourse made the West a "manly" space by excluding both Euro-Canadian and indigenous Native women. Gender divisions within this discourse came to define mixed heritage Métis women as different from white women if they refused to cut their ties to Native cultures. Once considered by settlers as valued members of fur-trading communities, who functioned comfortably in both Native and Euro-Canadian cultures, these Métis women now became "Native." Euro-Canadian women arrived and were described as "gentle tamers," which reinforced a definition of Native women as "uncivilized." A woman could be designated a "gentle tamer," and be included in the history of the West in a way women who needed "taming" were not. At the same time, this designation as "gentle tamers" excluded them from access to wealth, to opportunity, and to a place in history. In the 1990s, Cavanaugh argues, the same language was being used to exclude women from their rightful place in western history.

Jean Barman sharpens the focus still more in "Taming Aboriginal Sexuality: Gender, Power, and Race in British Columbia, 1850–1900." Here Barman explains how agents of colonization constructed roles and identities for Native women, then related them to sexual behavior and activity. This definition, in turn, became a critique of the way in which women lived and cared for their children. Like Cavanaugh, she finds these old attitudes persisting into the 1990s.

Using a wide array of sources, Mary Ann Irwin examines the formation of women's benevolence societies in San Francisco. She convincingly demonstrates that San Franciscans, between 1850 and 1880, mainly relied on women's charities to provide social services for women and children. Through these pioneering welfare programs, benevolent women were able to influence community politics, making their voices heard in the public arena. Gender ideology, Irwin believes, clearly contributed to benevolent women's success; their "identification with femininity and piety enabled them to draw on public support for their social welfare projects."

Lynn Hudson examines the clash of race, sex, gender, and power in a San Francisco courtroom. This focus on an 1884 San Francisco divorce case allows Hudson to examine issues of sexual power, interracial alliances, and public imagery of women in public places. Newspapers often portrayed the two major women involved, the African American entrepreneur Mary Ellen Pleasant and her Irish American protege Sarah Hill, as madam and prostitute. Yet Hill's lawyers countered with their own imagery, portraying the women in roles that white San Franciscans found non-threatening. Hudson's essay reminds us that courtroom dramas take on new meaning when race, class, and gender are the prime categories of analysis.

Laura Jane Moore writes of the Southwest in the early twentieth century in "Elle Meets the President: Weaving Navajo Culture and

Commerce in the Southwestern Tourist Industry." She explains how closely tied to national politics even Diné (Navajo) women were because of their participation in tourist sites. Here, Native women working in Native workplaces, were asked to participate in the "staged authenticity" of "idealized domestic tableaux." Moore argues that these workplaces became sites of "compromise and confusion, exploitation and resistance."

Margaret Jacobs has followed the lead of Pascoe and Brooks in discussing interracial marriages and relationships. Using case studies of marriages between white women and Native American men, Jacobs shows how these marriages helped to reshape gender and racial conventions. The Eastman marriage, taking place at the end of the 19th century, rested upon the premise that interracial marriage would foster assimilation of Indian people into white society. The Luhan marriage some thirty years later was fostered by the belief that Indian values and lifestyles might cure American societal ills and dysfunctions brought about by modernization and industrialization.

As these essays show, an increasing number of scholars are writing about western women, race, and gender. Whether from vantage points along the southern or northern borderlands, or from other frontiers where cultures meet, these studies are sharpening the ways in which historians research and describe women of the West. We urge others to do the same with the most critical minds, careful research, and most engaging styles possible. Our thanks to all involved in this project with us.

The Gentle Tamers Revisited: New Approaches to the History of Women in the American West

Joan M. Jensen and Darlis A. Miller

OVER twenty years ago, Putnam Press published Dee Brown's *The Gentle Tamers*, one of the first books to attempt an overview and analysis of the roles of women in the West. *The Gentle Tamers* elaborated and codified the assumption that white males "tamed" the West in its physical aspects and that white women, who followed the men, gently tamed the social conditions (including, of course, white men). By focusing on women as a group, Brown filled a major gap in western historiography, and because he provided a thesis and a framework, his book remains the most widely read book on women in the West. This essay is an attempt to place the concept of the "gentle tamers" in its larger historiographical context, to examine the ways in which women in the West have been viewed by historians, and to explore new possibilities for analysis.[1]

Brown's book essentially provided an elaboration of an older male image of western women, one which still dominates literature and the classroom. A newer, ethnically broader and more varied image of women in the West is today challenging that older view. This view rests on a

* Joan M. Jensen and Darlis A. Miller, "The Gentle Tamers Revisited: New Approaches to the History of Women in the American West," *Pacific Historical Review* 49:2 (1980). ©1980 Pacific Historical Review, Pacific Coast Branch, American Historical Association, University of California Press. Reprinted by permission.

multicultural approach which calls for an evaluation of the experiences of all ethnic groups of women within a historical framework incorporating women's history into western history.[2] This process will necessitate the rewriting of western history, a task which should be undertaken with an eye to other work now being done in women's history.

Since Fredrick Jackson Turner first presented his famous thesis to fellow historians in 1893, studies of the American frontier and westward expansion have issued forth in a steady stream. Although the master himself virtually ignored women's roles in conquering the frontier, other historians have made some attempt to include women in their studies of the American pioneering experience.[3] It is, of course, difficult to generalize about women on the frontier. The term has been used to refer to a sparsely populated area on the edge of settlement with its particular location changing as Euro-American settlement moved west across the continent.[4] For over three hundred years there were men and women in America experiencing frontier conditions. The frontier of Jamestown settlers was beyond the fall line; that of revolutionary America was beyond the Appalachians; and that for Americans living in mid-nineteenth century was beyond the Mississippi. So temporal and spatial considerations have complicated efforts to generalize about frontier women. Then, too, the frontier has been defined as process—the process through which a relatively primitive society is transformed into a more complex society.[5] It is generally in this area—frontier as process—that historians have inserted their comments about frontier women.

But students of American expansion and the pioneering process have never come to grips with terminology. "Frontier" and the "West" are terms frequently interchanged, and their temporal and spatial delineations remain imprecise and shrouded in confusion. There is general consensus among some observers that the trans-Mississippi region—or more specifically the area west of the ninety-eighth meridian—is the "real West," perhaps because it developed in more recent times or more likely because its physical and cultural characteristics differed so dramatically from areas to the east. Hence this vast territory is frequently referred to as the Far West or the New West to distinguish it from the earlier wests of colonial times.[6] When historians have turned their attention to western women, typically they have focused on women in this geographical region west of the Mississippi, though here again terminology and delineations are imprecise.[7]

After Herbert E. Bolton made borderland studies popular, the Spanish Southwest became a major field for study within the broader context of American western and frontier studies. Although Bolton was at ease in crossing the modern international boundary in his studies, later students of the Southwest generally limited their focus to Texas and the Mexican cession lands—New Mexico west to California. So southwestern women became a theme—really a whisper—in general studies of the American Southwest.[8]

Regardless of theme or approaches used by western historians, frontier women of the West and Southwest share certain characteristics as portrayed in traditional studies. They are invisible, few in number, and not important in the process of taming a wilderness. Or conversely, their role has been sentimentalized and given a rhetorical mystical importance approaching sainthood. As T. A. Larson pointed out in 1974, standard college textbooks used for courses in western history virtually ignore women, though they were written by men with impeccable professional credentials.[9] As recently as 1976, a textbook on the West listed only three women in the index: Helen Hunt Jackson, Queen Liliuokalani, and Sacajewea. The index also included an entry for frontier family, and, indeed, within the text one could find the better part of one page devoted to the life of women and children on the frontier. Characteristically, although the author elsewhere discussed George Rapp, Robert Owen, and utopian communities which they established in the Old West, he failed to mention Mother Ann Lee, founder of the well-known Shaker communities.[10]

Although women have remained invisible to most writers of western history, their scant numbers on the frontier have compelled a few historians to give them at least passing attention.[11] Richard A. Bartlett, who has published the most recent social history of the American frontier, emphasized the "overwhelming preponderance of males" in frontier regions. "No one has ever questioned, let alone analyzed," he stated, "the masculinity of the frontier society. Since it is as obvious as the sun in the daytime, the subject has not been discussed."[12] Moreover, chroniclers of mining and cattle frontiers invariably noted the scarcity of women and attributed the prestige and distinction accorded western women to that very scarcity.[13] As an example of special treatment allotted to women, one writer noted that bylaws were enacted in a Montana mining camp of 300 men and 15 women which decreed the death penalty "for murder, thieving, or for insulting a woman."[14]

By virtually excluding women from western studies on the one hand, and emphasizing their rareness on the other, the impression is left that women played insignificant roles in settling the American West. As the frontier advances with all its romance and color across the pages of Ray Allen Billington's monumental *Westward Expansion*, it is a robust masculine domain that emerges, and the few women who appear, Calamity Jane and Mary Lease, for example, do so on a masculine stage.[15] It has been observed by more than one investigator that women were not fur trappers, miners, assayers, explorers, pony express riders, cattle riders, military commanders, politicians, railroad builders, or Indian traders, and therefore presumably non-essential in the development of the West.[16] On the other hand, there has been a strong tendency to replace solid research on women's roles with lofty rhetoric distorting western women beyond recognition. In speaking of such women, Dee Brown wrote that "they attracted little attention individually . . . but as a mass maternal force their power was unmatched in the domestication process that transformed the wild frontiersmen into ordinary placid citizens."[17] Page Smith described women as "the shock-troops of Western migration."[18]

Where anything more specific has been attempted, investigators have described western women in stereotyped images and symbols. Although variations are many, these images can be assembled for convenience into four major categories: gentle tamers, sunbonneted helpmates, hell-raisers, and bad women. The gentle tamer category encompasses western women as civilizers, ladies, and suffragists. Countless students of western history identify women as the chief civilizing agents on the frontier, whether they lived in mining camps, ranches, or sod-house prairie shanties. They carried with them to their new homes as much of the trappings of civilization as possible and subsequently assumed major responsibility for establishing the social and cultural values once known in former homes. Dee Brown declared that the Wild West was tamed by its petticoated pioneers, while another writer observed that it was women who "reminded the men of the world of literature and arts."[19] Moreover, habits of language, dress, cleanliness, and morality were all reportedly improved once women arrived on the frontier.

Sometimes the gentle tamer was a lady—a chaste beautiful creature which cowboys placed on a pedestal and worshipped from afar—who received credit for improving manners and morals. Pious, pure, and submissive, the refined lady nevertheless administered constant pressure to respect the Sabbath, inhibit cursing and drinking, promote better grooming and more diversified diet and in general smooth rough edges from frontier society.[20] On the other hand, refined ladies frequently are depicted as having difficulty adjusting to new and rough surroundings, and those who could not adapt suffered intense mental and physical anguish.[21]

Suffragists are also depicted as women who, though not as gentle as their sisters, are still portrayed as improving the quality of frontier society. At the very least, suffragists argued, voting rights would induce women to migrate west, replacing a transient bachelor society with a stable family community. Moreover, it could be argued that enfranchised women would support legislation curbing less attractive appetites of strong willed and undisciplined westerners.[22]

Undoubtedly the most popular and enduring image of frontier woman is the subonneted helpmate so movingly depicted in 1921 by Emerson Hough who wrote:

> The chief figure of the American West, the figure of the ages, is not the long-haired, fringed-legging man riding a rawboned pony, but the gaunt and sad-faced woman sitting on the front seat of the wagon, following her lord where he might lead, her face hidden in the same ragged sunbonnet which had crossed the Appalachians and the Missouri long before there was the seed of America's wealth. There was the great romance of all America—the woman in the sunbonnet; and not after all, the hero with the rifle across his saddle horn.[23]

As helpmates, women carried out routine chores in addition to doing men's work when emergencies arose or their men were away.

Virtuous and strong both emotionally and physically, they endured pain and hardship with little complaint. As one researcher succinctly stated, "the primary defining feature of this group of women was their ability to fulfill their duties which enabled their men to succeed."[24]

Women as hell-raisers were not very common but they were widely talked about. These were the super cowgirls, the Calamity Janes, who acted more like men than women and became heroes of dime novels and wild west shows. James D. Horan called them "Desperate Women," while a second author called them "Wiley Women of the West."[25] Although they violated the mores of proper society and on occasion entered the criminal world, they were often depicted as good-looking and well-educated women who could outride, outshoot, and outcuss the best cowboys in the West.

The image of western women as bad women appears in a variety of forms, overlapping with the hell-raiser image, but generally associated with sex and raw nature. These were prostitutes, the soiled doves of all nationalities, who inhabited gambling saloons, dance halls, local cribs, and areas referred to as hogtowns. A variation on this theme is the harlot with a heart of gold—honest, loyal, generous, compassionate, and revered by admirers who accorded her status as a great lady.[26]

A new approach to women in the West has emerged in the past few years which refuses to accept the images of western women as portrayed by earlier historians and therefore promises a more accurate interpretation of this part of women's history. These scholars have attempted to analyze critically the images of western women: the authors have challenged the old images in various ways, either with literary criticism, by testing the reality of these images, or by attempting to create a new image through careful quantitative and archival research. The first method treats images in literature as just that, literary images to be examined with the tools of literary criticism. The second method tests the image against the reality of women's lives. The third approach, in careful case studies, provides new images which emerge from a large number of documents for a very limited geographical area.

A number of articles in literary criticism, especially those by Beverly Stoeltje and Beverly Trulio, have used the first method. Analyzing the accounts, primarily those by males, these authors have shown that what men described may have had no necessary relation to women but that their images reflected either literary types or cultural attitudes. Much can be gained from looking at literature in its literary and cultural context and from pointing out as Trulio did, for example, that racial stereotypes of New Mexico women were very pronounced in writings of Euro-American men.[27] To analyze the types of frontier female images and to show how they parallel and are defined by male frontier images, as Stoeltje has done, is also valuable.[28]

While these literary studies sharpen our perception about the context and limitation of these images, they do little to answer the question of how accurate these images are, or to what extent they reflect the reality of women's lives. The studies which do attempt to test images against realities seem to conclude that congruence between image and reality is almost nonexistent. Using various sources, authors have come up with uniformly consistent results. T. A. Larson, in analyzing women in relation to jobs, has concluded that if the reality of women's jobs outside the home was reflected in western literature, the western woman would be portrayed as a "domestic servant," an image almost never present.[29] Sheryll Patterson-Black, in examining the image of the reluctant woman pioneer, has found that, at least in Nebraska and Colorado, there is much contradictory evidence showing that a variety of pioneer women flourished on the frontier. Because under the Homestead Act of 1862, women could be homesteaders in their own right, many women enthusiastically pioneered alone or with sisters and mothers. In some areas of Colorado women were able to prove up, that is to establish a homestead and maintain occupancy for a certain number of months, more often than did men.[30]

In a recent review of Iowa pioneer women, Glenda Riley attempted to find four types of women often portrayed in western literature: The Calamity Janeite, the sex object, the frontier suffragist, and the saint in the sunbonnet. The women could not be found in Iowa. Looking at the period from 1833 to 1870, Riley found that while Iowa women may have been handy with a gun, they did this as part of their everyday life and not as Calamity Janes. Nor were women often defined strictly as "sexual women." Frontier suffragists all came from the East. And the image of the sunbonnet saint, the pioneer woman as wife and mother, was far too narrow to encompass the variety of women who homesteaded with other women, shared the enforcement of societal norms with men, and often wore eastern fashions rather than calico and sunbonnets.[31]

These studies are basically revisions of old images. The case study approach has produced at least three carefully researched and argued articles which attempt to create new images. Two quantitative studies have dealt with family structure. For Los Angles, R. Griswold del Castillo has argued that disintegration of the Chicano extended family followed the Euro-American invasion, and there were many female headed households in the years after the Civil War.[32] In San Antonio, according to Jane Dysart's research, daughters of more wealthy Chicano families often intermarried with Euro-Americans and their children passed into that culture, detaching themselves from the Hispanic heritage.[33] A third study examined the attitudes toward work of the Euro-American women on the trail to Oregon and California. It found the eastern traditions resilient to western experience. Women temporarily performed jobs traditionally assigned to males but refused to abandon permanently "women's work."[34]

Each of these case studies presents an important new image of women—moving out of the Chicano extended family, moving into the Euro-American culture, and refusing to abandon women's traditional work roles. Yet these new images are isolated images, like snapshots of single cultures without the context of relationships among them. Moreover, they remain nineteenth-century images with little attempt to link the nineteenth to the twentieth century. It is a nineteenth-century picture album of women in the West.[35] What we would like to propose here is a new multicultural framework as a focus for western women. Once refocused on cultures, many new insights, approaches, and questions immediately appear. We have chosen migration west; demography on both the rural and the urban frontier; relations among women of different cultures; politics; and occupations as examples of the possibilities for reevaluating the history of women in the West.

The term migration west, indeed the term "West" itself, masks the reality that for many western women the West was North or East. The major nineteenth-century migration westward followed a great increase in literacy rates for women in the Northeast. As a consequence, women left a trail of words behind. The accounts left by Euro-American women going West must number in the thousands. Southern white women and recent European immigrant women were much less literate and left far fewer accounts.[36] Even fewer are the written accounts by Hispanic women who moved north from Mexico and Asian women who later traveled east across the Pacific. Historians may never know what going north meant for Hispanic women of the earlier period but they can still document immigration of the late nineteenth and early twentieth century through oral history. The moving accounts by Chinese women who arrived at Angel Island in the 1930s indicate the importance of employing oral history to document the recent immigration process for western women.[37]

Although the experience of women traveling to a new home was different for each group, accounts of Euro-American women from the nineteenth century may suggest questions to be asked about migration by women of all cultures. These accounts indicate that work roles were often temporarily taken over by women on the way West, but women seldom moved into male work roles permanently.[38] Women with heavy family responsibilities went more reluctantly than daughters, the unmarried, or young married women.[39] Wives may have gone reluctantly because husbands made the decision to move while a wife may have preferred other alternatives, but single women often saw migration as an opportunity to better their condition.[40] The strain of peopling a new frontier may have caused tensions which were resolved by increasing traditional bonds between mothers and daughters. It may have also tightened the bonds of immigrant daughters to families as they moved into wage labor to help support foreign-born parents and siblings.[41] Lillian Schlissel has concluded that obedience and obligation "thrust daughters into the only frontier they were to know, the frontier of the wage-working class."[42] For Hispanic women, Asian women, and black women who arrived in the West in the largest numbers during the twentieth century, a place in the wage market was even more crucial.[43]

The study of twentieth-century immigration history would make the lives of Hispanic and Asian women much more visible in western history. Male-female ratios were high for Asians until after 1910. Then the number and proportion of women increased rapidly and Asian communities became increasingly urban. Today immigration from most Asian countries is fairly balanced sexually and predominantly urban. With Hispanic immigration, the balance has even swung toward women. Early twentieth-century immigration reports show predominantly male groups migrating to the Unites States from Mexico. That situation had begun to change by World War II. By the 1970s, Hispanic women outnumbered men as newcomers. More than two-thirds of the immigrants from Central and South America were women by 1977. Leaving children to be cared for by other females in their extended families, women came north by the thousands seeking urban wages as household and garment workers. They sent money home to support households left behind much as men had done earlier.[44]

Like reevaluation of the process by which women migrated west, demography or the study of population change can be an essential check on distorted western history. Density of population, gender balance, life cycle (especially marriage, age, and fertility) can tell us much about women's lives in the West, question old interpretations, and give direction to new studies. There have been almost no careful demographic studies on the far western states, but there have been studies on the rural frontier, especially for the West North Central states. Most of the studies deal with the nineteenth century, and many of them use only one census year rather than following a process through several decades. Nevertheless, they provide important information on women in the West.

Demographic studies do not support the common assumption made most often about women in the West, that they were scarce with single men far outnumbering them. Rather, studies show that gender balance differed according to area and time, indicating that the above generalization must always be qualified. Studies of the rural frontier (usually defined as an area with a density of two to five people per square mile) from Indiana to Nebraska show that these areas were most often settled by families and that there was not a large excess of single men. In studying a sample from 1840 to 1860 in a series of western frontiers, Jack Eblen concluded that not more than 25 percent of the adult males were single.[45] In Nebraska, in 1850, newly settled areas had a ratio of three men to two women.[46] Studies of Kansas and Iowa indicate a similar ratio.[47] While the earliest mining frontiers in Colorado and California do confirm a great sexual imbalance (23 to 1 in California and 34 to 1 in Colorado in 1860), this condition disappeared rather quickly. By 1870, the ratio of men to women in California was two to one. The same ratio existed in 1870 for the state of Oregon.[48] Because of the settled Hispanic population and the family migrations of Mormons, New Mexico and Utah had a sexually balanced population during most of the nineteenth century.[49] In other far western states, a gender imbalance still existed in 1870. The proportion was 4 to 1 in Arizona, 5 to 1 in Nevada, 6 to 1 in Wyoming, and 8 to 1 in Idaho and Montana. This great disparity by state indicates that a tendency still common in discussions of women in the West is to make a generalization based on an area or a time when males did predominate and then to exclude other areas and times as not typical of the West.

Demographic facts also disprove generalizations related to sexual imbalance. While births tended to be rather balanced in the second generation on the frontier, economic changes could affect the normal process of equalization of the sexes. Thus, a study of Iowa showed that the number of single males increased rather than decreased in the decades after settlement.[50] Migration of males to work in predominately male industries or in agriculture may have changed the sex balance fairly drastically not only among immigrant groups like the Chinese or the Mexicans, but also among the native-born populations.[51]

A third set of generalizations often made about women in the West, which demographic studies have qualified, is that because they were so out-numbered by males, they invariably married, usually younger than women in the East, and quickly remarried when widowed. By 1900, at least 1 in 4 women between 25 and 29 remained unmarried in the Far West. California had one of the highest rates of single women aged 25 to 29 in the country (33 percent), much higher than the national average (27.5 percent). On the other hand, New Mexico had a low 12 percent of women remaining single in this age group in 1900.[52] One study for Texas in 1850 indicates that even in the early settlement process many young people may have remained unmarried.[53] Such differences reflect a great variety in life styles of women in different areas.

If some women did not marry at all, others did not marry until they were much older than has been assumed. Many of the couples settling on farms were between 30 and 40.[54] The study of Texas in 1850 showed the average age for women to marry as 22 and the average age for men as 26.[55] The presence of eligible partners and presumably even the availability of land were not the only factors in determining the age at marriage in the West.

Although these western women may not have married as young as once assumed, two earlier generalizations seem to hold true—that women on the frontier had higher fertility rates than women behind the frontier, and that there were few older women in the frontier areas.[56] These facts indicate that the subjects of childbearing and childrearing in the rural West are important and unexplored areas needing examination. What did it mean for the frontier mother to have no older women nearby to assist in child birth and child care? Such generational discontinuity must have had a great effect on the first women in the West and may have affected the second generation as well. With more children to care for, both mothers and daughters had an extra burden without grandmothers. The presence of an older female generation and an extended family pattern for may Native American and Hispanic women may have made their experiences quite different from this first generation of eastern settlers and from later Hispanic and Asian immigrants.

There is some evidence that fertility rates may have increased rather than declined once an area became improved in the region behind the frontier. Thus, rural women in newly settled areas behind the frontier deserve more attention than they have received from historians.[57] Perhaps the frontier still exerted pressures on mothers, pressure no longer present for the daughters; or the availability of nearby land combined with improved farms made it desirable for women to have more children. Once land became less available, apparently the fertility rates dropped. Studies indicate that in some areas in the late nineteenth century, more children may have remained on the farms and parents may have spaced the birth of their children more closely.[58] Finally, at least one study shows that widows did not invariably remarry, especially when they held land in rural western areas.[59]

These studies can, of course, only question older generalizations. Before a new framework can be established, far more demographic analysis is necessary. But the studies cited above do indicate the large numbers of women present on the rural frontier, the variations in their life cycles, and the importance of future studies being well grounded in demography.

In addition to questioning old generalizations, demographic data on women of different ethnic groups can be utilized more effectively. The Spanish government conducted censuses in the late eighteenth century which can provide information on the living arrangements of early Hispanic women, and American censuses exist from 1850.[60] There were separate censuses taken of Native Americans in 1890 which tell much about women's life styles.[61] Other sources exist to identify the location of women of different cultures. There is no reason for historians to assume that the first Euro-American woman in an area was more important as a woman than the thousands of Native American women or Mexicanas who were already there. Estimates of the number of *criollas, mestizas,* and Native American women are available for the eighteenth century and need to be refined.[62] It is not enough to write about Sister Monica and the French nuns who arrived in Arizona in 1870. We need to know about the culture of the hundreds of Hispanic women already there, 79 of whom entered the convent which the nuns opened that year.[63]

Demography can also remind historians that the rural frontier was not necessarily the destination of the migrants to the West. Many women headed for the urban rather than the rural frontier. If a rural frontier is defined by low population density, an urban area is defined most simply by its high density. The importance of towns in settling the West has often been noted by historians but the relation of women to this urban process has seldom been studied. Gender is a basic element in any study of the urban process.[64] As early as 1899, Adna Weber noted that women migrated over short distances more often than men, particularly to nearby towns, and had longer lives than men once they arrived.[65] Sixty years later, Richard C. Wade, in *The Urban Frontier,* offered a view of the upper-middle-class woman's life in western cities.[66] Yet few historians have followed Wade's example in describing the lives of urban western women, and no theoretical framework has been developed which would include women as an integral part of the urbanization in the West. If the Pacific states have been more urban than the nation as a whole since the 1860s, as Earl Pomeroy notes, then women's urban history should certainly begin with these cities, even if the ratio of women to men in the major far western cities was low.[67] A state which had a predominance of men over women could still have cities in which proportionately more women than men lived.

The presence of "female cities" in the West—where females outnumbered males or where women were a higher percentage than in the state as a whole—needs to be studied. By 1900, St. Louis had a balanced sex ratio; Denver had 99 women for every 100 men and Los Angles 97. For reasons we do not know, the male fraction of the population increased rather than decreased between 1900 and 1910 in the major far western cities but it again dropped rapidly after 1910.[68] In the West North Central states, Kansas City, Minneapolis, St. Paul, and Des Moines became "female cites" between 1900 and 1930.[69]

Long before 1930, women were abandoning the country for the city in the Far West. In the nineteenth century, summer trips to San Francisco by the wives of army officers brought them into an urban center where, according to tourists, women seemed to display much more independence than women in the East.[70] When Gertrude Atherton began to describe women in her hometown of San Francisco at the end of the nineteenth century, easterners found her writing obscene and immoral. She wrote about independent young women who flaunted Victorian values.[71] Were these western urban women the same in their marital relations, life styles, and morals as women in the East? Or was Atherton's life and the lives of her heroines reflective of a different society in the West? Did these women already display a cluster of attitudes which foretold a western view of morals, which as one historian has recently suggested, later became the vanguard for the rest of the nation?[72]

Not only urban but small-town life remains unexplored in the history of women in the West. Few historians have attempted to explain the effect which ecological changes, like lumbering in northern New Mexico or mining in southern Colorado and Arizona, had on women's lives.[73] A woman's life in a twentieth-century company mining town in the West may have been very different from either city or farm life. Agnes Smedley, in *Daughter of Earth*, gave a devastating view of women's lives in Trinidad, Colorado, and Raton, New Mexico, but no one has tried to gauge its accuracy.[74] Only recently has there been sufficient interest in examining the lives of Chicanas who won the mine strike portrayed in the movie *Salt of the Earth*.[75] We still do not know how Chicanas in other mining towns lived or responded to conditions where wage labor existed primarily for males.

Black women in the West have also become increasingly urban during the twentieth century. Eliza, a cook who followed Elizabeth Custer west to Kansas after the Civil War, complained that she missed the picnics, the church socials, and the burials of the black community.[76] One look at the census records will explain why she was lonely. There were many black women in Louisiana, Texas, Missouri, and Arkansas: state estimates for 1900 range from 80,000 to 328,000 for these states. As one looks west, however, the number of black women drops and the proportion of black males goes up. In Kansas and Oklahoma, where many black families homesteaded after the Civil War, there were only 25,000 and 27,000 black women, respectively. California and Colorado had 4,000 and 5,000. The rest of the far western states had fewer than a thousand black women and the ratio of men to women reached a high of 281 men per 100 women in Arizona where many black soldiers and cowboys worked.[77]

Arizona is thus clearly not the place to look for black women in the Far West either in 1900 or later, although by 1930 there were over 4,000 there. The predominantly female black population in Colorado was also only slightly over 6,000 by 1930. The place to look for black women in the Far West is in California where the population reached 10,000 by 1910, almost 19,000 by 1920, and nearly 41,000 by 1930. And the place to look for black women in the Far West is in the cities. In 1930, black women in Louisiana, Texas, Arkansas, and Oklahoma were still 60 to 80 percent rural, and in Missouri and Kansas only 60 to 80 percent urban. In most Mountain and Pacific states (with the exception of Arizona and New Mexico where a majority of black women remained rural), the percentage reached 73 to 90 per cent urban, with

Colorado and California having the most urban population. Oral histories being conducted in Colorado are beginning to show the important role of women in small black communities, and in the highly segregated existence black families faced in cities like Denver.[78] Particularly after 1930, the historical frontier for black women lies in cities like Los Angles.[79]

Even more neglected than demography as a subject of historical inquiry are relationships among women of different cultures. Euro-American women who lived among Native American women as captives, missionaries, army and trading women, and anthropologists have left numerous if not unbiased accounts of their experiences. Captivity was perhaps the closest prolonged contact of Euro-American women with Native American cultures. Women were often allowed to live when men were killed because they were noncombatants who might be ransomed or who could perhaps be put to work without danger. Long before the Euro-American pioneers crossed the Mississippi these contacts had given rise to a large literature of captivity narratives, largely stylized accounts of indignities.[80] Some of these accounts were not told by the women captives themselves but by military officers, publicists, or others interested in convincing the public that any policy of leniency toward Indians was mistaken.[81] Others, however, are accounts by women themselves. Awareness of context, literary and political styles, and differences in Native American tribes is essential for any effective analysis of these accounts but they remain an important source for cross-cultural contact. Some Euro-American women emphasized the cruelty of Native American women to those captured; other accounts, like those of the Oatman girls in Arizona, indicated that relations between women could be very good when they worked together in the fields.[82] Many difficulties of women prisoners may have stemmed from life styles rather than simply being prisoners. Euro-American women were often expected to carry water and gather wood, chores which they could not or would not perform as efficiently as was expected of them. Studying patterns of expectation and response may be possible after careful examination of documents. Also, times changed. Indians who were friendly in the 1840s or 1850s were not as friendly after more contact with eastern settlers, a fact which needs to be considered in any analysis of Indian-white relations.[83]

Even more helpful, however, would be an attempt to compare the experiences of Native American and Euro-American women caught in the crossfire between desperate warriors and determined soldiers. To juxtapose, for example, the account by the Norwegian Guri Olsdatter, who escaped capture but left letters describing with horror her escape, against the account by the Cheyenne woman Iron Teeth, who saw soldiers killing women and children, may give a more balanced idea of the fortunes of women caught in the war zone than a view from only the side of Euro-American women.[84] Comparisons of how the women of white, Native American, and Mexican cultures were treated by men of war, how warfare affected their lives, and how they explained such actions will tell us more about the women and men of each culture than looking only at white women as captives.

Peaceful contacts between white women and Native American women need to be explored more carefully. Mormon women were one large group of white women who had contact for over a century with Native American women in the West. Although Mormon women did not function as official missionaries in the nineteenth century, their interactions with Native Americans were often important for peaceful relations. They acted as doctors and midwives to Native American women and took Indian children into their families. Adopting Native American orphans was not always a pleasure for Mormon women but most considered it a duty. These children were usually raised as a part of the family, although they often died young because of the changes of diet and life style.[85] From these contacts and others, Mormon women learned Indian dialects. Women performed an important role in feeding visiting delegations: Visiting whites might be told to wait while this important courtesy was completed, and women had often to deal with the demands of small groups of Native American males who overstepped the bounds of courtesy. It seems evident that Mormon women preferred dealing with Indian women rather than men. Women normally repaid Mormon sisters for food by carrying water or helping with chores while men simply expected to be fed. Once relief societies were formed in the 1860s, women developed programs to help Indian women in their regions. Such missionary work contributed to serious splits in Indian groups and sometimes provoked hostility, but some

Native American women undoubtedly welcomed the efforts of the Mormon sisters.[86]

Mormon women also went into Native American villages to minister to Indian women as doctors and midwives. The church encouraged medical training for women and was anxious to convince Indians that their medicine was more powerful than that of the Indians. One Mormon woman returned elated after spending several days treating an Indian woman because of the good effect this was expected to have on relations with the tribe.[87] These scattered examples indicate that a reexamination of the voluminous material on Mormon women would reveal additional cross-cultural contacts.

Although numerous published accounts exist by women of both Catholic and Protestant missions in the West, their role in cross-cultural relations has yet to be examined critically. This missionary work was, of course, a continuation of work done east of the Mississippi. Published accounts exist from the 1830s for the West, many by women who were teachers or wives of male missionaries but who functioned as essential members of the overall missionary programs.[88]

Some early army women like Mary H. Eastman wrote books about the cultures of the Native Americans among whom they lived. Many, like Martha Summerhayes, wrote memoirs which included references to Native American women. Alice Blackwood Baldwin, stationed with her husband at Fort Wingate, New Mexico, in 1868 noted that she made firm friends with nearby Navajo women and also established friendly relations with Hispanic women living in proximity to the fort.[89] Women traders, like Louisa Wade Wetherill, were early ethnologists. After the army and the trading women came women anthropologists whose work among Native Americans has influenced greatly the entire historical picture of Native American women.[90]

References to cross-cultural contacts in other situations need to be reexamined. Dee Brown, for example, who seldom mentioned Native American women in *The Gentle Tamers*, included one incident where Euro-American women pleaded with men of their party to save a starving Indian girl. The men (with one dissenting vote) determined to abandon the girl and the women stayed behind for a while to nurse her. Later one man went back and shot the girl.[91] Such incidents tell us a considerable amount about the difficulty of practicing female charity in situations dominated by male decisions. On the other hand, Dee Brown omitted a significant incident related by Martha Summerhayes in her memoir of army life. She described a visit from Native American women who brought a cradle board for her firstborn, cuddled the child, and then placed it gently in the cradle board.[92] Summerhayes noted that these were the "important" women in the tribe, but did not comment upon the expectations of these women. Did they expect sororal relations similar to the fraternal relations sometimes developed between male chiefs and officers?

Relations between Native American women and Hispanic women varied by area and circumstance. In some New Mexico villages, for example, Native Americans and Hispanos merged their cultures and intermarried forming an early Chicano population. In others, Native Americans and Hispanos remained separate and continued to identify primarily with one or the other culture.[93] Class may have cut across cultures bringing the rich Hispanic woman closer to wealthy American born women or an Indian woman with high status in her community than to poor Hispanic sisters.

Hispanic traders, cooks, *curanderas*, and laundresses also interacted with American-born women. Many Native Americans and Mexicanas sold or traded with American women in the nineteenth century and some of these commercial relations can still be traced. Native American women and Mexicanas taught Americanas about the use of herbs which they often collected and sold. Agnes Cleaveland, in *No Life for a Lady*, described herself working under the direction of a Mexicana who lived at her ranch to save the gangrened arm of a man. Work relations can be traced through oral histories of both employees and the employed. Questions of this type may lead not only to more careful analysis of interactions but also to greater precision in describing various cultures and how they changed. None of the cultures was timeless. They all changed in some ways over time.[94]

If relations among women of different cultures have been neglected, the politics of middle-class women in the West certainly have not. Suffrage has consistently engaged the interest of historians for almost a decade because its progress seems unique in the West. By 1914, women had gained suffrage in ten of the eleven states in the Far West and the Territory of Alaska. Such a clear-cut western success in electoral politics at a time when women's suffrage was receiving resounding defeats in the East was certain to evoke attempts at explanation. State studies have been published on some aspects of the suffrage battle for all of the western suffrage states with the exception of Oregon, Nevada, and the wayward New Mexico which did not endorse woman suffrage until 1920.[95]

There are three ways in which historians have interpreted the success of women's suffrage in the West: through analysis of economics, of ideas, and of political structures. Rather surprisingly, few historians have looked carefully at economics. The history of the West as a whole has had few Marxist interpreters. The weighing of economic considerations, except the availability of land and water, does not occur often in accounts of the West as a crucial factor in historical change. It has sometimes been argued that women were scarce, hence their economic value was greater; or that frontier women participated more than eastern women in agricultural production, but this argument is most often made as an assumption rather than as part of a thorough analysis. T. A. Larson dismissed out of hand the idea of frontier partnership in production with a reference to Abigail Scott Duniway's complaint that farmers were killing their wives with neglect and overwork. Even in Utah, where the link between the economic importance of Mormon women and the support which the Mormon church gave women's suffrage seems most evident, that link is not discussed by historians. Most historians prefer to discuss suffrage in the context of social relations or ideology.[96]

Ideology was, for a long time, the favorite explanation for western suffrage. Early accounts of western suffrage often assumed a positive frontier ideology as the cause. In the West, a "frontier spirit" promoted a sense of equality, of chivalry, or of women's role as "civilizer." This frontier sprit has been notoriously difficult to document and few recent historians have attempted to do so. Rather, they have usually questioned these assumptions and, when looking at ideology, have tended to find more conservative attitudes involved—as ideological underpinnings for suffrage in the West. A few have considered western progressive ideology as a positive force and recently Ronald Schaffer, in looking at

California, has stressed the importance of ideological change for suffrage tactics. In California, suffragists developed a new belief that only if women themselves wanted to vote could suffrage be obtained and a campaign was explicitly designed to inculcate that belief in masses of California women.[97]

More often, however, historians have looked carefully at western political structures for clues to the success of suffrage. One of the most important points made by T. A. Larson and the others in their examination of early suffrage is that small elite groups of males were most influential in the nineteenth-century territories which finally adopted suffrage. There was a strong movement in a number of territories for suffrage: in most it failed. In Montana, Utah, and Idaho, where it succeeded, religious and party politics most often determined success. The fluid political situation in the West made suffrage a possibility at a time when it could not be considered in the East.[98]

How the masses of western men reacted to demands for suffrage became much more important when state suffrage became an issue. Third party movements like the Populists and Progressives, general discontent or political apathy, the position of unions on suffrage, temperance issues, rural-urban splits, immigrants, and religious differences, all affected campaigns for state suffrage. What seems to have occurred in the West, earlier than in the East, was an urban swing to support suffrage which carried unions, middle-class reform leaders, and Socialists into the suffrage ranks. This swing began soon enough to undercut movements to repeal or restrict earlier suffrage extension by territorial governments and at the same time to push state suffrage through.[99]

Most important for carrying suffrage in the West, however, was the emergence of the women's movement as a mass movement among western urban middle-class women, who elaborated social group structures and then political structures. The active leadership and organizational activities of Mormon women in state suffrage campaigns in Utah, Idaho, and Arizona had important implications not only for the suffrage movement but also for the later movement for the equal rights amendment in the West. Mormon women had their own societies committed to women's suffrage, and allies in the male Mormon hierarchy. During the suffrage campaigns Mormon women worked with gentile (non-Mormon) women in important coalitions: in Utah, they campaigned hard to retain suffrage in 1895; in Idaho, they helped swing an entire section of the state to suffrage in 1896; and in Arizona, they provided leadership for the suffrage success in 1912. The absence of Mormon women from the pro–Equal Rights Amendment ranks has drastically changed the pattern of the women's movement in the West more recently and weakened it considerably.[100]

Women's clubs, temperance unions, and eventually Equal Suffrage Leagues paralleled Mormon organizational structures. These groups had enough money and expertise to launch widespread media campaigns which included newspapers with large circulations, vast numbers of pamphlets, and posters. Assistance from eastern suffrage organizations, either in the form of money or leadership or both, was often crucial. The establishment of political formations organized at the precinct level accounted for the final success in a number of states. Highly sophisticated political planning carried California, the first urban industrial state to enact women's suffrage.[101]

The richness of these suffrage studies seems to hide their limitations. Suffrage is virtually the only aspect of western women's political history yet studied in depth. This focus on suffrage as the most important aspect of the western women's movement has excluded a broader approach to women and politics in the West. It has excluded, for example, the question of what happened to the women's movement after suffrage. There are hints in several of the works on suffrage that coalitions which emerged early in the West to bring suffrage as a part of progressive politics also disintegrated early. Support for women's suffrage in the East and ratification of the Nineteenth Amendment were not easily obtained in the West once success at the state level had been achieved there. Repression of Socialist and militant labor movements in the 1920s sheared off potential support for women's issues.[102] Californians Annette Abbott Adams and Katharine Edson held federal office in the 1920s but we have no analysis of how many women held federal office and what this meant in terms of political power.[103] In some western states, women fought in the 1920s for the other rights still not granted by state laws. They also held a large number of state offices. The careers of Nellie Ross, first woman governor of Wyoming and first woman to hold gubernatorial office in the United States, and Miriam Ferguson, who was elected governor of Texas in 1924, need to be studied in the context of political activities of women in the West, not just in relation to the political careers of their husbands.[104]

Focus on suffrage has also led to neglect of other political movements in the West which interested women. Many were active in the pacifist movement in the 1920s and the 1930s. Hard battles were fought by women in political movements and in political parties on issues which were, at least in part, women's issues. The movement of women into the Republican and Democratic parties during the 1930s, and the activities of women in the Socialist and Communist parties, all need to be considered more carefully before any type of overall appraisal can be made about women's political power in the West.[105]

Political analysis has yet to go beyond the activities of the middle-class women in the West to include Afro-American, Hispanic, or Native American women. During the Montana suffrage campaign a woman dressed as Sacajawea, the woman who accompanied Lewis and Clark on their expedition to the Pacific, marched in a parade of suffragists who had adopted Sacajawea as a symbol of Native American women's importance in the early West. Yet the interest of Euro-American women seemed seldom to extend beyond interest in Sacajawea as a symbol to the political realities of Indian women who, as a whole, were disfranchised until 1924 or much later in western states. Western Native American women played important roles within their own tribes and in the last decade have emerged as political leaders in the West, but their political activities have yet to be studied systematically.[106]

Hispanic women are almost never discussed in relation to women's rights. Historians have sometimes attributed the lack of suffrage in New Mexico to Hispanic males, the assumption being that if they were opposed, then certainly the women were inactive. Male New Mexico politicians used the argument that Hispanic males would not accept women's suffrage to defeat a Populist women's suffrage resolution in the 1890s, but it is by no means clear that their argument was true. The governor later responsible for calling a special legislative session in 1920 to ratify the women's suffrage amendment was Hispanic. Although the Equal Suffrage League in New Mexico was dominated by women with non-Spanish surnames, Hispanic women were already active in local politics. How Hispanic women worked within the political structure with men of their culture needs to be more carefully analyzed. While economics and political repression of the Hispanic population in most states obviously retarded the movement of women into electoral politics, they have emerged in more recent campaigns as an important element in achieving political equality.[107]

The role of black women is equally neglected. The political tradition which allowed a Barbara Jordan in Texas and Yvonne Braithwaite Burke in California may be different from the tradition in the eastern and southern states. Studies of the crucial years between 1930 and 1960 may reveal the base of black women's political power in these states.[108]

While historians have found middle-class women an important and obvious part of western history, the history of labor politics is still dominated by male unionization. In the early twentieth century, garment manufacturers migrated into the Southwest specifically to take advantage of low wages being paid to Hispanic and Asian women in factories and sweatshops. The politicization of this industrialized female work force began in the Depression. Hispanic women struck and attempted to organize, often fighting union leaders from the East, and union structures with which they could not identify. Although women emerged as leaders in the garment industry as well as in farm worker struggles, in food processing strikes, and even occasionally in male miner's strikes, they could seldom maintain decision-making positions in the male-dominated labor movement as long as its power base remained in industries utilizing primarily male labor. The lack of success of western working-class women in molding unions into instruments for their own needs undoubtedly delayed the political education of larger groups of women to long-term political activity.[109]

What is most needed is a picture of how women fit into the economic structure in the West through their labor. Occupational or labor history is inadequately or insufficiently described by historians. This neglect is due only in part to the concentration on industries utilizing primarily male labor in the West, such as mining. It is also due to defects in the census system which often failed to record women's work, to an ideological framework which devalued women's work, and to the absence of conceptual frameworks to study women's labor history in the West.

Rural western women seem to have been particularly industrious yet were often excluded from census returns because their work on the farm was not considered a full-time occupation in the nineteenth century. Mormon women are one group of western women noted for their industriousness on the early frontier. Within a church which emphasized "busyness," Mormon women worked industriously in many occupations to contribute their share to the household economy.[110] Plural marriages, large families, and a religious community with an almost mercantilistic economic theory led women into hard and steady work during the nineteenth century, often at jobs not visible to the census takers. Not only census takers, but the ideology of an ethnic group itself could mask the work of women. Among Italian eastern urban immigrants, for example, a woman's work was often not defined as work at all. Among Polish immigrants, on the other hand, women proudly claimed the title of "worker." Such differences must have existed in the West as well.[111]

A variety of women's rural production activities never appeared on the census returns. Labor performed in the home for use and production of small quantities of goods for local markets continued far longer in the West than in the East. Butter production in the Midwest, sales of eggs, poultry, and vegetables gave farm families precious cash they needed to survive and to buy farm equipment and additional land.[112] Health care likewise continued to be handled by women in parts of the West. Mormon midwives, Hispanic *curanderas*, and Native American herbalists carried this tradition into the twentieth century.[113] The work of prostitutes who crowded into western mining and railroad towns was usually not enumerated as "wage-labor," yet thousands worked in San Francisco, in Denver, and in El Paso as well as in smaller towns. Often prostitutes were forced to pay "fines" to continue to practice. They provided thousands of dollars in revenues to cities. Like the foreign miner's tax which supported the state of California for nearly a decade, the fines on prostitutes allowed officials to avoid taxing the more affluent classes while maintaining control over a group of social outcasts. Immigrant women, especially Asian women, were condemned for this type of work, but foreign prostitutes were only a small proportion of the total number of women employed in this occupation in the West.[114]

Other kinds of work, like elementary school teaching, could also be underenumerated because of the high turnover. Historians have over-emphasized the higher education of women, neglecting to document the spread of elementary education and the teaching of elementary education by women. Far larger numbers of women had experiences in teaching than census returns indicate because they moved into and out of the teacher work force fairly rapidly. By the late nineteenth century, normal schools were beginning to appear in the West, and Euro-American women were moving into the last male teaching domains in the Southwest. Their dominance in the teaching profession, in an area where the federal and state governments were attempting to create political and cultural dominance for Euro-Americans, involved them in highly volatile situations. Segregation, the suppression of Native American and Spanish languages in the schools, and the substitution of eastern unified educational norms for community control were all part of a western educational system in which women were dominant at the lowest level.[115]

Of the jobs enumerated, historians agree that women in the West were little different in job patterns than women in the East. The easiest job for a woman to get was that of household worker, and if there was a typical western woman by occupation, she would be a woman who worked in a rural or urban household for another woman. No one has yet studied these most typical of western women who were of all ethnic backgrounds.[116]

In the West there were few female towns, like the textile mill towns of the East, where women sometimes composed 30 to 40 percent of the labor force or southern towns, where black women had high labor participation rates. In towns like Denver, Kansas City, and San Francisco, 10 to 14 percent of the labor forces was female by 1880, while in Minneapolis, St. Paul, and St. Louis, 15 to 19 percent of the labor force was female. Towns in the West remained service-based far longer than towns in the East, thus ensuring that a high proportion of employed women would remain in service industries, but the extent to which women have moved into the western labor force in the twentieth century is still often underestimated.[117] The range of work of Hispanic women has been particularly misrepresented by popular stereotypes. Today in the Far West there is little difference in the urban labor force participation of women of different ethnic groups. In Los Angles in 1975, employment statistics showed there was virtually no difference in the percentage of Hispanic, "white," and black women working. The main difference was that proportionately far more Hispanic women worked as operatives in manufacturing industries than did other women.[118]

Older working women can still fill in the context of their working lives through oral history programs now in progress. In New Mexico, for example, women who homesteaded in 1908 are describing their experiences. Chicanas who ran farms while their husbands worked in the mines before World War I and Apache women who tanned and sold hides are telling their stories. One Navajo woman interviewed recently talked about her grandmother's work as a medicine woman, her mother's work as a weaver, and her own work as a cook after being forced to attend a government boarding school.[119] The experiences of women in the West are alive in the memories of women living today, and through these experiences historians can begin to know the women of each of the cultures and how they together became the women of the West.

A multicultural approach need not eliminate class or politics from western women's history. Rather, it can insure that the problems of political power and the political dimensions of the social history are not ignored.[120] Women of the West were divided not only by culture but also by the conflicts among cultures. The point where women crossed boundaries to share common interests as women can be as carefully noted and analyzed as the points at which they remained separate. With a broader comparative perspective, many of the previous assumptions and generalizations about western history may be questioned. Some generalizations will prove adequate and survive; others will undoubtedly have to be abandoned. But out of the testing will come a more representative history of both men and women in the West.

The objection is still sometimes made to historians of women, as it was to historians of the black experience in America a decade ago, that the materials to answer questions about women simply do not exist.

One does have to know where and how to look for material, but the documents and artifacts left by women are immense. Oral history is rapidly expanding the body of documentary evidence. Interdisciplinary approaches, particularly anthropology and sociology, are providing methods by which the economic activities and social relations of large numbers of women who left no personal documents can become a part of written history. The case-study approach will continue to provide valuable insights about western women, but we need, above all else, studies firmly based on a comparative multicultural approach to women's history in order to understand fully the western experience. Women's history has developed sophisticated techniques of dealing with the reality of women's past. It is ready now to cross the reef and be anchored in the harbor of historical studies. Much of this work will have to take place in that historiographical area west of the Mississippi which we still designate western history.

---

* The authors are members of the history department at New Mexico State University.

Jensen-Miller
Prize
1990

'At Their Peril': Utah Law and the Case of Plural Wives, 1850–1900

Carol Cornwall Madsen

VARIOUS studies have examined the politics, the sociology, the economics, and the evolution of the relationship between the Mormon church and the federal government attendant to the Mormon practice of polygamy during Utah's territorial history. A relevant but lesser known aspect of the subject is the impact of Utah's domestic relations laws on plural wives, as these laws were shaped by polygamy and the federal efforts to abolish it. While all polygamists were at legal risk, plural wives were vulnerable not only to criminal prosecution but also to permanent legal discrimination because of their unorthodox marital choice.

Joseph Smith, Mormon church founder, introduced the practice of plural marriage in 1843 as a restored biblical principle in Mormon theology.[1] It was practiced privately until 1852, three years after the church settled in isolated Utah. Then it was publicly announced as a tenet of Mormon doctrine. While personal disputes arising from and within the practice were theoretically governed exclusively by ecclesiastical authority, the Mormon-dominated legislature sought to

★ Carol Cornwall Madsen, "'At Their Peril': Utah Law and the Case of Plural Wives, 1850–1900," *Western Historical Quarterly* 21 (1990). © 1990 Western Historical Society Quarterly, Western History Association. Reprinted by permission.

bring those issues under legal protection as well. Though never inserting the word "polygamy" into any statute, the Utah legislature framed laws that favored the practice without seeming unduly incongruent with the law in other states and territories, thus avoiding special scrutiny by the U.S. Congress.

Initial efforts to legally safeguard the practice were generally successful for several reasons. When Utah obtained territorial status in the Compromise of 1850, it became subject to the control of a federally appointed governor and judiciary. With the appointment of church president Brigham Young as first governor and the election of an all-Mormon legislature, however, Mormon legislative initiative was ensured. Secondly, an unusual, though not unique, legislative move attempted to place judicial control in Mormon hands as well. One of the first acts of the legislature in 1851 was to extend the prerogatives of the probate courts, which normally heard only civil cases. Broadly construing the meaning of the territorial Organic Act, which stipulated that the authority of the probate courts "shall be limited by law," the legislature granted original jurisdiction in both civil and criminal cases to the probate courts, whose officers the legislature was also empowered to appoint.[2] Thus, probate courts possessed concurrent jurisdiction with the district courts and offered an alternative to the federally appointed, non-Mormon officers of the district courts.[3]

Another effort by the territorial legislature to enact protective legislation was rejection of the common law in 1854. Since bigamy was prohibited by common law, this legislative act could be construed as permitting legal recognition of plural marriage.[4]

Thus, until Congress passed the Morrill Act in 1862, the first federal law specifically prohibiting bigamy, and the 1874 Poland Act restricting the jurisdiction of the Utah probate courts, the legal protection of Mormon institutions was relatively free of federal intervention.[5]

Most Mormons simply avoided the courts, as far as possible, by settling their disputes within an ecclesiastical court system established early in the history of the church. Presided over by bishops of each ward (ecclesiastical unit) at the first level, it provided an appellate system rising from the bishop's court to the high council court (comprising representatives from several wards), and ultimately reaching to the first presidency of the church (the president and two counselors).

On 4 February 1831, a year after the church was organized, Edward Partridge was appointed bishop over the church and empowered to "see to all things as it shall be appointed unto him" regarding the laws given to govern the church.[6] Four days later, Joseph Smith outlined the procedure for removing unrepentant members from the church in a statement embracing "the law and discipline" of the church. For murder, theft, and lying, the offender was subject to the law of the land, but for adultery and other domestic disputes, the case was to be brought before the elders of the church (ordained male members), including the bishop, if the dispute could not be settled privately.[7]

On 1 August 1831 the bishop was instructed that he was "to judge his people by the testimony of the just, and by the assistance of his counselors."[8] While this directive established the framework for what came to be known as bishops' courts, early practice varied as to the number of elders and church members who attended them. Disciplinary action was often interspersed with other church business and generally voted upon by all those assembled.[9]

On 17 February 1834 the first high council for the church was organized in Kirtland, Ohio, then church headquarters, to settle difficulties unresolved by the bishops' courts.[10] In the council minutes, additional procedural due process is detailed. Though intended to act as an appellate body to review decisions of the "bishop's council," in practice the high council often assumed original jurisdiction.[11] The first presidency of the church or a member thereof presided over the high council.[12] This pattern was further modified on 28 March 1835 when the first presidency was retained as the presiding quorum of the church; and the Quorum of Twelve Apostles, next to the first presidency in authority, was designated a "traveling Presiding High Council" to serve as a supervisory and appellate body above the "standing" high councils.[13]

Church leaders urged members to use ecclesiastical courts rather than traditional legal courts, even in Mormon-dominated Nauvoo, Illinois, where the church was headquartered from 1839 to 1846. Though the city court judge was a Mormon and the resident justice of the peace was a friend of the Mormons, later converting to Mormonism, church members settled most of their disputes in bishops' or high council courts, a situation which prefigured Utah practice.

With the exodus west, settlements were established along the way, complete with wards, bishops, and high councils (where appropriate), the most notable of which were at Winter Quarters, Nebraska, and Kanesville, Pottawattamie County, Iowa. In these frontier settlements, bishops' courts and high councils became, for the first time, the de facto civil, as well as ecclesiastical, tribunals.

A hearing held by the Pottawattamie high council on 9 July 1847, presided over by Apostle Orson Hyde, illustrates the informality of the procedure. The case involved a dispute between Joseph Meakam and William Carter. Testimony indicated that Carter had married or "covenanted" with Meakam's daughter, Cordelia, as a plural wife, and when she discovered him "to be a scoundrel," she had returned to her father's home, followed by Carter, who threatened that she and all wives who broke their covenants with him would be damned. Her father blamed her subsequent death on the stress she endured because of Carter's threats. Although Carter strenuously denied the charges, Apostle Hyde detected "a spirit manifest here for covering up facts."[14] Others testified to hearing William assert that covenant breakers would be damned, and Hyde reaffirmed "the spirit's prompting" to him in an interview with Carter that Carter was indeed untruthful.

Hyde then admonished Carter to confess, since he "had the witness within him," that Carter had lied in denying that he had preached false doctrine. When threatened with the loss of his church membership, his priesthood, as well as his wives, Carter finally confessed and pled for mercy. The unanimous vote of those assembled was to extend mercy to the defendant.[15]

Even though this court was the only governing judicial entity in Kanesville at the time, the sanctions it threatened to impose were ecclesiastical in nature. Though church courts were not uniformly consistent, the nature of the sanctions, the informality of the proceeding, and the presiding judge's reliance "on the spirit" for a just decision were generally typical of subsequent church court proceedings.[16]

Church courts were especially useful in settling domestic conflicts involving polygamy because of the practice's extralegal character.

Nevertheless, Mormon legislatures also attempted to protect the women and children involved in plural marriage by enacting laws based on principles governing church court decisions. Most of these protective laws fell into the category of domestic relations, including marriage, divorce, and succession or inheritance. Their checkered history illustrates the escalating tension between local attempts to preserve a religious practice and federal efforts to destroy it and the legal consequences for plural wives.[17]

For its first four decades, Utah law had no provisions for the civil licensing and registration of marriage. The only marriage law of the period was included in an ordinance incorporating the church, which authorized it to "solemnize marriages compatible with the revelations of Jesus Christ."[18] This ordinance provided for "a registry of marriages," but it was to be kept only in the branches or stakes of the church. No civil record was required until the Edmunds–Tucker Act established regulatory measures in 1887. Thus, polygamous alliances did not need to become a matter of public record. In 1862, the Morrill Act specifically declared bigamous marriages illegal, but not until 1876 did the church-owned *Deseret Evening News* concede that the practice was "not recognized by the law of the land."[19] Polygamy continued to be practiced by church members, however, for another fourteen years, until 1890, when church president Wilford Woodruff suspended the performance of any further plural marriages.

Though polygamy was denounced as a system of female bondage by non-Mormons, the liberality of Utah's divorce laws and the ease with which church divorces were granted belied this perception. As historian Lawrence Foster has noted, in polygamous Utah, contrary to prevailing opinion, women enjoyed more freedom in terms of marriage and divorce than women in other polygamous cultures.[20] Though easy divorce seems incongruous with the Mormon theological focus on the eternity of marriage and propriety of plural marriage, the religious faithfulness and mutual affection of the participants were the primary determinants of a successful union. As early as 1842, according to one account, Joseph Smith taught that marriage was a covenant between two people and if it had not been conducive of blessings and peace, they were free to separate since "it was a sin for people to live together and raise or beget children, in alienation from each other."[21] The sin, according to Mormon thought, was not in divorce but in perpetuating the form of marriage and the begetting of children without the cementing bond of affection. The decision in an 1847 divorce case brought before the high council in Winter Quarters, Nebraska, invoked this tenet: "No man or woman should ever be compelled to live together who cannot live in union. You two now are to separate and not come together again."[22]

In 1861, Brigham Young, successor to Joseph Smith, reiterated this principle. "When a woman becomes alienated in her feelings and affections from her husband, it is then his duty to give her a bill and set her free," he said in a church conference. To continue to live together when a wife had become alienated from her husband was to violate the marriage covenant. Moreover, if a man proved to be an "unworthy" husband and father, he automatically forfeited his marriage covenants, and his wife or wives were "free from him without a bill of divorcement."[23] The sanctity and perpetuation of a marriage, as a holy sacrament, were contingent on the righteousness of the couple and the retention of affection between them. Two cases brought before a Fillmore, Utah, bishop in 1883 illustrate the value placed on affection in marriage. "Although her [the applicant's] grounds are not just," the bishop reported to church president John Taylor (successor to Brigham Young), "in our opinion it would not be wise to compel her to continue to be the wife of her husband inasmuch as she claims that she does not now nor never did have any affection for him." In another instance, though the bishop again felt the complaining wife did not have sufficient grounds for divorce, she had expressed such hostility to her husband that he was willing to recommend a divorce and "leave the matter to the judgment of President [John] Taylor."[24]

Church leaders continually preached against divorce and urged the reconciliation of estranged couples, but when conciliatory efforts failed, then they advised an expeditious separation and settlement. "Parties should be advised to learn how to live together in peace," Brigham Young counseled in 1851, "but if it is best for them to separate," the husband should give the wife and children "a large proportion of the property."[25] Plural wives were particularly admonished to bear their burdens uncomplainingly and "not to expect heaven on earth but to prepare for it in due time."[26] Nevertheless, they were speedily granted divorces when desired. Extant records show that more than 1,600 applicants, most of them women, received ecclesiastical divorces before polygamy was suspended in 1890.[27]

While both men and women appealed to church courts for divorce, men were almost routinely refused, except in compelling circumstances, while women were seldom denied their requests.[28] In typical earthy imagery, Brigham Young told one male petitioner, "If you have drawn a red hot iron between your legs and scorched yourself, bear it without grunting, and if it smarts, grease it. . . . I want the brethren to stop divorcing their wives, for it is not right. I do not want to grant divorces."[29] The preferential treatment given women is consistent with Young's explanation of the sin of begetting children in alienation of affections and reflects the relative ease with which women could remarry in polygamous Utah, as well as the voluntary nature of the practice of polygamy. A church divorce confidentially and expeditiously released women unable to bear the emotional or physical burdens of plural marriage.

The governing policies for church divorces transferred into civil law in 1852, when the territorial legislature attached an incompatibility clause to the traditional grounds for divorce (impotency, adultery, desertion, habitual drunkenness, felony conviction, and abusive treatment). In words similar to those used in church divorce actions, the statute provided that divorce could be granted "when it shall be made to appear to the satisfaction and conviction of the court, that the parties cannot live in peace and union together, and that their welfare requires a separation."[30] The law also provided a minimal residency requirement. Anyone who was or "wished to become" a resident of Utah could invoke the jurisdiction of the court.[31] While various explanations have been tendered for Utah's adoption of such a liberal statute, it is consistent with Mormon legislative efforts to facilitate and protect the practice of polygamy with laws that reflected church court policies and practices.[32]

Although Utah was among the 20 percent of states and territories with the highest divorce rate, it was lower than nearly all of its western neighbors during the first twenty-year period for which national divorce statistics were compiled (1867–1887).[33] More than a third of Utah civil divorces during this time utilized the incompatibility clause, 71 percent of them granted during a single three-year period, 1875 to 1877. In fact, the total number of civil divorces granted in Utah more than tripled between 1875 and 1877, dropping back to its 1874 level in 1878. Four Utah counties registered precipitous increases, but the most dramatic occurred in the small southern Utah county of Beaver, where divorces jumped from two in 1874 to 108 in 1875 and 358 the next year. Of a total of 691 divorces in Beaver County during this twenty-year period, 91 percent were granted between 1875 and 1877. This aberration did not reflect an unusual season of marital discontent, but an exploitation of Utah's divorce law by non-Utah divorce lawyers, who found its open residency requirement and completion of the transcontinental railroad (in 1869) an irresistible combination. For example, of the 691 Beaver divorces, only seventy-five involved bona fide Utah residents. All the others were migratory divorces brought by residents of eastern states "wishing," for a day, to become residents of Utah.[34] The probate judges in these counties facilitated the use of their courts by eastern divorce lawyers, creating a short-lived, but active, divorce mill in Utah.

Alarmed at the flagrant abuse of Utah's divorce law, Governor George W. Emery strongly urged the legislature to amend the law in 1876, but not until a grand jury investigation the following year and another urgent appeal by Governor Emery, in 1878, did the Mormon legislature reluctantly eliminate the offending provisions.[35] A *Deseret News* article explained the reluctance: "Polygamy would be considered a system of bondage, if women desiring to sever their relations with a husband having other wives, were refused the liberty they might demand."[36] Though plural wives could not utilize civil courts for divorce, first wives could. Moreover, the liberal divorce law contradicted the popular image of the enslaved wife in Utah. Thus, Mormon legislators agreed to reformulate the law only when convinced its abuse by non-Mormons had overshadowed its value to Mormons.

Rigid jurisdictional distinctions were not always maintained in divorce suits. In 1872, when Emmaline Kesler elected to divorce her husband, Frederick, of thirty-six years, she filed in district court. Three weeks later, at her husband's urging, she withdrew her suit from the gentile-governed district court and refiled it in the Mormon-administered probate court, where the judge awarded her a bill of divorce three weeks later on the grounds that "said parties cannot live together in peace and union."[37]

Thirteen months later, Abigail Kesler, Frederick's plural wife of fourteen years, also left him. Informing Kesler by mail that she would not ask for a divorce for the sake of her children, she requested only a portion of his property to support them. Before receiving a reply, however, Abigail visited Brigham Young and secured a bill of divorce and his word that she was entitled to a third of her husband's estate, valued then at $12,000. In response to Kesler's inquiry about the matter, Brigham Young wrote: "Your wife Abigail called upon me, stated her feelings and requested a bill, which under the circumstances we thought proper to grant her, as is usual when a woman insists upon one. . . ."[38] While appeals for church divorces generally originated in bishops' courts, from which recommendations were sent to the first presidency for decisions, some applicants skirted this procedure and appealed directly to the church president. Moreover, Brigham Young sometimes suggested a choice of venue. In 1870, he advised Maria Jarman to apply "either to Bro. Elias Smith, Probate judge of Salt Lake County, or to this office, and procure a bill at any time." It is not clear whether Maria Jarman was a first or plural wife, but it is clear that Young and Smith did not have comparable jurisdiction. Young also occasionally instructed probate judges on the disposition of cases, as he did in the divorce suit of Sarah Hutchenson, advising Judge Elias Smith "that it would be proper" to grant Sarah a divorce from her long-absent husband.[39]

Numerous legal entanglements resulted from this blurring of jurisdictional boundaries. For example, in 1870 Eleanor and Elbridge Tufts decided to terminate their marriage of one year and were granted a church divorce. Both remarried. Upon learning twenty years later that the church divorce was not valid, Eleanor ceased living with John Wickel, her second husband, and sued Tufts for divorce. The divorce was still pending in 1895 when Tufts died. Eleanor then filed claim for a dower interest in his property as his only legal wife. The claim was granted by the trial court and affirmed by the Utah Supreme Court.[40] In a similar case decided three years later, John R. Park, an early Utah educator, married Annie Armitage, a young convert, in 1872 at her bedside, believing her to be on her death-bed but wishing to secure an eternal marriage for them both. When Annie unexpectedly recovered, the two agreed to separate and obtained a church divorce the following year. Park never remarried, but Annie married and bore ten children. At Park's demise in 1902, Annie sued to recover a dower interest in property conveyed by Park before his death, claiming her right as his widow, since her church divorce from him was not valid. Though she lost her case in trial court, the Utah Supreme Court reversed the decision and she recovered her widow's share.[41]

Divorce became less relevant following the 1890 suspension of church-sanctioned plural marriage, and a clear distinction between ecclesiastical and civil marriages and divorces took effect in Utah. The next several decades represented a period of legal adjustment for plural wives and children, many of whom found themselves in a state of legal limbo regarding their inheritance rights.[42]

Like Utah's early marriage and divorce laws, laws of succession also attempted to accommodate the needs of plural wives and children.[43] An 1852 statute rather ambiguously provided that in the absence of a will, and after payment of the liabilities of a man's estate, whatever property remained would "descend in equal shares to his children or their heirs; one share . . . through the mother of such children or if he has had more than one wife, who either died or survived in lawful wedlock, it shall be equally divided between the living and the heirs of those who are dead. . . ."[44]

Written ten years before passage of the Morrill Act outlawing bigamy, the phrase "lawful wedlock" as it referred to additional wives was not necessarily contradictory. The following section, however, went beyond the implied rights of plural wives in the first section to provide that "illegitimate children and their mothers" shall inherit "in like manner."[45]

Mary Ann Maughan, widow of Peter Maughan of northern Utah's Cache Valley, noted the inherent inequity in the "equal distribution to all heirs" of the property in a polygamous marriage. Though she was married thirty years and raised ten children, she was irked to learn that since it was ruled "best for all to share alike," the two-year-old son of her sister wife, Lissy, "was awarded just as much as I was."[46]

A further provision of the 1852 law allowed illegitimate children and their mothers to inherit from the father, whether acknowledged by him or not, if it could be demonstrated that he was the father. Succession cases indicate this was the statute that granted plural wives inheritance rights.

In 1876, at the urging of Governor George W. Emery, the legislature amended the statute to require that the father acknowledge the illegitimate heirs before they inherit to avoid the possibility of fraudulent claims and to prevent injustice to legitimate heirs. It also reluctantly removed the heritable rights of mothers of illegitimate children to conform to the requirements of the Morrill Act, which not only made bigamy a crime, but also nullified all territorial laws that appeared to "establish, support, maintain, shield or countenance polygamy."[47] Since the Mormon-controlled probate courts were allowed to retain jurisdiction in the settlement of estates after the federal Poland Bill of 1874 transferred all other civil and criminal jurisdiction to the district courts, succession claims could continue to be settled before sympathetic judges. Where succession or inheritance claims were heard, however, depended on the disposition of the first wife, who could press her legal claims in a territorial court or defer to an ecclesiastical court to decide the distribution of the estate. The Gunnell wives of Cache Valley, unlike Mary Ann Maughan, were subject to the later laws providing only for illegitimate children. When Francis Gunnell died in 1889, his second wife Emma "was left nothing, not being recognized by law as a wife. Everything was left to the first living wife, Aunt Esther, and some property divided among the children." The children combined their small inheritance and built a home for their mother.[48] The silence of the law on plural wives' inheritance from their intestate husbands required them to find relief primarily through church courts or through the generosity of their children. Even plural wives who were beneficiaries of a will found themselves in a state of dependency. Emily Dow Partridge Young, widow of Brigham Young, shared in his estate, but found the limitations of her widowhood demeaning. A widow "is left to the mercy of his [sic] children," she complained. "They are given preeminence, while the wife and mother is ignored. Even my home, that I hold the deed of," she angrily noted, "is given to my children and I am not allowed the right to own anything but am fed with a spoon like a baby."[49]

When prosecution of polygamists under the Morrill Act failed, Congress passed more stringent anti-polygamy legislation in 1882 (Edmunds Act) and 1887 (Edmunds-Tucker Act). The Edmunds Act affirmed the legality of the inheritance rights of illegitimate children born prior to January 1883, but did not acknowledge any rights of plural wives. In debate on the bill, Senator George F. Edmunds (R-VT) declared that "this bill does not leave any polygamous woman in any worse condition in point of law than she is at the moment, but it leaves her children in an infinitely better condition, because it makes them legitimate."[50] The Edmunds-Tucker Act, while annulling all laws providing for the capacity of illegitimate children to inherit, also included a "saving clause" as to those children legitimated by the Edmunds Act and all others born within twelve months after its own passage in 1887.[51]

In *Chapman v. Handley,* a suit brought in 1890 by the "illegitimate" offspring of George Handley, who died in 1874, and his plural wife Mary, the Utah Supreme Court held that the 1852 territorial law that gave illegitimate children the right to inherit from their fathers had been superseded by the 1862 Morrill Act, which disallowed any laws that supported polygamy. The Court thus denied the petitioners their claim of inheritance.[52] The United States Supreme Court, however, ruling on a similar case, *Cope v. Cope,* reversed the judgment of the Utah court and found that the legislature was free to provide for illegitimate children to inherit from their mother, father, or both, declaring that it was "unjust to visit the sins of the parents on the heads of the children."[53] The United States Supreme Court seemed more willing than Utah's judiciary to interpret the Morrill Act broadly, distinguishing between the rights of illegitimate children to legal protection and the illegal actions of their parents. The irony and ultimate tragedy, however, derive from the obvious disparity between the intent of Congress to protect the moral and social interests of Mormon women by freeing them from polygamy and its subsequent failure to protect their economic or legal status.[54]

Nor were plural wives given legal status by the first legislature of the State of Utah that, in 1896, passed a law legitimating *all* issue of bigamous and polygamous marriages contracted prior to that year and providing that such children could inherit from both parents, but making no provisions for plural wives.[55] The importance of writing wills was never so apparent. One astute daughter, Anne Leishman of Cache Valley, Utah, urged her father to make a will. "My mother would come in all right if he dies for a home and things," she explained, "but Aunt Betsy [his plural wife] would only be treated as a child. . . . . She can't write a check, she can't sign a deed, she can't do anything."[56] More than her husband or children, the plural wife experienced the penalities of living beyond the boundaries of the law.

The common law right of dower, granting a widow a one-third interest in her husband's real property, if he died intestate, and a one-third inchoate interest during his life-time, was obviously inoperative in polygamy, and the Utah legislature formally abolished dower in 1872.[57] Since dower had been abolished, never enacted, or modified in other areas in the United States, Utah's legislation could not be construed as a wholly unique accommodation to the imperatives of plural marriage, but was clearly enacted to equalize the claims of plural wives on their husbands' estates.[58] It also left polygamous husbands free to distribute their estates equitably by will. Mormon critics viewed the law as one more legal support of polygamy by breaking down the distinction between lawful and plural wives. One 1882 critic observed that abolition of dower rendered "a polygamous wife slavishly dependent on the husband's favor for any share of his property after his death" and urged repeal of the measure to protect the interests of the legal wife who, in polygamy, he said "is not the favorite as a general rule."[59] Absence of dower effectively diminished a legal wife's claim, by withdrawing her inchoate interest in her husband's property during his lifetime and granting her only an equal share with all of her husband's direct heirs at his death.

In 1887, dower was reinstated by the Edmunds-Tucker Act. Its reinstitution continued to work against the legal interests of plural wives, even as sole surviving wives of their husbands. In one case, for example, the first wife died and the surviving plural wife claimed at the death of her husband that she was entitled to dower as the legal wife under the principles of common law marriage. The court denied her claim, rejecting the evidence of common law marriage and ruling in essence that her original marriage as a plural wife was invalid and did not assume legality upon the death of the first or legal wife.[60] In another instance, Emily P. Raleigh sued for her dower right, as a sole surviving wife, in a piece of property willed by her husband to a mutual investment company. Though she had occupied the property for forty-six years and claimed it as a gift from her husband, the court ruled against her claim declaring that whatever misfortune she felt had befallen her was a result of her own volition. She made the choice to become a plural wife, the court asserted, "at her peril," failing thereby "to acquire the status of a lawful wife." She was, therefore, "without the pale of the law, of inheritance as to any property which her husband had acquired or might thereafter acquire."[61]

Polygamy impinged less directly upon the development of Utah's property law. While dower clearly mitigated the property claims of a plural wife, passage of a Married Person's Property Act at the same time dower was abolished in 1872 protected the property owned by all women at marriage. The act allowed each spouse to retain and control the property each brought to the marriage, as well as that acquired afterwards.[62] While the repeal of dower was opposed by non-Mormons, the Property Act was hailed by Mormon women as progressive and far more in keeping with the times respecting the advancing legal rights of married women.[63]

Utah law was amended by federal statute or judicial decree in two non-domestic areas that also affected the status of plural wives. In 1870, the territorial legislature enfranchised women, only the second legislature in the country to do so. Originally proposed by several members of U.S. Congress as a means of empowering plural wives to throw off the yoke of polygamy, woman suffrage was seized on by Mormon lawmakers to counteract the perception of the subjugated plural wife. From 1870 until 1887, woman suffrage was inextricably linked to polygamy by non-Mormons, who feared it would strengthen Mormon political hegemony. Every congressional measure proposed to curtail the practice included repeal of woman suffrage in Utah. Though eastern suffragists forcefully lobbied against repeal, the Edmunds Act finally denied polygamists the vote in 1882, and the Edmunds–Tucker

Act disenfranchised all Utah women in 1887. While a presidential amnesty in 1893 restored the vote to men who gave up polygamy, women were not reenfranchised until statehood in 1896.

A major tool in the prosecution of polygamists was the testimony of plural wives. But Utah's civil code, adopted in 1870, exempted husbands and wives from testifying against each other, unless the action involved one against the other. It was later amended to allow testimony against one by the other in cases of crimes committed by one on the other.[64] Federal prosecutors sought ways to circumvent this husband/wife privilege. While testimony from wives other than the first was admissible, since they were not legal wives, various approaches were applied to obtain testimony from first wives. In *United States v. Bassett,* in which the defendant's first wife agreed to testify, her testimony was ruled admissible by the Territorial Supreme Court, on the basis that polygamy was a crime against *her,* and, thus, under the civil code, she could testify. Moreover, it ruled that polygamy was also a crime of violence to her feelings, personal security, and her liberty, and she was, thus, allowed to testify under the criminal code as well. Since an exception to the husband/wife communication privilege was permitted under the criminal code when a "violent" crime was committed by one against the other, the prosecutors hoped to utilize that exception by declaring polygamy a crime of violence. When the case was appealed to the United States Supreme Court, however, it reversed the lower court's decision. It defined polygamy as a crime against the marital relation, rather than against the lawful wife and refused to acknowledge it as a crime of violence.[65] Thus, the right of immunity excused first wives from testifying, but not being subject to this law, plural wives were required to testify against their husbands. Those who refused were cited for contempt, and several women were imprisoned.[66] In one more instance, plural wives stood outside the boundaries of the law.

While in most respects the development of law in territorial Utah followed principles of the common law, despite legislative efforts to disclaim it, Mormon lawmakers attempted to shape the law, as far as possible, to fit the necessities of a unique family structure. Throughout Utah's territorial period, the law underwent repeated modification, as federal law and judicial decree reshaped it to match the legal contours of the larger society. The Mormon-federal conflict, among other things, demonstrated the fluidity of law in its response to the social factors influencing it. On the local level, Utah laws protecting Mormon interests continually met defeat by the federally appointed judiciary. Yet, on the national level, while congressional lawmakers carved away those protective statutes, the U.S. Supreme Court often exerted a meliorating influence. The weight of congressional legislation, however, ultimately prevailed. Though their children, as innocent victims, were granted legal protection, polygamous husbands faced criminal prosecution and their plural wives, legal discrimination. While many polygamists escaped federal prosecution altogether and others paid the requisite penalties of a fine and a relatively brief imprisonment, all plural wives experienced the legal consequences of living outside the protective limits of the law. Moreover, while polygamous husbands ultimately regained their legal and political rights through a presidential amnesty, plural wives did not. Because far more women than men practiced polygamy, the legal ramifications for women were not only more permanent, they were more pervasive.

While polygamy contributed to the shaping of Utah's territorial law, it is instructive to recognize that the law was so formulated as to accommodate a marital style involving only about 25 or 30 percent of Utah's residents. Rather than reflecting or regulating the practices of the larger population of the territory, the law, in this case, attempted to protect the rights of the minority, sometimes at the expense of the majority. Only when met by coercive measures did Utah/Mormon lawmakers finally "render unto Caesar" the legal prerogatives they had claimed for themselves in pursuit of the establishment of their religious commonwealth, yielding to federal measures to bring the territory into legal harmony with the rest of the nation.

★ Carol Cornwall Madsen is an associate professor of history and senior research historian in the Joseph Fielding Smith Institute for Church History at Brigham Young University.

Race, Gender, and Intercultural Relations: the Case of Interracial Marriage

Peggy Pascoe

FOR scholars interested in the social construction of race, gender, and culture, few subjects are as potentially revealing as the history of interracial marriage. Clearly, the phenomenon of interracial marriage involves the making and remaking of notions of race, gender, and culture in individual lives, as well as at the level of social and political policy. Yet, the potential of the subject has barely been tapped. The vast majority of studies have been carried out by social scientists, who search for laws of social behavior that might either predict or account for the incidence of interracial marriage.[1] The handful of historians who have taken up the topic use their insight into change over time to expose flaws in nearly every theory social scientists have proposed. But whether historians focus on the actual patterns of intermarriage or on the enactment of laws against it, they tend to accept the social-scientific assumption that race and sex themselves are immutable categories, the "givens" of historical analysis; they stop short of investigating historical changes in notions of race and gender.[2]

* Peggy Pascoe, "Race, Gender, and Intercultural Relations: the Case of Interracial Marriage," *Frontiers: A Journal of Women's Studies* 12:1 (1991). © 1991 Frontiers, University of Nebraska Press. Reprinted by permission.

Assumptions like these are distinctly at odds with the work of both the vast majority of feminist scholars, who see gender as a social construction, and a growing group of ethnic studies scholars, who challenge the notion that race should be conceived of as a biological category. When I started to think about writing a history of interracial marriage, I found the gap between these two sets of assumptions at first puzzling, then intriguing. Now, I think it is a vital clue to the way a study of interracial marriage might address three central conceptual challenges faced by women's historians seeking to write multicultural history:

1. the challenge of exploring the interconnections between gender and race relations;

2. the challenge of learning to see race, as well as gender, as a social construction, and

3. the challenge of choosing a definition of culture suitable for writing intercultural history.

In this rather speculative essay, I will use my preliminary research on the history of interracial marriage in the U.S. West to offer some thoughts on each of these challenges.

First, however, a little background is in order. Probably the most intriguing aspect of the history of interracial marriage in the United States is that, although such marriages were infrequent throughout most of U.S. history, an enormous amount of time and energy was nonetheless spent in trying to prevent them from taking place.

From the colonial period clear through the mid-twentieth century, state legislators made it their business to pass laws designed to prohibit what they came by the 1860s to call *miscegenation*, a term that means mixture of the races. The laws were enacted first—and abandoned last—in the South, but it was in the West, not the South, that the laws became most elaborate. In the late nineteenth century, western legislators built a labyrinthine system of legal prohibitions on marriages between whites and Chinese, Japanese, Filipinos, Hawaiians, Hindus, and Native Americans, as well as on marriages between whites and blacks. Legislators targeted both interracial sex and interracial marriage, but the latter drew the strongest prohibitions and the most litigation, largely, I think, because marriage involved property obligations. Although most northern states repealed their prohibitions after the Civil War, in the South and the West, laws against miscegenation remained in force through much of the twentieth century. Many were erased from the books only after the Supreme Court declared them unconstitutional in 1967.[3]

Interracial marriage has been studied far more often by social scientists than by historians, but both groups have seen it primarily as an issue of race relations. Yet, as any historian of women would suspect, interracial marriage is also an issue of gender relations, in obvious and not-so-obvious ways. The first challenge in writing its history is to learn to see interracial marriage as a matter of both gender and race relations.

To begin with the obvious, the campaign to prohibit interracial marriage reflects U.S. gender hierarchies, as well as racial hierarchies. One of the very first prohibitions on interracial marriage, passed in Maryland in 1664, was straightforwardly sex-specific: it prohibited marriages between "freeborne English women" and "Negro slaves."[4] Although most other colonies and states framed their laws in more generic terms, New Mexico followed the Maryland model as late as 1857, prohibiting marriage between, to use the language of the law, "any woman of the white race" and any "free negro or mulatto."[5] In conjunction with laws that defined the children of slave women as slaves and laws that denied legal legitimacy to slave marriages, miscegenation statutes contributed to a context in which white women's sexuality was firmly controlled even as white men were allowed a great deal of informal sexual access to black women.[6]

As it turns out, sex-specific miscegenation laws, unusual as they were, provide clues to the gender hierarchies structured by the majority of miscegenation laws, which were technically gender-blind.[7] In the United States, these laws were most likely to pass when legislators proposed them in the wake of scandals over white women's participation in interracial relationships. My research indicates that the laws were applied most stringently to groups like the Chinese, Japanese, and Filipinos, whose men were thought likely to marry white women. They were applied least stringently to groups like the Native Americans (who were inconsistently mentioned in the laws) and Hispanics (who were not mentioned at all), groups whose women were historically likely to marry white men.

Another side of these gender and race hierarchies can be seen in the miscegenation cases that ended up in appeals courts. Until the mid-twentieth century, only a few of these cases were brought either by interracial couples seeking the right to marry or by law enforcement officials trying to prevent them from doing so. Most of the court cases were ex post facto attempts to invalidate interracial marriages that had already lasted for a long time. Such cases were brought by relatives or by the state after the death of one spouse, most often a white man. The lawsuits were designed with a specific purpose in mind: to take property or inheritances away from the surviving spouse, most often a woman of color.

This is what happened, for example, in the 1921 Oregon case of *In re Paquet's Estate*.[8] In this case, decided after the death of Fred Paquet (a white man), Ophelia Paquet (his Native American wife) lost control of her husband's estate to her late husband's brother John (a white man), who challenged her for its control. The language of Oregon's miscegenation law was broad: it declared null and void marriages between "any white person" and "any negro, Chinese, or any person having one fourth or more negro, Chinese, or Kanaka blood, or any person having more than one half Indian blood."[9] Under the provisions of this law, the Oregon Supreme Court declared the Paquets' thirty-year marriage invalid. To do so, the court dismissed Ophelia Paquet's claim that the miscegenation statute denied Native Americans the same rights as whites. Echoing state courts all over the country, the Oregon court held that the statute did not discriminate against Native Americans because, as the judge said, "It applies alike to all persons, either white, negroes, Chinese, Kanakas, or Indians."[10]

The elements of this decision—the primacy of the issue of property, the tug-of-war between women of color and their white opponents for control of white men's estates, and the willingness of courts to invalidate long-term marriages in proceedings not directly related to the marriages themselves—were quite standard in miscegenation case law. The only unusual note in this decision was that, having deprived

Ophelia Paquet of her inheritance, the court went out of its way to express its sympathy for her, suggesting to the victorious John Paquet that because Ophelia had been "a good and faithful wife" to his brother "for more than 30 years," he should consider offering her "a fair and reasonable settlement." [11]

This intertwining of gender and race hierarchies is the most obvious aspect of gender relations in interracial marriage, but it is not the only aspect. A different kind of story, one as much about social construction as about hierarchy, can be seen in interviews conducted with participants in interracial marriages. There is an abundance of such interviews because, beginning in the early twentieth century, social scientists who studied race relations grew fascinated with interracial marriage, which they saw as a prime index of assimilation. Perhaps the best-known of these interview projects is the Survey of Race Relations carried out by University of Chicago sociologist Robert Park. The survey, conducted up and down the Pacific Coast in the 1920s, resulted in several hundred interviews, including many with participants in interracial marriages. [12] A host of somewhat lesser-known sociologists and anthropologists, from Romanzo Adams in Hawaii to Manuel Gamio in the Southwest, shared Park's fascination with interracial marriage and also conducted interviews with participants.

Like most researchers after them, these early twentieth-century social scientists saw interracial marriage primarily as a matter of race relations. What is, however, most interesting to me as I look at the interviews is that individual men and women's decisions to cross racial boundary lines were often rooted in conceptions of gender relations. Consider, for example, the Hawaiian woman who told Romanzo Adams why so many Hawaiian women married non-Hawaiian men. "The Hawaiian men," she said, "are not steady workers and good providers. The Chinese men are good to provide, but they are stingy. The white men are good providers and they give their wives more money." [13] Her comment, of course, expresses race and class hierarchies, but both of these hierarchies are rooted in comparative definitions of manhood: note that she emphasized above all the desire to marry men who fit the role of "good provider." In choosing men they hoped would fit this role over men who may not even have aspired to do so, Hawaiian women shaped gender relations by promoting a particular definition of manhood. Much the same might be said of the post–World War II white soldiers who married Japanese women because, they said, Japanese women were more "feminine" than white women.[14]

These examples of the social construction of gender are specific to the history of interracial marriage, but the general concept of the social construction of gender is a familiar one to historians of women, who have long distinguished between the notion of sex (a biological category) and gender (a social construction). Although a vanguard of feminist theorists have recently begun to argue that the distinction is an artificial one, it is significant that they make the case that both sex and gender are social constructions; in this sense, their arguments demonstrate that, within feminist history, the notion that gender is a social construction is now considered so obvious as to be beyond dispute.

Unfortunately, the same point cannot yet be made about race. Consequently, the second conceptual challenge of writing a history of interracial marriage is to apply the same sophistication that women's historians use in tracing reformulations of gender to the analysis of reformulations of race.

Perhaps the most surprising thing I've learned by studying interracial marriage is how reluctant historians are to see race as a social construction. On one level, of course, any historian knows that race is, as Barbara J. Fields argues, a social category without real content; that is, social attitudes and institutions, not biological difference, sustain white dominance.[15] Yet, at the same time, most histories of racial groups—and most considerations of the role of race in women's history—tend to treat race as if it were a fixed biological marker, a reliable index to an unchanging history of social hierarchy.

So, in the late twentieth century, at a time when biologists themselves maintain that racial categories are so arbitrary as to carry no useful meaning at all, historians continue to refer to "race" as a factor in history, to speak of people of different "races" and to regard "racism" as a sort of prejudice rooted as much in individual psychological needs as in social history. Historians have tended to view race relations as a superstructure built on a biological base. Because their viewpoint has prevented them from seeing that race, like gender, is a social construction (the contours of which have undergone significant changes over time), a reassessment is needed.

Part of the problem, I think, is the lack of a term for *race* that functions in the same way as the term *gender*, that is, to signal a social construction distinct from biological classification. In the absence of such a term, historians tend to use the term race to refer to both biological categories and social relations, conflating the two in a way that makes it difficult to see race as a social construction. In an attempt to avoid this problem, scholars in other disciplines have begun to experiment with new terminology. Literary critic Henry Gates, Jr. puts the word race in quotation marks whenever he uses it; ethnic studies experts Michael Omi and Howard Winant speak of "racial formations"; poststructuralists refer to ideas of "racial difference" analogous to ideas of "sexual difference."[16]

If the lack of a term for race analogous to gender is one roadblock to understanding the social construction of race, another is the historians' tendency to think of race relations primarily in terms of the African American experience. When we look at race relations through a multicultural lens, historical shifts in the meaning of the term race rise to the surface. Late nineteenth-century miscegenation laws in the West are a case in point; they provide a virtual map of the changing legal definition of race and offer clues to a major reformulation of the notion of racial difference that emerged in the late eighteen hundreds and solidified in the first half of the twentieth century.

During this period, western state legislators significantly expanded the original southern prohibitions on marriages between blacks and whites by adding new groups—first Native Americans and then Asian Americans—to the list of those prohibited from marrying whites. The banning of Asian Americans took various forms. In the 1860s, it was common for lawmakers to single out the Chinese, the first Asian group to immigrate to the United States in large numbers, for mention in miscegenation laws.[17] As Chinese immigrants were followed by Japanese immigrants, some states enacted miscegenation laws that made use of the catchall term "Mongolians," intended to cover both groups.[18] Even this expansion, however, did not satisfy legislators for long.

In 1933, for example, a California judge was presented with the issue of whether a Filipino man who wanted to marry a white woman should be classified as a member of the "Mongolian race" or the "Malay race."[19] After a lengthy discussion of racial classifications, the judge held that Filipinos could not be classified as "Mongolians" and so must be considered "Malays." Under California miscegenation law, "Mongolians" were prohibited from marrying whites, but "Malays" were not mentioned; therefore, the judge's decision paved the way for the couple in question to marry. The California legislature, however, promptly subverted the decision by passing a new law that added "Malays" to the list of those already forbidden to marry whites.[20]

This expansion of the definition of race in miscegenation law in the late nineteenth and early twentieth century contrasts sharply with late-twentieth-century developments, so much so that we can, I think, speak of another reformulation of the notion of racial difference in our own time. In 1967, after years of intermittent pressure, the U.S. Supreme Court declared miscegenation laws unconstitutional.[21] The Supreme Court decision in *Loving v. Virginia* marked a substantial shift in the social construction of race: by Supreme Court ruling, biological race is no longer a significant category in U.S. marriage law.

This recent shift may mark a point in U.S. history at which race proves to be an even more malleable social construction than gender for, at the same time that the notion of biological race was being removed from marriage law, the notion of biological sex was becoming more deeply embedded in it. In Utah, for example, the state legislature repealed its ban on interracial marriages in 1963, then, in 1977, it passed a ban on same-sex marriages.[22] In this case, Utah turns out to be more typical than exceptional. Fifteen of the nineteen states whose laws I have surveyed had, since their territorial periods, defined marriage as a contract between "parties," gender unspecified. Between 1970 and 1980, nine of these same states enacted a new definition, one that used sex-specific language, usually declaring that marriage was a contract between "a man and a woman."[23] To add insult to injury, sex-specific definitions of marriage were frequently passed as parts of bills intended to erase gender differences in marriage law. They were usually included in legislation designed to eliminate the difference in legal ages between men and women and to replace the generic pronoun "he" with "he and she." But that is, perhaps, another story.

For the moment, all I want to suggest is that the history of inter-racial marriage provides rich evidence of the formulation and refor-mulation of race and gender and of the connections between the two. With those points in mind, I will turn to the last of the three challenges I want to discuss, one that I might call the problem of the paradigm.

For a history of interracial marriage set in a multicultural arena and seen as a problem in intercultural relations, culture is as important a cat-egory of analysis as race and gender. Writing multicultural history requires a working definition of the term *culture*. Yet, at the present time, to study culture is to enter one of the most amorphous areas of histor-ical research. There is no shortage of possibilities. Although definitions of culture remain elusive, the concept of culture has become ubiqui-tous. Just think for a moment of some of the categories of culture cur-rently used by U.S. historians. There are, to begin with, the racial and ethnic categories: African American culture, Hispanic culture, Asian American culture, and so on. There are also economic categories: cor-porate culture, work culture, working-class culture, consumer culture. There are chronological categories: traditional culture, Victorian cul-ture, Modernist culture. There are even hierarchical categories: high cul-ture and popular culture. And I could go on, from women's culture to political culture to "the new cultural history."[24]

Scholars in a variety of disciplines are trying to make sense of this embarrassment of cultural riches. As I survey their work, it seems to me that we are witnessing a major shift in the reigning paradigm of cul-ture. The direction of change seems reasonably clear—it leads away from a paradigm of culture as a unified system of values and beliefs toward a paradigm of culture as a series of conflicts over meaning played out along such dividing lines as race, class, and gender.

The older paradigm, in which culture is seen as a relatively unified system of values and beliefs, was rooted in the kind of cultural anthro-pology usually identified with Clifford Geertz. For a couple of decades now, social historians have adopted this model of culture with enthu-siasm. They use it to emphasize the community strength, collective con-sciousness, and active agency of people in the various cultures they study.

In the most common work of this kind, social historians attach the term culture to one of the categories of race, class, or gender. When they do this, they end up with topics such as women's culture, working-class culture, or slave culture, all of which have become popular subjects in U.S. social history. The great strength of this kind of work is its "thick descriptions" of the central values and beliefs within each of these cultures. The great weakness is that its practitioners tend to encapsulate each culture, isolating it from its historical and social context. Power relations within each culture are de-emphasized, and power relations between cultures are ignored.[25]

The newer approach to studying culture, now rapidly becoming paradigmatic, focuses directly on power and conflict, though it more often highlights conflict within a given culture than conflict between cultures. This newer approach is most closely associated with the critical wing of the emerging discipline of cultural studies, those academics who call themselves "cultural critics."[26] Their approach has roots in critical theory, poststructuralist literary criticism, and postmodern anthropology. From the cultural critical perspective, culture is not, as many social historians would have it, the embodiment of community consciousness. Instead, culture is a site of conflict in which various groups struggle to control symbols and meanings.

Cultural critics take on the task of uncovering power relations in every aspect of life, from social institutions to the forms of knowledge to language itself. In the process, they emphasize the forces that limit human agency, they challenge the notion that identity is a unified phenomenon, and they assert that experience (a favorite category of social historians, feminists, and ethnic studies scholars) is not what it seems. The critics drive home their point by describing peoples' consciousness as, to use one of their favorite phrases, "always already" shaped by forces outside their control.[27]

The distance between the "old" and "new" paradigms of culture can be traced in a variety of disciplines. In anthropology, it is the distance between Clifford Geertz's "interpretation" of culture and James Clifford's critique of the "predicament" of culture. In history, it is the distance between social histories of working-class, slave, or women's cultures, on the one hand, and, on the other, Thomas Bender's call for the study of a "public culture" in which workers, slaves, and women are considered "parts" of a much larger cultural "whole." In feminist studies, it is the distance between Barbara Smith's call for a black feminist literary criticism and Gayatri Spivak's reflections on *whether* subaltern women can speak *at all*.[28]

For a history of interracial marriage, neither of these paradigms is completely sufficient. If I accepted the social historical model, my study of intermarriage could find no room to grow. Social historians keep relations between cultures on the margins (or perhaps I should say in the introductions, footnotes, or conclusions) of their studies. If, on the other hand, I framed my work according to the cultural critical model, my history of interracial marriage would emphasize large shaping forces and de-emphasize people as active agents. To adopt for a moment the language of cultural critics, my study would become the story of the cultural production of hegemonic definitions of racial and sexual difference embedded in legal discourse.[29]

The cultural critical model is becoming enormously popular among literary critics and postmodern anthropologists, but most social historians retain their dedication to unearthing the viewpoint of subordinate groups and their attachment to the triad of agency, identity, and experience that cultural critics attack so fiercely. Historians of women are, I think, positioned right in the middle of the two groups and therefore are exceptionally well placed to see the strengths and the weaknesses of the cultural critical paradigm.[30]

The great strength of cultural criticism is its attention to power relations within given cultures. Historians of women certainly understand the need to analyze these power relations; in fact, feminist scholars were instrumental in exposing the gender divisions that exploded the rather romantic social historical depictions of supposedly unified working-class, ethnic, and racial cultures.

But historians of women have also developed the notion of a powerful, albeit sometimes idealized, "women's culture," that has in some respects provided an affirming vision for subordinate groups.[31] Thus, historians of women should be especially alert to the dangers of adopting a critical cultural paradigm that builds its case by attacking the concepts of human identity, experience, and agency.

In trying to build a model that acknowledges the constraining power of structures over peoples' lives, cultural critics have created a paradigm that itself imposes significant constraints on our ability to understand peoples' active participation in building and challenging social structures. To return to my example for a moment, because a cultural critical study of interracial marriage would emphasize shaping forces, it would de-emphasize a central part of the story I want to tell: the active agency of the participants in interracial marriages. It would, in other words, limit my ability to understand participants' involvement in the reformulation of race and gender relations.

Such a paradigm is problematic no matter whom it is applied to, but it is especially troubling that cultural critics are deconstructing concepts of individual and community agency just at the point when feminist historians are extending their accounts of female agency from white middle-class women to women of color.[32] It might even be said, I think, that because cultural critics doubt that scholars can ever comprehend powerless groups, they have created something of a crisis among those who want to write the histories of subordinate peoples. The problem can most easily be seen by once again comparing the cultural critics to their social history predecessors. In essence, adopting the cultural critical approach means replacing the old social history project of reclaiming the voices of powerless peoples with a different project—that of critiquing dominant peoples' depictions of subaltern "others."

And there is another, related aspect of critical cultural studies that historians of women should worry about: the growing tendency to use the term cultural in the generic singular instead of in the plural.[33] Partly because of their doubts about the ability of scholars to understand subordinate groups, cultural critics are a particularly inward-looking group. When they do go so far as to critique power relations between cultures, they do this from a vantage point located (however ambivalently) within the dominant culture.

For a historian interested in writing a history of interracial marriage—or in developing a multicultural history of women—this simply won't do. If, as cultural critics would suggest, culture is a site from which to begin analysis, it makes a considerable difference which site we choose to begin from. To keep a firm eye on the tensions between the power of the dominant, on the one hand, and the agency of the oppressed, on the other, we must choose sites in which multiple cultures are present, and we must focus on the problem of recovering the perspectives of the powerless, as well as the powerful. And here we come back to the U.S. West for, with its remarkable history of cultural diversity, no area offers a better location for considering the theoretical questions of race, gender, and intercultural relations that are at the heart of the history of interracial marriage.

★ Peggy Pascoe holds the Beekman Chair of Northwest and Pacific History at the University of Oregon.

Women of Color and the Rewriting of Western History: The Discourse, Politics, and Decolonization of History

Antonia I. Castañeda

HISTORIANS have long struggled with the need to rewrite western history and to articulate a new, inclusive synthesis that fully incorporates the history of women of color.[1] In her concluding remarks at the Women's West Conference in Sun Valley, Idaho, in 1983, Susan Shown Harjo (identifying herself culturally as Cheyenne and Creek and politically as Cheyenne and Arapaho) charged that women of the West

> are still possessed of inaccurate information about who we are collectively, who we are individually, and who we have been. We view each other through layers of racial, ethnic, and class biases, perpetuated by the white, male ruling institutions, such as the educational system that teaches in the early years and controls later research in the history of women in the West.[2]

* Antonia I. Castañeda, "Women of Color and the Rewriting of Western History: The Discourse, Politics, and Decolonization of History," 61:4 *Pacific Historical Review* (1992). © 1992 Pacific Historical Review, American Historical Association, Pacific Coast Branch. Reprinted by permission.

This critique of the reigning historiography has changed little since then or since Joan Jensen and Darlis Miller first called for a multicultural, or intercultural, approach in their essay, "The Gentle Tamers Revisited: New Approaches to the History of Women in the American West."[3] A decade of "multicultural" historiography has still not come to terms with the historical, theoretical, political, and ideological issues raised by Harjo at Sun Valley.

This essay discusses the historiography that was written during the 1980s about women in the nineteenth-century West. It examines the issues, politics, concepts, methodologies, and language of the "multicultural" or intercultural approach first articulated by Jensen and Miller and the ways in which the intersection of gender, race, sexuality, ethnicity, class, and culture are described, theorized, and interpreted in the recent historical literature. The first section places in context the historiography of women of color in the decade before "The Gentle Tamers Revisited" was published, while the second places in context "The Gentle Tamers Revisited" itself.

THE HISTORIOGRAPHY OF WOMEN OF COLOR AND THE POLITICS OF HISTORY

The academic discourse on the historiography of women in the West still does not accept that studying and writing the history of racial ethnic people as well as of women in the United States are avowedly political acts.[4] Yet the political and intellectual roots of the contemporary historical study of women in the West were sown in the political struggles of the late 1960s and 1970s—in the case of white women, in the women's liberation movements; in the case of women of color, in the national third-world liberation movements.[5] These movements were at times related, but their political and intellectual origins, commitments, and ideologies were markedly different.

The women's liberation movement in the United States focused specifically on gender oppression. Never of one mind or one ideology, the women's movement was nevertheless fundamentally rooted in a middle-class political liberalism that subscribed to including the excluded as long as they fit within the existing norms. Its origins, identification, and praxis sprang from the suffragist movement of the mid-nineteenth century—a movement that never reconciled its origins in abolitionism with an abiding belief in white racial superiority.

The study of women began with the political struggles of the women's movements of the 1960s and 1970s and with the feminist theories and scholarship that grew from them. The women's movement was a middle-class, white women's movement, and until very recently, the historians who have researched and written the history of women in the West have been principally white women. Many of them participated in the women's movement or are members of the generation of scholars who struggled to found women's studies programs and departments in western colleges and universities. Most feminist scholars write the history not of women, but of white women in the West.

In contrast, most women scholars of color who research and write the history of women of color look not to the women's liberation movement, but to third-world liberation movements. These movements focused on the race and class oppression of African Americans, Chicanos, Native Americans, Puerto Ricans, and Asian Americans in the U.S. and identified with global struggles of third-world peoples for economic and political freedom.[6] They found their historical and cultural origins in indigenous, native worlds that antedated European imperialism, and they began to reclaim those origins, which had been devalued and suppressed in Euro-American institutions and society.[7] These national movements interpreted the exploitation and oppression of third-world peoples in the United States as an extension of the historical, global colonial, and neocolonial relationships that tied Europe and subsequently the United States to third-world countries.[8] Drawing upon theories of dependency and, in some cases, interpreting their reality in the United States as internal colonialism, these movements had a transnational identification and praxis. Although different ideologies, including cultural nationalism, prevailed, most national liberation movements supported a Marxist or neo-Marxist perspective that focused on class and racial oppression but ignored issues of patriarchy and gender oppression, gay and lesbian oppression, and the intersection of gender, race, sexuality, and class.

Women scholars of color, however, also struggled against the internal gender oppression of their own families, organizations, and communities and against a historical sexual exploitation rooted in the intersection of their gender with their race and class. This consciousness distinguished their gender oppression markedly from that of white women and distinguished their racial and class oppression markedly from that of men of color. It also differentiated the feminist ideologies of women of color from those of white women.

Individually and collectively, in conferences, presentations, and published works, feminists of color challenged male-dominated ethnic studies departments that ignored gender and sexuality and women's studies departments that ignored race and class.[9] In the case of the latter, they were highly critical of the assumptions, the universalizing tendencies, and the lack of consciousness about the dynamics of power and privilege rooted in race and class that informed white feminist scholarship. Drawing upon contemporary writers and political activists, including Angela Davis, Dolores Huerta, Janice Mirikitani, and Janet McCloud, as well as upon their own experiences, these writers and scholars initiated a new body of creative as well as academic literature.[10] Although few in number, they began to recover the voices, histories, cultures, literatures, and experiences of women of color in the United States and to teach courses on women of color. In the decade of the 1980s they published several collections of creative and critical writings by women of color.[11] These collections, however, did not include historical studies on women of color in the nineteenth-century West. This was due to the abysmally small numbers of professionally trained women scholars of color who might have produced these studies. Statistics reveal that between 1975 and 1988 there were 192 doctoral degrees in history awarded to women of color: 8 to Native Americans, 42 to "Asians," 101 to African Americans, and 41 to "Hispanics."[12]

MULTICULTURALISM AND ITS DISCONTENTS

With the publication of "The Gentle Tamers Revisited" in 1980, Jensen and Miller launched a new era in the field of women's history. Their essay provided Euro-American feminist and nonfeminist historians with a critical base from which to challenge the historiography in two subfields of U.S. history: the history of the American West and the history of women. For this group of scholars, Jensen and Miller's essay became the foundation on which to build a historiography of women in the West. It offered them a "new, multicultural" framework from which to contest both the East Coast focus of U.S. women's history and the biases of the male-centered frontier thesis.

Jensen and Miller called for a newer, ethnically broader, and more varied image of women in the West based on a multicultural approach that recognized and included the experiences of women from different races, ethnicities, cultures, and classes. They also stated that "a multicultural approach need not eliminate class or politics from western women's history" and that "women of the West were divided not only by culture but also by the conflicts among cultures."[13] Jensen and Miller's multicultural approach appeared to be the perfect base from which to include the excluded and thereby move women in the West from the periphery to the center of the history of both women and the American West. They did not, however, examine, analyze, discuss, or theorize about the conflicts and differences among cultures. Neither did they examine the applicability of the existing categories, concepts, and paradigms or redefine culture(s), politics, the parameters of cultural conflict, or sex-gender issues and women's roles within that cultural conflict. They also failed to analyze relations of power among women of different races, classes, and cultures.

Jensen and Miller's vague outlines for multicultural approaches to the history of women in the West have been uncritically appropriated, adopted, and applied, and in some cases extended or expanded, without question or analysis by feminist and nonfeminist historians alike. These scholars have begun to apply methods from numerous disciplines to research, write, discuss, anthologize, and publish a variety of works on gender, race, and class in the West.[14] Using a multicultural, intercultural, or, to a much lesser degree, comparative perspective, they have produced two principal types of work: descriptive studies and studies of the contact between white men or women and women of color.

The first type, principally journal articles and conference papers collected in anthologies, describes the experience of Euro-American, Spanish-Mexican, Indian, and, to a much lesser extent, African American women.[15] Asian and Asian American women—whether Chinese, Japanese, Korean, Filipino, South Asian, or Southeast Asian—appear in only one anthology, a multicultural reader published in 1990.[16] Although the early studies tend to focus on the nineteenth century— beginning with Euro-American westward expansion in the 1830s and ending with Frederick Jackson Turner's "closing of the frontier"—the study of women of color has of necessity pushed the time span back to the sixteenth and seventeenth centuries for Spanish-Mexican women and much earlier for Native American women.[17] Recent studies of workers from Asia and the Pacific Islands have also pushed it forward to the twentieth century and extended the geographic region to include Hawaii and Alaska.[18] Moreover, interest in particular themes, such as widowhood and women in prisons, is beginning to result in thematic works, including the important anthology *On Their Own: Widows and Widowhood in the American Southwest, 1848–1939*. These works offer significant possibilities for the development of comparative studies across race, class, cultures, and region.[19]

The second type, which includes books as well as journal articles, focuses on Anglo perceptions of racial ethnic women or on the contact and relationships between Anglos and racial ethnic women, usually Native American and Mexican women.[20] Generally, studies on interracial contact in the nineteenth century do not examine interculturalism, interracial unions, or *mestizaje* (racial and cultural mixing) in Mexico's northern territories prior to the arrival of Euro-Americans in the 1820s and thus do not recognize these as core elements in the history of the West.[21] Research on intercultural contact has recently begun to focus on prostitution, a form of labor in which women of all races and cultures participated in the postwar nineteenth-century West; interracial marriage; and the moral reform movements of Euro-American women.[22] The study of interracial marriage and Anglo reform movements now embraces the twentieth century and has begun to examine relations between Anglos and Asian and Asian American women.[23] Despite the exceptions, few studies analyze the historical gender, "racial," political, economic, and cultural issues and conflicts inherent in interracial marriage, assimilation, and acculturation.

DIVERSITY

The issue of diversity was, moreover, a reality for indigenous peoples in the Americas long before the arrival of Europeans. Although racial diversity in the West may be a relatively recent phenomenon (some two and four hundred years old in California and New Mexico, respectively), cultural diversity is not. Before the Spanish arrived in 1769, California was one of the most densely populated and culturally and linguistically diverse areas of the continent north of Mexico.[24] Precontact indigenous societies throughout the Americas included a broad spectrum of social structures ranging from the matrilineal and matrilocal societies of the Navajo and Western Apache to egalitarian, foraging bands in California to highly stratified, hierarchically organized social orders in central Mexico and Peru.[25]

Recognizing and according significance to cultural diversity are important for two reasons. First, the recent emphasis placed on the nineteenth- and twentieth-century West as, according to Peggy Pascoe the "most racially and culturally diverse region of the nation" merely reconfigures and perpetuates, in another guise, the earlier myth of western America's uniqueness. Indigenous cultural diversity was not unique to the West, and its decline in other regions of the country, the South and Southeast for example, was due precisely to the impact of European and Euro-American expansion and colonization. Moreover, although the diversity among indigenous groups declined, the importation of Africans from different parts of the continent added new elements of cultural, as well as racial, diversity to nonwestern regions. Diversity in the American West, then, merely reflects a pattern in place long before the arrival of Europeans, and the change in the composition of diverse groups across time—the decline of some groups and the addition of others—is a function of the political and economic developments occurring in a particular region.

Second, women's gender experiences and definitions were as

diverse as the cultures from which they came. Women apprehended knowledge and acted within their universe according to their culture and its particular economic and socio-politico-religious organization.[26] Understanding the nature of gender systems and experiences before contact is critical to understanding how those experiences changed with conquest and colonialism and why women responded and acted the way they did in intercultural settings and relationships. It is also critical to understanding how they maintained, adapted, and transformed their own cultural forms while resisting, adopting, adapting, and affecting those of other groups.

THE IDEOLOGY OF RACE

Jensen and Miller should not be faulted for being merely suggestive or for how their call is applied by others. They should, however, be criticized for organizing their essay and discussion around concepts, issues, categories, and language that belong to the history of middle-class white women and for not addressing how these may differ for women of color. Although ostensibly centering all women as historical subjects, "The Gentle Tamers Revisited" fundamentally centered only Euro-American women. Jensen and Miller's brand of multiculturalism kept middle-class white women as the subject and the normative group for description, analysis, interpretation, and comparison. They neither challenged nor altered the standard Eurocentric focus, methodologies, or paradigms of women's history. The multicultural approach to the history of women in the West reflects the critical problem in American historiography, which, to quote Ann DuCille's recent review, "is the continued marginalization of those historically constituted as 'other.'"[27]

Jensen and Miller encoded their discussion and analysis with a range of images and stereotypes applied to and reserved exclusively for white women in the West, beginning with the term "gentle tamers."[28] None of the historical literature—neither the documents of the Euro-American conquest nor studies by historians or other writers—refers to any women of color as gentle tamers, meaning bearers of culture and "civilization."

Thus Euro-American individuals or groups, both male and female, remain the true subject of multicultural studies.[29] Based principally on Euro-American, English-language sources, these studies explore Anglo perceptions of women of color and the Anglo side of the cultural equation. While some of these works, particularly the most recent ones, recognize the poststructuralist debate about the meaning and definition of culture and seem to disavow the earlier paradigm of culture adopted by social historians, theoretical approaches that incorporate the historical realities of people of color, and their own interpretation of their realities, are still wanting.[30]

While feminist scholars are beginning to examine race and miscegenation within a multicultural framework, most continue to ignore the complexities of multiple racial and cultural mixtures in the United States and to avoid examining how the prevailing construction of race has been applied differently to different racial ethnic peoples across time and space.[31] Mexicans (both native and foreign born), for example, were included in the 1920 U.S. federal manuscript census as part of the white population. In 1930, however, the U.S. Bureau of the Census classified them as nonwhite and set up "Mexican" as a race unto itself. Since Mexicans have been officially classified both as white and nonwhite, antimiscegenation laws sometimes applied to them and sometimes did not.[32] Nevertheless, as one early study of the Mexican American community concluded, irrespective of the official racial classification, intermarriage with Mexicans was disparaged, and "the Anglo member of an intermarrying couple . . . is classified as a 'Mexican' by the American community."[33]

Theories about the social construction of race do not yet examine or account for these kinds of complexities. Nor does the significance of interracial marriage and mixing among peoples of color, or the mestizaje of the Mexican population, form part of how the social construction of race and studies of miscegenation are conceptualized for nineteenth- or twentieth-century North American society. Acutely aware that the new theories remain constructed and defined by the same "hegemonic voices," scholars of color have vigorously critiqued the "rush to theory" that ignores, excludes, or does not comprehend the realities of people of color and, in this case, women of color.[34]

Jensen and Miller examined the ideology of gender, but not the ideology and politics of race, culture, class, and expansionism that produced and maintained stereotypic images of white women and women of color. They acknowledged the existence of racial stereotypes and cultural conflicts without placing racial contact and cultural conflict in their historical or political or ideological context. They assumed that concepts, categories, terminology, methodology, and language are universally applicable. By doing so they remained squarely within both the Turnerian tradition of frontier history and the tradition established early in the field of women's history. White women remain, as Chandra Mohanty states, the authorial subject, "the yardstick by which to encode and represent cultural others."[35] Jensen and Miller merely substituted the experience of white males with that of white women and thus reproduced the same relationships of power and authority that male historians used when writing the canon of history. The discussions and analysis of multicultural contact and relations remain skewed, centered on, and interpreted from the Euro-American side of the relationship.

Generalizations about women of color perpetuate pernicious stereotypes. Native American, Chicana, African-American, and Asian American scholars have identified two dichotomous images of women of color in the literature—"good" and "bad." These images vary among racial ethnic groups but are in all cases totally unrelated to the notion of "gentle tamers."[36] Within this dichotomy, "good" women of color are light-skinned, civilized (Christian), and virgins. They are "good" because they give aid, or sacrifice themselves, so that white men may live; white men marry them. "Bad" women are dark-skinned, savage (non-Christian), and whores; white men do not marry them.

In the case of Native American and Mexican/Mexican American women, these dichotomies translate into contradictory images of the "noble princess/savage squaw" and the "Spanish senorita/Mexican prostitute," respectively. The "noble princess" and the "Spanish senorita" are deracinated and converted into acceptable images of marriageable women. These "good" women are the "Indian princess" and the "Spanish" grandmother whom many white pioneer families proudly claim as ancestors. According to the mythology within which these stereotypes are steeped, such women reject their own kind, native men, in favor of their white saviors. Marriage to the blue-eyed strangers saves them from the oppression of their own men and thus from the savagery of their race, culture, group, and nation.

The negative stereotypes were applied to all Native American and Mexican women except those few belonging to what Euro-Americans considered the native ruling class, with whom they could form beneficial alliances, including marriage. They sexualize Indian and Mexican women, devaluing and dehumanizing them as women who give away or sell sexual intercourse. Within this stereotype, Indian women relate to "idle, shiftless, thieving, drunken" Indian men, while Mexican women are "fandango-dancing, monte-dealing consorts of Mexican bandits."

The historical literature presents stereotypic images of women that center on sexuality and the relationship that the particular women and their racial or national group, or both, have to the political economy. Moreover, the relation to the political economy informs the history of women of color and distinguishes the daughters of the country—Native American or Mexican women—from African American and Asian women.

During the first stages of contact and conquest, marriage to a Native American or a Mexican woman of a particular family or class had significant economic and political value. These marriages were often the vehicle by which Euro-American men gained access to land or other economic resources as well as to political and military alliances.[37] This was not the case with African American or Asian women in the nineteenth-century West. As enslaved or contract workers, African American and Asian women had neither economic nor political value as marriage partners. The miscegenation laws, which criminalized marriage to people of African descent, were later extended to Asians.[38]

Consequently, stereotypes of African and Asian women center almost exclusively on the pejorative "bad/whore." This image simultaneously sexualizes women and impugns their sexuality. The implicit sociopolitical message is clear: Women of color are immoral because their peoples, races, and nations are immoral.[39] Whereas the pejorative stereotype of African American and Asian women is rooted in sexuality, the positive stereotype, when it appears at all, is rooted in work and servitude. "Good" African American and Asian women serve their owners, or former owners, well. They do not run away, join or lead revolts, learn to read or write, or cause trouble.

THE POLITICS OF RACE AND POWER

Jensen and Miller did not analyze the relations of power among women of different races, classes, or cultures in the West. The devaluation of the sexuality of women of color, and by extension the devaluation of their people, was an important element in the rationale for war, conquest, exploitation, and subsequently exclusion.[40] It was—and remains—a central part of the racist argument that served the political and economic interests of an expansionist United States.

Anne Butler, for example, in her recent study of prostitution in the American West, paints Chinese and Mexican cultures as undifferentiated, static, and monolithic. She presents Mexican and Chinese women as unthinking, passive victims—entities with no agency. In this work, Mexican women come from a society and history of

> an unending cycle of victory and defeat, oppression and submission that comprise the history of the Southwest. . . . Oriental women carried with them to North America the societal hierarchy that they had lived with in China. . . . The emigrants . . . came from a life of control and rigidity, similar to the structure the Chinese merchants established. . . . These women simply moved from one controlling hierarchy to another without transformation in their own societal roles. Brought from a pre-industrial society and closeted in a minority subculture, Oriental prostitutes had little opportunity to develop changed self-concepts in their new environment.[41]

Butler judges Mexican and Chinese women and their cultures by traditional Euro-American norms of "progress" and ignores both the political economy of prostitution for women of color in the West and women's agency under extreme conditions of oppression and exploitation. Nor does she recognize, for example, that the "Chinese merchants who had a status in the U.S. they did not have in Chinese" society created the so-called minority subculture within a context of exclusion, racism, and inequality.[42]

Multicultural works about women written during the decade of the 1980s tend to emphasize harmonious, cooperative, mutually supportive relations between women of color and Anglo women in the American West.[43] Although they do not ignore the reality of racist attitudes among white women, their accounts are remarkably free of intercultural conflict in a land bloodied by three centuries of war and conquest.[44] Yet white women are "gentle tamers" because they are the female counterparts of white men who "tame the wild West." "Taming the West," gently in the case of white women and violently in the case of white men, is a metaphor for expansionism. Within their gender spheres and based upon the power and privilege of their race and class, Euro-American men and women expanded the geo-political-economic area of the United States and established Euro-American hegemony in the region. They did so by waging war, by displacing and removing the occupants, and by appropriating the land. By skirting the issue of conflict in expansionism, these studies perpetuate the myth of the "bloodless conquest" of California, the West, and the Southwest, one of the central tenants of the expansionist ideology that rationalized and justified war and conquest.

The multicultural approach also ignores the myriad roles which sometimes include cultural, ideological, social, and physical violence that women of the conquering group(s) assume in establishing hegemony over another group. It also ignores the economic and other privileges that women of the conquering group derive from the oppression of women and men of the group being oppressed. Ironically, by emphasizing the benign, conflict-free relationships between white women and women of color in the American West, multicultural studies reaffirm the notion that white women are the "gentle tamers." This harmonic view contrasts sharply with the reality. Rosalia Vallejo's reminiscences of the Bear Flag Revolt in California, court records of cases in which Mexican women were plaintiffs as well as defendants against Anglos, including women, accounts of the wholesale sexual violence against Indian women, the efforts of African-American women to free themselves from bondage, and the sexual exploitation of Asian women reveal the truth of those relations.[45]

The brutally violent conflicts engendered by expansionism and the establishment of Euro-American hegemony—including conflicts between white women and women of color—remain part of our daily lives and are expressed in the contemporary writing of women of color. According to Paula Gunn Allen, "like our sisters who resist in other ways, we Indian women who write have articulated and rendered the experience of being in a state of war for five hundred years."[46] Histories of the West in which women of color are the subject, have agency, and are located within their own culture are only now being researched, written, and published.

THE EMPIRE WRITES BACK: THE DECOLONIZATION OF WESTERN HISTORY[47]

The literature by contemporary women writers of color in the United States vividly depicts the conflicts, tensions, violence, and warfare—physical, ideological, psychological, and cultural—that affect their own lives and form part of the collective memories and lives of their female kin and communities. This new, immensely rich, powerful, and growing body of literature—such as the autobiographical, biographical, and fictionalized writings of Louise Erdrich, Gloria Anzaldúa, Amy Tan, and Toni Morrison—helps to offset the dearth of historical studies about women of color, at least for the twentieth century.[48] Women of color are at the center of these works, describing, analyzing, and expressing their own historical and cultural subjectivities. Rooted in what theorist Chela Sandoval terms oppositional consciousness, this literature offers a critical base for new definitions, forms, expressions, and theories of culture, that is, of what writers of color have, in their call for reimaging America, termed cultures of collectivity and struggle.[49] These cultures are rooted in knowledge and experience that both antedate and supersede—just as much as they are shaped by, adapted to, resistant to, and coexistent with—European and Euro-American cultures of colonial domination. Collected in a wealth of new anthologies by and about women of color, this oppositional literature blurs academic disciplines and literary genres and crosses national boundaries. It expresses the complex, multiple subjectivities that women of color have lived, which Shirley Geok-Lin Lim describes as "the plural singularity" of Asian

American women.[50]

This plural singularity refers to both the commonalities and the differences of gender, race, culture, class, and sexuality among women. It is present in the new historiography that examines women's history within the concepts and theories that frame the discourse of colonialism in historical studies, and discursive colonization in literary and cultural studies. Initially derived from the Marxist and neo-Marxist studies of Latin America, Africa, and India, this interdisciplinary approach draws upon methodologies and theories from cultural anthropology, ethnohistory, sociology, literature, and feminism to examine the conquest and colonization of the Americas. This approach, states Ramon Gutierrez, views history as a "dialogue between cultures, each of which had many voices that often spoke in unison, but just as often were diverse and divisive."[51] Conceptualizing the historical process "as a story of contestation, mediation, and negotiation between cultures and between social groups," this approach clarifies the power dynamics of the European conquests and the contest of cultures that began in 1492 and remains very much with us.[52]

Especially important to historical scholarship on women of color in the United States, including the West, is the work of third-world feminists and other third-world scholars and writers who employ critical theory, postmodern anthropology, and poststructuralist literary criticism to analyze how the colonizer represented African, Native American, mestiza, and Asian women.[53] Analyzing woman and the female body as a metaphor for conquest, these scholars interpret the white colonizers' appropriation of the native woman—by representing her as sexually available to the colonizer and as oppressed within her own culture—to be pivotal to the ideology and the political agenda of colonialism. In analyzing colonialism, Malek Alloula, for example, interprets the colonizer's possession of the native woman by constructing false images of her and her society as "less of a conquest than a deformation of the social order."[54]

These scholars not only examine the centrality of sex-gender to the politics of colonialism but also focus on the relations of power both among cultures and within cultures. They view scholarship and the production of knowledge as a political and discursive practice—it has a purpose and is ideological. Within this broad framework, third world feminists reexamine, reconstruct, and re-present native women within their own cultures as well as responding to colonialism. In doing so, they interrogate their own traditions from within. They call into question traditions, conventions, and contemporary relations of power and offer searching critiques of their own societies and historical conditioning.

This analysis, which examines both the historical and the contemporary writing on native African, Asian, and American women produced by westerners, criticizes feminist writing on third-world women. Placing western feminist writing within the context of a first/third world balance of power, Chandra Mohanty, for example, characterizes much of this work as rooted in "assumptions of privilege and ethnocentric universality, on the one hand, and inadequate self-consciousness about the effect of western scholarship on the 'third world' in the context of a world system dominated by the West, on the other."[55]

REWRITING THE NINETEENTH-CENTURY WEST

For the nineteenth-century West, historical studies on comparative frontiers that begin to examine frontier expansion within a global context of European colonization and capitalist development employ the dialogic framework.[56] These historians define the frontier as a territory or zone of encounter, interchange, and conflict between distinct societies—one indigenous and one intrusive. Taking a macrotheoretical approach, they argue that the "history of frontier expansion in the Americas is the history of the expansion of European capitalism into non-European areas."[57] Americanist Patricia Limerick interprets the history of the American West as one chapter in the global and bloody story of Europe's expansion and centuries-long contest for property, profit, and cultural dominance.[58] Similarly, historian Rosalinda Mendez González argues that if we are to understand the experience of all women we must study "the larger, more fundamental political-economic forces in the development of the West."[59] Scholars who study Native Americans and Mexicans include the resistance to domination, and those who examine the pattern of global frontier expansion concentrate on the differences specific to each nation, region, and frontier.[60]

Work in ethnic and women's history has added gender, race, sexuality, and culture to class as categories of historical analysis in studies of global capitalist development. Placing these at the center of historical examination—that is, using them as organizing principles—provides the basis for reconceptualizing and reanalyzing all aspects of history and the historical process. Chicana/Latina historians who study Spanish-Mexican women in eighteenth-century California and nineteenth-century New Mexico reveal, for example, that sex-gender, race, and culture are central to the politics and policies of conquest and colonization and to the sociopolitical and economic development of these regions as they changed from Spanish to Mexican to Euro-American rule.[61] Gender, race, culture, and class are political designations as much as they are social constructions.

This approach enables us to examine the specific realities in which women of different races, cultures, and classes live in any society at any given time. It also allows us to examine gender systems and women's experiences within the sociopolitical and economic context of local, national, and international developments at any given historical moment and to compare similarities and differences among women within one society and across societies. Most particularly, doing so allows us to study gender experiences, which are rooted in and intersect with race, culture, and class, within distinct economies and societies—both precapitalist and capitalist. In brief, it allows us to be historically specific, to recognize women's agency, and to understand, in Mohanty's words, "the contradictions inherent in women's location within various structures."[62]

Anthropological studies, for example, examine women's relations of production in precontact societies and refute earlier interpretations of Native American women.[63] They reject principal tenets of western feminism that had been applied to women worldwide, including the universality of male dominance and the dichotomy between public and private acts. These studies conclude that within egalitarian foraging band societies, women exercised control over their own lives and activities and operated formally and publicly in their own interest. Social and sexual relations were reciprocal and complementary. Human sexuality, but most particularly women's sexuality, was not controlled by males, and a broad spectrum of sociosexual relations existed. Moreover, each society had its own customs for marriage, divorce, polygamy, polyandry, the berdache, and cross-gender dressing.

Historians are also reexamining various dimensions of the issue of sexuality within the context of colonization. Focusing on the response of native women to sexual and other violence, Albert Hurtado, among others, is detailing the historical resistance of Native American women.[64] Similarly, anthropologist Patricia Albers concludes that despite the structural and other changes wrought by capitalism, Dakota women and their communities did not dramatically change their basic values of reciprocity, collectivity, and complementarity.[65] These and other values were central to their resistance to and survival of colonialism and its attendant oppressions.

Moreover, while earlier studies dealt with Native American sexuality principally in terms of the "unspeakable things" done to white women captives, historical documents reveal that different practices of war prevailed in the Americas and that female captives fared according to the practices of the victorious group. Some of the native Californian groups, for example, practiced ritual but not physical warfare; some warred not at all; and some practiced warfare and captured women and children but never sexually molested female captives. Such was the case with the Yuma, who believed that intimate contact with enemy women caused sickness.[66]

Focusing on women of color changes the discourse and enables historians to examine how those women responded to changes in the economic and social order—including the changes wrought by violence—based on their own values, norms, and circumstances. Deena González, for example, examines interracial marriages as part of Spanish-Mexican patterns of racial and cultural contact. She focuses on the culture-specific gender strategies that Spanish-Mexican women in Santa Fe, New Mexico, used to resist and subvert structures of Euro-American colonialism in the nineteenth century.[67] Using Spanish-language sources, González weaves her analysis with the women's own language, imagery, and consciousness, which reveal the subjectivities, complexities, tensions, strategies, conflicts, and contradictions of their lives,

as well as their sense of honor, propriety, justice, and right. Placing
Chicana history in time, space, and social relationships prior to the
arrival of Euro-Americans, González's work provides a critical new
point of departure for studies of nineteenth- and twentieth-century
Chicana/Latina history.

Likewise, Asian American historians, Sucheng Chan and Judy Yung,
among others, use Chinese and other Asian-language sources to recover,
reconstruct, and reinterpret the complex realities of Chinese, Japanese,
Korean, Filipino, South Asian, and Southeast Asian women in the
American West from the mid-nineteenth century to the present.[68] In
addition to cultural and class differences, asian-language sources, including oral history interviews, reveal that Chinese and Japanese women
who consented to come to the United States as workers and subsequently as picture brides had their own individual motives for doing
so. Some sought to contribute to the family economy; others wanted
to be educated and to see the world.[69] Once in the United States, Asian
women resisted marital and other conditions they did not like despite
the difficulties and lack of recourse.

In her recent work on the Chinese in California, historian Chan
studies gender issues imbedded in the Chinese Exclusion Laws of
1881–1882 and adds a vital new chapter to immigration history in general and to Asian American women's history in particular.[70] Shifting the
focus of earlier studies on migration from "Chinese patriarchal culture
and the soujourner mentality thesis" and centering on gender issues and
U.S. immigration policy, Chan chronicles how different groups of
Chinese women were targeted for exclusion and denied entry to the
United States. Examining the legislation from the 1870s to 1943, Chan
finds the sexuality of Chinese women to be a pivotal issue in legislative
hearings, committee meetings, and statutes as well as in municipal ordi-
nances. She concludes that

> contrary to the common belief that laborers were the target
> of the first exclusion act, the effort to bar another group of
> Chinese—prostitutes—preceded the prohibition against
> laborers. Given the widely held view that all Chinese females
> were prostitutes, laws against the latter affected other groups

of Chinese women who sought admission into the country as well.[71]

The stereotype that all Chinese women were prostitutes whose presence would corrupt the morals of the nation's youth can be traced to the 1850s and prevailed well into the twentieth century. The Page law, passed in 1875, was designed to end the threat of cheap Chinese labor and to prevent "immoral Chinese women" from landing in the United States. New laws passed in 1903, 1907, and 1917 were designed to deport alleged prostitutes, which included all Chinese women. According to Chan, "no Chinese woman, regardless of her social standing, was safe from harassment."[72]

Similarly, George Peffer argues that the government's targeted exclusion of Chinese women effectively prevented Chinese families from forming and thus kept a full-fledged Chinese/Chinese American society (or societies) from establishing itself in the United States during the nineteenth century.[73] Although Peffer's brief essay does not fully develop the relationship between sex-gender and economic issues, the links are certainly there to be examined and explored. That is, in Chinese contract labor, the expanding, postwar boom economy of the mid-nineteenth-century West found what it most needed: a large, mobile, exploitable, expendable source of cheap manual labor. Chinese laborers—both women and men—were brought in to do particular kinds of work in a segmented labor force that kept them mobile, transient, exploitable, and expendable.[74] Unlike men, Chinese women were also brought to perform sexual intercourse, and their sexuality could be and was impugned.

Moreover, the "sexuality/immorality" of Chinese prostitutes became the rationale for excluding not only all Chinese women, as Chan and Peffer demonstrate, but, with the beginning of the economic downturn of the 1870s, all Chinese.

The Chinese experience was not singular. Similar issues of sex-gender, contract labor, immigration policy, and exclusion prevail in the history of Japanese immigration to Hawaii and the mainland.[75] Hawaiian sugar planters began contracting Japanese laborers, both male and female, and importing Japanese women to Hawaii for purposes of prostitution beginning in the late 1860s. Agricultural interests in the West subsequently followed suit. In a pattern established earlier with the Chinese, the "sexuality/immorality" of Japanese women was a key element in the rationale for excluding the Japanese in the first decade of the twentieth century.[76]

The intersection of gender, race, and labor is also central in new studies of African-American women in the West. Historian Shirley Ann Moore examines these issues in her study reconstructing the experience of African-American women workers in Richmond, California, from 1910 to 1950.[77] Using extensive oral history interviews, family memoirs, documents, music, memorabilia, and other archival material, Moore explores the "development of strategies of economic empowerment of women who labored under the tripartite yoke of oppression and were compelled to develop resourceful, self-affirming strategies to carve out some measure of economic autonomy for themselves and their families."[78] This is the first study to examine the experience of the generation of African-American women who took part in the "great migration" in the prewar years of the early 1900s and who built and shaped African-American communities in the West.

Earlier studies of women and of African-Americans in the West discussed African-American women in general or focused on individual women such as Mary Ellen Pleasant and Biddy Mason; they did not use gender as a category of historical analysis or examine gender issues and women's experiences of slavery, freedom, or the boom-bust economy in the nineteenth-century West.[79] With the exception of Jack Forbes's work on Africans and Native Americans, no historians have focused on the nature of interracial marriage or other socio-sexual and political relationships among people of color. The recovery of factual information and the interpretation of African-American women's lives in the nineteenth- and early twentieth-century West, like that of Native American and Asian American women and Chicanas, is only now being undertaken.

★   ★   ★

In focusing on women of color as historical subjects in the nineteenth-century Euro-American West, and employing gender, race, class, culture, and sexuality as categories of analysis within the context of colonization, newer studies, principally by women historians of color, are reexamining old sources, discovering new sources, using new methodologies, and challenging earlier interpretations of women in general. They are also refuting previous interpretations of women of color in particular. These scholars, states historian Deena González, have found it necessary first to "deconstruct the racialized and sexualized history of women of color in order to reconstruct it."[80]

Their examinations reveal important commonalities and differences based on historical presence and on gender and its intersection with race, sexuality, culture, and class. These new findings form a critical new basis for reconceptualizing and reinterpreting not only women's and racial ethnic history, but the labor, economic, political, immigration, cultural, and social history of the West as well.

They have sketched some of the broad themes that are of importance to women of color, including sexual and other physical, as well as psychological, violence within the context of the politics of expansionism; devaluation of their sexuality by Euro-American society; discrimination based on race, culture, and class; resistance to oppression; use as labor (enslaved, contract, and wage); the mestizaje within Mexican communities as well as intermarriage and racial-cultural mixing among people of color; settlement; family; religion; and community building. Other themes, such as accommodation and adaptation to the Euro-American presence in their homeland; intermarriage with Euro-Americans; immigration; deportation; and the experience of slavery and freedom from bondage in the West, are more specific to one group or another.

Drawing upon new, interdisciplinary methodologies and frameworks defined in the scholarly studies of third world women, these studies examine and analyze women of color within their own cultures; in particular, they examine how these women responded to the alien, hostile, often violent society of the nineteenth-century American West. These studies focus on women's agency and on how women of color use their own culture and knowledge to sustain them, how they subvert and/or change the environment, and how they adopt or create new cultural forms. Further, these studies explore the multiple contradictions of women's lives in colonialism. They explore both the hegemonic and counterhegemonic strategies, roles, and activities that women, depending on their position in society, developed and employed in both the historical and contemporary period. Women of all races, classes, and cultures are active subjects, not passive objects or victims of the historical process.

Validating and drawing upon knowledge rooted in the experience of colonialism (but still manifest in their daily lives), and drawing as well upon knowledge antedating colonialism, these historians are examining both the historical and the contemporary writing of African American, Asian American, Chicana, and Native American women and their communities on the land base we now call the American West. They are deconstructing, reconceptualizing, and reconstructing the histories of women and communities of color in this region. Thus they are equally critical of the early historical literature and of the recent historical studies, including those employing the multicultural approach to the history of women in the West and feminist writings of women of color.

Historians, including feminist historians and other feminist scholars, must examine their assumptions as well as their racial, class, and gender positions as they redefine historical and other categories of analysis. The structures of colonialism are the historical legacy of the United States, and, as such, inform the profession of history and the production of historical scholarship as much as they do any other human relationship and endeavor. If western history is to be decolonized, historians must be conscious of their power and ideology within the structures of colonialism, and conscious as well of the ways in which historical scholarship has helped to sustain and reproduce those structures. The study of women of color requires us to reexamine, challenge, and change those structures. Only then will we decolonize western history.

★The author is a member of the Women's Studies Program and the Chicano Studies Department in the University of California, Santa Barbara.

I thank Deena Gonzáles and Emma Pérez for reading and commenting on this essay, and Elizabeth Forsyth for editorial assistance.

Jensen–Miller
Prize
1993

'A Memory Sweet to Soldiers': The Significance of Gender in the History of the 'American West'

Susan Lee Johnson

O F all the regions people have imagined within the boundaries of what is now the United States, no place has been
so consistently identified with maleness—particularly white
maleness—as the region imagined as the American West. There is something odd about attending to gender in such a historical place—a place
where the dominant popular culture suggests that white women were
civilizers, women of color were temptresses or drudges, and men of
color were foils for the inevitable white male hero, who is, after all, the
true subject of the history of the "American West." Studying women
there is like enlisting in the frontier regulars; when you do so, you
commit yourself to a battle-ready stance that wearies all but the strongest
of heart. Studying men there is like playing with fire; when you do so,
you face the engulfing flames of western-history-as-usual, which naturalizes and universalizes white manhood as quickly as you can strike
a match to a lodgepole pine.

★ Susan Lee Johnson, "'A Memory Sweet to Soldiers': The Significance of Gender
in the History of the 'American West'," *Western Historical Quarterly* 14:3 (1993). ©
1993 Western Historical Society Quarterly, Western History Association. Reprinted
by permission.

Yet these same perils mean that we can learn something new about gender from studying an imagined place like the American West—a place where customary gender relations were disrupted for many years by unusual sex ratios and a place around which cultural meanings have collected until it has become a sort of preserve for white masculinity. We can also learn something new about gender from studying a process like the conquest of the West, the consolidation of Anglo-American dominance, and the constant realignment of relations of domination in a multiracial and multiethnic social world. Conversely, if we attend relentlessly to racialized notions of gender, we are bound to learn something new about the West—itself not just the "American West," which too often is shorthand for an Anglo-American West, but all of the regions people have imagined in the western half of the North American continent.

I will not engage in all aspects of this larger project here but will take up those aspects that reflect my particular intellectual and political positioning. As a student, I came to western history first and women's history and women's studies second, and my training in these fields centered disproportionately on Anglo-American experience. I gained what limited knowledge I have of ethnic studies and feminist theory late and largely on my own in the formal sense, though informally, especially in ethnic studies, I have benefited from the training provided by patient and committed friends, colleagues, and students. In time these emphases congealed into a broader concern with questions of region, race, and gender. Ultimately, however, to engage in this larger project of mapping racialized notions of gender onto the field of western history, we will need a set of tools developed in a number of interconnected areas of inquiry: feminist theory, ethnic studies, women's and labor history, lesbian and gay studies, postcolonial and minority discourse, cultural studies, and queer theory, to name a few. I will take on just a piece of that project here, drawing from my own background in the study of region, race, and gender, to ask some questions about the "subject" of the history of the "American West." I see this, then, as a specific intervention in the rewriting of western history, one that is self-conscious of its historical and historiographical moment, rather than as the statement-of-the-century implied by the essay's subtitle, which commemorates, for better or worse, the centenary of Frederick Jackson Turner's frontier thesis.

In recent years, this "subject" has been jostled by the emergence of a small mountain of scholarship on women in the West, indicating deep and active fault lines in the terrain of western history as a whole. Review essays by Joan Jensen and Darlis Miller in 1980 and by Elizabeth Jameson in 1988 surveyed that new terrain as it emerged, and special sections and issues of *Montana The Magazine of Western History* and the *Pacific Historical Review* have brought the issues and concerns of western women s history up to date in the 1990s.[1] Despite this outpouring of scholarship, the truly earth-shattering potential of studying western women has not been realized; only a few groundbreaking works that are not women's history per se try to make gender a central category of analysis.[2] Books and articles about women proliferate; anthologies now include a requisite women's history chapter; and scholarly conferences feature separate panels on women's experiences. Most mainstream scholars, however, leave questions of gender to women's historians, who are also usually women historians. Although this turn of events is hardly unique to western history, it does have its peculiar "western" dimensions and may require peculiarly "western" efforts to change its course.

This is because the relationship between what is western and what is male is overdetermined.[3] That relationship, though it reaches back over the centuries of Anglo-American westward expansion on the North American continent, tightened into an almost impermeable bond by the end of the nineteenth century. The American West as a conceptual region, then, did not become such a stubbornly, almost belligerently, male preserve until, however ironically, as a demographic region it was ceasing to be disproportionately male. The construction of a masculine West was part of a larger late-nineteenth-century "crisis of manliness" in the United States—a crisis in which older definitions of white, middle-class manhood that emphasized restraint and respectability (manly men) gave way to newer meanings that focused on vigor and raw virility (masculine men).[4] That transformation was closely linked both to U.S. imperialism in the Pacific, the Caribbean, and Latin America and to stateside developments such as the rise of organized labor, the shifting tactics of African-American leaders from the late nineteenth to the early twentieth centuries, and the broadening and consolidation of the woman movement in the same period. It was perhaps most evident in the cultural resonance of such turn-of-the century phenomena as the fiction of Owen Wister, Theodore Roosevelt's advocacy of "the strenuous life," Buffalo Bill's Wild West Show, the art of Frederic Remington, and Frederick Jackson Turner's appeal to the western man of action.

For a hundred years now, many have struggled with the all-too-material legacy of that crisis—that is, the discursive decline of manliness and the concomitant rise of masculinity. This new, hegemonic masculinity has been contested, and in some cases transformed, by a number of twentieth-century social practices: western women's labor force participation during World War II; the growth of lesbian and gay communities in the urban West; and the continuing evolution of competing styles of gender relations among western American Indians, Mexican Americans, Asian Americans, and African Americans. But the discursive apparatus of white masculinity has not been dismantled, and the "American West" still exists as a sort of happy hunting ground for Anglo virility.

Nor, in the academic arena, have the practices of western women's history proved equal to the task; mainstream historians respectfully acknowledge the new scholarship without incorporating its imperatives into their own work.[5] Then too, the field of western women's history has developed with western-history-as-usual as its reference point, deriving part of the legitimacy it *has* achieved from its oppositional relation to the presumed white male subject of the history of the "American West." For this reason, despite constant calls for multicultural approaches, western women's history is slow to incorporate into its purview the imperatives of ethnic studies scholarship, as historian Antonia Castañeda so eloquently explains in her essay "Women of Color and the Rewriting of Western History."[6] As long as the close identification between the categories "white men" and the "American West" continues both in popular culture and in mainstream scholarship, the relationships among western-history-as-usual, (white) western women's history, western ethnic history, and the history of western women of color will remain brittle at best.

On the other hand, if we can problematize men and what is "masculine" or "manly" in the history of the American West, and if we can see such gendered imaginings in all their racial, ethnic, and economic dimensions, we stand to gain even more than an understanding of how various women and men lived the western past. It is a commonplace of women's and ethnic studies that, in the United States, women of all races and ethnicities and peoples of color, both women and men, constitute "marked" and white men "unmarked" categories of human experience—the unmarked category serving as the normative, the more inclusive, the less "interested" and particular. As historians, then, we must both illuminate female and non-Anglo-American lives and mark the category of white, male experience—show it to be as historically and culturally contingent, as deeply linked to conceptions of gender and race, and as limited in its ability to explain the past as that of any other group of westerners. Only then can we begin to deflate the overblown rhetoric of white masculinity that has long been associated with the "American West." That rhetoric not only has obscured the vast diversity and stubborn inequities of western life but also has informed configurations of power and politics from Hollywood to Washington, D.C., and has been exported by U.S. media to far corners of the globe.

My argument, then, runs like this: gender is a relation of difference and domination constructed such that it appears "natural" in day-to-day life. The West is historically a place of disrupted gender relations and stunning racial and ethnic diversity, a diversity structured by inequality and injustice. So, studying gender in the West holds promise for the project of denaturalizing gender and dislodging it from its comfortable moorings in other relations of domination, from small-town racism to worldwide imperialism. In short, we need to ask what studying gender can do for the history of the West and what studying the West can do for the politics of gender.

But where to begin? One place to start is with some of the work western historians know best, reading it anew with eyes trained to recognize the ways in which racialized notions of gender have created meaning and reinforced power relations in the Wests of academia and popular culture. Indeed, in the West as many scholars have represented it, gender has been among the great invisible creators of meaning, perhaps more invisible than race itself, which even in the most predictable, problematic winning-of-the-West narratives has been an explicit, if deeply offensive, analytical theme. To demonstrate this, I have chosen two texts for critical rereading: Henry Nash Smith's *Virgin Land* (1950) and Richard Slotkin's *The Fatal Environment* (1985). These works represent mainstream western intellectual history at its most sophisticated and provocative and are texts that I assume most students of the West have encountered in their academic careers.[7]

There are worlds of difference between *Virgin Land* and *The Fatal Environment*, differences that reflect not only scholarly developments during the thirty-five years that separate their publication dates but changes in the politics of gender as well. Nevertheless, they share the habit of bracketing gendered concerns and associating them primarily with things female, particularly with white women and, sometimes less consciously, with unconventionally gendered white men. As a result, female gender remains the marked category in the texts, a category unmarked by race. Men of color—primarily American Indians—are marked by race but not by gender, whereas women of color are nearly absent altogether. In these texts, white male gender, in all its anxious self-absorption, remains the unspoken but obstreperous subject of the history of the "American West."

First I turn to *Virgin Land*—a gendered appellation if ever there was one. In her appropriately titled book *The Lay of the Land* (1975), Annette Kolodny laid bare a crucial thesis of any feminist critique of Smith.[8] But my critique is not only this critique—that Smith repeats, indeed, takes problematic pleasure in, the land-as-woman metaphor that characterized white men's encounter with the frontier, particularly as earlier images of the land-as-mother gave way to later images of the land-as-virgin. As important as such an indignant slap at male presumption can be, it does not go as far as it might in confounding what historian Regina Kunzel has identified, in a different context, as the "old, old story" of male sexual aggression and female sexual passivity.[9] The gender trouble in *Virgin Land* is at once simpler and more complicated than its metaphoric association of the frontier experience with rape culture, at worst, or virgin fetish, at best. It is simpler because it is not just the monotonous hierarchy of conventional heterosexual relations that *Virgin Land* obscures (indeed, Smith naturalizes more than he obscures that hierarchy). What Smith obscures is that his account of the "impact of the West … on the consciousness of Americans" and of the "consequences of this impact in literature and social thought" is mostly concerned with the impact of the West on white men and the consequences of that impact on white male literary and scholarly production. I say "mostly" because Smith includes respectful, if ultimately depreciatory, readings of authors such as Caroline Kirkland and Alice Cary, whom he describes as clever if dowdy literary foremothers of the bright young men who established the frontier realist genre (Hamlin Garland, for example, and, tellingly, Kirkland's biological son, Joseph Kirkland). These nods to matronly white women writers aside, *Virgin Land* is by and large a paean to the extraordinarily rich, elastic, and complex set of meanings that white men have attached to what Smith calls "the vacant continent beyond the frontier." That definition of the West is itself telling, for if the "virgin land" was repeopled by Mexicans and American Indians, it would become clear not only what but who was unwillingly to play "woman" to westward movement. If Smith had been able to mark the experience that most enthralled him as white, as male, and as heterosexually oriented (but shot through with what Eve Kosofsky Sedgwick calls male homosocial desire), we would have read a quite different book.[10]

Still, the gender trouble in *Virgin Land* is more complicated than a lay-of-the-land thesis suggests, because of the brief, curiously situated chapter that Smith includes at the end of what he calls "Book Two: The Sons of Leatherstocking."[11] The final chapter in that "book" is entitled "The Dime Novel Heroine," and so from the start these gun-toting girls are making trouble under a sign that is clearly gendered white male. The "Dime Novel Heroine" is not only conceptually but physically central to Virgin Land—the text as a whole roughly straddles it. It is conceptually central because it marks a turning point in Smith's analysis from an earlier emphasis on the West as wilderness to a later emphasis on the West as garden.

For Smith, the emergence in late-nineteenth-century dime novels of the wild western heroine—cross-dressing hunk of a girl who could shoot from the hip like a man—marked the inevitable decline of the

wilderness metaphor and its ability to produce a hero suitable to a growing, civilized, democratic nation. From James Fenimore Cooper's
Leatherstocking, a man of nature with a perfect moral compass and deep
respect for women of culture, Smith traces the "progressive deterioration"
of the western hero to a self-reliant two-gun man who behaved . . . the
same . . . whether he were outlaw or peace officer." That deterioration
reached its nadir when the heroine too, "freed from the trammels of gentility, developed at last into an Amazon who was distinguished from the
hero solely by the physical fact of her sex."[12]

In this, then, gender becomes a distinction without a difference, as
Smith all but dismisses the physicality of the dime-novel heroine in a
move that prefigures feminist debates over the meanings of "sex" and
"gender," albeit for quite different rhetorical purposes. For Smith, once
the wilderness was peopled with similarly gendered toughs, whatever
their genitalia, the fate of the frontier hero was sealed. As the representative of his (white) race, the hero had no meaning in a world with one
gender, for a world with one gender was a world without gender. In the
absence of difference, who would birth the frontier hero? Who would
domesticate his increasingly savage soul?

The threat of race suicide, brought about by the collapsing of white
womanhood into white manhood, is also reflected in the illustrations
for the book, of which there are a dozen.[13] They begin with a beneficent
image of the goddess of agriculture in the Mississippi Valley, but they end
ominously with a dime-novel cover that features a phallic rendering of
Calamity Jane in buckskin, leveling not one but two guns (or, as the caption puts it, "a pair of cocked revolvers") at a frightened male foe. Her
enemy's name is Gardner (gardener? anyway, Ralph, to his friends), and
his only weapon, a fairly good-sized knife, is withdrawn from battle,
pointed away from Jane and toward his male companions. The image is
complicated further by the dime-novel title that runs in bold letters
above it: *Deadwood Dick in Leadville; Or, A Strange Stroke, for Liberty*.

Who *is* the subject of this pastiche? Why is Deadwood Dick absent
from the cover illustration, and why is Calamity Jane foregrounded?
What will happen to Deadwood Dick in Leadville, that rough-and-
tumble mining camp in Colorado? What "strange stroke for liberty" will
he take? The possibilities for Dick and Jane, deadwood and calamity, are

multiple. But evidence for a race-and-gender panic reading appears in the figure of the well-dressed, dark-skinned cardplayer in the lower righthand corner of the illustration. The gambler (the text reveals that this is "straight and honest" Carlos Cordova, who carries no gun) looks as if he stands to gain the most when Jane enacts this particular calamity; he sits waiting while the white men rise to meet their challenger.[14]

A full analysis of the fear of race suicide represented in such images and in such texts would require a thorough rereading of the genre, but even this brief glance at the dime-novel hero(in)es who bring up the rear for the sons of Leatherstocking reveals something more than a "progressive deterioration" of the western tale. Smith complains that after the 1880s, dime novels lost whatever literary merit they had once possessed and became locked into formulas that eventually came to characterize most western films and radio shows in the first half of the twentieth century as well. He thus forecloses analysis of such narratives at this curious moment in their evolving representations of gender and race, turning his attention from the seemingly bankrupt metaphor of the wilderness to the more promising metaphor of the garden. For myself, I would like to have lingered in the "wild" West a little bit longer.

Then again, if rough-and-tumble captures your fancy, there is always the work of Richard Slotkin. Despite the recent publication of *Gunfighter Nation* (1992), the third volume of Slotkin's "frontier myth" trilogy, I will focus on the second volume here, in part because it covers much of the same nineteenth-century ground as *Virgin Land*.[15] Written with the benefit of two decades of feminist ferment, *The Fatal Environment* is more self-conscious than *Virgin Land* about the maleness of the frontier myth it seeks to explicate, but only modestly so. It is a book concerned instead with how "the Myth of the Frontier" developed even as the "real frontier" passed away and the United States became increasingly urban, industrial, and class stratified.

Indeed, Slotkin capitalizes both "myth" and "frontier" and precedes these terms with "the," thereby hypostatizing "the Frontier Myth" as singular and univocal, a kind of pillar of stone that becomes an easy target for patricidal critique. This approach has its benefits; fortified with structuralist tools, Slotkin skillfully historicizes the frontier myth, leaning back as far as the Puritan wars with native peoples and forward to the 1876 Battle of the Little Bighorn, which, in its retelling as "Custer's Last Stand," takes its place as the centerpiece of *The Fatal Environment* (the title itself comes from a poem Walt Whitman first published as "Death-Sonnet for Custer"). Slotkin's purpose is to show how U.S. history was mythologized as an "Indian war" writ large even as mythmakers fretted over the closing of the frontier. The Last Stand story, Slotkin claims, fused these two processes (mythologizing the frontier and fretting over its passing) and thus became the "central fable" of the new, industrial "Myth of the Frontier."[16]

Slotkin shows how "Indian war"—especially the fight-to-the-last of the soldier so white he can dress like an Indian and still stand for his race—became a metaphor for a variety of social conflicts plaguing a newly industrialized nation that was also recovering from a catastrophic civil war. He argues that by the time of Little Bighorn, journalists had already developed the habit of juxtaposing stories of American Indian resistance in the West with articles on the problems of emancipated African Americans in the South and the struggles of organized white workers in the North. Newspapermen not only set these stories side by side but also used common verbal or thematic cues (such as "savage" or "race" or "war") to link the articles to one another, and they occasionally wrote editorials that made the analogies explicit.[17]

So when George Armstrong Custer and his troops met their fate at the hands of two thousand Lakota, Cheyenne, and Arapaho warriors amassed at the Little Bighorn River in June 1876, journalists soon began to see soldiers of civilization making last stands against all manner of savagery, not only in the West but in the North and the South as well. The Great Strike of 1877, in which railroad laborers resisted a nationwide rollback of their wages, is Slotkin's major case in point. As workingmen walked off their jobs and violence ensued, editors rushed in to announce, "The Great Railroad Strike Becomes a Savage War," and headlines about the "fighting strikers" ran cheek-to-cheek with those about "murderous reds" (here meaning Nez Perce Indians but recalling the Paris Communards as well).[18] Slotkin deftly demonstrates how white newspapermen saw class in racial terms during the nineteenth century and how Indian-white conflict, in particular, came to stand for battles between labor and capital.

The analysis falters, though, when Slotkin tries to juggle gender along with his concern for race and class.[19] When gender does trip onto the stage in *The Fatal Environment*, it often does so in the person of female characters in novels.[20] In fact, gender is always self-consciously at issue when Slotkin writes about women, and the presence of women, historical or fictional, often prompts him to think of the men he has put on stage as gendered beings too. But when women are nowhere to be found (and in the nineteenth-century West, this state of affairs was not rare), Slotkin's men often revert to their customary status as normative humans, unmarked by gender.

Still, there are exceptions. Slotkin's descriptions of Custer, for example, are probably more deeply gendered than they are racialized; Custer's race seems not at issue until he meets up with racialized "others"—American Indians, in particular—whereas his gender is at issue from childhood, as he seeks to accommodate motherly and fatherly influences. But when it came to Custer and gender, there was trouble afoot, trouble that Slotkin finds symbolized best in how the officer wore his hair: Custer would clip it short for a time, Slotkin observes, and then grow it out and "let his curls swing below his shoulders perfumed with cinnamon oil." Slotkin suggests that the long hair somehow reflected Custer's father's "flamboyance," but it also, the author acknowledges, made Custer "appear 'feminine.'" Furthermore, Custer apparently took sensual pleasure in this "feminine" appearance.[21]

Slotkin makes much of the ways that Custer used his seeming youth—he was, after all, regarded as Americas own "boy general"—to court the favor of older, more powerful men, be they military superiors, New York financial magnates, or Washington politicians.[22] But the author hesitates to explore the ways that Custer's variable gender performances worked to the officer's advantage. This is not to say that Slotkin ignores the evidence. He is quick to include an assessment of Custer by an aide to General Phil Sheridan, Custer's commanding officer. The aide characterized the relationship between Sheridan and Custer as grounded in difference: "While Sheridan was always cool, Custer was aflame." Custer's flaming tendencies, the aide went on to explain, were not hard to tolerate: "We all liked Custer and did not mind his little freaks . . . any more than we would have minded temper in a woman."[23]

For Slotkin, this characterization is an instance of Custer as a "liminal hero, the boy-man whose sexual character is on the border between masculine adulthood and the passionate nature of woman." As such, Custer embodies for Slotkin the key trait of a mythic hero, that is, the "incarnation of . . . polar oppositions." Moving swiftly from Custer's "little freaks" to his inevitable rise from the grave as the ultimate American hero, Slotkin concludes: "Custer is presented as the meeting point of the positive and negative forces in American culture—masculinity and femininity, adulthood and childhood, civilization and savagery, sanity and madness, order and disorder."[24] Never mind that each of these oppositions had very specific (and changing) meanings during the nineteenth century. Never mind that the masculine-feminine dichotomy in particular—which I see more as a twentieth-century construction—might be more usefully characterized as one between manliness and womanliness in this period. Never mind that these binaries were hotly contested not only within the white, Protestant, middle-class, male-dominated cultural ethos but also from the margins by people not privileged by race, religion, class, or gender.

I could put these critiques aside for a moment. I could even, grudgingly and temporarily, grant Custer the central place in U.S. history for which he so longed. But I would also want to linger a little longer than Slotkin does over how Custer inhabited a gender and how his way of doing gender (and how much of that way) was mapped onto a whole region and ultimately onto the imagined community of the nation.[25] In addition, I would want to consider, in the context of western history, what gender has to do with race wars and how it inflects class conflict as well. And I would want to think about how the scholarly impulse to find One Big Myth and to identify its One True Hero relates to the dominant cultural impulses that, by the twentieth century, turned the "American West" into a mirror for a particular white male subjectivity. This impulse more recently has led Slotkin to argue that a new, less politically problematic national myth "will have to respond to the demographic transformation of the United States and speak to and for a polyglot nationality," as if the old myth spoke for an actual past, before the fabled "demographic transformation," when the United States and its colonial predecessors were not troubled by the presence of women, peoples of color, and unmanly men.[26]

Much is held in abeyance when this impulse to find One Big Myth and to identify its One True Hero is indulged. There is the dime-novel heroine, whose brazen perversion of the heroic suggests that western heroism itself is a parody for which there is no original, only better and worse performances.[27] Recall that Smith's search for the ultimate American hero led him to abandon dime novels just as the she-man came into her pistol-packing own. Also held in abeyance are Custer's "little freaks," which Slotkin quickly positions in a larger symbolic universe of all the grand binary oppositions of modern Anglo-American culture. I am still curious, even after 532 pages of *The Fatal Environment*, to learn how a white man who took sensual pleasure in his cinnamon-scented locks and who seemed aflame in relation to more conventionally gendered men came to stand as the great tragic hero of Anglo America in the age of industrialization.

Not only is there little in *The Fatal Environment* to help me make sense of this, there is little in the whole of western historiography to which I can turn in beginning such a project. Even western women's historians have not offered much grist for this mill, except for a delightful disdain for Big Myths and True Heroes and a dogged devotion to the heroics of everyday life.[28] So although I might begin my inquiry into the gendering of the "American West" with the attitude of recent western women's history, for analysis I am more inclined to turn to current shifts in thinking about gender in the larger field of women's studies. Curiously enough, these two contemporaneous scholarly developments have proceeded relatively independent of one another.

The new work on western women that began to appear in the late 1970s opened up whole social and political worlds to view that had long been obscured by the stultifying maleness of the West as it had been represented in both academia and popular culture. *Frontier Women, Westering Women, The Women's West, Western Women: Their Land, Their Lives*—the book titles were bold and defiant, crafted as if to say: "The game's over, boys. It's my ball and I'm going home." The trouble was that the boys had balls too, and so instead of stopping the contest, the feminist retreat simply started a new, largely white, women's league—a sort of "our books, ourselves" approach to the game of historical scholarship.[29]

Meanwhile, back at the women's studies ranch, scholars in a variety of disciplines were busy lassoing the very category of "women" itself, tying it up in quotation marks, showing it to be not a transparent, self-evident denotation of people sexed female but, as Denise Riley puts it, a category "historically, discursively constructed . . . a volatile collectivity in which female persons can be very differently positioned, so that the apparent continuity of the subject of 'women' isn't to be relied on."[30] That is, whereas western women's historians took for granted that the subjects of their research and analysis were, in a word, "women," other women's studies scholars (a few of them historians) marveled at how we have come to see women and men at every academic turn. So while the women of western women's history trudged matter-of-factly across the Overland Trail gathering buffalo dung for fuel, the "women" of women's studies got all dressed up and stepped out on the town to a dizzying gender-bender ball, where anything could—and did—happen.

Though inconsistently acknowledged by women's studies scholars privileged by race, ethnicity, class background, or sexuality, the original invitations to try out these new dance steps came disproportionately from scholars, writers, and activists marginalized by those very same social constructions.[31] As Evelyn Brooks Higginbotham has recently argued, white feminist theorists, in particular, have nodded curtly at the overtures of feminists of color while going on "to analyze their own experience in ever more sophisticated forms." Similarly, Norma Alarcón and Chela Sandoval have demonstrated the difficulties that hegemonic feminism has had in incorporating the insights of U.S. Third World feminist theories, insights that necessarily undermine understandings of gender as a binary opposition isolated from other social and discursive categories such as race and culture.[32] To me, this conversation about gender and politics among differently situated feminists, a heated conversation characterized by inequalities of power among speakers, holds as much promise for thinking about what gender might mean in the history of the West as does the literature that seems to formulate such questions most explicitly—the historiography of western women. For my purposes here, then, I will step back from that place called the "Women's West" and survey instead the terrain of gender itself. What is gender, anyway, and how can attending to it transform our thinking about western history?

One clear trajectory in feminist theory—if I may collapse a series of complex and often contradictory moves into a general, unidirectional trend—has been from structuralist to poststructuralist thinking, from singular to multiple explanations for gender difference and gender hierarchy, and from a self-evident, self-confident agreement on social constructionism to an increasingly complicated inquiry into just what it *means* to say that gender is socially (or culturally or historically) constructed.[33] An original insight of women's studies in the 1970s was the distinction between sex and gender, with "sex" standing for the biological givens that distinguish female from male and "gender" the cultural elaborations based on the givens of biological sex. Anthropologist Gayle Rubin developed the most stunning explication of this distinction in her essay "The Traffic in Women: Notes on the 'Political Economy' of Sex," which set a high standard for both rigor and wit in feminist scholarship.

Poking fun at how fast and loose some had been with the term patriarchy, for example, Rubin reminded feminists to maintain a sense of historical specificity. "Abraham was a Patriarch," she quipped, "one old man whose absolute power over wives, children, herds and dependents was an aspect of the institution of fatherhood."[34] Substituting the term "sex/gender system" for obfuscating terms like "patriarchy" or "mode of reproduction," Rubin wove together insights from Marx and Engels, Freud and Lacan, and Levi-Strauss to postulate systematic ties among the creation of two dichotomous genders from the givens of sex, the ubiquity of sexual divisions of labor, and obligatory heterosexuality. Explaining that gender presumes not only identification with one sex but also sexual desire for the other, she invoked the book of Genesis once again: "The sexual division of labor is implicated in both aspects of gender—male and female it creates them, and it creates them heterosexual."[35] If this set of insights alone became commonplace in studies of western places and peoples—insights that refuse to take male-female differences, couplings, and divisions of labor for granted—the field would take a great leap forward.

But there is more. In the last decade, the feminist credo of the distinction between sex and gender has fallen on hard times as some scholars have argued that no real substance of biological sex necessarily lies beneath the cultural elaborations of gender. Thus whereas Smith describes the devolution of the dime-novel heroine into an "Amazon who was distinguished from the hero solely by the physical fact of her sex," some feminist theorists would dispute the "physical fact" itself. As Riley puts it, "Nothing is assumed about an underlying continuity of real women, above whose constant bodies changing aerial descriptions dance."[36] The work of Judith Butler has been particularly revealing on this point. She suggests, first, that even if we assume the stability of male and female bodies, there is no reason that the construction "men" will always follow from male bodies and the construction "women" from female bodies. Nor is there any reason that the seeming binariness of sex (its splitting into two dichotomous categories) will necessarily lead to two, and only two, genders. Second, Butler argues that the duality of sex, far from being an immutable "fact of life," is itself historically constructed through various scientific and other discourses that have worked together to make us see natural male and female bodies even if we are skeptical about "natural women" and "natural men." In this reading, sex was "always already gender," masked as biology's last stand— and sex will presumably go the way of Custer when faced with the warrior wisdom of feminist theory.[37]

For some scholars of the last decade, then, gender is not so much a noun as it is a verb. Butler argues that "gender is always a doing," and Riley speaks of the act of inhabiting a gender, notions I used earlier in my reading of Slotkin's Custer. In this vein, Butler suggests that gender is performative—again, an analysis I drew on in thinking about Custer. Thus, "gender is the repeated stylization of the body, a set of repeated acts . . . that congeal over time to produce the appearance of substance, of a natural sort of being."[38] (And if that still seems abstract, just think of how it worked for John Wayne or how it works for you.) Other scholars, Joan Scott among them, have looked beyond the ways in which people "do" gender to analyze how sexual difference creates meaning in situations in which individual human bodies and their stylization are less at issue.[39] The nineteenth-century creation of the working class on male terms is one case in point; so too, I would contend, is the consolidation of the "American West" as a masculine preserve.

Yet these scholars are among those to whom Higginbotham refers when she notes that the "new wave of feminist theorists finds little to say about race."[40] To the extent that this is true, this "new wave" will prove of limited use to western historians, for whom analysis of racial difference and racial domination must be a key mode of inquiry. And indeed, although most white feminist scholars acknowledge the importance of race somewhere in their work, few follow through with a thoroughgoing analysis of how gender is racialized and race is gendered, even in relationship to white women. In fact, race is perhaps least often invoked as a category of analysis when white experience is at issue. This has prompted historian Elsa Barkley Brown to argue, "We have yet to accept the fact that one cannot write adequately about the lives of white women in the United States in any context without acknowledging the way in which race shaped their lives."[41]

Nevertheless, it is work by and about women of color that routinely recognizes, as bell hooks puts it, that "none of us experiences ourselves solely as gendered subjects."[42] Higginbotham, in particular, has explored race as a metalanguage that obscures other social relations such as gender and class. Such insights resonate with Slotkin's work on the racializing of class tensions in the nineteenth century but are largely absent in his attempts to analyze gender.[43] Alarcón has gone further to examine the differences between the theoretical subject of Anglo-American feminisms and that of women-of-color feminisms. The Anglo subject of knowledge is "autonomous, self-making, self-determining"; she pursues her own identity largely in opposition to Anglo men. This should sound familiar because it is work like Alarcón's that has informed my thinking not only about the presumed white male subject of the history of the "American West" but also about how western women's history has suffered from its overidentification, in oppositional terms, with western-history-as-usual.

Third World feminisms have developed more diffuse and complex notions of identity and subjectivity, acknowledging multiple referents for consciousness that explode the neat dichotomies of Anglo feminist theories of gender. As Alarcón points out, for example, the existence of class and racial hierarchies often means that one may "'become a woman' in opposition to other women." Such notions of multiple consciousness derive from the historically and culturally specific struggles of U.S. women of color. Gloria Anzaldúa's borderlands consciousness, "*la conciencia de la mestiza*," is a case in point especially relevant to western historians, arising as it does in part out of Anzaldúa's South Texas roots. Her consciousness of the borderlands encompasses a sense of self and a politics antithetical to binary thinking that opposes Indian to Mexican, Mexican to Anglo, female to male, gay to straight, and south-of-the-border to north-of-theborder.[44]

From these historical and cultural specificities and their resulting notions of consciousness, Sandoval has developed a synergetic theory of "differential consciousness," one that emphasizes the importance of shifting tactics, which enables political coalitions to resist relations of domination in their myriad incarnations. In what is easily one of the most visionary sentences in any recent work of feminist theory, Sandoval explains the grace, flexibility, and strength required of those who would practice this differential consciousness: "enough strength to confidently commit to a well-defined structure of identity for one hour, day, week, month, year; enough flexibility to self-consciously transform that identity according to the requisites of another oppositional ideological tactic if readings of power's formation require it; enough grace to recognize alliance with others committed to egalitarian social relations and race, gender, and class justice, when their readings of power call for alternative oppositional stands."[45]

This is a program for political change on a grand scale, but its implications, I think, are relevant on the relatively smaller scale of transforming the field of western history. It will require grace, flexibility, and strength, and it will require working in alliance with those whose training and commitments differ from our own, to recognize and refuse the ways that racialized notions of gender have created meaning and reinforced relations of domination in the American West as constructed by both scholarship and popular culture.

This much we have learned: first, gender is what one does rather than what one is. That is, it is not so much that boys will be boys as it is in that being boyish, one becomes a boy in a given context. Second, gender creates meaning quite apart from the practices by which individuals become gendered. That is, political cultures, presidential administrations, social classes, and regions themselves, at certain historical moments, will seem to some to be saturated with womanliness or manliness, femininity or masculinity. Third, gender never exists as a simple binary that can be disaggregated from other constructed relations of difference and domination such as race. As Brown puts it, "All women do not have the same gender."[46] Neither do all men, as suggested by soldiers' perceptions of Custer and Sheridan and by the competing styles of manhood represented in the dime-novel cover for Deadwood Dick in Leadville.

What happens when we take these insights back to the land of Big Myths and True Heroes? We do not necessarily stop studying myths, or cultural memories, and their heroes. As a region historically in a colonial relationship with the dominant Northeast, the West, like the South, has produced more than its share of larger-than-life legends who tell us a great deal not only about gender and race relations within particular regions but also about how regions themselves become imagined as gendered and racialized places. Hopefully, though, we can learn to attend to legends less celebrated than Custer and to see the ways in which cultural memory and cultural amnesia among the dominant and the nondominant have helped to create all of the regions people have imagined in western North America.

As a California historian, I am reminded of particular examples. What of Joaquín Murrieta, the supposed scourge of the Southern Mines, who has been remembered by Chicano scholars and activists alike as symbolizing a history of resistance to Anglo domination but who is mostly forgotten in mainstream accounts of the Gold Rush? What of Babe Bean (later known as Jack Garland), who was heralded in the turn-of-the-century press as the "trousered puzzle" of Stockton? This passing woman has been reclaimed by lesbian and gay historians, who discovered that s/he had been born in 1870 as Elvira Virginia Mugarrieta, of Mexican and Anglo parentage. But Babe Bean and many other westerners who engaged in gender and ethnic passing have been largely ignored by western-history-as-usual. Attending to such characters will not advance the study of One Big Myth and its One True Hero, but it will represent an attempt to listen in on a many-voiced conversation about cultural memory of a multiracial, once disproportionately male historical place—in this case, California.[47]

Yet even if we turn back to Big Myths and True Heroes from time to time, we need to stop privileging aspects of those myths and characteristics of those heroes that fit most comfortably with dominant cultural notions of how white manhood is embodied in the "American West." I am struck, for example, by the lines of Walt Whitman's "Death-Sonnet for Custer" from which Slotkin chose the title of *The Fatal Environment*.[48] They are bellicose lines that fight to the last until Custer and his entourage finally fall:

> The battle-bulletin,
> The Indian ambuscade, the craft, the fatal
>   environment,
> The cavalry companies fighting to the last
>   in sternest heroism,
> In the midst of their little circle, with their
>   slaughter'd horses for breastworks,
> The fall of Custer and all his officers and men.

My own eyes, though, are drawn to Whitman's last stanza, where an interestingly gendered and unambiguously sexualized Custer, now an object of desire for his officers and men, relinquishes symbols of his power and rests in the sweetness of defeat. Imagine, then, a different title for a book about the myth of the frontier in the age of industrialization, a title drawn instead from these lines of Whitman's:

> Thou of the tawny flowing hair in battle,
> I erewhile saw, with erect head, pressing ever
>   in front, bearing a bright sword in thy hand,
> Now ending well in death the splendid fever of
>   thy deeds,
> (I bring no dirge for thee, I bring a glad
>   triumphal sonnet,)
> Desperate and glorious, aye in defeat most
>   desperate, most glorious,

After thy many battles in which never yielding up
  a gun or a color,
Leaving behind thee a memory sweet to soldiers,
Thou yieldest up thyself.

I imagine that many of us want to say and do something new about the significance of gender in western history and to say and do it without assuming old postures of domination—without striking a pose, if you will.[49] If that is what we want, then some among us will have to yield up guns and colors, quietly, without trying to become anybody's heroes.

---

* Susan Lee Johnson is Associate Professor of History at the University of Wisconsin-Madison.

This essay first appeared the *Western Historical Quarterly* 24 (November 1993): 495–517. It also appeared in *A New Significance: Re-envisioning the History of the American West*, ed. Clyde A. Milner II (New York: Oxford University Press, 1996, pp. 255–278, and was accompanied there by two helpful commentaries: Albert L. Hurtado, "Staring at the Sun," pp. 279–283, and Deena J. González, "A Regendered, Reracialized, Resituated West," pp. 283–288. The version published here reproduces the updated endnotes that appeared in the 1996 reprinted version.

Many people have read various drafts of this essay and given me suggestions for revision or otherwise offered encouragement, including Nancy Cott, William Cronon, Laura Downs, Yvette Huginnie, Albert Hurtado, Kali Israel, Regina Kunzel, Howard Lamar, Karen Merrill, Clyde Milner, Kathryn Oberdeck, Peggy Pascoe, Mary Renda, Vicki Ruiz, Barbara Savage, and colleagues in the women's junior faculty reading group of the University of Michigan's history department. Five friends and colleagues have been particularly unstinting with their time, their criticism, and their warm support: Deena González, Camille Guerin-Gonzales, David Gutiérrez, Yukiko Hanawa, and Katherine Morrissey.

Gender, Race, Raza

Amy Kaminsky

S INCE the publication of *This Bridge Called My Back: Writings
of Radical Women of Color* (1981) and *All the Women Are White,
All the Blacks Are Men, but Some of Us Are Brave* (1982), scholarship by and about women of color has become increasingly central
to the project of academic feminism in the United States.[1] Many white
academic feminists have, for their part, made a concerted effort to pay
attention to issues of race in their theoretical, critical, and pedagogical
work.[2] This important and necessary change is increasingly affecting the
way gender itself is understood. Nevertheless, the acknowledgment of
racial difference and even the publication of important feminist/wom-
anist work concerning women of color has not meant that race has been
sufficiently theorized in the context of feminism. Here I am referring
not simply to challenging the homogeneity of a racial community, or
to looking simultaneously at race and gender, but, rather, to analyzing
the instability of race itself and the part gender plays in naturalizing
what gets called "race" in and across cultures.[3] In an attempt to do some
of this work here, I use a comparative, gender-conscious approach to

---

★ Amy Kaminsky, "Gender, Race, *Raza*," *Feminist Studies*, 20: 1 (Spring 1994).
©1994 Feminist Studies, Inc. Reprinted by permission.

examine configurations of race as they occur in and between Spain, Spanish America, and the United States. I name and discuss three discrete but overlapping moments of Hispanic racial formation: the Imperial, the postcolonial, and the expatriate. The Imperial moment occurs between 1492 (when the last Moslem kingdom in Spain was defeated by Ferdinand and Isabella and Columbus landed in America) and the mid- to late-nineteenth century, when Spain lost its American colonies. The postcolonial moment begins with that nineteenth-century independence from Spain and continues through the present. It refers geographically to Spanish America. The expatriate moment is primarily a late-twentieth-century phenomenon marked by the emigration of Spanish Americans to Europe (including Spain) and the United States. My discussion elaborates the notion that as a cultural construction race is unstable and has different meanings and different purposes in different times and places and that gender is fundamental in making those meanings and revealing those purposes.

The ease with which so many North Americans can cross most geographical borders too easily deceives us into thinking that we are able to cross all borders—linguistic, cultural, historical—with similar ease. The average English speaker's faith in literal translation, together with the belief that race is biologically determined, creates the illusion that when we talk about racial difference across cultures and over time we mean the same things. Yet the differing linguistic-geographical axes in English and Spanish have a profound effect on meanings of crucial categories of analysis. Like the Spanish *género*, whose primary meanings of genre and grammatical gender make it a false cognate for "gender" as it is used in English, *raza* does not quite mean "race."[4]

"Race" in English has polished its veneer of scientific objectivity, but raza still relies on affective connotations of culture and affinity. In the politicized borderlands of the United States that were formerly northern Mexico, raza means "Chicano." For the Chicano movement, which takes language itself as a vehicle for constituting an oppositional culture, the very Spanishness of the word is an irreducible part of its meaning. In this context, raza, unlike "race," is not a category that may include many possible variants. Heavy with connotations of Chicano family, history, and politics, raza actively resists translation.

In another use of the term, originating in Spain, the Imperial Spanish *Día de la Raza* (Columbus Day, literally "Day of the Race") celebrates an expansionist consolidation of race by means of conquest and colonization, the drive toward a great and inclusive Hispanic race, first under the protection of Empire (as Jose Piedra argues), and later as an affirmation of independence.[5] Its goal—and enabling belief—has been the assimilation of difference into a homogenizing *hispanidad*, a term that might provisionally be translated as "Hispanicity." Hispanidad wills a whitening first of Spain and then of what Carlos Fuentes has called Afro-Indo-Ibero-America.[6] The purifying noun, hispanidad, suggests the promise of supremacy for all those who submit to inclusion under its rubric. The English word "Hispanic," on the other hand, is an adjective signifying a form of non-whiteness, a marker of difference with implications of inferiority.[7]

As a U.S. racial term, "Hispanic" is a relatively new, vague, and contested category.[8] Its emergence marks the third moment of racial formation I discuss in this article. This expatriate moment is characterized by a shift from a position of dominance and majority status, particular to the Imperial and postcolonial moments, to a position of subordination and minority status. The term "Hispanic" is imposed by a hostile dominant culture in the United States and derives from a history of colonialism, insofar as it refers to people whose ancestors lived in areas of the Americas colonized by Spain, including descendants of the Spaniards themselves. It is largely linguistic, with Spanish a cultural connector, even if—as is often the case among third-generation Chicanos, for example—the language is no longer spoken. It even sometimes includes Asians and Jews, as well as the descendants of those Blacks and Native peoples forcibly melted into the pot of hispanidad under Empire. Not least problematically, it collapses particular national identities and cultural heritages into a single, undifferentiated category.[9]

Feminists in the United States tend to treat race as a stable (if complex) category. Among white feminists, moreover, there is a danger of fetishizing, and thereby immobilizing, race in the desire to engage in responsible feminist practice. One manifestation of this phenomenon can be found in anthologies of feminist literary criticism which consist of large numbers of essays on white writers that pay little attention to race, overshadowing a single article on a racially identified writer or subject.[10] As a fetish, race becomes a receptacle for meaning instead of a locus of the production of signification. At its worst, the reification of race creates the expectation that women of color will write only from a fixed standpoint and a demand that they be spokespeople for a group, writing from an "experience" that is uniform and already known.[11] This sort of essentialism limits agency, negates change, and stunts theoretical growth. As long as race is assumed to be a monolithic category, and as long as only people of color are assumed to "have" race, it will be the lump in the batter of feminist theory; and all our adding and stirring will be futile. Only when we conceptualize race as mutable and multi-valenced can we hope to make sense of the ways in which it interacts with the differently nuanced category of gender.

Race, like gender, can be thought of as a cluster of characteristics that are explained in terms of purported biological difference. (And in Spanish America there is far less resistance than in the United States to the notion of biological gender.) Both gender and race, as sets of behavioral expectations rationalized through biology, are hard categories to shake loose from beliefs about the constraints of biology. The inherited traits of race would seem to adhere to one another, as if hair texture, say, were only the visible sign of other, hidden, properties. Moreover, the absence of revealing physical characteristics are understood not to negate the existence of these deeper truths: blood will tell. Racial metaphors range from the invisibly internal (the aforementioned blood, particularly dear to sixteenth- and seventeenth-century Spaniards bent on proving the "purity" of theirs) to the blatantly external (skin "color," the favorite of contemporary North Americans). In all cases the referent is something of which only traces remain in the individual: her or his parentage. Even in English, race is, ultimately, less about science than social organization, more about lineage than gene pool, while hierarchized racial difference is a function of conditions of political and economic dependency. Race is legitimated by something that looks like biology, made scientific in the nineteenth century by the newly developing field of physical anthropology.[12] It is constituted through a cluster of prescribed, proscribed, or permitted behaviors not unlike those associated with a feudal notion of social organization. Unlike laws of nature, however, rules of behavior can be transgressed. When they are, authority takes care that the transgressor is either punished or pardoned, so that through its intervention the fundamental structures of racially or gender-appropriate behavior can be recovered.

For example, in 1797, after his father petitioned the king of Spain to allow him to continue his studies and attain a formal degree, activities prohibited to Blacks in the Spanish colonies, José Ponciano de Ayarza was granted permission to attend the University of Santa Fe in Bogotá (Colombia) and become a lawyer. The king wrote that "the character of mulatto being held extinguished in him, he be admitted, without its serving as precedent, to the degrees he may seek in the university...."[13] Similarly, when the pope allowed Catalina de Erauso (1585-?), who had lived much of her life as a soldier of the Conquest in the New World, to resume her masculine clothing and way of life, he did not repeal the laws of gender-appropriate behavior of his day but instead reasserted them by the very act of granting Catalina her singular privilege.[14] These exceptions to authorized gender and race behaviors quite explicitly do not unmake the rule.

Unlike gender in Western culture, which breaks down into a pair of bipolar opposites, where male/female is another way of saying male/not male, race cannot be split neatly in two.[15] As defined by the U.S. Bureau of the Census, for example, race is a melange of governmentally determined classifications that follow no particular pattern. The 1990 U.S. Census designates the following racial categories, in the following order: White, Black or Negro, Indian (Amer.), Eskimo, Aleut, Asian or Pacific Islander (with a series of geographical locators).[16] There is a mechanism for refusing any of these classifications: the slot designated "Other race." Even so, these categories are clearly insufficient. Ashkenazi Jews often classify themselves as white in relation to African Americans but as racially different in relation to white gentiles. Arab Americans, like Latinos, are increasingly identified and identifying in ways that are part ethnic and part racial, a phenomenon no doubt intensified by the current political climate in the Middle East. "The Black or Negro category," according to the census material, "also includes persons who identify as African-American, Afro-American, Haitian, Jamaican, West Indian, Nigerian, and so on."[17] That is, the category contains anybody who has African ancestry, and who, if light skinned, chooses to self-define. American Indian includes anyone of a bureaucratically designated percentage of Native American ancestry, whose self-identification is ratified by a tribal group.

The racial categories defined by the U.S. Bureau of the Census may be bureaucratically consolidated, but they derive in part from the individual's sense of identity within community and subsequently modify the community's perception of itself. This perception is affected, in turn, by the dominant culture's participation in the naming process. Racial identification, then, rests on multiple factors, including self-definition, external attribution, and political exigency, in different proportions, and resulting in a gaggle of official racial groupings. Despite this pileup of color-coded categories—black, red, brown, white, yellow—there remains a tendency in the United States to think of race in terms of white/not-white, where not-white oscillates between Black and a litany of othernesses.[18]

Although "female" and "not-male" are pretty much coterminous, "Black" is merely one version of "not-white." The tendency in the United States to categorize racial "others" in relation to whiteness, and to elide the differences among these others, serves to maintain the symbiotic fictions of "white" as norm and "Black" as race. The emerging racial category "Hispanic" easily disappears into the realm of "non-white," eliding the multiple differences in U.S. society, all the while burying ever more deeply the differences within "Hispanic." In the Census material, interestingly, "Hispanic" is not classified as a race. It is, instead, a specially designated ethnic classification, unique among all U.S. ethnicities in appearing on the form.[19] "Hispanic" itself is broken down into four categories: Mexican, Mexican-Am, Chicano; Puerto Rican; Cuban; other Spanish/Hispanic (including the rest of Spanish America and Spain). The officially recognized internal differences are geographical and, astonishingly, political (namely, Chicano and Mexican-Am). Despite the fact that the Census does not classify Spanish/Hispanic under "race," but rather gives it its own slot on the form, in the popular imagination "Hispanic" is a racial classification, insofar as it is invoked along with African American, American Indian, and Asian as a designated minority group. Stuart Hall's observation that whereas racial identity was once tied to nationality it is now tied to ethnicity is perfectly congruent with the argument I am making here.[20]

The construction of "Hispanic" as race in the first, Imperial, moment and in the second, postcolonial, moment is nicely illustrated in two unselfconsciously gendered tales of racial formation under the sign of hispanidad, one Spanish, the other Mexican. In the third, expatriate, moment, the stories no longer unconsciously reproduce cultural givens concerning gender in their production of racial formations but, rather, interrogate both gender and race. I invoke these stories not as magic mirrors that reflect without distortion the essence of their moment, nor as signposts pointing baldly to turns in the road, but rather as texts in a larger discursive field that serve as catalyst and reference point for my discussion. The Spanish story is from the anonymous picaresque novel, *Lazarillo de Tormes* (c. 1554). What characterizes the picaresque, and its prototype, *Lazarillo de Tormes*, is its caustic and purportedly didactic representation of the underside of society during the time of the consolidation of the Spanish empire. In the following passage the title character recalls his mother, in the first-person narration typical of the Spanish picaresque:

> My widowed mother, finding herself without a husband or anyone to take care of her, decided to [ally herself with good folk in order to] be like them. So she came to the city to live. She rented a little house and began to cook for some students. She washed clothes for some stable-boys who served the Commander of La Magdalena, too, so a lot of time she was around the stables. She and a dark man—one of those who took care of the animals—got to know each other. Sometimes he would come to our door and wouldn't leave till the next morning; and other times he would come to our door in the daytime pretending that he wanted to buy eggs, and then he would come inside.
>
> When he first began to come I didn't like him; he scared me because of the color of his skin and his [evil aspect]. But when I saw that with him around the food got better, I began to

like him quite a lot. He always brought bread and pieces of
meat, and in the winter he brought in firewood so we could
keep warm.

So with his visits and the relationship going right along, it happened that my mother gave me a pretty little black baby, and
I used to bounce [him] on my knee and help keep [him] warm.

I remember one time when my black stepfather was playing
with the little fellow, the child noticed that my mother and I
were white but that [he was not, and, frightened, he shrank
from him and toward my mother and pointing his finger said,
"Mama, bogeyman!"] And my stepfather laughed: "[Son-of-
a-bitch]."

Even though I was still a young boy, I thought about the word
my little brother had used, and I said to myself: How many
people there must be in the world who run away from others
[because] they don't see themselves.[21]

In the underclass world of the Lazarillo, there is a rough equiva-
lency between the parents: the gender role of one and the race of the
other are both markers of subordination. The white mother is a widow
who needs to feed her family, the Black father is a slave; gender and
race meet on the common ground of poverty. The woman without a
husband to provide for her finds her counterpart in the Black who is
made to serve a master in a discourse in which his unmarked, dominant, gender meets up with her unmarked, dominant race.[22] The
sexual relationship between Zaide and Lazarillo's mother is a matter
of mutual agreement.

In the next generation, race as hispanidad emerges from the resolution of the fear of difference. Both Lazarillo and his brother dread
what is unfamiliar in the Black father. The baby is afraid only of Zaide's
color; Lazarillo, who is old enough to recognize culturally appropriate
behavior, is frightened of both his stepfather's color and his unfamiliar
countenance, which he calls "evil." But Zaide is a good man who

provides for his family, a kind father who plays with his child. Lazarillo's fear disappears when he connects Zaide's presence to food and warmth in the house. When the baby shows fear of his father's color, Zaide responds with good humor. Not incidentally, this baby recognizes racial difference at the point when he enters into language—that is, when language makes it possible for him to articulate difference. At the same time, the sentence that tells of this differentiation is ambiguous and in need of some disentangling to get to which "he" is the stepfather and which is the baby. That is to say, differentiation threatens to collapse back into sameness even as it is being articulated.

Lazarillo would have his audience believe that he is telling this tale for its moral: that many people fear in others what they do not see in themselves. The baby assumes he is white, because white is standard in the household (Lazarillo and his mother stay, Zaide comes and goes), but he cannot see his own dark face. Lazarillo has to overcome a fear of the other, but the baby has to get over what amounts to a fear and ignorance of the self. That Lazarillo then generalizes the baby's response suggests that this racial splitting and lack of self-awareness is a societal problem, not a question of individual childhood development. Although we cannot know whether Lazarillo's mother entered into a relationship with Zaide for reasons of pure survival, Lazarillo tells us that Zaide is motivated by love, and we see that theirs is a stable, long-term relationship.[23] Zaide and Lazarillo's mother part only because the state separates them, denying Lazarillo's mother contact with Zaide after the two are caught and punished for his crime of stealing and hers of possessing stolen goods:

> As luck would have it, talk about Zaide [. . .] reached the ears of the foreman, and when a search was made they found out that he'd been stealing about half of the barley that was supposed to be given to the animals. He'd pretended that the bran, wool, currycombs, aprons, and the horse covers and blankets had been lost; and when there was nothing else left to steal, he took the shoes right off the horses' hooves. And he was using all this to buy things for my mother so that she could bring up my little brother. [. . .]

And they found him guilty of everything I've said and more.
[...]

They whipped my poor stepfather and scalded his wounds
with boiling fat, and they gave my mother a stiff sentence
besides the usual hundred lashes: they said that she couldn't go
into the house of the Commander (the one I mentioned) and
that she couldn't take poor Zaide into her own house.[24]

Here gender and racial difference are imposed from the outside, by
the authorities; for although the crimes the couple commits are not
specifically racial or gendered, the penalties are. To suffer whipping and
scalding with boiling fat, as Zaide does, is a penalty reserved for slaves.
The mother is punished beyond the hundred lashes that any white, male,
Christian criminal would get; she is deprived both of her source of
income doing domestic work for the commander's stable hands and of
the company and support of her child's father.[25] After the forced separation of the parents, the child, who earlier had to learn he was Black,
is simply absorbed into the white family. Once the authorities banish
Zaide, effectively erasing his (further) presence in the text, the child
becomes a Spaniard, like any other. After this incident, Lazarillo refers
to the child only once again and with no racial reference whatsoever.
Ironically, it is language, which enabled Lazarillo's baby brother to articulate difference, that also subsumes him into the sameness offered by
Hispanidad.

"Language has always been the companion of empire."[26] So wrote
Antonio de Nebrija in 1492, in dedicating his Grammar of the Spanish
Language to Queen Isabella. José Piedra recalls Nebrija in his assertion
that hispanidad is a linguistic contract, consolidated in and through
Empire, at a time of Spanish sovereignty and power:

The unification of all races into the Text [the Castilian of
Nebrija's 1492 Grammar] was propelled by many social, religious, and historical circumstances, chief among which were
Spain's own racially ill-defined origins, its occupation by
lighter and darker-skinned conquerors who imported their

own black slaves and citizens, and the rest of Europe's prejudices about Spain's imprecise racial heritage. This constellation
of circumstances led to a theoretical welcoming, on paper, of
black newcomers under the far-reaching umbrella of a
"Hispanic" race.[27]

This Imperial incorporation of the racial other, begun in 1492 and
continuing until the Spanish empire was dissolved, is the first of three
moments of the elaboration of hispanidad I have mentioned. The second
moment, which registers the separation of the countries of Spanish
America from Spain, is expressed in Octavio Paz's story of Mexican
racial formation, "*Los hijos de la Malinche*" (The sons of Malinche), in
his influential 1950 book of essays on the Mexican national character,
The Labyrinth of Solitude. Here Paz identifies the common epithet with
the historical figure of Malinche, the indigenous woman who served as
Hernan Cortés's translator and sexual partner during his conquest of
Mexico.

This story, unlike the *Lazarillo* episode, is a tale of racial and sexual
plunder in which there is no reconciliation.[28] In it power relations are
exaggerated, and gender and race are called into play as markers of
oppression in an unbalanced equation, where the father is the white
European male who rapes the racial and gendered other, the Indian
woman. She is shamed, as women often are in rape stories: pitied for
the violation of her body, blamed for betraying her people. The child
of this union is the *mestizo*, the mixed-race Mexican who still needs to
come to terms with his violent beginnings:

If the *Chingada* is a representation of the raped Mother, it does
not seem to me forced to associate her with the Conquest,
which was also a rape, not only in the historical sense but in
the very flesh of Indian women. The symbol of surrender is
Doña Malinche, the lover of Cortés. It is true that she gives
herself voluntarily to the Conqueror, but he, once she stops
being useful to him, forgets her. Dona Marina has become a
figure that represents Indian women, fascinated, or violated,
or seduced by the Spaniards. And in the same way that the

child does not forgive his mother for abandoning him to seek his father, the Mexican people do not forgive Malinche her betrayal. She incarnates what is open, what is fucked, in contrast to our Indian men, stoic, impassive and closed.

When he repudiates Malinche [. . .] the Mexican breaks his ties with the past, renounces his origins, and enters history alone.[29]

In this account the child is not ignorant of his origins (as is Lazarillo's brother), nor is racial identity incorporated into the healthy self. Rather, the racially mixed offspring repudiates—or represses—his parentage, denies his history, and is in need of something like psychoanalysis to come to terms with the lacerating violation that produced him. Racial identity, a matter of self-definition mediated by sociocultural attribution, requires a conscious desire for self-awareness. At the same time, gender oppression is validated and naturalized by Paz's transformation of the rape of the mother into a voluntary act of sexual submission, which he asserts with some vehemence. "It is true," Paz affirms, on no particular evidence, "that she gives herself voluntarily to the Conqueror."[30] Unlike Lazarillo's mother, with whom the narrator sympathizes, Paz's Malinche, unceremoniously abandoned by her bored "lover" rouses little compassion. Moreover, it is not only Cortés, but also Paz, who abandons Malinche. Lazarillo's mother is present in the text both before Zaide enters the scene and after he is banished from it; Malinche is invoked only as an effect of Cortés's actions. Her sexuality is no more than a function of his desire—including his desire that she be a willing participant—unlike Lazarillo's mother who is in control of her body, and who, whether for love or more practical motives, enters into a mutually satisfying sexual arrangement with Zaide.

Bringing the Spanish and Mexican stories together, and remembering what Jose Piedra calls "Spain's own racially ill-defined origins," we are reminded how shaky is the story of a single, monochromatic Hispanidad. The child of Zaide and the widow, born in the late fifteenth or early sixteenth century, could easily have grown up to be one of Cortes's soldiers. The pure European conqueror was more than a little

African, and racial differentiation in Europe as well as America turns out not to be binary but multiple.

Piedra claims that the consolidating device the empire would impose to mask racial difference was language itself. Equally important in the Hispanicization of the other, however, was the imposition of religious homogeneity. In the Lazarillo episode, for example, although no overt mention is made of it, race is closely tied to religion. Like the Jews, the Moors, understood as both Black and Muslim, were considered dangerous to Catholic Spain, and that danger derived equally from religion and race, because the two were constructed as inseparable. The instability of racial incorporation is, in fact, most visible in the Inquisition, which regularly routed out those newly Christianized (read Hispanicized) subjects who were insufficiently incorporated into an *hispanidad* that Piedra defines as "a grand metaphor for unrealized promises of universal harmony."[31] To this day, Spaniards tie language to religion. As a student, when I rudely spoke English in front of my Spanish friends they would tell me in no uncertain terms, "*Habla cristiano*"— talk Christian—benignly oblivious to the complexity of such a demand on a Jew.

By the end of the nineteenth century, all that was left of the Spanish empire was language. As Miguel de Unamuno proudly, pathetically, claimed: "To speak of the Spanish race is not to know what one is talking about. . . . The language is the race."[32] As power shifted in Europe, Spain became insignificant, starting in the late seventeenth century and culminating in the nineteenth with the loss of its last American colonies. Until the final quarter of the twentieth century Spain was out of step with the rest of the continent—the Spanish Civil War anticipated the Second World War but also precluded Spain from acting in it, and when the rest of Europe was rebuilding, Spain under Franco stagnated. During the same period, the countries of Spanish America were consolidating their own identity, while becoming increasingly important to, and dominated by, the United States. Hispanidad now changed meaning, as it shifted its center from Spain to its former colonies. It took on the theme of a unified Spanish America, with the linguistic and cultural bond of a colonial past against which to define itself. At the same time, it was challenged by racial and national differences within.

This second, postcolonial, moment in the formation of hispanidad consists of the forging of new nationalities within Spanish America in opposition to the European colonizer. This gesture fluctuates between asserting national and pan-American identities, and it relies on the difference from the former colonizer, whether idealized, as in Jose Vasconcelos's *Cosmic Race* or troubled, as in Paz's *Labyrinth of Solitude*.[33] Ironically, however, the stabilization of race as a function of nationality, which a number of countries have addressed via the ideology of mestizaje, results in a mystification of racial hierarchy and difference that mimics the colonial gesture of Imperial incorporation. The principle of mestizaje, because it tacitly justifies colonization in the forging of a new race/nation that blends conqueror and conquered, materially threatens indigenous people who resist assimilation in the new nation/race.[34] Furthermore, Paz's mestizaje symbolically erases women as products of the new racial blend. In his account, all women are sexually available to men and as such occupy the space of the conquered Indian mother.

Two and a half decades after Paz invoked the rape of Malinche as the engendering moment of a Mexican race, Victoria Ocampo wrote what would be one of many feminist revisions of the Malinche story, echoing the victimization theme but rescuing the Indian woman from what Ocampo believed to be ill-deserved scorn and censure.[35] Unlike Paz, feminist writers do not blame Malinche for her "betrayal" of her people but, rather, sympathize with her position and admire her ability to survive enslavement in two oppressive cultures. A frequent theme in the feminist retellings of the story is Malinche's betrayal by her people. Ocampo, writing from an upper-class, but also pan-American position in Argentina, a country whose national identity is not built on an ideological foundation of mestizaje, invokes Malinche as an example of mistreated, misunderstood womanhood. Rosario Castellanos, writing from within Mexico just a few years before Ocampo, not only absolves Malinche of blame but also downplays her victimization and dilutes her symbolic role as the nation's mother. In Castellanos's play, *The Eternal Feminine,* Malinche is one of a group of female figures from Mexico's past for whom the writer is creating a revisionist history.[36]

A significant number of feminist-revisionist Malinche stories are written by Chicanas on the other side of the Mexico/United States divide. As the frontier is crossed, a subtle change takes place in these retellings: The border is a geographical sign separating the postcolonial from the expatriate moment in racial formation. However, the border, as Gloria Anzaldúa has perceptively noted, is not a one-dimensional line but an inhabited space that joins as well as divides. The Chicanas who rewrite Malinche are deeply marked by a U.S.-style racial consciousness, and by their feminism, which is played out in most of their accounts by an exploration of the mother/daughter relationship. They are also marked by Paz's canonical Mexican version of the story.

Historian Cordelia Candelaria considers Malinche a "feminist prototype, a girl-child

> given away by her mother who sought to gain control of her daughter's inheritance for a son by her second husband. . . . Malinal was given to itinerant traders who eventually sold her to the ruling cacique of Tabasco. . . . After his takeover of Tabasco, and in keeping with age-old historic traditions, Cortes received from the cacique a gift of twenty maidens to serve as domestic labor for the warrior's adventurers. Malinal was part of the group.[37]

Along the same lines, Adelaida R. Del Castillo frames the story as a New World version of Snow White, with the mother as primary villain.[38] Cherríe Moraga echoes Gloria Anzaldúa's implication that the mother may not have been the one to decide her daughter's fate and that holding her responsible is just another version of woman blaming.[39]

Most of the Chicana writers, like Castellanos, contest the portrayal of Malinche as helpless victim, and the majority reclaim her as a sexual subject. Del Castillo takes Paz to task for equating women's sexuality with passivity and violation and suggests that Malinche was a willing sexual partner. Poet Alma Villaneuva's Malinche, in contrast, denounces her rape, and as an angry goddess she demands retribution, while Margarita Cota-Cárdenas writes a Malinche who loves Cortés but defies all attempts to pin her down to a single interpretation.[40]

The Chicanas who write as the spiritual daughters of Malinche as part of a resistance to an oppression in which race and gender are inextricably intertwined displace the paradigmatic male child of the conquest and interpose a female subject. This subject sustains the vision of gender evoked and then suppressed in Paz's version. Nomenclature helps reveal the story's racial subtext: Paz usually calls the woman Malinche, which is how the Spaniards rendered her name; but many Chicana writers, recuperating the story still further as one of racial as well as gender revindication, insist on the indigenous form, Malinal, Malinalli, or Malintzín. Despite the differences between the female- and male-centered versions of these stories, what they all share is the extreme polarization that disallows the nuance of intersecting identities. The result is that the mestiza daughter holds fast to her Indian identity, while the father is the irredeemably white oppressor. "My Chicana identity is grounded in the Indian woman's history of resistance," Anzaldúa writes.[41] This declaration of Indian strength is a source of pride, and in Moraga's case it figures a lesbian feminist reading of the contemporary Chicana who claims her heritage through her mother.

Yet this polarization, whereby race is marked by and as gender, cannot be sustained. The figure of Malinche has been injected with multiple and contradictory meanings precisely because the racially marked other she represents has been overly simplified. As Norma Alarcón has perceptively noted, "issues of 'class' and 'color' [. . .] per se have not entered the [Chicana] reappropriation [of history, sexuality, and language] because [. . .] the person and symbol of Malintzín—indigenous female slave in her own society as well as in the one taking shape under the Spaniards—implicitly subsumes those as part of her condition, hence the possibility of her suppression as feminine/maternal speaking subject."[42]

Malinche, as she is written by Paz, oscillates between betraying and founding "the race," or "her people." But there are two different races/peoples here: the betrayed Indian and the rounded *mestizo*. The latter contains and transforms the former and can only exist without anguish if the idea of racial purity is discarded as a possibility, or at least as an ideal. Adelaida R. Del Castillo, whose self-described "mystical interpretation" of Malinche is grounded in historical sources, points out that there was no single people for Malinche to betray. To accuse Malinche of betraying her people is to project her into the future, to have her betray the very *mestizo* nation that she begot: the betrayal is in the begetting itself.

Del Castillo's account is compelling for the way it fuses (and refuses) the various Malinche stories. Melodramatically, she repeats the story of Malinche as the mother of a race: "In the midst of the horror of destroyed bodies, of disease and wounds and the stench of decaying corpses of both men and animals, Marina shed her own blood with that of the men. In the midst of all this death, she made love to a decaying Cortés, thus giving birth to a new people." Del Castillo abandons her purple prose to report the death and displacement of Malinche's actual mestizo children. The Spaniards killed her son: hers was not to be the first of a new race. The dispossession of Malinche's daughter tragically parodies her own childhood experience. But this time it is the father who is solely to blame for the daughter's fate: "Don Martín Cortés Tenepal, natural son of Hernán Cortés and Doña Marina, was accused of treason and tortured by the Spaniards to obtain a confession, after which he was executed. María Jaramillo, legitimate daughter of Don Juan Jaramillo and Doña Marina, was robbed of her inheritance of land and money by her own father soon after Doña Marina's death."[43]

The tale of Malinche's children anticipates the future. Her son is literally accused of the treason that she has come to stand for, and he is annihilated. Her daughter's fate becomes that of the contemporary mestiza, Mexican or Chicana, who, robbed of her patrimony, is denied the full meaning of her mestizaje. But this child cannot simply claim her identity as an Indian either. The Chicana is not Malinche's daughter but her daughter's daughter: Moraga writes that she comes from "a long line of *vendidas*."[44]

The third-moment Chicana inclination to identify with the Indian mother (which is not only a feminist gesture but also one that marks the Chicano movement in general) undermines the second-moment Mexican nationalist project of the mestizo as alloy, a fully blended and fully stable being. This identification is, I think, both a form of solidarity with the growing international indigenous movements and a testament to the force of racial formation in the United States, which seeks ontological singularity.

Like the Spanish empire, the U.S. empire has its reasons for maintaining the fiction of a Hispanic race. The unified identity of the attributed Hispanic label serves to provide an "other" that consolidates North American (and European) white supremacy. This monolithic Hispanicity obscures racial classifications within Spanish American countries.[45] Alongside the early, careful, measuring-cup terms that denote the amount of one's African ancestry in Spanish America, there are myriad terms, not all of them benign, for various racial ancestries and mixtures, from *criollo* and mestizo to *mulato* and *zambo*. (In the United States terms like "half-breed," "octaroon," and "mulatto" are not only racist but antiquated. Moreover, the resolution of the concepts they denote into absolute racial categories testifies to how U.S.-style dominant whiteness demands sharp divisions.) Class differential plays an important role in racial attribution within many Spanish American societies, where such markers of superior economic and social class as the wearing of business attire and the use of standard speech are perceived as markers of whiteness as well. This more fluid approach to race does not mean that differentiation and hierarchy do not exist, only that they are expressed in other ways.

In Puerto Rico, the question of national identity as it is tied to racial difference is a central issue in such major twentieth-century writers as Francisco Arriví, Luis Palés Matos, and René Marqués, who often lodge this theme in stories of sexuality and reproduction. Younger Puerto Rican writers like Rosario Ferré and Ana Lydia Vega explore the same conjunction of elements from a decidedly feminist perspective. But as a person crosses over onto the U.S. mainland, Puerto Rican intracultural differences are supplanted by a unitary racial attribution. Aurora Levins Morales describes the shock of "white" Puerto Ricans from the island who come to the mainland and find they are "brown."[46] In a parodic echo of Nebrija's unifying grammar, the Spanish language, or its residual mark, the accent, is a determinant, now marking the outsider instead of the insider.[47]

Feminists from other parts of Spanish America also note this linguistically charged racialization. María Lugones, for example, is a philosopher and social activist from Argentina, of European background and living in the United States, who tells of experiencing the expatriate moment of Hispanicization when she entered the United States. Lugones's strategy has been to embrace this racial assignment and use it in opposition to the system that imposes it. Identifying politically with Chicanos and other Latinos, Lugones speaks specifically as a Latina in her scholarship.[48] She simultaneously theorizes and enacts this position by writing bilingually, thereby inverting the insider/outsider dichotomy imposed by the dominant culture and empowering the bilingual reader by injecting Spanish into the prestigious venues of what had been English-only academic journals.

Lugones plays successfully with markers of status, but on the whole, class in the United States is masked. For this reason, class differences are suppressed in the transformation of racial classifications in the border crossing. What seems to remain is the differing ability of distinct Latino groups to assimilate or to prosper. Cubans, for example, for reasons of politics and class, have tended to the latter but not the former. Class and race overlap: Many of the middle-class Cubans who came to the United States after the revolution were white, and many of the poor, who remained because their lives were improved, were Black. On the other hand, certain words associated with nationality can carry both class and racial meanings in the United States. For some Midwesterners, "Mexican" is marked by class to mean "migrant worker." An upper-class, light-skinned "Mexican" is unthinkable; such a person would be reinvented, not "Mexican," but "from Mexico."[49] The prepositional phrase makes nationality seem contingent, unlike the adjectival noun, which is marked indelibly. To be Mexican is to be "other" in racial and class terms. To be "from Mexico" is to have something interesting to add to a Minnesota evening's conversation. This distinction is a liberal gesture that may begin to de-essentialize racial categories but at the high cost of perpetuating class divisions and toying with national and ethnic identities.

The racial construction characteristic of the expatriate moment— a consolidation of Hispano-American otherness defined not from within but from without—derives in part from a simplified version of postcolonial national/racial identity, which in turn has roots in Imperial *hispanidad*. It occurs in Europe as well as in the United States. Cristina Peri Rossi's short story, "*La influencia de Edgar A. Poe en la poesía de*

Raimundo Arias" (The influence of Edgar A. Poe on the poetry of Raimundo Arias), serves as an illustration.[50] In Peri Rossi's tale of racial unhinging, Alicia, the child of America, a girl whose particular heritage is apparently Caucasian, takes advantage of the European assumption that all Spanish Americans are the exotic "other." The story takes place in Spain, the site chosen for exile in Alicia's father's mistaken belief that a common language would mean a relatively painless assimilation, and where, since 1972, Peri Rossi has been living out what began as her own exile from Uruguay. In effect, Alicia's father anachronistically pins his faith on the promise of Imperial *hispanidad*; Alicia quickly learns better. Dressed in what in her own country was a costume for a school play in which the audience would recognize her as a white child disguised as an Indian, she begs for money from a European public that sees her as foreign and exotic. Alicia gets away with this impersonation because, as far as her audience is concerned, it is no impersonation. It is not the outlandish costume, which is blatantly phony (it looks like early Hollywood Indian), that allows the urban Europeans to see Alicia as racially other but her Spanish American-ness that makes the costume credible. Her father, on the other hand, who tries to assert the sameness promised by the Imperial contract, is rendered invisible. He fails at even the deracinated version of modern commerce—selling soap out of a briefcase—that is the parodic sign of participation in First World modernity. It is only as racial (and therefore cultural) other that the child of Spanish America can be seen at all. The act of dressing up may be a falsification of what she knows to be her identity, but it confirms the European version of the racial identity now ascribed to the undifferentiated Spanish American. The European response to the racialized Spanish American other is chronicled by exiles like Peri Rossi, forced to leave their countries during the military dictatorships of the 1970s and early 1980s. Other Peri Rossi stories return to the exile either as invisible or as the exotic other. In "La ciudad" (The city), for example, a European woman figures Spanish America as the other to Europe: dirty, dangerous, exotic.[51] "*Las estatuas, o la condicion del extranjero*" (Statues, or the foreigner's condition) evokes the foreigner whose presence is simply not acknowledged.[52] Peri Rossi's stories return the once-colonized figure to Spain for redefinition. The process of homogenization and racialization of Spanish America that these stories represent highlights the radical failure of the Imperial gesture. This process also occurs in the United States, which similarly creates an undifferentiated Spanish American, whom it calls "Hispanic" once she or he crosses the border into this country. Ironically, although Spain now participates in the othering of Spanish America, Spaniards who come to the United States are not exempt from the racializing Hispanicization that Spanish Americans undergo. In a classic example of chickens coming home to roost, first moment hispanidad (the Spanish empire's colonizing notion of a people) converges with Hispanicization—the desire of dominant U.S. society to racialize this particular other.

The United States is coming to categorize Hispanic as race as a way of invoking a purported biological border at a time when the geographical border between North and South America is more and more permeable, and when there are as many Spanish Americans or their descendants living in the United States as in some Spanish American countries. Like the two earlier moments in Hispanic moments of racial formation discussed in this article, the current one relies on a form of homogenization. Although each of these homogenizing gestures has its own distinguishing features, each is the work of a dominant group representing state power, and each has been resisted by those on whom it has been imposed.

Whereas the Imperial moment is characterized by the incorporation of the racial other into the expansionist Imperial body and the postcolonial moment by assimilation into the new national body, the expatriate moment is characterized by the crossing—or shifting—of boundaries so that "Hispanic" becomes the name of the alien, menacing the body. The term "expatriate," when applied to Puerto Ricans, whose nation remains a virtual colony, is almost wishful. When applied to Chicanos, it is grimly ironic. It is not they who have been removed from their land, but their land whose identity has been changed via appropriation by another power, turning them, its previous inhabitants and their descendants, into strangers in what was once their home. The Chicano is no longer Mexican but is not fully expected to be at home in the United States either. We have already seen how the daughters of Paz's Malinche are thrown back to the precise moment of contact between Spain and America, recalling the violated essential other. This is not just an effect of the identification of the mother with the Indian but also of the anomalous position of the Chicana (and also the Chicano), still colonized, in a post-colonial world.

Nevertheless, the Chicanas who claim a revindicated Malinche as mother have also chimed themselves as mestiza. Standing in contrast to the Anglo colonizer, the colonized mestiza occupies the position of indigenous other, which is already, but only, one of her components. In Mexico, postcolonial mestizaje is the creation of a new race on which to found new nations. Functioning as a dominant discourse of national identity, the invocation of mestizaje often threatens indigenous cultures. In Mexico "Indian" stands in opposition and resistance to mestizo. In the United States, in contrast, mestizo is an oppositional racial fiction, barely recognized by the dominant culture, for whom mixed ancestry originating elsewhere resolves into simple "otherness." Meanwhile, for the classes of people who invoke it for its oppositional value, mestizaje risks absorption into a form of indigenousness.

The oppositional borderland mestizaje that such writers as Anzaldúa and Moraga invoke is superimposed on normative Mexican mestizaje. The expatriate *mestiza/o* is composed of the (already otherwise, and not fully homogenized, mestiza/o) Mexican and the North American (assumed to be European but of course also racially diverse).[53] Both these writers confront the indigenous woman who challenges their right to claim a purely Indian identity. Anzaldúa faces the fact that "living in the Borderlands means knowing/that the *india* in you, betrayed for 500 years,/is no longer speaking to you," and she postulates a multivalenced borderlands.[54] Moraga is saddened and resigned: "She's right [. . . .] In her world, I'm just white."[55] Moraga now avoids collapsing india and "woman" by emphasizing the gender distinctions within precontact indigenous culture. Drawing on Aztec female deities who struggle against their male counterparts, Moraga refashions the trope of the weak Indian-as-woman into the figure of the powerful woman Indian. Other Latina feminists, occupying two "impure" cultures that they themselves embody, are also addressing this complexity. Levins Morales incorporates Jew and Puerto Rican, and Maria Lugones theorizes the impossibility and limitations of purity, even in separation.

Lugones conceptualizes mestizaje as multiplicity, never resolving into one or another of its parts and never blending them into an homogenous whole. For Lugones, mestizaje is another name for impurity, and it is to be deployed as a form of resistance.[56] Her formulation, derived from a U.S. Latino context, and also from a feminist reading of gender and a lesbian theory of sexuality, is applicable broadly to a whole range of differences and stands as a direct challenge to a notion of racial or ethnic fixity.

Imperial and nationalist "hispanidad" and expatriate "Hispanicity" are fictions of purity, the first two based on the promise of assimilation into the dominant culture, the last based on an equally false premise of exclusion. For the first and second moments of Hispanic racial formation to occur—in order to (re)produce the new race—the heterosexual female body must be conscripted. This attempt was certainly resisted—by Jews and Muslims in Spain, and by indigenous peoples on this continent. A major distinguishing feature of the current form of resistance is the different discursive location gender has assumed in the late twentieth century. Gender difference was formerly invoked as a kind of conscripted female heterosexuality to be utilized literally and figuratively in naturalizing racial fictions. It functioned as an unremarked marker, part of a God-given or scientifically proclaimed order, and it depended on women's silence. Race was naturalized via gendered sexuality that, in turn, was always already naturalized. Now, race is only residually about naturalized difference, and the contemporary bureaucratization of race stands as its own accusation, a technology that produces, reproduces, and shores up the shaky edifice of racial differentiation. Previous bureaucracies of race erected by Empire, the Inquisition, and the modern nation state, which had the same function, were not thought of as doing anything but revealing an existing truth.

Current feminist consciousness brings gender to the surface in the first- and second-moment origin narratives of racial formation, and it reconfigures gender itself in the third-moment stories. Peri Rossi's Alicia is a daughter in relation to a father, an inversion of the time-honored mother/son dyad that also questions generational roles. Along the same lines, much Chicana feminist work is interested in women-to-women relationships cross-generationally.

Women who come out of a history of compulsory, and racialized, heterosexuality are foregrounding gender and historical race, and dislodging both—excavating them, making them visible, and exploding them. They are likely to invoke race as a political mechanism or as a complex, fraught multiplicity of meanings—Anzaldúa's *frontera*, Moraga's exploration of her multiracial family, Levins Morales's self-conscious position as Jewish Puerto Rican, metropolitan Lugones's alliance with Chicanos of rural New Mexico. It is also not a coincidence that many of the best-known of the theorists doing this work are lesbians who are simultaneously reconfiguring women's sexuality. For—to give an example—although lesbian motherhood is also a reality, it is not the same old naturalized story and in fact is profoundly upsetting to patriarchal desire and expectation; it disrupts the culturally determined natural order. The resisting Chicana/Latina, who in her most radical and theoretically promising form is lesbian, refuses complicity with any racializing project that demands her sexual complicity. Lugones, Moraga, and Anzaldúa all resist the smoothing out of difference and find strength in their own multiplicity as they engage in struggle, within and with the culture.

The differences within an emerging racial category like "Hispanic," the struggle over the very nomenclature of race, and the unpredictability of racial difference are reminders that race cannot be taken as a simple variable in the cultural equation that feminism and other oppositional politics are trying to solve. When the meanings of racial categories change, and when racial attribution disengages from identity, race enters a state of flux that best serves liberatory ends if it refuses stability.

* Amy Kaminsky is Professor and Chair of the Women's Studies Department at the University of Minnesota.

I wish to thank Cheri Register, Naomi Scheman, Joanna O'Connell, Elaine Johnson, and the *Feminist Studies* editors and reviewers, who read earlier drafts of this article and pushed and prodded me to make it better than it was.

Jensen-Miller
Prize
1995

Texas Newspapers and Chicana
Workers' Activism, 1919–1974

Irene Ledesma

URING the 1935 organizing of Dorothy Frocks workers in
San Antonio, Mexican women, members of the
International Ladies Garment Workers Union (ILGWU)
advertised for a fund-raising dance in the local labor-union paper. In
the advertisement, union leaders described the women workers as
"some of the most comely of the female sex to be found anywhere.
They are good seamstresses besides."[1] Although the editors of the paper
recognized the women's struggle, they portrayed the dance merely as a
social event. This incident was not unique. The press image of Mexican
women workers frequently diverged from the women's pronouncements and actions.[2] In this article, I would like to show that Texas-press
images of Mexican-American strikers depended on Anglo, "American,"
and male criteria, and therefore touched only peripherally on the
women's experiences.

This essay critiques the coverage of strikers in local, labor, and
Spanish newspapers during four periods of Chicana labor militancy in

★ Irene Ledesma, "Texas Newspapers and Chicana Workers' Activism, 1919–1974,"
Western Historical Quarterly 15:3 (1995). © 1995 Western Historical Society
Quarterly, Western History Association. Reprinted by permission.

El Paso and San Antonio. Coverage of the strikers was tainted by popular notions of gender, class, and ethnicity. The Chicana strikers' situation was often at variance with these images.

Scholars of women's history have shown that prescribed roles for women, compared to their real actions, were often inconsistent and were burdened by existing gender prejudices. Recently, historians have extended their analysis in two ways: by examining the language of ordained gender agendas and by observing how language proscribes women's behavior. In an essay on gender and language, Joan Wallach Scott argued that language theorists believe "words acquired meaning by implicit or explicit contrasts established in specific contexts." Thus, words used to define a group imply or differentiate the speaker's or writer's (or his/her group's) political relation to his/her subject. Elizabeth Faue, in her article on gender and solidarity, illuminated Scott's point. She showed that the use of male terminology in union acts of strike activity in the 1930s in Minnesota effectively dismissed women's contributions, even though the women's actions were often similar to those of male union members. Nancy Hewitt's critique of news accounts about Hispanic cigar workers in Florida shows similar patterns of bias. Newspapers advocated an Anglo, male sense of solidarity to lure a Cuban work force away from a vision of "brotherhood" that included women.[3]

Historians have shown little interest in the work experiences of Mexican-American women. They have focused on males or Anglo-American women. In the last twenty years, however, Mexican-American historians have begun to study the union activity of California Mexican-American women. Some described these women as activists with supportive union leadership. Others showed them as innovative participants in benignly neglectful unions. A few questioned union motives. In Texas, Mexican-American women strikers were as activist and innovative as union members anywhere, despite tremendous odds: hostile owners, city officials, laborites, or a Mexican-American community holding certain expectations of them.[4]

Texas newspapers reported numerous union disputes and constructed images of Chicana strikers. To name four significant examples: In El Paso, in 1919, Mexican laundry women protested the firing of two workers for union activity. During the 1930s, Mexican women in San Antonio—cigarmakers, pecan shellers, and dressmakers—went on strike for higher wages and for improved working-conditions. Chicanas also played a significant role in the 1959 Tex-Son strike in San Antonio and the 1972–1974 strike at Farah in El Paso.

The Mexican women strikers in El Paso contended with a particularly antagonistic, Anglo-dominated economy. World War I anti-foreign propaganda and Pancho Villa raids into New Mexico generated hostile anti-Mexican sentiments. Accordingly, in 1919, the Anglo-American population of El Paso generally viewed Mexican immigrants as an alien force. This hostility was compounded by the anti-labor sentiments of local officials, who expressed themselves by creating an ordinance against picketing.[5]

Organized labor also resented Mexican immigrants. Union officials blamed them for low wages, claimed they took jobs from Americans, and declared that they served as strikebreakers. El Paso's light industrial economy and the discriminatory practices of American employers placed unskilled Mexican workers in low-paying, segmented, and stratified jobs. Married Mexican immigrant women usually did not work; young, single Mexican women were employed in domestic service and in laundries.[6]

When the Mexican women's laundry strike broke out, however, xenophobic labor leaders momentarily stopped their racially-based campaigns against the employment of Mexicans. The story of the laundry workers is a good example of how labor leaders seemingly change their attitudes toward Mexican workers. On 24 October 1919, Mexican women workers organized a local of the International Laundry Workers Union. Soon after, the Acme Laundry of El Paso fired two veteran workers—one sorter and one marker—because they were recruiting new members to the union. According to sorter Francisca Saenz, the remaining Mexican women at Acme then refused to cooperate with Acme's attempt to send their work to other local laundries. Within a few days, almost five hundred laundry women walked out of the six laundries in the city.[7]

On the evening of the walkout at Acme, several hundred Mexican laundry women voted to stay out until the company reinstated the two fired workers. Subsequently, William Moran, editor of the labor paper and head of the Central Labor Union (CLU), the labor leadership in El Paso, assumed control of the strike. He took responsibility for all public statements on the strike and created a fund-raising committee from the CLU membership. A few Mexican women were assigned the task of persuading strikebreakers to refrain from taking the places of union members; all other Mexican women union members were relegated to the union hall.[8] The CLU leadership takeover reflected a belief generally held among unionists that working women could be dominated by male leaders. The takeover further suggested that Anglo CLU leaders perceived Mexicans as docile people.

From previous experience, labor leaders understood the difficulty of presenting a favorable image of Mexican immigrants to the Anglos in El Paso. Like many Progressive reformers of the era, the editors of the *El Paso City and County Labor Advocate* called on employers to prevent vice among the unmarried Mexican women workers. Labor leaders focused on the low wages of the laundry strikers, asking, "What chance has a girl or woman to live a decent respectable life at the wages of this kind?" In another article concerning wages, the union leadership claimed that many of the laundry stockholders were two-faced in calling for "clean-up campaigns" while "breeding prostitution and every thing that can possibly be vicious" and by paying a four dollar a week wage.[9] As the strike intensified, the paper attempted to counter El Pasoans' notions that Mexicans were morally lax. To do this, they imposed on the public images of the women's vulnerability.

In this attempt to help, the labor leadership itself ignored other roles of the Mexican women unionists. In November, a Texas Welfare Commission study of wages—in a variety of industries—revealed that many of the laundry women supported their families. One laundry worker told the committee, "I find it difficult to live on my wages, which I turn in to the family budget." Despite the report and personal testimony, union leaders continued to portray these workers as women in need of moral protection and guidance. Emphasizing once again Progressive interest in working women's morality, an editorial asked, "Does the public believe that a woman can live on less than $1 per day and be possessed of a properly nurtured body or mind morally nurtured?"[10] By focusing on working women's alleged immorality and vulnerability, unionists sought to overcome resentment of the image of Mexicans as scabs and cheap labor, an impression that they themselves had cultivated in previous years during anti-alien campaigns.

In their attempt to create new images of the women, the labor press fought employer practices that were acceptable to business-dominated civic leaders. The labor paper raised the issue of the women's citizenship, hoping to turn the public against the practice of hiring Mexican aliens to replace strikers. Labor leaders intended to reach any reform-minded unionist through the use of Progressive rhetoric. These leaders emphasized that the striking women were asking for fundamental rights expressed in the Constitution. They admitted, too, that many Americans regarded all Mexican Americans as Mexicans. However, they reminded the public:

> True it is, they are nearly all of Mexican origin, but they are by no means all of Mexican citizenship. The large majority are residents of El Paso and citizens of the nation.[11]

Acknowledging members' prejudices, the labor paper sought its members' support by defining Mexicans in a manner consistent with Progressive ideals.

Labor leaders used the citizenship angle to reverse other working El Pasoans' chronic antagonism toward Mexican immigrants. Pressing the issue, the *Labor Advocate* insisted that "nothing will be left undone to see that they receive just treatment and a square deal . . . which the Constitution of the American government guarantees to its every citizen."[12] Fortunately for El Paso labor leaders, Theodore Roosevelt's Progressive language and Americans' ideal vision of the Constitution proved perfect for turning Mexicans from aliens into American citizens.

The laborites did not limit to editorials their representation of the strikers. Having banished the Mexican women strikers to the union hall or to the picket line, the CLU leadership sent out agents to garner support from other locals, Mexican-American civic groups, and Anglo-American organizations. The American Federation of Labor (AFL) sent in C. N. Idar to help. Idar, in a speech before the El Paso Ministerial

Alliance, took the opportunity to impress upon his listeners the image of the strikers as both morally vulnerable women and as citizens. He told the group that prevailing wages did not permit the Mexican laundry women to "live decent and respectable lives as American citizens."[13] Both appeals succeeded: locals sent funds totaling more than $3,000. Local ministers promised to look into the situation.

But union leaders' appeals on the issue of morality posed a problem. When Mexican women strikers positioned themselves at the El Paso-Ciudad Juarez border bridge to prevent Mexican citizens from taking their places, they contradicted union images of vulnerability. Those that remained picketing at plant sites issued verbal threats. They told one worker they would "pull her hair out if she crossed the line." They also knitted and sold items for strike coffers, even as a male unionist took a leave of absence from his job to raise strike funds.[14] Such actions clearly contradicted the prevailing image of these workers as defenseless women.

On the issue of anti-Mexican biases, the union faced overwhelming obstacles. In 1919, Anglo El Pasoans regarded Mexicans as foreigners, regardless of their citizenship status. Anglos saw non-English speaking Mexicans as unlikely Americans. They perceived a link between corrupt local government officials and Mexican votes. Protestant Anglos considered Catholics non-Christians, and Mexicans were mostly Catholic. These Protestants also held Mexicans responsible for bootlegging and for the excessive drinking in the area. And Anglos believed that Mexicans, as dark-skinned people, expressed a threatening sexual licentiousness through prostitution. Clashes between Mexican revolutionaries and American citizens in Columbus, New Mexico, added to Anglo El Pasoans' convictions that Mexicans spelled trouble.[15] Despite Anglo preconceptions, the Mexican strikers in El Paso saw themselves to be Americans, and they viewed those crossing over from Juarez to be the "aliens."

Laundry owners rallied, turning the tables on their opponents by seizing these negative preconceptions and applying them to union members. The daily press was quick to echo the owners' cause. Reiterating that the strike had no effect on his business, the owner of the Excelsior Laundry boasted in the *El Paso Herald,* "[S]ome of my

Mexicans quit and I put Americans in their place. The American used just half as much materials as the Mexican. The work was cleaner and whiter and better in every way." In a news advertisement in the same paper, the owner of the Elite Laundry reinforced notions of Mexican workers as less capable of good work. He argued that the walkout had started when a girl was fired for not doing her work. The *El Paso Herald* added to the negative image by describing strikers as "Mexican girls" who "are enjoying their vacation." The paper declared, "At the central Labor Union hall the girls are singing and dancing." In these depictions, the Mexicans seemed childlike. As one school principal said of them, "The Mexicans are particularly gifted in art work and music."[16]

Without evidence, the commercial press disparaged the Mexican strikers by linking them to radical groups. The *Herald* published the mayor's instructions to the police chief "to permit no disorders of rioting in this city no matter what the cause." The *El Paso Morning Times,* at least, noted that the women had acted peacefully during the strike.[17] The press gave inordinate attention to materials written in Spanish that had been seized from the Industrial Workers of the World (IWW). The daily papers played up the actions of scab laundry drivers as a first blow against Bolshevism.[18] Although the Mexican women strikers had not gone beyond verbal jousting against strikebreakers, the daily press insisted on associating them with so-called un-American activities.

The daily press fueled ethnic slurs by quoting employers. One such quote included the Acme Laundry owner's pernicious statements on wages to the Welfare Commission. In his testimony, he argued that Mexican women worked too slowly, lacked interest in their work, and completed less items than American employees. He referred to twenty striking women from his plant as, "the cheaper sort of work." He said he found it difficult to find workers for the better jobs because Mexican women could only do routine back labor. Although the two Mexican women he fired had worked (one as a sorter and one as a marker) for at least six years, he testified that American women served better at those positions.[19] Such public observations fueled existing prejudices, intensifying the image of the Mexican women strikers as "un-American," subversive, or inept.

The sentiments of Anglo-American society complicated the strike situation for the women. These El Pasoans seemed to share with other Americans a fear that organized labor might lead the way to Bolshevism. The local American Legion members searched the city for "Reds" but found none. The press, meanwhile, exploited strike stories involving the IWW, and the hysteria reached such heights that the press interpreted unintelligible graffiti found in a men's room as the advance guard of the IWW.[20] Stories such as these gained credibility in light of the other negative images of Mexicans.

The Spanish-language press, with its largely Mexican audience, was enthusiastic, but patronizing, in its portrayal of laundry strikers. The paper covered the visit of Mexican women strikers to local Mexican civic groups, proudly and frequently referring to the women's Mexican antecedents and emphasizing their goals as a struggle for respect for their rights. Stressing the women's peacefulness, the press claimed, "pero no han pasado de eso [shouting at scabs]," the papers expressed outright admiration for them, saying "nuestras mujeres estan dando un ejemplo de caracter, energia y solidaridad racial." Interestingly, the Mexican umbrella union that supported the women declared itself the voice of the Mexican community, announcing that the latter was "muy dignamente representada en las sociedades."[21]

For all its posturing in support of the laundry strikers, *La Patria* was often condescending. An article calling the women "compatriots" expressed appreciation to all who had helped the women in their struggle and exhorted the latter to remain united in the view of the union's efforts on their behalf. Earlier in the article, *La Patria,* recounting how the mayor had ordered the police to enforce peace on both sides, considered the situation grave. The journalist stressed that the women "se han portado con toda correccion." This writer added that the violence would be eschewed by the organizers and indicated that any violence would undercut the women's final goal.[22] The ones who wrote these words offered solidarity only because the strikers behaved correctly, and such writers took upon themselves the task of showing to whom the women ought to be grateful as well as what the women's goals should be.

Editors of *La Patria,* and others, appeared intent on educating the women on the conduct of labor disputes. In a discussion of the problems facing the strikers, they predicted the negative outcome of the strike. With a hint of censure, they concluded that too many unemployed women resided in El Paso and Ciudad Juarez. Both strikers and the union realized the extent of the unemployment problem. The CLU sought a solution, asking city officials to demand that laundry owners not hire alien labor. The effort was rebuffed. Another Mexican-American organization added a *machismo* element. In calling for a conference on the strike, the umbrella civic group noted the high percentage of *women* [my emphasis] strikers and asked that "no por esa misma razon [deben] abandonarlas en este momento." Thus, they implied the women needed their help.[23] Mention of the strike by the press had diminished by early December, an indication that the prediction of the Spanish press that the strike would fail had been realized.

Those civic groups to whom *La Patria* appealed clearly reflected the class interests of the Spanish press and of their own membership. In particular, the Mexican Alliance's denial of rumors that it was contemplating supporting a general strike by Mexican workers showed the members' eagerness to appease the owners. When questioned on the issue, members responded that "they were in full sympathy with the striking girls [but] no proposition of a sympathetic strike by local Mexican workers was favored or had even been considered."[24] Seeing themselves as representatives of El Paso's Mexican community, the Mexican Alliance quickly discounted any connection to extremist actions.

By 1920, many CLU members withdrew into an alliance with a Ku Klux Klan-dominated good-government movement.[25] With this retreat, organized labor and Mexican immigrants lost the opportunity for an alliance. Nativism in the 1920s and bad economic conditions in the 1930s widened the rift. It would not be until the 1950s that organized labor in El Paso allied itself once again with those workers of Mexican heritage.

Labor union activity in the United States increased enormously in the 1930s because of economic conditions and encouragement from the national government in the form of the Wagner Act. The creation of the Congress of Industrial Organization (CIO) made trade unionism possible to the "unorganizable." In San Antonio, between 12,000 and 15,000 mainly unorganized pecan shellers worked in the pecan industry. Pecan shelling was normally a young, single woman's job, but Depression conditions had forced men into the industry, and home-shelling by entire families became common. When the CIO began unionizing efforts among the shellers, business and community leaders, who touted the city as a haven of cheap labor and who relied on bought Mexican votes, worried that the Chicano masses might become politically conscious.[26]

Conditions and pay in pecan plants in San Antonio early in this century can best be described as poor, but the economic situation of the 1930s made it worse. Workers sat in filthy rooms on backless benches with boxes of pecans in front of them. They were surrounded by the dust from broken shells, and they cracked the nuts by hand. The average weekly wage was $2.25. In 1934, and again in 1935, the pecan shellers forced companies to rescind pay cuts. The owner of Southern Pecan Shelling Company solved this problem by funding the president of the largest local, making it, for all intents and purposes, a company union. In 1936, the president of Southern Pecan proclaimed that five cents a day was plenty for the shellers, who, he said, daily consumed nuts as they worked. That year the company made a profit of $500,000.[27]

On 1 February 1938, thousands of pecan shellers walked out in protest of yet another wage reduction. The pecan shellers chose a non-sheller, twenty-three-year-old Emma Tenayuca, as strike committee chair. The shellers told the Spanish paper that, "la repetida líder no ha tomado participacion en este movimiento de manera espontanea, sino obedeciendo la persistente solicitud de los obreros." Tenayuca had earned the Mexican-American workers' respect through her activities as secretary of the local chapter of the Workers' Alliance. During the 1937 winter layoff of relief recipients on public works projects, Tenayuca and the Alliance staged a workers' protest in front of city hall. Additionally, in Tenayuca's words, "the Workers' Alliance continued, carrying grievances, meeting on Sunday." According to Tenayuca, the Alliance "had more than 10,000 members," and its attempts to inform Mexican-American workers of their rights and to alleviate their work-related problems angered city government officials. For years, they had counted on an acquiescent Mexican-American work force to prop their political machine.[28]

In support of city government's contention that no strike existed, police committed violence on the picket line almost daily. San Antonio did not have Mexican policemen in the 1930s, but strikers, and most of their leaders, came from the Mexican community. Both male and female strikers were arrested during the strike, although on occasion police released from jail women with children. The governor of Texas initiated an investigation on blatant police harassment after the Mexican consul and a U. S. congressman protested the worker's treatment.[29]

Police used lawful and unlawful means to suppress the strike. Capturing national attention with their actions, they tear-gassed pickets indiscriminately, jailed pecan shellers for days without charging them, and took workers outside city limits, forcing them to walk miles back to town. At one point, the police chief doused male strikers with hoses for protesting jail conditions. A local study by a woman's group revealed that Mexican women strikers were crowded into cells with prostitutes. The treatment of the women reflected city officials' bias in categorizing women into what historians call the whore/Madonna complex. The police chief justified his handling of the strike situation by claiming, "It is my duty to interfere with revolution, and communism is revolution." The archbishop of San Antonio, Arthur Drossaerts, praised the chief's efforts.[30]

Fearing the political consequences of a successful strike, the Democratic machine at city hall denounced the strikers and their leaders as outsiders and Communists. The local papers published the police chief's comment that no strike existed because Communist leaders— and he named Tenayuca and Minnie Rendon, the local's secretary— duped the Mexican-American workers. In addition, the mayor and the head of the city vigilance committee questioned the credentials of Cassie Jane Winifree, state chairperson of the Women's National League for Peace and Freedom, after she requested approval to seek funds for strikers' meals. The daily paper wrote approvingly of the mayor's visit to pecan sheds, where he told workers,

> I am convinced that you will not be able to receive calm and dispassionate hearing if you permit Communistic leaders to excite and agitate your people . . . I have reference to such well-known Communistic leaders as Mrs. Emma Tenayuca Brooks, Jim Sager and their co-workers and advisors in the Communist or Red movement.[31]

The police chief told a state inquiry commission, "if the [Mexican] westside workers were organized by UCAPAWA [United Cannery, Agricultural, Packing and Allied Workers of America], 25,000 persons would be lost to the 'Red Banner.'" The daily press accepted the mayor's and the chief's characterizations and disseminated them without further inquiry.[32] Refusing to consider the frustrations of a destitute people, the mayor and chief gave voice to Anglo San Antonians' views of Mexican immigrants as ignorant, tractable people open to subversive influences.

Daily press accounts of the strike focused on similar allegations about Tenayuca. They centered on Tenayuca's connections to Communism. Even after UCAPAWA's national president, Donald Henderson, took over the strike, the papers continued to allude to Tenayuca's Communist affiliations. The journalists concentrated on her marriage to Homer Brooks, onetime candidate for governor on the Communist ticket. Tenayuca's marriage to an Anglo failed to endear her to other Anglos, not only because she was breaking a social taboo with the marriage but because the marriage reflected her ties to outsiders and Communists. The Mexican community preferred to see her in terms of her activism on their behalf. It typically referred to her as "la pasionaria" rather than by her married name.[33]

In addition to frequent references of her marriage to a Communist, the press detailed Tenayuca's protest activities as chair of the state chapter of the Workers' Alliance. The *San Antonio Express,* reporting the findings of the state industrial commission on police harassment, noted that she had previously been "acquitted of a charge of unlawful assemblage and disturbing the peace."[34] In this article on police wrong-doing, the journalist discredited Tenayuca by associating her with anarchy, lawlessness, and even subversion.

In contrast to the obviously hostile attitude of the Anglo press and aggressive actions of the police, the middle-class Spanish-language paper *La Prensa* expressed some support for the Mexican strikers. The paper approvingly described them as "los miembros de la Texas Pecan Shelling Workers Union han guardado completo orden durante sir huelga, sin recurrir a actos de violencia." The journalist at *La Prensa* attempted to dilute the negative images of the strikers by noting that "unos cuantos radicales, sin coneccion alguna con la industria de nuez, intentaron de tomar parte en la huelga y algunos fueron aprehendidos." The paper, however, also noted that two Mexican-American civic groups—the League of Loyal Americans and the Mexican Chamber of Commerce—demanded that strike leaders sign a loyalty pledge. These groups proclaimed, "We are interested in Mexican workers getting a living wage because we want them to be loyal and progressive citizens of the United States." Two weeks later a worker's rally featured the archbishop, a University of Mexico student, and two representatives from Mexican civic groups. Speakers denounced Communist support and reinforced middle-class Mexican-Americans' stance.[35]

At the same time, the paper offered stories on other aspects of the strike that showed the Mexican unionists' viewpoint. The paper published the workers' defense of Tenayuca and a statement of their intent to protest her arrest. *La Prensa* also published references to the strike that the daily press ignored, such as a charge by Henderson that city opposition was racially motivated. In addition, *La Prensa* proudly noted that the Mexican vice-consul defended the rights of arrested Mexican strikers by attending their court appearances.[36] As had *La Patria* in El Paso in 1919, *La Prensa* offered support only when the women behaved according to middle-class standards. Additionally, by the 1930s, the owner of the paper, favoring American citizenship, lost interest in returning to Mexico. His editors reflected this shift in mindset by emphasizing that the Mexican strikers were peaceful, citizenship-worthy people.

The Anglo-labor leadership in San Antonio shared city government fears that the Mexican masses might revolt. This concern explained the labor paper's lack of coverage of the shellers' strike. In the four years prior to the 1938 strike, the labor press occasionally expressed its dismay over work conditions in the pecan industry, and referred to the Mexican strikers as "that class of citizenship that are located on our West side."[37] This was a weak gesture made to represent the strikers as Americans. Laborites knew that during a depression American workers' resentment of aliens increased. In the case of Mexicans, this animosity was so intense that repatriation efforts in some cities had succeeded.

When the unionist newspaper did take up the topic, labor leaders' resentment was clear. The paper had indicated its biases in the 1934 strike by declaring that a "more intelligent class of workers" would not have brooked the interference that the sheriff had inflicted on the Mexican strikers' rights. The attorney for the ILGWU may have expressed local labor leaders' attitude most cogently by saying that the pecan strike concerned "un grupo de radicales que se declararon en huelga bajo la gufa de Emma Tenayuca de Brooks y Homer Brooks." During the dispute some presidents of locals joined pecan-sheller representatives at behind-the-scenes meetings with town officials. But, in fact, by 1938, the AF of L leadership had done nothing to organize the largely female shellers, and it expressed surprise and perturbation in the *Weekly Dispatch* over CIO efforts to do so that year.[38]

The Mexican pecan shellers won the dispute. Three Mexican women—Amelia De La Rosa, Natalia Camareno, and Velia Quiñones—served on the committee arranging for an arbitration board settlement that restored wages to pre-strike levels. Other women did not fare as well. Tenayuca left San Antonio in 1939 when in August a mob stormed the city auditorium in a successful effort to prevent an Alliance rally. Tired of her protest activities, city leaders advised her to leave or face the consequences. Pecan-shelling companies reverted to machine labor in 1939 to avoid paying the wage rates of 25 cents an hour that had been set by Fair Labor Standards Act. This measure reduced the work force in the sheds by thousands.[39]

In addition to the 1938 pecan shellers' action, three other brief dressmakers'-strikes took place in the decade. In the post–World War period, strikes in San Antonio and El Paso also concentrated in the garment industry, an important source of employment for Chicanas in Texas. Mexican immigration into the U.S. increased after 1950, resulting in a pattern of urbanization. Unskilled, uneducated Mexican laborers in search of jobs moved into San Antonio, Corpus Christi, Houston, Dallas, and El Paso. Two major strikes occurred in the post-war period. The ILGWU lost contracts at Texas Tiny, Texas Infants, Jay-Ann, and Juvenile in San Antonio in the early 1950s. They then fought a do-or-die battle at Tex-Son in 1959. The Amalgamated Clothing Workers of America (ACWA) in El Paso, with contracts only at Levi-Strauss and

Hortex in 1972, tried to solidify the union with a win against Farah Manufacturing Company.[40] Farah had five plants—making it the largest garment firm in the city.

The 1930s pattern of garment strikes continued after World War II. They included much violence, bread and butter demands, and many Mexican-American women in low-level, union positions. The long history and deep roots of the male hierarchy at both the ILGWU and AWCA made for strict control of events at the local level by a similarly male-organized management staff. However, the 1959 strike at Tex-Son also saw the ILGWU's use of a Chicana organizer for the first time.

In the winter of 1959, approximately 185 Chicanas and Anglo women workers at Tex-Son went on strike to protest the company's policy of sending out work to Mississippi. In actuality, at the time of contract negotiations, Tex-Son owner Harold Franzel hired former Chamber of Commerce president and alleged union-buster Theo Weiss as company attorney. A fairly stable union-management relationship turned into a battle for the ILGWU's survival. For two years the Chicana strikers picketed Tex-Son. They experienced two violent confrontations with non-strikers and participated in a regional boycott. Franzel outlasted the women by replacing them from a readily available pool of unemployed Chicana workers.[41]

The regional boycott of Tex-Son products required an extensive propaganda campaign. The union made appeals for support based on family and motherhood. It effectively reproduced a $9.12 check made out to Helen Martinez, with an accompanying photograph of her child. The union questioned whether anyone thought they could feed their family on such wages. The emphasis on motherhood continued in the union paper. It distributed a photograph of Martinez and her family and included a discussion of the film, "Mother is on strike."[42] The domestic ideology of the period identified women as wives and mothers. The union focused on that role despite the earlier attempt to depict the women as breadwinners.

In 1947, Texas demonstrated its labor conservatism with the passage of a right-to-work law. In the 1959 strike, the union portrayed an image of family togetherness to ward off the appearance of disorder that striking workers might conjure in the minds of the San Antonio community. Discussing the 1959 strike, a union paper columnist described "a real union Santa" from other union locals distributing Christmas presents for children whose "mothers are on strike." Union members in other industries in the Midwest and Southwest, as well as in San Antonio, distributed flyers directed at shoppers. They presented pictures of strikers' children and their letters written to other children urging the latter's parents not to buy Tex-Son goods. In a handbill to retailers and buyers, strikers' pleaded, "For OUR children's Sake Please Don't Buy Tex-Son Products for YOUR Customers' Children."[43] Domestic ideology of the 1950s portrayed the family as a bulwark against foreign influences and Communistic social chaos. The union, therefore, referred to strikers' children in press stories. While these appeals served to allay Anglo Texans' prevailing anti-unionism, nativism, and conceptions of the Chicanas as migrants and alien, they did little to enhance the women's identity as working people.

The union pushed the mother propaganda so hard, it lost sight of Chicanas as workers. The labor paper, for example, devoted an article to Dolores Herrera's work as chair of the kitchen committee. The writer extolled her cooking skills, claiming strikers found hers better than those in most San Antonio restaurants. The article focused on her sacrifice in cooking breakfast and lunch everyday in a hot, enclosed room. At a mass rally attended by over one thousand fellow unionists at the Alamo, an AFL-CIO organizer had promised strikers, "You will discover capabilities you never thought you had." Herrera seemingly already had done so before the strike. She had worked at TexSon since 1953. She had also served as vice-president of the San Antonio Joint Board of the ILGWU, on negotiating committees, and as shop committee member.[44] In the article, however, Herrera lost her identity as Tex-Son employee and ILGWU striker. The writer depicted her, instead, as a 1950s self-sacrificing American mother personified, albeit in reduced circumstances and of a browner hue.

By the fall of 1961, the ILGWU curtailed benefits to pickets due to rising costs. Eighty strikers chose to continue despite this signal of defeat. The labor press, unable to resist the season's sentiments, provided the most moving picture of them in a comparison with Mary, Mother of Jesus:

Many of these strikers are mothers, and they too wanted to be able to buy pretty clothing for their own children. . . . If they fainted from hunger on the picket line, that would be one thing. But, if they quit, they couldn't face themselves. That was why these mothers of San Antonio were walking a picket line before Christmas on St. Mary's, the street named for the Mother of Jesus.[45]

Union insistence on portraying the Chicana strikers as mothers, while true to a large extent, placed the women in an extremely limiting role. Women were presented either as bad and promiscuous or as good and virginal. In a period tainted by McCarthyism, images of virginity, motherhood, and peace and quiet worked better for the union than allusions to citizenship.

The commercial media presented a less generous view of the Chicana ILGWU strikers. It exaggerated the sensational elements whenever possible. On 26 and 27 February, the first week of the strike, angered by seeing police escort workers out, strikers attacked them; patrolman Manuel Garza said: "[Women] swung purses, threw eggs, cursed, kicked, pulled hair, kicked and clawed." The *San Antonio Express* splashed front page photographs of the arrests, in which the police had used unnecessary force, leaving women with rucked up clothing exposing thighs and legs. The paper headlined the events as riots and focused on police charges of drunkenness and disorderly conduct.[46] Apparently the press understood that the strikers' "unwomanly" behavior during the melee, and perhaps their ethnicity, generated negative publicity for strikers who dared challenge the status quo.

The daily press showed their tendency to offer mixed and biased messages in an article on Sophie Gonzales, the first Chicana ILGWU organizer in Texas. Gonzales picketed sites from six in the morning until five in the afternoon. When Tex-Son employees tried to hex strikers with voodoo dolls, she kept her composure and pronounced, "Voodoo is for the birds!" The writer, however, focused on Gonzales's family life, inquiring about her husband's opinion of her work, and the expectations she had for her son's future. As always, Gonzales used her public relations talents effectively: "My boy wants to be a union organizer when he grows up. But I'd rather see him become a road engineer." The writer described Gonzales as "a large but well-proportioned woman with light black hair and high school girl eyes." A pretty woman, Gonzales, dressed in a black skirt, white blouse, heels, and carrying a parasol, offered a pleasing picture of womanhood to the public. Her picture graced the pages of the paper several times, despite the generally negative attitudes of the commercial papers toward the strike.[47]

The Chicanas' situation at Tex-Son followed a much more mundane path than the press indicated. Knowing the stakes were high, the ILGWU kept a tight lid on the course of the dispute. Except for the incidents of 26 and 27 February, the daily activities associated with a prolonged strike and boycott were characterized by routine behavior. For the first time in ILGWU's history in Texas, Chicanas dominated the union local and chaired strike committees. They spent the majority of their time organizing strike parades, picketing stores, making a film, writing letters, and raising funds. Gonzales, the organizer, and Gregoria Montalbo, the local's president, devoted most of their efforts to acquiring financial and moral support from the community. Striking Chicanas at Tex-Son showed that they were more than the "mothers" and "rioters" that the press portrayed them to be.

Even more directly than daily press stories, Tex-Son company owner Franzel provided negative images of the strikers in his many press releases. After he failed to compromise with the strikers at the urging of a federal conciliator, Franzel told reporters that the events of 26 and 27 February showed evidence of the strikers' "evil conduct." He called on "high thinking people" to "join with us in condemning the shameful depths to which the strike has sunk" and promised never to rehire the strikers who had "stooped to such a cowardly and dastardly level."[48] Franzel clearly tried to portray the strikers as degenerate, untrustworthy people, and nothing like ordinary, good, happy Americans.

Franzel went further, employing a tactic well known in American history. After he read about a strikers' parade attended by thousands of other unionists, Franzel linked it with an earlier news story on Communism. "We have no direct evidence that there is any connection between the parade which occurred and this communist directive," he reported, "but it is [an] interesting coincidence."[49] As had city officials in the 1930s, Franzel was determined to separate the strikers from the community at large and to make them appear disloyal.

The strikers' resolution to continue picketing proved insufficient after the ILGWU quit. They could not succeed against the hundreds of dollars that Franzel used for a union-busting attorney or against the great availability of inexpensive labor in the garment industry. Though women pickets continued into the winter of 1962, monetary resources dwindled and the union could provide little support. The women eventually conceded the situation.

The 1972 Farah strike in El Paso was the other major garment dispute in the post-war period. The labor disagreement between Farah Manufacturing Company and the Chicana members of the ACWA lasted two years. It centered on an owner determined not to accept the union, and included a nationwide boycott of Farah slacks. The union relied on prevailing ideologies based on ethnicity in garnering support for the women strikers and frequently turned for aid to the Chicano civil rights movement, which had begun more quietly, but lasted longer than the Black civil rights movement. In the beginning, the local news media ignored the strike. As the editor of the *El Paso Times* put it, "I am for Farah; he is a good citizen and he has done a lot for El Paso."[50]

Because of Willie Farah's virulent anti-unionism, he forbade labor activism, and ACWA recruitment in 1969 was clandestine. By 1972, the ACWA planned to challenge Farah before the National Labor Relations Board (NLRB), and thus it was unprepared for the walkout in May. On the day of the walkout, Farah employees at the San Antonio plant walked out protesting the firing of a machinist for union activity. Led by veteran women workers, thousands from El Paso joined their *companera* unionists from San Antonio. The two-year long labor dispute became characterized by Farah's unbridled public pronouncements, the national boycott, and a suit/countersuit battle before the NLRB.[51]

By 1972, the labor newspaper played a lesser role in strike events. The ACWA used pamphlets, leaflets, cards, and especially, personal appearances in the strikers' cause. The popularity of the sunbelt areas of the Southwest created a growing El Paso community that was more diverse and more likely to read the *New York Times* than a union paper.

Furthermore, the union surely found the new electronic media appealing in touting the strike. Other media picked up the story nationally, mitigating the labor paper's already diminished role.

But, the labor union had a second image of the strikers to disseminate. The Chicano movement in Texas crystallized in 1966–67 during a farmworkers' strike in Rio Grande City. The 1969 high school students' walkout in Crystal City expanded the movement by including state and national issues, as well as local matters of concern. With this expansion in mind, and perhaps to offset any ideas that their first message might seem too radical, the union developed a second message to temper any conception that the strikers were only violent reactionaries. It enhanced the public image of the Chicana strikers by portraying them as family-oriented. The union happily helped the national papers carry both messages—as a Chicana struggle for human dignity and justice and as a family issue.

In their boycott campaign against Farah slacks, union publicists played on the two themes of family and social justice with success. In 1973, the Committee for Justice for Farah Strikers created a Christmas card showing a female child clinging to an adult hand and explaining that her father was a Chicano striker "struggling to attain simple human rights." A union leaflet for shoppers portrayed a young female with arm raised in a clenched fist, representing, the inscription said, a minority group seeking to end its oppression. The legend on a handout to students containing a child's picture and a male picket against a fence topped by jagged wire spikes emphasized, "We are striking for our rights as American citizens . . . for our dignity as human beings, for our self-respect as proud Mexican Americans."[52]

In their propaganda against Farah, the union betrayed their basic underlying insensitivity to issues of gender and ethnicity. The inscription on the leaflet of a young woman with raised fist seemed to imply that Chicanos had previously never protested their oppression, although the ACWA itself had led strikes of Chicanas in 1953, 1965, and 1971 in El Paso. Unable to forego its image of workers and unionists as men, the union in the Christmas card poster of 1973 pictured a male hand for the child to hold on to, and the legend discussed the striking parent as "her father." Yet, the majority of workers at Farah and on strike were women. Even the union emphasis on the nuclear family seemed questionable. According to women strikers at Farah, many of them were single female parents with children.[53]

Initially, the union kept women strikers limited to picketing and clerking tasks, while men made public statements. According to a woman striker, however, the ACWA was forced to send Chicanas on speaking tours, locally and nationally, after repeated public requests. Women strikers created their own group known as Unidad Para Siempre (Unity Forever) to better utilize their own talents. They organized speaking and television engagements, facilitated resources to supporters, and developed a strike fund directed from a local church. One striker noted that Unidad offered women the sense of mutual understanding that Amalgamated seemed to lack. In her words, "[W]e used to meet once a week and talk about the struggle, the rank and file being more supportive and that's why we met."[54]

As unrealistic as were the union depictions of the Farah strikers, they did garner a tremendous positive response. Local unions not only participated in picketing, parading, and boycott activities, but some, like the meat-cutters union, funneled into the coffers a thousand dollars a week to cover expenses. Likewise, on the national level, unions like the United Auto Workers offered funds as well as experienced personnel to head boycott actions in other cities. Even the football players' union publicly expressed support for the Farah strikers. International unions proclaimed their solidarity by joining in the boycott of Farah products.[55]

From the beginning, Farah publicly and privately opposed the ACWA with every available means. He humiliated women by making them sweep floors, and he fired others suspected of union activity. To stop the walkout, Farah secured an injunction resulting in the arrests of hundreds. He placed barbed wire fences around his five plants and hired security guards with dogs to protect them. In his most pernicious pronouncement, he used the old charge of subversion, telling the *Los Angeles Times* that the strikers were Communists, and the union "had done him a favor by getting rid of that filth." By quoting Farah, the *LA Times,* long a self-admitted voice for the California elite, continued that policy in Texas.[56]

In 1972, the local press's limited coverage of the strike illustrated Farah's importance to the business community of El Paso. The Chamber of Commerce president and owner of one bank considered himself Farah's best friend and frequently served as spokesman for him. Not only did Farah own ten plants employing 22 percent of the city's work force, but he served on the board of one of the oldest and most established banks in El Paso with the *El Paso Times's* publisher. Although strikers complained that the media underestimated the size of crowds at rallies, the paper's representation of them consisted more of omission than commission. For example, in a series of articles on the strike, the *Herald Post* led each segment with Farah's point of view, leaving out the strikers' perspective.[57] Like the *LA Times,* the two commercial papers in El Paso showed no hesitancy to express their partiality to Farah. The papers may have felt that their only option was to protect the local son. The boycott had garnered immense support from unions, churches, political figures like Edward Kennedy, and international unions for the strikers.

With their pro-Farah stance, the local press published many of Farah's public statements unchallenged. In an article on continuing production during the strike, the paper accepted company claims that "94% of its workers[—]including supervisors, executives, and officers[—]have Spanish surnames," never once noting, that, if true, it was a very recent phenomenon.[58] By accepting uncritically Farah claims and by bypassing the position of the strikers, the press made clear the reality that the latter did not matter politically or otherwise in El Paso.

Besides omitting the strikers' sides of the stories, the *Herald Post* gave favorable accounts of Farah's activities. For example, when the Texas Conference of Churches cut short Farah's speech, the paper accepted his explanation that it was "strictly a point of order." Other papers made it clear that he had been stopped because he chastised the churches' support of the strikers. The press included positive physical descriptions of Farah such as "youthful looking."[59] If the press sought to show Farah so favorably, it must have realized that doing so might cause readers to view strikers negatively.

The ACWA survived Farah's determined efforts to keep the union out because of the tremendous success of the national boycott of Farah pants. Farah stock plummeted from $39.50 in 1972 to $8 in February

1974. The "don't buy" campaign cost the company about $8 million in 1972 and $2.5 million in the last quarter of 1973.

After two years, Farah agreed to the original demands for job security, arbitrable quotas, a grievance system, and a company-paid health plan, as well as agreeing to recognize the union and rehire the strikers. While the company implemented the new policies, management carried out most of them half heartedly and used others, like the grievance plan, to punish the most activist strikers now back on the payroll.[60]

The union was influenced by Farah's faltering finances in the settlement terms. Many union members felt alienated by the sudden end of the strike and others by the fast-hand vote on the contract. Workers complained, "All of a sudden the strike was over. . . . We really didn't know what was going on . . . I didn't like it." Another described the decision on the contract: "[S]o he read the contract real fast and then he asked, 'Does anybody disapprove?' and then a few of the people raised their hands and they were ignored . . . he said, 'Oh, this means we go back to work.' We didn't vote on it." The ACWA resorted to calling union dissenters Communists and greedy troublemakers.[61] In union representations, the Chicana strikers at Farah changed from Chicanas fighting for justice and honor to union-busters.

Guided by accepted ideas of gender, class, and ethnicity in American society, Texas newspapers expressed unwarranted assumptions in their representations of the Chicana strikers. The daily, local papers maintained a consistent profile of the strikers as outside mainstream America—as Bolsheviks, Communists, and as evil and filthy foreigners. When the local press was not focusing on the alleged anti-social and anti-American behavior of the women, it tended to ignore them and concentrate on the males instead. San Antonio and El Paso papers emphasized the Mexican heritage of the strikers in negative ways, usually through the comments of company owners or city officials. These papers pictured the Chicanas as lazy, impressionable, and stupid—or simply as "Mexicans." The daily paper's representations illustrated their bonds with Anglo government at the local level.

The daily press did not seem bothered by their contradictory depictions of the strikers. Their efforts *meant* to alienate the women from the rest of the community. At times, the papers portrayed the women as the antithesis of American good. In the next breath, the papers called them gullible and too indolent even to realize the American work ethic. Anglo readers could be comfortable with these representations because they fit into the accepted notion of Chicanas as an alien and unassimilable element. It was with this shared understanding with other establishment institutions that the commercial press pushed incomplete images of the striker.

To gain support, the labor press would periodically change its image of the Chicana strikers. It would select what was socially palatable in an effort to make acceptable a group of strikers who stood on the margins of society. In 1919, the 1930s, and 1959, the labor papers overlooked the Mexican heritage of the strikers to stress their American citizenship and their roles as vulnerable women and mothers. In the 1970s, with ethnic movements "in," the ACWA exploited the Chicana identity of the Farah strikers to gain boycott support nationwide.

Labor editors operated with many of the same prejudices as the rest of the community. In 1919, the labor paper pulled back from earlier anti-Mexican diatribes and supported the Mexican women strikers only to retreat into a KKK alliance by 1920. In the pecan strike of 1938, the labor paper, run by AFL leaders, gave coverage only in reaction to CIO interest or involvement in it. Only after World War II did mainstream labor provide less hesitant support to striking Chicanas—and they still continued to create narrow depictions of these women workers.

Spanish-language papers virtually disappeared after World War II, but in the earlier strikes, the papers, caught between their Mexican origins and ties to Chicana strikers and their hopes of becoming Americans, tried to play it both ways by stressing the Mexican heritage of the women in a positive way and at the same time stressing their good behavior. By emphasizing proper behavior, the Spanish press, with its own middle-and-upper class management, clearly exhibited patronizing attitudes towards the strikers as women and as working-class people.

In reality, the seeming ambivalence of the Spanish press lay purely on the surface. Its concerns over its own status in the U. S. inhibited its sense of solidarity, as evidenced by the civic club's attitude in 1919 that the women's good behavior had earned them the former's support as representatives of the Mexican community. The striking women's often violent responses served to place them beyond the pale of traditional middle-class ideology, and the male hierarchy in the Spanish-language press preferred instructing the women on strategy and conduct. Particularly after the 1920s, the middle- and upper-class Mexican immigrant embraced American ideals, and they pushed their ideals on their less well-placed ethnic sisters.

The distorted press portrayals of Mexican-American women strikers contain implications for all women workers. What the papers noted about the women revealed more about the journalists' inclinations and societal expectations of women than any meaningful delineation of the women's experiences. Women never did fit journalists' standards, whether based on class or ethnic definitions—because both or either were seen in male terms. All three press institutions expected certain behavior from women strikers, after having already designated them as the "other." This designation of otherness might well explain women strikers' actions, which are often defined as fierce, aggressive, and extreme. If they were already beyond the rules, why not act that way? For each woman striker, it was another woman striker who acted as her guide. The women's sense of striker solidarity became heightened when the local press, the labor papers, and the Spanish press deemed them as different.

The newspapers in El Paso and San Antonio proved unable to move beyond established notions of gender, class, and ethnicity in their coverage of the Chicana strikers between 1919 and 1974, but in the process, the press provided information on the overwhelming forces the women faced during protest situations. The Chicanas fought not only great opposition from the companies, but a powerful daily press ready to condemn their actions in support of the established order. Even their supporters, the unions and Spanish-language papers, expected certain behavior from them based on each paper's particular agenda in a given period. Despite these complex odds arrayed against them, Chicanas in Texas demonstrated the power of persistence in the battle for labor justice.

ABBREVIATION GUIDE

ILGWU	International Ladies Garment Workers Union
CLU	Central Labor Union
AFL	American Federation of Labor
IWW	Industrial Workers of the World
CIO	Congress of Industrial Organizations
UCAPAWA	United Cannery, Agricultural, Packing and Allied Workers of America
ACWA	Amalgamated Clothing Workers of America
NLRB	National Labor Relations Board

★ The late Irene Ledesma was an assistant professor in the Department of History and Philosophy at the University of Texas-Pan American in Edinburgh, Texas.

For their assistance with the citations, thanks are extended to Jane Boley, archivist in the University of Texas at Arlington, Special Collections; Tab Lewis, archivist, Textual Reference Branch of the National Archives; and Gerrianne Schaad, curator of manuscripts, University of Texas at El Paso, Special Collections.

Jensen-Miller
Prize
1996

'This Evil Extends Especially . . . to the Feminine Sex':
Negotiating Captivity in the New Mexico Borderlands

James F. Brooks

L ATE in the summer of 1760, a large Comanche raiding party
besieged the fortified home of Pablo Villalpando in the
village of Ranchos de Taos, New Mexico. After a daylong
fight, the Comanches breached the walls and killed most of the male
defenders. They then seized fifty-seven women and children, among
whom was twenty-one-year-old María Rosa Villalpando, Pablo's
second daughter, and carried them into captivity on the Great Plains.
María's young husband, Juan José Xacques, was slain in the assault, but
her infant son, José Juliano Xacques, somehow escaped both death and
captivity.

The Comanches apparently traded María shortly thereafter to the
Pawnees, for by 1767 she lived in a Pawnee village on the Platte River
and had borne another son, who would come to be known as Antoine.
In that year, the French trader and cofounder of St. Louis, Jean Salé dit
Leroie, visited the Pawnees and began cohabiting with María. About
one year later, she bore Salé a son, whom they named Lambert. Perhaps
this arrangement suited Salé's trading goals, for it wasn't until 1770 that

---

★ James F. Brooks, "'This Evil Extends Especially . . . to the Feminine Sex':
Negotiating Captivity in the New Mexico Borderlands," in *Feminist Studies* 22:2
(1996). ©1996 Feminist Studies, Inc. Reprinted by permission.

he ended María's Indian captivity and brought her to St. Louis, where they married.

Jean and María (now Marie Rose Salé) had three more children, when, for unknown reasons, Jean returned to France, where he remained the rest of his life. María stayed in St. Louis to become the matriarch of an increasingly prominent family. Her New Mexican son, José Juliano, would visit her there, although we will see that the reunion proved bittersweet. María finally died at the home of her daughter, Hélène, in 1830, at well over ninety years of age. For María Rosa Villalpando, captivity yielded a painful, yet paradoxically successful, passage across cultures into security and longevity.[1]

Long understood as a volatile and complex multiethnic borderland, greater New Mexico presents an intriguing problem to scholars of Indian-Euroamerican relations. Despite the reality of Spanish colonialism and the notable success of the Pueblo Revolt (1680–93), the region remained a "non-dominant frontier" in which neither colonial New Mexicans nor the numerically superior indigenous peoples proved able(or willing) to dominate or eject the other completely.[2] This article takes one step toward a deeper understanding of the question, by exploring the role captive women like María Rosa played in promoting conflict and accommodation between colonial Spanish (and later Mexican) society and the indigenous people of greater New Mexico. During the Spanish and Mexican periods (c. 1600–1847), thousands of Indian and hundreds of Spanish women and children "crossed cultures" through the workings of a captive-exchange system that knit diverse communities into vital, and violent, webs of interdependence. These captives, whether of Spanish origin, or Native Americans "ransomed" by the Spanish at *rescates* (trade fairs), seem crucial to a "borderlands political economy" that utilized human beings in far-reaching social and economic exchange.[3]

Developing in the wake of Spanish slave raids and Indian reprisals, over time this commerce in captives provided the basis for a gradual convergence of cultural interests and identities at the village level, emerging in "borderlands communities of interest" by the middle years of the nineteenth century. Seen as both the most valuable "commodities" in intersocietal trade *and* as key transcultural actors in their own right, captive women and children participated in a terrifyingly, yet at times fortuitous, colonial dialectic between exploitation and negotiation. Until now, their histories have lain in the shadows of borderlands historiography.[4] Although firsthand accounts are rare, and other evidence must be used with caution, an examination of their experience may contribute to our understanding of colonial processes in New Mexico and elsewhere in North America.

Whatever the large-scale antagonisms between Spanish colonists and Native Americans, problems of day-to-day survival required methods of cross-cultural negotiation. Prolonged, intensive interaction between New Mexican *pobladores* (village settlers) and nomadic or pastoral Indian societies required some mutually intelligible symbols through which cultural values, interests, and needs could be defined. Horses, guns, and animal hides spring immediately to mind as customary symbols of exchange, but women and children proved even more valuable (and valorized) as agents (and objects) of cultural negotiations. In New Mexico, as elsewhere in North America, the "exchange of women" through systems of captivity, adoption, and marriage seem to have provided European and Native men with mutually understood symbols of power with which to bridge cultural barriers.[5]

Rival men had seized captives and exchanged women long before European colonialism in North America. The exogamous exchange of women between "precapitalist" societies appears to represent a phenomenon by which mutual obligations of reciprocity are established between kindreds, bands, and societies, serving both to reinforce male dominance and to extend the reproductive (social and biological) vigor of communities.[6] This essay approaches the issue from a variety of sources and perspectives. Combining Spanish archival research with some of the classics of North American Indian ethnology, and viewing both through the lens of feminist critiques and extensions, I suggest that the capture and integration of women and children represented the most violent expression along a continuum of such exchange traditions. The patriarchal subordination of women and children, it has been argued, served as a foundation upon which other structures of power and inequality were erected. Gerda Lerner contends that the assertion of male control over captive women's sexual and reproductive services provided a model for patriarchal ownership of women in "monogamous" marriages by which patrilineal bloodlines remained "pure." From this sense of proprietorship grew other notions of property, including the enslavement of human beings as chattels.[7]

In New Spain, under the *Recopilacion* of 1680 (a compendium of laws governing colonial/Indian relations), Spanish subjects had been encouraged to redeem indigenous captives from their captors, baptize them into the Catholic faith, and acculturate them as new "detribalized" colonial subjects.[8] These redemptions occurred in roughly two forms—either through formal "ransoming" at annual trade fairs (*ferias* or *rescates*) or small-scale bartering (*cambalaches*) in local villages or at trading places on the Great Plains. Trade fairs at Taos, Pecos, and Picuris Pueblos had long fostered the exchange of bison meat for corn, beans, and squash between Plains Indians and the Río Grande Pueblos and had probably included some exchanges of people as well.[9]

These seasonal events continued after the Spanish reconquest of New Mexico in 1692–96. Throughout the eighteenth century, Spanish church and secular authorities vied to gain control of this trade, variously blaming each other or local *alcaldes* (village mayors) for "the saddest of this commerce." In 1761 Fray Pedro Serrano chided Spanish governors, who "when the fleet was in" scrambled to gather as many horses, axes, hoes, wedges, picks, bridles, and knives in order to "gorge themselves" on the "great multitude of both sexes offered for sale."[10] Fifteen years later, Fray Anatasio Domínguez reported that the Comanches brought to Taos for sale "pagan Indians, of which held quite steady until the mid-nineteenth century, was "two good horses and some trifles" for an "Indian girl twelve to twenty years old." Male captive boys usually brought a "she mule" or one horse and a "poor bridle . . . garnished with red rags." The general atmosphere, according to Domínguez, resembled a "second hand market in Mexico, the way people mill about."[11]

After 1800 these formal rescates decline, replaced with smaller, more frequent on-the-spot bartering. This seems due to several factors—Plains Indians wishing to avoid possible exposure to Euroamerican disease, a desire on the part of New Mexican villagers to escape taxation of their Indian trade, and a geographical expansion of the borderlands economy. By the 1850s local traders like José Lucero and Powler Sandoval would purchase Mexican captives from Comanches at Plains outposts like "Quitaque" in Floyd County, Texas, giving, for example, "one mare, one rifle, one shirt, one pair of drawers, thirty small packages of powder, some bullets, and one buffalo robe" in exchange for ten-year-old Teodoro Martel of Saltillo, Mexico.[12]

Judging from extant New Mexican parochial registers, between 1700 and 1850, nearly 3,000 members of nomadic or pastoral Indian groups entered New Mexican society as *indios de rescate* (ransomed Indians), *indios genízaros* ("slaves"), *criados* (servants), or *huérfanos* (orphans), primarily through the artifice of "ransom" by colonial purchasers.[13] Ostensibly, the cost of ransom would be retired by ten to twenty years of service to the redeemers, after which time these individuals would become *vecinos* (tithes-paying citizens). In practice, these people appear to have experienced their bondage on a continuum that ranged from near-slavery to familial incorporation, an issue that will be addressed at length in this work.

Ransomed captives comprised an important component in colonial society, averaging about 10 to 15 percent of the colonial population, and especially in peripheral villages, where they may have represented as much as 40 percent of the "Spanish" residents.[14] Girls and boys under the age of fifteen composed approximately two-thirds of these captives, and about two-thirds of all captives were women "of serviceable age" or prepubescent girls.[15]

This commerce in women and children proved more than a one-way traffic, however. Throughout the period under consideration, nomadic groups like Comanches and Navajos made regular raids on the scattered *poblaciones* (settlements), at times seizing as many as fifty women and children.[16] In 1780, Spanish authorities estimated that the *Naciones del Norte* (Plains tribes of the northern frontier) alone held more than 150 Spanish citizens captive, and by 1830 the figure for the Comanches alone may have exceeded 500.[17] Among the Navajos, as late as 1883 U.S. Indian agent Dennis M. Riordan estimated that there were "300 slaves in the hands of the tribe," many of whom were "Mexicans captured in infancy."[18] Like their Indian counterparts, these women and children found themselves most often incorporated into their host society through indigenous systems of adoption. As fictive kin, they too experienced a range of treatment. Although impossible to arrive at precise numbers of New Mexican captives in Indian societies, their representation becomes increasingly significant in a discussion of the workings of the captive system and the personal experience of captives themselves.

The captive-exchange system appears overwhelmingly complex when examined through particular cases, but certain overall patterns seem consistent. First, captive taking and trading represented the most violent and exploitative component of a long-term pattern of militarized socioeconomic exchange between Indian and Spanish societies. Second, it seems that New Mexican captives and *indios de rescate* generally remained in their "host" societies throughout their lifetimes. Third, female captives often established families within the host society, and their descendants usually became full culture-group members. Male captives, on the other hand, suffered either a quick retributive death or, if young, grew to become semiautonomous auxiliary warriors within their new society. Finally, it appears that many captives found ways to transcend their subordinate status by exercising skills developed during their "cross-cultural" experience. In doing so, they negotiated profound changes in the cultural identity of the societies within which they resided, changes which continue to reverberate in the borderlands today.

THE CAPTIVE EXPERIENCE

Torn from their natal societies in "slave" raids, treated like *piezas* ("coins," a common term in New Spain for slaves, both Indian and African) in a volatile system of intercultural exchange, and finally the "property" of strangers, captive and ransomed women seem unlikely subjects as historical actors. But the experiences recounted henceforth show these women and children negotiating narrow fields of agency with noteworthy skill. From positions of virtual powerlessness, captive women learned quickly the range of movement allowed by the host culture, especially in regard to adoption and *compadrazgo* (god-parenthood) practices.[19] This first phase of integration gave them "kin" to whom they could turn for protection and guidance. But this security remained limited, and many faced coercive conjugal relationships, if not outright sexual exploitation by their new masters.

Whether of Spanish or Indian origin, two factors are essential to our understanding of the captive experience in greater New Mexico and perhaps to similar cases in other periods and regions. First, captives' status and treatment within the host society would establish the structural constraints (culturally specific customs and laws governing rights and obligations) within which individuals might pursue their goals.[20] Second, sheer luck and the individual captive's personal resources determined much of her actual lived experience, ranging from terror and exploitation to a few remarkable cases of deft negotiation and good fortune, into which María Rosa Villalpando's story certainly falls. Overall, the interplay of structural constraints, contingency, and skills can be seen in most captives' lives. Another captive woman, Juana Hurtado Galván, proved so adept at the cross-cultural enterprise that her story exemplifies successful adaptation.

Early in the summer of 1680, shortly before the conflagrations of the Pueblo Revolt, a band of *Apaches del Nabajo* ("Navajos") swept down upon the *rancho* of Captain Andrés Hurtado and took captive his seven-year-old daughter, Juana.[21] For the next twelve years, her life among the Navajos lies concealed, a blank in the historical record that can only be reconstructed by inference and imagination. But those years of captivity seem to hold the key to understanding much of Juana's subsequent life, a long and controversial career that ended in 1753. When she died, Juana owned her own rancho with three houses and managed extensive herds and flocks. Her illegitimate son, Juan Galván, served as the *teniente* (assistant magistrate) of the Zia district.[22] Nativity had given Juana linkages to both Spanish and Pueblo society, and in her captivity she developed linguistic and kinship ties with the Navajos. Throughout her life, her experience as a captive woman would afford her special negotiating skills with which she pursued security for her lineage.

Juana's mother had come from the Pueblo of Zia, probably as a *criada* (domestic servant) of Captain Hurtado, but we know little more about her life.[23] No doubt sexually used by Hurtado, the daughter she bore in 1673 was just one among hundreds of such *coyotas* (children of mixed Spanish/Indian parentage) resulting from the Spanish colonization of

New Mexico. The mother's connection with Zia Pueblo, however, remained central to her daughter's story. After Juana's halfbrother, Martín, a soldier in the Spanish *reconquista* of 1692, ransomed Juana from captivity, the young woman petitioned for and received a private *merced* (land grant) at the northwest corner of the Zia Pueblo lands, near the village known today as San Ysidro.[24] This rancho proved a key locus of trade among Navajos, Pueblos, and Spanish villagers for the next half-century and was the source of Juana's wealth and influence.[25]

Although restored to colonial society, Juana never severed connections with her onetime captors. Frequent visits by Navajos to her rancho suggest that she had experienced adoption into a Navajo clan. She may even have married in captivity, as she never formalized any future conjugal relationship. Kinship aside, her trilingual skills and cultural intermediacy facilitated economic exchanges between potential enemies. Her affinity with Navajos remained so close that Fray Miguel de Menchero commended her usefulness in assisting proselytization efforts: "They had kept her for so long [that] the Indians of said Nation make friendly visits to her, and in this way the father of the said mission has been able to instruct some of them."[26]

Juana's conduct, however, also attracted criticism from church authorities. Throughout her life, she persisted in maintaining a long-term liaison with a married man of Zia, presumably named Galván. By 1727, this relationship had resulted in four children and charges of scandalous behavior leveled against her by Franciscan *padres*. When authorities sought to place Juana in stocks, however, the people of Zia "threatened that the whole pueblo would move to the mesa tops, rather than have her mistreated."[27] Like the Navajos, the people of Zia apparently saw tangible benefits in the presence of this kinswoman on their borders. Defining kinship more broadly than did the Spanish, they seemed willing to provoke conflict in defense of their relationship with someone who provided a bridge across three cultures. As she drew upon her qualities and talents as a negotiator, Juana "La Galvana" utilized her experience as a captive to carve out an intermediate niche in the complex power relations of colonial New Mexico.

Juana's intermediacy was accentuated by her mixed-blood status, and her paternal linkage to a Spanish *encomendero* (holder of tributary rights to Indian labor) probably allowed her the opportunity to occupy a privileged niche compared with many captives. Because one side of the captive system originates in indigenous, precontact exogamous exchange traditions, we need to look at gender and social hierarchies within Native American societies to begin to understand the structural constraints that Juana and other captives might have experienced. Although they display variation, women's and captives' status within Indian societies of the borderlands (Navajo, Apache, Ute, and Comanche) may be generally described as subordinate to men and holders of the "cultural franchise" but enhanced by traditions of matrilineality and social mobility.[28]

Navajo patterns of gender and social hierarchies show a blending of southern Athabascan systems and cultural adaptations to Spanish colonialism near their homelands. Navajo women owned the flocks of sheep and wove the textiles that formed the core of their pastoral economy. Matrilineal descent, therefore, conferred important productive resources as well as kin-reckoning through women. Navajo men, however, prevailed in "public" decisions involving warfare and diplomacy.[29]

Captives taken in warfare with other tribes or raids on Spanish settlements again experienced a range of treatment. If not killed in vengeance satisfaction, the captive invariably suffered a period of harsh and terrifying ritual abuse. This "taming" process probably formed the first phase in adoption ritual.[30] After "taming," most captives became inducted into the clan of their captor, or the "rich man" who purchased them from the successful warrior. Once a clan member, it seems few barriers stood in the way of social advancement. The New Mexican captive Nakai Na'ddis Saal, raised in a clan on Black Mesa, "became a singer of the Nightway," an important Navajo ceremony. The Sonoran captive Jesus Arviso, taken by Chiricahua Apaches in 1850 as a boy and traded to the Navajo Kla Clan, served as the principal interpreter for his host society throughout the Fort Sumner "Long Walk" era. Marrying into the Nanasht'ezhii Clan, he chose to remain a Navajo, welcoming a congressional delegation to Fort Defiance in 1919 and living at Cubero until his death in 1932.[31]

Captive women usually became clan members and married exogamously. Even if not inducted into clan membership, their children by Navajo men were considered members of the father's clan.[32] Although we can only speculate, these clan and kin affiliations probably provided Juana Hurtado with the networks that allowed her to act as an intermediary between Zia Pueblo and Spanish society. Indeed, Juana seems noteworthy among captives for having chosen to return to her birthright, for some sources indicate that most captives, when "set free . . . immediately took the shortest trail back to the hogans of their masters."[33]

Captives seem to have fared less well among the Jicarilla Apaches, a semi-sedentary people who practiced a seasonal economy that balanced hunting and collecting with extensive horticulture. Apache women, however, benefited from matrilineality and ownership of fields and crops which "were planted, weeded, and harvested by the joint labors of the entire family." This gender-integrated labor diverged when men hunted or raided and women engaged in the life-cycle labor of family reproduction. Although subordinate to men, women made important ritual contributions to the success of hunters: "a man and his wife pray together and smoke ceremonially before the husband leaves for the hunt. After his departure the woman continues a series of ritual duties." Similarly, before men departed for warfare or raiding, "a woman [was] chosen to represent each man to serve as proxy in group decisions, [and she] obeyed many restrictions in matters of dress, food, and behavior to ensure his safe return."[34]

Warfare among the Jicarillas often involved the seizure of captives, either for vengeance satisfaction or cultural integration. Adult male captives "were tied to posts and slain by women with lances," but captive women and children found themselves incorporated into the band. A captive woman "could not be molested until she had been brought back and a ceremony . . . performed over her," probably some form of adoption that established her subordination within the Apachean levirate. Even with this adoption, captive women "were not considered fit wives. They were sexually used, and sent from camp to camp to do the heavy work. Their children by Apache men, however, were recognized as Jicarilla" and "accepted into Apache life."[35] We shall see that this second-generation integration appears nearly universal among the indigenous groups in question and provides another constraining structure in captive women's decisions to remain within the host society even when offered their "freedom."

These patterns of gender and social subordination, mitigated by adoption and generational enfranchisement, are reiterated in an examination of Comanche society. Drawing largely upon ethnographic data gathered in the 1930s, Jane Fishburne Collier has argued that women's status in pre-reservation (c. 1875) Comanche society, as reflected through the dynamics of bride-wealth marriage, "may best be understood in the context of relations between men."[36] Certainly, the Comanches seem to represent the most noteworthy case of Plains Indian individualism and status competition between men, where wife-stealing often served as an intraband expression of a general cultural pattern. One of Collier's sources (E. Adamson Hoebel), pointed out, however, that although "before the law, [the] Comanche woman was a quasi-chattel," social custom allowed women a considerable degree of choice in extra-legal activity.[37]

Surprisingly, first Hoebel then Collier overlooked evidence of women-centered status competition, a stretching of patriarchal structural constraints. In one-half of the marital disputes Hoebel recorded, women had left their husbands for other men, often joining their lovers on war parties. In one case, the couple stayed away from the band for two years, and when they returned, the woman had fifteen horses in her personal string.[38] Women could also obtain horses (next to captives the most prestigious "commodity" in Comanche society) through the institution of the "Shakedown Dance," whereby successful raiders were shamed into giving a part of their herd to young, unmarried women.[39] Status and prestige also accrued to women through the matrilineal transfer of medicine powers, as in the case of Sanapia, a Comanche Eagle Doctor.[40] These examples suggest that within male-defined cultural limitations, Comanche women exploited opportunities for competitive mobility and status enhancement. Captives, although initially lower in status, appear to have negotiated similar avenues toward social mobility.

No other Plains society engaged in captive raiding as vigorously as did the Comanches. This seems a result of both individual status competition and the need to replace a population ravaged by warfare and epidemic disease.[41] Comanche society offered several social locations into which captives could be integrated, ranging from chattels to kins-men and women.[42] Ralph Linton suggests that the prestige value of captives reflected their "importance in the social and economic life of the tribe. Mostly Mexican, they tended the horse herds and practiced most of the specialized industries such as gun repairing and saddle-making." The honored position of center-pole cutter in the Comanche Sun Dance went either to a "virtuous Comanche woman, a virtuous captive woman, [or] a captive man who had a number of war-deeds to his credit."[43] Among the Kiowas, a Plains people closely allied with the Comanches after 1805, captives like Loki-Mokeen, a Mexican mulatto, could become officers of the Sun Dance and protectors of the sacred *Taim* Bundle.[44] Andrés Martínez, called by the Kiowa "Andali," was seized from his family's pastures near Las Vegas, New Mexico, and grew to adulthood as a Kiowa warrior. In 1889 he converted to Methodism and told his story to the Reverend J. J. Methven.[45] Similarly, the "cap-tive-friend" who fought alongside his Comanche warrior-brother, appears prominently as a type in Hoebel's ethnography.[46]

Captive women often found themselves under the protection of Comanche women. Rosita Rodrigues, writing in 1846, reported she "remained a prisoner among the Comanche Indians about one year, during which time I was obliged to work very hard, but was not oth-erwise badly treated as I became the property of an old squaw who became much attached to me."[47] Similarly, Sarah Ann Horn, taken cap-tive in 1837, reported that she was taken in "by an old widow woman . . . a merciful exception to the general character of these merciless beings." Although she was "set to work to dress buffalo hides," she did not suffer sexual abuse.[48] It appears that at least some captive women were informally adopted by older women, by which action they received the protection of the Comanche incest taboo.[49] By extension, it bears consideration that in some cases, Comanche women may have identified and acted upon interests counter to those of Comanche men, protecting captive women either for their value as "chore sisters" or through human empathy.

Rodrigues and Horn are among the very few women who, when repatriated, wrote of their experiences among the Comanche. Most captive women seem to have remained with their captors, marrying and establishing families in the host society.[50] Rodrigues herself left a son behind among the Comanche, reporting that she "heard from him a short time ago—he is well and hearty but he is pure Indian now."[51] Josiah Gregg noted the presence of Mexican women among the Comanche when he began traveling the Santa Fe Trail in the 1830s. He remarked with surprise that some of these "preferred remaining with [their captors], rather than encounter the horrible ordeal of ill-natured remarks on being restored to civilized life." One woman refused to return even after the offer of $1,000 for her ransom. She sent word that the Comanche "had disfigured her by tatooing; that she was married, and perhaps *enceinte* (pregnant), and she would be more unhappy returning . . . under these circumstances than remaining where she was."[52]

These women had good reason to fear social opprobrium if they returned to Spanish society. When authorities introduced an alms-gathering plan in 1780 to raise funds for the ransom of Spanish captives, Teodoro de Croix declared with alarm that "this evil [captivity] extends especially . . . to the feminine sex . . . on account of the lascivious vice of sensuality in which they are now afforded the greatest liberty to indulge themselves."[53] This may have been a rhetorical flourish to heighten interest in the plan, but it suggests that the conjugal arrangements of Comanche women might entail certain attractions to captive Spanish women as well.

Spanish concerns about the influence of Indian life-ways on their subjects went beyond anxieties about the behavior of "their" women in captivity. The simple fact that thousands of Indian captives and their descendants now resided in "Spanish" society stimulated a growing polemic of caste-conscious distancing by elite *españoles* vis-à-vis the culturally mixed people in the border villages. Elite anxieties were provoked by evidence that border villagers often exhibited behavior and pursued interests more in tune with their Indian neighbors than those contained in policy directives from Santa Fe or Mexico City. Gradual movement toward "borderlands communities of interest" linking New Mexican villagers with contiguous Indian groups emerged as one consequence of the presence of captive Indian women in colonial New Mexico.

Recently, Ramón Gutiérrez addressed one aspect of this cultural complexity, arguing that eighteenth-century New Mexico developed as a "timocracy," where "differences between aristocrats and landed peas-ants were of degree rather than kind. Spaniards, whatever their estate, were men of honor in comparison to the vanquished Indians." Gutiérrez contends that the *genízaro* (slave) caste, formed from the mass of indios de rescate obtained by the Spanish through ransom, constituted a "dis-honored" status against which all Spanish, regardless of economic posi-tion, could define their *calidad* (rank).[54]

Although Gutiérrez offers strong evidence for this honor/dishonor distinction among elite españoles, his use of prescriptive sources gener-ated by these elites tends to leave on-the-ground relations between *mes-tizo pobladores* (mixed descent settlers) and their genízaro neighbors somewhat obscure. As we will see, by the end of the eighteenth cen-tury, Spanish ecclesiastics and administrators spoke of their colonial vil-lagers in terms usually associated with *los indios bárbaros*, often referring to them as "indolent," "rude," "independent," and "lewd." Captive exchange lay at the heart of this blurring of cultural boundaries.

New Mexico appears similar to other colonial borderlands, where patterns of cultural accommodation appear ongoing beneath longer-term themes of cultural conflict, and the exigencies of day-to-day sur-vival promoted periods of relatively peaceful coexistence.[55] Always uncertain, and often punctuated by violent exchanges, relations between village-level New Mexicans and their nomadic-pastoral Indian neighbors may be viewed in like terms, but with heightened focus on exchanges of women and children as central objects and agents of intercultural negotiation. Locally constructed communities of inter-est were designed to foster mutual exchanges (economic and cultural) with a minimal loss of life. By late in the eighteenth century particu-lar aspects of these relations received higher recognition in formal negotiations surrounding Spanish, Comanche, Ute, and Navajo peace treaties. The movement toward local mixed-cultural communities, however, distanced the village people of New Mexico from their colo-nial administrators, a trend that would lead to internal conflict by the nineteenth century.

Foreshadowing this turmoil, in 1794 Don Fernando de la Conchá complained to incoming Governor Don Fernando Chacón that the vil-lage people of the province seemed "indolent": "They love distance which makes them independent; and if they recognize the advantages of union, they pretend not to understand them, in order to adopt the liberty and slovenliness they see . . . in their neighbors, the wild Indians."[56] Concern on the part of Spanish administrators had increased throughout the preceding decades. In 1776 Antonio de Bonilla had found the "settlements of the Spaniards . . . scattered and badly defended," protecting neither themselves nor "contributing to the defense of the province."[57] Two years later, Fray Juan Augustín de Morfi attributed this situation to the fact that the "pobladores liked to live apart, far from the prying eyes of neighbors and the restraining influence of authorities," where they could "commit with impunity all manner of immoral and criminal acts, and . . . were not ashamed to go about nude so that lewdness was seen here more than in the brutes."[58]

Like Morfi, Concha felt that social intercourse with the *Indios bárbaros* lay at the heart of this problem. Life in the villages, he told his successor, had become so distanced from colonial control that he recommended "the removal of more than two thousand [villagers]," whose "bad upbringing results from . . . the proximity and trade of the barbarous tribes." This trade appears to have become increasingly a part of the borderlands economy in New Mexico and one which villagers sought to conceal from colonial control. Concha complained that the villagers, "under a simulated appearance of ignorance or rusticity . . . conceal the most refined malice."[59]

A decade later, Chacón would note that the villagers were "little dedicated to farming," surviving instead on a vigorous trade with nomadic Indians. In exchange for the settlers' manufactured goods and agricultural products, nomads like the Comanches gave them "Indian captives of both sexes, mules, moccasins, colts, mustangs, all kinds of hides and buffalo meat."[60] As the Bourbon Reforms brought efforts to incorporate New Mexico within the economic sphere of New Spain, especially in a developing sheep and textile industry, the informal economic autonomy of villagers seemed a barrier to progress.[61]

Tensions between administrators in Santa Fe and their backcountry subjects exploded in August 1837. The villagers of Río Arriba descended upon the *villa* and seized the government, executing Governor Albino Pérez in the process.[62] Infuriated by rumors of direct taxation under Santa Ana's centralizing Constitution of 1835, which threatened to interfere with their autonomous indigenous trade, the rebels identified themselves "with the savage tribes . . . making the same cause and their same interests."[63] Mexico restored central authority by 1838, but communities of interest between New Mexican villagers and their Native neighbors persisted. In 1847 the villages again rose in rebellion, this time against the American military government of occupation. Pueblo Indians and New Mexican allies killed Governor Charles Bent in Taos, while Manuel Cortés of Mora joined with Apache and Cheyenne allies to raid U.S. military and commercial supply lines on the eastern frontier.[64] This ability to build strategic linkages across cultural boundaries was a consequence of long experience in economic and human exchange.

The seeds of these linkages were both cultural and biological, which we see revealed in a village-level intermingling of status groups. In Ranchos de Taos, for example, the Spanish census of 1750 reported nine Spanish households of fifty-seven persons, six *coyote* households of fifty-five persons, and eight genízaro households of twenty-five persons. Even the Spanish households showed a blurring of caste category; the house of Antonio Atiensa included his *coyota* wife, María Romero; their *castizo* (*español* and coyota) son, Domingo Romero; and the widow, Juana, with her daughter, Manuela, no doubt *criadas*. Similarly, the house of Juan Rosalio Villalpando, an important español, included his wife, María Valdes, and their six children, all of whom are termed coyote, suggesting that María may have been an *india de rescate*. Pablo Francisco Villalpando's household, from which María Rosa would be seized ten years later, contained three female and two male *servientes*, two of whom carry the family name. Mixing may have crossed class as well as caste lines in some village families.[65]

The fact that the census arranged households by caste category reveals a conscious concern about caste status on the part of Spanish administrators, but the data also demonstrate how informally these categories might be arranged at the village level. Census findings from a cluster of Plazas at Belén show a somewhat different, yet consistent, pattern. In 1790 the third Plaza, "Nuestra Señora de los Dolores de los Genízaros," contained thirty-three households, all designated as genízaro, a strong indication that in some cases true communities developed among some indios de rescate. But the adjacent second Plaza of Jarales held thirty Spanish, twelve mestizo, four coyote, and two genízaro households. The marriage patterns from these communities reveal little caste-anxious endogamy; of the twenty-eight unions, only one is *español-española*. Six marriages involved *genízaro-genízara,* and five *mestizo-mestiza*. The remaining sixteen show a crossing of caste lines. In most of these, hypogamy seems the rule, with women marrying men of "lower" status. Children of these unions, for example, *genízaro-coyota*, follow the father's status and are later enumerated as *genízaros*.[66]

By the late eighteenth century, however, this designation for children born of captive Indian women may not have carried only the "dishonored" quality that Gutíerrez proposes. Instead, it may indicate a movement toward identity formation on the part of the *genízaros*. As early as 1744, sources report that genízaro men played an important role as military auxiliaries for the Spanish.[67] By 1780, a group of thirty-three *genízaros* negotiated with Spanish authorities from a position of some power, threatening that if their lands in the Barrío de Analco in Santa Fe were not protected, they might go "in search of relief to our lands and nation."[68] Governor Joaquin del Real Alencaster organized an official *Tropa de Genízaros* (militia troop) in 1808 to patrol the eastern frontier of New Mexico, in response to Zebulon Pike's adventurism of the previous year.[69] And in 1837, following the Río Arriba rebellion noted earlier, the revolutionary government elected José Gonzales, a *cibolero* (bison hunter) from Taos who may have been a genízaro, as their new governor.[70] As subordinate, yet militarily skilled members of New Mexican society, genízaro men found themselves valued in a colony always in need of men-at-arms. Once established on the outer marches of the province, they managed to assert an intermediate negotiatory identity.

Initially little more than pawns in a distinctive "slave trade," captive Indian women and children established families within New Mexican society whose members eventually owned land, served in the military, and even led major rebellions. In their cases, maternity provided avenues of agency, especially as they manipulated structural constraints to establish increasing security for their offspring and, consequently, for themselves.

Two such constraints applied particularly to women in colonial New Mexico: marriage and *compadrazgo* (godparent) relations. For Spanish women, and mixed-blood or captive women who had internalized their conversion to Christianity, the dictates of the Catholic Church structured their agency within marriage. Gutíerrez has shown how caste-endogamous marriages served to "purify" the bloodlines of New Mexico's ruling elite.[71] The gender hierarchy of the church also firmly established women's subordination as dependents under the patriarchal authority of husbands and the church, with preservation of family honor through legitimate offspring their principal social role. Unlike women in the English colonies, however, Spanish women maintained separate property throughout their marriage(s) and could bequeath their estates independent of their husbands' wills.[72]

Spanish women's "property" often included *indias de rescate*, who found themselves transferred to daughters as servants, or "emancipated" with the condition that they continue to "watch over and assist my daughter as if she were her mother."[73] Others received clear title to parcels of land "in appreciation of years of service to me without salary."[74] When José Riano contested the will of Gregoria Gongora in 1739, he explicitly excepted from the disputed property "a piece of land for the india who raised my youngest and other children."[75]

Although these cases suggest a familial quality to the relations between Spanish and Indian women, few masters or mistresses actually formalized this quality in godparent relations. Of the 3,294 "slave" baptisms in New Mexico between 1693 and 1849, only 14 percent feature "owners" as *padrinos* (godparents), and the vast majority (65 percent) show "no apparent relationship," simply members of the local Spanish community. Gutíerrez argues that these figures reflect the internal contradictions between the benign character of compadrazgo and exploitative character of master-slave relations.[76]

An alternative explanation, and one more in keeping with the argument herein, might see these baptismal data as representative of mutually supportive relationships between the New Mexicans and indios de rescate, a variation upon traditions of adoption that we have seen as ubiquitous in nomadic and pastoral Indian society. Frances S. Quintana argues that in New Mexico, compadrazgo relations show two patterns, an "old world" tradition that "intensified existing kin relationships" among colonial elites, and a "new world" innovation that "helped to stabilize relationships between native Indian populations and Spanish and mestizo groups."[77]

In addition to the baptisms of indios de rescate noted above, during the same period we see the baptism of 1,984 "illegitimate" children born of the women of the genízaro caste. In fact, Gutíerrez has recorded only twenty church-sanctioned marriages among members of this group and suggests that this reveals the continuing control of masters over the sexual services of "slave" women.[78] Certain of his cases support Gutíerrez's conclusion, but we should also recognize that refusal to "consecrate" a conjugal union also served as an act of resistance among both Pueblo and nomadic Indian groups.[79] At Zia Pueblo, and among the Navajo, a refusal to name the parents of "illegitimate" children continually frustrated Spanish authorities.[80] It seems reasonable to conclude here a mixed pattern of sexual exploitation of indias de rescate by Spanish masters, and a collective strategy of identity maintenance that, by refusing Catholic structures, retained the offspring of those and voluntary unions with Indian men as members of the cultural community.

Conceived in grossly unequal relationships, the children who resulted from unions with captors often served, ironically, to strengthen the status of captive women. As full culture-group members of either Indian or genízaro communities, these daughters and sons provided social access and security to their mothers. As Marietta Morrissey has found for slave women in the Caribbean, concubinage with dominant men often involved a painful balancing of shame and hope. If they acceded to sexual relations with masters, their children were born free, and in a position to assist in the dream of manumission.[81] In some cases as well, real bonds of affection and respect developed between sugar planters and slave women, a factor that seems likely in some of the New Mexican examples.

Although the creation of kinship seems the primary avenue by which captive women sought security and identity, we may also discern other facets of their lives from within the historical record. In addition to the life-cycle labor of family reproduction, these women engaged in subsistence and market production. The eighteenth and nineteenth centuries

saw dramatic shifts in the status and work of Plains Indian women as peoples like the Comanches, Kiowas, and Cheyennes began participating in
the European fur and hide trade. With the horse and gun, one Indian man
could procure fifty to sixty buffalo hides per season, twice as many as one
Indian woman could tan for use or exchange. An increase in polygamy,
and raiding for captive women, served to counteract this labor shortage.[82]
The captivity narratives quoted earlier make it clear that captive women
were "set to work to tan hides" almost immediately. The appearance of
polygamous households probably made this work more efficient, for "co-
wives" might process hides while the "first-wife" performed higher-status
production and distribution like cooking, clothing manufacture, and cer-
emonial activities.

Indias de rescate appear most often as household servants, but to
consider their work entirely "domestic" is probably misleading. Because
both Apache and Navajo captive women came from societies in which
women were the principal horticulturists, they may have found themselves gardening and even tending flocks in New Mexican villages. We
are only beginning to develop an understanding of women's economic
life in colonial New Mexico, but Angelina F. Veyna's work with women's
wills suggests that both Spanish and Indian women may have been more
involved in farming than previously thought. The fact that women
owned *rejas* (ploughshares) and willed them not to their sons but to
their daughters suggests either a farming orientation or a means of
attracting potential husbands.[83]

Navajo and Apache women held captive in New Mexican households also worked as weavers, both of basketry and textiles. H. P. Mera
has described the nineteenth-century "Slave Blanket" as a crossover style
between Navajo and New Mexican techniques, using New Mexican
yarns and designs, but produced on the distinctive upright looms of
Navajo women.[84] These early New Mexican *serapes* became important
trade items at rescates, given in exchange for buffalo hides and dried pem-
mican. Although today in villages like Chimayo, men weave the distinctive Río Grande blankets, this seems the result of a concerted effort early
in the nineteenth century to develop a commercial textile industry.[85]

Captive women and children played important roles in one last
area, that of Spanish-Indian diplomacy. Their cross-cultural experience

made them valuable as interpreters, translators, and envoys for Spanish military leaders. By 1750 the Comanche had obtained French guns, and Governor Vélez declared that unless a peace were negotiated they might prove "the ruin of this province." In order to communicate with several Comanche hostages held in Santa Fe, Vélez utilized the interpretive services of a Kiowa woman who had been captured by the Comanche, lost to the Utes in a raid, then purchased as a *criada* by Antonio Martín. This negotiation resulted in a temporary truce, sealed by the exchange of several prisoners.[86]

When the peace collapsed in 1760, captive women again served in a diplomatic capacity, this time as emissaries. Unable to find the appropriate Comanche leaders with whom to bargain, Vélez "dispatched six Comanche women prisoners as ambassadors to their nation." Within a month, four of the women had returned, along with nine Comanche captains, and another truce was affirmed by the return to the Comanche of "thirty-one women and children, among whom, fortunately, were their relatives."[87] Similarly, when Governor Juan Bautista de Anza and Ecueracapa (Leather Jacket) negotiated the Spanish-Comanche Peace of 1786, which lasted until 1846, they sealed their agreement by exchanging a Comanche boy, "José Chiquito," for Alejandro Martín, "eleven years a captive among the band of Captain Tosapoy."[88]

NEGOTIATING CAPTIVITY IN THE NEW MEXICO BORDERLANDS

Often deemed invisible commodities in the "slave trade" of the Spanish borderlands, the captive women and children discussed here emerge as human actors engaged in a deeply ambivalent dialectic between exploitation and negotiation. Their stories begin in a moment of abject powerlessness, where subordination serves as a substitute for violent death. But from that moment forward, we see them taking tentative steps toward autonomy and security. Captive women worked within the limits set by their captors, yet through the creation of kinship, their daily labors, and their diplomatic usefulness, they managed to carve out a future for themselves and their lineages. Although fewer in number, captive boys became men who utilized their military skills to attain status and limited autonomy.

Beginning with an indigenous tradition of captive taking, and intensified by Spanish military and economic exploitation, the captive-exchange system developed as one important component of a border-lands political economy that produced conflict *and* coexistence. Maria Mies has conceptualized the interlinkage of men's militarism and the forcible exchange of women as a universal "predatory mode of appropriation," a paradigm for "all exploitative relations between human beings."[89] In New Mexico, Spanish and Indian men found that even more than horses, guns, or hides, their counterparts valued women and children; and they established some nominal agreement that these would serve as objects and agents of intersocietal exchange. Conflict and accommodation patterns, therefore, between these rival societies may represent attempts by differing forms of patriarchal power to achieve external economic and military objectives while reinforcing the stability of internal social and gender hierarchies.

Of course, the social consequences of exchanging women and children across ethnic boundaries proved difficult to contain, and both New Mexicans and their Indian neighbors found customary relations unsettled by cultural hybridity. In time, the mixed-blood descendants of captive women and children exhibited new collective interests that influenced their choice of cultural identification. The collective interests of second- (and subsequent-) generation descendants blurred the boundaries between New Mexican villagers and their Indian neighbors. Plains Indian societies became increasingly militarized and market oriented during this period, and New Mexican villagers increasingly mobile. By the 1830s, New Mexican *ciboleros* (bison hunters) and *comancheros* (traders and raiders) appeared regularly in travel accounts.[90] Plains Indian societies displayed new forms of collective action, and villagers rose in radically democratic rebellions.

Despite the exploitative quality of the captive-exchange system, its victims found ways to exercise agency and achieve some measure of security and comfort for themselves and their descendants. Within the structural constraints considered here, there lay some opportunity, especially when captives found it possible to use newly acquired cross-cultural skills to their advantage. For example, Juana Hurtado received the support of the Zias and Navajos in her role as cultural center-person. A Crow woman might be sold at a *rescate* by some Comanches, escape to find her way homeward, and end up leading a French trading expedition back to New Mexico.[91] A Pawnee woman in Santa Fe could discover that her master had settled land upon her in his will, for the consideration that she continue to serve as criada to his son.[92] Finally, María Rosa Villalpando of Taos, whose story opened this article, found herself traded to the Pawnee, married there, then remarried to become the "matriarch" of a French fur-trading enterprise in St. Louis. Her New Mexican son, José Juliano, visited her there in 1802 and attempted to establish a claim as her heir. Perhaps conflicting maternal sentiments forced María into a hard choice—she paid José Juliano 200 pesos to relinquish his claim and sent him packing. José Juliano took a long route home, for in 1809 New Mexican authorities contacted Spanish administrators in San Antonio, Texas, and suggested José be forcibly sent home, for he had a wife and children "without support" in the village of Ojo Caliente.[93]

Although the American conquest of 1846–48 resulted in the erosion of shared values and interests between New Mexicans and southwestern Indians, vestiges of the borderlands communities of interest still survive. Miguel Montoya, historian of the village of Mora, defines the historical identity of his neighbors in this way: "We were Spanish by law, but Indian by thought-world and custom. We respected *los viejos* (the elders), who looked after our spiritual health. We have relatives in the Pueblos, and out there, in Oklahoma (pointing east, to the reservations of the Comanches, Kiowas, and Southern Cheyenne)."[94]

★ James F. Brooks is a member of the research faculty and Director of the School of American Research in New Mexico.

'No Place for a Woman': Engendering
Western Canadian Settlement

Catherine A. Cavanaugh

I N March 1996, Madeleine Gould's nine-year quest for recognition as a Yukon pioneer ended in defeat when the Supreme
Court of Canada upheld the right of the Territory's fraternal
Order of Pioneers to exclude women from its ranks. In their majority
decision, the seven male justices in the nine-member highest court noted
the long history of the all-male organization, "formed in 1894 by the
Forty Mile community . . . for the purposes of establishing a police force"
and providing mutual support and protection to its members:"male persons of integrity and good character who met a ten-year residency
requirement."[1] By the early 1900s, the order's policing activities were no
longer necessary, and it became a social organization primarily concerned with preserving local history. Noting this shift in activities, Mister
Justice La Forest upheld the order's right to exclude women on the basis
that it was a private organization dedicated to "preserving the moral
values, male camaraderie and mutual respect, traditions and secret rites
that were engendered by and formed the fabric of a Klondike brotherhood of the 1890s."[2]

* Catherine A. Cavanaugh, "'No Place for a Woman': Engendering Western
Canadian Settlement," *Western Historical Quarterly* 28 (1997). © 1997 Western
Historical Society Quarterly, Western History Association. Reprinted by permission.

The court's two female justices disagreed, stressing both the order's public function to preserve history and its private function to maintain the status and prestige bestowed on its members. Noting a range of public benefits membership conferred, including "a respect in the community" as a "'modern' pioneer, part of the select society of past pioneers," Madame Justice Beverley McLachlin pointed out that "[t]he order has assumed an important role in defining the pioneers of the Yukon, and that recognition as a member of the order and recognition of a person as a Yukon pioneer are largely synonymous in the mind of the public." "Can it be right then," she asked, "that [membership] is denied to one-half of the Yukon population, its women?"[3] Siding with the Yukon Human Rights Commission in its original decision, Madame Justice Claire L'Heureux-Dubé also rejected the "male camaraderie" argument, adding that the exclusion of women from the order distorted the history it created because it left women out. Quoting from the evidence presented in the case, L'Heureux-Dubé concluded that as a result "[t]oday, these women have been all but forgotten, with not even their names recorded."[4]

In *Gould v. Yukon Order of Pioneers* the court was asked to rule on a narrow question of Canadian human rights legislation regarding sex discrimination, but the case is also a sharp reminder of the legacy of settlement. The issues before the court highlight the ways in which gender—in this instance, "male camaraderie" and "Yukon brotherhood"—continues to be used to naturalize male privilege as founding fathers while excluding women from that history.

This paper argues that the gender division the case reflects was established early in settlement discourse and perpetuated in both the official and popular mind. It begins with an exploration of settlement discourse and the ways Victorian gender ideology was used to provide the conceptual framework, or mental map, upon which European colonization and settlement took place.[5] It goes on to suggest that in constructing and reconstructing the West—from wilderness wasteland to economic hinterland to agrarian paradise—expansionist discourse perpetuated the myth of the West as a "manly" space, assigning to it a moral and political force that underwrote élite Anglo-Canadian men's hegemony in the territories.[6] Finally, the implications for women of this masculinist cultural context are considered using three examples.

The first example is taken from the so-called Foss-Pelly scandal that gripped the Red River colony in 1850. It examines the role of Sarah Ballenden, a métis daughter of the fur trade, in the events surrounding the scandal to show how gender was used to construct categories of race in the new West. The second example explores the campaigns to extend married women's property rights in the three prairie provinces in the 1910s and 1920s. Women won important legislative changes, but the cultural assumptions that underwrote men's control of land, and therefore wealth, in the new provinces remained intact. The third example considers women's engagement with electoral politics in the years immediately following the extension of provincial suffrage in 1916–1917. It illustrates how the legacy of settlement continued to shape prairie women's political opportunity during the inter-war period.

This analysis shows that during the settlement period gender ideology was integral to cultural constructions of the West. It underwrote institutional practices and conventions ranging from the sexual division of labor, economic opportunity, and political rights to what Sarah Carter terms "the categories and terrains of exclusion" constructed along racial and class lines.[7] This study suggests that while the possibilities for women (and men) were shaped by a masculinist cultural context, in the shifting realities of the turn-of-the-century, Euro-Canadian women's responses to cultural constructions of the West as a manly space were neither inevitable nor always predictable.

Studies of settlement discourse focus primarily on the American settlement frontiers and the place of the West as a dominant symbol of nation-building and the opportunity for conquest.[8] As Richard Slotkin so expertly argues for the United States, "this myth-historiography" of frontier was variously used to underwrite American colonialism and to explain the nation's distinctive culture and emergence as a world power.[9] Within this tradition, the significance of "wilderness-going" as a source of individual and national regeneration owes much to Frederick Jackson Turner and his disciples who argued that American democracy was forest-born, emerging out of the individual (male) pioneer's struggle to subdue the wilderness—and its native inhabitants—and wrest a living from the land.[10] But, as Slotkin points out, while Turner assigned to "yeoman farmers" the leading role in American development, it was Theodore Roosevelt's *The Winning of the West* (New York, 1897) that elevated the frontiersman to the legendary hunter/Indian-fighter, representing him as the ideal of American manhood.[11]

North of the forty-ninth parallel, the American frontiersman's Canadian counterpart labored in comparative obscurity. Historians of the Canadian West tended to minimize the symbolic role of the frontier in nation-building, favoring instead explanations of national differences between the counties. In Canada, patterns of western settlement are taken as further evidence of the development of a unique political culture, characterized by peace, order, and good government. Even when Canadian scholars document similar perceptions of the significance of western settlement to national identity—even national destiny—the uses of masculinity in constructing a mythical West remain largely unexplored.[12]

To be sure, Canadian dreams of empire fell far short of the American achievement of world power status, but a brief examination of the contemporary Canadian literature reveals striking parallels with American expansionist discourse. Canadians too saw the West as a source of national regeneration and spiritual renewal through a reinvigorated manhood. Consider, for example, what the popular writer Ralph Connor says about the West and the men who settled it.[13] Connor's early novels, *Black Rock* (Toronto, 1896) and *The Sky Pilot* (Toronto, 1899), were both run-away best sellers based on his experiences as a Presbyterian missionary in western Canada during the mid-1890s.[14] In his novels, Connor's frontiersmen stand as the salvation of a "worn-out civilization."[15] Having turned away from what was widely perceived at the time as the moral decline of urban, industrial society, he explains that these "hardy soul[s] . . . pitched their camp, and there, in lonely, lordly independence, took rich toll of prairie, lake, and stream as they needed for their living."[16] For Connor, the "untrammelled, unconventional mode of life" of the frontier had transformative power: "Freed from the restraints of custom and surrounding," even the most "high bred . . . young lads . . . soon shed all that was superficial in their make-up and stood forth in the naked simplicity of their native manhood. The West discovered and revealed the man in them."[17]

By assigning masculinity to the expansionist enterprise, settlement discourse used gender to support Euro-Canadian nation-building and buttress the claims of competing white male élites in the political and economic skirmishes for dominance in the territories following the annexation of the Hudson's Bay Company lands in 1870. Expansionists touted the manly West as more democratic than the East, uncorrupted by the influences of industrialization and urbanization, or the emasculating effects of "overcivilized" domesticity, casting the West's wide open spaces and bracing climate as sources of moral and spiritual uplift.[18] In the West, a man was thought to be freed from the oppressive gentility of the urban East and the alienating influences of modern bureaucratization and industrial capitalism's wage labor. In his physical struggle in an alien and hostile environment, the frontiersman/farmer/rancher supposedly reasserted his "natural" independence and manly dignity. So, in 1873, George M. Grant, an advocate of western settlement, could claim that in the West, "a man feels like a young giant," and "cannot help indulging in a little tall talk, and in displays of his big limbs." Thomas Spence (1880) could confidently predict that the only capital a homesteader needed to succeed in the West was "brawny arms and a brave heart," and Nicholas Flood Davin (1891) readily assert that just "three years" in the Northwest would raise a prairie farmer "higher on the scale of manhood." Emily Murphy shared these views, but attributed the physical and moral qualities of the pioneer to both men and women. "It is a great place, the Canadian West," she boasted as Janey Canuck, "the country of strong men, strong women, straight living and hard riding."[19]

In the discourse of western expansion Murphy is an exception. Typically, women are represented as existing outside of the masculine enterprise of settlement. When women do appear, it is more often as "civilizers" or "gentle tamers."[20] Created in opposition to the middle-class ideal of active, conquering manhood, civilizing womanhood is made passive and disembodied, thereby guaranteeing representations of men's dominance. This relationship is captured in the following newspaper account published in 1891. Assuming that western settlement was an exclusively male experience, the author explains that as European men traveled west:

all that was independent and self-assured in them was developed.... Men weak and impractical were hardened into sterner stuff.... Sentiment and weakness were discarded; laziness fled utterly. Each was anxious to rifle nature, and that, too, as quickly as possible. Caste and social distinction were blotted out. All men were equal in that strange pilgrimage. Strength was capital then.... Women's part in this strange existence was an influence for the good. Rough and godless as were these men, woman was still enshrined in their hearts, in the tender memory of mother, sister, sweetheart. And so they idolized and worshipped faraway woman ... good or bad she saved those wicked men from a hardness scarcely less than that of the rocks they crushed.[21]

Or, consider Ralph Connor's introduction to *The Sky Pilot*, "a story," he writes:

of the people of the Foothill Country ... those men of adventurous spirit, who left homes of comfort, often of luxury, because of the stirring in them to be and to do some worthy thing ... freed from all the restraints of social law, denied the gentler influences of home and the sweet uplift of a good woman's face.[22]

Literary constructions of the West as a "manly" space often contradicted the reality of settlement and were primarily intended for Eastern audiences. But they also worked to shape newcomers' responses to their new environment and give meaning to the settlement enterprise. For example, after spending his first winter homesteading in the Buffalo Lake district of the Northwest Territories (east of present-day Lacombe, Alberta) in 1893–1894, John Wilcox associated himself with the hearty band of pioneers at the centre of Connor's stories. In a letter to his cousin Jack in Ontario, Wilcox praises the exceptional beauty and abundant resources of western Canada. The West, he reports, is truly a land of promise: It is "the best country for stock I have seen ... there is everything here a man wants, plenty of hay, water, wood and mountains of coal . . . [t]he lakes and creeks are full of fish . . . this is the home for geese and ducks. . . . I have a splendid good gun. I tell you it is great fun hunting here." "[B]ut God help it for lonesomeness," Wilcox added, "It is so lonesome I don't know how to live. . . ." "Dear Jack," he continues, "I wish you lived here so I could have an old friend to talk to." But ending his letter on a melancholy note, Wilcox recognizes that his cousin probably would not want "to leave civilization" to come west.[23]

Wilcox's letter echoes expansionist literature in the way he uses gender to make meaning of space. On first reading, his approach seems contradictory. He admits that he is alone and isolated—"10 miles to . . . [the] nearest white bachelor," and "27 miles to a white woman"—but concludes that the West is "all right for a man to come [to] . . . to make money." His cousin is a man, but Wilcox assumes Jack would prefer the comforts of the developed East. While confessing that he does not "know how to live" beyond the reach of "civilization," Wilcox asserts that in the West there is "all that a *man* wants." His own feelings of isolation and loneliness lead him to conclude that the West "is no place for a *woman*/there is no Sundays here."[24] In part at least, these contradictions were reconciled by symbolic constructions of the West as a place of mythical masculine renewal.

Indeed, Connor and Wilcox are engaged in a similar project. By staking his claim to the future in the West, Wilcox is imaginatively joined to the manly struggle for survival in the harsh prairie wilderness. Framed as a masculine enterprise, the promise of the West is much more than the making of money. The search for wealth becomes a struggle for essential manhood. In both the official and popular mind, this idea was fundamental to the way in which the West was conceived, organized, and incorporated into the national dream. For example, when two of the largest areas of the Northwest Territories were joined to confederation as the provinces of Alberta and Saskatchewan, Prime Minister Wilfred Laurier considered it a symbolic coming of age. Self-government, he told the nation, reflected the West's "state of manhood" in 1905.[25]

The antecedents of the manly West of colonization and settlement are found in the imaginary landscapes of the fur trade. In popular literature this mythical country is populated by gentlemen adventurers, staunch missionaries, hardy traders, and backwoodsmen whose exploits served symbolically to underwrite imperial masculinity. Abjuring the comforts of European civilization was as crucial to the heroic test of their masculine mettle as was their mastery over the "barbarous" conditions of Indian country and its indigenous peoples.[26] Over time, the boundary between these two worlds shifted, but to the Euro-Canadian mind the characteristics that separated them remained clear. When Frances Simpson, the English wife of Governor George Simpson, first encountered the "boundless Wilderness" of the Northwest in 1830, she thought that "the boundary between the Civilized and the Savage Worlds" lay roughly two days by canoe from Montreal. Her journals capture her mounting sense of danger as she traveled deeper into the territories, although she seems uncertain as to whether the greater threat lay with "Nature in her grand, but Savage and uncultivated state," or in the "wild & savage habits of the Aborigines."[27]

Simpson's trepidation underscores the political significance of European constructions of the West as simultaneously "alien" and "manly." While his western odyssey was thought to be the making of British manhood, entering this "wild & savage" land was assumed to have the opposite effect on genteel women. As recent studies argue, the "Frail Flower" of Victorian womanhood, assumed to be physically and emotionally weak, was supposedly more vulnerable then her male counterpart to the dangers of the "untamed" West. Seen as powerless and unable to adapt to this alien environment, she was considered to be entirely dependent on the protection of European men.[28] This unreflective view of sex difference has persisted in the historical literature so that the arrival of European women in the West is seen to disrupt two hundred years of relatively peaceful relations based on marital alliances between European men and Aboriginal women. In this analysis, the events surrounding the Foss-Pelly trial, which began in Red River on 16 July 1850, mark a racial divide in the history of the Canadian West, precipitated by the appearance of white women in the colony.[29]

The Foss-Pelly sex scandal has been described in detail by historian Sylvia Van Kirk and need be outlined only briefly here.[30] The case involved Captain Christopher Foss, a British army officer newly arrived in Red River, and Sarah Ballenden, the métis wife of the Hudson's Bay Company's Chief Factor, John Ballenden.[31] For about a year, rumour had circulated throughout the colony that Ballenden and Foss were involved in a relationship "of such a character as to entitle Mr. B(allenden) to a divorce."[32] Hoping to put an end to the gossip, Foss sued three company employees and their wives, including the clerk, A. E. Pelly, and his wife Anne Clouson Pelly, for instigating a defamatory conspiracy. The ensuing trial focused on Sarah Ballenden's moral character and sexual behaviour. Much of the testimony consisted of suspicion and innuendo and the jury quickly found no basis for the charges of sexual misconduct. Ballenden was completely exonerated and heavy damages found against the defendants. But, as Van Kirk points out, this did not end the matter. The trial and its aftermath divided the colony along racial lines. Ballenden's supporters, largely drawn from the Indian and métis population, continued to assert her innocence while her accusers and their supporters, predominantly white Protestants backed by the local clergy, persisted in their attacks on her character and standing in the community. Vilified as a fallen woman and suffering ill health, Ballenden was ultimately driven from the colony in social disgrace. She died of consumption three years later at the age of thirty-five.

Van Kirk's argument that Sarah Ballenden was the victim of white women's racism rests on the role of two British women, both recently arrived in the colony, Anne Clouson Pelly and the sister of Reverend David Anderson, Anglican Bishop of Rupert's Land, Margaret Anderson, who Van Kirk describes as "the epitome of the strait-laced, sharp-tongued spinster."[33] Van Kirk identifies Pelly and Anderson as Bellenden's chief accusers, arguing that they were motivated by a sense of racial superiority and a perception that inter-racial marriages threatened the future welfare of white women. Viewed as agents of empire, but limited to a narrowly defined competition as the preferred wives of white men, the actions of these newcomer women appear petty and vindictive.

There can be little doubt that white women were often just as eurocentric as their male counterparts. Indeed, it would be unusual if they were not equally embedded in the cultural assumptions of nineteenth-century imperialism. Moreover, as wives, sisters, and daughters of imperial officers and company officials, the work of enforcing social hierarchies often fell to colonizing women, making them more visible in the process.[34] But, as Margaret Strobel has pointed out, the tendency in imperial histories to interpret white women's actions as more aggressively racist than those of white men, perpetuates Victorian gender ideology. The myth of the destructive female preserves nineteenth-century assumptions of a dependent femininity and white women's moral superiority, while exaggerating their social power.[35] Blaming Anglo-Canadian women for the deterioration of race relations at Red River may be convenient, but it obscures the reality of gender roles in the colony and misses their political significance. In large part, white women's influence in colonial settings was derived from their marital status to imperial men. Circumscribed by official opinion, their influence could not be exercised directly or independently.[36] As white settlement increased, political and economic power at Red River became concentrated in the governing class of élite Euro-Canadian men. Ultimately, Sarah Ballenden's position in the colony—and, as it turned out, her life—depended upon the goodwill of the newly appointed Associate Governor of the territories, Eden Colvile. Colvile and his British wife protected Ballenden for a short time, but when the governor withdrew his patronage in the winter of 1850, the ailing Ballenden was left to her unhappy fate.

Characterizing the Foss-Pelly scandal as a struggle between two groups of women for status as the preferred brides of European men distracts us from the crucial question of social formation during a critical period in the development of western Canada. The scandal offers compelling evidence that a shift in favour of white institutions and conventions occurred in the northwest as early as 1850. Understanding the nature of this change requires a fuller appreciation of the ways in which gender was used to construct relationships of power, between men and women, but also between classes and races.

The question of rank was alive in the events at Red River, serving to further inflame the racial attacks aimed at Ballenden, wife of the chief factor, and the highest ranking woman in the colony at the time. But rank failed to protect her from imperial and patriarchal goals that rested on complimentary assumptions of British racial superiority and white male dominance. If Sarah Ballenden had been the wife of a rank-and-file trader it is quite likely that she would have avoided censure altogether or at least managed to negotiate the crisis more successfully. As it was, her social status, which devolved from her family relationships to two white men, was doubtless a contributing factor in the effort to discredit her. But once her reputation as a respectable lady was called into question even her husband's loyal support proved insufficient protection. This suggests that in the shifting interests of Euro-Canadian expansion some men (notably, those married to Aboriginal or métis women) also experienced a sharp decline in status and power.

Ballenden's mixed-race heritage was central to the charges of sexual misconduct which formed the basis of the attack on her respectability. Fraternization with Aboriginal (or métis) women could be tolerated, even advocated, within the context of the fur trade, on the grounds that it enhanced company profits. But, the collapse of the Hudson's Bay Company trade monopoly in the territories in the 1840s, combined with a rapidly expanding American frontier to the south (the neighbouring Minnesota Territory was established in 1849), presaged great changes in the established order at Red River. Western expansion held the promise that great fortunes might be made. Indeed, the success of the colony itself, which boasted a population of 172,000 by 1860, more than that of the entire Hudson's Bay territories, only fuelled expansionists' dreams. A realignment of political and economic forces dictated a shift in the social order, one that would ensure élite Euro-Canadian men's hegemony in the new West.

The Foss-Pelly scandal illustrates the ways in which imperial and patriarchal goals were joined in the cause of establishing a new Euro-Canadian male élite in western Canada. After about 1850, when there was the prospect of more wealth to be had, élite men had greater concern to marry women of their own race and class whose children would be their legitimate heirs.[37] Under the conditions of colonization and settlement, métis women who, like Sarah Ballenden, had successfully adapted to European culture in the context of fur trade society, were made especially vulnerable to these new imperatives. In the European drive to clearly demarcate social categories, these women were caught in an ambiguous—and, to the official mind, socially disruptive—space

defined by newcomers as neither white nor Indian. Thus, the charge of
sexual misconduct levied against Ballenden served a dual purpose.
Underwritten by the widely held Euro-Canadian belief that Indian
women were, by nature, promiscuous and therefore a social danger, it
attempted to resolve Ballenden's racial ambiguity by denying her élite
or respectable status. This had the effect of insisting upon her Indian
identity.[38] In the new order that increasingly defined the West from the
mid-nineteenth century, acculturated métis women would be forced to
choose between their heritages. This point is underscored by the fact
that Ballenden's younger sisters resolved the dilemma by settling among
the English in Quebec.

Imperialists' constructions of aboriginal peoples as the "uncivilized" Other—what scholar Edward Said terms "orientalism"—were
interwoven with representations of the West as a vast, untamed wilderness, unsuited to white settlement and to white women in particular.
As the geographic frontier continued to push inland during the closing decades of the nineteenth century, the well-established divide
between Canada and the territories remained intact. By 1870, William
Francis Butler, a British army officer, drew this imaginary line between
the civilized and uncivilized world in the prairie grassland immediately
west of Winnipeg. Setting out to investigate the western territories for
the federal government, Butler wrote:

> [on] the 24th of October I quitted Fort Garry at ten o'clock
> at night, and, turning out into the level prairie, commenced a
> long journey towards the West. . . . Behind me lay friends and
> news of friends, civilization, tidings of a terrible war, firesides,
> and houses; before me lay unknown savage tribes, long days of
> saddle-travel, long nights of chilling bivouac, silence, separa-
> tion, and space.[39]

Expansionists saw this widespread perception of an uninhabitable
West as a serious impediment to their purposes and set out to reconstruct the western prairies of the fur trade as a commercial and agricultural Eden. As outlined above, the ideological uses of gender reached
a high point in the excesses of their booster literature, which took as a

central theme the reconfiguration of the ideal frontiersman from social renegade to domesticated man, head of the farm family.

Connor's hardy band of ranchers and cowboys now stood in opposition to successful settlement which dictated that western man accept limitations on his freedom. In exchange, expansionists held out an "offer of free land . . . and the prospect of a competence acquired through industry."[40] In their vision of a new, agricultural West, manly virtue was preserved in the enterprising farmer who was willing to trade on his wit and brawn to "make good." As one official from the Department of the Interior put it, "the men of good muscle who are willing to hustle."[41] In these new masculinist definitions of the ideal settler, women's exclusion continues to be so taken for granted that it seems to be less an idea than the natural order of things. On the question of preferred immigration, the first man in charge of populating Butler's "great lone land," Minister of the Interior Clifford Sifton, was emphatic, stating: "[w]e do not want anything but agricultural labourers and farmers or people who are coming for the purpose of engaging in agriculture, either as farmers or laborers."[42] When pressed in the House of Commons on whether or not the government would grant homesteads to women, Sifton's successor, Frank Oliver, was equally unequivocal, noting that "the department does not recognize the right of a woman to take up homesteads."[43] The only exception to this rule was in the case of a widow with dependent children, but this regulation was given the narrowest interpretation, making it difficult, even impossible, for women to qualify. Elaborating on his position five years later, Oliver explained that "the object in giving homesteads is to make the land productive, and this would not be the case if [they were] held by women."[44] When Cora Hind, Manitoba journalist and wheat crop forecaster, objected to the decision, Oliver protested that "to admit [women] to the opportunities of the land-grant would be to make them more independent of marriage than ever." And Oliver felt this would defeat the government's purpose of recreating the middle-class domestic ideal on the prairies. As Hind explained, by "granting a land-gift to men" the minister intended "to induce them to make home on the prairie—home in the centre of their agricultural pursuit."[45]

The push to domesticate the West meant that official attitudes toward women settlers were contradictory. On one hand, Ottawa recognized that its vision of placing "a large producing population upon the Western prairies . . . to wholly transform the financial difficulties of the country" would not be achieved without women's productive and reproductive labour.[46] Indeed, the government implicitly recognized what was obvious when it established a fee of two dollars paid to immigration agents for each woman who settled in the West.[47] On the other hand, the assumption that agriculture was an exclusively male enterprise had the effect of making women's work invisible. Women, of course, did "make the land productive," but the ground they tilled was not a *tabula rasa*. Just as a masculinist cultural context sharply narrowed the possibilities for aboriginal women in the new West, it also shaped the contours of the lives of newcomer women. By inscribing the West with meaning that relied on Victorian gender ideology, settlement discourse worked simultaneously to include Aboriginal women as the exotic "other" and exclude them as "uncivilized" and therefore unwomanly. It had a similar, if opposite, effect on Euro-Canadian women. Cast as "civilizers," Anglo-Canadian women in particular were assigned the privileges that were assumed to accrue to their race, but race privilege rested on sex difference and was hedged around by dominant notions of ideal femininity.[48]

Evidence of the power of masculinist conventions to exclude Euro-Canadian women on the basis of their sex is apparent in the attenuated voices of newcomers. The high-born Frances Simpson, for example, found the myth of the "manly" West so compelling that she failed to count herself among those European influences making themselves felt in the Northwest from the mid-nineteenth century. Only where European men were present at "a Trading Post of the Honourable Hudson's Bay Company . . . [or] small [American] Garrison" was she "reminded . . . of the enterprise of Europeans . . . providing employment for thousands, taming the ferocious lives of the Indians, and gradually introducing the peaceful occupation of husbandry; the first step towards civilization.[49] Years later, when another genteel Englishwoman, Irene Parlby, minister without portfolio in the United Farmers' Government of Alberta, was asked to recall her pioneering experiences for *The Canadian Magazine,* she wrote instead of the "clear-eyed man, the real pioneer type . . . content to travel with a good stout axe, and make his road as he went along."[50] Elizabeth Hanson remembered that when she arrived in Alberta in 1911, it was a "wild country . . . nothing was completed. It was a raw, man's world, not for women."[51]

For other Anglo-Canadians just being a woman in the West seemed to disrupt old gender conventions, making new ones possible. Agnes Higginson Skrine, for example, included herself in the settlement project on the same basis as men. Writing in 1898, she asserted that "[s]peaking as a . . . female, I like the country . . . I like the simplicity, the informality of the life . . . I like both the work and the play here, the time out of doors and time for coming home, I like the summer and the winter, the monotony and change. Besides, I like a flannel shirt, and liberty."[52] For Anglo-Canadian women, the private sense of sex-defiance that came with being a woman in a manly country provided a critical counter-narrative to the myth of the womanless West. In the early decades of the twentieth-century West, the "girl of the new day" adopted the stand of the sex renegade not because she had entered manly work in the factory or professions, but because she stood in a new, more equitable relationship to man as his partner in the settlement enterprise. But, when the idea of a pioneering partnership was used to underwrite western women's bid for public authority in the new West, it had the effect of reinforcing dominant gender conventions despite reformers' implicit challenge to élite men's arbitrary privilege.

Like their male counterparts, women reformers in western Canada drew upon settlement discourse to advance their political aims. As partners in nation-building, they accepted their mission to clean up society, but their vision of the future West differed sharply from men's. They sought to reconcile the contradictions inherent in social and symbolic constructions of the West as a manly country that ignored women's contribution to settlement even as they were called to populate the West and make it productive. They began by demanding legal recognition of the value of their labor in the home and on the farm. Their approach was twofold: to gain access to homesteads on the same basis as men and to win legal recognition of their economic contribution to the family farm. Questions of citizenship and constitutional status became the focus of reform only after initial efforts to renegotiate the social relationship between men and women failed.

On the question of homesteads for women, male legislators stood their ground and used their power to say no. The issue remained largely dormant for twenty-five years, as a result of federal-provincial disputes over jurisdiction of crown land, but women did continue to press forward on their demands for parental rights and homestead dower.[53] The dower campaign began modestly. Initially, western women sought what eastern women already had; the right of the wife to a portion of her husband's estate following his death.[54] When this was denied, they took the more radical step of insisting that the law guarantee the wife ownership during the husband's lifetime. This became the principal distinguishing feature of homestead/dower legislation once it was enacted.[55]

By 1920, all three prairie provinces had introduced a dower law but the legislation was subsequently seriously eroded by judicial interpretation. Specifically, the decisions of the male court put in question the wife's ownership when it upheld the right of the husband to sell, mortgage, or otherwise encumber the homestead without his wife's consent. This was a disappointing set back for prairie women, who sought to protect their home and livelihood against speculation and sale during a period of rapidly escalating land prices. Recognizing that the new law did not give them and their children the security they sought, reformers began to see dower itself as a stumbling block to women's economic independence. As one commentator put it, women were no longer content to accept "little bits of favouritism in legislation" in the form of "relief provisions" to the wife and insisted that the "interests of the two home builders . . . [be] fully recognized in law."[56] The ensuing debate, public and within the ranks of organized women, underscored male intransigence on the question of a pioneering partnership, moving organized women to claim an equal share in property they had helped to build up. In 1925, Irene Parlby introduced a matrimonial property bill which anticipated joint ownership in both husband and wife.[57]

Matrimonial property on the basis of joint ownership marked a dramatic shift in women's demands. Coupled with a call for equal custody rights for the mother, it attacked the age-old principle of male authority in the family by asserting the legal personality of the wife. In Alberta, organized farm women played a crucial role in guiding the matrimonial property bill to the floor of the provincial legislature. The bill received second reading before it was turned over to a legislative committee charged with investigating married women's property rights and recommending appropriate legislative changes.[58] Parlby headed the committee of two men and four women, including Henrietta Muir Edwards, Emily Murphy, and Gwendolyn Duff (committee secretary and a lawyer). Parlby, Edwards, and Murphy were already active in lobbying for legal reforms for women. Edwards published an account of the legal status of women in Canada in 1908 and a review of Alberta law as it affected women and children in 1917.[59]

Murphy was a magistrate of the provincial court and was actively pursuing the question of Canadian women's constitutional status as persons under the British North America Act. As President of the United Farm Women of Alberta from 1916 to 1920, Parlby took a lead in provincial debates on women's legal status. She personally promoted changes to the Alberta law along the lines of the then-existing Swedish legislation, which recognized the economic value of women's domestic labor and provided for mediation in the event of a dispute between husband and wife.[60] But, following extensive enquiry into Canadian and European law as it affected women during marriage, the committee recommended against substantive changes.

That the committee's final report fell so far short of the actions and public statements of three of its leading members suggests that its authorship lay elsewhere. No record exists of the committee's deliberations, but there is every reason to believe that the members reported privately to the government, which was responsible for the document as it appeared in its final form. Indeed, it is entirely likely that Premier John E. Brownlee had a direct role in writing the report. Certainly such an action would be consistent not only with Brownlee's reputedly heavy-handed approach to governing but also with his past relationship with the United Farm Women of Alberta.[61] As legal advisor to the United Farmers, Brownlee frequently attended United Farmers of Alberta (UFA) conventions, where he participated in discussions on the legal reform resolutions brought by the women. He worked closely on early drafts of the Farm Women's proposals for matrimonial property legislation. For example, when the convention members failed to agree on the women's 1920 resolution calling for "Equal Custody and Equal

Property Rights," it was tabled—along with delegates' instructions that the UFA executive together "with Mr. Brownlee, could deal with [it] more deliberately."[62] When it reappeared at the 1922 meetings, additions included a legal definition of community of property similar to that in the matrimonial property bill of 1925, and an entirely new clause that established the husband as "head of the community" with the sole right to manage the family property but "restricted as to selling or mortgaging real estate, or leasing it for more than one year, without the concurrence of his wife."[63] This provision also appeared in Parlby's bill. Brownlee again made his position clear when, under his direction as Attorney General in 1923, the department issued a statement opposed to joint ownership. Government lawyers explained that despite the "inequality" and "apparent injustice" in the law as it affected married women, any remedy would require "community practically on the basis of partnership" (which was the essence of women's demands) and this would be too costly, too radical, inconvenient, unjustifiable, as well as generally too disruptive to the economy, and therefore bad for business.[64] This was Brownlee's opinion in 1927 when his government submitted its final report.

Taken together, the campaigns for homesteads for women, custody, and dower struck at the very heart of the manly West. They challenged men's control of land, and therefore wealth, in the predominantly agricultural West and men's sole authority as *paterfamilias,* or head of the prairie household as Minister of the Interior Oliver envisioned it.[65] Having breached the masculinist convention of the West, women began to make themselves visible by contesting male authority and intervening in public discourse on their own behalf. But, because women had no vote or power to initiate change, male legislators could readily refuse their demands. The limited success of their early reform campaigns led directly to prairie women's call for suffrage. Emily Murphy, suffragist, novelist, and social reformer, put the need succinctly when she explained that "because women had no votes their going to the Legislature was not taken seriously . . . all that was considered necessary [by provincial legislators] was respectful treatment."[66] As events would show, formal recognition of women's citizenship also proved inadequate to curb males acting on their own interests.[67]

Winning the vote did open the door to a second manly space: the territory of high politics. During the years immediately following the extension of the provincial franchise in 1916, women eagerly took up the challenge of elected office although their representation among sitting members of western legislatures remained small.[68] By the 1930s, women had all but disappeared from the ranks of prairie legislators. Understanding how a masculinist culture shaped the conditions of women's entry into public life in western Canada also illuminates the contours of their exclusion from political power.

On the prairies, women's organized reform was closely linked to the "farm revolt." The Alberta Non-partisan League gave Canada its first woman legislator when Louise McKinney was elected to that province's legislature in 1917. And, in the run-up to the Alberta provincial election of 1921, all political parties actively recruited female candidates, hoping to win the support of the new woman voter. That year, eight women candidates, representing six political parties, entered the field; two were elected.[69] On the day before the election, one of the capital city's leading newspapers proudly boasted that "Thirty-One Thousand Voters . . . Will Elect Five Men To Legislature."[70] Following the headline, the paper printed a list of the candidates running in the constituency of Edmonton. They included four men and one woman, the popular novelist, temperance activist, and social reformer, Nellie McClung. What McClung thought of the editors' assumption that politics was an exclusively male domain we do not know. The paper's view, however, was widely shared. Critics claimed that the new woman voter took little interest in politics and lacked the independence necessary for the responsibility of citizenship. The editorial opinion of the *Calgary Western Standard* was typical, declaring "women in politics are a failure." According to the editors

> [v]ery few of the women voters understood who and what they were voting for. They were in most cases biased in their opinions being persuaded entirely by the opinions of their husbands or sweethearts. . . . The Standard will also wager that a majority of these women voters were disgusted with their time spent in the booths and would much preferred to be

down town shopping. . . . It is all very well and highly complimentary to give the lady-folk the right to vote but seriously politics is a man's game and it is just as easy to make a woman a politician as it is to make a lady's hat-maker out of the average man. It isn't in the calibre of the being.[71]

This was not the official view of organized farmers who were among the earliest supporters of women's suffrage. Farm men argued that women's moral leadership in public life was crucial to social improvement. William Irvine, a leading spokesman of the UFA and author of *The Farmers in Politics*, explained that on the social question, farm women were "in the van[guard] . . . in education, health, home life, the development of the young . . . and in raising the moral standard" of the community. Moreover, when he urged that the "farmer and his partner stand shoulder to shoulder in the great political and economic struggle that is ahead," the agrarian leader, Henry Wise Wood, instructed his members that women should be seen as "an active, necessary part" of the farm movement and not "merely . . . [as] lending their silent moral support" to the men.[72] Irvine credited women with broadening the social vision of the UFA, explaining that:

the farmer's organization was primarily economic in origin and aim. In the earlier stage, it did not see much beyond the price of wheat, the lowering of freight rates, and the abolition of the tariff. But men, in their struggle against the evils of commercialism have been commercialised. . . . Plutocratic organizations are dominated by the desire for higher profit, labor organizations concentrate on higher wages, and farmer organizations, too, began by seeking higher prices. . . . [But] the United Farm women have helped greatly to save the United Farmers' movement from the usual fate of male movements. The male mind, during the individualistic system of society, went to seed on commercialism; and the human values . . . have been choked out. . . . To remedy this state of affairs was the work which the United Farm Women undertook first.

According to Irvine, the women's campaigns revitalized the farm movement, taking it into a "larger world of thought and action."[73]

As a political manifesto, *The Farmers in Politics* was intended to present the movement as a united front in the battle against eastern interests. Published in 1920 at the height of the agrarian revolt, it also sought to establish the UFA as the official voice of reform in the western provinces. By invoking conventional notions of women's moral authority, Irvine hoped to buttress the UFA's political claims. But the alliance between farm men and women was never as smooth as Irvine suggested. Based on the politics of separate spheres, which positioned women as the moral guardians of national life, it confined women to a narrow sphere of influence—what Irvine called the "spiritual side of life."[74] This delicate alliance was also subject to the political settlement that signaled the collapse of western progressives as a national force by 1925. Having won major concessions from Ottawa, including guaranteed transportation rates and control of wheat marketing, organized farmers retreated from electoral politics. Only the UFA continued in government until the mid-1930s. Still, the skirmishes for political ascendancy that marked the early decades of the twentieth century did open a space for organized farm women to intervene directly in political life. They used this opportunity to press for social reforms. In much the same way as an earlier generation of newcomer women had taken up their assigned civilizing mission, a political generation of prairie women accepted the social question as their special mandate.

When they responded to the call for social improvement, prairie women took their hope and inspiration from the settlement project. For example, Irene Parlby saw women's settlement work as the basis of their claim to a voice in the future of the West. She argued that just as women had been prepared to "follow their men into the wilderness, to share with them its privations, so they were prepared to take their part actively, in the new work to be done" to build up prairie society.[75] In her view, questions of social and economic justice arose naturally from settlement and the "cultivation of the land must be followed by the cultivation of a worthy social and economic system of living."[76]

By drawing on settlement discourse women reformers sought to establish their authority to share in determining the future direction of the country and make governments accountable to them. They argued that women's contribution to settlement, specifically their farm and domestic labour, entitled them to look to public institutions to ameliorate the harsh conditions they faced on western homesteads, calling on legislators to "consider the real value of the human being, particularly women and children, in equal degree to that of property."[77] The Saskatchewan feminist, Violet McNaughton, pointed to the link between women's private concerns and public campaigns when she explained the origin of her long-held commitment to improving public health care on the prairies. While recuperating from surgery in a Saskatoon hospital in 1911, she heard "the echoes of the real estate boom" in the city and thought of "the only solid thing back of the boom, the homesteads of Saskatchewan. Back of these homesteads were the frozen noses, long travail on the trail, the grain in the bedrooms" (a reference to her first bedroom in Canada which doubled as a granary). "Here was I," she wrote, "a part of this one solid thing—and I had to come 65 miles for medical treatment." As unnecessary deaths of rural mothers and their infants mounted, McNaughton redoubled her resolve to see nursing care established in every rural district. "I am going right after this medical aid question," she declared in 1916, "I am going to make it my subject."[78]

Prairie women sought to relieve the hardships farm families faced by redressing the economic inequalities between urban and rural populations, but they also pointed out that farm women and their children suffered disproportionately compared with men. As Parlby put it, "no group of women [worked] so hard, so ungrudgingly and so unselfishly. And yet we know for a fact that in many instances, not even the produce that they raise by their own labor, can be sold and claimed as their own."[79] Parlby argued that any economic improvements brought about by what she described as "the dollars and cents side" of the Farmers' platform should not sit as increased profits in the pocket of individual farmers, but must benefit rural families generally through improved services, education and health care.

The problem, as organized farm women saw it, was that they were excluded from a share in the benefits of settlement. Vulnerable to arbitrary male power, they sought to curb men's authority and win greater autonomy by urging that benefits should be more broadly distributed.

Parlby thought that the "socially minded man and woman will think almost identical thoughts," but counted progressive men in the minority. As she saw it, "male selfishness" and "drive to dominate" were the main obstacle to social equality. For Parlby and others, evidence of the failure of male authority to govern lay in the death and destruction of the war of 1914–1918. They concluded that "in the interest of civilization the future centre of power must rest not in the fighting male of the race but in woman."[80]

Reformers viewed the social experiment taking place on the prairies, with their "many races, many tongues, many creeds," as proof of the possibilities for bridging "human barriers," including those that divided men and women, and for building a safer, more tolerant, more just society.[81] They were not so naive as to believe that social harmony was a simple matter of sympathetic understanding, rather, they argued that understanding was a necessary precondition for achieving their goal. Anglo-Canadian women activists did not always live up to their own ideals. Moreover, there was no inevitable trajectory from women's reform activities to equality for all women. By demanding greater equality with men, middle-class women intended to extend their own authority. This had the effect of excluding other women on the basis of race, class, and ethnicity or because they were relative latecomers to the West and therefore not part of a select group of founders.[82] Still, women's challenge to the idea of the West as an exclusively male space did shift political discourse, offering a broader social vision than masculinist conventions alone would allow.

When women put their social vision to the test in the years immediately following suffrage, becoming pioneers in a second gendered space, that of "high" politics, they understood what was at stake. McClung went to the heart of the matter when she summed up the challenge confronting women in the 1920s: "I knew the whole situation was fraught with danger," she wrote. If a woman "failed, it would be a blow to women everywhere." If she "succeeded, her success would belong to her as an individual. People would say she was an exceptional woman. She has a 'masculine' mind."[83] This was indeed what happened to the Saskatchewan reformer Violet McNaughton. Describing McNaughton's ability to hold a convention floor, one reporter observed that she "fights as a man fights. There have been rare moments on the floor of a convention when [McNaughton] has argued her case against that of a masculine opponent with a wit so subtle that he has turned, half expecting to see her exercise that prerogative of her sex and duck under his elbow, but he finds her standing in her place."[84] According to Parlby, women entering politics faced a hostile environment. "To-day women are on trial in the political field," she explained, "[e]very false step they take, every little remark which may sound foolish, is eagerly discussed, and widely heralded abroad with the cynical sneer:'What else can you expect of a woman?!'"[85]

Parlby entered public life because she believed that prairie society needed women's "intuition, their idealism, their willingness to sacrifice their individual interests, their willingness to give service without thought of personal gain."[86] McClung also saw women as "cleaning up politics," but in her view corruption in public life was not the central question for the future. Rather, it was "the problem of living together." Any effective solution must include women at all levels of society since, in McClung's view, "the world has suffered long from too much masculinity and not enough humanity."[87] McNaughton looked to the day when "an army of women workers . . . women on every executive and every committee . . . women organizers and women speakers" would transform prairie politics.[88] But when McNaughton's efforts to penetrate the ranks of the male-dominated Progressive Party collapsed, along with the party, in the mid-nineteen twenties, she retreated from high politics, focusing on her work as an editor writing in the pages of *The Western Producer.*[89]

For this generation of activists, the formal political field remained a manly preserve. Even McClung, who was especially skilled at the political joust, had surprisingly little to say about her legislative career.[90] Her silence speaks loudly of her frustrations and disappointments in public life. Five years after entering the Alberta legislature, she welcomed the defeat that allowed her to return to her first love. Writing and publishing provided a degree of independence, freedom, and authority denied her as a woman in politics. Parlby was the more reluctant politician, but she remained in office for thirteen years.[91] Her election in 1921 was greeted with wide-spread speculation that she would be appointed minister of health.[92] Instead, she was named minister without portfolio, with no salary, no budget, and no department of her own.[93] Publicly, she accepted her appointment with grace, but complained privately that "Minister without Portfolio is a stupid position."[94] She was right. In the absence of any specific government initiatives on social reform, her mandate to inform ministers on issues of particular concern to women and children could bring few concrete results. Her position as the "Women's Minister" was more symbolic than real, giving her influence at the table but no direct power to set the government's legislative agenda.

Historians explain the slim record of achievements for prairie women reformers in the early decades of the century as conservative middle-class women's betrayal of an earlier generation of more radical feminists or as the result of deep disillusionment following the high expectations that marked the votes-for-women campaign.[95] Having exaggerated the power of a few newcomer women to act in the interests of their class and race during the early period of colonization and settlement, scholars then subordinated a later generation of political activists to class interests or fractious feminist politics. This paper suggests that the contours of prairie women's politics were shaped more broadly by the ways in which gender was used to inscribe meaning on the West as social space. While settlement stimulated new debates (such as "how to live" in the West), by demarcating and privileging a mythical pioneering brotherhood, and the values it represented, expansionist discourse circumscribed the possibilities for change.

By intentionally foregrounding gender as a primary way in which social relationships were organized under the conditions of western expansion, we begin to see the ways in which women were both bound and freed by colonization and settlement even as they were divided from each other by race and class. The cultural construction of the West as "no place for a woman" represented Aboriginal women as a threat to the social order Europeans deemed necessary to their imperialist project, positioning them outside the boundaries of "civilized" society. It had a similar, if opposite, effect on Euro-Canadian women. By casting newcomer women as gentle tamers, it positioned them as the antithesis of a rough and ready, independent West that underpinned capitalist

expansion. In settlement discourse, middle-class white women embodied everything that the frontiersman had rebelled against. Men, like John
Wilcox, might lament the loss of Sundays and all that they represented
of the comfort and society of home, but their self-assigned task of manly
conquest and regeneration relied upon the absence of the very thing
they most urgently sought.

The difficulty for women reformers in the West was that by
definition, *they* were the social problem. Opposition to women's full
inclusion in the civic life of the country was not unique to western
Canada. But in the West, where gendered categories and terrains of
exclusion were a legacy of recent settlement, women activists continued
to be seen as interlopers in a manly country and a drag on western man.
Moreover, by transforming the search for wealth into a quest for
manhood, settlement discourse marginalized the social question of how
to live in the harsh reality that was the turn-of-the-century West. Cast
as an individual problem, the social question remained beyond the reach
of political reform. Attempts by agrarian reformers like William Irvine
to unite the two in the 1920s failed because the political debate was
bound by masculinist conventions that placed individual independence
above social community. But claims to independence rested on gender
asymmetry that mediated race and class hierarchy. Despite Agnes
Higginson Skrine's bid for freedom in the wide open spaces of the
prairies, that place was culturally inscribed in ways that worked to
frustrate her expectation. A manly West dictated that "a flannel shirt and
liberty" remain the exclusive rallying cry of a specific prairie manhood.

While some women saw the West as liberating them from
conventional femininity, their assertions of equal status with the frontiersman had the opposite effect. By denying the differences sex difference made, women were drawn further into dominant gender
conventions. Those who attempted to transcend the boundaries of
middle-class femininity found themselves adopting a masculine stance,
which, implicitly at least, denigrated their femaleness. On the other
hand, when women like Parlby and McClung insisted upon their female
specificity (and the values that were assumed to accrue thereto) they
were barred from an autonomous political authority on the grounds of
that very specificity. By focusing on the ways in which a gendered West

constructed relationships of power by hierarchically organizing access to wealth and opportunity, we begin to see the history of western Canadian settlement more fully. Only then can we appreciate its legacy.

---

* Catherine A. Cavanaugh teaches history and women's studies at Athabasca University in Alberta, Canada.

Taming Aboriginal Sexuality: Gender, Power, and Race in British Columbia, 1850–1900

Jean Barman

I N July 1996 I[1] listened in a Vancouver court room as Catholic Bishop Hubert O'Conner defended himself against charges of having raped or indecently assaulted four young Aboriginal women three decades earlier. His assertion of ignorance when asked what one of the complainants had been wearing on the grounds that, "as you know, I'm a celibate man" encapsulated his certainty that he had done nothing wrong.[2] He admitted to sexual relations with two of the women, but the inference was clear: they had made him do it. They had dragged him down and led him astray. The temptation exercised by their sexuality was too great for any mere man, even a priest and residential school principal, to resist.

I returned home from that day, and subsequent days in the courtroom, deeply troubled. I might have been reading any of hundreds of similar accounts written over the past century and more about Aboriginal women in British Columbia. This essay represents my first attempt to come to terms with Bishop O'Conner and his predecessors, made more necessary on reading the National Parole Board's

---

* Jean Barman, "Taming Aboriginal Sexuality: Gender, Power, and Race in British Columbia, 1850–1900," *BC Studies* 115/116 (1997/98). ©1998 BC Studies. Reprinted by permission.

decision of March 1997. The Board denied Bishop O'Conner parole, subsequent to his conviction on two of the charges, because "your recent psychological assessment indicates that you hold your victims in contempt," and "at your hearing today . . . you maintain that . . . you in fact were seduced."[3] If I earlier considered that my response to my days in the courtroom might have been exaggerated, I no longer did so. My interest is not in Bishop O'Conner's guilt or innocence in a court of law, but, rather, in tracing the lineage of his attitudes in the history of British Columbia.

The more I have thought about Bishop O'Conner, the more I realize that those of us who dabble at the edges of Aboriginal history have ourselves been seduced. However much we pretend to read our sources "against the grain," to borrow from the cultural theorist Walter Benjamin, we have become entrapped in a partial world that represents itself as the whole world. Records almost wholly male in impetus have been used by mostly male scholars to write about Aboriginal men as if they make up the entirety of Aboriginal people.[4] The assumption that men and male perspectives equate with all persons and perspectives is so accepted that it does even not have to be declared.[5] Thus, an American researcher wanting to find out about her Aboriginal counterparts discovered that "indigenous communities had been described and dissected by white men—explorers, traders, missionaries, and scholars—whose observations sometimes revealed more about their own cultural biases than about Native people. Misperceptions of Indian women were rampant because they were held up to the patriarchal model."[6]

So what happens when we turn the past on its head and make our reference point Aboriginal women instead of Aboriginal men? We come face to face with Aboriginal sexuality or, more accurately, with male perceptions of Aboriginal sexuality. The term 'sexuality' is used here in its sociological sense as "the personal and interpersonal expression of those socially constructed qualities, desires, roles and identities which have to do with sexual behaviour and activity," the underlying contention being "the social and cultural relativity of norms surrounding sexual behaviour and the sociohistorical construction of sexual identities and roles."[7] In a useful summary of recent scholarship, English sociologist Gail Hawkes tells us that the word sexuality "appeared first in the nineteenth century," reflecting "the focus of concerns about the social consequences of sexual desire in the context of modernity." Christian dogma defined sexual desire "as an unreasoned force differentially possessed by women, which threatened the reason of man" and the "inherent moral supremacy of men." According to Hawkes, "the backbone of Victorian sexuality was the successful promotion of a version of women's sexuality, an ideal of purity and sexual innocence well fitted to the separation of spheres that underpinned the patriarchal power of the new ruling class."[8] Sexuality, as Hawkes contextualizes the term, helps us better to understand the half century in British Columbia, 1850- 1900, when newcomers and Aboriginal peoples came into sustained contact.

Everywhere around the world Indigenous women presented an enormous dilemma to colonizers, at the heart of which lay their sexuality.[9] Initially solutions were simple and straightforward. During conquest local women were used for sexual gratification as a matter of course, just as had been (and still are) female victims of war across the centuries. If unspoken and for the most part unwritten, it was generally accepted that, so long as colonial women were absent, Indigenous women could be used to satisfy what were perceived to be natural needs.[10] No scruples existed over what the pioneering scholar on race Philip Mason has termed "the casual use of a social inferior for sexual pleasure."[11] The growth of settler colonies changed the "rules of the game." As anthropologist and historian Ann Laura Stoler astutely observes, drawing from her research on colonial Asia, "while the colonies were marketed by colonial elites as a domain where colonizing men could indulge their sexual fantasies, these same elites were intent to mark the boundaries of a colonizing population, to prevent these men from 'going native,' to curb a proliferating mixed-race population that compromised their claims to superiority and thus the legitimacy of white rule."[12]

In British Columbia gender, power, and race came together in a manner that made it possible for men in power to condemn Aboriginal sexuality and at the same time, if they so chose, to use for their own gratification the very women they had turned into sexual objects. While much of what occurred mirrored events elsewhere, some aspects were distinctive.[13] Colonizers never viewed Aboriginal men as sexual threats,[14] whereas attitudes toward women acquired a particular self-righteousness and fervor. The assumptions newcomers brought with them shaped attitudes, which then informed actions. By the mid-nineteenth century Europeans perceived all female sexual autonomy to be illicit, especially if it occurred in the public sphere, considered exclusively male. Aboriginal women in British Columbia not only dared to exercise agency but often did so publicly, convincing men in power that their sexuality was out of control. To the extent that women persisted in managing their own sexual behaviour, they were wilded into the 'savages' that many newcomers, in any case, considered all Indigenous peoples to be.[15] That is, until Aboriginal women acceded to men in power by having their sexuality tamed according to their precepts, they were for the taking, an equation of agency with sexuality that encourages Aboriginal women's portrayal, even today, as the keepers of tradition. As noted about American anthropological writing, "Native women are pictured as unchanging—clinging to a traditional way of life that exists outside the vicissitudes of history."[16] To avoid the image that men like Bishop O'Conner continue to project on them, Aboriginal women have had to be stripped of their agency, past and present.

PROSTITUTION

Indigenous sexuality struck at the very heart of the colonial project. British historian Catherine Hall has noted, in reference to Victorian England, that "sex was a necessary obligation owed to men and not one which women were permitted to talk or think about as owed to themselves."[17] Sexual independence, or circumstances where that possibility existed, was the ultimate threat to the patriarchal family. Children were considered to belong to their father, who had to have the assurance that they were indeed his biological heirs. As succinctly summed up by George Stocking in his history of Victorian anthropology, "if the ideal wife and mother was 'so pure-hearted as to be utterly ignorant of and averse to any sensual indulgence,' the alternate cultural image of the 'fallen woman' conveys a hint of an underlying preoccupation with the threat of uncontrolled female sexuality." By the time Victoria came to the throne in 1837, "the basic structure of taboos was already defined: the renunciation of all sexual activity save the procreative intercourse of Christian marriage; the education of both sexes in chastity and continence; the secrecy and cultivated ignorance surrounding sex; the bowdlerization of literature and euphemistic degradation of language; the general suppression of bodily functions and all the 'coarser' aspects of life – in short, the whole repressive pattern of purity, prudery, and propriety that was to condition sexual behavior for decades to come." Counterpoised to this stereotype were "savages," who were by definition "unrestrained by any sense of delicacy from a copartnery in sexual enjoyments."[18]

Any interpretation of events during the half century 1850-1900 must adopt the language of colonialism as it was applied to Aboriginal women's sexual independence. Around the colonized world the charge of prostitution, engaging in a sexual act for remuneration, was used by those who sought to meddle in Indigenous lives. Sexuality was not to be talked about openly, but prostitution and all that it implied could be publicly condemned. In other words, sexuality had wilded into prostitution or possibly concubinage, cohabitation outside of marriage, in order for it to be tamable. Hawkes traces the fervor over prostitution back to Christianity, which both gave it prominence and held out promise for "the redemption of the prostitute, the personification of polluting and uncontrolled women's sexuality." Moving to the nineteenth century, "Victorian sexual morality was focused on, and expressed through, the 'social evil' of prostitution. Prostitution was discussed in such diverse venues as popular journalism, serious weekly reviews, medical tracts and publications from evangelical organizations devoted to the rescue of fallen women . . . prostitution provided a forum within which to express, covertly, anxieties about, and fascination with, the characteristics of women's sexuality."[19]

No question exists but that Aboriginal people in British Columbia viewed their sexuality differently than did colonizers. It is difficult, if not impossible, to reconstruct gender relations prior to newcomers' arrival, nor is it necessary to do so in order to appreciate the enormity of contact. The scholarship is virtually unanimous in concluding that, traditionally, marriages were arranged with goods passing to the woman's family.[20] Intrusions of European disease, work patterns, and economic relations unbalanced Aboriginal societies and tended to atomize gender relations. Women possessed opportunities for adaptation not available to their male counterparts.[21] Many of the taboos normalized and universalized by Europeans simply did not exist in Aboriginal societies. If for Europeans sexuality had to be strictly controlled in the interests of assuring paternity, the link may have been less critical for Aboriginal people in that the group, rather than the immediate biological family, was the principal social unit.

To grasp the rapidity with which Aboriginal women became sexualized as prostitutes in colonial British Columbia, it is instructive to go back in time to another bishop, George Hills, first Anglican bishop of Vancouver Island. Arriving in Victoria in January 1860, he encountered a figurative tinder box, a fur-trade village which in just twenty months had been turned upside-down by the gold rush, bringing with it thousands of newcomers from around the world, almost all of them men. Bishop Hills was almost immediately condemning "the profligate condition of the population." "The Road to Esquimalt on Sunday is lined with the poor Indian women offering to sell themselves to the white men passing by—& instances are to be seen of open bargaining."[22] Bishop Hills's Methodist counterpart Thomas Crosby, who arrived in the spring of 1862, was similarly struck by "the awful condition of the Indian women in the streets and lanes of Victoria."[23]

What newcomers constructed as prostitution did become widespread during the gold rush, just as it had existed to some extent during the fur trade. The evidence may be largely anecdotal, but it is consistent and, for some times and places, overwhelming.[24] Virtually all of the descriptions come from a colonial male perspective, but they are so graphic and diverse as to leave little doubt as to the circumstances. The most visible sites were seasonal dance halls where for a price miners could while away "the long winter evenings" by interacting socially with Aboriginal women.[25] A New Westminster resident evoked its "Squaw Dance-House" frequented by miners "hastening to throw away their hardly earned gold." Her description is graphic: "As soon as eight or half-past struck, the music of a fiddle or two and the tramp of many feet began. Later on the shouts of drunken men and the screams of squaws in like condition made night hideous. Each man paid fifty cents for a dance, and had to 'stand drinks' at the bar for himself and his dusky partner after each."[26] Bishop Hills described "houses where girls of no more than 12 are taken in at night & turned out in the morning—like cattle."[27] Even while acknowledging dance halls' contribution to urban economies, the press repeatedly denounced the Aboriginal women whose presence made them possible, as in an 1861 editorial charging that "prostitution and kindred vices, in all their hideous deformity, and disease in every form, lurk there." In their San Francisco counterparts "the females were at least civilized," but "here we have all the savagery of the ancient Ojibbeways [sic], with all the vice of a reckless civilization."[28] If the decline of the gold rush from the mid-1860s put an end to dance halls' excesses and dampened down excitement over prostitution,[29] the wildness associated with Aboriginal sexuality had permeated settler consciousness.

FEMALE AGENCY

Turned on their head, contemporary portrayals of Aboriginal women during the gold rush affirm their agency. Agency is by its very nature relational and interactive. Just as occurred during the fur trade[30] and in traditional societies,[31] Aboriginal women both initiated and responded to change. They scooted around, they dared, they were uppity in ways that were completely at odds with Victorian views of gender, power, and race. Some likely soon realized that, however much they tried to mimic newcomers' ways, they would never be accepted and so might as well act as they pleased.[32] An Aboriginal woman "dragged" the friend of a man who had assaulted her to a nearby police station "to be locked up as a witness," only to have him seek "the protection of the police, which was granted" until she left.[33] The jury in a court case against a Victoria policeman accused of "having attempted to ravish the person of an Indian squaw" was told that the verdict hinged on whether "you believe the simple evidence of the three Indian women" and, "after consulting together about one moment, [the jury] returned a verdict of

'Not guilty.'"[34] In some cases Aboriginal women were encouraged or forced by the men in their lives. References abound to fathers selling their daughters "for a few blankets or a little gold, into a slavery which was worse than death,"[35] exchanges likely viewed by some as only continuing traditional marital practices. Yet even missionary accounts hint at female agency, as with Bishop Hills's comment after unsuccessfully remonstrating with "a woman making up a dress" for the dance house that night: "Poor creatures they know these things are wrong—but the temptations are too strong."[36]

Perhaps the most telling evidence of Aboriginal women's management of their sexual behaviour are the numbers who chose to live, at least for a time, with non-Aboriginal men. The nature of some decisions is suggested by Crosby's account of a twelve-year-old girl who, having "refused at first to follow a life of sin," "was visited by a great rough fellow who, with his hand full of money and with promises of fine clothes and trinkets and sweets, coaxed her and finally prevailed upon her to come and live with him."[37] Although referring to a later point in time, Emily Carr's observations in her fictionalized memoirs are particularly evocative, as in a conversation between two Aboriginal women whom she almost certainly knew personally. "'We got a house with three looms, and a sink and kitchen tap. Jacob and Paul go to school with white children. Too bad you not got white man for husband, Susan.'"[38] Aboriginal women caught in the tumultuous world that was the gold rush sometimes had to make hard decisions, whether for material goods or personal safety. In such circumstances a lonely miner's entreaties could be persuasive.

Non-Aboriginal men had their own reasons for entering into relationships. During the heady years of the gold rush, at least 30,000 White men and several thousand Chinese and Blacks sought their fortunes in British Columbia. Most soon departed, for the difficulties of getting to the gold fields were horrendous, but however long they stayed, their utter loneliness in a sea of men cannot be discounted. The most fundamental characteristic of non-Aboriginal women in gold-rush British Columbia was their paucity.[39] A Welsh miner reported back to his local cleric how "considerable value is placed on a good woman in this country."[40] An Englishman who had already tried his hand in Australia lamented: "The great curse of the colony so far, as it must always be the curse of any colony in which such a want exists, is the absence of women . . . there must be at least two hundred men to every woman. . . . I never saw diggers so desirous of marrying as those of British Columbia. If it is one thing more than another a miner sighs for after a hard day's work, it is to see either his tent, or his log hut, brightened up by the smiles of a woman, and tidied up by a woman's hand. . . . The miner is not very particular—'plain, fat, and 50' even would not be objected to; while good-looking girls would be the nuggets, and prized accordingly."[41] When a non-Aboriginal man saw an Aboriginal woman, what he may have perceived was not so much her Aboriginality as her gender and, certainly, her sexuality.

Structural factors specific to British Columbia encouraged couplings. At the level of everyday life Aboriginal people were not nearly so alien as sometimes portrayed, or as they became in the American Pacific Northwest.[42] Relations were generally peaceful, and many miners and settlers survived only because of local largesse. A German visiting the gold fields in 1858 reported that "many Indians lived in the neighborhood, who on the whole are on friendly footing with the Whites."[43] A guide to prospective settlers published a quarter of a century later asserted: "The intending settler may depend on finding the Indians peaceable, intelligent, eager to learn and industrious to a degree unknown elsewhere among the aborigines of America."[44] Another factor was ease of communication through common knowledge of the Chinook trading jargon. Containing about 600 words and a large variety of non-verbal additions, Chinook facilitated conversations across the races. People could talk to each other on an ongoing basis, and sometimes they did more than just talk.

Although some of the relationships spawned by the gold rush extended through the couple's lifetime, many were fairly transient, two persons cohabiting for a time until one or the other decided to move on.[45] In most cases it was the man who did so, and, as one Aboriginal woman recalled,

> Oh, it was hard on Indian wives, I guess,
> But they always managed

To raise their children
Even if their husbands finished with them.[46]

Women might end relationships, as in the gold-rush town of Lytton in 1868 where a man "lately left by his Indian wife who had had two children by him . . . confesses having sown the seed he has reaped."[47] Other women simply ensured that their husbands knew that they could leave if they wished to do so. An early novel depicted a saloon keeper with a "squaw wife" named Desdemona whose independent character drew on the author's many years in British Columbia.

> All who know the habits of the squaws married to white men, especially if they lived in one of the towns, will remember the overmastering desire they occasionally developed for a return to their tribe, and a resumption of their old life for at least a time. To fish all night from a light cedar canoe, with no thoughts of the white man's scorn, to pick berries, cut and dry fish till their garments were saturated with the odour of salmon, gather roots, herbs, and the bark of trees for baskets, the rushes also for klis-klis or mats. To extract the beautiful and durable reds and blues from certain plants and berries, and generally to revel in God's great temple of nature.

So it was with Desdemona. "One of these calls from the wild had taken Desdemona, and when her *tenase tecoup* man (small white man) came in one night, the house was dark, and she and the children gone." She had "stepped into a canoe, paddled across the wide [Fraser] river, and up the salmon stream," and only when it suited her fancy did she return home to her husband.[48]

The various data from personal accounts, church records, and the manuscript censuses suggest that, in those areas of British Columbia opened up to Europeans during the gold-rush years, about one in ten Aboriginal women cohabited at some point in her life with a non-Aboriginal man.[49] The prevalence of such unions even caused the first session of the new provincial legislature, following entry into Confederation in 1871, to pass a bill, subsequently disallowed by the federal government, to legitimize children of unions between Aboriginal women and non-Aboriginal men whose parents wed subsequent to their birth.[50]

TAMING ABORIGINAL SEXUALITY

By the time British Columbia became a Canadian province in 1871 Aboriginal women had been almost wholly sexualized.[51] The perception of widespread prostitution, and if not prostitution then concubinage, gave men in power the freedom to speak openly about matters that otherwise would have been only whispered.[52] Newcomers took for granted the fall as depicted in the Bible. Human nature was weak, and the biological man could easily be tempted to evil by his female counterpart, just as Bishop O'Conner considers himself to have been a century later. It was woman's place to be docile and subservient so as not to provoke man. For all those seeking to control Aboriginal peoples, women who exercised sexual autonomy had to be subdued. Conversion to Christianity held the key, for "woman was always the slave or burden-bearer until the Gospel came and lifted her into her true social position," which was essentially as man's handmaiden.[53] Whether missionaries, government officials, or Aboriginal men, the common perception was that the only good Aboriginal woman was the woman who stayed home within the bosom of her family. So an informal alliance developed between these three groups to refashion Aboriginal women.

This tripartite alliance, wherein men in power buttressed and comforted each other, was grounded in mutual expediency and, to some extent, in mutual male admiration. With entry into Confederation, responsibility for Aboriginal people shifted to the federal government under the terms of the British North America Act, and it did not take long for newly appointed officials to realize the enormous benefit to be had from establishing cordial relations with missionaries, who were already at work across much of the sprawling province. Officially, missionaries had no status, but unofficially they became the government's foot soldiers, and its eyes and ears. Aboriginal policy, as it developed in

British Columbia, was to minimize official involvement in everyday affairs, which effectively meant letting missionaries have a free hand.[54] If disagreeing in many areas, including Aboriginal people's right to an adequate land base, government officials repeatedly commended missionaries for having "taught, above all, the female portion of the community to behave themselves in a modest and virtuous manner."[55] The other prong of the alliance crossed racial boundaries in the interests of gender solidarity and mutual self-interest. Members of the Indian Reserve Commission active across British Columbia in the mid-1870s left an extensive paper trail and repeatedly expressed approval of Aboriginal "manliness" and of "the industry of the men."[56] Similarly, in missionary accounts it is almost wholly Aboriginal men who are given individuality and personality.[57] Men, particularly those who emulated colonial ways, needed to have suitable spouses, and for this reason too Aboriginal women had to have their sexuality tamed.

As for Aboriginal men, they were likely motivated by a shortage of women and also, some of them, by a desire to please their colonial mentors. Reports of a shortage are sufficiently widespread to be convincing. As early as 1866 Bishop Hills observed "a scarcity of wives" among the northern Tsimshian, many of whose members camped in Victoria on a seasonal basis.[58] The Indian Reserve Commission's census of a decade later counted 1,919 Aboriginal persons in the area extending from Burrard Inlet north to Jervis Inlet, across to Comox, and down through the Saanich peninsula, including the Gulf Islands; of these, 979 were adult males compared with 919 adult females, and 94 male youth compared with 84 female youth.[59] The enumerator of the southern interior, extending from Lytton through the Nicola Valley, counted 884 adult males compared with 803 adult females and lamented "the absence of females both adults and youths – those who should have been the future mothers of the tribe."[60] Some Aboriginal men, in effect made deals to behave in accord with missionary aspirations for them in exchange for getting wives.[61] Crosby described a visit to a Queen Charlottes village in about 1885, where local men promised him: "Sir, if you will come and give us a teacher, we will stop going to Victoria. Victoria has been the place of death and destruction to our people, as you see we have no children left to us. All our young women are gone;

some of our young men can't find wives any more; and we wish that you could help them to get wives among the Tsimpshean people."[62]

The tripartite campaign to tame the wild represented by Aboriginal sexuality had two principal goals. The first was to return Aboriginal women home. The second was to desexualize Aboriginal everyday life, in effect to cleanse it so that the home to which women returned would emulate its colonial counterpart.

RETURNING ABORIGINAL WOMEN HOME

Marriage lay at the heart of newcomers' morality and, as anthropologist George Stocking concludes, "it is perfectly clear that 'marriage proper' meant proper Victorian marriage" whose "purpose was to control human (and especially female) sexuality, so that there might be 'certainty of male parentage.'"[63] As summed up by historians Leonore Davidoff and Catherine Hall for England between the late eighteenth and mid-nineteenth centuries, "marriage was the economic and social building block for the middle class." "Marriage became both symbol and institution of women's containment. It was marriage which would safely domesticate the burgeoning garden flower into an indoor pot plant; the beautiful object potentially open to all men's gaze became the possession of one man when kept within the house like a picture fixed to the wall."[64]

In theory, two marital strategies could have tamed Aboriginal sexuality. One was to encourage non-Aboriginal men to wed their Aboriginal partners, the other to return Aboriginal women home to wed Aboriginal men. Either would have satisfied Victorian notions of marriage, but the alliance of interests that existed among men in power combined with growing racism to ensure that the second option would be favoured. As early as 1873 an agitated provincial official pointed to the federal government's responsibility for "the care and protection of the native race in this Province, [and] so long as this shameful condition of things is suffered to continue unchecked, the character of that race in the social scale is practically a delusion."[65] Reserve commissioners reported on conversations with chiefs at Nanaimo, where "the evil of concubinage of their young women with the white men around were specially pointed out."[66] By 1884 an Indian agent with an Aboriginal wife and grown daughters felt able to argue, perhaps with a touch of self interest, that "with the present state of civilization in the country and the abundance of white and educated half breed women— such a practice should be put a stop to in future."[67] Aboriginal women were needed at home to service their menfolk.

For men in power, gender and race neatly dovetailed. Within the mix of pseudo-scientific ideas associated with Social Darwinism, new-comers accepted, as seemingly demonstrated by the triumph of colonialism and technological advances, that mankind had evolved into a hierarchy with Whites on the top and Aboriginal people near the bottom.[68] Persons of mixed race ranked even lower, for, to quote a colonial visitor, "half-breeds, as a rule, inherit, I am afraid, the vices of both races."[69] Concerns grew over "a class of half-breed children . . . who, under the bond of illegitimacy, and deprived of all incentives in every respect, will in course of time become dangerous members of the community."[70] During the late 1870s such fears were exacerbated by a murderous rampage by the young sons of a Hudson's Bay trader and Aboriginal woman,[71] and given a sexual edge by female mixed-race students at a public boarding school becoming pregnant by their male counterparts.[72] While some encouragement was given to non-Aboriginal men to marry Aboriginal women with whom they were cohabiting, this was, for the most part, done somewhat grudgingly.[73]

Petitions became a favoured means to compel Aboriginal women back home. The tripartite alliance developed a dynamic whereby Aboriginal men signed petitions orchestrated by missionaries who then dispatched them to government officials to justify their taking action.[74] Both Catholic and Protestant missionaries participated, as did Aboriginal men across much of the province and numerous officials at various levels of government.

In 1885 Oblates missionaries stage-managed two identical petitions to the governor general affirmed with their mark by 962 Aboriginal men, including at least eighteen chiefs, from across the Cariboo and south through the Lower Fraser Valley. In the best English prose the petitions "beg[ed]" to lay before your Excellency" that a "great evil is springing up amongst our people" whereas "on a dispute between a married couple, the wife leaves her husband and goes off the Reservation, and takes up with a bad white man, China man, or other Indian, and [they] live together in an unlawful state." The men sought permission to "bring back the erring ones by force if necessary."[75] Caught up in the rhetoric to tame Aboriginal sexuality, the Ministry of Justice drafted an even broader regulation for consideration by the chiefs, one which made it possible to "bring back to the reserve any Indian woman who has left the reserve and is living immorally with any person off the reserve." The proposal was only derailed by the Ministry of Justice's suggestion, made almost in passing, that the Department of Indian Affairs should "consider before it is passed whether or not the putting of it in force will lead to riots and difficulties between the Indians and the white people and others with whom the Indian women are said to be living immorally."[76] Three of the four Indian agents consulted considered that this might well happen were chiefs given such authority. One of them acknowledged female agency in his observation that, "while in some cases the Indian woman might be brought back without trouble, it would be impossible to keep her on a reserve against her will."[77] The project was shelved, even though the Catholic Bishop at New Westminster intervened directly at the federal ministerial level in an attempt to bypass the bureaucrats.[78]

The campaign to tame Aboriginal sexuality was not to be thwarted, and the Oblates were almost certainly behind a bolder petition dispatched in 1890 to the Governor General. The chiefs of fifty-eight bands, again extending from the Cariboo through the Fraser Valley, indicated by their marks that they were "much aggrieved and annoyed at the fact that our wives, sisters and daughters are frequently decoyed away from our Reserves by ill designing persons." No means existed to return "these erring women," but, even were this possible, "in most cases these women are induced to return again to their seducers." Fearing that "some of our young men who are sufferers will certainly take the law into their own hands and revenge themselves on the offending parties," the petition sought "a law authorising the infliction of corporal punishment by the lash."[79] The advisability of "legislation, making it an offence for a white man to have sexual intercourse with an Indian woman or girl without Christian marriage," was referred to the Ministry of Justice,[80] which in this case pulled the plug. The Ministry considered the legislation unnecessary, since "the laws relating to the protection of females and for the punishment of persons who seduce or abduct them, apply to Indian women as well as to white women."[81] Yet the campaign persisted, and later in 1890 the Indian agent at Lillooet urged, on behalf of "the Chiefs of the numerous Bands around here," that "a severe penalty should be imposed upon any person, not an Indian, who, harbouring an Indian woman, does not deliver her up to the Chief of the Reserve."[82]

At this point the enthusiasts may have stumbled. Acting largely independently of civil authority, the Oblates had allied themselves across much of the Interior with local Aboriginal men in order to effect control over everyday life.[83] As one Indian agent noted in the early 1890s, although the "flogging habit has been abandoned for some years past" and fines are not so common as they once were, "considerable sums of money are annually collected by the chiefs and their watchmen for the benefit of the churches whose functionaries attend to their spiritual welfare."[84] In the spring of 1892 the Oblate missionary at Lillooet, the chief, and four other Aboriginal men were brought before the local magistrate, convicted, and given jail sentences for "flogging a young girl . . . on the report only of a fourth party" for some unspecified sexual activity. "Without investigation *he* [priest] *ordered* 15 lashes. His plea was 1st ancient customs of the Indians & 2nd necessity for such punishment in order to suppress immorality." The Indian agent who made the report considered both that the "ancient customs" were not as portrayed by the missionary and that the local men should not have been punished so severely, since they "believed the Priest to be their Commander in all Church matters—and that consequently they were obliged to obey him."[85] The incident appears to have cooled the alliance between the Oblates and local men, who "were astonished at the extent of the jurisdiction of the Courts of law, when even the dictates of a Priest should be upset and the Priest himself held accountable."[86]

The Protestants could be just as enthusiastic as the Catholics in allying themselves with local men to keep women at home and then calling on federal officials to enforce what they could not effect by their own devices. In 1889 the Indian agent at Alert Bay, acting in concert with the local Anglican missionary, stopped a group of women from boarding a steamer to Victoria. His justification was that they "went with the avowed purpose of prostituting themselves" and he "had previously been requested by numbers of young men to prevent if possible their wives and sisters from going to Victoria."[87] Reflecting the tripartite alliance's perspective, the Indian agent considered that "nearly all the young women, whenever they leave their homes, whether ostensibly for working at the canneries or at the Hop Fields, do so with the ultimate idea of making more money by prostitution."[88] The steamboat company vigorously protested and the provincial Indian superintendent was luke-warm to the action, astutely observing that "the Indian women and their friends come to Victoria, and other places, in their canoes," making their restriction practically impossible.[89] Nonetheless, the Indian agent and Anglican missionary did such a successful end run to federal officials as to persuade them to propose legislation to keep at home, by force if nec-essary, "Indian women from the West Coast of British Columbia, who are in the habit of leaving their Villages and Reserves by steamers and by other mode of transport with the object of visiting the Cities and Towns of that Province for immoral purposes."[90]

The proposed legislation hit a snag only after the federal Minister of Justice indicated "that there is not at present sufficient material on hand to permit of the drawing up of a Bill fully dealing with the ques-tion."[91] The Minister requested the provincial superintendent to circu-larize Indian agents around the province. Even though the agents would likely have found it far easier to acquiesce to expectations than to dis-pute them, they were all, apart from those at Alert Bay and Babine in the Northern Interior, remarkably sanguine. On the west of Vancouver Island, "I do not know of a single instance on this Coast where a young girl has been taken to Victoria or elsewhere for the purposes of prosti-tution."[92] His neighbour was "not aware of any Indian women belong-ing to the Cowichan Agency who leave their Reservations for immoral purposes."[93] In the Fraser Valley and Lower Mainland, "there are very few immoral women."[94] As for the Central Interior, "the practice of Indian women leaving their Reserves for the purpose of leading immoral lives is not common in this Agency."[95] The Southern Interior agent offered a general observation: "Indians are in their nature, in consequence of their training, habits and surroundings, far less virtuous than the average whites. Their morality should not therefore be judged by the standards of the white people. The Indian woman, although, as above stated, inclined to be worse in her morals, is naturally modest."[96] The North Coast agent considered that the "Indians have learned from sad experience the effects of immorality in the cities and are rapidly improving their conduct."[97] Summarizing the responses, the provincial superintendent concluded that "the few Indian women who may be found living an immoral life in our towns and Cities are less in number as a rule than of their white sisters."[98]

Nonetheless, the depiction of Aboriginal sexuality as out of control was too attractive an explanation for missionary and government failings to be abandoned. Just three years later, in 1895, a petition signed by thirty-four men from central Vancouver Island, all but one with their marks, demanded legislation to prevent "our wives and daughters and sisters" from being "carried to Victoria for illegitimate purposes."[99] The British Columbia senator to whom the petition was addressed took its claims at face value and demanded that steps be taken to "prevent the deportation of Indian women," seeing that "Indians are wards of the government under tutelage and not qualified to manage their own affairs wisely." The senator, who simply assumed that Aboriginal women's sole role was to service their menfolk, emphasized that an "increase, instead of a decrease, is much to be desired" in the Aboriginal population.[100] The federal response is interesting because, rather than quoting from the Indian agents' reports in their files, officials emphasized the difficulties of securing legislation. In doing so, they revealed, perhaps inadvertently, that women were de facto having their travel restricted by local Indian agents "when requested by the husband or brother or anyone having proper authority, to stop a woman from going away, and so the men have the prevention of that of which they complain almost entirely in their own hands."[101] The sexualization of Aboriginal women had far less to do with reality than with the needs, and desires, of men in power. So long as settler society perceived a need to tame Aboriginal sexuality, men in power could reorder Aboriginal society with impunity.

REORDERING ABORIGINAL SOCIETY

Over time virtually every aspect of Aboriginal everyday life acquired a sexual dimension, thereby justifying its reordering. Aboriginal sexuality, or perhaps more accurately the fear of Aboriginal women's agency, became a lens through which traditional preferences in housing, social institutions, and child care were critiqued and found wanting.

The rhetoric condemning the "big houses" inhabited by Coastal peoples made explicit Victorian fears of the body and of human sexuality. It also reflected Social Darwinian notions of the hierarchy of species, at the top of which lay Western societies premised on the monogamous conjugal family. The very existence of sites where more than a single family lived together was equated with immorality. No doubt existed but that, given the opportunity, men and women would act on their impulses. Davidoff and Hall have linked the subordination of women to the private home: "Woman had been created for man, indeed for one man, and there was a necessary inference from this that *home* was 'the proper scene of woman's action and influence.' . . . The idea of a privatized home, separated from the world, had a powerful moral force and if women, with their special aptitude for faith, could be contained within that home, then a space would be created for true family religion."[102] So also in British Columbia, the single family home came to be seen as a necessary prelude to Christian conversion.

Men in power repeatedly lauded the single-family house, as in side notes on the Reserve commission's census of Aboriginal people. At Burrard Inlet: "The houses at this place have a pleasing appearance when viewed from the sea. They are mostly of the cottage style, white washed and kept cleaner in this than is usual with most Indians." In contrast, along the Fraser River: "Most of the houses of this tribe are of the primitive style. There are however several cottages kept and fitted up in a neat manner." At Cowichan on Vancouver Island: "There are a few tidy cottages – what they require is a desire and encouragement."[103] Missionaries like Crosby were even more fervent and repeatedly linked housing to sexuality. "The old heathen house, from its very character, was the hot-bed of vice. Fancy a great barn-like building, . . . occupied by as many as a dozen families, only separated from each other by low partitions." The interior seemed made for naughty deeds. "Picture such a building, with no floor other than the ground, no entrance for light except the door, when open, and the cracks in the walls and the roof. Around the inside of such a building were ranged the beds, built up on rude platforms." "Is it any wonder that disease and vice flourished under such favorable surroundings?"[104] In sharp contrast stood "the Christian home." Crosby considered that "the only way to win the savage from his lazy habits, sin and misery" was to "be able and willing to show how to build a nice little home, from the foundation to the last shingle on the roof."[105]

Fear of Aboriginal sexuality became frenzied in the rhetoric around the institution of the potlatch. Missionaries led the campaign against this social activity practiced across most of the province, garnering support from government officials and over time from some younger converted Aboriginal men. Initially arguments focused on the event itself as being "demoralizing," leading to "debauchery."[106] Federal legislation banning the potlatch took effect at the beginning of 1885, but did not bring about wholesale conversion to Christianity. Missionaries soon sought both allies in Aboriginal men in search of wives and reasons, apart from themselves, to explain their failure to live up to their expectations for themselves.[107] The ethnographer Marius Barbeau concluded in 1921, after examining federal files on the potlatch, that, "as the Church has not succeeded in making converts to any material extent . . . there must be found a scapegoat, and as the potlatch already had a bad name, it was blamed."[108]

The sexualization of the potlatch had a number of components, but centred on the supposed sale of Aboriginal women as wives or prostitutes to get the money to potlatch.[109] In 1893 a Toronto newspaper reported that a group of missionaries had witnessed "blankets for potlatch procured at the expense of the virtue of women," an event which the local Indian agent determined was sensationalized.[110] By the end of the century the press was convinced that "the potlatch is the inciting cause of three-fourths of the immorality that exists among Indian women."[111] Writing shortly thereafter, the Indian agent at Alert Bay asserted that the younger generation of Aboriginal men supported his attempt to persuade his superiors in Ottawa to act against potlatching:

"It looks cruel to me to see a child 13 or 14 years of age put up & sold just like sheep or a nanny goat, to a bleary eyed siwash old enough to be her grand-father, for a pile of dirty blankets, which will in turn be Potlatched to the rest of the band, and all to make the proud Father, a big Injun," rather than "let her marry a young man whom I am sure she wanted."[112] The Indian agent quoted a longtime missionary to make his point that "the girls die off and the young men for the most part cannot get wives because as a rule they have no blankets or money unless they are sons of chiefs and the others cannot get wives until they are able to command a certain sum which is so difficult as they have to compete with the older men who hold the property."[113]

The unwillingness to tolerate Aboriginal women's agency was a major factor in the determination to replace familial child care with residential schools operated by missionaries under loose government oversight. As attested by the scholarship, schools sought total control over pupils' sexuality, particularly that of girls.[114] The twinned concepts of Christian marriage and the Christian home depended on young women remaining sufficiently unblemished so that they could become good wives according to Victorian standards of behaviour. The attitudes and actions of Thomas Crosby and his wife Emma are instructive. Crosby considered that parents, "though kind and indulgent to their children, are not capable of teaching and controlling them properly" and "something must be done to save and protect the young girls . . . from being sold into the vilest of slavery."[115] "On account of the prevalence of this traffic in Indian girls, many of the early missionaries were led to establish 'Girls' Homes' for the rescue and further protection of these poor victims of this awful system."[116] The taming that went on in the Crosbys' girls' home, as in residential schools across the province, left no doubt as to Aboriginal agency. As remembered by a Crosby school matron in the early 1880s, the girls required "a great deal of Grace, Patience and determination, they were so obstinate and disobedient."[117]

The wildness associated with Aboriginal sexuality explains attitudes toward a girl's transition from pupil to wife. Reflecting the assumptions of the day, the superintendent of the Children's Aid Society in Vancouver expressed relief that "the savage was so thin and washed out" of two young women of mixed race, so that they were able to find happiness with their White lovers. Yet this represented "only a glimmer of light in the darkness."[118] According to Crosby's biographer, "girls stayed at the Home until they were married, at which time a new girl would be admitted."[119] The full extent of missionaries' distrust of their charges is evident in the musings of another Crosby matron regarding the potential marriage of a fourteen-year-old student: "It would seem sinful to allow such things to be mentioned if they were white girls, but here they are safer when married young."[120]

Here again the informal alliance operated. Schools measured their success by numbers of girls who "have married Christian Indians, have helped to build up Christian homes, to civilize the people generally and to aid in developing their own neighborhood." "Instead of a young man with his friends going with property and buying a wife, as was done formerly, many of our brightest young men tried to make the acquaintance of the girls in the Home." Women might no longer be sold by their fathers, but they were no less commodities when it came to marriage. The Crosbys, like other missionaries, put a romantic spin around what was, in effect, a good being made available to a handful of men considered suitably Christian. "There was no doubt in our minds that real, true love again and again developed between the young people who thus became acquainted. This acquaintance finally resulted in their marriage and the happy life that followed."[121]

CONSEQUENCES

By the end of the nineteenth century settler society took for granted the interpretation that men in power put on Aboriginal women's agency. The ongoing frenzy over the potlatch is indicative. The press became ever more determined to expose its supposed basis in Aboriginal sexuality. "Indian girl sold for 1,000 blankets" hit Vancouver streets in 1906.[122] The story makes clear that the supposed revelation about "the awful Indian practice of potlatch" originated with an Anglican missionary who was disgruntled because a pupil had married someone other than the man she had selected for her. Later in the year both Vancouver and Ottawa newspapers trumpeted "Five Indian Girls

Sold,"[123] a report that, on investigation, proved to be groundless.[124] A Vancouver paper headlined a year later, "Squaw sold for $400.00 at Alert Bay to a grizzled Chief from Queen Charlottes."[125] It turned out that, while two marriages had occurred, neither involved "a grizzled chief," and the local Indian agent considered the article to be "very misleading."[126] The press coverage prompted a host of women's voluntary associations across the country to demand legislation to "put an end to this great blot on the Civilization and Christianity of Canada."[127] Writing in 1921, a barrister who was the son of the former Indian agent at Alert Bay and who represented Aboriginal people opposed to the potlatch ban, considered that "the strongest reason for enforcing the law against the Potlatch is the question of Indian marriages. . . . It is also contended that women are bought and sold, [but] this is not true."[128] Had the potlatch not been so successfully sexualized, it is doubtful that opponents could have maintained its illegality into the mid-twentieth century. The taming of Aboriginal sexuality had become a means to an end, as well of course as an end in itself, but the effects were no less detrimental to Aboriginal women.

For Aboriginal women, the consequences of the ceaseless rhetoric of scorn heaped on them in the interests of men in power were enormous. Some women acquiesced and returned or remained at home,[129] and the Crosbys delighted "in visiting around among the villages, to pick out these Christian mothers who had the privilege of the 'Home' life and training."[130] In a broad sense, Aboriginal societies did come to mimic their colonial counterparts, which is not unexpected given federal policies and the material advantages to be got from doing so. An Aboriginal informant explained in 1950 how "converts were sometimes termed 'made white men', as they used different types of houses and they dressed in white men's clothes, while their heathen brothers . . . indulged in all of the old rituals."[131] Some women had the decision taken out of their hands. As more marriageable White women became available and attitudes hardened, numerous non-Aboriginal men shed their Aboriginal partners. The manuscript censuses for the late nineteenth century indicate that, while some of these women did return home and enter into new unions with Aboriginal men, others scraped along at the edges of settler society.

Other women continued to dare.[132] Many inter-racial unions survived the campaign to tame Aboriginal sexuality, in some cases by the partners legally marrying or retreating outward into the frontier, or by simply standing their ground.[133] The encouragement that missionaries and government officials gave to Aboriginal men may have caused some women to disengage from their home communities in search of more satisfying life opportunities. To the extent that traditional patterns of gender relations gave way to male mimicry of European practices, so the social distance between the sexes may have widened. Women still married out, as indicated by the 1901 manuscript census[134] and evoked in a Carr vignette about a woman who had "married white" and "both loved her husband and gloried in his name," for "it was infinitely finer to be 'Mrs Jenny Smith' than to have her name hitched to an Indian man's and be 'Jenny Joe' or "Jenny Tom.'"[135]

Most important, the campaign to tame Aboriginal sexuality so profoundly sexualized Aboriginal women that they were rarely permitted any other form of identity. Not just Aboriginal women but Aboriginal women's agency was sexualized. In the extreme case their every act became perceived as a sexual act and, because of the unceasing portrayal of their sexuality as wild and out of control, as an act of provocation. By default, Aboriginal women were prostitutes or, at best, potential concubines. Their actions were imbued with the intent that men in power had so assiduously ascribed to them, thus vitiating any responsibility for their or other men's actions toward them. Sexualization of Aboriginal women's agency occurred within a context in which they were already doubly inferior by virtue of their gender and race, thus virtually ensuring that any Aboriginal woman who dared would become colonialism's plaything. Again, the stories are legion, be it the Okanagan Valley in the 1880s, Vancouver Island in the 1920s, the North Coast in the 1960s, or Bishop O'Conner. Sometimes the accounts embody a strong element of bravado, in other cases the wish fulfillment of lonely men, but in yet others a strong dose of action, as with O'Conner.

A young Englishman who arrived in the Okanagan Valley shortly after the completion of the transcontinental railroad in 1886 exemplified a generation of newcomers who took for granted Aboriginal women's sexualization. "Most of these girls were graceful, some even pretty; clear, light bronze skins with just a touch of color in the cheeks, even teeth and glossy jet black hair, that had almost a tinge of blue in it; their black eyes would be modestly cast down in the presence of white men. And sometimes a shy upward glance of coquetry – but not if there were any bucks in sight." He recalled a contemporary who, "fed up with batching, had disturbed the monastic peace of the community by taking unto himself a dusky mistress." The sexualization of Aboriginal women's agency removed any sense of responsibility. Even as his friends were deciding whether to be jealous, "he and his lady had a bad row, and realizing that his little romance was ended he fired her out, and as none of the rest of the old boys were gallant enough to take a chance on her, the lady returned to the bosom of her tribe, and once more there was peace on earth in the little community."[136]

Even persons who supported Aboriginal people, as did the lawyer representing them in the 1920s against the potlatch ban, persisted in seeing women in sexual terms, considering that "contact between Indians and loggers has always been fraught with dire results—particularly to the Indian women." This assessment was in sharp contrast to his view of Aboriginal men: "The Indian man in his own environment is a man of dignity, big and venerable."[137]

In a generally sympathetic account of a summer sojourn in 1966 at Telegraph Creek on the North Coast, a young American made clear that Aboriginal women's agency remained sexualized. "More than they would have in the old days, I'm sure, they make fun of the Indians to me ... [for] their limber-limbed promiscuity." A friend "eats supper with me, chatting about the morals of the Indian girls ('No morals at all if you scratch their stomachs a minute')." Their every action became a sexual action, thus his vignette relating how "earlier in the spring a girl appeared in the store, sent by her parents, and took up the broom and began to sweep, after the historical fashion of a squaw proposing to a white man." For this young man, the wild which was Aboriginal sexuality remained mythic. Noting that "in New York to dream of a woman is an unremarkable event" but "here it invests the whole night with sexual urgency," he repeatedly found himself tempted, as after "I've had a day hearing stories of. . . . Indian women being mounted and screwed." He resisted, but precisely because he did accept the equation of

234

Aboriginal female agency with sexuality: "Of course these Indian girls are too vulnerable to fool with, so I have only the past to keep me company in bed."[138]

Hence we come full circle to Bishop O'Conner who at virtually the same time that this young American was fantasizing acted on his impulses. Like so many men before him, he still considers himself to have been "seduced" and, a full generation later, remains in his heart "a celibate man." I have no doubt that O'Conner feels himself to be sincere, just as I now have no doubt of the importance of newcomers' construction of Aboriginal women's sexuality for understanding events during that critical half century, 1850–1900, when your, my, and Bishop O'Conner's British Columbia came into being.

---

* Jean Barman is Professor of Educational Studies of the University of British Columbia, Vancouver, Canada.

'Going About and Doing Good':
The Politics of Benevolence, Welfare, and
Gender in San Francisco, 1850–1880

Mary Ann Irwin

I N keeping with the Progressive era's faith in solving social problems scientifically, newly founded Stanford University began
collecting data in 1893 for an analysis of welfare in San Francisco,
California. The published report contained a detailed list of the 204
public and private agencies providing social welfare services in the city,
along with their expenditures for the year. The report revealed that, in
1893 alone, the sum expended on social welfare services in San Francisco
came to just over $1,380,500.[1] The amount perplexed author Charles
K. Jenness, who considered it "an enormous charity bill for a city so
young as San Francisco, and whose entire population numbers scarcely
300,000." By comparison, Jenness mused, "Baltimore, with 100,000 more
inhabitants, expended in 1892 about $50,000 less." He concluded that
"the cost of relieving the poor in San Francisco is undoubtedly more in
proportion than any other young and prosperous city."[2]

The Stanford report provides a valuable "snapshot" of San
Francisco's social welfare system in 1893. It is the earliest detailed picture
we have of the city's sprawling, evidently chaotic mass of social services,

* Mary Ann Irwin, "'Going About and Doing Good': The Politics of Benevolence,
Welfare, and Gender in San Francisco, 1850–1880," *Pacific Historical Review* 68:3
(1999). ©1999 Pacific Historical Review, American Historical Association, Pacific
Coast Branch. Reprinted by permission.

both public services funded and administered by the city of San Francisco and services funded and managed by private citizens. This "snapshot" quality is also the report's most frustrating aspect. Because it only captures a moment in time, it neither explains how San Francisco's welfare system developed nor illuminates the social, economic, and political forces behind that development.

This study unravels the complex forces shaping local welfare provision in California during the formative period between 1850 and 1880. Because the key component of local welfare was charity, and because local women were at the forefront of charity work, this history centers on woman-led charities. Studies of nineteenth-century American women's benevolence have paid relatively little attention to western women; much more is known about women's associations in the East than the West.[3] Likewise, recent scholarly studies of "maternalism" focus on women and organizations east of the Mississippi River, despite the keen interest of western women in maternal and infant health, pure food, sanitation, and so forth. This literature, moreover, concentrates almost exclusively on the Progressives and gives little attention to the maternalist activities of nineteenth-century women.[4] In turn, while Western historians have studied the lives and struggles of women in the West, they have emphasized, for the most part, formal politics, especially efforts to gain the franchise.[5] In California, where sixty-two years elapsed between statehood and woman suffrage, focus on the vote misses a potent form of social and political power available to California women—the collection and distribution of public and private funds for social welfare.

The very newness of San Francisco offered a space in which benevolent women could influence community politics through pioneering social welfare programs. Examination of women's charities illuminates the process by which San Francisco's welfare system emerged and how women's charities fit—economically, socially, and politically—into the city's evolving municipal structure. The central fact of poor relief in San Francisco in the period 1850–1880 was the city's substantial reliance on women's charities for social services, especially for women and children. Yet, despite the attention historians have given local politics and to the role of private organizations in poor relief, very little has been said about the impact of women's charities on municipal welfare policy and practice.[6] In overlooking the crucial factor of gender, historians miss the critical differences between public and private models of welfare—that is, differences between male and female modes of political action in the nineteenth century.

Gender is central to the history of welfare in San Francisco. Gender ideology supported women's entry into local benevolence work, and it lay at the heart of differences between public and private welfare. Operating at the vague frontier between "public" and "private," women's charities served the community at a variety of levels. Poor families relied on benevolent women for services the city did not provide, especially services to women and children. As leaders of charities, benevolent women found a medium through which to pressure community members and state and local policy-makers to consider the needs of children and women. They earned public accolades for their piety and femininity while avoiding the hostility aimed at organizations with less traditional goals. The city also benefited from women's charity work: Public officials relied on women's privately-funded services to avoid higher taxes and voter wrath. Indeed, the economy and efficiency of their work allowed officials to escape the cost and burden of some forms of relief well into the twentieth century. Citizens supported women's charity because it limited public welfare spending and avoided the corruption that seemed inevitably to follow expansion of the public sector. Women's charities were thus not only key components of the city's welfare system but a central feature of the local political economy.

Why did a city as "young" and "prosperous" as San Francisco develop an extensive public-private welfare system, as described in the 1893 Stanford report? The most obvious answer, of course, is the Gold Rush. The city's meteoric growth is well known. From about 800 souls in 1848, San Francisco's population soared to over 36,000 in 1852. Between 1860 and 1870, San Francisco's population increased by 163 percent, from 56,800 to 149,500. In the 1870s, the city's population grew to nearly 234,000.[7] Such rapid growth naturally created severe social problems, and Forty-Niners turned to the characteristic nineteenth-century solution: the benevolent association. These private associations met the everyday health and welfare needs of the community, as well as its emergencies. During the cholera epidemic of 1850, for example, the Odd Fellows spent $27,000 of their own money setting up a temporary hospital; members prepared meals, nursed the sick, and buried the dead. Private groups acted as lobbyists as well, pressuring officials to improve public welfare services in the makeshift jails and City Hospital.[8]

The harshness of San Francisco's economic cycles also made private charity a continuing necessity. Through the 1850s and 1860s, the city experienced epic cycles of boom-then-bust. The situation only grew worse in the 1870s. Early in the decade, the recently completed transcontinental railroad simultaneously wrecked the local economy and doubled the city's population. By the winter of 1875, the effects of a national depression finally filtered west to San Francisco.[9] In 1876, 7,000 San Franciscans were receiving help from a private charity, the San Francisco Benevolent Society (SFBS). Two years later, when an estimated 15,000 men were out of work, the SFBS and local churches fed more than 2,000 people a day.[10]

Try as they might, local officials simply could not keep up with constantly escalating demands for relief. Like most American cities at mid-century, San Francisco possessed little in the way of a formal public welfare system.[11] Prior to completion of the Alms House in 1867, the indigent could only apply for room and board in the jail or City Hospital. San Francisco's only other public welfare institution, the Industrial School, limited admission to juveniles.[12] Not surprisingly, these facilities were no match for the hardships caused by the city's recurring economic crises.

Despite the volatility of the city's economy, political considerations made expansion of public welfare impractical. As in other cities of the period, taxpayers demanded inexpensive, efficient municipal government.[13] Indeed, allegations of public waste and corruption toppled San Francisco's government in the mid-1850s. Local businessmen-turned-vigilantes claimed that the politicians were squeezing "outrageous taxes . . . from the citizens" and spending them on "fine horses" and "luxurious living."[14] When the vigilante phase ended, the businessmen went into politics. Calling themselves "the People's party," they won key municipal offices in the elections of 1856 and immediately cut taxes by 40 percent. As a result, municipal funding for social welfare fell steadily as a proportion of the city budget, from 14 percent in 1860, to 11 percent in 1880, and to 8 percent by 1898.[15] From the "Revolution of '56" through the end of the century, public welfare expenditures consistently failed to keep pace with the city's growth. The dominant political ethic of "no-growth" compelled local politicians to prevent the expansion of public services, including welfare.[16] Instead, local officials relied on private charities to provide the lion's share of poor relief.

San Francisco's reliance on private charity was not unusual. As Mary Ryan observes, most of the urban public's needs were not met directly by city hall in the nineteenth century, but rather by a network of private companies and voluntary associations "that passed around and through the formal government."[17] Americans at mid-century had minimal expectations of city governments: They were to tax, prevent riots, regulate piers, streets, and fences, and occasionally construct public buildings. Except in extreme emergencies, urban residents viewed poor relief as a private rather than a public responsibility. American cities could thus avoid responsibility for welfare because an alternate system existed—private charity.[18]

There were cultural as well as practical reasons for the prevalence of private charity in San Francisco. Religious beliefs encouraged service to the poor. Evangelical Protestantism, for example, urged Christians to aid the needy. Press and pulpit continually urged men of wealth to be Christian gentlemen and serve the communities in which they had prospered. Women were exhorted to good works as well. Indeed, women were disproportionately active in charity work throughout America. Many accepted society's estimation of their sex as naturally pious and pure, taking on the prescribed role of benefactor to the poor.[19] Through charity work, Christian women could both *do* good and *be* good.[20] The women of San Francisco's Union Missionary Society were clearly acting on religious belief when they vowed to "follow the example of our Savior by going about and doing good" among the city's poor.[21]

Influential as religious precepts were in urging women into charity work, gender ideology was also important. The social ethic that Barbara Welter called "the Cult of True Womanhood" encouraged women to devote themselves to the private sphere of home and family, leaving the public sphere of commerce and politics to men. Benevolence work, however, blurred the distinction between the two domains. Church programs to feed and clothe the poor, tend the sick, or raise money to spread the gospel all opened the door to public action without flouting the cultural demands of femininity, piety, and gentility.[22] Significantly, women in rough frontier communities found the ideology of separate spheres as relevant to their lives as did eastern women. If anything, western women may have felt the demands of feminine propriety even more keenly. As Julie Roy Jeffrey found, many women emigrated to the frontier believing that it was their special mission to "civilize" the West.[23] Not surprisingly, those arriving in San Francisco in the 1850s, 1860s, and 1870s found the exuberantly male community badly in need of a woman's touch. To the seventeen or more benevolent societies formed in the 1850s, the newcomers added at least a half-dozen more of their own, ranging in purpose from spreading the gospel to tending the sick. The number of female-led charity organizations continued to grow over the next three decades, becoming, to no small degree, the city's welfare system.[24]

Judging by the enthusiasm with which they greeted the newcomers' organizations, San Francisco men approved wholeheartedly of women's charity work. In the summer of 1853, the *San Francisco Alta California* applauded "the intelligence and enlightenment" of the women who formed the San Francisco Ladies' Protection and Relief Society. The *Alta* urged Christian gentlemen to aid unfortunate women "who left home wives and mothers but arrived widows," finding themselves "destitute in our city by the decease of their natural protectors on their passage hither."[25]

Like the Forty-Niners before them, white, middle-class Protestant women arriving in San Francisco after the first frantic years of the Gold Rush brought with them the habit of association.[26] Although women's associations followed familiar patterns, there were distinct differences between local male- and female-led charities. Male-led charities were primarily for men; the separation of spheres made it unlikely men would directly provide the services women and children required. Women's charities observed the same etiquette and provided services exclusively for children and their own sex. Gendered distinctions applied to public services as well. Many of California's earliest county hospitals, for example, accepted neither women nor children as patients. Only specialized private hospitals admitted children but, prior to 1875, San Francisco did not have one.[27] The only other type of unofficial public aid that might have been available to women and children—political patronage—was usually reserved for voting-age males.[28] Local women's charities therefore filled a critical gap in public and private welfare services. Beginning with the first woman-led organization formed in 1850, San Francisco women practiced what might be called "lifeboat benevolence," a particularly feminine version of charity in which women and children always came first.

A closer look at the origins and activities of several key women's charities in the period 1850 to 1880 reveals how religion, gender ideology, and material circumstances interacted in San Francisco's welfare history. San Francisco's first social welfare institution—indeed, the first in California—was an orphanage founded by women. The total number of children in the city was only 1,000 or so in 1851, but the needs of those left orphaned still required immediate attention. As Ruth Shackelford found, the general vulnerability of children in nineteenth-century America was intensified by the unhealthy conditions of Gold Rush San Francisco. Forty-Niners arriving by ship periodically unleashed malaria, cholera, and smallpox on the overcrowded city, which, along with natural disasters, severe overcrowding, and inadequate public services, left a considerable number of children without one or both parents to care for them. According to Shackelford, what was unique about San Francisco was how quickly these children became a problem.[29] In 1850, Elizabeth Waller, wife of superior court judge Royal Waller, learned of a family devastated by cholera en route to San Francisco. Their parents' death left five children orphaned and alone in the city. Waller called a meeting of churchwomen to consider the best means of caring for these and other dependent children, and the San Francisco Protestant Orphan Asylum (SFPOA) was born.

The form of their organization followed the pattern of women's voluntary associations throughout the country. The women drafted a constitution and elected a slate of Lady Managers; local businessmen were enlisted as trustees to act in legal matters. Then the women got down to the serious business of raising funds and building an orphanage.

The results were impressive. By 1853 they had a substantial stone structure costing $22,658.65 and built entirely by private donations. Founders also showed an enviable talent for managing money: When the building was finished, the women had exactly $1.50 left in their treasury.[30] The SFPOA soon proved the city's need for such a facility. It opened with twenty-six children in 1853, and within three years its population had more than doubled.[31]

The Ladies' Depository, another local woman's charity, was formed in 1866. Although there were other needlework associations in the country, what may have been unusual about this and other local women's organizations was its target population.[32] Where later generations organized to aid those beneath them, the first generation of benevolent women founded institutions that they themselves might need.[33] Managers of the Ladies' Depository aimed to serve women like themselves, ladies unaccustomed to waged labor "who, by reverse of fortunes are unexpectedly obliged to rely on the work of their own hands for their support . . . whose delicacy would deter them from seeking assistance in any more public way."[34] While the reference to "delicacy" and "sudden reversals of fortune" betrays an awareness of caste, it also reveals the founders' appreciation of the precariousness of class in San Francisco, where the comfortable lifestyles of middle- and upper-class women could—and often did—evaporate overnight. To meet the needs of such women, the founders combined a work-relief program with a woman-led commercial venture, the Ladies' Depository Co-Operative Store. Managers took donations from "subscribers," or private contributors, and used the money to purchase sewing materials. These materials were given to "depositors," or seamstresses seeking work, and were returned as completed articles for sale in the store. The managers returned 90 percent of the sale price for each article to the woman who had made it, retaining only 10 percent to cover their costs. Along with the income provided to needleworkers, the Co-Operative Store provided additional women with wages as clerks. Given the few forms of employment then open to San Francisco women, the Ladies' Depository served a real need.[35]

The practical wisdom of combining charitable projects with the services all women needed is especially evident in the area of medical philanthropy. In 1867 the wives of several prominent businessmen

founded the San Francisco Female Hospital (SFFH), a hospital spe-
cializing in gynecological and obstetrical care. Like the Ladies'
Depository, founders had San Francisco's youth and instability in mind;
as the secretary explained, the facility was intended for the woman who
found herself "deprived of the comforts to which, perhaps, she had
long been accustomed, often, too, a stranger in a strange land."[36]
Because founders believed that all women needed competent medical
care, the hospital accepted all applicants, regardless of nativity, race, religion, or marital status. Despite these charitable aims, SFFH founders
encountered opposition from the community, perhaps over the promise to treat all women—even unwed mothers—humanely. In their
second annual report, SFFH surgeon C. T. Deane admitted that, in the
beginning, "there were not wanting prophets of evil, who foretold the
failure and misrepresented the object for which the charity was inau-
gurated."[37] Despite the murmurings, founders proceeded with their
plans. Their perseverance was rewarded: In its initial year of operation
the SFFH served 198 women, which proved San Francisco's need for
such a facility at the same time it silenced those predicting failure. By
the end of its second year, the hospital had treated 384 sick and pregnant women and delivered 214 babies. Not only did the SFFH provide
a high volume of medical care, it also appears to have provided high-
quality care: In the same two years, only five babies were lost and not
one mother died.[38]

The San Francisco Ladies' Protection and Relief Society
(SFLP&RS), organized in 1853, addressed a wider variety of needs than
those already discussed. Tradition holds that the SFLP&RS began when
a young woman came to San Francisco in search of a gold-hunting
brother. Her letters evidently never reached him because he failed to
meet her ship. A fellow passenger directed her to a house on Minna
Street that turned out to be a brothel. Alone and friendless, the young
woman wandered the streets in mounting panic until she saw a woman
observing her from the window of her home. Trusting to the solidarity of her sex, the girl ran to the door begging for protection, and the
SFLP&RS was born.[39]

Her benefactor, the wife of Presidio Commissar A. B. Eaton,
promptly called a meeting of churchwomen to consider the needs of

respectable women who found themselves alone and unprotected in the city. The SFLP&RS initially aided women and children by paying their board in the homes of poor families, a strategy that benefited both groups. In addition, the society opened an "intelligence office" to help women find lodging and employment. Like other women's groups of the era, SFLP&RS strategies evolved with experience. In 1857 the women decided they could improve their operations with a shelter. The "Home" accepted paying and non-paying adult women and their children, and it boarded local children regardless of whether their parents could pay. Like the SFPOA, the women soon proved the community's need for such a facility: By 1869 the Home was caring for 173 children between the ages of eight months and twelve years. By 1884 the facility was overcrowded, with 212 children.[40]

The SFLP&RS also served a genuine need among the poor. Through the Home and members' outreach efforts, local women and children found resources for surviving the vicissitudes of urban life. In 1858, for example, Mrs. Mulcahy asked for medical care for her children, who were sick with whooping cough. When a member found Mrs. Garvie and her children destitute and homeless, the SFLP&RS agreed to provide the mother "with what may be necessary for her present wants" and to find her a job.[41] In 1860 the Christy family was overwhelmed by misfortune: "Mrs. Christy appeared to be in consumption, and Mr. Christy crippled by a fall, & unable to walk. The children ragged and hungry." The member assigned to follow their progress reported the aid given the family: "Mrs. Reese had been to see them, & had expended $17.50 for them, had engaged a nurse, at $1.00 per day, Mrs. Sneath had sent them a bag of flour, & Mr. Selby had liberally donated $7.50 toward paying rent."[42] With each local economic catastrophe, demand for SFLP&RS services multiplied. During the depression years of 1876 and 1877, for example, the Home housed and fed an average of 196 women and children per month, schooled an average of 272 children per month, found homes for 17 orphans, and distributed money, fuel, and provisions to an unspecified number of women and children living outside the Home.[43]

For each of the organizations described here, it is difficult to reconcile the depth and breadth of their charity work with the tendency of some historians to depict women's benevolence as hollow rituals of noblesse oblige rather than meaningful service.[44] Such depictions miss the value of benevolent women's services to the poor themselves as well as to the larger community. Moreover, the emphasis on "social control," or the opportunity for charity leaders to condition aid on the adoption of middle-class values, deflects attention from the ways in which middle- and upper-class women used their connections in service of the poor. In a very real sense, it was benevolent women's class identities that made their organizations possible. As in other American cities of the period, the directors of local women's charities were often the state's most influential citizens.[45] Editors of the *San Francisco Alta California* were quick to point out that "the intelligen[t] and enlighten[ed]" women who founded the SFLP&RS were "the wives of some of our most respectable citizens," including Thomas O. Larkin, first American consul to (then-Mexican) California, and James King of William, reformer-editor of the *San Francisco Bulletin*.[46] The original board of the SFPOA were the wives of San Francisco's first Protestant clergymen; over the years, its trustees included pioneer banker Darius Ogden Mills, superior court judges David Shattuck and Royal Waller, city supervisor and mayor James Otis, and San Francisco supervisor and future California governor Henry H. Haight. The endorsement these women received made sense. Community leaders were those who brought wives and families to San Francisco, and these were the women who organized the city's most enduring—and influential—benevolent societies.[47]

Given their often intimate connections to state and local politicians, the ease with which founders raised funds and smoothed out legal difficulties is not surprising. In January 1855, for example, the SFPOA convinced city leaders to allocate $125 per month in public funds to the orphanage.[48] In the 1850s Mayor C. K. Garrison more or less gave two city blocks to the SFPOA for $100; building materials for the asylum were then donated by the municipal stone quarry. When the women discovered that construction could not begin until side streets were surveyed, Supervisor Henry Haight ordered surveys and then, as a bonus, had two streets named after managers Elizabeth Waller and Anna Haight (his wife).[49] Local women also had success with state officials. In 1855 the legislature gave the SFPOA $5,000 in state funds. The SFLP&RS requested and received $6,000 from the state for their new Home in 1863. In 1878 the woman-led Children's Hospital sought and received $1,000 from the legislature. In 1870 legislators gave the SFFH $5,000, and over the next eleven years, state and local officials annually contributed between $3,000 and $5000 to it.[50] The success of these organizations in obtaining public funds for services to women and children shows that women could be quite successful in putting the issues of greatest concern to them on the public agenda.

But even with the generosity of state and local officials, women's charities would not have survived without the broad support of all classes of San Franciscans. Contrary to their depiction as "reluctant citizens," San Franciscans responded generously to appeals for aid.[51] Records of the SFPOA, SFLP&RS, and Children's Hospital reveal that citizens supported women's charities enthusiastically. Elites bestowed gifts of cash, stocks, bonds, gold bullion, goods, and real estate on all three organizations. In 1855 alone, the SFPOA collected over $10,000 in private donations. In 1860, Horace Hawes gave the SFLP&RS an empty lot in the area bounded by Van Ness, Geary, Franklin, and Post Streets. When the Sansome Hook and Ladder Company gave the SFPOA its building at Montgomery and Jackson in 1860, James Lick donated the land on which it stood. James Donohue, a prominent Irish Catholic businessman, gave the Protestant orphans twenty years' interest income from stock in his gas company. In 1886 Nathaniel and Emmaline Gray helped defray Children's Hospital's building costs by donating a fifty-vara lot on the corner of California and Maple streets. The following year, W. K. Van Allen sold the hospital the lot next door at half its value.[52]

Support for women's charities was not limited to the elite. The Catholic Laborers Union Association donated $500 to the Roman Catholic Orphan Asylum in 1854, and, a few days later, a group of Protestant laborers donated $200 to the SFPOA. White-collar workers gave as well; when two SFPOA Lady Managers made a walking canvass of the business district in 1854, they found even the clerks begging to contribute: "We visited every place of business in town, offices, banks and stores, asking always for the head of the firm, who not only responded liberally, but other gentlemen happening to be present, and men and clerks, would say, 'Are you not going to ask me to give?' or, 'Won't you allow me to contribute?'"[53]

Although some women's charities were quite successful in enlisting community support, business and political leaders nonetheless controlled the context in which their organizations operated. Despite the city's wild and woolly reputation, San Francisco elites tended to be political conservatives. Civic leaders generously supported benevolent women's organizations, but that support was denied organizations with more controversial goals. The tiny Woman's State Suffrage Association, for example, could count on little in the way of public or even private funding.[54] Because local women's benevolent organizations focused on caring for women and children—areas traditionally within the feminine sphere—their leaders walked the fine line between acceptable female activism and intolerable feminist stridency. Gender ideology thus promoted some women's entry into the public sphere, but it limited others hoping to expand women's political and economic opportunities.[55]

This constraint is particularly apparent in the activities of San Francisco's Hospital for Children and Training School for Nurses (Children's Hospital). Originally known as the Pacific Dispensary, the facility was begun by three women doctors in 1875. Its mission was to provide affordable medical care to women and children and—equally important to its founders—to establish a medical institution "for women, controlled by women, with women physicians."[56] Female physicians, residents, interns, and matrons filled the majority of the hospital's posts and jealously guarded against male encroachment. In their fund-raising appeals, however, Lady Managers carefully avoided even the hint of feminism. Instead, leaders consistently described the facility's work in terms of Christian duty and feminine service to the broader family of mankind. President Mrs. W. B. Harrington, for example, explained that the work of the hospital was "an abiding lesson of the supreme value of human love and sympathy, of the indissoluble tie which binds together rich and poor, happy and unhappy, and which NOT to recognize is to fall short of our duty."[57] In order to legitimate their public relationships with business leaders and politicians, as well as their highly visible role in civic affairs, charity leaders were compelled to extol the private, feminine virtues of piety and domesticity. In their carefully worded reports and petitions, benevolent women took care to reaffirm the male/public, female/private dichotomy of separate spheres, glossing over not only subversive goals but also the basic day-to-day business and political skills required to manage their institutions. Ironically, charity leaders were expanding women's sphere at the same time they confirmed its limits.[58]

Of course, the line between public and private spheres was illusory. The metaphor of separate spheres was a useful construction, a social ideal, not a description of reality.[59] Women often crossed the line into what was, essentially, the masculine sphere. And, as the Forty-Niners demonstrated, nineteenth-century men often displayed the qualities of sympathy and selflessness attributed to women. During the cholera epidemic of 1850, for example, one observer noted that the Odd Fellows and Free-Masons "contributed money and exertions as freely as if their lives had been devoted to the exclusive function of human kindness."[60] It was the flexibility of sphere ideology that allowed women to operate so successfully on the broad plane of community action without appearing to leave their appropriate sphere. At the same time, the pervasiveness of sphere ideology underlay the genuine differences between public and private welfare in San Francisco.

The most obvious difference between local public and private welfare was in the kinds of services provided, especially "indoor" and "outdoor" relief. Indoor relief meant custodial care of the poor in institutions; outdoor relief was aid to the poor in their own homes. Like many cities of the period, it was San Francisco's policy to provide only indoor relief.[61] From 1850 to 1880 (and well beyond), the only public welfare offered by San Francisco required institutionalization in either the jail, City Hospital, Industrial School, or Alms House. There were only two exceptions to this policy: In 1870 the city began donating half of all fines received to the male-led San Francisco Benevolent Society (SFBS) for distribution as outdoor relief.[62] Thereafter, the SFBS received a maximum of $5,000 a year to distribute to the poor. The only other public outdoor relief was the Robinson Bequest: In 1881, a wealthy citizen left $40,000 to the city with the request that the annual interest be given to poor women and children. Like the SFBS allocation, this sum was quite small; in 1893 the interest came to only $2,395.80. The city made no other allocations for outdoor relief from 1850 to 1906.[63] Private charities, on the other hand, provided both indoor and outdoor relief. Between 1863 and 1873, for example, the SFLP&RS paid rents, bought provisions, provided nurses, medical attention, clothing, and fuel for fifty-one families living outside the Home.[64] The availability of outdoor relief was critically important to poor mothers and fathers, since outdoor relief allowed families to stay together while institutionalization generally split adults and children among different facilities.

The gap between public and private spending on welfare could be quite dramatic. In 1893, the only year for which relatively complete figures exist (and the first year of the country's worst depression to date), the city expended a total of $7,395.80 in outdoor relief. In contrast, private charities distributed more than $308,500 in outdoor relief—forty-one times as much as the city. When indoor and outdoor relief are considered together, the gap between public and private spending was still substantial. In 1893 the city spent a total of $57,601 on poor relief, while private charities expended $503,622—nearly nine times as much.[65]

Aside from differences in kind and quantity of aid given, there were also qualitative differences between private and public welfare. Even where public and private agencies offered identical services, contemporary observers considered private facilities superior. The California Society for the Prevention of Cruelty to Children (CSPCC) devoted much of its energies to retrieving children from public institutions, a fate CSPCC leaders evidently equated with cruelty. City administrators seemed to agree. In May 1877 the CSPCC removed thirteen-year-old William Reagan from the city jail and sent him to St. Vincent's Orphan Asylum. That same month the CSPCC found Mary Walker and her child Lizzie in the city jail, "where they had applied for lodging, perfectly destitute"; Lizzie was sent to the SFLP&RS Home.[66] In 1877 the Probate Court placed a total of fifty-eight abandoned, abused, or neglected children under CSPCC jurisdiction. Of these, twelve children were placed in families, five were returned to their parents, and one was sent to the Alms House. The remaining forty children were divided between two private institutions.[67]

Two years later, city officials again followed CSPCC recommendations in placing the majority of its wards of court (forty-one out of sixty) in private institutions. Out of forty-one children for whom adoptive families could not be found, only six were sent to public institutions (one to the City Hospital, four to the Industrial School, and one to the Alms House). Of the remaining thirty-eight children, all were placed in private facilities managed by women: Sixteen were sent to the SFLP&RS Home, eleven to Mt. St. Joseph's Infant Asylum, ten to the Roman Catholic Orphan Asylum, and one to the Presbyterian (Chinese) Mission Home. Women's facilities also dominated in medical placements: In the same group, three of the four children placed in hospitals were sent to the woman-run Children's Hospital.[68]

The records of other public agencies reveal the same preference for private institutions. In the 1870s, when Elizabeth Armer began an informal day-care center in a working-class neighborhood, police and criminal courts lost no time in sending children "up to Miss Armer's to be looked after."[69] Likewise, in 1868 Industrial School officials sent a number of children to the SFPOA and the SFLP&RS Home.[70] Such transfers suggest an agreement that women's facilities came closer than public institutions to the desired ideal, the private family. Of course, public officials also had practical reasons for preferring women's institutions: Their inmates were supported by private donations, rather than tax dollars.

Perhaps the most profound difference between private and public forms of welfare was in the care with which managers shepherded their financial resources. The San Francisco Female Hospital (SFFH) again illustrates the point. In their first year, founders raised $13,037 in private donations and netted another $230 in a fund-raising fair. With this total capital, they rented two large houses, purchased furnishings and bedding, hired a physician, matron, nurses, and servants, and provided free medicines, food, medical care, and accommodations to 198 women. Having done all this, the women showed a balance of $5,000 in the Savings Bank and held Spring Valley Water Company stock worth $3,148 at the end of their first year.[71]

As contemporaries saw it, the skills required to run social welfare institutions economically came naturally to women. Indeed, as the leaders of a New York hospital explained, "there were many household details in a large hospital *only* understood by women."[72] San Franciscans evidently agreed: In March 1869, while citizens were anxiously calculating the cost of operating the new Alms House and reading daily newspaper accounts of scandal at the Industrial School, editors at the *San Francisco Daily Bulletin* were praising the efficiency and economy of the SFFH.[73] "It is gratifying," they wrote, "to find that money given for charitable purposes has been well spent." In an acidly acute analysis of the difference between public welfare and private charity, the editors observed that:

> It too often happens that the managers of institutions supported by other peoples' money, without intending to be extravagant, think it necessary to spend more liberally or provide more substantively, to furnish more luxuriantly, or build more costly than they would if it was for a private concern and all the little bills had to be paid out of their own pockets. [74]

As the *Bulletin* saw it, public institutions were profligate because they were spending "other peoples' money." In contrast, private charities paid "all the little bills" from their own pockets; thus the *Bulletin* could reassure San Franciscans that "every one who gave a dollar, or who may give a dollar to this institution, has the pleasure of knowing that not only has a great amount of good been done, but has been done wisely and well."[75]

The emphasis on economy was not limited to the SFFH but seemed to be characteristic of local women's organizations. The observed differences between public and private institutions derived, in large part, from the different models each used. Lady Managers drew upon the domestic model with which they were most familiar: that of the well-ordered, middle-class home. The SFPOA orphanage and SFLP&RS shelters consistently referred to their facilities as "home" and residents as "family." Even SFFH managers thought of their maternity hospital as "a quiet and comfortable home" to which women could turn in their hour of need. These values carried over into management. In their weekly visits to the SFLP&RS Home, board members were lavish in their praise of thrift and good order; a visiting delegation in February 1870, for example, "found everything neat and orderly & evidences of Miss Harmon's thrift and economy on all sides."[76] But discovery of vegetables rotting in the pantry provoked instant rebuke and changes in Home practices: "Henceforth," managers agreed, "the cook was to purchase produce only from the daily peddlar [sic] and only in quantities sufficient for the day's needs."[77] Evidently, such lapses were rare. One manager seemed almost disappointed after her inspection in January 1871, when "the testamony [sic] was uniformly of neatness and good order and general good management. Not enough to critacise [sic] to make a written report interesting."[78] Although residents may have found Lady Managers' middle-class standards intrusive, or even oppressive, the insistence upon comfort and economy brought obvious benefits.

In contrast, public welfare facilities of the period seemed unable to offer either comfort or economy.[79] Comparison of public and private operating costs may suggest why this was so. The closest parallels are between the woman-led SFLP&RS Home and the city-managed Industrial School and Alms House. The institutions were not entirely analogous, in that they catered to different clienteles: The SFLP&RS Home accepted only infants, children, and adult women; the Industrial School served only juvenile males, and the Alms House accepted children and adults of both sexes and all ages.[80] On the other hand, the three institutions were similar in that they each provided custodial care of varying lengths to a shifting population, operated in the same political and social climate, and spent dollars of equal value. As Table 1 demonstrates, in each of the years examined, the cost of maintaining an inmate in the Alms House or Industrial School was higher—in some cases, two to three times higher—than in the SFLP&RS Home.[81]

Table 1: Approximate Cost of Maintenance Per Inmate Per Month,
SFLP&RS Home, Alms House, and Industrial School, 1872–1879

YEAR	SFLP&RS HOME	(N)★	ALMS HOUSE	(N)	INDUSTRIAL SCHOOL	(N)
1872–1873	$7.80	(170.5)	$21.92	(290)	$13.09	(258.5)
1873–1874	6.68	(169)	22.11	(319.5)	19.22	(249.5)
1874–1875	8.56	(170)	19.63	(363)	13.23	(231)
1875–1876	7.33	(186.5)	14.36	(370.5)	14.51	(394)
1876–1877	7.82	(196)	21.79	(395)	12.79	(202.5)
1877–1878	6.10	(206.5)	20.95	(437)	13.03	(221.5)
1878–1879	6.60	(212.5)	20.73	(472)	10.51	(205.5)

★(N) = *Average number of residents per month.*

Sources: San Francisco Ladies' Protection and Relief Society, "Minutes,"
1872–1879; San Francisco Supervisors, "Alms House Reports," "Industrial
School Reports," in *Municipal Reports*, 1872–1879.

The superior economy of the SFLP&RS over public facilities
partly reflects the charity's different status in the community. Whereas
the city was compelled to purchase everything its institutions required,
woman-run organizations regularly reaped the benefits of community
support. As seen above, the dollar value of such support could be substantial. But the primary reason women's charities operated with greater
economy than their public counterparts was the voluntary labor of the
Lady Managers themselves. This was, in fact, the most significant cost
difference between women's charities and public institutions. Charities
could operate their institutions less expensively than public facilities
because managers were not paid for their labor, typically the most
expensive item in the budgets of public institutions. Over its first eleven
years of operation, the largest expense item for the Industrial School
was always salaries. In all but two years of the period 1872 to 1880, the
city spent more on Industrial School salaries than it did on food and
provisions for inmates.[82] Thus, a larger percentage of public funds ear-

marked for the poor went to those providing aid, rather than to those needing it.

One might argue that the difference between public welfare and women's charities derived from the differences between men and women. However, the evidence from San Francisco suggests that the main difference between public and private welfare was not due to gender *per se*. Private, male-led charitable organizations could also operate with greater efficiency than public programs, for much the same reason: More of the dollars earmarked for the poor actually reached them through private organizations than through public institutions, because fewer dollars were consumed by overhead, especially the salaries of administrators. Rather, the key distinction between women's benevolence and public welfare derived from the sexual division of labor dictated by nineteenth-century gender ideology: Private charities relied upon volunteers, often women, whereas public institutions paid their workers, usually men.

Given San Francisco's refusal to provide outdoor relief and the close watch taxpayers kept on municipal spending, one might expect that the city expended very little on public welfare. Actually, San Francisco spent hundreds of thousands of dollars on institutional care for the poor. From 1859 to 1880, taxpayers spent close to $1.5 million for the Alms House and Industrial School alone.[83] Whatever the deficiencies of local public welfare, the problem was not solely lack of funds. Rather, the flaws may have been inherent in the nature of nineteenth-century public administration, a system Theda Skocpol has characterized as "patronage democracy" and Sam Bass Warner, Jr., has called "privatism." Traditionally, municipal government blended public service with private economic aspirations. Municipal strategies for meeting such urban needs as public transit, garbage collection, and poor relief—for example, the franchise system and public alms houses—frequently provided politicians and entrepreneurs with opportunities for personal financial gain. Evidently, San Francisco's public welfare institutions were just as prone to corruption as those in other American cities of the period.[84] Local welfare administrators manipulated supply contracts for personal profit, and the budgets of public welfare facilities were used for political patronage. According to Roger Lotchin, Democratic machine functionaries diverted $166,000 from the State Marine Hospital for patronage and gifts to prostitutes and mistresses in the 1850s. On election day, the entire medical staff and all the Hospital's movable patients were required to get out and "vote 'the ticket'—as many times as they could."[85] Leontina Murphy found evidence of fraud among food contractors at City Hospital during the period 1849 to 1936. In 1872 San Francisco Alms House Superintendent M. J. Keating admitted that unscrupulous businessmen were supplying rotten meat and short-weighted goods to the facility; as a result, Alms House inmates were slowly starving to death.[86]

In contrast, women's charities operated outside the system of patronage and public-service-for-profit. Benevolence, the primary mode of political participation for nineteenth-century women, blended the traditional values of Christian charity with the virtues of the private sphere: femininity and domesticity. The well-ordered Christian home was both model and creed for local women's institutions. The Women's Christian Association, for example, ran their institution as "not only a home but a 'Christian Home'." Like the woman-led facilities discussed above, managers vowed to "do all that was necessary to make the Home in every respect a happy Christian family."[87] Because benevolent women's politics were shaped by the values of piety and domesticity, their institutions rose above self-interested partisanship to create, in James T. Kloppenberg's words, a political ethic "based on responsibility rather than cupidity."[88]

It is no wonder that San Franciscans were eager to support private charities, especially those led by women. Citizens must have felt themselves fortunate indeed to possess a supplemental welfare system managed, in large part, by individuals believed to be immune to greed and corruption. From the community's perspective, the superiority of women's charities derived from their exclusion from formal municipal politics. Any discomfort citizens may have felt over women's excursions into the masculine sphere were easily outweighed by the benefits of retaining control over social welfare spending. San Franciscans found benevolent women's services so useful precisely because they operated at the indistinct boundary between "public" and "private." Their services allowed citizens to avoid expansion of the public sector, with its associated risks of higher taxes, waste, and political corruption.

By the early 1880s women's charities and church groups faced new challenges. The brick-and-mortar institutions erected by the women studied here represented entrenched tradition in the 1880s and 1890s, when a new generation of reformers began vying for control of the city's welfare system. Orphanages and shelters, for example, were criticized by reformers favoring outdoor forms of relief for children, such as foster homes and boarding-home care.[89] Independent agencies faced pressure to join the local "charity organization society," the Associated Charities, which sought to streamline and rationalize local charity efforts. Joining, however, meant private organizations would lose their autonomy and perhaps their distinct character as women's charities.[90] A new generation of college women likewise scoffed at benevolence work as sentimental and old-fashioned; instead they placed their faith in settlement houses and the new science of social work.[91] While reformers of the Progressive era retained their mothers' and grandmothers' faith in the special virtues of women, they directed their attack on what they saw as the causes, rather than the effects, of poverty.[92] The foothold gained by women's charities from 1850 to 1880 provided the foundations for what the latter group would call "municipal housekeeping" but, at the same time, set the stage for intergenerational conflicts over ideology, methods, and (perhaps most importantly) access to public and private financial support.[93]

Looking back at the period 1850 to 1880 it is clear that issues of gender continuously shaped the context in which local women operated, affecting both the strategies they devised and the responses they received. Benevolent women's identification with femininity and piety enabled them to draw on public support for their social welfare projects. At the same time, their place outside formal politics made possible the superior economy of their institutions. For their part, San Franciscans were eager to support women's private ventures, which simultaneously satisfied charitable impulses while guarding against municipal waste and corruption. The result was a system of public and private welfare that bore the clear imprint of benevolent women's values, interests, and concerns. Leaders of local women's charities thus played an active—if forgotten—role in local politics.

This study suggests a number of further lines of inquiry. In the West, discussion of women's presumably greater freedom has typically been tied to early suffrage,[94] yet a great deal remains to be learned about the opportunities western women enjoyed in the realm of maternalist politics. The principal form of public power exercised by women in the presuffrage era was that of lobbyist, fund-raiser, and resource redistributor. The evidence from San Francisco shows that this power was substantial. The extent to which this city was unique remains to be seen, but additional studies of women's charity work throughout the United States will make meaningful comparisons between regions possible. By the same token, inclusion of western women in studies of "maternalism" will help develop a genuinely national image of women's social politics.

For urban historians and students of Progressivism, the evidence from San Francisco demonstrates the potential value of an expanded time frame for research. The findings of Seth Koven and Sonya Michel regarding women's politics in the Progressive era apply to San Francisco in the period 1850 to 1880 as well: Where state welfare structures and bureaucracies remained rudimentary, women exerted their influence to define the needs of mothers and children and design programs to meet them.[95] San Francisco women shaped state and local welfare policy long before the club movement, woman suffrage, or the phenomenon Paula Baker has called the "domestication of politics."[96] Despite the gap of several decades, benevolent women's approaches to poor relief have much in common with the strategies of Progressive-era reformers. In fact, nineteenth-century concerns echo resoundingly in current discussions of welfare reform.[97] Rather than limiting discussions of benevolence or maternalism to a specific time or generation, scholars need to see both as part of a continuum in women's political concerns. Locating maternalist politics in an era when welfare essentially meant charity will lead to a fuller and more illuminating picture of women's participation in politics, not only in the West but in American politics as a whole.

★ Mary Ann Irwin is an independent scholar, writing and teaching history in the San Francisco Bay area.

The author wishes to thank Karen J. Blair and Robert W. Cherny for reading and commenting on several versions of this article.

'Strong Animal Passions' in the Gilded Age: Race, Sex, and a Senator on Trial

Lynn M. Hudson

AT the height of Gilded Age splendor, San Francisco witnessed the fall of one of its wealthiest robber barons, William Sharon, former United States Senator of Nevada. Sharon's offense, according to a Superior Court judge, stemmed from his inability to control his "strong animal passions." Two women, an African American entrepreneur, Mary Ellen Pleasant, and an Irish American and purported prostitute, Sarah Althea Hill, orchestrated Sharon's demise. This racialized and sexualized scandal tantalized San Franciscan and national audiences for years as two lawsuits, *Sharon v. Sharon* (1884) and *Sharon v. Hill* (1885), captured the public imagination.[1] It is no wonder the pundits took such pleasure in the cases. The *Sharon* trials had all the ingredients for a Victorian drama: voodoo spells, stolen underwear, voyeurism, venereal disease, a secret marriage, a passionate or prurient widower, and unrequited love. The courtroom narratives that surfaced provide ample opportunities to view anxieties about sex, power, color, property, and wealth and their instability in Gilded Age America.[2]

This is partly a story about what constitutes marriage and what constitutes prostitution at the end of the nineteenth century. The

★ Lynn M. Hudson, "'Strong Animal Passions' in the Gilded Age: Race, Sex, and a Senator on Trial," *Journal of the History of Sexuality*, 9:1–2 (2000). © 2000 Journal of the History of Sexuality, University of Texas Press. Reprinted by permission.

demarcations between these arrangements appear to blur, not only in this trial, but increasingly so across the nation.[3] Sarah Hill claimed she married William Sharon; Sharon insisted he paid Hill for sex. Whether Hill acted as a wife or a prostitute preoccupied judges, attorneys, and the press. Mary Ellen Pleasant's high visibility as a key witness for Hill, and the presence of other African Americans in the courtroom, ensured that the trials—and the discourse inside and outside the courtroom— would also hinge on issues about race. But more, Pleasant's capital and her financial support of Hill's case disrupted dominant assumptions about the place of African Americans in post-Reconsruction America. San Francisco, like other United States cities, rendered many of its black citizens powerless through *de jure* and *de facto* segregation and discrimination. The enracing of Pleasant in this case is more complicated than assigning to her the role of mammy, voodoo queen, or madam, though all of these stereotypes applied liberally. The knowledge about white men's secrets that Pleasant controlled, combined with her wealth, made her threatening in ways that mere blackness does not alone explain.[4] The legal contest between Sharon, Hill, and Pleasant, then, is also about Western wealth and capital; both Sharon and Pleasant had profitted mightily from gold and silver mining and real estate speculation. Their wealth helps to explain why they could afford such a public and lengthy legal contest in the first place. The price of financial success for both Sharon and Pleasant intensified during the trials. But while Sharon's heirs would eventually reap the rewards of his millions, Pleasant and Hill paid dearly for trafficking in sexual secrets.

This article focuses on the 1884 divorce trial *Sharon v. Sharon*. It also considers the impact of the trial on the culture of San Francisco and the West. The key players in this case inspired myriad narratives about sex and power articulated through headlines, cartoons, editorials, and public speech. Newspapers in particular were preoccupied with the Senator's sexual behavior. This fascination, however, has obscured the other meanings imbedded in the case: women's bargaining position in sexual relationships with men, the vulnerabilty of maculinity and robber barons in the West, the fear of wealthy African Americans and the power they could acquire.

THE ARREST

When William Sharon, lounging in his lavish personal suite at the Palace Hotel, was arrested on September 8, 1883 for adultery, most wondered how the wealthy widower—who had so successfully manipulated his financial affairs and those of others—could be taken to jail on those charges. In the months that followed, Sarah Hill 's original charge of adultery was thrown out of district court on technical grounds, and her attorney George Washington Tyler filed a new suit on November 1, 1883 in San Francisco's Superior Court. This suit, *Sharon v. Sharon*—which captured the limelight for years—was Sarah Althea Hill Sharon's request for divorce. Sarah Althea Hill Sharon claimed that the two had been secretly married in 1880 and charged William Sharon with desertion and adultery committed with nine women.[5]

Mary Ellen Pleasant had already made her fortune in San Francisco by the time of Sharon's arrest.[6] Like Sharon, Pleasant had profited from the enterprises that shaped the Western economy in the second half of the nineteenth century. Her financial holdings included investments in quicksilver mines and California real estate. Unlike Sharon, Pleasant also profited from a range of smaller enterprises including laundries and exclusive boardinghouses that were home to many of Sharon's associates in city finance and politics. Pleasant may have provided her boardinghouse guests with prostitutes or female companions. Prostitution was central to the mining economies of California, Nevada, and other Western states, and most likely, some of Pleasant's patrons expected sexual service along with room and board.[7] Whether or not men paid for sex in her boardinghouses, however, is less important than the way sex became so central to Pleasant's legacy. The legend of Pleasant as black madam serves to obscure the most prominent aspect of her career: entrepreneurial activity that absorbed profits from miners, politicians, and bankers, and channeled them into her vast financial enterprise. The obfuscation of Pleasant's entrepreneurial success has served different functions in different eras: during her own lifetime it may have served to limit her access to certain circles of the black elite, and it may have sullied her reputation among the state's lawyers and judges.

Pleasant was well-known when she arrived in the courtroom for the Sharon trial; she also stood on familiar ground. In the 1860s she filed two lawsuits challenging segregation on San Francisco's streetcars. Like many other African American women, Pleasant drew attention to Jim Crow and the plight of black urbanites in the years after the Civil War.[8] Members of Sharon's defense team saw Pleasant as the evil mastermind behind Sarah's case.[9] One judge claimed, "Pleasant . . . was forced to admit after much evasion [that] she has advanced more than $5,000 [to Sarah's cause]."[10] The implication that Sarah worked as a prostitute and Pleasant as a madam informed much of the discourse in the courtroom. Proof that this was indeed the arrangement never materialized. Nevertheless, Pleasant's income—much of it obtained indirectly from secrets revealed in her establishments—caused quite a stir. Reporters consistently drew attention to Pleasant's assets, and her property in particular: "[She] derives a good income from eight homes, situated on Octavia, Clara, Stone, Scotland and Harrison streets, added to which is the revenues of a large ranch near San Mateo, besides that of $100,000 in bonds of the United States, while a ready sum awaits her call in our city banks."[11] Pleasant's capital and stature prompted suspicion. African American capitalists, often the target of brutal violence in the post-Reconstruction era, rarely appeared in court as key witnesses for white plaintiffs.

Sharon v. Sharon took place against a backdrop of 1880s abundance in California. It was an era of unprecedented wealth as well as scandal for investors and entrepreneurs.[12] Railroad and mining monopolies squeezed tremendous profits out of the West. And few profited more than city-builder William Ralston's right-hand man, William Sharon.[13] Sharon served as United States Senator from Nevada between 1875 and 1881, but lived in San Francisco after 1872.[14] As the owner of the Palace Hotel, reputedly the largest hotel in the world when it was built in 1875, he was at the center of San Francisco's elite social circle. Sharon's background reflected a life of privilege and to some extent, luck. Born in Smithfield, Ohio in 1820, Sharon studied law with Lincoln's future Secretary of War, Edwin M. Stanton in Steubenville, Ohio. Tempted by stories of the Gold Rush, Sharon took the overland route West in 1849. In San Francisco Sharon became partners with the men who controlled the Bank of California, the largest bank West of the Mississippi. Sharon's association with this circle of bank men—known as Ralston's Ring—led to his appointment as agent of the Nevada City branch of the Bank in 1864. Together the San Francisco and the Nevada offices controlled much of California finances and some of the most lucrative mining territory in the world—the Comstock Lode. Not known for his charm or good looks, Sharon was described by one reporter as "a pale little man with a large head, ladylike hands and feet, and cold blue eyes."[15] With accusations of effeminacy such as this, journalists hoped, perhaps, to belittle Sharon's status. By the time he was elected to the Senate in 1875 he controlled the Comstock Lode, the richest silver mining region of the country, owning at least seven active silver mines.[16] Sharon also owned the Reno-Virginia City Railroad and in the year he was elected to the Senate he acquired Nevada's most influential paper, *The Territorial Enterprise*. His worth was estimated to be between twenty and thirty million dollars in 1875.[17] Sharon's wife, Maria Ann Mulloy, died that same year, and Sharon later stated under oath that he began paying women monthly salaries to have sex with him in his apartment at the Palace Hotel.[18] Sarah Hill, he claimed, was one of those women.

CONFIDING IN A NEGRO

Born in Cape Girardeau, Missouri, Sarah Althea Hill moved to San Francisco in 1871 following her parents' death.[19] Hill's exact age at the time of the trial is not known but she was probably in her early twenties when she moved West. She lived for some time with her aunt and grandfather, then moved on her own from boardinghouse to hotel.[20] Sarah Althea Hill's background is rather sketchy. She was of Irish descent; her great grandparents probably migrated from County Antrim in the 1770s.[21] Her body, not her background, drew much more attention from the press: "[Her] face is shapely and oval, the features are regular, the mouth is well cut, the lips are rather full and are the most expressive feature. They look resolute, but betray also that their owner has a temper."[22] Her hair, described alternately as auburn or strawberry blonde, also elicited commentary. One reporter wrote blithely, "Her hair

is auburn, and, if it is not false, is of luxuriant growth. That portion growing above the forehead is devoted to curls and ringlets, which fall in
profusion over the dome of thought."[23] The press's earliest portraits of
Sarah wavered on the brink of harlotry. Sarah countered this characterization with her own claims of blue blood stock. Before the trial, the
San Francisco Bulletin printed a letter from a friend of Sarah's family,
claiming that Sarah was a descendent of Revolutionary heroes. Even
Sharon's millions, "would hardly compensate a handsome and accom-
plished young woman for his age and reputation and certainly no one
can have a higher family connection than she has." Sarah and her family
thought Sharon "of very low birth" and not equal to her social standing, according to the letter.[24]

On the morning of March 10, 1884, the divorce trial began in
Department Two of the Superior Court in the San Francisco City Hall
with Judge Sullivan presiding. The public had already been treated to a
few scandalous pretrial tidbits collected during the depositions, and, as
a result, the courtroom was packed on opening day.[25] From the onset,
the case raised the specter of the Senator's uncontrolled passions and
interracial alliances between women. Technically, the case hinged on the
question of whether or not Sharon and Hill had been legally married
in 1880. Many key witnesses for both the plaintiff and the defendant
were African American women. On the first day of the trial it was clear
that Sarah's interracial relationships and her alleged use of voodoo would
be substantial issues for the defense in their attempt to discredit her.
Sharon's lead attorney, William Barnes, made the following promise:

> We will show how [Hill] visited the sanctums of fortune
> tellers, negroes, Germans, French and every race. We shall show
> how she obtained a pair of Sharon's dirty socks, had them
> charmed by a negro, and then wore them upon her limbs to
> charm him. How she wore one of his soiled undershirts and
> how she paid $25 for a pinch of pepper and salt a negro gave
> her to charm Mr. Sharon. She disclosed her secrets to a col-
> ored woman and did not confide in a relative. She had no one
> to confide in but a negro.[26]

The defense concentrated much of their efforts on proving that Sharon had been tricked into "strong animal passions" through charms or voodoo. Questioning Pleasant's role as confidant also formed a central part of the defensive attack. "Will anybody tell me," begged Barnes in his argument to the state Superior Court, "why it was that this unfortunate woman never confided the secret of her marriage to one respectable person of her own color, class, or rank in life?"[27] Pleasant occupied a conspicuous place in the courtroom from the first day. She sat behind Sarah in the first row of spectators. At seventy years of age, Pleasant appeared elderly yet stately in her seat at the City Hall. Her presence—and that of the other black witnesses—marked the courtroom as a site where racialized fantasies and fears played themselves out publicly.

The courtroom scenario—of Sharon, the white patriarch, Sarah, the desirable young belle, and Pleasant, the desexualized elderly black woman—also resonated with American cultural icons rooted in the system of slavery. As long as these familiar roles were maintained by the principal actors in the case, and Pleasant played the role of the mammy, her danger to white San Franciscans, and especially white men, would be diminished.[28] At least that was what Sarah's attorneys were hoping; drawing on a familiar story line, that of the faithful mammy, the counsel planned to elicit sympathy for Sarah's case.[29] The other possibility raised by the specter of Sarah and Pleasant, was that Pleasant was a madam—as many San Franciscans believed—and Sarah her employee. That, too, represented a familiar narrative, but one that Sarah's legal team hoped to avoid. Investing Pleasant with mammy-like characteristics and portraying Sarah as the helpless victim of Sharon's sexual desire, became the chief legal strategy for Hill's attorneys.

HOTEL SEX

For Sarah to elicit sympathy as a scorned wife, she must first show that Sharon had in fact married her. To do this, Sarah explained to the Judge that she hid her friend, Nellie Brackett, behind a bureau in William Sharon's room in the Palace Hotel so that Nellie might hear Sharon's promise of marriage. Miss Brackett—who testified that she heard more lovemaking than conversation—did vouch for the existence of a marriage. She testified that Sharon cooed "Who is my own little wife and nobody knows about it?"[30] When Sarah was asked why she hid Nellie in the bureau, she responded, "Well, I wanted to prove to her that I was married to Mr. Sharon." The examiner asked, "You didn't want it for the purpose of proving it to anybody else?" Sarah answered, "I wanted her to tell Mammie Pleasant what she had heard and how he had talked to me."[31] Sarah testified that Pleasant encouraged her to pursue the Senator for the alimony payments he owed her. Sharon, according to Hill, fell behind in his payments. In a heartless move, Sarah explained, Sharon had her evicted from the room he had secured for her at the Grand Hotel. Sharon's suite at the Palace Hotel and Hill's room at the Grand Hotel were connected by a foot bridge that came to be known as "the bridge of sighs."[32] When Sharon had the carpet removed from Sarah's hotel room, she began writing a letter to Sharon about their arrangements, under the advice and counsel of Mary Ellen Pleasant, she told the Judge.

Sharon's attorneys found Sarah's testimony implausible on several counts. Why did Sharon kick her out if they were actually husband and wife? And why did Sarah not mention the marriage or the marriage contract when she penned the letters to Sharon? In answer to the latter, Sarah replied, "I did not mention my contract, or the fact that I was his wife, because I did not want to anger him. . . . Mrs. Pleasance [sic] me to do so."[33] These remarks and others Hill made on the stand testified to Pleasant's central role in Sarah's life and in her case. Whereas Hill's attorney would emphasize the natural affinity between a young woman and her mammy, the story that Sharon's attorney would tell was one of unnatural affinity: "Mrs. Pleasance occupies a very peculiar relation to the respondent in this case, one utterly inexplicable upon ordinary principle or upon any reasonable ground. Her intimacy with Miss Hill, as now related, was one that ought not to have existed. . . . They were together daily according to the present story."[34] Intimacy between Sharon and Hill was the explicit text of the trial; but intimacy between Pleasant and Hill was no less at issue.

Sarah's bad judgment could be measured, according to Sharon's attorney, by witnessing her descriptions of Mary Ellen Pleasant:

Miss Hill's descriptions of the woman to whom she attributes supernatural power must be given in her own language. She says: "Mammie Pleasant was old and had the experience, and she had the experience of lots of girls and women;" "had the experience of the world, of being a servant, and being a wife, and being the head of families."[35]

Sarah's portrayal of Pleasant reveals a conscious effort to cast Pleasant in acceptable roles for a black woman: as a wife, nurturer, and servant. But it was the mammy image that rang true to most observers of the trial. Many San Franciscans believed that Pleasant worked as a servant for a family named Bell, and now some believed that she was mother and mammy to young girls like Sarah.[36] Sarah's case hinged on representing her relationship with Pleasant in this way; were they to be seen as protégé and advisor—a more accurate description of their relationship—Sarah's argument would weaken.

STOLEN UNDERWEAR AND VOODOO SPELLS

Stolen underwear was the topic of extensive discussion in the second week of the trial.[37] The San Francisco *Chronicle*, which displayed sensational headlines since the trial began, ran the following on March 19, 1884: "Sharon's Dirty Duds, Sarah Althea's 'Hoodoo': Socks and Shirts to Rekindle Love's Flame in Sharon's Bosom." Evans, one of Sharon's attorneys, "pulled out of the wrappers a sock so dirty and ill-smelling that Sarah Althea was compelled to hold her nose."[38] Sarah adamantly denied ever using the dirty underwear to put a spell on Sharon and asked Evans, "Are you through with your dirt?"[39]

There can be no doubt that the public—both in and out of the courtroom—was as titillated by the mention of voodoo as they were by the presence of Sharon's socks and undershirt. That there were "at least thirty women" in the audience the day the smelly socks were unveiled, a fact most reporters found remarkable. The San Francisco *Chronicle* described a room full of "fortune tellers, all witnesses in the case in connection with Sarah Althea's alleged devotion to Voudou."[40]

Potions, charms, and voodoo, were referred to throughout the proceedings. Attorneys for both sides spent countless hours questioning black women who might have used, sold, or heard of charms, potions, or spells. On April 14, 1884, Frances Massey, an African American woman, testified that Sarah had come to her and requested aid and had brought her a pair of socks to charm. Mrs. Massey heard Sarah claim that she had also charmed Sharon's food. "Who told her to do that," asked Barnes. "Oh, I would not like to tell; it is a lady I respect very much," answered Massey. Then the witness announced that the culprit was Mrs. Pleasant.[41]

One of the more intriguing twists of the trial was the way in which both attorneys tried to use Sarah's involvement with voodoo as part of their argument. Barnes, who revealed a particular distaste for Sarah's black acquaintances, nevertheless called in a host of black witnesses who testified that Sarah had visited them for charms. He argued that by consulting voodoo practitioners Sarah was conducting herself as a single woman who "did not occupy the place of a loving, trustful wife."[42] Tyler seemed to vacillate between dismissing "hoodoo" as irrelevant to the case and hoping to prove that Sarah was manipulated by sorceresses like Mrs. Massey. Neither side disputed the validity or power of voodoo or spiritual practitioners. Many nineteenth-century Americans subscribed to various forms of spiritualism and the occult—voodoo was just one of the many. But voodoo signified blackness, and that fact was not lost on the participants, the observers, or the recorders of the case. Contact with voodoo, whether by Sarah or any other white person, signaled poor judgment and criminality.[43]

Trying to ferret out the "truth" about voodoo in a courtroom proved as farcical as hiding Nellie Brackett in a closet. Actual voodoo practitioners, those who drew on the traditions of the African diaspora, took a vow of silence as part of their beliefs. What these women described in the San Francisco courtroom sounded less like voodoo and more like love potions. But charms or potions touched by brown hands became voodoo in Victorian America. And the image of Pleasant running some kind of voodoo racket appealed to many, as it only served to underscore the blackness and the danger of Pleasant.[44]

Both sides of the divorce trial knew very well that Sarah's

relationship to African Americans—and particularly to black women—was a key element of the trial. Barnes argued that Pleasant was responsible for most of the black witnesses who appeared in court. Pleasant, according to Barnes and many others, single-handedly launched Sarah's case and gathered her witnesses. In his argument before Judge Sullivan, Barnes exclaimed:

> She is the best all-round witness Mr. Tyler ever had. She is a glorious old woman. I do not wonder that he loves her. I am not surprised that he canonized her. . . . She proved the existence of a contract in 1882. . . . She has produced a noble army of martyrs in the cause of Miss Hill. I do not wonder that Mr. Tyler expresses such sentiments of affection towards Mrs. Pleasance. Where would he have been without her?[45]

Mary Ellen Pleasant's testimony had nothing to do with potions or spells. She took the witness stand five times and offered significant testimony regarding the existence of a marriage contract. Since much of the case rested on the contract, her testimony shaped the outcome of the trial. But her actual statements on the stand prove rather bland compared to other witnesses who confessed to selling potions, being in love with Sarah, or listening to Sarah and the Senator have sex.[46] This blandness was an excellent strategy as it helped take the wind out the defense's sails; Pleasant appeared calm and subdued as Sarah's friend and helpmate.

When she first took the witness stand Pleasant testified that she found Miss Hill weeping at the Grand Hotel because Mr. Sharon had had her ousted from the premises. When Sharon kicked Sarah out of the Grand Hotel, after their marriage had soured, explained Pleasant, Hill was desperate to find a room.

> I have lived in San Francisco since 1849. I met the plaintiff in the Grand Hotel about two years ago. She wanted me to furnish a house for her. I asked to see the marriage contract to see if she had any guarantee for her money. The plaintiff showed the contract, and then I went to Mr. Sharon. I told

him that I heard he had some kind of relation with Miss Hill and owed her money, and asked him if it would be all right if I furnished the house. Mr. Sharon said all right, go ahead and furnish it and he would pay the bills.[47]

The encounter in the Grand Hotel in January 1882, Pleasant claimed, was the first time she and Sarah had met. This contradicted the defense's claim that the two had concocted the marriage contract two years earlier. Surprisingly, Pleasant was barely cross-examined by Sharon's attorneys.

Pleasant's claim that Sarah had told her about the marriage contract at this meeting became a pivotal issue in the case. Rather than focus on the contract itself, Sharon's attorneys would argue that Pleasant was hardly a trustworthy confidante for such an important piece of news:

> Mrs. Pleasance became the receptacle of the respondent's [Hill's] entire confidence. She was not only told of her marriage—informed her of her relations with Mr. Sharon generally—but when it came to the critical moment of expulsion from the hotel the respondent took the direction—think of it!—took the sound direction of this old negro diplomatist as to the character of the letters she should write to her husband![48]

Pleasant's character as well as Sarah's was on trial, and Pleasant's first appearance in court whetted the appetites of a hungry press corps.

SELLING BABIES

From the outset, courtroom discourse raised questions about the power of Mary Ellen Pleasant. Did she have an "unnatural" power over Sarah Hill? Did she operate a clandestine organization of women who made a career of tricking San Francisco men? As the trial progressed, other questions about Pleasant's presumably illicit activities surfaced. In particular, the framing of Pleasant shifted to include her role as a so-called baby-seller.

Pleasant's name is first associated with procuring homes for babies in April 1884, the second month of the trial.[49] An astrologist, Mrs. Wanger, a "not unpleasant-looking woman of middle age," testified that, in 1882, Miss Hill planned to acquire a baby that she would use to blackmail Mr. Sharon. "How was she to get the baby?" Mrs. Wanger was asked. "Why, the same as other women; she said she would pull the wool over Sharon's eyes. The lady that gets the baby is here," announced Wanger. "Who was it?" Tyler asked. "Mrs. Pleasance; yes, she said that Mrs. Pleasance got the babies for Mrs. Bell, and Mrs. Bell pulled the wool over Tom Bell's eyes."[50]

Thomas Bell, long-known in San Francisco for his involvement in the Bank of California and his reputation as a quicksilver king, had a strange but significant role in the trial. His testimony was required to prove that Sarah Althea Hill was indeed at his home on May 1, 1883. Another witness, a gravedigger by the name of Gillard, had testified that he saw Sarah Hill using charms in a graveyard (presumably to put a spell on Sharon) on the first of May 1883. Bell testified that he had been in Mexico on a trip but arrived home to Octavia Street at eleven o'clock on May first to have lunch and Miss Hill was in attendance.[51]

Bell and Pleasant both claimed that Sarah was at the house that day, although Pleasant herself was on an outing with the Bell children. In her testimony on July 22, 1884, Pleasant stated, "I have lived at Mr. Bell's for nine years. On the first of May, 1883, I went to Patterson's ranch; I used Mr. Bell's team that day; I did not use my own; when I returned to Mr. Bell's the plaintiff was not there." In addition to Bell and Pleasant, four other witnesses testified that they knew Sarah had taken lunch at the Bell/Pleasant household. Pleasant most likely secured these witnesses as it was in Sarah's interest to provide a solid alibi.

It was in the best interest of the defense, however, to draw attention to Pleasant's involvement in baby selling and bring the conversation back to that topic. Barnes attempted to do this by drilling one of the witnesses about the ages and names of the Bell children. One author describes the scene as follows: "Barnes and one of the witnesses were locked in a confused and heated exchange about the number and description of the Bell children as the time for adjournment arrived, and Judge Sullivan said pleasantly, if wearily, 'We'll give the babies a rest until tomorrow at ten o'clock.'"[52]

Indeed when the trial resumed the next day, July 23, 1884, the press had a field day over missing babies. Whereas the previous days' headlines read: "An Alibi for Sarah: Where She Spent May Day of 1883," the San Francisco *Chronicle's* headline of the 24th asked: "Where is Bertha's Baby?" A German-American woman, Mrs. Weill, testified that Pleasant, at her request, had placed a certain Bertha Bonsell's baby in a "good home." Thus began a lengthy discussion in the press about baby selling—including a front-page cartoon of Pleasant in the political journal, *The Wasp*. The caption of cartoon, "When I was young and charming, I practiced baby farming," leaves no doubt as to the opinion of this particular journal.

Mrs. Weill had been brought into court by Tyler to testify that she too had seen Sarah at the Bell household on the first of May. But Barnes began his cross examination in a different vein: "Do you know a girl named Bertha Bonstell?" asked Barnes. "Yes sir, she is in San Jose," answered Weill. "Do you remember when she was in the Lying-In Hospital and had a baby there?" pressed Barnes. Tyler objected immediately. And Barnes chimed:

> We claim that this woman, Mrs. Pleasance, is at the bottom of what I shall claim is this mass of perjury that is being committed by these people. I want to show the relation between this woman on the stand and Mrs. Pleasance, and I want to ask her if she did not get this girl's baby from . . . the Lying-In Hospital and give it to Mrs. Pleasance to palm off on Thomas Bell.[53]

Judge Sullivan allowed Barnes to further question Mrs. Weill, at which point Barnes asked her if one of the Bell twins was Bertha Bonsell's babies. Mrs. Weill replied, "Not to my knowledge." But Mrs. Weill did explain that Pleasant helped her find a home for Bertha's baby and that the baby was "in a house on Bush Street." While Barnes had not succeeded in proving that the Bell children were "palmed off" on

Bell, he had introduced solid evidence that Pleasant was in the business of finding homes for newborns.

The next day, Tyler called Pleasant back to the stand: "Did you ring in Bertha's baby on Mr. Bell?" he queried. "No sir," Pleasant responded. In a revealing yet nonchalant exchange, Pleasant chats with Tyler about the babies:

> "Mrs. Weill asked me to get a home for Bertha's baby; I told her I would, and Mrs. Weill said she would get me a wet nurse for Mrs. Bell's twins; our babies were born ten or fifteen days before Bertha's; Bertha's baby was adopted by a lady on Bush street."
> "Whose babies do you mean when you say 'our babies'?"
> "I mean Mr. Bell's babies."[54]

In this light Pleasant's work placing babies in homes looked more like charity or reform and less like black market baby selling or blackmailing. The image of Pleasant saving unwanted babies and placing them in good homes also conformed to the image of elderly black women—mammies—doting over white babies.

Pleasant's veracity continued to be dismissed with utmost scorn by Sharon's legal team. In their final arguments Tyler and Barnes made much of Pleasant's role in the case. On August 12, 1884, Tyler, "in a fury" let loose "his hot invective against Sharon." In his attempt to prove Sharon to be a perjurer, Tyler concentrated on Pleasant's testimony:

> I claim that Mr. Sharon's statement to Mrs. Pleasance is a virtual admission that he signed the contract. He told her when she was talking about the case with him that he could prove that the plaintiff had been intimate with a dozen men since the contract was signed. If your Honor believes Mrs. Pleasance, this is an acknowledgment of the making of a contract.[55]

Tyler placed before the Judge a test of Pleasant's character and trustworthiness. Judge Sullivan was asked to weigh the faithfulness of this black servant: Was she a true mammy? Tyler made his plea very directly:

Allow me to call attention to the character and testimony of Mrs. Pleasance. Mr. Barnes will no doubt try to malign her character; yet, while she was on the stand, he did not cross-examine her. Mr. Barnes adopted the most contemptible manner to discredit her and to shake her testimony in your Honor's mind. He said that Mrs. Pleasance had been ringing in other people's babies on Tom Bell; but what proof did he bring to prove any such outrageous statement?[56]

The baby selling accusation clearly worried Tyler. A baby-selling mammy was not an image Tyler wanted before the Judge. A defensive Tyler pleaded: "Mrs. Pleasance found a home for Bertha's baby. She has found homes for other unfortunate girls' babies. Is that anything against her?"[57]

Representations of Pleasant shifted considerably during the trial. In the early days of the trial Pleasant was described by the press as a "colored peddler of white laces."[58] She "first visited [Sarah] for the purpose of making a sale of some luxurious articles of female underwear which she habitually peddled to the class of white women with whom she associated," according to Sharon's attorneys.[59] But the image of underwear-selling mammy unraveled during the course of the case, and Pleasant was eventually described by Barnes as "the sole financier of the anti-Sharon syndicate."[60] The shift in emphasis is noteworthy; initially the defense employed the slave-like imagery of a lace-peddling mammy to describe Pleasant. But by 1885 this had been replaced by the image of a voodoo priestess deviously manipulating the unsuspecting Sarah with charms and potions as well as financial wizardry.

STRONG ANIMAL PASSIONS

In spite of Barnes' best efforts—and a final argument that took six days in court—many observers sided with Sarah when all was said and done. The Judge, however, had given no indication of his opinion. Thus his verdict, delivered on December 24, 1884, came as a surprise to everyone. The opinion took two and a half hours to read, during which Mr.

Sharon did not fare well, "The defendant was a man of unbounded wealth," the Judge pronounced, "possessed of strong animal passions that, from excessive indulgence, had become unaccustomed to restraint."[61] Clearly, this judge did not look favorably on the millionaire's inability to control his sexual appetite. The contract was deemed to be valid and Sarah was thus entitled to a divorce and alimony. Sullivan awarded Sarah $2500 a month and $55,000 in attorneys fees.[62] When Sharon heard the announcement of Sarah Althea Hill's award he told reporters that the Judge placed a much higher value on Sarah than she did: "When she and I had to fix her value, she rated it at $500 a month."[63] This verdict privileged the madam's word over that of the client's, in this case Sharon's, at least in the eyes of many contemporary observers. One judge went to so far as to describe Pleasant as a "magician and tamer of wild animals," crediting her with considerable power over the ex-Senator's "strong animal passions."[64]

While awaiting her payments, however, Sarah appeared in the next courtroom drama: the federal case brought by Sharon, that began in February 1885—*Sharon v. Hill*. The federal case seemed like a repeat performance of the previous year's drama, only with a few new twists. Sarah was arrested and spent twenty-four hours in San Francisco's Broadway jail for refusing to deliver the necessary documents to Judge Sawyer of the United States District Court. Pleasant visited Sarah in jail bringing her a basket of food. A crowd cheered when Sarah left the jail and she took the opportunity to recite a poem she composed for Judge Sawyer.[65] This was not Sarah's only dramatic performance during the federal case: She also accepted the role of Portia in the San Francisco Grand Opera's production of *The Merchant of Venice* that year.[66] Sarah's exuberance would be short-lived.

Judge Sawyer was joined by Judge Deady of Oregon, and when they delivered their opinion on December 26, 1885, the rosy future that Pleasant and Hill had no doubt imagined shattered. The women had expected large sums of money from Sharon's estate given the earlier verdict. This time, however, the contract was determined to be invalid. Deady, in particular, focused on the sexual improprieties committed; and although they had nothing to do with weighing the validity of the contract they were a blight on Sarah's character not Sharon's. As he explained, "the sin of incontinence in a man is compatible with the virtue of veracity and does not usually imply the moral degradation and insensibility that it does in a woman."[67]

Deady also made his opinion of Pleasant quite clear. She was a "shrewd old negress of considerable means" with a "conspicuous and important" role in the case. Without Pleasant, he claimed, the case "never would have been brought before the public." "For my judgment," he wrote, "this case, and the forgeries and perjuries committed in its support, have their origin largely in the brain of this scheming, trafficking, crafty old woman."[68]

Though the federal case was not by any means the end of the legal skirmishes—appeals and ancillary cases waged on—it was, in many ways, the end of the partnership of Pleasant and Hill.[69] Following Sharon's death in 1885, Sarah married one of her lawyers, David S. Terry.[70] Terry, well-known in San Francisco as the former Chief Justice of the State Supreme Court, was murdered in 1889, and that precipitated a rapid decline in Sarah's mental health. By 1892, Pleasant was taking care of the widow whom the papers described as "hopelessly insane."[71] Mrs. Terry told reporters that Pleasant's house at Octavia and Bush streets was her only sanctuary.

On March 9, 1892, however, Pleasant signed a petition for the health commissioners and had Sarah Althea Terry committed to the state institution for the insane. According to the *Chronicle*, "Mammy Pleasant appeared at once as complainant and friend, and of all the people present, male and female, was the only one who showed any sympathy for the demented creature."[72] Pleasant no doubt felt defeated. Her efforts to wrest Sharon of his fortune had failed and she had not fared well in the courts. As Pleasant entered into another series of lawsuits with Teresa Bell over her own property in the 1890s, she would feel the scars from this tiresome effort.

Pleasant's participation in the litigation was probably part of a complicated financial scheme that involved not just Sarah but many players among San Francisco's elite. Some authors believe that Pleasant's involvement in the case can be explained through a closer look at the Bank of California fiasco and the intertwined finances of Thomas Bell, William Sharon, and Mary Ellen Pleasant. When the Bank of California failed and Ralston resigned as president, Thomas Bell and William Sharon were stockholders. Both Bell and Sharon desperately hoped to restore the Bank to its glory days and save their own fortunes. Sharon maneuvered his way to the top of the Bank's chain of command and bought up most of the shares. He also accepted responsibility for Ralston's debts and acquired Ralston's assets.[73]

Sharon's success cost Bell prestige and capital.[74] Pleasant's finances were certainly connected with those of the Bells, and it is likely that when Bell lost out to Sharon as President of the Bank both Bell and Pleasant also lost considerable capital and power as chief share holders. Records do not reveal how much of Pleasant's money was tied up in Bell's shares or how much she stood to gain or lose when Bell's worth shifted. Nevertheless the theory that Pleasant was out for "triple revenge," as one author calls it, may have some validity.[75]

CONCLUSIONS

The trials mark a site where power is made visible: Pleasant's, Hill's, and Sharon's.[76] For that reason it is a useful episode in which to examine how that power operated and how it was contested. Pleasant's power was contested by attorneys, reporters, and judges, who employed stereotypes, and a range of images from the pilfering mammy to the money-grabbing madam, to discredit her status and power. But the courtroom narratives also reveal that power for women in the Victorian era was located in different places depending on age, race, and class. For Sarah, power emanated from her ability to portray Sharon as an adulterer unable to control his sexual impulses and herself as scorned wife. Pleasant's power emanated from her wealth, her secrets, and the comfort white America invested in the role of the mammy. Pleasant played her part well, on the stand she called herself Thomas Bell's servant, when in fact she was a business partner and co-mortgage holder.

For nearly a year, Pleasant rose every morning, dressed for court, took a team of horses downtown and sat next to Sarah Althea Hill. During the trials she never spoke publicly about the state of her finances or her contribution to Sarah's case. But her behavior indicates that she cared deeply about the outcome. After Sarah's brief victory was over-turned in federal court, Pleasant took her under her wing again and Sarah lived her last weeks in Pleasant's mansion on Octavia Street before being institutionalized. Since Sarah was admittedly broke and not entitled to alimony Pleasant stood to gain nothing from these acts of kindness.

The trials made public the female friendships and homosocial net-works in San Francisco. When Sarah was on the stand she testified that Pleasant "guided her through difficulties . . . but only as a great and true friend, you understand. Mammy expected nothing in return; absolutely nothing."[77] At least one titillated reader wrote that there was something "outré" and "sapphic" in the relationship between Pleasant and Hill.[78] Reading sexual intimacy into the relationship is to misunderstand their bond, forged, at least partially, on the basis of their perception of het-erosexual relations in Victorian San Francisco. Pleasant and Hill shared a desire to make men—in this case Sharon—pay for sexual favors.

In his final argument, Barnes reveals the relationship to be more dangerous than one of mere confidantes: "Mrs. Pleasance occupies a very peculiar relation to the respondent in this case, one utterly inex-plicable upon any ordinary principle or upon any reasonable ground. Her intimacy with Miss Hill . . . was one that ought not to have existed."[79] Their relationship proved threatening for a variety of rea-sons; that it was interracial was probably chief among the qualities that Barnes found so peculiar. And the intimacy between them became part of the discourse of the trials. Suggesting that it was a sensual or inti-mate relationship may not have single-handedly discredited Sarah, but the defense obviously thought that it might help to do so. As Martha Hodes has made abundantly clear, interracial intimacy and its policing defined Reconstruction politics.[80]

The meanings that can be deduced from the trials, however, are not merely about personal relationships. The political implications of the relationships between Pleasant, Sharon, and Hill, and of the trials themselves, are vast. Sharon and Pleasant were players in San Francisco's world of high finance, stock speculation, and silver mining entrepreneurs. Their names were well-known when the first trial began. But women—even famous ones like Pleasant—encountered risks in public space that men did not. As Mary P. Ryan argues, women entered a world of sexual objectification when they participated in public life in a city like San Francisco.[81] Further, since African Americans were denied access to most public arenas and institutions—from restaurants to juries—the risk to Pleasant and the significance of her presence in court cannot be exaggerated.

Until very recently, evidence of women's political culture in the nineteenth-century has most often been located in abolitionist activities and suffrage campaigns not boardinghouses or bordellos. Recent studies, however, find women engaged in political work outside of these arenas; Evelyn Brooks Higginbotham, for example, points to the political significance of black women's church work.[82] Pleasant and Hill's experience also indicates that women infiltrated more traditional political arenas: places marked off as male domains. San Francisco's public sphere was more integrated—in terms of gender and race—than previous studies of the city have indicated.[83] Black women in San Francisco were often seen in public spaces. But most likely they would have been seen performing service sector jobs: as a maid in the Palace Hotel, for instance.[84] The elite black women of the city would attend church functions, literary societies and the like, but a courtroom was public in a way that these spaces were not.[85]

This public arena made women easy prey for journalists. In the pages of the newspapers and magazines Pleasant and Hill were described and displayed. During the course of *Sharon v. Sharon*, Pleasant would be depicted as a mammy and a baby-seller. She would be associated with the practice of voodoo, magic, and witchcraft. The risks to her career and reputation were far greater than those to Sharon, because as Judge Deady pronounced, male sexual misconduct could be expected and therefore tolerated. Pleasant was aware of the risks and careful to construct an unthreatening appearance and testimony. Yet the public scrutiny of the 1880s—the racialized and scandalous cartoons and headlines included—contributed to her financial decline. Hill's association with Pleasant taints her and marks her as dirty. Whether she is paid for sex or demands a marriage contract for sex, matters less than the "fact" that she inhabited a deviant underworld of black women.[86]

In the Gilded Age, as these trials show, racial and sexual tensions continued to intrude upon—if not define—national debates over the power of the state, unregulated capitalism, and westward expansion. In an age when men like Sharon plundered the West's landscape, helping themselves to resources with reckless abandon, his adultery seemed in keeping with his public practices of greed and exploitation. Sharon's inability to control his sexual appetite merely provided another example of the excessive and unregulated behavior of robber barons. Pleasant's and Hill's attempt to control Sharon and make him accountable for this behavior ultimately failed.

* Lynn M. Hudson is Assistant Professor of History at California Polytechnic State University at San Luis Obispo.

Elle Meets the President: Weaving Navajo Culture and Commerce in the Southwestern Tourist Industry

Laura Jane Moore

DURING the spring of 1903, President Theodore Roosevelt included a two-hour stop in Albuquerque while on a speaking tour through the western territories. The Commercial Club of Albuquerque chose a Navajo woman, called Elle of Ganado, to weave a gift for the president—a textile rendition of his honorary Commercial Club membership card. Club members provided the design, which Elle wove quickly in hand-spun red, white, and blue yarn. During his tour of Albuquerque, Roosevelt visited the Commercial Club, where he received Elle's blanket, and he stopped by the Alvarado Hotel's Indian Building, where he met the weaver herself. An Albuquerque newspaper reported that upon meeting the weaver, the "president gave her a hearty shake and told her how much he appreciated her work. The little speech was interpreted and pleased the Indian woman beyond expression."[1]

Although her own thoughts were apparently "beyond expression," Elle's image spoke volumes to turn-of-the-century Americans, showing

---

* Laura Jane Moore, "Elle Meets the President: Weaving Navajo Culture and Commerce in the Southwestern Tourist Industry," *Frontiers: A Journal of Women's Studies* 22:1, (2001). ©2001 Frontiers, University of Nebraska Press. Reprinted by permission.

New Mexico as not only conquered but commercialized, safe for investment and safe for statehood. Indeed, Commercial Club members orchestrated this performance as part of a statehood campaign, a drive for integration into the social, economic, and political life of the United States, an effort that would not pay off for nearly ten more years. Elle and the president's meeting suggests ways in which race and gender, regional and national politics, culture and commerce interacted and were inextricably linked as the twentieth century began. The pivotal role that Elle played in Roosevelt's visit reveals that while we tend to think of women like Elle as marginalized historical figures, they were far from peripheral to the unfolding of twentieth-century American history. Not only can we better understand such women by placing them within the larger economic, cultural, and political context of their times, but we can better understand that context by putting a woman like Elle at its center.

Elle of Ganado, also called Asdzaa Lichii' (Red Woman) in Navajo, was born to the Black Sheep Clan and lived in the southern part of the Navajo Reservation near the Hubbell Trading Post in Ganado, Arizona. She might have been about fifty years old at the time she met Roosevelt, and she lived until 1924. At the suggestion of trader John Lorenzo Hubbell, she and her husband Tom began spending substantial periods of time in Albuquerque beginning in 1903 after the Fred Harvey Company opened its Indian Building as part of the Alvarado Hotel complex at the Santa Fe Railroad depot. Together with other Navajo and Pueblo families, they worked as arts and crafts demonstrators within the burgeoning southwestern tourist industry.[2]

Most scholarly literature on southwestern tourism examines the ironies and complexities of images of Indians portrayed as purely non-industrial producers of "traditional" handcrafts, "outside history, outside industrial capitalism" that had begun to emerge at the turn of the century.[3] Elle's Commercial Club blanket, however, unabashedly declared the link between Indian art and turn-of-the-century capitalism. It is a reminder that those who worked as demonstrators were, like all Americans at the time, entering new kinds of economic relationships that would affect their work and their communities in profound ways. Beyond their ideological implications, then, these tourist sites were workplaces to which a number of Native Americans agreed to travel for extended periods of time. The sites were also cultural crossroads at which negotiations took place between employers and employees, between young corporate and rural America, between white men and Indian families, between metropolitan and peripheral economies. This essay explores the contours of these crossroads, the compromises demanded and the benefits promised various participants.[4]

The Fred Harvey Company, it has been said, "invented" the Southwest as "America's Orient." Fred Harvey was an English immigrant who opened his first restaurant along the Santa Fe Railroad line in 1876 in Topeka, Kansas. From there the company grew into the first chain of restaurants and of railroad hotels. Harvey built his company's reputation on the notion of civilizing rail travel to the West by selling good food served by respectable young, white, single women called "Harvey girls." Combining hot meals, Harvey girls, and Indian images in their advertising, the company presented the West as an exotic but accessible tourist paradise. By the time of Harvey's death in 1901, his empire consisted of twenty-six restaurants, sixteen hotels, and twenty dining cars.[5]

The Harvey Company went into the Indian art business at the instigation of Harvey's daughter, Minnie Harvey Huckel, an avid Indian art collector. In 1902 she suggested that a display of Indian art be included in Albuquerque's new Harvey hotel, the Alvarado. Her husband, J. F. Huckel, a New Yorker who had been in the publishing business and was now a Fred Harvey vice president, began to commute from Harvey headquarters in Kansas City to Albuquerque, where he created the Fred Harvey Indian Department. The Huckels' collaboration with Harvey employee Herman Schweizer ensured the success of this venture. Schweizer, a German immigrant, had found his way to the Southwest in the 1880s, had jobbed silver and turquoise to Navajo silversmiths, and while working at the Harvey restaurant in Coolidge, New Mexico, had begun buying and selling Navajo arts and crafts—a successful sideline that caught Minnie Huckel's attention. Schweizer spent the rest of his life managing the Fred Harvey Indian Department. He had an eye and a taste for the Indian art business and soon built the Harvey Indian collection into a premiere showcase. This success was further facilitated by the architect Mary Colter who helped to design the Indian Building at the Alvarado and subsequently went to work full time for the company. Colter was an important force in developing a regional architectural style inspired by local, native design—spaces for the "staged authenticity" that became fundamental to southwestern tourism, and spaces designed for commercial transactions that also offered a seemingly behind-the-scenes view of Indian homelife.[6]

The development of southwestern tourism thus depended on diverse players who illustrate the various and complex forces at work at the turn of the century: Minnie Huckel, a wealthy woman and art patron; Mary Colter, a professional woman finding a career in the Southwest; J. F. Huckel, an elite eastern businessman; Herman Schweizer, a young, ambitious, Jewish immigrant; and a number of Native American artists, including Elle, worked together to invent the modern Southwest and to find a place for themselves within it. Each brought her or his own goals, background, and economic and cultural logic to their meeting. They did not always act out of positions of equality, but each were crucial players in the story. Most analyses of the Harvey Company and southwestern tourism in general tell the story from the Anglo participants' point of view, even when critiquing their use of Indians and Indian imagery. Although the individual, private thoughts and reactions of Indian workers such as Elle may never be known, careful reading of sources left mostly by those Anglo participants can help us examine their roles and experiences within the larger context of turn-of-the-century Navajo and American history.

Much recent scholarship has explored the elevation of Indian imagery in this period, even as Native Americans remained culturally, politically, and economically marginalized. Indian artisans were central figures in the invention of the Southwest. Traveling in the comfort of a berth on the Santa Fe railroad, white Americans could see exotic pockets of the nation where the industrialization, urbanization, and bureaucratization of the era had not yet, it seemed, taken hold. Yet in this period, as industrial capitalism spread and the Southwest was incorporated into the nation and the national market economy, it became, as Leah Dilworth explains, "increasingly clear that the development of the American West would depend on the metropolis for capital and cheap immigrant labor." Ironically, she continues, "The spectacle of Indian artisanal labor resurrected an ideology that declared precisely the opposite: That the rural artisan and the farmer were the backbone of the nation's economy."[7] The presence of hardworking, artistic Indians provided tourists with a heavily mediated—indeed artificially constructed—arena in which to feel they had safely encountered the real West through a glimpse of Indian homelife. Barbara Babock, Marta Weigle, and others have shown that the prominent place of female Indian artisans and their children in locales like the Fred Harvey Indian Building was crucial to the domestication of the image of the "wild" West. They call such sites "ethnic sets for exotic performances" or "human showcases" where "the companies staged authenticity by controlling the architectural setting, 'live' demonstrations and other expressive performances, museum and sales displays, publications, and virtually all associated exegesis."[8]

Tourists viewed Indians purportedly practicing their naturally artistic, premodern everyday lives, but the artists, too, were travelers who had moved from their rural homes to these tourist spaces in order to incorporate income from such work into their families' economic strategies. The idealized domestic tableaux offered at a Harvey House obscured a gender organization and economic system that differed markedly from that of Euro-Americans. It also ignored the cultural meanings that the Diné, or Navajos, themselves found in their textiles. Weaving was, and is, a highly respected activity that reflects and reinforces Navajo women's economic, cultural, and social centrality.[9] Navajo textiles had long been both market objects and unique cultural expressions embodying *hozho*, the central Navajo philosophical concept that connotes harmony, balance, goodness, and beauty. Weaving also reflects the power of thought and the combination of autonomy and cooperation that is so important to the Diné. Husbands build looms for their wives, and weavers sometimes work side by side at the same loom. At the same time, the design of a rug, as one weaver explains, "just has to be you," and, to quote weaver Mary Lee Begay, "takes a lot of hard thinking."[10] Weavers do not generally sketch out designs but rather conceive and then hold them in their minds as they work. A leading scholar of contemporary Navajo textiles, Ann Lane Hedlund, explains that weaving "represents a proper way to make a living or, putting it more exactly, to live"; weavers practice their art while "caring for their families, homes, and herds . . . and remembering the sacred stories, prayers, and songs that 'go with the weaving.'"[11]

Those "familes, homes, and herds" are organized around the principle of motherhood, a term that refers not just to biological mothers, but to the women of one's clan, the family's sheep herd, and the family's land. The Diné are matrilineal, tracing descent from the female side of the family, and matrilocal, with daughters living with their husbands and children near their mother. The primary familial bond is between a mother and child (not between a husband and wife); Navajos belong or are "born to" their mother's clan; and other clan members are their closest relatives. Individual women, men, and children own livestock and other property but share the care of herds and fields. Women generally control range land, and land use is typically inherited from mothers. Weaving, too, has always been dominated by women (though men can, and some do, weave), and weaving knowledge passes from generation to generation through kinship bonds.[12]

At the turn of the twentieth century, livestock products were the primary source of subsistence and of income, supplemented by farming and by trading other items, most importantly textiles, at the local trading post. Living in an often harsh and unpredictable environment, the Diné pooled resources along kinship lines. Economic specialization was not practical, but varied economic strategies and adaptability to changing environmental and historical forces were. Even while becoming more dependent on the national market economy, the Diné did not abandon their diversified subsistence economy or reciprocal economic expectations revolving around matrilineal kinship ties.[13]

Long before trading posts or Harvey houses, weaving had been one of many activities through which women contributed to the household economy. Between the seventeenth and nineteenth centuries, the Diné had increasingly oriented their economy and culture around sheep herds while developing much of what is now considered traditional Navajo culture. Navajo women used their sheep's wool to weave blankets and clothing for family use and for inter- and intratribal trade. By the early nineteenth century, Navajo blankets were prized within a wide regional market for their quality—so tightly woven they were water-proof—and their beauty.[14]

In 1865 U.S. troops that had wrested control of the region from Mexico two decades earlier implemented a scorched-earth policy, massacring herds and burning crops, in order to impoverish and defeat the Diné. Elle probably joined the approximately eight thousand Navajos who were moved to a tiny reservation near Fort Sumner in southeastern New Mexico called Bosque Redondo, or *Hweeldi* in Navajo. There they faced disease, death, and emotional and economic turmoil. Even though they were short on wool and given manufactured blankets and clothing, Navajo women nevertheless "set up looms and created blankets of strength and beauty."[15]

To the army officers at Bosque Redondo, Navajo women's commitment to their looms appeared not as evidence of resilience but proof of conquest. Long accustomed to the association of femininity, domesticity, and textile production, Anglo observers thought weaving augured well for Navajos' ability to adopt "civilized" gender roles. When American officials offered Navajos Anglo-style looms and spinning wheels, however, the Navajo women refused to use them or to work with the white women hired to instruct them, insisting on continuing with "their old plan of spinning and making blankets."[16] Weavers readily adopted some newly available materials, including commercial dyes and yarns, but insisted on controlling the means of production. Nor did they adopt Euro-American gender roles, but continued to ground their social organization and identity in matrilineal kinship relations. Despite cultural misreadings of the Navajo, weaving became a critical point of contact, valued by both groups but for different reasons.

After four years, American officials decided that relocating the Diné to Bosque Redondo had been a costly mistake, making a once self-sufficient tribe an unnecessary economic burden on the federal government. In 1868, eager to return home, a group of Navajo headmen signed a treaty establishing a reservation carved out of their traditional homeland. As soon as they returned, they set about resurrecting a pastoral economy using sheep and goats provided by the federal Office of Indian Affairs and taking advantage of a national boom in the wool market. White traders appeared in Navajo country to broker the sale of wool from Navajo herds to eastern markets. Trading posts sprouted along the new railroad lines and deeper within Navajo country. The Diné traded wool, sheep, textiles and other products for flour, coffee, sugar and other items they could not produce at home. Traders thus helped introduce the national market economy to the Diné while becoming cultural brokers as well. During the 1890s drought and a severe national depression lowered wool prices and ended the Diné's economic recovery, but they continued to center their lives around their sheep herds, grafting elements of the national market economy onto their subsistence economy.[17]

Weavers left traces of these historical changes and continuities in their textiles. They adopted designs from manufactured Pendleton blankets from Oregon that they bought at trading posts, experimented with serrate style designs inspired by Hispanic weaving, and increasingly used commercial yarns and dyes. The Indian Office provided finely spun yarn manufactured in Germantown, Pennsylvania, that allowed weavers to develop ever more intricate and complex designs. Some weavers began to include figurative elements such as trains in their textiles in a new "pictorial" style. When wool prices dropped in the 1890s, women apparently turned increasingly to weaving as a way to increase the value of their wool. New designs reflected changing concerns of the weavers and the changing market. Traders encouraged weaving styles they thought would sell well and regional styles named after neighboring posts emerged. For the most part, Navajos stopped weaving clothing and instead created what would come to be called rugs, meant not to be worn, but to be souvenirs of the West. Military personnel were among the first Anglo collectors, followed by growing numbers of explorers, scientists, government personnel, and finally tourists arriving with the new railroads.[18]

Railroads altered the economic, cultural, and social contours of the region. By the turn of the century, the Santa Fe dominated Albuquerque's economy and had practically built a whole new town around its depot. Railroads also shifted the region's perspective from a local economy oriented along a north–south axis facing Mexico to an east–west trajectory incorporated into the U.S. national economy. One of the byproducts of this process was the introduction of wage work and migrant labor to Native American communities. Many Navajo and other Indian men added income from railroad work to the contributions they made to their household economy. Meanwhile, as the Navajo economy became increasingly incorporated into the modern industrial economy of the United States, the inter- and intratribal blanket trade evaporated as southwestern Indians adopted white-style clothing and factory-made blankets. Navajo weavers adopted their art to a new and changing market that, though it did not generally pay producers well, yet could be crucial to the household economy. Navajo textiles had become a key commodity in southwestern economic development and were central to the income of traders and the growing tourist economy.[19] One of the most famous and successful trading posts, for example, was John Lorenzo Hubbell's in Ganado, Arizona, in the southern part of Navajo country near the New Mexico border. The Hubbell family eventually opened several other posts and became the main suppliers for the Harvey Company. They also became employment brokers, recruiting Navajos and Hopis, including Elle and Tom of Ganado, who were willing to work at Harvey houses as arts and crafts demonstrators.[20] Within the growing trading post economy, Navajo weavers found new and different customers, and they experimented with new materials and designs while maintaining traditional production techniques and continuing to create uniquely Navajo textiles. While the railroad introduced industrial capitalism to the rural Southwest, it also introduced the Southwest, or a particular image of the Southwest, to the world. Ironically, while some Indian men learned to participate in industrial wage work, the Santa Fe's tourist business perfected the image of Indians as naturally artistic pre-industrial craftspeople. Upon disembarking at Albuquerque, train travelers passed through the Harvey Indian Building on the way to the Alvarado lobby. The first thing they saw were weavers, potters, silversmiths, and basket makers, and Fred Harvey sales increased appreciably as a result of this encounter.

The Indian workers' primary job was to be on display for the tourists. In making arrangements for the demonstrators, Harvey Indian Department manager Herman Schweizer explained to the trader John Lorenzo Hubbell that "the principal thing [is] for them to be at work when trains are in. They should be working from 7:30 a. m. to noon.

They can work as much or as little as they want to in the afternoon but must come back after supper for about one hour for evening trains." In exchange the Harvey Company provided room and board and on at least one occasion Schweizer promised "double of what they are getting for their stuff on the reservation." This was a good enough deal, apparently, to entice a number of artists and their families away from their homes, farms, sheep, corn, and kin for two or three months at a time, long enough for good weavers to complete a large weaving project "if they bring blankets already started."[21]

Schweizer and Huckel always preferred a mix of women, men, and children to provide scenes of domestic, familial, artistic comradery. The ideal Navajo couple would include a weaver and a silversmith. Navajo women would weave, care for the children, cook, and perform janitorial duties, though accomplishing the latter out of the view of tourists.[22] Navajo silver work was still a somewhat new craft, and silversmiths were harder to find than weavers. Back in Navajo country, economic specialization in weaving or silversmithing would be unusual. Instead, arts and crafts work was integrated into diversified economic strategies. Even the Harvey men did not rely on their demonstrators for quality silver work. More important to them was to have a man who knew enough to act like a silversmith while being "a good man," that is, reliable, honest, and hardworking. His tasks would include cleaning and upkeep on the buildings and usually translating.[23]

Many Indian artists worked at some point for the Fred Harvey Company. The San Ildefonso Pueblo potter Maria Martinez and her husband Julian worked as Harvey demonstrators early in their careers, before developing the black pottery style that brought so much fame. The Hopi-Tewa potter Nampeyo also worked for the Harvey Company on a few occasions, demonstrating her Sikyatki revival style. Nampeyo had already begun to make a name for herself, which the Harvey Company cashed in on when they hired her.[24] Elle, in contrast, was not well-known until her work for the Harvey Company made her one of the only other Indian artists with name recognition in the early twentieth century. Elle's willingness to stay away from home for long periods of time and to be photographed over and over again made her one of the Harvey Company's favorite employees.[25] She and her husband were local celebrities in Albuquerque, their activities documented regularly in the town's newspapers. They met and were photographed with numerous national celebrities, too, from the Chicago Cubs to "America's sweetheart," Mary Pickford. Encouraged by their success in Albuquerque, the Harvey Company began employing demonstrators for other sites as well. Elle and other artists traveled around the country representing the company at expositions in San Francisco, Chicago, and elsewhere. They also worked in other Harvey houses, most notably at the Grand Canyon, where living exhibits of Indian "homelife" were built into the tourist spaces.[26]

Architect Mary Colter based the architecture of the Grand Canyon's Hopi House on that at Oraibi, one of the oldest inhabited villages in the United States. Hopi demonstrators lived upstairs, Navajos camped nearby, and downstairs salesrooms also invoked Indian "homelife." By emphasizing art, and deemphasizing other economic activities carried out in actual Hopi villages, the Hopi House helped to define Native American culture narrowly by its marketable, artistic products. While Harvey publications extolled the Hopi House as a "reproduction of the homes of this tribe as they are found on their reservation," it was not a reproduction but an interpretation of Indian life in which certain characteristics stood in for Indian culture. The inaccuracy of this "staged authenticity" is highlighted by the number of Navajos who enacted their artistic domestic life at the *Hopi* House, where Navajo weaving and silver were especially important commodities.[27]

Authenticity was itself historically constructed, and it changed over time. At the Grand Canyon, Huckel insisted that Navajo women "have and *use* some of their homemade pots to cook." At the same time, Schweizer and Huckel solicited Hubbell's help in securing an "old Navaho forge . . . perhaps a piece of steel rail or whatever there may be that is homemade" for silversmiths working at the Hopi House.[28] Authenticity, then, did not require the complete rejection of technology or industrialization; Navajo silver work, in fact, was not a traditional craft and relied on modern technology, in this case steel. What seemed to be most important in indicating authenticity was the word "homemade," which suggested self-sufficiency: that a Navajo man could build a forge out of a piece of steel rail; that a Navajo woman could feed her family out of homemade pots; that for these Indians art and labor were integrated into everyday life. Such items as Navajo pottery might merely serve as decoration in modern white American homes in which the art of self-sufficiency had been lost, but for Indians they must still be *used*. Harvey images of Indian artisans played off concerns emerging from the arts and crafts movement about the alienation of art from labor in the modern industrial world, the growing dichotomy between the traditional and the modern, and a nostalgia for a mythological past.[29] Still, the art itself did not (yet) have to be so pure: "Modern" designs were especially popular, and weavers could use manufactured yarns and dyes as long as they wove them by hand.

As for the Diné, their identity was less tenuously tied to material objects such as stoves or pots than was the Anglo definition of an "authentic" Indian. On one occasion Tom and Elle asked a Harvey manager to provide buckskin and other materials so that Tom could make moccasins for Elle.[30] This story suggests an impressive level of self-sufficiency that might reinforce Anglo understandings of Indian authenticity: Even if they did not hunt the buck and cure the hide themselves, they also did not buy the manufactured product. But the cost of a pair of shoes may have been less of an issue for the couple than a deeper cultural undercurrent. As a Navajo woman interviewed in the 1990s explained, moccasins "were first worn by the holy people and reflect our culture and our identity as Diné. . . . It is by a Navajo's moccasin the Holy People recognize that a person is a Diné and who that person is." Indeed, establishing this identity may have been especially important to demonstrators like Elle who had journeyed so far from home. Moreover, the construction of the moccasins is critical because the sole "represents mother earth" and the top, which is "dyed red to represent the rainbow . . . is father sky." The sinew that ties together the sole and the top represents lightning and thus the "union of mother earth and father sky [which] brings forth all life." As when a Navajo weaves, the process of making moccasins expresses hozho, harmony between nature and the supernatural, and the power of thought: "We think about how we are going to make the moccasins, we plan out how best to make the moccasins, we use our thinking and planning put into action when we make the moccasins, and when we are done we have moccasins to protect our feet and give us comfort."[31] In other words, the material, the color, and the process of constructing the moccasins would have been more important to Elle and Tom than that the finished product was "homemade."

Diné identity depended on relationships to land, kin, and livestock, relationships that income from weaving could help maintain. In contrast to Elle and Tom, most weavers were unwilling to stay away from home for long periods of time. For that reason, most of the rugs sold in Harvey houses were woven not by demonstrators, who could not in any case have produced the necessary volume, but by women back in Navajo country who combined weaving with their other daily activities. Often these weavers bought packaged dyes at their trading post. Sometimes they spun and carded wool from their own sheep, but often they received wool from a trader as an advance on their rug, or perhaps they paid another woman to process wool for them. Weaving was thus part of both a local and national economy, combining traditional means of production with materials and marketing strategies made available by industrial capitalism.

Presenting "authentic," "traditional," "ancient" Indian culture to the tourist market was crucial to the economic development of the Southwest, yet in both practical and ideological ways it could clash with official federal Indian policy. In day-to-day business practice, for example, the Harvey people took Navajo polygamy—the bane of Christian missionaries—in stride. In fact, polygamy might have made Harvey managers' job easier by providing more adults, especially weavers, per family to take care of various chores. Similarly, the disjuncture between educating Indian children in the Protestant, individualistic, capitalist work ethic that lay at the heart of assimilationist policy ran counter to Huckel and Schweizer's desire for demonstrators to bring along their children who were "one of the chief attractions to the traveling public."[32] The Harvey men had to obtain Indian agents' permission for the children to accompany their families. The agents were employees of the federal Indian Office whose policy was to wean Indian children *away* from traditional culture, the very culture that was being preserved, commodified, and marketed at the Grand Canyon.

Meanwhile, Harvey managers also found some elements of traditional culture trying, and they worried frequently about "spoiled"

Indians having a bad influence on other demonstrators.[33] While Indians were asked to demonstrate the appearance of self-sufficiency, attitudes of independence could get them sent home. Demonstrators were to be viewed by, but not interact with, tourists, except within prescribed limits. Most importantly, the Harvey employers wanted demonstrators to act as passive producers rather than active participants in the Indian art market. As anthropologist John Hudson explained to his wife Grace Hudson about the Pomo demonstrators he helped the Harvey Company hire, what "the Harvey's [*sic*] want is the attraction to visitors and monopoly of all work done."[34]

Demonstrators who tried to take business into their own hands, as did a silversmith called Taos, threatened this monopoly. "He is making silver for other Indians and they are selling it," Huckel complained to Hubbell. "He is going over town and selling it and also selling it to our guests on the quiet. Taos has been spoiled by his experience at St. Louis" during the world's fair and, though a "silversmith is quite an attraction," he was becoming uncontrollable. In the end, they sent him home with his wife even before she had completed the blanket she was weaving, which they bought for twenty dollars. Taos received thirty-one dollars, although he asked for $36.50. Harvey manager Snively refused him the additional five-fifty "as I thought he was trying to skin me." He also refused "to pay him $12.50 for putting Pins in 50 buttons for Hat Pins which was about two days' work" but "compromised with him at 12 1/2 cents each."[35]

The dispute with Taos was not the only time that these tourist spaces, primarily dedicated to the commodification of women's work, became arenas for conflicts among men. Shortly before sending Taos home, another Navajo, called Long Man, who in Schweizer's opinion had not been working out well anyway, was "getting troublesome and stubborn. . . . He is pretty much of a mischief maker."[36] "I've had a lot of trouble with the Indians lately in little petty ways," Schweizer wrote Hubbell late in May of 1905 from the Grand Canyon. "The Longman sort of queered the whole bunch, he seems to be a sort of evil spirit reads the stars and all that sort of thing."[37]

This last complaint indicates that although demonstrators willingly traveled into these white tourist sites, they maintained ways of looking at the world that did not always mesh well with their employers' assumptions about market forces and employee responsibilities. Elle and Tom may have been the Harvey Company's favorite employees, but they were not particularly acculturated. Although willing to stay for several months each year, they would go home for reasons that mystified the Harvey people, for example, when Schweizer wrote Hubbell that, "Elle has rheumatism and Tom says Long mans saw the sign and she'd die if she didn't get medicine."[38] In this case, Tom, Long Man, and Elle did not mean western medicine to be found in pills or at hospitals, but the Navajo medicine around which their religious beliefs were organized. Indeed, because the Navajo worldview centers on maintaining well-being through hozho, cultures could clash most irrevocably around the issue of health.

At Harvey houses different worldviews grounded in different economic and gender systems collided. Within this context, it should come as no surprise that even a woman's body could become the site of conflict, as happened to one of the favorite demonstrator families headed by Maria Antonio and Miguelito during the summer of 1905. In May the family began planning to return to the reservation in anticipation of another of Miguelito's wives, Agippa, giving birth. Huckel and Schweizer were not happy with their decision to leave. In a letter to Hubbell, Huckel wrote: "It seems to me he would be much better off if he stays where he is. He is earning a pretty fair salary," and the family was "doing well." Their young daughter, Tonsi-pah, also a weaver, had been ill, but was "quite recovered. Of course, if he is set on going home, I presume it is not advisable for us to object or persuade him not to."[39] The timing was not good for the Harvey Company, as other demonstrators were also "restless," "lonesome," and "homesick," and Elle and Tom were also away.[40] During June, Schweizer and Huckel, with Hubbell's help, tried to make arrangements for replacements while waiting eagerly for Elle and Tom's return.[41]

Then in mid-June Agippa gave birth, probably prematurely. The Harvey people called in a Dr. Pearce who had attended demonstrators before with success. This time he predicted that the baby would not live a month. Huckel told Hubbell, "Agippa was not very ill in Dr. Pearce's opinion, but he would be obliged to attend to her and take her to the hospital."[42] Later Huckel explained, "We have had so much hospital and other work connected with Migelito's family that I think he believes thoroughly in the 'white man's' doctor."[43] They did not anticipate any problems. Still, Huckel suggested that the family return to the reservation once Agippa was well enough: "I feel if this baby should die at Albuquerque or Agippa should get very ill there the Indians might think it was on account of their living there." He apparently had some understanding of Navajos' need to avoid places associated with death and realized that a death at a Harvey House could be disastrous for the demonstrator program. But Agippa never recovered sufficiently to return home, and, as she got sicker, the limits on this family's acceptance of white ways were severely tested. Schweizer informed Hubbell, "Migelito took his wife out of the hospital and he has her down by the river in a grove of cottonwoods where he built a temporary shelter for her and says he is going to cure her."[44]

Though angry at Miguelito and reprimanded by his boss, Schweizer apparently did not know how to stop this retreat to traditional medicine. In fact, the Harvey men knew that Miguelito was a singer, that is, a Navajo doctor and religious leader. Just the previous fall he had performed a healing ceremony for Tom when doctors at Albuquerque's St. Joseph's Hospital failed to cure his pneumonia. On that occasion Miguelito and Tom's traditional ways brought Fred Harvey good publicity as the Albuquerque paper followed Tom's progress.[45] Born during the Navajos' confinement at Bosque Redondo in the 1860s, Miguelito must have been about forty in 1905.[46] During the 1930s, he and his family would act as important informants for the anthropological work then undertaken with increasing frequency in Navajo country. In her classic studies from that period, anthropologist Gladys Reichard would celebrate Miguelito's knowledge of Navajo religion and Maria Antonio's knowledge of weaving.[47] In the summer of 1905, Miguelito knew what he was doing in that cottonwood grove on the banks of the Rio Grande, although a full-scale sing back home surrounded by a crowd of relatives and friends would surely have been more effective.

When Agippa died, Schweizer, furious, wrote Hubbell, "You can tell Miguelito when he returns that there is no one to blame for her dying but himself." Schweizer insisted that the doctors had told them that she "was bound to die unless she was operated on *immediately.*" In fact, Schweizer finally got her to the hospital, but "It was too late. . . . Dr. Pearce told me that there was no excuse whatever for her dying." He insisted that from then on, they would have a stricter policy in which demonstrators "will have to take [their] physician[']s orders or go back to the reservation on the first train."[48]

Miguelito, Maria Antonio, and Tonsi-pah hurried home after Agippa's death, "too nervous" even "to finish their blankets."[49] But they soon returned. As demonstrators, they moved between their rural homes and Harvey houses and occasionally on longer trips to expositions, integrating demonstration work into their diversified economy. Their movement provides yet another example of the back and forth between "farm and factory" that marked the daily lives of so many Americans in the early twentieth century. But Harvey houses were unusual factories. Rather than wholesale celebrations of technological progress, they were meant to be oases from the modern world. More than mere workplaces, they presumed to display the artistic homelife of what the Harvey Company termed "America's First Families." But for the Indian demonstrators, home was not the Hopi House.[50]

Because the Harvey Company's business *was* tourism, the demonstrator program was, in a sense, far more important to them than to their Native American employees. Schweizer liked "to see my factory in full blast," but he constantly struggled to keep enough demonstrators on hand: "Everybody going to the Hopi House is asking where the Hopi Indians are," he moaned to Hubbell on one occasion, ignoring the fact that many of his favorite Hopi House demonstrators were Navajo. With Miguelito's family gone after Agippa's death, only Tom and Elle remained at the Grand Canyon, making "the Indian proposition . . . really a farce." He pleaded with Hubbell to persuade Miguelito to return or to make some other, really "any arrangement," just, "get some Indians to the Canyon at once."[51]

"It was up to the family when they wanted to quit and go home," remembered one woman who as a child had accompanied her mother to Albuquerque for two months.[52] And so they did, for dramatic reasons such as Agippa's death or in response to more quotidian or seasonal necessities—to plant their corn, check in with family and friends, attend ceremonies, take care of business, because they just wanted to, or, in the case of one man called the "Old Silversmith," because "people are bothering too much trying to take his picture."[53] Demonstrator work provided some welcome income as well as travel and adventure. It may even have appealed to a few demonstrators as a way to practice and preserve traditional crafts. Most demonstrators, however, were likely less concerned with facilitating cross-cultural exchange than in the satisfaction of earning decent money for work that was of both economic and cultural value to them and their communities. For some, such as Agippa, this decision could lead to tragedy. For others, such as Elle, it may also have entailed sacrifice that was deemed worthwhile. In any case, in the early twentieth century such craftwork was integrated into Navajos' diversified subsistence economy even when practiced in the "staged authenticity" of Albuquerque's Indian Building or the Grand Canyon's Hopi House.

While the Diné brought economic assumptions based on that diversified subsistence economy and reciprocal economic obligations to Harvey houses, their employers maintained faith in market forces and economic specialization. Part of the justification for the marketing of tradition was, according to the Harvey people, that it would benefit all concerned: "The railroad company is very much interested in the success of this project," Huckel wrote Hubbell, "and the tourists are as much so, and I think it will help eventually the.... Indians by creating a market for their goods."[54]

Through their art, it seemed, Indians could be incorporated into the national market economy and could find a future in modern America, as long as there was a market for their goods. "Staged authenticity" thus suggested an alternative to assimilation: Indian cultures had unique contributions to make, and perhaps they were worth preserving, at least in part. It also served to define Indians as "naturally artistic," a positive but ultimately constraining view.

The conquest of Indian America included not only military force and boarding schools but also the ideological reduction of native cultures to their marketable artistic products—an example, perhaps, of what Barbara A. Babcock calls "modern power," replacing "violence and force with the 'gentler' constraint of uninterrupted visibility, 'the gaze.'"[55] A woman like Elle would not languish in prison like Geronimo, but she was captured many times—on film.

Yet, while in the tourist literature Indians were presented as silent, "beyond expression," a woman like Elle was hardly mute, even if she did not speak English. Remembered decades later as "the boss of the weaving outfit in Albuquerque"[56] she, like her husband Tom and Miguelito and Maria Antonio, found a role in the modern world and a way to support herself by embodying the traditional Indian artisan yearned for by modern Americans. She took on that employment and even met the president without abandoning her ties to her rural home, her kin, her language, her Navajo name, or her religion. In his speech in Albuquerque the day they met, Roosevelt praised those with "adventurous temper and . . . iron resolution . . . who first tempted the shaggy wilderness and turned it into habitations for man." His meeting with Elle is a reminder that the West had been inhabited by "man"—men and women—long before the Anglo conquest, and that diverse groups would continue struggling to make a home there in the twentieth century, a task that might take an even stronger resolution and more adventurous spirit than those manly pioneers Roosevelt had in mind.[57] Historically and historiographically, we have tended to examine more closely the perspective that Roosevelt brought to his meeting with Elle, but just because we do not know what Asdzaa Lichii' said about this encounter does not mean that she said nothing. Despite the lack of written sources from her perspective, we can shift our frame of reference to make the central actor in the story the weaver instead of the president. In doing so, we can deepen our understanding of the ways in which diverse Americans entered the twentieth century and forged our common history.

Much rural women's history has analyzed how women adopted products of domestic labor to the early twentieth century's expanding national industrial economy. The Navajo rug trade fits neatly into this larger historiographical context, but it is worth remembering that Navajo textiles had always been commodities as well as cultural expressions. As Navajo weavers became symbols of the modern Southwest, Navajo women who wove found new markets for their craft. Such marketplaces were sites of compromise and confusion, exploitation and resistance. But, as Diné, weavers continued to expect both financial remuneration and cultural respect for their work. One professional weaver, following in Elle's footsteps, explained in 1986: "Your mind and prayers are connected" to weaving; a rug "just has to be you. . . . I want the Navajo weaver to get lots of money for their weaving. I go several places to teach that." Weaving remains a good way to help face difficult economic circumstances, despite the low return per hour of labor. Younger women, she predicted, will continue to take up weaving because if "there are no jobs for them . . . they think about weaving." Echoing the words of many Navajo weavers over the centuries, she explained, "I raised my children" with weaving, and "with my weaving I get what I want."[58]

★ Laura Jane Moore is an Assistant Professor of History at the University of Georgia.

Laura Jane Moore's essay is drawn from research she did for her dissertation, "The Navajo Rug Trade: Gender, Art, Work, and Modernity in the American Southwest, 1870s–1930s." She received a Ph.D. in U.S. History in 1999 from the University of North Carolina at Chapel Hill. Most of her research and writing has focused on connections between women's history and Native American history, including an M.A. thesis on the Omaha LaFlesche sisters and a recent article on the Apache woman warrior Lozen.

I first told the story of Elle meeting the president at the Fifth Annual Conference on Rural and Farm Women in Historical Perspective held in 1995 in Chevy Chase, Maryland. I would like to thank Lu Ann Jones and Anne Effland for making my participation there possible. Since then the paper has been through many permutations. My thanks go to Jacquelyn Hall, Nancy Hewitt, John Kasson, Marla Miller, and Molly Rozum for their help on the dissertation chapter from which this article is drawn. Participants in the Duke-UNC Feminist History Group and Nancy Shoemaker, as panel commentator, at the 1999 Western History Association meeting provided useful suggestions and lively discussions of earlier versions. Finally, I am grateful to Kathleen Howard, Joan Jensen, Marla Miller, Kathleen Tabaha, and an anonymous outside reader for their thoughtful comments on drafts of the present article and to John Moore and Roberto Mosheim for crucial aid in its completion.

The Eastmans and the Luhans:
Interracial Marriage between White Women
and Native American Men, 1875–1935

Margaret D. Jacobs

T a lavish wedding and reception in New York City in
1891 Elaine Goodale, daughter of a prominent New
England family, married Charles Eastman, a member of
the Wahpeton band of the Santee Sioux (Dakotas). Writing in her
memoirs, Elaine declared, "I gave myself wholly in that hour to the
traditional duties of wife and mother, abruptly relinquishing all
thought of an independent career for the making of a home. At the
same time, I embraced with a new and deeper zeal the conception of
life-long service to my husband's people." Charles, a medical doctor,
described himself a few months before their marriage by writing, "I
was soon to realize my long dream—to become a complete man! I
thought of little else than the good we two could do together."[1] Both
Charles and Elaine were members of a group of reformers who sought
to solve the so-called Indian problem through assimilation, and they
portrayed their marriage as a natural means to overcome Indian
"backwardness" and poverty. The white woman would further uplift

---

★ Margaret D. Jacobs, "The Eastmans and the Luhans: Interracial Marriage between
White Women and Native American Men, 1875–1935," *Frontiers: A Journal of
Women's Studies* 23:3 (2002). © 2002 Frontiers, University of Nebraska Press.
Reprinted by permission.

her already civilized Dakota husband, and the couple would work diligently to serve his people.

Fifty years later New York socialite Mabel Dodge moved to Taos, New Mexico, with her Russian émigré husband, the painter Maurice Sterne. Mabel soon became entranced with Tony Luhan, a Taos Pueblo Indian. Describing her feelings, Mabel wrote in her memoirs,

> I had a strange sense of dislocation, as though I were swing-
> ing like a pendulum over the gulf of the canyon, between the
> two poles of mankind, between Maurice and Tony; and
> Maurice seemed old and spent and tragic, while Tony was
> whole and young in the cells of his body, with his power
> unbroken and hard like the carved granite rock, yet older than
> the Germanic Russian whom the modern world had
> destroyed.[2]

Mabel and Tony eventually divorced their respective spouses and married each other in 1923. In this case Mabel saw herself as a bridge between Tony's people and her own; she envisioned her marriage not as a vehicle by which to uplift and "serve her husband's people," but as a means to save her own race from the destruction wrought by the modern world.

The stories of the Eastmans' and Luhans' marriages contain all the necessary ingredients for two "racy" novels, but they also provide more than voyeuristic romances. As Peggy Pascoe has written, "For scholars interested in the social construction of race, gender, and culture, few subjects are as potentially revealing as the history of interracial mar-riage."[3] Both the Eastmans and the Luhans operated at the outer bound-aries of American racial norms. Yet, through writing and speaking about their marriages, both couples worked to transform the racial ideologies of their times. Similarly both couples were bound by the gender norms of their respective eras but they also actively reshaped gender and sexual conventions. The great majority of literature on interracial marriage has focused on laws forbidding interracial marriage and the court cases that ensued to challenge these laws. Another large part of the literature focuses on European and/or white American social attitudes toward interracial marriages. Until recently most studies of interracial marriage also focused almost exclusively on couples designated as white and black.[4] This essay differs from such previous work in two important ways. First, I examine a little-studied configuration—white women and Indian men—and its changing meaning in American society.[5] And second, rather than asking what white Americans thought about such liaisons, I instead consider how interracial couples themselves defended their choices and navigated the often-hostile terrain upon which they lived. I also examine the role interracial couples themselves played in reshaping public attitudes toward their marriages. It is, of course, impossible to generalize from only two such interracial marriages; this article should be viewed less as a definitive statement on the subject and more as a tentative step into the shallow end of a deep pool of material on the interplay between social currents, ebbing and flowing notions of gender and race, and interracial couples' own actions and movements to stay afloat.

Analyses of interracial unions comprise but one part of a new intellectual pursuit—critical race theory, an exploration of the changing racial categorization of ethnic "minorities" in the United States. Bolstering the work of scientists who have found no genetic or biological basis for racial categorization, critical race theorists have analyzed the adaptable, dynamic, and fabricated quality of race by studying how certain groups who were once considered non-white eventually became white, enjoying all the privileges that attended advancement in the racial hierarchy.[6] Studies of interracial love, sex, and marriage between peoples categorized as Asians, American Indians, African Americans, Mexicans, and whites have complicated our understanding of the way that racial categories are constructed, dismantled, and reassembled.[7]

Such studies have made it increasingly difficult to use racial terms such as "white," "black," and "Indian" without quotation marks or tedious sentence structures. Yet if such terms have no objective basis, they nevertheless retain their power as terms derived from historical and social processes. As George Frederickson puts it, "It would be a mistake to infer that, once invented, [race does] not become durable and enormously influential."[8] I use such racial terms to denote socially and culturally contrived designations that have deep historical roots in American society.

As Pascoe argues, a study of interracial marriage can also yield a greater understanding of the construction of gender norms as well. Just as with the study of race, women's historians and other feminist theorists have for decades documented the fleeting nature of gender norms and argued that gender is not a fixed set of notions that directly correlates with biological differences between the male and female sex.[9] Many scholars of intermarriage have ignored gender; they have made little distinction between attitudes toward and laws aimed at relationships between white men and non-white women and those directed toward unions between white women and non-white men.[10] But, as a growing number of other historians have shown, American society has had markedly different attitudes toward interracial marriage depending on the gender of the white person involved. In general, interracial relationships between white men of the colonizing, dominant group and nonwhite women of colonized, conquered, and/or enslaved groups have been tolerated. Although laws in many colonies and states forbid interracial marriage between white men and black women, for example, many white slave owners commonly engaged in forced sex, concubinage, and informal relationships with their female slaves without social opprobrium.[11] As we shall see, relationships between white men and Indian women were similarly tolerated within American society. Liaisons between white men and nonwhite women did not violate the hierarchical order that developed between European Americans, African Americans, and American Indians. Rather, they represented extensions and reinforcements of colonialism, conquest, and domination.

As David Fowler, Kathleen Brown, and Martha Hodes have pointed out, however, white Americans were much more threatened by interracial sex and marriage that involved white women and non-white men. Where there was a higher incidence of such liaisons, as in Virginia and Maryland, colonies and states were much more likely to pass laws against interracial marriage.[12] When white women and non-white men engaged in sexual relationships or married, they violated the colonial, racial, and patriarchal order. Within this order, white men dominated both their daughters and wives as well as groups of subjugated peoples such as American Indians and African Americans. By law, white women were economic, social, and sexual possessions of white men, therefore a nonwhite man who "possessed" a white woman undermined the gendered and racialized dominance of white men. The children of such unions also threatened the social order, especially since southern colonies had conveniently passed laws establishing that children followed the condition of their mothers. Thus a union between a white woman and a nonwhite man could allow a child of a "Negro" or Indian man to be legally white.

In the history of the mainland United States, forty-two states, colonies, or territories passed laws against marriage between people categorized as belonging to different races. Most legislatures focused on relationships between whites and "Negroes" or "mulattos," but three colonies and fourteen states prohibited marriages between whites and Indians. Louisiana and North Carolina also banned marriages between Indians and "Negroes." Twelve states or territories forbid marriages between "Orientals" and whites.[13] Yet if laws against interracial marriage were not as common for Indian-white couples as for black-white couples, social taboos could be as powerful as legislative acts in shaping the lives of white women and their Indian husbands or lovers.

In the colonial era in American history there was widespread opposition to marriage between white women and Native American men. In fact, it was assumed that, as Brian Dippie explains, "The white woman would ordinarily be the unwilling victim in a union consummated through force—that is, as the captive ravished by her Indian captor, her body defiled, her spirit still pure."[14] According to historians Native Americans did use captivity to avenge the deaths in war of tribal members or to replace lost family members. Some captives were tortured and put to death; others were ritually adopted and could become full-fledged members of the tribe. Captive girls and young women were more likely to be adopted than killed, and many went on to marry and raise families among their captors. English colonists were surprised and alarmed by the numbers of English captives who chose to remain with their Indian captors, even when given the chance to be "redeemed." In one famous case in 1703, Eunice Williams was captured at age seven along with her entire family from Deerfield, Massachusetts. At age sixteen she married a converted Catholic Mohawk Indian from the Kahnawake Mission in Canada and the couple had at least two daughters who married Indian men. Until her death at age ninety-five, Eunice "preferred the Indian mode of life, and the haunts of Indians, to the unutterable grief of her father and friends."[15]

Significantly, white opposition in the colonial period to marriages between white women and Indian men seemed to have centered more on differences of religion than on conceptions of race or skin color. Eunice Williams's family objected to her marriage to a Mohawk man more because he did not share the Puritan religion than because he was Indian. Her family repeatedly sought to "redeem" her, that is, to bring her back into the Puritan fold.[16] From the late eighteenth through the nineteenth centuries, however, new objections by whites surfaced that were based more on a belief in insurmountable biological and physical differences between Indians and whites. This change in attitudes is well illustrated in an episode that occurred in Cornwall, Connecticut, in the 1820s. Two young Cherokee men, John Ridge and Elias Boudinot, had converted to Christianity and been sent to study at the Cornwall Foreign Mission School. Both men fell in love with and eventually married white women. The townspeople were incensed and demanded that the Foreign Mission School close. After their wedding Ridge and his bride, Sarah Northrup, had to be hustled into a coach and at every station stop from Cornwall back to Cherokee country in present-day Georgia crowds of angry people jeered the young couple. The editor of one Connecticut newspaper remarked that some people believed Sarah "ought to be publicly whipped, the Indian hung, and the [girl's] mother drown'd." Once news of Elias Boudinot and Harriet Gold's engagement leaked out, Harriet had to be hidden in a neighbor's house for protection. On the village green, in full view of both her hiding place and her parents' home, two young men laid an effigy of Harriet on a funeral pyre; her own brother lit the fire.[17]

In contrast, white American attitudes toward white men who took Indian concubines or wives in the period before the Civil War were much more lenient. The attitude toward such men was a sense of mild disapproval and sympathetic understanding; since these men lived in remote frontier outposts where there were few white women, they simply had to take Indian women as last resorts.[18] According to Richard Slotkin, white Americans gradually transformed the white frontiersman who consorted with Indian women into a "hero rather than a racial traitor." Because these frontiersmen were so integral to English colonization of the North American continent eventually their liaisons with Indian women were excused and even largely ignored.[19]

In contrast, why were unions of white women and Indian men seen as so scandalous, so threatening? Clearly it was no longer a religious issue. John Ridge and Elias Boudinot were practicing Christians who were training to convert other Cherokees to Christianity. By the 1820s a notion had emerged that there was an essential biological difference between Indians and whites, and it made many whites recoil in disgust and dismay from such marriages. A white woman who preferred a "savage" over one of her own "blood" upset the supposedly natural racial order, that the "civilized," white conqueror maintained superiority over the "savage red-skinned" Indian.

Interracial relationships between white women and Indian men also threatened predominant nineteenth-century American views of gender relations. America still operated under the notion of the *feme covert*; when a woman married she became entirely "covered" by her husband. Any property she brought to the marriage as well as her legal identity became subsumed under her mate's. As Linda Kerber has shown, a married woman possessed no independent relationship to the state; her position was constantly mediated through that of her husband's. Thus, to a society that adhered to the feme covert, a white woman who married an Indian would become Indian. The local Cornwall newspaper editor, in fact, argued that through marrying John Ridge, Sarah Northrup "had thus made herself a squaw."[20] White men would lose their patriarchal power over a white woman who married an Indian, and, in the process, Indian men would gain a power and a prerogative that many white men believed should be theirs alone. The status of any children born to such interracial couples also troubled white Americans. As with the children of white masters and their black slave women, it was assumed that the children of white men and Indian women were Indian. But what of the children of white women and Indian men? Should they follow the condition of their mother? Should such mixed-race children be granted the status and privilege of whiteness? Neither white nor Indian, such children made a mockery of racial categories, revealing their instability and impermanence.

Yet not all white Americans subscribed to these views. A sizable number of social activists and other public figures embraced a more environmentally and culturally determined view of racial difference. In the meeting between white women and Indian men, they suggested that Indian men might be positively influenced to move toward "civilization." Lydia Maria Child, abolitionist and women's rights advocate, published *Hobomok* in 1824. This novel was set during the first decades of the Massachusetts Bay Colony, in which the heroine of the story, Mary Conant, marries an Indian. Although Mary's father disapproves of her choice of mate, her white friend Sally believes Hobomok "was the best Indian I ever knew. . . . He seems almost like an Englishman."[21] Child's novel intimated that intermarriage between whites and Indians could serve as a positive force for transforming Indians into Englishmen or whites. As a feminist, Child did not adhere to the notion that a white woman who married an Indian man would take on his condition, that is, become an Indian. Instead, the woman would maintain her civilized position and serve as a guiding influence on her Indian husband.

By the second half of the nineteenth century, Child's belief that white women might civilize Indian men through marriage had gained greater currency. After the Civil War a movement of white reformers emerged that had become intensely interested in righting the wrongs that had been inflicted upon American Indians. This group of reformers quickly became convinced that isolating Native Americans on reservations was not the solution to the "Indian problem." Rather, they insisted, assimilation was the answer. If Indians could be uplifted and civilized, they believed, the United States would no longer have a significant number of impoverished, backward, and wronged people living off the government.[22] To some reformers, adopting Child's view, interracial marriage between white women and Native American men offered a "natural" way of assimilating Native Americans. Elaine Goodale seems to have grown to share this viewpoint.

Elaine had been raised in a stable, middle-class home in New England. As a young adult she went to work at Hampton Institute,

General Samuel Armstrong's school in Virginia for newly emancipated African Americans and newly conquered Plains Indians. Teaching English to former Lakota warriors, Elaine became convinced that the only way Indians could survive in the modern world was through education.[23] In 1885, longing to see the Indian country where many of her students came from, she set off on a tour of the Dakota Territory. At the age of twenty-two Elaine convinced the Episcopal Bishop in Dakota Territory to allow her to set up a school in the White River Camp on the Lower Brulé Sioux reservation. In 1889 she took a respite from her work among the Lakotas and returned home to write articles and give paid lectures regarding her experiences and perspectives on Indian life and policy. When Thomas Morgan became the commissioner of Indian affairs he favored a more systematic system of government-run day schools and appointed Elaine Supervisor of Education in the Dakotas where she was responsible for overseeing sixty schools spread out across hundreds of miles.[24]

In 1890, as a new Ghost Dance movement spread to the Plains Indians, local whites and the new Indian agent reacted with alarm because they believed the Ghost Dancers were preparing for war rather than praying for a return to their traditional way of life. As white concern grew into hysteria the government agent closed all the schools and ordered all government employees, including Elaine, and "friendly" Indians to report to the Pine Ridge Agency. Feeling that they were unnecessarily being held under martial law, Elaine pleaded with agency officers to let the so-called "Friendlies" return home and to reopen the day schools. Instead, white alarm over the Ghost Dance increased. Elaine busied herself by preparing a Christmas celebration for the Lakotas at the agency.[25] In the meantime, she also met the new agency physician, Dr. Charles Eastman.

Charles Eastman, named Ohiyesa by his Lakota family, was a member of the Wahpeton band of the Santee Sioux (Dakotas) who lived in present-day Minnesota. His mother died shortly after his birth, leaving him to be raised in a very traditional manner by his paternal grandmother. In 1862 a band of disgruntled Santee Sioux rose up in rebellion and killed many white settlers in the area when the Indian agent failed to deliver rations on time but prohibited the starving Sioux from hunting game off the reservation. After this incident, known as the Minnesota Massacre by local white families, Ohiyesa fled with his uncle and grandmother across the Canadian border and lived in Manitoba until he was fifteen. Both Ohiyesa and his uncle believed that Ohiyesa's father, Many Lightnings, had been captured by the U.S. Army and executed. However, Many Lightnings had been pardoned by President Lincoln. Shortly thereafter he converted to Christianity, changed his name to Jacob Eastman, and took up a homestead in Flandreau, South Dakota.[26]

When Ohiyesa was fifteen and just completing a coming-of-age vision quest, his father came to retrieve him in Manitoba. Believing it part of his destiny, Ohiyesa returned to Flandreau with his father and became Charles Eastman. From there he embarked on a journey from Santee Normal School to Beloit College, Knox College, Dartmouth College, and finally to Boston University Medical School. Shortly after Charles graduated from medical school, he secured a position with the Bureau of Indian Affairs (BIA) and was sent to Pine Ridge Indian Agency. He arrived in 1890 in the midst of the growing hysteria over the Ghost Dance.[27] As the crisis grew Charles and Elaine became acquainted and soon fell in love. Charles was attracted to Elaine's sincere interest in Indians and her ability to speak Dakota fluently. He felt a commonality with her that transcended their different cultural backgrounds. Her ideals, he said, "seemed very like my own," and her childhood had been spent "almost as much out of doors as mine."[28] They announced their engagement on Christmas Day, 1890.

Four days later, hundreds of Lakotas were killed at the Wounded Knee Massacre. As agency doctor Charles attended the victims and few remaining survivors of the massacre, while Elaine assisted as his nurse. The tragedy seemed only to bring them closer, and they married six months later. She gave up school teaching and her reform work to bear and raise their six children and keep house. He alternated over the next several decades between practicing medicine, organizing Indian affiliates for the YMCA, and working for the Bureau of Indian Affairs. He also became a frequent lecturer and prolific writer on Indian affairs and culture.[29]

Charles and Elaine seem to have been motivated to marry by powerful physical, intellectual, and spiritual attractions. In Charles's books, *Old Indian Days*, he related the story of a man named Antelope who fell in love with a woman from the enemy tribe. As he described it, "Their marriage, they believed, was made by a spirit, and it was holy in their minds. Each had cast away his people and his all for the sake of this emotion which had suddenly overtaken them both with overwhelming force." Antelope and his bride planned to live in seclusion away from each of their people. However, once they had a son, each wanted him to be part of their own tribe's people. Eventually the couple determined to return to her people.[30] This tale may convey some hint of how the Eastmans saw their own marriage.

While their marriage appears to have been truly based on mutual attraction, the couple may have often been compelled to justify themselves to a hostile and intolerant public. Imperialism, social Darwinism, nativism, and the emerging "science" of eugenics all spurred white supremacy in this period.[31] In its American form, eugenics originated in the late nineteenth century but became increasingly popular in the first decades of the twentieth century. At the First Universal Races Congress held in London in 1911 one eugenicist asserted that "mankind can solely or mainly be improved in the only manner that animals can— that is, by careful selection or breeding."[32] Eugenicists at the Universal Races Congress divided over the advisability of race mixing between "whites" and "non-whites." Already ranking Indians and blacks far below whites, some theorists believed race mixing would result in progeny with even worse genetic makeups than full-blood Indians or pure blacks. Others believed that "half-breeds are not able to compete [in many qualities] with the stronger races of the Aryan stock, [but] . . . it is none the less certain that we cannot place [them] at the level of really inferior races."[33] A rare few asserted that race mixing resulted in a "superior type."[34] Sharing the common eugenicist view many white Americans looked askance at marriages between white women and Indian men, primarily because they believed the "Indian problem" to be a problem of biology. To this group of Americans Indians were biologically inferior to and different from native-born, white Protestant Americans, and segregation (or sometimes extermination) appeared to them to be the only solution to the Indian problem.

This was the controversial climate into which the Eastmans married and bore six mixed-race children. To defend themselves, the couple justified their marriage publicly as a natural means to assimilate the Indian. In a speech at the First Universal Races Congress, Charles articulated this philosophy. "Since it is admittedly impossible for the Indian to continue to exist as a separate race, with his proper racial characteristics and customs, within the limits of the United States," he asserted, "race amalgamation is the only final and full solution of the problem, and only in this sense, implying no lack of vitality, but quite the reverse, is the American Indian a 'dying race'."[35] Many missionaries and reformers concerned with Indian affairs shared this view, perceiving the "Indian problem" primarily as a matter of environment rather than a biological problem.

The couple's support for amalgamation took on a very personal as well as a very public dimension. Charles remarked in his memoirs that "our greatest personal concern [was] the upbringing and education of our children."[36] It must have been difficult for him to listen to the myriad academic theories and eugenic pronouncements at the Universal Races Congress. In his own speech, he vigorously defended interracial marriage and the children these unions produced.

> The common slur which attributes to the mixed-blood the "vices of both race and the virtues of neither" is absolutely unjust. . . . Within the past twenty or thirty years . . . there have been a great many inter-marriages . . . between educated Indians and Caucasians; and whereas in the early days only Indian women contracted these alliances, of late years almost as many Indian men choose Anglo-Saxon wives. Such marriages, based upon mutual sympathy and affection, have been generally happy and have had the best results.[37]

Charles was not being quite truthful. He and Elaine were having troubles. As early as 1894 there were rumors of incompatibility between the two.[38] Both chose not to write about these troubles or to destroy all record of them. Perhaps, as a couple who upheld themselves as an example of the assimilating power of interracial marriage, they did not wish to illuminate their difficulties. Yet stories that the two coauthored seem to provide important hints regarding the ups and downs of their cross-cultural marriage. In *Wigwam Evenings*, one story concerns a man who married a Bear Woman, was deceived by her, and almost eaten by her relatives. Were the Eastmans referring to their own marriage and the possible feeling of being eaten up by each other's communities when they wrote, "This story is told for a warning to those who wish to marry among strangers"?[39]

In 1921, after thirty years of marriage (many of which appear to have been unhappy), the Eastmans separated for good. Charles divided his time between a cabin in Ontario and his son's home in Detroit. Elaine lived out the remainder of her life in Massachusetts. Based partly on interviews with Eastman descendants, Charles's biographer Raymond Wilson asserts that Charles resented his wife's interference in his writing and her supposedly domineering manner. Wilson also discovered that Charles was known as a philanderer.[40] Beyond these highly personal conflicts, I believe there were also more philosophical differences between the two.

When the couple married, they seemed to share a view of the proper roles of men and women and a view of the best solution to the so-called Indian problem. Over time, however, Elaine seems to have become embittered by the sacrifices she felt that she made to carry out the proper role of a woman. She also seems to have grown angry with her husband for failing to live up to her vision of the male role. Charles seems to have become resentful of the demands of Christianity and civilization and the loss of many aspects of his cultural heritage. Foremost among these was his sense that he had lost his manhood. As I explore below, it appears that his vision of manhood significantly conflicted with Elaine's.

By virtue of her childhood and her early career as a schoolteacher, writer, and Indian reformer, Elaine seemed destined to join the large number of white women reformers of the late nineteenth and early twentieth centuries who made new public spaces and careers for themselves.[41] Yet she claims that, ironically, her feminist mother withheld her support for Elaine's career plans. "Mother failed, indeed, to sympathize with my plans or my enthusiasm," Elaine lamented, "but neither she nor any one else proposed a satisfying alternative."[42] Even without her mother's support Elaine might have attained the public career she craved. But her course was altered further when she met and married Charles. Elaine said and wrote little about her marriage at the time, but one speech she made to the Lake Mohonk group of reformers in 1895 is perhaps revealing. Speaking of Indian women she remarked, "What I like about the Indian woman is that she is so womanly. I hope it will be a long time before she becomes so advanced as to desire any better career than that which culminates in motherhood."[43] At the time, Elaine may have willingly sacrificed her burgeoning career to marry and to raise six children.

Charles had his own ideas about how women should behave, from both his own culture and from his inculcation in white American social values. In Part Two of *Old Indian Days*, called "The Woman," Charles conveyed these ideas: "The Indian woman in her quiet way preserves the dignity of the home. From our standpoint the white man is a law-breaker!. . . . [The woman] is the foundation of man's dignity and honor. Upon her rests the life of the home and of the family."[44] At least at the beginning of their marriage, Charles's view of the proper role of a woman meshed with Elaine's.

In later years, however, Elaine developed a different view of her marriage and her role within it. In several articles and her autobiography she writes with an unmistakable bitterness about her marriage. She asserts that "for fifteen years I handled nearly all the correspondence and publicity incident to twenty-five or more annual appearances" of her husband. Furthermore, she claims to have cowritten every book attributed to Charles alone. In a 1939 letter, she asserted, "Dr. Eastman's books left his hand as a rough draft in pencil, on scratch paper. From this I made two or three typed copies, revising, omitting and re-writing as necessary."[45] In her autobiography, she revealed how much her backstage role frustrated her:

No, I won't say that the adjustment was easy or that I was never lonely, restless, and haunted by a secret sense of frustration. Every woman who has surrendered a congenial task and financial independence will understand. Saving the joys of motherhood, my pleasures must be vicarious ones. He traveled widely, . . . and met hosts of interesting people. I was

inevitably house-bound. . . . For many a year every early dream
and ambition was wholly subordinated to the business of helping my talented husband express himself and interpret his
people. Whether or not this was wise is perhaps an open question. Obviously, it was far from modern.[46]

Elaine might have been happy to play the role she felt was appropriate to her sex had Charles been playing the role she felt was appropriate to his, that of breadwinner. At several points in her autobiography and articles she lets slip her disappointment in his inability to fulfill
this role. She had to write a "few 'pot boilers' for our income was never
at all adequate to the family needs." She also accused her husband of
engaging in a "series of dubious experiments." Charles did, indeed, have
difficulty holding down a steady job, at least partly due to the prejudice against him as well to his own growing disillusionment with the
BIA. After the couple married he returned to his position with the
BIA at Pine Ridge but when he protested that many of the reservation's inhabitants had been cheated out of their depredation claims, he
was transferred. Instead of accepting the transfer, he resigned from the
BIA and started a private medical practice in St. Paul, to which he
attracted few patients. Thereafter, he worked in numerous capacities,
including as a recruiter with the YMCA and the Boy Scouts, as a public
speaker and writer, as a lobbyist for the Sioux, as a collector of ethno-
logical specimens, and again for the government to revise Sioux allotment rolls. He and Elaine later opened a summer camp in New
Hampshire for girls.[47] Charles himself admitted that the family struggled financially. In a letter to his friend, fellow doctor and activist Carlos
Montezuma, Eastman declared, "It seems you and I are brought into
this life—to exert ourselves for a cause. Therefore, we must not give
up. I have a large family to support, but they are great inspiration to
me. I never have . . . left my quiver empty. It seems that I am getting
accustom[ed] to emergencies."[48] Elaine, however, did not sympathize
with the limited options that Charles faced in his work. Instead her
vision of womanhood and manhood began to veer away from that of
her husband's.

At the same time Charles and Elaine might have evolved

differently regarding racial and cultural views. Although in her memoirs she critiques those "strait-laced individuals" who rejected everything Native in the late nineteenth century, Elaine nevertheless supported the cornerstones of assimilation policy—Christian conversion, American education, and allotment of communally owned Indian lands. "Having lived at the heart of the issue for half a century," she wrote, "I deeply regret the folly of holding the tribes together in compact masses and teaching them dependence upon the federal government. It has, quite unnecessarily, kept the majority of Indians children and wards to this day."[49] In the 1890s Charles seems to have agreed with his wife. For example in 1895 he worked for the YMCA on the Pine Ridge Agency in South Dakota to encourage young Sioux Indians to accept Christ. He noted, "There are 7000 Indians on this reservation, and the wild dances and many of the degrading things are still in full force, and unchecked, to drag these young men down." He hoped to replace the traditional dances of the Sioux with "scientific and systematic sports."[50]

As Charles aged, however, he rediscovered his Indian religious roots and became more critical of Christianity. In fact, by 1911, when he published *The Soul of the Indian*, he suggested that traditional Indian religion was truer to Christ's teachings than Christianity as practiced by most Americans. "It is my personal belief, after thirty-five years' experience of it," wrote Charles, "that there is no such thing as 'Christian civilization.' I believe that Christianity and modern civilization are opposed and irreconcilable, and that the spirit of Christianity and of our ancient religion is essentially the same."[51] Indeed, in Charles's view,

> It appears that not freedom or democracy or spiritual development, but material progress alone, is the evidence of 'civilisation'. The American Indian failed to meet this test, or rather, he made no attempt to meet it, being convinced that accumulation of property breeds dishonesty and greed, while concentration of population is abnormal and the mother of many evils, both physical and moral.[52]

As we shall see, Charles's opinion of Christianity and civilization would come to predominate in the 1920s among a group of white primitivists.

Charles seemed particularly concerned that American civilization had unmanned Indian men. In fact, his writing is laden with references to manhood and manliness. As he defined it, "true manhood" meant a life of "physical activity and endurance."[53] He sought to rejuvenate Indian manhood and make known to Americans that the Indian "race has contributed some sterling traits to the American ideal," including "a model physique." He believed that if reformers "could awaken the old idea that no man can be a man without sound muscle, that no warrior can be a warrior, no hunter can properly be a hunter, without good, sound muscle," they could improve the lives of Indian men. He hoped that young Indian men would "hold together for developing their manhood, their character." Charles practiced what he preached. At Beloit College he spent three hours a day in physical exercises to keep himself fit.[54]

Clearly the Eastmans had veered apart from one another and not just for personal reasons. Elaine remained faithful to a vision of Indian assimilation that Charles outgrew and eventually challenged. Elaine became embittered by playing a backstage role once married. Similarly, Charles could not completely conform to Elaine's ideal of what a man should be, a provider for his wife and children. Instead, he defined manhood first as developing one's physical body so as to be a strong modern-day warrior.

Charles's view that Indian men embodied a true manhood became a powerful notion in the 1920s. This perspective became popular among a group of bohemian antimodernists who romanticized primitive people. Disillusioned with modern American society, they looked to primitive societies as model communities that could restore some of the values and lifestyles supposedly lost by modernization and industrialization. This group included writers and artists, many of whom settled in Taos and Santa Fe, New Mexico, in the years surrounding World War I.[55]

One of the most famous of the antimodernist refugees of this era was Mabel Luhan, born to a wealthy and prominent Buffalo family. After the death of her first husband, the birth of her only son, and a scandal involving an affair with her married gynecologist, Mabel traveled to Italy, where she married Edwin Dodge, a man she met on board ship. In the 1910s, Mabel returned to New York City and became active in the radical politics of her day. She opened a salon in her Fifth Avenue apartment where the great intellectuals and activists of the day regularly gathered. In 1917, having divorced Edwin and broken off her love affair with John Reed, Mabel rashly married the Russian-born painter Maurice Sterne.[56]

Mabel shortly regretted her hasty marriage and packed Maurice off to the Southwest on a solitary honeymoon where she had "heard there are wonderful things to paint. Indians." While Maurice honeymooned alone in Santa Fe, Mabel visited a medium in New York City who envisioned her "surrounded by many people . . . dark people . . . dark faces—they are Indians." The psychic told Mabel, "You are to help them—you are for them." One night Mabel dreamed she "saw a large image of Maurice's head," and as she gazed at his face, it "began to fade and another face replaced it, . . . a dark face with wide-apart eyes that stared at me with a strong look, intense and calm. This was an Indian face." A few days later a letter arrived in the mail from Maurice, asking Mabel, "Do you want an object in life? Save the Indians, their art-culture—reveal it to the world!"[57]

Taking these developments as a mystical sign, Mabel soon joined her new husband in New Mexico. But Mabel disliked the company of other artists in Santa Fe and was intrigued instead by Taos, seventy-five miles to the north. Impulsively, on their first visit and before even viewing Taos in daylight, Mabel insisted that the couple rent part of a house there. Once settled into her new home, she walked daily to Taos Pueblo. One day a Pueblo woman, Candelaria Luhan, invited Mabel, Maurice, and Mabel's son into their home. Candelaria's husband, Tony, was playing a drum, his head bent over it intently. When he looked up, Mabel "saw his face was the face that had blotted out Maurice's" in her dream. Mabel grew infatuated with Tony, and Tony returned her interest. Throughout Mabel's first winter and spring in Taos Tony often came to drum in her home. In the spring and summer Tony took Mabel and her family and friends on tours of the area. He encouraged her to buy a home and property in Taos.[58]

In August of 1918 Maurice returned to New York, leaving Mabel and Tony free to pursue their burgeoning romance. The new couple lived openly together, their unabashed adultery causing scandal in both white and Pueblo societies. When Mabel became involved in a nation-wide effort to save Pueblo lands in the 1920s, her affair threatened to undermine the campaign. In 1923, at the urging of their white friends, Mabel and Tony divorced their spouses and married one another. Revealingly, it was more their adultery and cohabitation without mar-riage than the interracial quality of their liaison that caused many white Americans to view Mabel and Tony's relationship as scandalous. This suggests that a great shift in attitudes had occurred among at least some white Americans.[59]

Taos Pueblo, on the other hand, did take offense at Tony's rela-tionship with a white woman and his abandonment of Candelaria. Once divorced from Tony, Mabel agreed to pay Tony's former wife thirty-five dollars a month for the rest of Candelaria's life. The Taos tribal council punished Tony in other ways; although he was permitted to keep his position on the tribal council, he was barred from participa-tion in religious kiva ceremonies. Not until 1935 did Taos's *cacique*, or religious head, reverse this position.[60] Taos Pueblo's reaction to the rela-tionship suggests an important area for further research. So often focused on how white Americans viewed interracial marriage, scholars have not yet excavated the ways in which Indian communities and other non-white communities perceived and regulated such relationships.

In her memoirs Mabel presented her courtship with Tony in glowing, romantic terms, but she actually experienced many troubled times with him. In her book on the British writer D. H. Lawrence, *Lorenzo in Taos*, she dramatically lamented, "What incomprehensible aloneness for the white woman / Who crosses over into the Indian heart!" She confided to Lawrence that Tony gave her zest in life, "but so much spoils it. I suppose we must admit our different cultures—our surface lives—have taken different directions. So that there is practically nothing for us unavoidably to *do* together. . . . If we sit in a room, it is silence."[61] She also revealed to her Jungian therapist, Frances G. Wickes, that Tony had pursued affairs with other women, including the painter Georgia O'Keefe. For her part Mabel also sought to seduce other men, including Lawrence and Jean Toomer, a mystic and writer connected with the Harlem Renaissance.[62] Historians are at a loss to know how Tony perceived his relationship with Mabel because, unlike Mabel, he did not write his memoirs or leave behind any written evidence of his perspectives. We can only surmise from Taos Pueblo's actions that Tony sacrificed a great deal of his tribal affiliation due to his marriage to Mabel. Despite their troubles, however, the couple remained married the rest of their lives.

The symbolic power of their marriage may have sustained Mabel through the hard times. Unlike Elaine Goodale, who had accepted and promoted unions between white women and Indian men as a means to assimilate Indians into white society, Mabel rejected the goal of assimilation, both personally and politically. As an advocate for the Pueblos and other Indians in the 1920s she condemned the federal policy of assimilation and campaigned for indigenous land rights and religious freedom. In order to preserve Pueblo culture she promoted Pueblo arts and crafts and sought to insulate the Pueblos from the "corrupting" influences of modern white society.

On a personal level Mabel wished to purge herself of "her people." "Was it possible for me to get away from [my people]," she queried, "and wash away from myself the taint of them, the odor of their sickness and their death? . . . I hated them in myself and myself in them, and I longed to blot them out in this other."[63] She sought to emulate the Pueblo Indians by cutting her hair in the fashion of Pueblo women and wearing a shawl about her shoulders Pueblo-style. When she returned from one of her visits to Taos Pueblo, she "assumed a bright noncommittal expression which I supposed was the way Indians looked. I wanted to be like them and felt, in an obscure way, that if I looked and acted the way they did, I would be."[64] As defined by Mabel, a marriage between an Indian man and a white woman no longer functioned as a means for the white woman to assimilate the Indian man and his race. Instead the Indian man might now save his white wife and her decaying society.

Despite her desire to marry Tony, to "go Native," and to heal modern American society with the values of Indian culture, Mabel did not wholeheartedly favor marriage between Indians and whites, not because it would sully the white race but because it would, in her mind, ruin the Indian race. In 1933 she confided to her old friend John Collier, an antiassimilationist reformer who became commissioner of Indian Affairs in the 1930s, "Although I married an Indian I did not do so when we were both young (and I don't believe in it for others). I cannot bring myself to change from my previous hope that the Indian culture may be saved as it cannot be if he [sic] becomes absorbed into the Mexican or the white races."[65] Mabel's note to Collier reveals just how muddled her view of race was. In Mabel's view, it seemed to be "blood" that determined Indianness. Nevertheless Mabel believed that she could virtually become an Indian through adopting Indian dress and hairstyle and by marrying an Indian man. She lived in an era in which the progressive faith in environmental nurture had waned and in which eugenics gained in popularity (even among leftists). Thus she could construct a contradictory view of race as determined by blood for Indians but volitional for whites.[66]

There are other documented examples of white women who found intimacy and companionship with Indian men in the 1910s and 1920s. In 1913 Maria Keller, an immigrant from Romania, married Carlos Montezuma, a Yavapai medical doctor and activist who was a close associate of Charles Eastman's. When Montezuma died in the 1920s, Maria married William Moore, a Pima man.[67] Edith Warner, who in 1928 became a caretaker of a railway station at Otowi Bridge in New Mexico, befriended many Indians at nearby San Ildefonso Pueblo. An Indian man, Tilano, who helped her with projects around her home and the station, eventually came to live with her. Although Warner's biographer claims that "they were not man and wife," Edith and Tilano lived together in the same home and were clearly close companions, if not sexual partners, for the remainder of their lives.[68] Carobeth Laird, while married to the anthropologist John Peabody Harrington, met and fell in love with George Laird, one of her husband's Chemehuevi informants. In the early 1920s Carobeth divorced her husband and married George.[69]

In the 1920s other white women merely flirted with the idea of a sexual liaison with an Indian man. According to writer and New Mexico tour guide Erna Fergusson, it was common in the 1920s to see "women novelists picturesquely distributing peacock-feathers among good-looking young Hopis" at the Hopis' Snake Dance. Erna Fergusson herself, if not openly pursuing young Indian men, saw the attraction. As she viewed an Indian dance Fergusson "watched one beautiful young dancer, posed perfectly on the balls of his feet, his body slim and straight like an arrow, wild and fawn-like even under baggy . . . trousers." In dismay, Fergusson "turned to an Indian Service man" sitting near her. "Why, oh why, does he wear trousers?" Fergusson wailed. "His body is so beautiful." The Indian Service man rebuked her sternly, "Young lady, . . . don't talk like that to me. I've spent the best years of my life trying to get these fellows into pants."[70]

The allure of Indian men seems to have affected not just an elite group of bohemian women but other women as well. In a revealing letter to Maria Montezuma Moore, Gladys Brown, a woman who appears to have been a passing acquaintance, remarks on Moore's recent remarriage to "another Indian!" "How could it be otherwise?" speculated Brown. "You had such a wonderful Indian in Montezuma how could you marry a plain White Man, of course not. (I hope my father never sees that line)." Brown proceeded to share with Moore a "secret" that only her mother knew. "Sometime when you find a real honest to goodness Indian who is *good* capture him for me. Will I ever be so lucky not even being able to know any or to live near them and being so dreadfully backward in the bargain." Brown also told Moore that she loved Indian pictures but she only had two that were framed. "I cut all the Indians pictures out of papers and magazines that I see the big ones I tack up on the walls of my bedroom . . . every inch of wall covered.[71]

Such interest in and flirtatiousness with Indian men by white women annoyed Mabel, who complained to her therapist that "Tony is so attractive to women. . . . You cannot imagine how almost all women turn to him. He looks (and is) so somehow spiritual and magnetic at the same time. . . . They are attracted to him like bees to honey."[72] White reformers who were opposed to any such unions also noticed this phenomenon. Using a derogatory term for Indian men, in 1926 Clara True ridiculed these flirtatious white women as a "party of buck-struck society women."[73]

Why did Mabel Dodge Luhan and a significant number of white women suddenly become so openly passionate about Indian men?

Much of their new orientation can be attributed to the influence of an emerging anthropological theory—cultural relativism—that had been pioneered by Franz Boas and Elsie Clews Parsons, as well as a growing primitivist sentiment among many white Americans in the 1920s. Cultural relativists deemed Indian and other supposedly "primitive" cultures to be equal, not inferior, to white, Anglo-Saxon Protestant culture. Primitivists went even further; they regarded many Indian societies as superior to modern American society. Freud's new theories about sexuality and a loosening of late-Victorian sexual mores also coupled with changing notions of race to influence the new orientation of these white women. Building on Freud's theories, Mabel and other white women contended that modern Americans and Europeans had repressed their natural sexual instincts while primitive peoples suffered from no such unhealthy inhibitions. Describing a group of Taos Indians who came to dance at her house Mabel wrote, "Their brown bodies are beautiful, for every inch of them has a gleaming awareness as though their flesh is wholly awake." Mabel lamented that among whites, "Our bodies are deserted. We do not live in them and they are like abandoned houses."[74]

Mabel and, seemingly, other white women, also adopted a view of Indian manhood that closely correlated with Charles Eastman's. As she watched her first Pueblo dance Mabel asserted that "the sonorous drum fused the voices of the men and the volume of it all together was strong and good and very masculine." Mabel found this strong masculine essence lacking in modern white men, as she demonstrated in her portrayal of Maurice, her modern man, as "old and spent," his masculinity diluted. However, Tony, her "primitive," was "whole," "young" and "hard," his "power unbroken." Thus Luhan equated masculinity with primitiveness and emasculation with modernity. In a letter to her friend Elizabeth Shepley Sergeant, Mabel in fact asserted that there was an "incompatibility between those emasculated religions and the virile religion of the Indian that has retained its vigor and its life just because it has, symbolically, a sexual basis."[75] Not only were individual Pueblo men more masculine, but their entire religion was "virile." Interestingly, Charles Eastman's contention that Indian manhood was more masculine than white "civilized" manhood had become a commonly held assumption of the early twentieth century among some white women, particularly those of a bohemian background who were active in challenging and overturning the gender and race strictures of the late nineteenth century. In an era which extolled heterosexual sexuality, white women who took Indian lovers gave notice that they were no longer bound by the sexual inhibitedness of their race and era.

In the cases presented here what might appear to be simple human attraction between individuals who happened to be classified as two separate races actually illuminates shifting conceptions of race and gender in the period from 1875 to 1935. Up until the late nineteenth century, powerful social taboos, if not legal restrictions, proscribed marriages between white women and Indian men. Changes in ideas about race and gender in the late nineteenth century, however, opened the door a crack to more such unions. The notion that grew in popularity among most missionaries and reformers, in which perceived Indian inferiority was only due to environment and not to biology, made interracial marriage more thinkable, even desirable. The concurrent belief among reformers in white women's moral authority and ability to uplift "backwards" people further justified such marriages. But inherent contradictions within these two intertwined ideologies may have led not only to the downfall of the Eastmans' marriage but also to the creation of another set of notions about gender and race. As a reformer in the late nineteenth century Elaine Eastman had created a stimulating and fulfilling career for herself. Part of the message she was to convey to Indian families, though, was the ideal of the male as breadwinner and the female as homemaker. When she married Charles Eastman, the glaring contradiction between her actions and her pronouncements eventually came to haunt her. It can also be said that even as the ideology and policy of assimilation brought Elaine and Charles together, it also tore them apart. Charles became disenchanted with civilization and Christianity while Elaine generally maintained support for the assimilation agenda.

The breaking down of assimilation and moral authority that seems to have become embodied in Elaine and Charles's crumbling marriage opened the door wider for interracial marriages based on new notions of race and gender. A growing primitivist sentiment, a loosening of Victorian sexual mores, and a breakdown of the notion of female moral authority created a new justification for marriage between white women and Indian men. Mabel would not assimilate Tony; rather, she would learn from him and translate his Indian values to a failing American society. Further, Mabel would liberate herself as a woman through her connection with a truly masculine man.

The Eastmans' and the Luhans' marriages functioned not only as private affairs but as public embodiments of changing notions of race and gender. Studying how interracial couples presented themselves to a sometimes hostile, sometimes curious and voyeuristic American public can further enrich our understanding of the complex inter-workings of racial and gender construction in American history.

---

* Margaret D. Jacobs is Professor of U.S. Women's History at New Mexico State University.

Notes

Joan M. Jensen and Darlis A. Miller, The Gentle Tamers Revisited: New Approaches to the History of Women in the American West

1. We will use the following terms in distinguishing among various ethnic groups of women: Native Americans or Indian; Hispanic, Mexicana, or Chicana depending on the context; Afro-American or black; Asian-American; and Euro-American. We have included only published material in this survey.

2. The recent bibliography by Sheryll and Gene Patterson-Black, *Western Women* (Crawford, Neb., 1978) is the most complete available. There is no bibliography on Native American women in the West, but Beatrice Medicine, "The Role of Women in Native American Societies: A Bibliography," *Indian Historian*, VIII (1975), 50–54, contains a preliminary listing. For Chicanas, see Robert Cabello-Arandona, Juan Gómez-Quinoñes, and Patricia Herrera Duran, *The Chicana: A Comprehensive Study* (Los Angles, 1975). For black women, see Lenwood G. Davis, *The Black Women in American Society: A Selected Annotated Bibliography* (Boston, 1975). There is no published bibliography on Asian women, but see Verna Abe *et al.*, *Asian American Women* (Palo Alto, 1976); *Asian Women* (Berkeley, 1971; and Emma Gee *et al.*, *Counterpoints* (Asian American Studies Center, University of California, Los Angeles, 1979). Rodman W. Paul and Richard W. Etulain, comps., *The Frontier and the American West* (Arlington Heights, Ill., 1977) has a useful section on "Women, the Family, and Women's Rights in the West," 130–34.

3. Fredrick Jackson Turner, "The Significance of the Frontier in American History," in *The Frontier in American History* (New York, 1920), pp. 1–38. Some writers prior to 1893 attempted to emphasize women's contributions on the frontier. See Elizabeth F. Ellet, *Pioneer Women of the West* (New York, 1852); William W. Fowler, *Woman on the American Frontier* (1879; reprinted, Detroit,

1974). Among the earliest attempts in the twentieth century to write histories of women in the West are Nancy Wilson Ross, *Westward the Women* (New York, 1944) and William Forrest Sprague, *Women and the West: A Short Social History* (Boston, 1940). See also Mattie Lloyd Wooten, ed., *Women Tell the Story of the Southwest* (San Antonio, 1940). Among the first to question the application of Turner's thesis to women's experiences was David M. Potter in "American Women and the American Character," a lecture presented at Stetson University in 1959. In his lecture, Potter asked significant questions about male and female work roles in American society. See Don E. Fehrenbacher, ed., *History and American Society: Essays of David M. Potter* (New York, 1973), 277–303. For a recent account, see Julie Roy Jeffrey, *Frontier Women: The Trans-Mississippi West, 1840–1880* (New York, 1979).

4. Ray Allen Billington, *America's Frontier Heritage (New York, 1966)*, 25.

5. *Ibid.*

6. Walter Rundell, Jr., "Concepts of the 'Frontier' and the 'West,'" *Arizona and the West,* I (1959), 15–19; Arrell Morgan Gibson, *The West in the Life of the Nation* (Lexington, Mass., 1976), ix, 5–6.

7. Dee Brown, *The Gentle Tamers: Women of the Old Wild West* (Lincoln, 1958, reprinted 1968); Dorothy Gray, *Women of the West* (Millbrae, Calif., 1976). Some historians are beginning to include Hawaii and Alaska in their definitions of the American West. Although most histories of these areas place little emphasis on women and their contributions, two authors—Gavan Daws and Ted Hinckley—include scattered references to women missionaries and wives of missionaries. See Gavan Daws, *Shoal of Time: A History of the Hawaiian Islands* (New York, 1968) and Ted C. Hinckley, *The Americanization of Alaska* (Palo Alto, 1972). For an interesting account of one woman's life in central Alaska during the first four decades of the twentieth century, see Jo Anne Wold, *This Old House: The Story of Clara Rust* (Anchorage, 1976).

8. See, for example, Lynn I. Perrigo, *The American Southwest: Its People and Cultures* (New York, 1971), 9–13, 85, 196, 226, 318, 378–79, 407–408.

9. T.A. Larson, "Women's Role in the American West," *Montana, The Magazine of Western History,* XXIV (Summer 1974), 4.

10. Gibson, *The West in the Life of the Nation,* 207. Many textbooks are male-oriented and have only scattered references to women. See, for instance, Robert Athearn and Robert Riegel, *America Moves West* (5th ed., New York, 1971); Thomas D. Clark, *Frontier America* (New York, 1969); Ray Allen Billington, *Westward Expansion* (4th ed., New York, 1974); LeRoy Hafen, W. Eugene Hollon, and Carl C. Rister, *Western America* (3rd ed., Englewood Cliffs, 1970). Texts by John Hawgood, *America's Western Frontiers* (New York, 1967) and Robert V. Hine, *The American West: An Interpretive History* (Boston, 1973) are slightly better than others and include in their indices the activities and names of several women. Specialized studies of the West which are frequently used in college classrooms are also male-oriented and depict women in traditional roles. See particularly two books by Everett Dick, *The Sod House Frontier*

(Lincoln, 1954) and *Vanguards of the Frontier* (1941; reprinted, Lincoln, 1965).

11. Larson, "Women's Role in the American West," 5.

12. Richard A. Bartlett, *The New Country: A Social History of the American Frontier, 1776–1890* (London, 1974), 343.

13. Lewis Atherton, *The Cattle Kings* (Lincoln, 1961), 80; Duane Smith, *Rocky Mountain Mining Camps: The Urban Frontier* (Bloomington, 1967), 22, 188. Numerous works are available, however, describing the hardships, experiences, and adjustments of women who settled on cattle or sheep ranches in the West. Among the better examples of this genre are Nannie T. Alderson and Helena Huntington Smith, *A Bride Goes West* (Lincoln, 1942); Mary Hudson Brothers, *A Pecos Pioneer* (Albuquerque, 1943); Junietta Claridge, "We Tried to Stay Refined: Pioneering in the Mineral Strip," *Journal of Arizona History,* XVI (1975), 405–26; Agnes Morley Cleaveland, *No Life for a Lady* (1941; reprinted, Lincoln, 1977); Sallie Reynolds Matthews, *Interwoven: A Pioneer Chronicle* (3rd ed., Austin, 1974); Dorothy Ross, *Stranger to the Desert* (New York, 1959). Two good accounts of women who entered the cattle business are Emily J. Shelton's "Lizzie E. Johnson: A Cattle Queen of Texas," *Southwestern Historical Quarterly,* L (1947), 349–66; and Carrie Miller Townley's "Helen J. Stewart: First Lady of Las Vegas," *Nevada Historical Society Quarterly,* XVI (1973), 214–44, XVII (1974), 2–32. For the story of a woman who operated and expanded a sheep ranch in northwestern Colorado over a period of half a century, see Margaret D. Brown, *Shepherdess of Elk River Valley* (Denver, 1967).

14. Bartlett, *The New Country,* 349. Although their numbers may have been few, women did go to the mines and on occasion prospected and mined themselves. Harriet Rochlin tells the story of Nellie Cashman who became the West's most famous woman mining expert in "The Amazing Adventures of a Good Woman," *Journal of the West,* XII (1973), 281–95; while Duane A. Smith tells the story of Elizabeth "Baby Doe" Tabor with compassion in *Horace Tabor: His Life and the Legend* (Boulder, 1973). Many women participated in the Klondike Gold Rush in the 1890s and they are ably described by Laurie Alberts, "Petticoats and Pickaxes," *Alaska Journal,* VII (1977), 146–59. Some of the most perceptive first-person accounts of life in mining camps have been written by women, including Dame Shirley [Louise A.K.S. Clapp], *The Shirley Letters from California Mines in 1851–52* (San Francisco, 1922); Ralph Henry Gabriel, ed., *Frontier Lady: Recollections of the Gold Rush and Early California* (New Haven, 1932); Rodman W. Paul, ed., *A Victorian Gentlewoman in the Far West: The Reminiscences of Mary Hallock Foote* (San Marino, 1972); Mollie D. Sanford, *Mollie: The Journal of Mollie Dorsey Sanford in Nebraska and Colorado Territories, 1856–1866* (Lincoln, 1959); James L. Thane, Jr., *A Governor's Wife on the Mining Frontier: The Letters of Mary Edgerton from Montana, 1863–1865* (Salt Lake City, 1976). For additional information on the Montana gold rush, see S. Lyman Tyler, ed., *The Montana Gold Rush Diary of Kate Dunlap* (Denver, 1969). On the mining regions of Central Nevada, see Marvin Lewis, *Martha and the Doctor: A Frontier Family in Central Nevada* (Reno, 1977). Memoirs of

life as a miner's wife in Telluride, British Columbia, Idaho, and Leadville are presented by Harriet Fish Backus in *Tomboy Bride* (Boulder, 1969).

15. Ray Allen Billington, *Westward Expansion* (4th ed., New York, 1974).

16. Larson, "Women's Role in the American West," 4; Barlett, *The New Country*, 344.

17. Brown, *The Gentle Tamers*, 284.

18. Page Smith, *Daughters of the Promised Land* (Boston, 1970), 223.

19. Brown, *The Gentle Tamers*, 297; Bartlett, *The New Country*, 356. Rarely do authors of western textbooks view women as writers and artists in their own right, yet the literature on such women is extensive. On Helen Hunt Jackson as writer and reformer, see Evelyn I. Banning, *Helen Hunt Jackson* (New York, 1973); John R. Byers, "Helen Hunt Jackson," *American Literary Realism*, VI (1973), 197–241; Virginia McConnell, "H.H., Colorado, and the Indian Problem," *Journal of the West*, XII (1973), 272–80. Mary Hallock Foote as writer and illustrator is treated with understanding and insight in Rodman W. Paul's introductions to *A Victorian Gentlewoman in the Far West*. But see also Mary Lou Benn, "Mary Hallock Foote, Early Leadville Writer," *Colorado Magazine*, XXXIII (1956), 93–108; and Richard W. Etulain, "Mary Hallock Foote (1847–1938)," *American Literary Realism*, V (1972), 144–50. For novelist Gertrude Atherton, see Carolyn Forrey, "Gertrude Atherton and the New Woman," *California Historical Quarterly*, LV (1976), 194–209; and Elinor Richey, "The Flappers Were Her Daughters: The Liberated, Literary World of Gertrude Atherton," *American West*, XI (July 1974), 4–10. For Mary Hunter Austin's career as a journalist and novelist, see J. Wilkes Berry, "Mary Hunter Austin (1868–1934)," *American Literary Realism*, II (1969), 125–131; T. M. Pearce, *Mary Hunter Austin* (New York, 1965); and Donald P. Ringler, "Mary Austin: Kern County Days, 1882–1892," *Southern California Quarterly*, VL (1963), 25–63. Writings on novelist and short-story writer Willa Cather are numerous, but see E. K. Brown and Leon Edel, *Willa Cather: A Critical Biography* (New York, 1953); David Daiches, *Willa Cather: A Critical Introduction* (New York, 1962); Bernice Slote and Virginia Faulkner, eds., *The Art of Willa Cather* (Lincoln, 1974); and James L. Woodress, *Willa Cather: Her Life and Art* (New York, 1970). For a fine discussion of Mari Sandoz and her writings, see Mamie J. Meredith, "Mari Sandoz," in Virginia Faulkner, ed., *Roundup: A Nebraska Reader* (Lincoln, 1957), 382–86. Ina Agnes Graham sketches the life of San Francisco's pioneer poet-laureate in "My Aunt, Ina Coolbrith," *Pacific Historian*, XVII (1973), 12–19; while Rebecca Smith Lee presents the life of the woman who wrote the first history of Texas in English in *Mary Austin Holley: A Biography* (Austin, 1962). For a sketch of Arizona poet and historian Sharlot Hall, see Lawrence Clark Powell, "Letter from the Southwest," *Westways*, LXVII (January 1975), 24–27; and for one of H. H. Bancroft's writers, see Hazel Emery Mills, "Frances Fuller Victor, 1826–1902," *Arizona and the West*, XII (1970), 111–14. For additional writers and poets of the Southwest, see Miriam B. Murphy, "Sarah Elizabeth Carmichael: Poetic Genius of

Pioneer Utah," *Utah Historical Quarterly*, XLIII (1975), 52–66; Paul T. Nolan, "The Boomers: Oklahoma Playwrights Opened the Territory," *Chronicles of Oklahoma*, XLI (1963), 248–52; Thomas M. Pearce, *Alice Corbin Henderson* (Austin, 1969); and Raye Rice, "Utah's Leading Ladies of the Arts," *Utah Historical Quarterly*, XXXVIII (1970), 65–85. Twentieth-century Native American artists are described by Judy Casey in "She Speaks in Poetry," *Nevada Magazine*, XXXV (1975), 22–23, a sketch of Mabel Fillmore, Washo-Paiute basketweaver; and by Alice Marriott in *María: The Potter of San Ildefonso* (Norman, 1948), the story of María Martinez. For other artists and writers in twentieth-century New Mexico, see Dorothy Brett, "Autobiography: My Long and Beautiful Journey," *South Dakota Review*, V (1967), 11–72; Emily Hahn, *Mabel: A Biography of Mabel Dodge Luhan* (Boston, 1977); Mabel Dodge Luhan, *Movers and Shakers* (New York, 1936); Claire Morrill, "Three Women of Taos: Frieda Lawrence, Mabel Luhan, and Dorothy Brett," *South Dakota Review*, II (1965), 3–22; Claire Morrill, *A Taos Mosaic* (Albuquerque, 1973); and Georgia O'Keefe, *Georgia O'Keefe* (New York, 1976).

20. Beverly J. Stoeltje, "A Helpmate for Man Indeed': The Image of the Frontier Woman," *Journal of American Folklore*, LXXXVIII (1975), 27–31; Atherton, *The Cattle Kings*, 81–82.

21. Stoeltje, "A Helpmate for Man Indeed," 31.

22. Brown, *The Gentle Tamers*, 247–48, 251.

23. Emerson Hough, *The Passing of the Frontier* (New Haven, 1921), 93.

24. Stoeltje, "A Helpmate for Man Indeed," 32.

25. James D. Horan, *Desperate Women* (New York, 1952); Grace Ernestine Ray, *Wily Women of the West* (San Antonio, 1972). Other works of this genre include Duncan Aikman, *Calamity Jane and the Lady Wildcats* (New York, 1927); Harry Sinclair Drago, *Notorious Ladies of the Frontier* (New York, 1969); Richard Kyle Fox, *Belle Starr, the Bandit Queen, or the Female Jesse James* (1889; reprinted, Austin, 1960); John Marvin Hunter, *The Story of Lottie Deno* (Bandera, Texas, 1959); and Burton Rascoe, *Belle Starr, The Bandit Queen* (New York, 1941). Peggy Robbins shows, however, in her study of Calamity Jane that women could assert themselves in male–dominated society by establishing a unique character. Peggy Robbins, "Calamity Jane: 'Hellcat in Leather Britches'," *American History Illustrated*, X (June 1975), 12–21.

26. Stoeltje, "A Helpmate for Man Indeed," 38; Brown, *The Gentle Tamers*, 81–85. For popular accounts of prostitution in the West, see Kay Reynolds Blair, *Ladies of the Lamplight* (Leadville, 1971); Curt Gentry, *The Madams of San Francisco* (Garden City, 1964); Ronald Dean Miller, *Shady Ladies of the West* (Los Angles, 1964); and Joseph W. Snell, "Painted Ladies of the Cowtown Frontier," *The Trail Guide*, X (Dec. 1965), 3–24. Cy Martin's *Whiskey and Wild Women: An Amusing Account of the Saloons and Bawds of the Old West* (New York, 1974) is marred by its sexist overtones and callous treatment of women. In "An Inning for Sin: Chicago Joe and Her Hurdy-Gurdy Girls," *Montana, The Magazine of Western History*, XXVII (Spring 1977), 24–33, Rex C. Myers points

out that Montana dance hall girls were rarely prostitutes—most hoped to marry and become respected members of the community. For an interesting account of women depicted as temptresses in western songs, see Austin and Alta Fife, "Pug-Nosed Lil and the Girl in the Blue Velvet Band: A Brief Medley of Women in Western Song," *American West*, VII (March 1970), 32–37.

27. Beverly Trulio, "Anglo-American Attitudes toward New Mexican Women," *Journal of the West*, XII (1973), 229–239.

28. Stoeltje, "A Helpmate for Man Indeed," 25–41.

29. Larson, "Women's Role in the American West," 3–11.

30. Sheryll Patterson-Black, "Women Homesteaders on the Great Plains Frontier," *Frontiers*, I (Spring 1976), 67–88. For additional accounts of women homesteaders, see Eliza W. Farnham, *California In-Doors and Out: Or, How We Farm, Mine and Live Generally in the Golden State* (1856; reprinted, 1973); Joseph W. Snell, ed., "Roughing It on Her Kansas Claim: The Diary of Abbie Bright," *Kansas Historical Quarterly*, XXXVII (1971), 223–268, 394–428; Elinore Pruitt Stewart, *Letters of a Woman Homesteader* (Boston, 1914). Women not infrequently made "runs" to acquire land for themselves. See Lonnie E. Underhill and Daniel F. Littlefield, Jr., "Women Homeseekers in Oklahoma Territory, 1889–1901," *Pacific Historian*, XVII (1973), 36–47; Lynette Wert, "The Lady Stakes a Claim," *Persimmon Hill*, VI (Spring 1976), 18–23. The latter tells the story of Laura Crews, who made an 1893 Oklahoma run; her mother had made a similar race into Iowa in earlier years.

31. Glenda Riley, "Images of the Frontierswomen: Iowa as a Case Study," *Western Historical Quarterly*, VIII (1977), 198–202. Riley has been extremely active in recovering the history of Iowa pioneer women. See particularly her "The Memoirs of Matilde Peitzke Paul," *Palimpsest*, LVII (March/April 1976), 54–62; "Women Pioneers in Iowa," *ibid.*, 34–53; "Family Life on the Frontier: The Diary of Kiturah Penton Belknap," *Annals of Iowa*, XLIV (1977), 31–51; "A Prairie Diary," *ibid.*, (1977), 102–17; "Pioneer Migration: The Diary of Mary Alice Shutes," *ibid.*, XLIII (1977) 487–514; and "Civil War Wife: The Letters of Harriet Jane Thompson," *ibid.*, XLIV (1978), 214–231.

32. R. Griswold del Castillo, "La Familia Chicana: Social Changes in the Chicano Family of Los Angles, 1850–1880," *Journal of Ethnic Studies*, III (Spring 1975), 41–58.

33. Jane Dysart, "Mexican Women in San Antonio, 1830–1860: The Assimilation Process," *Western Historical Quarterly*, VII (1976), 365–75.

34. Johnny Faragher and Christine Stansell, "Women and Their Families on the Overland Trail to California and Oregon, 1842–1867," *Feminist Studies*, II (1975), 150–66; John Faragher, *Women and Men on the Overland Trail* (New Haven, 1979).

35. Traditional biographies and autobiographies which contribute to this picture album of women are nonetheless valuable and available in relatively large quantity. In addition to works already cited, see two books on pioneer women in New Mexico: Lily Klasner and Eve Ball, eds., *My Girlhood among Outlaws*

(Tucson, 1972); and Eve Ball, *Ma'am Jones of the Pecos* (Tucson, 1969). Fabiola Cabeza de Baca writes of four generations of the Cabeza de Baca family living on the Llano Estacado of New Mexico in *We Fed Them Cactus* (Albuquerque, 1954). DeWitt Bodeen and Horace Wyndham have concentrated on biographies of famous western actresses: Bodeen, *Ladies of the Footlights* (Pasadena, 1937); and Wyndham, *The Magnificent Montez* (New York, 1935). Short sketches of professional women in the West include Malcolm H. Clark Jr., "The Lady and the Law: A Portrait of Mary Leonard," *Oregon Historical Quarterly*, LVI (1955), 126–139, concerning the first woman lawyer in Oregon; G. Thomas Edwards, "Dr. Ada M. Weed: Northwest Reformer," *ibid.*, LXXVIII (1977), 5–40, about a doctor and advocate for women's rights; Douglas C. Jones, "Teresa Dean: Lady Correspondent among the Sioux Indians," *Journalism Quarterly*, XLIX (1972), 656–62, about the only woman correspondent to cover the Ghost Dance phenomenon in South Dakota and the aftermath of the Wounded Knee Massacre; James C. Malin, *Doctors, Devils and the Woman* (Lawrence, Kan., 1975), focusing on Sarah C. Hall and the fight to enlarge rights of women generally and in the professions. For a survey of women as journalists in Missouri, see Alma Vaughan, "Pioneer Women of the Missouri Press," *Missouri Historical Review*, LXIV (1970), 289–305. Mildred Crowl Martin, *Chinatown's Angry Angel: The Story of Donaldina Cameron* (Palo Alto, 1977) tells the story of a woman who fought the slave trade in Asian women in San Francisco. Several state history journals have included "First Ladies Series" concerning wives of governors. See particularly "The First Ladies of South Dakota," *South Dakota History*, III (1973), 156–68; and Helen Cannon, "First Ladies of Colorado: Nellie Martin Orman," *Colorado Magazine*, L (1973), 57–65.

Short sketches of western women as well as their recollections have been collected in a number of volumes. See especially Cora M. Beach, *Women of Wyoming* (2 vols., Casper, Wyo., 1927–29); Elinor Bluemel, *One Hundred Years of Colorado Women* (N.p., 1973); Vicky Burgess-Olson, *Sister Saints* (Salt Lake City, 1978); James Day, *et al.*, *Women of Texas* (Waco, 1972); Christiane Fischer, ed., *Let Them Speak for Themselves: Women in the American West* (Hamden, Conn., 1977); Dorothy Gray, *Women of the West* (Millbrae, Calif., 1976); Anne D. Pickrell, *Pioneer Women in Texas* (Austin, 1970); and Elinor Richey, *Eminent Women of the West* (Berkeley, 1975). This list of biographies and vignettes of western women is by no means exhaustive.

36. Maris A. Vinovskis and Richard M. Bernard, "Beyond Catherine Beecher: Female Education in the Antebellum Period," *Signs*, III (1978), 856–69. For an overview of ethnic groups' settlement on the Great Plains, consult Frederick C. Luebke, "Ethnic Group Settlement on the Great Plains," *Western Historical Quarterly*, VIII (1977), 405–30. Luebke notes that there are almost no studies of Irish immigrants on the plains; similarly, there are few studies focusing on immigrant women. Helen Z. Papanikolas, however, tells the fascinating story of a Greek woman immigrant who became a midwife and legend

in Utah in "Magerou, the Greek Midwife," *Utah Historical Quarterly*, XXXVIII (1970), 50–60. Scattered references to Italian women in the West can be found in Andrew F. Rolle's *The Immigrant Upraised: Italian Adventurers and Colonists in an Expanding America* (Norman, 1968), whereas little or no emphasis is given to German women in Terry G. Jordan's *German Seed in Texas Soil: Immigrant Farmers in Nineteenth-Century Texas* (Austin, 1966). Works which provide insight into the western experiences of Scandinavian women immigrants are Janice Reiff Webster, "Domestication and Americanization: Scandinavian Women in Seattle, 1888 to 1900," *Journal of Urban History*, IV (1978), 275–90; Arnold H. Barton, "Scandinavian Immigrant Women's Encounter with America," *Swedish Pioneer History Quarterly*, XXV (1974), 37–42; Theodore Blegen, *Land of Their Choice: The Immigrants Write Home* (Minneapolis 1955); and Olaf H. Olseth, *Mama Came from Norway* (New York, 1955). Robert E. Levinson provides a good overview of western Jewish settlement in "American Jews in the West," *Western Historical Quarterly*, V (1974), 285–94; while Harold Sharfman presents a patriarchal history in his *Jews on the Frontier* (Chicago, 1977). The *Western States Jewish Historical Quarterly* frequently publishes articles describing activities and experiences of western Jewish women. See, for example, Al Alschular, "The Colmans and others of Deadwood, South Dakota," IX (1977), 291–98; Henry and Lea Fine, "North Dakota Memories," *ibid.*, 331–40; Alice G. Friedlander, "A Portland Girl on Women's Rights— 1893," X (1978), 146–50; and Michael L. Lawson, "Flora Langermann Spiegelberg: Grand Lady of Santa Fe," VIII (1976), 291–308.

37. Judy Yung, "'A Bowlful of Tears': Chinese Women Immigrants on Angel Island," *Frontiers*, II (Summer 1977), 52–55. Historical material on Asian women is still scarce, partly because earlier researchers explicitly excluded women. See for example, John Modell, "Japanese American Family: A Perspective for Future Investigations," *Pacific Historical Review*, XXXVII (1968), 70, who explained that women were omitted in a sample of 1,047 interviews with Issei because men had to confront American institutions to a greater extent than women. A recent exception is Lucie Cheng Hirata, "Chinese Immigrant Women in Nineteenth-Century California," in Carol Ruth Berkin and Mary Beth Norton, eds., *Women of America: A History* (Boston, 1979), 223–44. See also the sections on Asian American women in *Bridge: An Asian American Perspective*, VI (Fall–Winter 1978), 16–53, VII (Spring–Summer 1979), 9–48.

38. Faragher and Stansell, "Women and Their Families on the Overland Trail," 150–66.

39. Ruth Barnes Moynihan, "Children and Young People on the Overland Trail," *Western Historical Quarterly*, VI (1975), 279–294; and Lillian Schlissel, "Mothers and Daughters on the Western Frontier," *Frontiers*, III (Summer 1978), 29–33. See also Barbara Laslett, "Social Change and the Family: Los Angeles, California, 1850–1870," *American Sociological Review*, XLII (1977), 268–91. The fictional portrayal of mother-daughter ties by several western authors is per-

ceptively analyzed in Judith Kegan Gardiner, "Wake for Mother: The Maternal Deathbed in Women's Fiction," *Feminist Studies*, IV (1978), 146–65; and Gardiner, "The Heroine as Her Author's Daughter," in Dana V. Hiller and Robin Ann Sheets, eds., *Women and Men: The Consequences of Power* (Cincinnati, 1977), 140–48. For Asian mother-daughter relations, see Maxine Hong Kingston, *The Woman Warrior: Memoirs of a Girlhood among Ghosts* (New York, 1976); and Woon-Ping Chin Holaday, "From Ezra Pound and Maxine Hong Kingston: Expressions of Chinese Thought," *Melus*, V (Summer 1978), 15–24.

40. Patterson-Black, "Women Homesteaders on the Great Plains Frontier," 67–88.

41. Elaine Silverman, "In Their Own Words: Mothers and Daughters on the Alberta Frontier, 1890–1929," *Frontiers*, II (Summer 1977), 37–44.

42. Schlissel, "Mother and Daughters," 32.

43. See, for example, Maria Linda Apodaca, "The Chicana Woman: An Historical Materialist Perspective," *Latin American Perspectives*, IV (Winter & Spring 1977), 70–89; various essays in *Asian Women*; and Sue Armitage, Theresa Banfield, and Sarah Jacobus, "Black Women and Their Communities in Colorado," *Frontiers*, II (Summer 1977), 45–51.

44. Lucy M. Cohen, "The Female Factor in Resettlement," *Sociology*, XIV (Sept./Oct. 1977), 27.

45. Jack E. Eblen, "An Analysis of Nineteenth-Century Frontier Populations," *Demography*, II (1965), 413.

46. David J. Wishart, "Age and Sex Composition of the Population on the Nebraska Frontier, 1860–1880," *Nebraska History*, LIV (1973), 109.

47. James C. Malin, "The Turnover of Farm Population in Kansas," *Kansas Historical Quarterly*, IV (1935), 339–372; and Mildred Throne, "A Population Study of an Iowa County in 1850," *Iowa Journal of History*, LVII (1959), 305–30.

48. Larson, "Women's Role in the American West," 5.

49. *Ibid.* Orval F. Baldwin II, "A Mormon Bride in the Great Migration," *Nebraska History*, LVIII (1977), 53–71, describes the migration of 1852 when ten thousand people, most of them in family groups, migrated en masse to Utah. For later sexual balance, see Dean L. May, "People on the Mormon Frontier: Kanab's Families of 1874," *Journal of Family History*, I (1976), 169–92.

50. Rodney O. Davis, "Prairie Emporium: Clarence, Iowa, 1860–1880: A Study in Population Trends," *Mid America*, LI (1969), 133.

51. Mexican immigrants had a sex ratio of 135.8 males to 100 females in the West North Central States in 1930. Wilson Cape, "Population Changes in the West North Central States, 1900–1930," *North Dakota Historical Quarterly*, VI (1932), 280. In Texas in 1910, the ratio among Chinese immigrants was 4,476 males to 100 females. Edward J. M. Rhoads, "The Chinese in Texas," *Southwestern Historical Quarterly*, LXXXI (1977), 5. See also Norman S. Haynor and Charles N. Reynolds, "Chinese Family Life in America," *American Sociological Review*, II (1937), 630–37; and Rose Hum Lee, "The Recent Immigrant Chinese

Families of the San Francisco-Oakland Area," *Journal of Marriage and Family Living*, XVIII (1956), 14–24. In California, first generation East Indian males married Hispanic women, but after immigration of East Indian women was allowed the next generation married back into the East Indian culture. Husuf Dadabhay, "Circuitous Assimilation among Rural Hindustanis in California," *Social Forces*, XXXIII (1954), 138–41. See also *Asian Women* (Berkeley, 1971).

52. Larson, "Women's Role," 9.
53. Blaine T. Williams, "The Frontier Family: Demographic Fact and Historical Myth," in Harold M. Hollingsworth and Sandra L. Myres, eds., *Essays on the American West* (Austin, 1969), 55.
54. Throne, "Population Study," 305–30.
55. Williams, "The Frontier Family," 64.
56. John Modell, "Family and Fertility on the Indiana Frontier 1820," *American Quarterly*, XXIII (1971) 625; and Richard A. Easterlin, "Factors in the Decline of Farm Family Fertility in the United States: Some Preliminary Research Results," *Journal of American History*, LXIII (1976), 603.
57. *Ibid.*, 604.
58. Susan E. Bloomberg, *et al.*, "A Census Probe into Nineteenth Century Family History: Southern Michigan, 1850–1880," *Journal of Social History*, V (1971), 26–45.
59. Williams, "The Frontier Family," 59.
60. Gilberto Espinosa and Tibo J. Chávez, *El Rio Abajo* (Pampa, Tex., 1967) contains an example of one of these early censuses.
61. U.S. Dept. of the Interior, Census Office, *Report on Indians Taxed and Indians Not Taxed* (Washington, D.C., 1894). Earlier census returns often included some of the Native Americans, and mission records also included numbers for early settlements.
62. Oscar Martínez, "On the Size of the Chicano Population: New Estimates, 1850–1900," *Aztlán*, VI (1975), 43–67.
63. According to the *Arizona Citizen*, Oct. 4 1879, p. 4, Tucson had a population of seven to eight thousand by 1879, three-fourths of it Mexicano, of which almost half must have been Mexicanas. In the Euro-American population there were very few women. Josephene B. Hughes, who arrived shortly after the nuns, also opened a school in 1873 for young Mexicanas. The role of nuns as teachers and health-care workers needs careful reevaluation. Much material is available. See Beth Hill, "The Sisters of St. Ann," *Alaska Journal*, VII (1977), 40–45; Sytha Motto, "The Sisters of Charity," *New Mexico Historical Review*, LII (1977), 228–36; Thomas Richter, ed., "Sister Catherine Mollon's Journal," *New Mexico Historical Review*, LII (1977), 135–55, 237–50.
64. Eric E. Lampard, "The Dimensions of Urban History: A Footnote to the 'Urban Crisis,'" *Pacific Historical Review*, XXXIX (1970), 272.
65. Adna Weber, *The Growth of Cities in the Nineteenth Century* (1895; reprinted, Ithaca, N.Y., 1965), 276.
66. Richard C. Wade, *The Urban Frontier* (1959; reprinted, Chicago, 1964), 207–09.

67. Earl Pomeroy, "The Urban Frontier of the Far West," in John G. Clark, ed., *The Frontier Challenge: Responses to the Trans-Mississippi West* (Lawrence, Kan., 1971), 13.

68. Figures in Robert M. Fogelson, *The Fragmented Metropolis: Los Angles, 1850–1930* (Cambridge, Mass., 1967), 82–83.

69. Cape, "Population Changes," 281.

70. Oscar Lewis, ed., *This Was San Francisco* (New York, 1962), 167–254.

71. Richey, "The Flappers Were Her Daughters," 4–10, 60–63. For an argument that the Portland Community was conservative, see Paul G. Merriam, "Urban Elite in the Far West: Portland, Oregon, 1870–1890," *Arizona and the West*, XVIII (1976), 41–52.

72. D'Ann Campbell, "Was the West Different? Values and the Attitudes of Young Women in 1943," *Pacific Historical Review*, XLVII (1978), 453–63.

73. Olen E. Leonard, *The Role of the Land Grant in the Social Organization and Social Process of a Spanish-American Village in New Mexico* (Albuquerque, 1970), 150. Marriott, *María, the Potter of San Ildefonso*, describes the disruption caused by lumbering, one result of which was to encourage women to make pottery for the market.

74. Agnes Smedley, *Daughter of Earth* (New York, 1973), 100–101, for Trinidad; and 123–36 for Raton, which she calls "Tercio" in her account.

75. Deborah Silverton Rosenfelt, ed., *Salt of the Earth* (New York, 1978) contains the film script and a commentary. For other accounts of mining towns, see Elizabeth Jameson, "Imperfect Unions: Class and Gender in Cripple Creek, 1894–1904," *Frontiers*, I (Spring 1976), 89–117; Philip Stevenson, "Deporting Jesus," *Nation*, CXLIII (July 18, 1936), 67–69; and Margerie Lloyd, "This Was Madrid," *New Mexico Magazine*, XLII (Nov./Dec. 1964), 14–16, 44.

76. Elizabeth B. Custer, *Following the Guidon* (Norman, 1966), 238. Earlier black families in the West were often enslaved, killed, or forced to flee. Daniel F. Littlefield and Mary Ann Littlefield, "The Beams Family: Free Blacks in Indian Territory," *Journal of Negro History*, VI (1976), 16–35.

77. The statistics on black population are from Charles E. Hall, *Negroes in the United States* (1935; reprinted, New York, 1969).

78. Armitage, Banfield, and Jacobus, "Black Women and Their Communities in Colorado," 45–52; and George H. Wayne, "Negro Migration and Colonization in Colorado, 1870–1930," *Journal of the West*, XV (1976), 102–20. Works by William Loren Katz, *The Black West* (New York, 1971); Glen Schwendermann, "Nicodemus: Negro Haven on the Solomon," *Kansas Historical Quarterly*, XXXIV (1968), 10–31; Mozell C. Hill, "The All-Negro Communities of Oklahoma: The Natural History of a Social Movement," *Journal of Negro History*, XXXI (1946), 254–68; and W. Sherman Savage, *Blacks in the West* (Westport, Conn., 1976) discuss the hopes and motivations of western migrants. For small town Texas, see Adah DeBlanc Simon, "The Discovery of Being Black: A Recollection," *Southwestern Historical Quarterly*, LXXVI (1973), 440–47.

79. Julia Kirk Blackwelder, "Women in the Work Force: Atlanta, New Orleans, and San Antonio, 1930 to 1940," *Journal of Urban History*, IV (1978), 331–58; Lawrence B. de Graff, "The City of Black Angels: Emergence of the Los Angeles Ghetto, 1890–1930," *Pacific Historical Review*, XXXIX (1970), 323–352, does not mention women. An article on Los Angeles which examines the social role of black women is badly needed.

80. Richard Slotkin, *Regeneration through Violence: The Mythology of the American Frontier, 1600–1860* (Middletown, Conn., 1973).

81. Lonnie J. White, "White Women Captives of Southern Plains Indians, 1866–1875," *Journal of the West*, VIII (1969), 327–54.

82. A.L. Kroeber and Clifton B. Kroeber, "Olive Oatman's First Account of Captivity," *California Historical Society Quarterly*, XLI (1962), 309–17.

83. White, "White Women Captives," 333, 342; Moynihan, "Children and Young People on the Overland Trail," 279–294.

84. Theodore C. Blegen, "Immigrant Women and the American Frontier," *Norwegian-American Studies and Records*, V (1930), 26–29; and Thomas B. Marquis, "Red Ripe's Squaw: Recollections of a Long Life," *Century Magazine*, CXVIII (June 1929), 201–202, 206–207.

85. Elizabeth Wood Kane, *Twelve Mormon Homes Visited in Succession on a Journey through Utah to Arizona* (Salt Lake City, 1974), 13, 33; Juanita Brooks, "Indian Relations on the Mormon Frontier," *Utah Historical Quarterly*, VII (1939), 27–47; and Beverly P. Smaby, "The Mormons and the Indians: Conflicting Ecological Systems in the Great Basin," *American Studies*, XVI (1975), 35–48.

86. Leonard J. Arrington, "Blessed Damozels: Women in Mormon History," *Dialogue*, VI (1971), 24.

87. Kane, *Twelve Mormon Homes*, 38.

88. See, for example, Cornelia Pelham, *Letters on the Chickasaw and Osage Missions* (Boston, 1833); and T. F. Morrison, "Mission Neosho: the First Kansas Mission," *Kansas Historical Quarterly*, IV (1935), 227–34. Standard sources for the Oregon missions are two works by Clifford Drury: *First White Women over the Rockies* (3 vols., Glendale, Calif., 1963–66); and *Marcus and Narcissa Whitman and the Opening of Old Oregon* (Glendale, Calif., 1973). The experiences of Margaret Jewett Bailey at the Oregon missions is explored in Janice K. Duncan, "'Ruth Rover'—Vindictive Falsehood or Historical Truth?" *Journal of the West*, XII, (1973), 240–53. See also Michael C. Coleman, "Christianizing and Americanizing the Nez Perce: Sue L. McBeth and Her Attitudes to the Indians," *Journal of Presbyterian History*, LIII (1975), 339–61. Insight into women's missionary work elsewhere in the West can be gained from the following: Elizabeth H. Hunt, ed., "Two Letters from Pine Ridge Mission," *Chronicles of Oklahoma*, L (1972), 219–25; Amy Passmore Hurt, "Life among the Apaches," *New Mexico Magazine*, XL (March 1962), 15–17, 35; Lilah Denton Lindsey, "Memories of the Indian Territory Mission Field," *Chronicles of Oklahoma*, XXXVI (1958), 181–98; Sister Blandina Segale, *At the End of the Santa Fe Trail* (Columbus, Ohio, 1932); and Sytha Motto, *No Banners Waving*

(New York, 1966), 38–39. For an interesting account of a black woman's experiences as missionary to Hawaii, see John A. Andrew III, "Betsey Stockton: Stranger in a Strange Land," *Journal of Presbyterian History*, LII (1974), 157–66.

89. Mary H. Eastman, *Dahcotah; or, Life and Legends of the Sioux around Fort Snelling* (New York, 1849); Martha Summerhayes, *Vanished Arizona: Recollections of My Army Life* (1908; reprinted, Glorieta, N.M., 1976); and Robert C. and Eleanor R. Carriker, eds., *An Army Wife on the Frontier: The Memoirs of Alice Blackwood Baldwin, 1867–1877* (Salt Lake City, 1975), 68, 79. Among other valuable memoirs written by military women are the following: Ellen M. Biddle, *Reminiscences of a Soldier's Wife* (Philadelphia, 1907); Mrs. Orsemus B. Boyd, *Cavalry Life in Tent and Field* (New York, 1894); Frances Carrington, *My Army Life and the Fort Phil Kearney Massacre* (Philadelphia, 1910); Lydia Spencer Lane, *I Married a Soldier* (Albuquerque, 1964); Sandra L. Myres, ed., *Cavalry Wife: The Diary of Eveline M. Alexander, 1866–1867* (College Station, Texas, 1977); Frances Roe, *Army Letters from an Officer's Wife* (New York, 1909); Mrs. Hal Russell, "Memoirs of Marian Russell," *Colorado Magazine*, XX (1943), 81–94, 140–54, 181–96, 226–38, XXI (1944), 29–37, 62–74, 101–12; and Teresa Viele, *Following the Drum: A Glimpse of Frontier Life* (New York, 1846). In addition to *Following the Guidon*, Elizabeth B. Custer wrote two books: "*Boots and Saddles," or Life in Dakota with General Custer* (1885; Norman, 1961); and *Tenting on the Plains, or General Custer in Kansas and Texas* (1889; Norman, 1971). Merrill J. Mattes tells of a frontier officer's wife in Wyoming and Montana in *Indians, Infants, and Infantry: Andrew and Elizabeth Burt on the Frontier* (Denver, 1960); while John R. Sibbald provides a summary of the lives of army women, including information on laundresses, in "Camp Followers All: Army Women of the West," *American West*, III (Spring 1966), 56–67. Other works which provide some insight into relations between Anglo women and Native American women include Donald K. Adams, ed., "Journal of Ada A. Vogdes, 1868–1871," *Montana*, XIII (Summer 1963), 2–17; Catharine Weaver Collins, "An Army Wife Comes West," *Colorado Magazine*, XXXI (1954), 241–73; and Alice M. Shields, "Army Life on the Wyoming Frontier," *Annals of Wyoming*, XIII (1941), 331–43.

90. Frances Gillmore and Louisa Wade Wetherill, *Traders to the Navajos: The Story of the Wetherills of Kayenta* (Albuquerque, 1953); and Hilda Faunce, *Desert Wife* (Boston, 1934). We have made no attempt to review the vast amount of material written by women anthropologists, but several studies are especially valuable. See Laura Thompson, "Exploring American Indian Communities in Depth," in Peggy Golde, ed., *Women in the Field: Anthropological Experiences* (Chicago, 1970), 47–66; Margaret Mead, *Blackberry Winter* (New York, 1972); and Helen Addison Howard, "Literary Translators and Interpreters of Indian Songs," *Journal of the West*, XII (1973), 214–17.

91. Brown, *Gentle Tamers*, 217. See Fred Lockley, "Recollections of Benjamin Franklin Bonney," *Oregon Historical Society Quarterly*, XXIV (1923), 50–51, for the original account.

92. Summerhayes, *Vanished Arizona*, 112–113.

93. Evon Z. Vogt and John M. Roberts, "A Study of Values," *Scientific American*, CXCV (July 1956), 25–32, remains one of the best attempts to compare values of different southwestern cultures, but it does not explore gender differences or change over time. For cultural contact, see Marta Weigle, ed., *Hispanic Villages of Northern New Mexico* (1935; reprinted, Santa Fe, 1975). Military pension records housed in the National Archives contain information relating to intermarriage, particularly marriages involving Euro-American men and Hispanic women.

94. Despite her negative stereotyping, Susan E. Wallace in *The Land of the Pueblos* (New York, 1888), 68, has a fine description of the Santa Fe washerwomen. Cleaveland, *No Life for a Lady*, 147–48.

95. Alan P. Grimes, *The Puritan Ethic and Woman Suffrage* (New York, 1967); and T. A. Larson, "Woman Suffrage in Western America," *Utah Historical Quarterly*, XXXVIII (1970), 7–19, have attempted to survey the entire West, but neither are detailed studies. T. A. Larson, "Dolls, Vassals, and Drudges—Pioneer Women in the West," *Western Historical Quarterly*, III (1972), 5–16, is primarily a study of Wyoming and Utah. For studies of individual states consult the following: *Wyoming*—T. A. Larson, "Woman Suffrage in Wyoming," *Pacific Northwest Quarterly*, LVI (1965), 57–66; *Utah*—Thomas G. Alexander, "An Experiment in Progressive Legislation: The Granting of Woman Suffrage in Utah in 1870," *Utah Historical Quarterly*, XXXVIII (1970), 20–30; Jean Bickmore White, "Woman's Place Is in the Constitution: The Struggle for Equal Rights in Utah in 1895," in Thomas G. Alexander, ed., *Essay on the American West, 1973–1974* (Provo, 1975), 81–104; and Beverly Beeton, "Woman Suffrage in Territorial Utah," *Utah Historical Quarterly*, XXXXVI (1978), 100–120; *Colorado*—Billie Barnes Jensen, "Colorado Woman Suffrage Campaigns of the 1870's," *Journal of the West*, XII (1973), 254–71; and Jensen, "Let the Women Vote," *Colorado Magazine* XLI (1964), 13–25; *Idaho*—T. A. Larson, "The Women's Rights Movement in Idaho," *Idaho Yesterdays*, XVI (Spring 1972), 2–15, 18–19; "Idaho's Role in America's Woman Suffrage Crusade," *Idaho Yesterdays*, XVIII (Spring 1974), 2–15; *Washington*—T. A. Larson, "The Woman Suffrage Movement in Washington," *Pacific Northwest Quarterly*, LXVII (1976), 49–62; *California*—Ronald Schaffer, "The Problem of Consciousness in the Woman Suffrage Movement: A California Perspective," *Pacific Historical Review*, XLV (1976), 469–93; and Jean Loewy, "Katherine Philips Edson and the California Suffragette Movement, 1919–1920," *California Historical Society Quarterly*, XLVII (1968), 343–350; *Oregon*—Abigail Scott Duniway, *Path Breaking: An Autobiographical History of the Equal Suffrage Movement in Pacific Coast States* (1914; reprinted, New York, 1971) remains the best available source; *Arizona*—Meridith Snapp, "Defeat the Democrats: The Congressional Union for Woman Suffrage in Arizona, 1914 and 1916," *Journal of the West*, XIV (1975), 131–59; *Montana*—Ronald Schaffer, "The Montana Woman Suffrage Campaign, 1911–14," *Pacific Northwest*

Quarterly, LV (1964), 9–15; T. A. Larson, "Montana Women and the Battle for the Ballot," *Montana, the Magazine of Western History*, XXIII (Jan. 1973), 24–41; John C. Board, "Jeanette Rankin: The Lady from Montana," *ibid.*, XVII (July 1967), 2–17; *New Mexico*—the best source is Ida Husted Harper, *History of Woman Suffrage* (6 vols., New York, 1969), VI, 434–39.

96. Larson, "Dolls, Vassals, and Drudges," 13. Leonard Arrington, "The Economic Role of Pioneer Mormon Women," *Western Humanities Review*, IX (1955), 145–64, does not relate economic roles to political participation.

97. Grimes, *The Puritan Ethic*, 101; Schaffer, "Problem of Consciousness," 469–93.

98. Larson, "Woman Suffrage in Western America," 10.

99. White, "Woman's Place," 84–104; Grimes, *The Puritan Ethic*, 101; Schaffer, "Problems of Consciousness," 483; Jensen, "Let the Women Vote," 23; and Larson, "Dolls, Vassals, and Drudges," 16.

100. White, "Woman's Place," 81–104; Larson, "Women's Rights Movement in Idaho," 15; and Judith Rasmussen Dushku, "Feminists," in Claudia L. Bushman, ed., *Mormon Sisters: Women in Early Utah* (Cambridge, Mass., 1976), 177–98. It seems likely that Mormon women also influenced the suffrage movement in Nevada.

101. See the following articles by Larson: "Women's Rights Movement in Idaho," 15; "Woman Suffrage in Western America," 19; and "The Woman Suffrage Movement in Washington," 61. In addition, consult Schaffer, "Problem of Consciousness," 482–83; and Schaffer, "The Montana Woman Suffrage Campaign," 9; as well as Jensen, "Let the Women Vote," 18.

102. Snapp, "Defeat the Democrats," 159; Larson, "Idaho's Role," 13. There is no study of the ratification of the Nineteenth Amendment in the West. Utah, Montana, California, and Colorado ratified it before January 1, 1920. Idaho, Arizona, and New Mexico ratified it early in 1920.

103. Loewy, "Katherine Philips Edson," 343; Joan M. Jensen, "Annette Abbott Adams, Politician," *Pacific Historical Review* XXXV (1966), 185–201. New Mexico progressives finally pushed through an amendment to the New Mexico constitution in 1921 which gave women the right to hold office at the state and local level. Frank D. Reeve, *History of New Mexico* (3 vols., New York, 1961), II, 353. See also Necah Stewart Furman, "Women's Campaign for Equality: A National and State Perspective," *New Mexico Historical Review*, LIII (1978), 370.

104. Carol Easton, "Honorable Nellie," *Westways*, LXVIII (Nov. 1976), 22–25, 70–71. See also Ingrid Winther Scobie, "Helen Gahagan Douglas and her 1950 Senate Race with Richard M. Nixon," *Southern California Quarterly*, LVIII (1976), 113–26.

105. Although large numbers of women joined the Communist party in California (and Mary Inman made important contributions to Socialist feminism), this movement has been neglected. For a brief discussion of Inman's work, see Ronald Schaffer, "Women and the Communist Party, USA," *Socialist Review*, XLV (May-June 1979), 83–87.

106. Carolyn Niethammer, *Daughters of the Earth: The Lives and Legends of American Indian Women* (New York, 1977), 143–45, discusses early western chiefs.

107. Cabeza de Baca, *We Fed Them Cactus*, discusses participation in local politics. William B. Faherty, "Regional Suffrage and the Woman Suffrage Struggle," *Colorado Magazine*, XXXIII (1956), 212–17, has argued that the Mexican vote had little effect on the outcome of the unsuccessful 1877 woman suffrage campaign in Colorado.

108. For Texas, see Elizabeth W. Fernea and Marilyn P. Duncan, *Texas Women in Politics* (Austin, 1977); and Wendy Watriss, "It's Something Inside You," *Southern Exposure*, IV (1977), 76–81. For California, see Gerald R. Gill, "Win or Lose— We Win: The 1952 Vice Presidential Campaign of Charlotta A. Bass," in Sharon Harley and Rosalyn Terborg-Penn, eds., *The Afro-American Woman: Struggles and Images* (New York, 1978), 109–118.

109. Victor B. Nelson-Cisneros, "La clase trabajadora en Tejas, 1920–1940," *Aztlán*, VI (1975), 239–65; George N. Green, "ILGWU in Texas, 1930–1970," *Journal of Mexican American History*, I (1971), 144–63; Rose Pesotta, *Bread upon the Waters* (New York, 1945); Dean Lan, "The Chinatown Sweatshops: Oppression and an Alternative," *Amerasia Journal*, I (1971), 40–57; Victor Nee and Brett DeBary Nee, *Longtime California: A Documentary Study of an American Chinatown* (New York, 1972); Patricia M. Fong, "The 1938 National Dollar Store Strike," *Asian American Review*, II (1975). For a recent account of Chicanas in the garment industry, see Laurie Coyle, Gail Hershatter, and Emily Honig, *Women at Farah: An Unfinished Story* (El Paso, 1979).

110. Arrington, "Economic Role of Pioneer Mormon Women," 145–64.

111. Corinne Azen Krause, "Italian, Jewish, and Slavic Grandmothers in Pittsburgh: Their Economic Roles," *Frontiers*, II (Summer 1977), 18–28.

112. Viola I. Paradise, "Maternity Care and Welfare of Young Children in a Homesteading County in Montana," in *Child Care in Rural America* (New York, 1972).

113. Chris Rigby Arrington, "Pioneer Midwives," in Bushman, ed., *Mormon Sisters*, 43–66; and Joan Jensen, "Politics and the American Midwife Controversy," *Frontiers*, I (Spring 1976), 19–33.

114. Martin, *Whiskey and Wild Women*, mentions in a number of places the high fines paid by prostitutes in western towns. See also George M. Blackburn and Sherman L. Ricards, "The Prostitutes and Gamblers of Virginia City, Nevada: 1870," *Pacific Historical Review*, XLVIII (1979), 239–58.

115. Jill C. Mulvay, "Zion's Schoolmarms," in Bushman, ed., *Mormon Sisters*, 67–87; Ronald E. Butchart, "The Frontier Teacher: Arizona, 1875–1925," *Journal of the West*, XVI (1977), 54–67; Joan M. Jensen, "Women Teachers, Class, and Ethnicity: New Mexico, 1900–1950," *Southwest Economy and Society*, IV (Winter 1978/79), 1–13; David B. Tyack, "The Tribe and the Common School: Community Control in Rural Education," *American Quarterly*, XXIV (1972), 2–19.

116. Blackwelder, "Women in the Work Force," 331–358.

117. Ronald L. Davis and Harry D. Holmes, "Studies in Western Urbanization," *Journal of the West*, XIII (1974), 1–5

118. Calif. Dept. of Employment Development, *Los Angles County: Manpower Information for Affirmative Action Programs* (Mimeographed, March 1975), gave the percentages as white 43.6, Spanish surname 42.7, black 50. Spanish surname women had much higher unemployment rates than white women. See also Laura Arroyo, "Industrial and Occupational Distribution of Chicana Workers," *Aztlán*, IV (1973), 343–381.

119. Yvonne Ashley, "That's the Way We Were Raised: An Oral Interview with Ada Damon," *Frontiers*, II (Summer 1977), 59–62. See also Sherna Gluck, "What's So Special about Women? Women's Oral History," *Frontiers*, II (Summer 1977), 3–17.

120. Elizabeth Fox-Genovese and Eugene Genovese, "The Political Crisis of Social History: A Marxian Perspective," *Journal of Social History*, X (1976), 205–19; Laurence Veysey, "The 'New' Social History in the Context of American Historical Writing," *Reviews in American History*, VII (1979), 1–12. Both of these essays warn about the dangers of a social history which is not integrated into the larger political economic context of history.

Carol Cornwall Madsen, 'At Their Peril': Utah Law and the Case of Plural Wives, 1850–1900

1. Joseph Smith also taught that marriages performed by the proper ecclesiastical authority, namely the current church president or one of his assignees, would be binding in heaven as well as on earth, a principle known as "eternal marriage" and considered an essential saving ordinance in Mormon doctrine. Marriages performed without this authority endured for time only, that is, until death separated the couple.

2. An Act Providing for a Probate Court, Section 30, 4 February 1852, 1851–52 Laws of Utah 42.

3. Nebraska, Colorado, Montana, Idaho, and Nevada also awarded their probate courts extended jurisdiction, but none as extensively as Utah. See Earl S. Pomeroy, *The Territories and the United States, 1861–1890* (Philadelphia, 1947). For an overview of Utah's probate courts see James B. Allen, "The Unusual Jurisdiction of County Probate Courts in the Territory of Utah," *Utah Historical Quarterly*, 36 (Spring 1968), 132–41. Detailed studies of two probate courts are Jay E. Powell, "Fairness in the Salt Lake County Probate Court," *Utah Historical Quarterly*, 38 (Summer 1970), 256–62; and Elizabeth D. Gee, "Justice for All or for the 'Elect'? Utah County Probate Court, 1855–1872," *Utah Historical Quarterly*, 48 (Spring 1980), 129–47.

4. 14 January 1854, Section 1, 1853–54 Laws of Utah 16. Utah and New Mexico were the only two Rocky Mountain territories to initially reject the common law, but most western states altered or adapted it to suit their own conditions,

when its precedents proved to be inapplicable. See Gordon M. Bakken, "The English Common Law in the Rocky Mountain West," *Arizona and the West*, 11 (Summer 1969), 109–28, and Bakken, *The Development of Law on the Rocky Mountain Frontier*, (Westport, CT, 1983). For a more detailed view of Utah, see Shane Swindle, "The Struggle Over the Adoption of the Common Law in Utah," *The Thetean: A Student Journal of History (May* 1984), 76–97; and Michael W. Homer, "The Judiciary and the Common Law in Utah Territory, 1850–61," *Dialogue, a Journal of Mormon Thought,* 21 (Spring 1988), 97–108.

5. Throughout this period, numerous Utah Supreme Court cases resulted in conflicting opinions regarding the applicability of the common law in Utah, until the Poland Act affirmed its validity. See Swindle, 94–97.

6. *The Doctrine and Covenants of the Church of Jesus Christ of Latter-day Saints* (Salt Lake City, 1957) (hereafter D&C), 41:10. This is a book of revelations, doctrine, and commandments accepted as scripture by Mormons.

7. *D & C,* 42:79–93.

8. *D & C,* 58:18.

9. Donald Q. Cannon and Lyndon W. Cook, eds., *Far West Record: Minutes of the Church of Jesus Christ of Latter-day Saints, 1830–1844* (Salt Lake City, 1983), 35–67.

10. *D & C,* 102.

11. Stephen J. Sorenson, "Civil and Criminal Jurisdiction of LDS.Bishops' and High Council Courts, 1847–1852," *Task Papers in LDS History,* No. 17, Historical Department, Church of Jesus Christ of Latter-day Saints (Salt Lake City, 1977), 21–7.

12. *D & C,* 102:3, 11.

13. *D & C,* 107:33.

14. Minutes, Pottawatamie High Council, 9 July 1847, LDS Church Archives, Salt Lake City, Utah (hereafter LDS CA).

15. Ibid.

16. For detailed studies of church courts see Sorenson, "Civil and Criminal Jurisdiction"; R. Collin Mangrum, "Furthering the Cause of Zinn: An Overview of the Mormon Ecclesiastical Court System in Early Utah," *Journal of Mormon History* 10 (1983), 79–90; and Raymond T. Swenson, "Resolution of Civil Disputes by Mormon Ecclesiastical Courts," *Utah Law Review,* no. 3 (1978), 573–95. A recent book-length study of Mormon courts is Edwin Brown Firmage and Richard Collin Mangrum, *Zion in the Courts, A Legal History of the Church of Jesus Christ of Latter-day Saints, 1830–1900* (Urbana, 1988).

17. Non-Mormon Utah residents found these laws particularly irksome. As quoted in Orson F. Whitney, *History of Utah,* 4 vols. (Salt Lake City. 1893), 3:61, in an 1878 appeal to Mrs. Rutherford B. Hayes, the newly organized Anti-Polygamy Society protests that the Utah legislature, "composed almost entirely of polygamists and members of the Mormon priesthood," has "thrown around polygamy every possible legislative safeguard in their power."

18. An Ordinance, Incorporating the Church of Jesus Christ of Latter-day Saints,

6 February 1851, 1851–52 Laws of Deseret 66. The ordinance did not prohibit any other ecclesiastical or legal entity from performing marriages. As a result of the lack of marriage registration, it is difficult to trace marriages performed in Utah between 1847 and 1887, except through ecclesiastical records and the personal papers of ecclesiastical and civil authorities, most of which are incomplete. See Lyman D. Platt, "The History of Marriage in Utah, 1847–1905," *Genealogical journal,* 12 (Spring 1983), 32–33.

19. Journal History of the Church (a chronological manuscript collection of journal entries and newspaper articles) 3 May 1876, LDS CA.

20. Lawrence Foster, "A Little Known Defense of Polygamy," *Dialogue, a Journal of Mormon Thought,* 9 (Winter 1974), 29.

21. Recorded in his journal and later printed in John D. Lee, *Mormonism Unveiled: Or the Life and Confessions of the Late Mormon Bishop, John D. Lee* (St. Louis, 1877), 146; see also Faster, "A Little Known Defense," 29.

22. Ecclesiastical Court Cases Collection, General Court Trials 1847, Fd. 17, LDS CA, quoted in Sorenson, "Civil and Criminal Jurisdiction," 32.

23. "Few Words of Doctrine given by President Brigham Young in the Tabernacle in Great Salt Lake City," reported by George Watt, 8 October 1861, LDS CA. Also reported in J. Beck, I Notebook, 1859–65, 8 October 1861 and 11 December 1869, Special Collections, Marriott Library, University of Utah. The case of Emma and Alisha Mallory is illustrative, though Emma desired a certificate of divorce, which was granted her on 1 August 1862 "because her husband . . has been cut off from the Church of Jesus Christ of Latter-day Saints for apostasy, and therefore *forfeited his privileges and blessings*" (author's emphasis). Brigham Young Papers, Box 64, Reel 99, LDS CA.

24. Ecclesiastical Court Cases Collection, 1880, Fd, 6; 1883, Fd. 6, LDS CA, noted in Firmage and Mangrum, *Zion in the Courts,* 327.

25. Sorenson, "Civil and Criminal Jurisdiction," 31.

26. Brigham Young Office Journals, 1857–1860, 19 April 1858, 21, LDS CA, quoted in Linda P. Wilcox, "Brigham Young as a Domestic Counselor," 15, unpublished paper in possession of author. See also Firmage and Mangrum, *Zion in the Courts,* 322–36 for examples of the efforts made by bishops and other ecclesiastical officers at reconciling couples and resolving family difficulties.

27. An analysis of these certificates of divorce is found in Eugene E. Campbell and Bruce L. Campbell, "Divorce Among Mormon Polygamists: Extent and Explanations," *Utah Historical Quarterly,* 4 (Winter 1978), 4–23.

28. The opportunity through polygamy for a dissatisfied husband to take an additional wife mitigated the necessity of divorce for men. Firmage and Mangrum's survey of LDS ecclesiastical court records (since closed to researchers) and Wilcox's survey of Brigham Young's letterbooks (copies of outgoing correspondence, LDS CA) show that divorces were granted primarily to wives, although a male applicant was expected to pay a fee of ten dollars "for his foolishness." *Journal of Discourses* (1875; Salt Lake City, 1966) 17:119. The liberal attitude toward female applicants is demonstrated in such

statements of Young's as, "When women tease for a divorce, and are determined to have one, what can be done better than to give them one?" Brigham
Young to Benjamin F. Johnson, 20 March 1865, Brigham Young Letterbook
7:517; or " . . . I should feel a little ashamed to require a wife to ask me twice
for a bill of divorce, or to refuse signing and paying for it at once"; or "If the
brethren were but a small part as anxious, diligent and prompt in this particular, [agreeing to divorce] as they are in having women scaled to them, it
would prevent much needless annoyance and perplexity to the sisters," Young
to Bishop Philo T. Farnsworth, 22 November 1859, Letterbook 5:132, quoted
in Wilcox, "Brigham Young," 16–17.

29. Brigham Young to Jonathan Pugmire, Jr., Journal History of the Church, 17
December 1858, LDS CA.

30. An Act in Relation to Bills of Divorce, Sections 2, 3, 1851–52 Laws of Utah
82.

31. Ibid., Section 2.

32. See, for example. Richard I. Aaron, "Mormon Divorce and the Statute of
1852: Questions for Divorce in the 1980s," *Journal of Contemporary Law,* 8
(1982), 20–22; and Firmage and Mangrum, *Zion in the Courts,* 324–27. Utah's
divorce laws were not so unusual as to provoke undue interest by Congress.
Other states that had similar provisions at that time were Indiana, North
Carolina, Illinois, Connecticut, Iowa (which had almost the exact wording as
the Utah law), and Maine, Arizona, Louisiana, South Dakota, and Washington
followed Utah in adopting similar "omnibus" clauses. The others, however,
did not include both an incompatibility clause and an open residency requirement as did Utah. For a general discussion of early divorce laws see George
Elliott Howard, *A History of Matrimonial Institutions,* 3 vols. (Chicago, 1904),
3:3–106. A brief, comparative analysis of these divorce laws is in Aaron,
"Mormon Divorce," 10–12.

33. Carroll D. Wright, *Marriage and Divorce in the United States, 1867–1886* (1889;
New York, 1976).

34. Divorce Docket, Beaver County Probate Records, 1856–1882, copy in LDS
Church Family History Library, Salt Lake City, Utah.

35. An Act Amending Sections 1151 and 1154 of the Compiled Laws of Utah,
Section 1, 2 February 1878, 1878 Laws of Utah 1. See also *Journals of the
Legislative Assembly of the Territory of Utah,* (Salt Lake City, 1876), 31 and (1878),
44–45; and report of grand jury, "Divorce," *Salt Lake City Deseret News Weekly,*
3 October 1877. The grand jury report indicated that of 300 divorces under
investigation, 80 percent were applied for by non-residents who never
appeared in court. Attorneys appeared for only sixty-seven of 150 of the cases.
Decrees were granted before defendants had had time to respond and sometimes with complete disregard for contested suits.

36. "Divorce," *Salt Lake City Deseret News Weekly, 3* October 1877.

37. Frederick Kesler Papers, Special Collections, Marriott Library, University of
Utah, Salt Lake City, Utah.

38. Ibid.
39. Brigham Young to Maria Jarman, 15 January 1870, "Brigham Young Letterbook" 11:954; Brigham Young to Elias Smith, 19 January 1870, "Brigham Young Letterbook" 11-959, LDS CA.
40. *Norton v. Tufts*, 19 Utah 470 (1899).
41. *Hilton v. Roylance,* 25 Utah 129 (1902).
42. Polygamy continues to be disallowed in the church and those Mormons who currently practice it, known as fundamentalists, are excommunicates or out of fellowship. A more detailed discussion of some of these cases is in Lois J. Kelly, "Polygamy and the Law, the Legal Status of Polygamous Wives After the Manifesto of 1890," unpublished paper in possession of author.
43. These laws were established to protect the property interests of the heirs of a husband or father who died intestate.
44. An Act in Relation to the Estates of Decedents, Section 24, 1876 Compiled Laws of Utah 268.
45. Ibid., Section 25. In *Cain Heirs v. Young,* 1 Utah 361 (1876) the court construed a widow's interest (in a monogamous marriage) to be "a child's part during her life or widow-hood," which in this case amounted to a one-third interest since there were two children.
46. Journal of Mary Ann Weston Maughan," in *Our Pioneer Heritage,* ed. Kate B. Carter, 20 vols. (Salt Lake City, 1959) 2:396.
47. "Acknowledgment" was a common law doctrine and assumed formal requirements in some jurisdictions. These later acts also provided that the mother was the intestate heir for an illegitimate child. See An Act Relating to Estates of Decedents, Sections 30, 32, 28 February 1876, 1876 Compiled Laws of Utah 276; see also An Act Relating to Estates of Decedents, Sections 4, 5, 13 March 1884, 1884 Laws of Utah 75.
48. Ruth Victor, "Emma Jeffs Gunnell," and Louis Jeffs Gunnell, "Lewellyn (Louis) Jeffs Gunnell," TS in possession of author.
49. Emily Dow Partridge Young, "Autobiography and Diary," TS, 28 February 1880, LDS CA.
50. U. S. Congress, *Congressional Record,* 47th Cong., 1st Sess. (1881–82), 1213.
51. Section 11, 24 Statutes at Large 637. The Edmunds Act amended the Morrill Act by changing the crime designated as bigamy to polygamy, making cohabitation a criminal offense, and legitimating children born of polygamous marriages, enabling them to inherit. The 1887 Edmunds-Tucker Act, which amended the Edmunds Act, among other provisions disallowed the right of illegitimate children born after March 1888 to inherit from either mothers or fathers. In 1891, however, the Utah Supreme Court in *Pratt v. Pratt* found that "A statute enacting that illegitimate children and their mothers inherit from the father is not repealed by the Act of Congress which annuls all acts and parts of acts of the Legislative Assembly of Utah Territory . . ." 7 Utah 278 (1891).
52. *Chapman v. Handler,* 7 Utah 49 (1890).

53. *Cope v. Cope,* 137 U.S. 832 (1890) In *Re Estate of Thomas Cope,* 7 Utah 63 (1890). See also In *The Matter of the Estate of Orson Pratt,* 7 Utah 278 (1891).

54. While plural wives had no legal rights, the government did not entirely leave them without recourse. In 1886, at the urging of moral crusader Angelia (Angie) Thurston Newman of the Methodist Woman's Home Missionary Society, Congress appropriated $40,000 for the construction of the Industrial Christian Home for Women in Utah, a refuge for unsupported or discontented plural wives. For varied reasons few women availed themselves of this sanctuary and its offer of industrial training and economic rehabilitation. For more details see Peggy Pascoe, *Relations of Rescue: The Search for Female Moral Authority* in *the American West, 1874–1939,* (New York, 1990).

55. An Act Relative to the Heritable Rights of Issue of Polygamous Marriages, 9 March 1896, 1896 Compiled Laws of Utah 128. An attempt to allow new trials in those cases decided adversely to the offspring of polygamous marriages was declared unconstitutional by the Utah Supreme Court.

56. Anne W. G. Leischman Oral History, Interview by John Stewart, 1973, TS, 6, Utah State University Voice Library Interview, LDS CA.

57. An Act Concerning the Property Rights of Married Persons, 16 February 1872, 1876 Compiled Laws of Utah 342. Since dower was implicitly abolished by the 1854 statute abrogating the common law in Utah, the "equitable right of a married woman to a separate estate" was legally recognized early. Subsequent court cases, however, continually raised questions about the validity of the statute. See *Hatch v. Hatch,* 46 Utah 116 (1915); and Swindle, "The Struggle," 94–97.

58. Some of the states that did not recognize the common law right of dower were Texas (dower repealed in 1840), Arizona (1865), Colorado (1868), Kansas (1879), Mississippi (1880), California (community property state), and Louisiana (never had dower). In place of dower, laws of succession were enacted providing for the descent and distribution of property. For an extensive nineteenth-century analysis of dower laws in the United States see Charles Scribner, *A Treatise on the Law of Dower,* 2 vols. (Philadelphia, 1883), 1:22–58. A comparative historical review of married women's legal rights in four western states, including Utah, is Helen S. Carter, "Legal Aspects of Widowhood and Aging," in *On Their Own, Widows and Widowhood in the American Southwest, 1848–1939,* ed. Arlene Scadron (Urbana, 1988), 271–300.

59. As quoted in Jennie Anderson Froiseth, *The Women of Mormonism or the Story of Polygamy* (Detroit, 1882), 360–61.

60. *Beck v. Utah-Idaho Sugar Company,* 59 Utah 314 (1921).

61. *Raleigh v. Wells,* 29 Utah 217 (1905).

62. An Act Concerning the Property Rights of Married Persons, 16 February 1872, 1876 Compiled Laws of Utah 342.

63. Many Mormon women viewed dower as a form of "vassalage" and "relic of the old common law" and acclaimed the passage of a married person's property act as more reflective of social and economic change. See "Woman's

Right of Dower," *Salt Lake City Woman's Exponent*, 1 December *1882;* see also "A Woman's Assembly," *Salt Lake City Woman's Exponent, 1* March 1894. Nineteenth-century feminists generally welcomed the proliferation of married women's property acts as a major step forward in the emancipation of women. By 1850, at least 17 states had some form of legislation that enabled married women to control their property, a number that expanded to 29 by 1865. See Lawrence M. Friedman, *A History of American Law* (New York, 1973), 186; and Norma Basch, *In the Eyes of the Law: Women, Marriage, and Property in Nineteenth Century New York* (Ithaca, 1982), *28.*

64. An Act Regulating Proceedings in Civil Cases in the Courts of Justice of this Territory and to Repeal Certain Acts and Parts of Acts, Section *379,* 17 February 1870, 1876 Compiled Laws of Utah 506, An Act to Amend Title XX, Section 30, 9 March 1882, 1882 Compiled Laws of Utah 79.

65. *Basset v. United States,* 137 U. S. 762 (1890).

66. See "A Few Facts," *Salt Lake City Woman's Exponent,* 15 July 1885, which lists Annie Gallifant, Belle Harris, Nellie White, Lydia Spencer, Elizabeth Ann Starkey, and Lucy Devereux among those who were charged with contempt of court and who were willing to be imprisoned rather than testify against their husbands. Belle Harris kept a journal, located in the LDS CA, of the three months she served in the Utah prison.

Peggy Pascoe, Race, Gender, and Intercultural Relations: the Case of Interracial Marriage

1. For a thorough review of these studies, see Paul R. Spickard, *Mixed Blood: Intermarriage and Ethnic Identity in Twentieth-Century America* (Madison: University of Wisconsin Press, 1989), pp. 6–17.

2. On the patterns of interracial marriage, see Spickard, *Mixed Blood;* Joel Williamson, *New People: Miscegenation and Mulattoes in the United States* (New York: Free Press, 1980); Rebecca McDowell Craver, *The Impact of Intimacy: Mexican-Anglo Intermarriage in New Mexico, 1821–1846,* Southwestern Studies #66 (El Paso: Texas Western Press, 1982); Darlis A. Miller, "Cross-Cultural Marriages in the Southwest: The New Mexico Experience, 1846–1900," *New Mexico Historical Review* 57 (October 1982): 335–59; Tanis C. Thorne, "People of the River: Mixed-Blood Families on the Lower Missouri" (Ph.D. diss., University of California, Los Angeles, 1987); Sylvia Van Kirk, *Many Tender Ties: Women in Fur Trade Society, 1670–1870* (Norman: University of Oklahoma Press, 1980); Jennifer Brown, *Strangers in Blood: Fur Trade Company Families in Indian Country* (Vancouver: University of British Columbia, 1980); Jacqueline Peterson and Jennifer Brown, eds., *The New Peoples: Being and Becoming Metis in North America* (Lincoln: University of Nebraska Press, 1985); Jacqueline Peterson, "Women Dreaming: The Religiopsychology of Indian-White Marriage and the Rise of Metis Culture," in Lillian Schlissel, Vicki L. Ruiz,

and Janice Monk, eds., *Western Women: Their Land, Their Lives* (Albuquerque: University of New Mexico Press, 1988), pp. 49–68; and John Faragher, "The Custom of the Country: Cross-Cultural Marriage in the Far Western Fur Trade," in Schlissel, Ruiz, and Monk, eds., *Western Women*, pp. 199–226. On miscegenation law, see Robert J. Sickels, *Race, Marriage, and the Law* (Albuquerque: University of New Mexico Press, 1972); Byron Curti Martyn, "Racism in the United States: A History of the Anti-Miscegenation Legislation and Litigation" (Ph.D. diss., University of Southern California, 1979); David H. Fowler, *Northern Attitudes Towards Interracial Marriage: Legislation and Public Opinion in the Middle Atlantic and the States of the Old Northwest, 1780–1930* (1963; New York: Garland, 1987); Megumi Dick Osumi, "Asians and California's Anti-Miscegenation Laws," in Nobuya Tsuchida, ed., *Asian and Pacific American Experiences: Women's Perspectives* (Minneapolis: University of Minnesota, Asian/Pacific American Learning Resource Center, 1982), pp. 2–8; Roger D. Hardaway, "Prohibiting Interracial Marriage: Miscegenation Law in Wyoming," *Annals of Wyoming* 52 (Spring 1980): 55–60; and Roger D. Hardaway, "Unlawful Love: A History of Arizona's Miscegenation Law," *Journal of Arizona History* 27 (Winter 1986): 377–90.

3. *Loving v. Virginia*, 388 US I, 18 L ed 2d 1010, 87 S Ct 1817 (1967).

4. William H. Browne, ed., *Archives of Maryland*, I, 533–34, cited in Fowler, *Northern Attitudes*, appendix, p. 381. For interpretations of these early laws, see A. Leon Higginbotham, Jr., and Barbara K. Kopytoff, "Racial Purity and Interracial Sex in the Law of Colonial and Antebellum Virginia," *Georgetown Law Journal* 77 (August 1989): 1967–2029; George Fredrickson, *The Arrogance of Race: Historical Perspectives on Slavery, Racism, and Social Inequality* (Middletown, Conn.: Wesleyan University Press, 1988), pp. 195–96; and Barbara J. Fields, "Slavery, Race, and Ideology in the United States of America," *New Left Review* 181 (May-June 1990): 95–119. As Fields points out on p. 107, the fact that the Maryland law of 1664 referred to "Freeborne English women" rather than "white" women suggests that the law does not so much reflect racial categories as it does "show society in the act of inventing race."

5. *New Mexico Terr. Laws*, chap. 20, secs. 3, 4, cited in Martyn, "Racism in the United States," p. 459.

6. John D'Emilio and Estelle B. Freedman, *Intimate Matters: A History of Sexuality in America* (New York: Harper and Row, 1989), pp. 92–97, 100–104; Jacquelyn Dowd Hall, "'The Mind that Burns in Each Body': Women, Rape, and Racial Violence," in Ann Snitow et al., eds., *Powers of Desire: The Politics of Sexuality* (New York: Monthly Review Press, 1983), pp. 328–49; Thelma Jennings, "'Us Colored Women Had to Go Through A Plenty': Sexual Exploitation of African-American Slave Women," *Journal of Women's History* 1 (Winter 1990): 45–74.

7. On this point, see esp. Higginbotham and Kopytoff, "Racial Purity."

8. *In re Paquet's Estate*, 200 P. 911.

9. *Oregon Code*, 1887, sec. 1927. "Kanaka" refers to native Hawaiians.

10. *In re Paquet's Estate*, 200 P. 911, 913.

11. *In re Paquet's Estate*, 200 P. 911, 914.

12. The Survey of Race Relations is housed in the Hoover Institution Archives at Stanford University.

13. Romanzo Adams, *Interracial Marriage in Hawaii: A Study of the Mutually Conditioned Processes of Acculturation and Amalgamation* (New York: Macmillan, 1937), p. 48.

14. On white soldiers who married Japanese women, see Spickard, *Mixed Blood*, chap. 5, pp. 123–57.

15. Barbara J. Fields, "Ideology and Race in American History," in J. Morgan Kousser and James M. McPherson, eds., *Region, Race, and Reconstruction: Essays in Honor of C. Vann Woodward* (New York: Oxford University Press, 1982), pp. 143–78, esp. p. 151. See also Fields, "Slavery, Race and Ideology."

16. Henry Louis Gates, Jr., *"Race," Writing, and Difference* (Chicago: University of Chicago Press, 1986); Michael Omi and Howard Winant, *Racial Formation in the United States: From the 1960s to the 1980s* (Boston: Routledge & Kegan Paul, 1986). For examples of poststructuralist discourse, see Homi K. Bhabha, "The Other Question . . . Homi K. Bhabha Reconsiders the Stereotype and Colonial Discourse," *Screen* 24 (1983): 18–36, and Joan Wallach Scott's definition of gender as "knowledge about sexual difference" in *Gender and the Politics of History* (New York: Columbia University Press, 1988), p. 2. A useful recent collection of articles on the social construction of "racisms" is David Theo Goldberg, ed., *Anatomy of Racism* (Minneapolis: University of Minnesota Press, 1990).

17. "Chinese" were mentioned in the miscegenation laws of Nevada (1861–1912), Idaho (1864–1887), Oregon (1866–1951), Montana (1909–1953), and Nebraska (1913–1963).

18. "Mongolians" were mentioned in the miscegenation laws of Arizona (1865–1962), Wyoming (1869–1882 and 1913–1965), California (1880–1959), Utah (1888–1963), Oregon (1893–1951), Nevada (1912–1959), South Dakota (1913–1957), and Idaho (1921–1959).

19. *Roldan v. Los Angeles County*, 129 Cal. App. 267 (1933).

20. *Statutes of California*, 1933, p. 561. Five other states also prohibited whites from marrying "Malays": Nevada (1912–1959), South Dakota (1913–1957), Wyoming (1913–1965), Arizona (1931–1962), and Utah (1939–1963).

21. *Loving v. Virginia*, 388 US 1, 18 L ed 2d 1010, 87 S Ct 1817 (1967). The major precedent for Supreme Court action was a 1948 case, *Perez v. Sharp*, in which the California Supreme Court had declared its state miscegenation statute unconstitutional. *Perez v. Sharp*, 32 Cal, 2d. 711, 198 P. 2d 17 (1948). In the years between the *Perez* and *Loving* decisions, most western state legislatures repealed their miscegenation laws: Oregon (1951), Montana (1953), North Dakota (1955), Colorado (1957), South Dakota (1957), California (1959), Idaho (1959), Nevada (1959), Arizona (1962), Nebraska (1963), Utah (1963), and

Wyoming (1965). Miscegenation legislation in two western states (Oklahoma and Texas) and a number of southern states remained in force until the *Loving* decision.

22. *Utah Laws*, 1963, p. 163; *Utah Laws*, 1977, 1st S S, p. 2.

23. The states that defined marriage in terms of "parties" or "persons" were Arizona, California, Colorado, Idaho, Kansas, Montana, Nebraska, Nevada, New Mexico, North Dakota, Oklahoma, Oregon, South Dakota, Texas, and Wyoming. Those (besides Utah) that adopted sex-specific definitions were Colorado (1973), Montana (1973), Texas (1973), Nevada (1975), North Dakota (1975), California (1977), Wyoming (1977), and Kansas (1980). Only two states, Washington (1970) and Alaska (1983), moved in the opposite direction, replacing definitions of marriage that originally spoke of "males and females" with definitions that spoke of "persons." These changes, however, offered same-sex couples little protection. In *Singer v. Hara,* a 1974 case, the Washington State Court of Appeals refused to allow a same-sex couple access to a marriage license, ruling that the introduction of the word "persons" in the state's new definition of marriage had been intended only to eliminate different age requirements by sex. *Singer v. Hara,* 11 Wn. App. 247 (1974).

24. On this last, see esp. Lynn Hunt, ed., *The New Cultural History* (Berkeley: University of California Press, 1989).

25. For analyses, see Thomas Bender, "Wholes and Parts: The Need for Synthesis in American History," *Journal of American History* 73 (June 1986): 127–32, and Peggy Pascoe, *Relations of Rescue: The Search for Female Moral Authority in the American West, 1874–1939* (New York: Oxford University Press, 1990), pp. 208–12.

26. See Richard Johnson, "What Is Cultural Studies Anyway?" *Social Text* 16 (Winter 1986–87): 38–80; Lawrence Grossberg, "Formations of Cultural Studies: An American in Birmingham," *Strategies* 2 (1989): 114–48; Victor Burgin, "Cultural Studies in Britain: 'Two Paradigms,'" *Center for Cultural Studies Newsletter* (University of California, Santa Cruz), Spring 1990; and Scott Heller, "Cultural Studies: Eclectic and Controversial Mix of Research Sparks a Growing Movement," *Chronicle of Higher Education,* January 31, 1990.

27. For a fine critique of deconstructionist use of the phrase "always already," see Diana Fuss, *Essentially Speaking: Feminism, Nature, and Difference* (New York: Routledge, 1989), p. 17.

28. Clifford Geertz, *The Interpretation of Cultures* (New York: Basic Books, 1973); James Clifford, *The Predicament of Culture: Twentieth-Century Ethnography, Literature, and Art* (Cambridge, Mass.: Harvard University Press, 1988); Bender, "Wholes and Parts"; Barbara Smith, "Toward a Black Feminist Criticism," *Conditions: Two* 1 (October 1977), reprinted in Elaine Showalter, ed., *The New Feminist Criticism: Essays on Women, Literature, and Theory* (New York: Pantheon, 1985), pp. 168–85; Gayatri Chakravorty Spivak, "Can the Subaltern Speak?" in Cary Nelson and Lawrence Grossberg, eds., *Marxism and the Interpretation of Culture* (Urbana: University of Illinois Press, 1988), pp. 271–313.

29. For an example of this approach, see Eva Saks, "Representing Miscegenation Law," *Raritan* 8 (Fall 1988): 39–69.

30. For a parallel argument about the significance of intellectual history, see John Toews, "Intellectual History After the Linguistic Turn: The Autonomy of Meaning and the Irreducibility of Experience," *American Historical Review* 92 (October 1987): 879–907.

31. On the concept of women's culture in women's history, see Ellen DuBois, Mari Jo Buhle, Temma Kaplan, Gerda Lerner, and Carroll Smith-Rosenberg, "Politics and Culture in Women's History: A Symposium," *Feminist Studies* 6 (Spring 1980): 65–75; Nancy Hewitt, "Beyond the Search for Sisterhood: American Women's History in the 1980s," *Social History* 10 (October 1985): 299–321; Linda Kerber, "Separate Spheres, Female Worlds, Women's Place: The Rhetoric of Women's History," *Journal of American History* 75 (June 1988): 9–39; Cecile Dauphin et al., "Women's Culture and Women's Power: An Attempt at Historiography," *Journal of Women's History* 1 (Spring 1989): 63–102.

32. For a parallel argument on this point, see Nancy Hartsock, "Foucault on Power: A Theory for Women?" in Linda J. Nicholson, ed., *Feminism/Postmodernism* (New York: Routledge, 1990), pp. 163–164.

33. Note, for example, that Thomas Bender reserves the use of the term culture for his discussions of U.S. "public culture," thereby demoting all the "cultures" social historians have unearthed—women's culture, slave culture, and so forth—to the status of "groups" within the larger public culture. For an argument for the need to resuscitate the notion of a national culture (but one that retains the concept of multiple cultures within U.S. society), see Elizabeth Fox-Genovese, "Between Individualism and Fragmentation: American Culture and the New Literary Studies of Race and Gender," *American Quarterly* 42 (March 1990): 7–34.

Antonio I. Castañeda, Women of Color and the Rewriting of Western History: The Discourse, Politics, and Decolonization of History

1. I use the term women of color to refer collectively to African American, Asian American, Mexican American/Chicana, and Native American women in the United States. I use the terms third world, third world woman/women, and third world movements with knowledge of the problems associated with the terms as discussed in Chandra Talpade Mohanty, Ann Russo, and Lourdes Torres, eds., *Third World Women and the Politics of Feminism* (Bloomington, Ind., 1991), ix-x. I use the terms raced ethnic and racial ethnic interchangeably with the term people of color to refer to the larger community that includes both men and women. For the term raced ethnic, see Norma Alarcón, "Chicana Feminism: In the Tracks of 'the' Native Woman," *Cultural Studies,* IV (1990), 248–256; for the term racial ethnic, see Evelyn Nakano Glenn, "Racial Ethnic Women's Labor: The Intersection of Race, Gender,

and Class oppression," *Review of Radical Political Economics,* XVII (Fall 1985), 86–108.

For a brief synthesis of some of the central issues in the recent historical literature on women in the West, see "Historical Commentary: The Contributions and Challenges of Western Women's History-Four Essays by Sarah Deutsch, Virginia Scharff, Glenda Riley, and John Mack Faragher," *Montana, the Magazine* of *Western History,* XLI (Spring 1991), 57–73.

For scholarly discussion of the debates and the historiography of frontier history/history of the West, generally exclusive of the issue of gender, see Patricia Limerick, *The Legacy of Conquest: The Unbroken Past of the American West* (New York, 1987); Roger L. Nichols, ed., *American Frontier and Western Issues: A Historiographical Review* (Westport, Conn., 1986); Michael P. Malone, *Historians and the American West* (Lincoln, Neb., 1983); "Historical Commentary: Western History, Why the Past May be Changing—Four Essays by Patricia Nelson Limerick, Michael P Malone, Gerald Thompson, and Elliot West," *Montana, the Magazine of Western History,* XL (Summer 1990), 60–77; Brian Dippie, "The Winning of the West Reconsidered," *Wilson Quarterly,* XIV (Summer 1990) 70–85; Sandra Myres, "What Kind of Animal Be This?" *Western Historical Quarterly,* XX (1989), 5–17; Charles S. Peterson, "The Look of the Elephant: On Seeing Western History," *Montana, the Magazine of Western History* XXXIX (Spring 1989), 69–73; Arnoldo De Leon, "Whither Borderlands History? A Review Essay," *New Mexico Historical Review,* LXA' (1989), 349–60; William G. Robbins, "Western History: A Dialectic on the Modern Condition," *Western Historical Quarterly,* XX (1989), 429–49; Martin Ridge, "The American West: From Frontier to Region," *New Mexico Historical Review,* LXIV (1989), 125–42; Gerald E. Poyo and Gilberto M. Hinojosa, "Spanish Texas and Borderlands Historiography in Transition: Implications for United States History," *Journal of American History*, LXXV (1988) 393–416; Donald Worster, "New West, True West: Interpreting the Region's History," *Western Historical Quarterly,* XVIII (1987), 141–56; David J. Weber, "John Francis Bannon and the Historiography of the Spanish Borderlands: Retrospect and Prospect," *Journal of the Southwest,* XXIX (1987), 331–63; Gerald D. Nash, "Where's the West?" *Historian,* IL (1986), 1–9; Richard White, "Race Relations in the American West," *American Quarterly,* XXXVIII (1986), 396–416; Gene M. Gressley, "The West: Past, Present, and Future," *Western Historical Quarterly,* XVII (1986), 5–23; Walter Nugent, "Western History: Stocktaking and New Crops," *Reviews in American History,* XIII (1985), 319–29; Rodman W. Paul and Michael P Malone, "Tradition and Challenge in Western Historiography," *Western Historical Quarterly,* XVI (1985), 26–53; David Weber, "Turner, the Boltonians, and the Borderlands," *American Historical Review,* XCI (1986), 66–81; Gene M. Gressley, "Whither Western American History? Speculations on a Direction," *Pacific Historical Review,* LIII (1984), 493–501; John W. Caughey, "The Insignificance of the Frontier in American History," *Western Historical Quarterly,* V (1974), 6–15; W. N. Davis, Jr., "Will the West Survive as a Field in American History?," *Mississippi Valley Historical Review,* L (1964), 672–85; Jack Forbes, "Frontiers in American History," *Journal of the West,* I (1962), 63- 73.

2. Susan Shown Harjo, "Western Women's History: A Challenge for the Future," in Susan Armitage and Elizabeth Jameson, eds., *The Women's West* (Norman, Okla., 1987), 307. After the first conference at Sun Valley in 1983, three additional conferences were held during the 1980s and one, entitled "Suspect Terrain: Surveying the Women's West," is being planned for 1992 at Lincoln, Nebraska. Issues of race and class bias surfaced at each of the conferences both in discussions of the new historiography of women in the West as well as in the conceptualization and organization of the conferences themselves. These same issues will inform the 1992 conference.

   The conferences of the 1980s were "Western Women: Their Land, Their Lives," Tucson, Ariz., January 12–15, 1984; "'The Women's West, 1984," Park City, Utah, July 11–14, 1984; "The Women's West: Race, Class, and Social Change," San Francisco, Calif., August 13–15, 1987. Two edited anthologies of works presented at the first two conferences have been published: Armitage and Jameson, eds., *Women's West,* and Lillian Schlissel, Vicki Ruiz, and Janice Monk, eds., *Western Women: Their Land, Their Lives* (Albuquerque, 1988).

3. Joan M. Jensen and Darlis A. Miller, "The Gentle Tamers Revisited: New Approaches to the History of Women in the American West," *Pacific Historical Review,* XL (1980), 173–214.

4. Rodolfo Acuña, *Occupied America: A History* of *Chicanos* (3d ed., New York, 1988), 307–62; Joan Wallach Scott, *Gender and the Politics of History* (New York, 1988); Gary T. Okihiro, ed., *In Resistance: Studies in African, Caribbean and Afro-American History* (Amherst, Mass., 1986); Gary T. Okihiro, "Education for Hegemony, Education for Liberation," in Gary Y. Okihiro, ed., *Ethnic Studies* (2 vols., New York, 1989), I, 3–10.

5. Adela de la Torre and Beatriz Pesquera, "Introduction," in Adela de la Torre and Beatriz Pesquera, eds., *Building with Our Own Hands: New Directions in Chicana Scholarship* (Berkeley, forthcoming 1992); Cheryl Johnson-Odim, "Common Themes, Different Contexts: Third World Women and Feminism," in Mohanty, Russo, and Torres, eds., *Third World Women and the Politics of Feminism,* 314–27; Alarcón, "Chicana Feminism," 248–56; Alma García, "The Development of Chicana Feminist Discourse, 1970–1980," in Ellen Carol DuBois and Vicki L. Ruiz, eds., *Unequal Sisters: A Multicultural Reader in US. Women's History* (New York, 1990), 418–31; Esther Ngan-Ling Chow, "The Feminist Movement: Where Are All the Asian American Women?" in Asian Women United of California, ed., *Making Waves: An Anthology of Writings by and about Asian Women* (Boston, 1989), 362–76; Nancy Diao, "From Homemaker to Housing Advocate: An Interview with Mrs. Chang Jok Lee," *ibid.,* 377–87; Teresa de Lauretis, "Feminist Studies/Critical Studies: Issues, Terms, and Contexts," in Teresa de Lauretis, ed., *Feminist Studies / Critical Studies* (Bloomington, 1986), 1–19; Linda Gordon, "What's New in Women's History,"

ibid., 20–30; Marilyn J. Boxer, "For and about Women: The Theory and Practice of Women's Studies in the United States," in Nannerl O. Keohane, Michelle Z. Rosaldo, and Barbara C. Gelpi, eds., *Feminist Theory: A Critique of Ideology* (Chicago, 1982), 237–372; Patricia Hernández, "Lives of Chicana Activists: The Chicano Student Movement (A Case Study)," in Magdalena Mora and Adelaida R. Del Castillo, eds., *Mexican Women in the United States: Struggles Past and Present (Los* Angeles, 1980), 7–16; Roxanne Dunbar Ortiz, "Toward a Democratic Women's Movement in the United States," *ibid.,* 29–36.

6. For representative descriptions and discussions of the various national liberation movements, see *The Struggle for Chicano Liberation* (New York, 1972); Armando B. Rendón, *Chicano Manifesto* (New York, 1971); Alvin M. Josephy, Jr., ed., *Red Power: The American Indians' Fight for Freedom* (New York, 1971); Vine Deloria, *Custer Died for Your Sins: An Indian Manifesto* (New York, 1969); Julius Lester, *Revolutionary Notes* (New York, 1969); Stokley Carmichael, *Black Power: The Politics of Liberation in America* (New York, 1967).

7. I use the terms native and indigenous to mean belonging to a particular place by birth. For an examination of the problems associated with the use of these terms, see Trinh T. Minh-ha, *Woman, Native, Other* (Bloomington, 1989).

8. Daniel Offiong A., *Imperialism and Dependency: Obstacles to African Development* (Washington, D.C., 1982); Ronald H. Chilcote and Joel C. Edelstein, eds., *Latin America: The Snuggle with Dependency and Beyond* (Cambridge, Mass., 1974); Ronald H. Chilcote, *Dependency and Marxism: Towards a Resolution of the Debate* (Boulder, Colo., 1982).

9. For early critiques by women of color of the biases of feminist theories and the politics of what Chandra Talpade Mohanty has termed "imperial feminism," as well as for unexamined philosophical positions in feminist and other scholarship, see Chandra Mohanty, "Under Western Eyes: Feminist Scholarship and Colonial Discourses," *Boundary 2: A Journal of Post-Modern Literature and Culture* (Spring/Fall 1984) 333–58; Adaljiza Sosa Riddell, "Chicanas en el Movimiento," *Aztlán,* V (1974), 155–65; Cherríe Moraga and Gloria Anzaldúa, eds., *This Bridge Called My Back: Writings by Radical Women of Color* (Watertown, Mass., 1981) *xxii-xxvi;* Barbara Smith, "Racism in Women's Studies," in Gloria T. Hull, Patricia Bell Scott, and Barbara Smith, eds., *But Some of Us Are Brave* (New York, 1982), 48–56; Hazel V. Carby, "White Woman Listen: Black Feminism and the Boundaries of Sisterhood," in Center for Contemporary Cultural Studies, *The Empire Strikes Back: Race and Racism in Seventies Britain* (London, 1982), 212–235; Bonnie Thorton Dill, "Race, Class and Gender: Perspectives for an All-Inclusive Sisterhood," *Feminist Studies,* IX (1983) 131–50; Mujeres en Marcha, *Chicanas in the 80s: Unsettled Issues* (Berkeley, 1983), 130–50; Bell Hooks, *Feminist Theory: From Margin to Center* (Boston, 1984); Alice Y. Chai, "Toward a Holistic Paradigm for Asian American Women's Studies: A Synthesis of Feminist Scholarship and Women of Color's Feminist Politics," *Women's Studies International Forum,* VIII (1985), 59–66;

Cynthia Orozco, "Sexism in Chicano Studies and the Community," in Teresa Córdova, Norma Cantu, Gilberto Cárdenas, Juan García, and Christine M. Sierra, eds., *Chicana Voices: Intersections of Class, Race, and Gender* (Austin, 1986), 11–18; Alma Garcia, "Studying Chicanas: Bringing Women into the Frame of Chicano Studies," *ibid.*, 19–29; Barbara Christian, "The Race for Theory," *Feminist Studies*, XIV (1988), 67–70; Jonella Butler, "Difficult Dialogues," *Women's Review of Books*, VI (February 1989), 16; Bell Hooks, *Talking Back: Thinking Feminist, Thinking Black* (Boston, 1989).

For the critiques of the 1990s, see "Editor's Note," and "Speaking for Ourselves: From the Women of Color Association," *Women's Review of Books*, VIII (February 1990), 27–29; Gloria Anzaldúa, "Introduction" and "Section 7: 'Doing' Theory in Other Modes of Consciousness," in Gloria Anzaldúa, ed., *Making Face, Making Soul: Haciendo Caras* (San Francisco, 1990), xv–xxviii and 335–402; Emma Pérez, "Sexuality and Discourse: Notes from a Chicana Survivor," in Carla Trujillo, ed., *Chicana Lesbians: The Girls our Mothers Warned Us About* (Berkeley, 1991), 159–84.

10. For a discussion of gender in the historiography of colonial and nineteenth-century California, including early studies in Chicano history, see Antonia I. Castañeda, "Gender, Race, and Culture: Spanish-Mexican Women in the Historiography of Frontier California," *Frontiers: A Journal of Women's Studies* [a special issue on Chicanas] XI (1990), 8–20. For feminist activist-scholar-philosopher Angela Davis, see Angela Davis, *With my Mind on Freedom: An Autobiography* (New York, 1974); for Dolores Huerta, vice-president of the United Farm Workers Union, see the UFW newspaper *El Malcriado* (published at Delano and Keene, California, from the mid-1960s to the 1970s); for Janet McCloud, a Tulalip woman who was one of the founders and leaders of the Survival of American Indians Association, Inc., and a leader in the struggle for Native American fishing rights in Washington state, see Laura McCloud, "Is the Trend Changing," in Alvin M. Josephy, Jr., ed., *Red Power: The American Indians' Fight for Freedom* (New York, 1971), 99–104; for activist-poet Janice Mirikitani, see Janice Mirikitani, *Awake in the River* (San Francisco, 1978) and Mirikitani, *Shedding Silence* (Berkeley, 1987).

11. Moraga and Anzaldúa, eds., *This Bridge Called My Back,* Hull, Scott, and Smith, eds., *But Some of Us Are Brave,* Gretchen M. Bataille and Kathleen Mullen Sands, eds., *American Indian Women: Telling Their Lives* (Lincoln, Neb., 1984); Shirley Geok-lin Lim, Mayumi Tsutakawa, Margarita Donnelly, eds., *The Forbidden Stitch: An Asian American Women's Anthology* (Corvallis, Ore., 1989); Asian Women United, ed., *Making Waves;* Anzaldúa, ed., *Making Face, Making Soul.*

12. American Historical Association, *Guidelines on Hiring Women Historians in Academia* (3rd ed., Washington, D.C., 1990). The guidelines homogenize distinct populations into broad "Asian" and "Hispanic" categories. See also, Joan M. Jensen, "Committee on Women Historians, 1970–1990: A Twenty-Year Report," *Perspectives: American Historical Association Newsletter*, XXIX (March

1991), 8–9; Deena J. González, "Commentary: The Rose Report, the Twenty-Year Report of the Committee on Women Historians, and National Ethnic Minority Women in the Professions" (Comments prepared for the American Historical Association Roundtable, Washington, D.C., Dec. 1990).

13. Jensen and Miller, "The Gentle Tamers Revisited," 212–13.

14. Peggy Pascoe, "At the Crossroads of Culture," *Women's Review of Books,* VII (February 1990), 22–23, raises critical questions about feminist theory, ideology, and politics. Although Pascoe argues for multiculturalism and inclusion of women of color in the women's history curriculum, she neither questions nor analyzes the concepts and assumptions of multiculturalism. Pascoe, in "Gender, Race, and Intercultural Relations: The Case of Interracial Marriage," *Frontiers: A Journal of Women's Studies, XII* (1991), 5–18, argues for the social construction of race and raises critical questions about historical scholarship and paradigms of culture but accepts uncritically Euro-centered notions of multiculturalism. Elizabeth Jameson, in "Toward a Multicultural History of Women in the Western United States," *Signs: Journal of Women in Culture and Society,* XIII (1988), 761–91, expands and updates the categories of a multicultural approach but does not analyze the concepts or theories and thus reaffirms Euro-centered definitions of multiculturalism. Sarah Deutsch, in "Women and Intercultural Relations: The Case of Hispanic New Mexico and Colorado," *ibid.,* XII (1987), 719–39, and in her subsequent book (cited below) conceptualizes "intercultural" and issues of assimilation, acculturation, and resistance for Nuevo Mexicanas as originating with the arrival of Euro-Americans and ignores the historical reality of Mexican/Native American interculturalism as well as the significance of this history in the subsequent relations with Euro-Americans. For troublesome generalizations about women of color rooted in unexamined concepts and assumptions about culture and people of color, see Deutsch, No *Separate Refuge: Culture, Class, and Gender on an Anglo-Hispanic Frontier in the American Southwest, 1880–1940* (New York, 1987); and Anne M. Butler, *Daughters of Joy, Sisters of Misery: Prostitutes in the American West, 1865–90* (Urbana, 1987). For a similar critique of Deutsch's *No Separate Refuge,* see Rodolfo Acuña, "The Struggles of Class and Gender: Current Research in Chicano Studies," *Journal of American Ethnic History* VIII (Spring 1989), 134–35. Marion Goldman, *Gold Diggers and Silver Miners: Prostitution and Social Life on the Comstock Lode* (Ann Arbor, 1981), examines prostitution within the boom-bust economy of the Comstock Lode and discusses racial and class hierarchies in prostitution within an economic, not a cultural or multicultural, framework.

15. Schlissel, Ruiz, and Monk, eds., *Western Women: Their Land, Their Lives,* Armitage and Jameson, eds., *Women's West;* Joan M. Jensen and Darlis A. Miller, eds., *New Mexico Women: Intercultural Perspectives* (Albuquerque, 1986); Cathy Luchetti in collaboration with Carol Olwell, *Women of the West* (St. George, Utah, 1982), a pictorial history with a section on "Minority Women" and photographs of African American, Chinese, and Native American

women—but no Mexican women; Janet Lecompte, "The Independent Women of Hispanic New Mexico, 1821–1846," *Western Historical Quarterly,* XII (1981), 17–35.

16. DuBois and Ruiz, eds., *Unequal Sisters.* Much of the periodical literature on Asian women has been collected in anthologies by and about Asian American women that are not conceptualized within the framework of the multicultural approach examined here.

17. Rosalind Z. Rock, "'Pido y Suplico': Women and the Law in Spanish New Mexico," *New Mexico Historical Review,* LXV (1991), 145–60; Jameson, "Toward a Multicultural History"; Cheryl J. Foote and Sandra R. Schackel, "Indian Women of New Mexico, 1535–1680," *New Mexico Historical Review* LXV (1991), *1–16;* Salomé Hernández, "Nueva Mexicanas as Refugees and Reconquest Settlers, 1680–1696," *ibid.,* 17–40; Sylvia Van Kirk, *Many Tender Ties: Women in Fur-Trade Society, 1670–1870* (Norman, Okla., 1980).

18. Mary Paik Lee, *Quiet Odyssey: A Pioneer Korean Woman in America,* edited by Sucheng Chan (Seattle, 1990); Ronald Takaki, *Strangers from a Different Shore: A History of Asian Americans* (New York, 1989); Yuji Ichioka, *The Issei: The World of the First Generation Japanese Immigrants, 1885–1924* (New York, 1988); Evelyn Nakano Glenn, *Issei, Nisei, War Bride: Three Generations of Japanese American Women in Domestic Service* (Philadelphia, 1986); Akeme Kikumura, *Through Harsh Winters: The Life of a Japanese Immigrant Woman* (Novato, Calif., 1981); Judy Yung, "The Social Awakening of Chinese American Women as Reported in Chung Sai Yat Po, 1900–191," DuBois and Ruiz, eds., 195–207. See the following essays, all of which are contained in Asian Women United of California, ed., *Making Waves:* Dorothy Córdova, "Voices from the Past: Why They Came," 42–49; Sun Bin Yum, "Korean Immigrant Women in Early Twentieth-Century America," 50–61; Marcelle Williams, "Ladies on the Line: Punjabi Cannery Workers in Central California," 148–58; Barbara Posadas, "Mestiza Girlhood: Interracial Families in Chicago's Filipino Community since 1925," 273–82. See also David Beesley, "From Chinese to Chinese American: Chinese Women and Families in a Sierra Nevada Town," *California History,* LXVII (1988), 168–79; Joan Hori, Japanese Prostitution in Hawaii during the Immigration Period," Nobuya Tsuchida, ed., *Asian and Pacific American Experiences: Women's Perspectives* (Minneapolis, 1982), 75–87; Alice Y. Chai, "Korean Women in Hawaii, 1903–1945," *ibid.,* 56–65; Yuji Ichioka, *"Amerika Nadeshiko:* Japanese Immigrant Women in the United States, 1900–1924," *Pacific Historical Review,* XL (1980), 339–57.

19. Arlene Scadron, ed., *On Their Own: Widows and Widowhood in the American Southwest, 1848–1939* (Chicago, 1988); Anne M. Butler, "Still in Chains: Black Women in Western Prisons, 1865–1910," *Western Historical Quarterly,* XX (1989), 19–36.

20. Sherry L. Smith, "A Window on Themselves: Perceptions of Indians by Military Officers and Their Wives," *New Mexico Historical Review,* LXIV (1989), 447–62; Sherry L. Smith, "Beyond Princess and Squaw: Army Officers'

Perceptions of Indian Women," Armitage and Jameson, eds., *Women's West*, 68–75; Lisa Emmerich, "Civilization and Transculturation: Field Matrons and Native American Women, 1891–1938" (Paper presented at the conference, "The Women's West: Race, Class, and Social Change," San Francisco, Calif., Aug. 13–15, 1987); Glenda Riley, *Women and Indians on the Frontier, 1825–1915* (Albuquerque, 1984); Annette Kolodny, *The Land before Her: Fantasy and Experience of the American Frontiers, 1830–1860* (Chapel Hill, N.C., 1984); Darlis A. Miller, "Cross-Cultural Marriages in the Southwest: The New Mexico Experience, 1846–1900," *New Mexico Historical Review* LVII (1982), 335–59; Sandra L. Myres, "Mexican Americans and Westering Anglos: A Feminine Perspective" *ibid.*, 414–30; Rebecca McDowell Craver, *The Impact of Intimacy: Mexican-Anglo Intermarriage in New Mexico, 1821–1846* (El Paso, 1982).

21. Susan L. Johnson's "Sharing Bed and Board: Cohabitation and Cultural Difference in Central Arizona Mining Towns, 1863–1873," Armitage and Jameson, eds., *Women's West*, 77–92, addresses the specific Mexican history of informal unions in its discussion of cohabitation among Mexican women and Anglo men as well as their conflicting values concerning informal unions. Johnson, however, generalizes about Mexican culture, Mexican women, and Mexican communities in Arizona mining towns without any gender-centered primary research on the issue of informal unions in Mexican culture and without any substantive evidence upon which to base her generalizations.

22. Butler, *Daughters of Joy;* Goldman, *Gold Diggers and Silver Miners,* Darlis A. Miller, "Foragers, Army Women, and Prostitutes," *New Mexico Historical Review, LXV* (1991), 141–68.

23. Peggy Pascoe, *Relations of Rescue: The Search for Female Moral Authority in the American West, 1874–1939* (New York, 1990); Pascoe, "Gender, Race, and Intercultural Relations"; Posadas, "Mestiza Girlhood," 273–82.

24. Joseph L. Chartkoff and Kerry Kona Chartkoff, *Archaeology of California* (Stanford, 1984); Robert E. Heizer and Albert B. Elsasser, *The Natural World of the California Indian* (Berkeley, 1980); Sherburne F. Cook and Woodrow Borah, *Essays in Population History: Mexico and the Caribbean* (3 vols., Berkeley, 1971–1979); Sherburne F. Cook, *The Population of the California Indians, 1769–1970* (Berkeley, 1976).

25. Irene Silverblatt, *Moon, Sun, and Witches: Gender Ideologies and Class in Inca and Colonial Peru* (Princeton, NJ, 1987); June Nash, "Aztec Women: The Transition from Status to Class in Empire and Colony," Mona Etienne and Eleanor Leacock, eds., *Women and Colonization: Anthropological Perspectives* (New York, 1980).

26. Ramón A. Gutiérrez, *When Jesus Came, the Corn Mothers Went Away: Marriage, Sexuality, and Power in New Mexico, 1500–1846* (Stanford, 1991), xvii–36; Sarah M. Nelson, "Widowhood and Autonomy in the Native American Southwest," in Scadron, ed., *On Their Own,* 22–41; Alice Schlegel, "Hopi Family Structure and the Experience of Widowhood," *ibid.,* 42–64; see the following essays in

Eleanor Leacock and Richard Lee, eds., *Politics and History in Band Societies* (Cambridge, Mass., 1982): Eleanor Leacock and Richard Lee, "Introduction," 1–20; Lee, "Politics, Sexual and Non-Sexual, in an Egalitarian Society," 23–36; and Leacock, "Relations of Production in Band Society," 159–70. See also June Nash, "A Decade of Research on Women in Latin America," June Nash and Helen I. Safa, eds., *Women and Change in Latin America* (South Hadley, Mass., 1986), 3–21; Etienne and Leacock, eds., *Women and Colonization*, 1–24; Eleanor Burke Leacock, *Myths of Male Dominance: Collected Articles on Women Cross-Culturally* (New York, 1981); Eleanor Leacock, "Women, Development, and Anthropological Facts and Fictions," *Latin American Perspectives*, IV (Winter-Spring 1977), 8–17; Eleanor Leacock, "Women in Egalitarian Societies," Renate Bridenthal and Claudia Koonz, eds., *Becoming Visible: Women in European History* (Boston, 1977), 11–35.

27. Anne Ducille, "Othered Matters: Reconceptualizing Dominance and Difference in the History of Sexuality in America," *Journal of the History of Sexuality*, I (1990), 102–27 (quote is from page 103).

28. Dee Brown, *The Gentle Tamers: Women of the Old Wild West* (New York: Bantam Books, 1974). Although Brown may have coined and been the first to use the term "gentle tamers," the concept of Euro-American women as the gentle, genteel bearers of "civilization" across successive frontiers is standard fare in the historical literature.

29. For an earlier, succinct critique of this approach, see Deena González, "Commentary [on a paper by John Mack Faragher, "The Custom of the Country: Cross-Cultural Marriage in the Far Western Fur Trade"]" *Western Women*, 217–22.

30. Rayna Green, ed., *Native American Women: A Contextual Bibliography* (Bloomington, 1983), 1–19; Green, "Native American Women," *Signs: Journal of Women in Culture and Society*, VI (1980), 248–67; and Green, "The Pocahontas Perplex: The Image of Indian Women in American Culture," *Massachusetts Review*, XVI (1975), 698–714; Antonia I. Castañeda, "The Political Economy of Nineteenth Century Stereotypes of Californianas," in Adelaida del Castillo, ed., *Between Borders: Essays in Mexicana/Chicana History* (Los Angeles, 1990), 213–36; Castañeda, "Gender, Race, and Culture: Spanish-Mexican Women in the Historiography of Frontier California."

31. For a discussion of the new approaches to culture in literature and history, see Lynn Hunt, ed., *The New Cultural History* (Berkeley, 1989). For a discussion of the issues in anthropology, see James Clifford, *The Predicament of Cultures* (New York, 1988); for the earlier approaches in social history, see Peter N. Stearns, "Social History and History: A Progress Report," *Journal of Social History*, XIX (1985), 319–34.

32. Richard Griswold del Castillo, *The Los Angeles Barrio, 1850–1890: A Social History* (Berkeley, 1979), App. A, 180–81; Leo Grebler, Joan W. Moore, and Ralph C. Guzmán, *The Mexican-American People: The Nation's Second Minority* (New York, 1970); José Hernández, Leo Estrada, and David Alvírez, "Census

Data and the Problem of Conceptually Defining the Mexican American Population," *Social Science Quarterly,* LIII (1973), 671–87. See also Ricardo Romo, "Southern California and the Origins of Latino Civil-Rights Activism," *Western Legal History,* III (1990), 379–406; Ramón A. Gutiérrez, "Ethnic and Class Boundaries in America's Hispanic Past," in Sucheng Chan, ed., *Social and Gender Boundaries in the United States* (Lewiston, N.Y., 1989), 37–53; Gloria A. Miranda, "Racial and Cultural Dimensions of Gente de Razon Status in Spanish and Mexican California," *Southern California Quarterly,* LXX (1988), 265–78.

33. Grebler, Moore, and Guzmán, *Mexican-American People,* 322.
34. Alarcón, "Chicana Feminism"; Christian, "The Race for Theory"; Henry Louis Gates, Jr., ed., *Race, Writing, and Difference* (Chicago, 1986); Mohanty; "Under Western Eyes"; Cornel West, "Minority Discourse and the Pitfalls of Canon Formation," *Yale Journal of Criticism,* I (Fall 1987) 173–200.
35. Mohanty, "Under Western Eyes," 336.
36. Deena J. González, "La Tules Image and Reality: Euro-American Attitudes and Legend Formation on a Spanish Mexican Frontier" in De la Torre and Pesquera, eds., *Building with our Own Hands;* Patricia Albers and William James, "Illusion and Illumination: Visual Images of American Indian Women in the West," in Armitage and Jameson, eds., *Women's West,* pp. 35–50 examine the unrealistic images of American Indians produced for postcards for the tourist trade; Green, ed., *Native American Women,* 1–19; Green, "Native American Women," 248–67; Green, "Pocahontas Perplex," 698–714; Maryann Oshana, "Native American Women in Westerns: Reality and Myth," *Frontiers: A Journal of Women Studies,* VI (Fall 1981), 46–50; Castañeda, "Political Economy of Nineteenth Century Stereotypes," 213–36; Castañeda, "Gender, Race, and Culture"; Renee E. Tajima, "Lotus Blossoms Don't Bleed: Images of Asian Women," Asian Women of California, ed., *Making Waves,* 308–17; Paula Giddings, *When and Where I Enter: The Impact of Black Women on Race and Sex in America* (Toronto, 1984), 31.
37. Castañeda, "The Political Economy of Stereotypes"; Green, "The Pocahontas Perplex."
38. Megumi Dick Osumi, "Asians and California's Anti-Miscegenation Laws," in Tsuchida, ed., *Asian and Pacific American Experiences,* 1–37; Akemi Kikumura and Harry H. L. Kitano, "Interracial Marriage: A Picture of the Japanese Americans," *ibid.,* 193–205. The Kikumura and Kitano essay was first published in 1973. Although California was a "free" state, slave owners still brought slaves to it and other western territories, and Euro-Americans still tried to enslave Indians. The fact that enslaved black people were able to win their freedom in California if they could get their case heard does not obviate the reality of enslavement in the West nor the need to examine it.
39. Castañeda, "The Political Economy of Stereotypes."
40. For a discussion of the devaluation of the sexuality of women of color as central to imperialism, with a specific focus on Native American women in

California, see Antonia I. Castañeda, "Sexual Violence in the Politics and Policies of Conquest," in De la Torre and Pesquera, eds., *Building with Our Own Hands.*

41. Butler, *Daughters of Joy,* 11–12.

42. *Ibid.,* 12.

43. Armitage, "Through Women's Eyes," in Armitage and Jameson, eds., *Women's West,* 9–19; Kolodny, *The Land before Her,* Riley, *Women and Indians on the Frontier,* Myres, "Mexican Americans and Westering Anglos."

44. For discussion of sexual and other violence toward women of color in frontier California, see Albert Hurtado, *Indian Survival on the California Frontier* (New York, 1989), 169–92; Castañeda, "Sexual Violence in the Politics and Policies of Conquest" and "The Political Economy of Nineteenth-Century Stereotypes"; Giddings, *When and Where I Enter,* Lucie Cheng Hirata, "Chinese Immigrant Women in Nineteenth-Century California, in Tsuchida, ed., *Asian and Pacific American Experiences,* 38–55; and Hirata, "Free, Indentured, Enslaved: Chinese Prostitutes in Nineteenth-Century America," *Signs: Journal of Women in Culture and Society,* V (1979), 3–29.

45. Rosalia Vallejo de Leese, "History of the Bear Flag Party," Manuscript Collection, Bancroft Library, University of California, Berkeley; Hurtado, *Indian Survival in California;* Giddings, *When and Where I Enter;* Hirata, "Chinese Immigrant Women," 1.

46. Paula Gunn Allen, ed., *Spider Woman's Granddaughters* (New York, 1989), 2.

47. The first part of this subtitle is derived from Bill Ashcroft, Gareth Griffiths, and Helen Tiffin, eds., *The Empire Writes Back: Theory and Practice in Post-Colonial Literatures* (New York, 1989).

48. For representative works, see Gloria Anzaldúa, *Borderlands-La Frontera: The New Mestiza* (San Francisco, 1987); Amy Tan, *The Joy Luck Club* (New York, 1989); Toni Morrison, *Beloved* (New York, 1987); Louise Erdrich, *Love Medicine* (New York, 1984).

49. Chela Sandoval, "U.S. Third World Feminism: The Theory and Method of Oppositional Consciousness in the Postmodern World," *Genders,* X (Spring 1991), 1–24; Bernice Johnson Reagan, "Forward: Nurturing Resistance," in Mark O'Brien and Craig Little, eds., *Reimaging America: The Arts of Social Change* (Philadelphia, 1990), 1–8.

50. Shirley Geok-lin Lim, "Introduction: A Dazzling Quilt," in Lim, Tsutskawa, Donnelly, eds., *Forbidden Stitch,* 12; Alarcón, "Chicana Feminism."

51. Gutiérrez, *When Jesus Came,* xvii–xviii.

52. *Ibid.*

53. See the excellent collection of essays in Mohanty, Russo, and Tomes, eds., *Third World Women;* Kumkum Sangari Sudesh Vaid, eds., *Recasting Women: Essays in Indian Colonial History* (New Brunswick NJ., 1990); Minh-ha, *Woman, Native, Other;* Malek Alloula, *The Colonial Harem,* translated by Myrna Godzich and Wlad Godzich (Minneapolis, 1986).

54. Alloula, *Colonial Harem,* xiv.

55. Mohanty, "Under Western Eyes," 335.

56. Howard Lamar and Leonard Thompson, eds., *The Frontier in History: North America and Southern Africa Compared* (New Haven, 1981).

57. *Ibid.*, 7.

58. Limerick, *Legacy of Conquest,* 26–27.

59. Rosalinda Méndez González, "Distinctions in Western Women's Experience: Ethnicity, Class, and Social Change," in Armitage and Jameson, eds., *Women's West,* 237–52.

60. Deena J. González, *Resisting the Favor: The Spanish-Mexican Women of Santa Fe, 1820–1880* (New York, forthcoming); Hurtado, *Indian Survival;* Victoria Brady, Sarah Crome, and Lyn Reese, "Resist! Survival Tactics of Indian Women," *California History,* LXIII (1984), 140–49; Lamar and Thompson, *Comparative Frontier History;* George Harwood Phillips, *Chiefs and Challengers: Indian Resistance and Cooperation in Southern California* (Berkeley, 1975); Jack Forbes, *Apache, Navaho, and Spaniard* (Norman, 1960).

61. Helen Lara-Cea, "Notes on the Use of Parish Registers in the Reconstruction of Chicana History in California Prior to 1850," in Del Castillo, ed., *Between Borders,* 131–60; González, *Resisting the Favor,* Angelina Veyna, "A View of the Past: Women in Colonial New Mexico, 1744–1767," in De la Torre and Pesquera, eds., *Building with Our Our Hands;* Antonia I. Castañeda, "Presidarias y Pobladoras: Spanish Mexican Women in Frontier Monterey, California, 1770–1821" (Ph.D. dissertation, Stanford University, 1990).

62. Mohanty, "Under Western Eyes," 346; Chandra P. Mohanty and Saya P. Mohanty, "Review: Contradictions of Colonialism," *Women's Review of Books,* VIII (March 1990), 19–21.

63. Etienne and Leacock, *Women and Colonization;* Leacock and Lee, *Politics and History in Band Societies;* Evelyn Blackwood, "Sexuality and Gender in Certain Native American Tribes: The Case of Cross-Gender Females," *Signs: Journal of Women in Society and Culture,* X (1984), 27–42.

64. Hurtado, *Indian Survival in California;* Brady, Crome, and Reese, "Resist!"

65. Lois Riding, "Native Women in California" (Paper presented at the Huntington Library Seminar in Women's Studies, San Marino, Calif., Jan. 20, 1991); Patricia Albers, "Autonomy and Dependency in the Lives of Dakota Women: A Study in Historical Change," *Review of Radical Political Economics,* XVII (Fall 1985), 109–34; Patricia Albers and Beatrice Medicine, eds., *The Hidden Half: Studies of Plains Indian Women* (New York, 1983); see Gutiérrez, *When Jesus Came,* for a discussion of socio-sexual reciprocity among the Pueblos of New Mexico.

66. On the Yuma, see Hugo Reid, "Letters on the Los Angeles County Indians," Susana Dakin, ed., *A Scotch Paisano: Hugo Reid's Life in California, 1832–1852* (Berkeley, 1939), app. B, 215–16, 240; see also Castañeda, "Presidarias v Pobladoras," 63–113.

67. González, *Resisting the Favor.* For a discussion of Nuevo Mexicanas and widowhood in the postwar period, see Deena J. González, "The Widowed Women

of Santa Fe: Assessments on the Lives of an Unmarried Population, 1850–80,"
in Scadron, ed., *On Their Own*, 65–90.

68. Sucheng Chan, "The Exclusion of Chinese Women, 1870–1943," in Sucheng
Chan, ed., *Entry Denied: Exclusion and the Chinese Community in America,
1882–1943* (Philadelphia, 1991), 94–146; Ichioka, *The Issei;* Marion & Hom,
Songs of Cold Mountain: Cantonese Rhymes from San Francisco Chinatown
(Berkeley, 1987); Judy Yung, *Chinese Women of America: A Pictorial History*
(Seattle, 1986); Judy Yung, "The Social Awakening of Chinese American
Women," in DuBois and Ruiz, eds., *Unequal Sisters*, 195–207; the following
articles appear in Tsuchida, ed., *Asian and Pacific American Experiences:* Hirata,
"Chinese Immigrant Women in Nineteenth Century California," 53–55;
Hirata, "Free, Indentured, Enslaved," 3–29; Hori, "Japanese Prostitution in
Hawaii," 56–65, and Emma Gee, "Issei Women," 66–74.

69. Gail M. Nomura, "Issei Working Women in Hawaii," in Asian Women United
of California, ed., *Making Waves*, 135–47; Ichioka, Issei, 164–175; Glenn, *Issei,
Nisei, War Bride*, 42–66.

70. Chan, "Exclusion of Chinese women," 94–146.

71. *Ibid.*, 95.

72. *Ibid.*, 132.

73. George Anthony Peffer, "Forbidden Families: Emigration Experiences of
Chinese Women under the Page Law, 1875–1882," *Journal of American Ethnic
History*, VI (Fall 1986), 28–46.

74. Lucie Cheng and Edna Bonacich, eds., *Labor Immigration under Capitalism:
Asian Workers in the United States before World War II* (Berkeley, 1984; Mario
Barrera, *Race and Class in the Southwest* (Notre Dame, Ind., 1979).

75. Nomura, "Issei Working Women in Hawaii," 135–147; Ichioka, *Issei*, 28–90;
Ichioka, *Amerika Nadeshiko*, 339–57; Ichioka, "Ameyuki-san: Japanese
Prostitutes in Nineteenth Century America," *Amerasia Journal*, IV (1977), 1–21;
Glenn, *Issei, Nisei, War Bride*, 3–20; Hori, "Japanese Prostitution in Hawaii,"
56–65.

76. Ichioka, *Issei*, 20–39.

77. Shirley Ann Moore, "Not in Somebody's Kitchen: African-American Women
Workers in Richmond, California, 1910–1950" (Paper presented at the
Huntington Library Seminar in Women's Studies, San Marino, Calif., Jan. 19,
1991); Shirley Ann Moore, *To Place Our Deeds: The Black Community in
Richmond, California, 1910–1963* (Chicago, forthcoming).

78. Moore, "Not in Somebody's Kitchen."

79. Joan Jensen and Gloria Ricci Lothrop, *California Women: A History* (San
Francisco, 1987), 32, 37; Rudolph M. Lapp, *Afro-Americans in California* (2d ed
San Francisco, 1987); William Loren Katz, *The Black West: A Pictorial History*
(3d ed., Seattle, 1987); Lawrence B. de Graaf, "Race, Sex, and Region: Black
Women in the American West, 1350–1920," *Pacific Historical Review*, XL (1980),
285–313; Delilah L. Beasley, *The Negro Trail Blazers of California* (1919; New
York, 1969).

80. Deena J. González, "The Spanish-Mexican Women of Santa Fe: Mocking the Conquerors" (Paper presented at the Writing on the Border Conference, Claremont Colleges, Oct. 27, 1989).

Susan Lee Johnson, 'A Memory Sweet to Soldiers': The Significance of Gender in the History of the 'American West'

1. Joan M. Jensen and Darlis A. Miller, "The Gentle Tamers Revisited: New Approaches to the History of Women in the American West," *Pacific Historical Review* 49 (May 1980): 173–213; Elizabeth Jameson, "Toward a Multicultural History of Women in the Western United States," *Signs* 13 (Summer 1988): 761–91; "The Contributions and Challenges of Western Women's History: Four Essays by Sarah Deutsch, Virginia Scharff, Glenda Riley, and John Mack Faragher," *Montana: The Magazine of Western History* 41 (Spring 1991): 58–73; "Western Women's History Revisited," *Pacific Historical Review* 61, special issue (November 1992).

2. I am thinking here of Ramón A. Gutiérrez, *When Jesus Came, the Corn Mothers Went Away: Marriage, Sexuality, and Power in New Mexico, 1500–1846* (Stanford, 1991); Albert L. Hurtado, *Indian Survival on the California Frontier* (New Haven, 1988); John Mack Faragher, *Women and Men on the Overland Trail* (New Haven, 1979) and *Sugar Creek: Life on the Illinois Prairie* (New Haven, 1986).

3. For related arguments, see Katherine G. Morrissey, "Engendering the West," in *Under an Open Sky: Rethinking America's Western Past*, ed. William Cronon, George Miles, and Jay Gitlin (New York, 1992).

4. Despite its North-South definition of regionalism, the provocative session entitled "Region, Race, and Gender: The 'Masculinity Crisis' and Realignments of Power in Late-Nineteenth-Century America" at the Eighth Berkshire Conference on the History of Women, Douglass College, 10 June 1990, has most influenced my thinking here. Respondents Henry Abelove and Drew Gilpin Faust commented on Nina Silber, "The Romance of Reunion: Northern Conciliation with the South and the Metaphor of Gender," and Gail Bederman, "Ida B. Wells-Barnett's Anti-Lynching Campaign and the Northern Middle Class's 'Crisis of Masculinity.'" Bederman's essay has since been published as "'Civilization,' the Decline of Middle-Class Manliness, and Ida B. Wells's Antilynching Campaign (1892–94)," *Radical History Review* 52 (Winter 1992): 5–30, and Silber's arguments appear in *The Romance of Reunion: Northerners and the South, 1865–1900* (Chapel Hill, 1993). See also Clyde Griffen, "Reconstructing Masculinity from the Evangelical Revival to the Waning of Progressivism: A Speculative Synthesis," in *Meanings for Manhood: Constructions of Masculinity in Victorian America*, ed. Mark C. Carnes and Clyde Griffen (Chicago, 1990).

5. Sadly, the most exciting and engaging work on the American West to appear in decades represents this tendency: Patricia Nelson Limerick, *Legacy of*

Conquest:The Unbroken Past of the American West (New York, 1987). For a recent textbook that tries harder to incorporate the insights of western women's history, see Richard White, *"It's Your Misfortune and None of My Own": A New History of the American West* (Norman, 1991). The special-chapter approach is represented by Michael P. Malone, ed., *Historians and the American West* (Lincoln, 1983), and Gerald D. Nash and Richard W. Etulain, eds., *The Twentieth-Century West: Historical Interpretations* (Albuquerque, 1989).

6. Antonia I. Castañeda, "Women of Color and the Rewriting of Western History: The Discourse, Politics, and Decolonization of History," *Pacific Historical Review* 61 (November 1992): 501–33. On the calls for multiculturalism, see Jensen and Miller, "The Gentle Tamers," and Jameson, "Toward a Multicultural History." A good example of a multicultural approach is Peggy Pascoe, *Relations of Rescue:The Search for Female Moral Authority in the American West, 1874–1939* (New York, 1990).

7. Henry Nash Smith, *Virgin Land:The American West as Symbol and Myth* (1950; reprint, Cambridge, Mass., 1970); Richard Slotkin, *The Fatal Environment:The Myth of the Frontier in the Age of Industrialization, 1800–1890* (New York, 1985). See also Richard Slotkin, *Regeneration through Violence: The Mythology of the American Frontier, 1600–1860* (Middletown, Conn., 1973) and *Gunfighter Nation: The Myth of the Frontier in Twentieth-Century America* (New York, 1992).

8. Annette Kolodny, *The Lay of the Land: Metaphor as Experience and History in American Life and Letters* (Chapel Hill, 1975).

9. Regina G. Kunzel, *Fallen Women, Problem Girls: Unmarried Mothers and the Professionalization of Social Work, 1890–1945* (New Haven, 1993).

10. Smith, *Virgin Land*, 4, 224–49. Compare Smith's reading of Kirkland and Cary to Annette Kolodny's in *The Land before Her: Fantasy and Experience of the American Frontiers, 1630–1860* (Chapel Hill, 1984), 130–58, 178–90. See also Eve Kosofsky Sedgwick, *Between Men: English Literature and Male Homosocial Desire* (New York, 1985).

11. Smith, *Virgin Land*, 112–20 (emphasis mine).

12. Ibid., 119. As for the physical positioning of the "Dime Novel Heroine" chapter, although the text is divided into a prologue and three "books," the prologue and the first two books constitute the first half, and the third book forms the second half of the volume. The chapter in question appears at the end of the second book.

13. Ibid., see illustrations following p. 98.

14. See Edward L. Wheeler, *Deadwood Dick in Leadville; Or, A Strange Stroke for Liberty* (New York, 1879).

15. Slotkin, *Fatal Environment*, and Slotkin, *Gunfighter Nation*.

16. Slotkin, *Fatal Environment*, 32.

17. Ibid., 336. For an especially satisfying account of related themes, particularly of the construction of western heroes, see Alexander Saxton, *The Rise and Fall of the White Republic: Class Politics and Mass Culture in Nineteenth-Century America* (London, 1990).

18. Ibid., 477–98, quotations on 484.

19. Although I invoke the "race, class, gender" trinity here, there are, of course, other recent claimants to the status of central categories of historical analysis; in the academic circles in which I move, sexuality and the environment are big contenders. I remain ambivalent about the latter, especially until environmental history begins to take race, class, and gender more (and "nature" less) seriously. Though we no doubt differ on what "more" and "less" would look like in scholarly practice, William Cronon has made a related call in his "Modes of Prophecy and Production: Placing Nature in History," *Journal of American History* 76 (March 1990): 1122–31, esp. 1130–31. I am even more taken with the notion of considering sexuality a separate category of analysis, though where gender leaves off and sexuality begins is always a hard call for me. For an earlier argument, see Gayle Rubin, "Thinking Sex: Notes for a Radical Theory of the Politics of Sexuality," in *Pleasure and Danger: Exploring Female Sexuality*, ed. Carole S. Vance (Boston, 1984). See also John D'Emilio and Estelle B. Freedman, *Intimate Matters: A History of Sexuality in America* (New York, 1988); and new work in lesbian and gay studies represented by Martin Bauml Duberman, Martha Vicinius, and George Chauncey Jr., eds., *Hidden from History: Reclaiming the Gay and Lesbian Past* (New York, 1989); Diana Fuss, ed., *Inside/Out: Lesbian Theories, Gay Theories* (New York, 1991); and Teresa de Lauretis, ed., "Queer Theory: Lesbian and Gay Sexualities" *Differences* 3, special issue (Summer 1991).

20. The other way women routinely appear in Slotkin's *Fatal Environment* is in their proximity to dominant nineteenth-century notions of savagery and disorder. In this, women occupy the same conceptual ground as people of color and the working class in Slotkin's analysis. Slotkin, *Fatal Environment*, 336, 342–43, 348, 478.

21. Ibid., 375.

22. Ibid., 381, 385–87, 390, 405–6. For analysis of such male homosocial ties and their links to homoeroticism and homophobia, see Sedgwick, *Between Men*, and Michael Moon, "'The Gentle Boy from the Dangerous Classes': Pederasty, Domesticity, and Capitalism in Horatio Alger," *Representations* 19 (Summer 1987): 87–110.

23. Quoted in Slotkin, *Fatal Environment*, 454.

24. Ibid., 454–55.

25. See Benedict Anderson, *Imagined Communities: Reflections on the Origin and Spread of Nationalism* (1983; 2d ed., rev., London, 1991).

26. Slotkin, *Gunfighter Nation*, 655. Slotkin goes on to say, "Historical memory will have to be revised, not to invent an imaginary role for supposedly marginal minorities, but to register the fact that our history . . . was shaped from the beginning by the meeting, conversation, and mutual adaptation of different cultures." To me, this indicates an unresolved tension in Slotkin's work over the relationship between dominant and nondominant myths, histories, and peoples.

27. See Judith Butler, *Gender Trouble: Feminism and the Subversion of Identity* (New York, 1990), 31.

28. See, for example, Susan Armitage, "Women and Men in Western History: A Stereoptical Vision," *Western Historical Quarterly* 16 (October 1985): 381–95.

29. For a thorough review, see Jameson, "Toward a Multicultural History." Major titles include Julie Roy Jeffrey, *Frontier Women: The Trans-Mississippi West, 1840–1880* (New York, 1979); Sandra L. Myres, *Westering Women and the Frontier Experience, 1800–1915* (Albuquerque, 1982); Susan Armitage and Elizabeth Jameson, eds., *The Women's West* (Norman, 1987); and Lillian Schlissel, Vicki L. Ruiz, and Janice Monk, eds., *Western Women: Their Land, Their Lives* (Albuquerque, 1988). (Sandra Myres disavowed a "radical" feminist approach in her work, though what was "radical" about contemporaneous scholarship is open to question.) The "our books, ourselves" phrase is a play on *Our Bodies, Ourselves,* the title of the many-editioned bible of the women's health movement. The most recent edition is Boston Women's Health Book Collective, *The New Our Bodies, Ourselves* (New York, 1992).

30. Denise Riley, *"Am I That Name?" Feminism and the Category of "Women" in History* (Minneapolis, 1988), 1–2.

31. I'm thinking here of earlier works such as Cherrie Moraga and Gloria Anzaldúa, eds., *This Bridge Called My Back: Writings by Radical Women of Color* (1981; 2d ed., rev., New York, 1983); Gloria T. Hull, Patricia Bell Scott, and Barbara Smith, eds., *All the Women Are White, All the Blacks Are Men, but Some of Us Are Brave: Black Women's Studies* (Old Westbury, N.Y., 1982); Evelyn Torton Beck, ed., *Nice Jewish Girls: A Lesbian Anthology* (1982; 2d ed., rev., Boston, 1989); Barbara Smith, ed., *Home Girls: A Black Feminist Anthology* (New York, 1983). Another key set of readings came out of the feminist sex wars of the late 1970s and early 1980s, one major skirmish of which took place at the "Towards a Politics of Sexuality" conference at Barnard College, New York, N.Y., on 24 April 1982, the proceedings of which were eventually published in Vance, *Pleasure and Danger*. See also Estelle B. Freedman and Barrie Thorne, eds., "The Feminist Sexuality Debates," *Signs* 10 (Autumn 1984): 102–35. Katie King usefully ties together some of the sex war literature with earlier women-of-color publications in "Producing Sex, Theory, and Culture: Gay/Straight Remappings in Contemporary Feminism," in *Conflicts in Feminism*, ed. Marianne Hirsch and Evelyn Fox Keller (New York, 1990).

32. Evelyn Brooks Higginbotham, "African American Women's History and the Metalanguage of Race," *Signs* 17 (Winter 1992): 251–74, esp. 252; Norma Alarcón, "The Theoretical Subject(s) of *This Bridge Called My Back* and Anglo-American Feminism," in *Making Face, Making Soul/Haciendo Caras: Creative and Critical Perspectives by Feminists of Color,* ed. Gloria Anzaldúa (San Francisco, 1990); Chela Sandoval, "U.S. Third World Feminism: The Theory and Method of Oppositional Consciousness in the Postmodern World," *Genders* 10 (Spring 1991): 1–24.

33. The following survey is not intended to serve as a comprehensive guide to

recent feminist theory. It neglects key thinkers, texts, and points of view. It is intended to suggest a few feminist avenues of inquiry that I think would be especially useful to western historians.

34. Gayle Rubin, "The Traffic in Women: Notes on the 'Political Economy of Sex,'" in *Toward an Anthropology of Women*, ed. Rayna R. Reiter (New York, 1975), 168 (emphasis mine). I rarely use the word patriarchy, for the reasons Rubin suggests, but am sympathetic to other ways of thinking about the term. As Mary Childers says: "For a lot of people who know what it is to have a daddy who beats everybody in the family, patriarchy is a great word. . . . And for all of us who work in institutions where there are inaccessible, controlling men at the top, patriarchy is a damn good word." See Mary Childers and bell hooks, "A Conversation about Race and Class," in Hirsch and Keller, *Conflicts in Feminism*, 68.

35. Rubin, "Traffic in Women," 180. See Gen. 1:27, "So God created man in his own image, in the image of God he created him; male and female he created them."

36. Riley, "Am I That Name?" 7.

37. Butler, *Gender Trouble*, 6–7. Just as this essay was going to print, Butler's response to critics of *Gender Trouble* appeared: *Bodies That Matter: On the Discursive Limits of "Sex"* (New York, 1993).

38. Butler, *Gender Trouble*, 24–25, 33; Riley, *"Am I That Name?"* 6.

39. Joan Wallach Scott, *Gender and the Politics of History* (New York, 1988).

40. Higginbotham, "African-American Women's History," 251.

41. Elsa Barkley Brown, "Polyrhythms and Improvisation: Lessons for Women's History," *History Workshop Journal* 31–32 (1991): 85–90, esp. 88. See also Hazel V. Carby, *Reconstructing Womanhood: The Emergence of the Afro-American Woman Novelist* (New York, 1987), 18.

42. Childers and hooks, "A Conversation about Race and Class," 68.

43. Higginbotham, "African-American Women's History," 255.

44. Alarcón, "The Theoretical Subject(s) of *This Bridge*," 357, 360, 361; Gloria Anzaldúa, *Borderlands/La Frontera: The New Mestiza* (San Francisco, 1987). Chandra Talpade Mohanty, "Cartographies of Struggle: Third World Women and the Politics of Feminism," and Lourdes Torres, "The Construction of Self in U.S. Latina Autobiographies," both in *Third World Women and the Politics of Feminism*, ed. Chandra Talpade Mohanty, Ann Russo, and Lourdes Torres (Bloomington, 1991), 1–47, 271–87. For excellent historical overviews of some of these struggles, which stress the relational nature of differences among women, see Brown, "Polyrhythms and Improvisation," and Evelyn Nakano Glenn, "From Servitude to Service Work: Historical Continuities in the Racial Division of Paid Reproductive Labor," *Signs* 18 (Autumn 1992): 1–43.

45. Sandoval, "U.S. Third World Feminism," 15.

46. Brown, "Polyrhythms and Improvisation," 88.

47. On Murrieta, see Pedro Castillo and Albert Camarillo, eds., *Furia y Muerte: Los Bandidos Chicanos* (Los Angeles, 1973), esp. 32–51, and Rodolfo Gonzales,

I am Joaquín/Yo soy Joaquín: An Epic Poem (1967; reprint, New York, 1972). I have written on the historical memory of Murrieta in "'The Gold She Gathered': Difference and Domination in the California Gold Rush, 1848–1853" (Ph.D. diss., Yale University, 1993). On Babe Bean, see San Francisco Lesbian and Gay History Project, "'She Even Chewed Tobacco': A Pictorial Narrative of Passing Women in America," in *Hidden from History*, ed. Duberman, Vicinius, and Chauncey, which is based on the video by Liz Stevens and Estelle B. Freedman titled "She Even Chewed Tobacco" (1983), produced by the History Project and distributed by Women Make Movies (225 Lafayette St., New York, NY 10012); and Louis Sullivan, *From Female to Male: The Life of Jack Bee Garland* (Boston, 1990).

48. Whitman's "Death-Sonnet for Custer" was first published in the *New York Tribune* days after the Battle of the Little Bighorn. It is reproduced in Slotkin, *Fatal Environment*, 10–11; it also appears in later editions of *Leaves of Grass* under the title "Far from Dakota's Cañons." See Walt Whitman, *Complete Poetry and Collected Prose* (New York, 1982), 592–93.

49. The phrase "striking a pose" is derived from Madonna, "Vogue," *The Immaculate Collection*, compact sound disk (New York, 1990).

Amy Kaminsky, Gender, Race, *Raza*

1. Cherríe Moraga and Gloria Anzaldúa, *This Bridge Called My Back: Writings of Radical Women of Color* (Watertown, Mass.: Persephone Press, 1981; reprint, Kitchen Table, Women of Color Press, 1983); and Gloria T. Hull, Patricia Bell Scott, and Barbara Smith, eds., *All the Women Are White, All the Blacks Are Men, but Some of Us Are Brave* (Old Westbury, N.Y.: The Feminist Press, 1982). Work by and about African American women is, not surprisingly, the most visible. Consider the prophetic title of bell hooks's text on African American feminism, *Feminist Theory: From Margin to Center* (Boston: South End Press, 1984). See Patricia Bell Scott, Beverley Guy-Sheftall, and Jacqueline Jones Royster, "The Promise and Challenge of Black Women's Studies: A Report from the Spelman Conference, May 1990," *NWSA Journal* 3 (spring 1991): 282–88, for a report on the growth of Black women's studies as a vital academic field.

2. See, for example, Elizabeth V. Spelman, *Inessential Woman: Problems of Exclusion in Feminist Thought* (Boston: Beacon Press, 1988); and Teresa de Lauretis, "Feminist Studies/Critical Studies: Issues, Terms, and Contexts," in *Feminist Studies/Critical Studies*, ed. Teresa de Lauretis (Bloomington: Indiana University Press, 1986), 1–19. This change is by no means complete, and according to some has barely begun. Norma Alarcón, "The Theoretical Subject(s) of *This Bridge Called My Back* and Anglo-American feminism," in *Criticism in the Borderlands: Studies in Chicano Literature, Culture, and Ideology*, ed. Héctor Calderón and José David Saldívar (Durham, N.C.: Duke

University Press, 1991), 28–39, for example, argues that white feminist theory remains unmoved insofar as the subject of feminism is still white.

3. Differences within racial categories have, of course, been dealt with by feminist scholars. To name a very few examples: Hortense Spillers, "Notes on an Alternative Model: Neither Nor," in *The Difference Within: Feminism and Critical Theory*, ed. Elizabeth Meese and Alice Parker (Philadelphia: John Benjamin, 1989), 164–87, discusses the tragic mulatta figure, an "other," defined by whites, within Blackness; and Patricia J. Williams's extraordinary study, *The Alchemy of Race and Rights* (Cambridge: Harvard University Press, 1991), never loses sight of gender. The recent anthology, *Breaking Boundaries: Latina Writing and Critical Readings*, ed. Asuncion Horno Delgado et al. (Amherst: University of Massachusetts Press, 1989), is structured along the divisions within the U.S. Latino community; and Patricia Zavella, "Reflections on Diversity among Chicanas," *Frontiers* 12, no. 2 (1991): 73–85, argues that cultural coherence is belied by the differing social location among Chicanas. On the other hand, discussions such as British Marxist Mike Cole's "'Race' and Class or 'Race,' Class, Gender, and Community? A Critical Appraisal of the Radicalised Fraction of the Working-Class Thesis," in the *British Journal of Sociology* 40 (March 1989): 118–29, focusing on the instability of race, barely touch on gender.

4. Amy Kaminsky, "Translating Gender," in *Reading the Body Politic: Latin American Women Writers and Feminist Criticism* (Minneapolis: University of Minnesota Press, 1993), 1–13.

5. José Piedra, "Literary Whiteness and the Afro-Hispanic Difference," *New Literary History* 18 (Winter 1987): 303–32.

6. Fuentes used this deliberately clumsy term, or some permutation of it, in a lecture at Macalaster College, St. Paul, Minnesota, in 1989. The fiction of assimilation, of course, is belied by the extreme othering first of indigenous people and later of Africans brought to the Americas as slaves.

7. Similarly, Rey Chow, "The Politics and Pedagogy of Asian Literature in American Universities," *Differences: A Journal of Feminist Cultural Studies* 2 (fall 1990): 29–51, cites Vine Deloria, Jr. on the "[relegation of] minority existence to an adjectival status within the homogeneity of American life" (45).

8. Laura E. Gomez, "The Birth of the 'Hispanic' Generation: Attitudes of Mexican-American Political Elites toward the Hispanic Label," *Latin American Perspectives* 19 (fall 1992): 45–58, notes that the English term "Hispanic" to designate a U.S. population was popularized in the 1980s. She points out that the term had its roots in the U.S. Bureau of the Census and represents a mainstream political viewpoint. Cherríe Moraga, in "Art in America Con Acento," in Moraga's *The Last Generation: Prose and Poetry* (Boston: South End Press, 1993), 57, lays blame for the term, and by extension the effects of, "Hispanicization" on Reagan-era bureaucrats.

9. "Hispanic" also collapses class differences. In the popular North American imagination, "Hispanic" is a sign of poverty. Yet the first wave of Cubans

fleeing Castro's revolution and the Somocistas who left Sandinista Nicaragua were hardly members of the underclass.

10. This observation is not meant to be an attack on white feminists' attempts to acknowledge racial difference but a recognition of the difficulties one faces when trying to theorize a number of variables at once. Historian Peggy Pascoe, "At the Crossroads of Culture: Decentering History," *Women's Review of Books* 7 (February 1990): 22–23, suggests that the best way to get at gender oppression is by focusing on what happens where different ethnicities, cultures, and classes meet; however, political scientist Barbara Cruikshank's unpublished paper on building women's coalitions, read at the University of Minnesota's Center for Advanced Feminist Studies' Theorizing Diversity Seminar in 1988, outlines the difficulty of reconciling different feminist agendas.

11. Mae Gwendolyn Henderson, "Speaking in Tongues: Dialogics, Dialectics, and the Black Woman Writer's Literary Tradition," in *Changing Our Own Words: Essays on Criticism, Theory, and Writing by Black Women*, ed. Cheryl A. Wall (New Brunswick, N.J.: Rutgers University Press, 1989; reprint, London: Routledge, 1990), 16–37, argues that African American women's standpoint is itself unstable because it represents two constituencies, each of which has a political claim that renders the other partial. Nevertheless, the term "standpoint" itself promises stability. Multiple "standpoints" certainly exert pressure requiring movement from spot to spot, but beyond that, the categories that define the so-called standpoints are constantly in flux, dissolving any possibility of fixity.

12. Anthropology is still invoked to legitimate racism, although contemporary anthropologists are quick to dissociate themselves from such use of their discipline. In a recent incident, a suburban Minnesota high school teacher justified racial categorizations by invoking "anthropology." Anthropologists at the University of Minnesota responded with a letter in the Minneapolis-St. Paul daily newspaper saying that anthropology most certainly is not about establishing racial categories.

13. "The Case of Jose Ponseano de Ayarza: A Document on the Negro in Higher Education," *Hispanic American Historical Review* 24 (August 1944): 448–49; and James F. King, "The Case of Jose Ponciano de Ayarza, a Document on Gracias al Sacar," *Hispanic American Historical Review* 31 (November 1951): 640. I use Piedra's translation (p. 321, emphases added). Piedra, following King, attributes the 1944 article to the journal's managing editor, John Tate Lanning.

14. My method throughout this article is to consider both historical and literary texts as part of the discursive field that produces and inscribes cultural practice. The distinction between the two is not rigid. Catalina de Erauso has only recently been reassigned to the category of historical personage. For many years this remarkable woman was assumed to have been a product of literary imaginations that invented an autobiography of her and wrote a play about her exploits.

15. Suzanne J. Kessler and Wendy McKenna, in *Gender: An Ethnomethodological*

Approach (New York: Wiley, 1978), demonstrate the alignment of female and not-male in contrast to male.

16. U.S. Bureau of the Census, Official 1990 U.S. Census Form (D-1, OMB No. 0607–0628), 2.

17. U.S. Bureau of the Census, Your Guide for the 1990 U.S. Census Form, 3.

18. This is not surprising, given the racial history of the United States. Until Emancipation, the United States, and particularly the slave states, encouraged the birth of Black babies, often in the most brutal ways. Currently, poor Black women are excoriated for their fertility. At the same time, white America apologizes for having exterminated the Indians, a gesture which simultaneously begs to excuse Euroamericans for the actual destruction of so many lives and masks the reality of a growing Indian population with vital cultures and political, moral, and legal claims to make on the dominant society.

19. Paul Bohannan defines ethnicity as "identity with or membership in a particular cultural group, all of whose members share language, beliefs, customs, values, and identity," in *We the Alien: An Introduction to Cultural Anthropology* (Prospect Heights, Ill.: Waveland Press, 1992), 321. This is a serviceable enough definition, although I would argue with the "all."

20. Stuart Hall "Minimal Selves," *ICA (Institute of Contemporary Arts) Document 6* (London: Free Association Press, 1987), 44–47. The American Heritage Dictionary, Third Edition, lists both racial and national heritage among the elements that can be, but are not necessarily, held in common by an ethnic group.

21. Mi viuda madre, como sin marido y sin abrigo se viese, determino arrimarse a los buenos por ser uno dellos, y vinose a vivir a la ciudad, y alquilo una casilla, y metiose a guisar de comer a ciertos estudiantes, y lavaba la ropa a ciertos mozos de caballos del comendador de la Magdalena, de manera qu fue frecuentando las caballerizas.

Ella y un hombre moreno de aquellos que las bestias curaban vinieron en conocimiento. Este algunas veces se venia a nuestra casa y se iba a la manana. Otras veces, de dia llegaba a la puerta, en achaque de comparar huevos, y entrabase en casa. Yo, al principio de su entrada, pesabame con el y habiale miedo, viendo el color y mal gesto que tenia; mas de que vi que con su venida mejoraba el comer, fuile queriendo bien, porque siempre traia pan, pedazos de came y, en invierno, lenos, a que nos calentabamos.

De manera que, continuando la posada y conversacion, mi madre vino a darme un negrito muy bonito, el cual yo brincaba y ayudaba a calentar.

Y acuerdome que estando el negro de mi padrastro trebejando con el mozuelo, como el nino veia a mi madre y a mi blancos y a el no, huia del, con miedo, para mi madre y, senalando con el dedo, decia: '!Madre, coco!'

Respondio el, riendo, '!Hideputa!'

Yo, aunque bien muchacho, note aquella palabra de mi hermanico, y dije entre mi '!Cuantos debe de haber en el mundo que huyen de otros porque no se ven a si mismos!'

See *Lazarillo de Tormes*, in *La novela picaresca española*, ed. Angel Valbuena Prat (Madrid: Aguilar, 1962), 85. According to Valbuena Prat, the three earliest known editions of this text are dated 1554. The translation is *The Life of Lazarillo of Tormes, His Fortunes and Misfortunes*, trans. Robert S. Rudder (New York: Unger, 1973), 5–6. I have modified the translation and marked my changes by brackets where I believe Rudder's translation altered the meaning of the original in important ways.

22. Angela Davis, in *Women, Race, and Class* (New York: Random House, 1981), argues that under slavery women and men were equals. The structure of slavery in early modern Spain was sufficiently different from the U.S. form Davis discusses to make it possible to talk about gender hierarchy in the Spanish instance. Furthermore, by no means all people of African heritage in sixteenth-century Spain were, or ever had been, slaves.

23. We need not depend on the notoriously unreliable Lazarillo's interpretation here, although we do rely on him for our knowledge of events.

24. From *The Life of Lazarillo of Tormes*, 6–7.

   Quiso nuestra fortuna que la conversacion del Zaide [. . .] llego a oidos del mayordomo, y hecha pesquisas, hallose que la mitad por medio de la cebada que para las bestias le daban hurtaba, y salvados, lena, almohazas, mandiles y las mantas y sabanas de los caballos hacia perdidas, y cuando otra cosa no tenia, las bestias desherraba, y con todo esto acudia a mi madre para criar a mi hermanico. [. . .]

   Y probose cuanto digo, y aun mis [. . .].

   Al triste de mi padrastro azotaron y pringaron, y a mi madre pusieron pena por justicia, sobre el acostumbrado centenario, que en casa del sobredicho comendador no entrase, ni al lastimado Zaide en la suya acogiese. (*Lazarillo de Tormes*, pp. 85–86)

25. Ruth El Saffar has pointed out to me that the widow's punishment was the penalty for incest. El Saffar suggests that because her relationship with Zaide exists outside the symbolic order, as the joining of "same," it might be figured as incestuous. In my reading, which I do not see as at odds with El Saffar's, the economy of sameness derives from social location.

26. "[S]iempre la lengua rue companera del imperio," in Antonio de Nebrija, *Gramatica de la lengua castellana,* ed. Antonio Quilis (Madrid: Editoria Nacional, 1980), 97, my translation.

27. Piedra, 307.

28. Cortés and Malinche differ from the characters in the *Lazarillo* in that they are historical personages. Nevertheless, the story of their relationship, based on the very sketchy contemporary accounts of *Cartas de relación* by Cortés and Bernal Díaz del Castillo's *Verdadera historia de la conquista de Nueva Espana* have been reworked by numerous historians, poets, playwrights, and fiction writers. See Sandra Messinger Cypess, *La Malinche in Mexican Literature* (Austin: University of Texas Press, 1991).

29. Si la Chingada es una representacion de la Madre violada, no me parece

forzado asociarla a la Conquista, que fue tambien una violacion, no solamente
en el sentido historico, sino en la carne misma de las indias. El simbolo de la
entrega es dona Malinche, la amante de Cortes. Es verdad que ella se da vol-
untariamente al Conquistador, pero este, apenas deja de serle util, la olvida.
Dona Marina se ha convertido en una figura que representa a las indias, fasci-
nadas, violadas o seducidas por los espanoles. Y del mismo modo que el nino
no perdona a su madre que lo abandone para ir en busca de su padre, el pueblo
mexicano no perdona su traicion a la Malinche. Ella encarna lo abierto, lo
chingado, frente a nuestros indios, estoicos, impasibles y cerrados.[. . .]

Al repudiar a la Malinche [. . .] el mexicano rompe sus ligas con el pasado,
reniega de su origen y se adentra solo en la vida historica.

See Octavio Paz, "Los hijos de la Malinche" (The sons of Malinche) in *El
laberinto de la soledad* (Mexico: Cuadernos Americanos, 1950; reprint, Mexico:
Fondo de Cultura Economica, 1959), 77–78, my translation.

30. Ibid., my emphasis.
31. Piedra, 308.
32. "Hablar de raza espanola es no saber lo que se dice . . . El lenguaje es la raza."
    Miguel de Unamuno, "Espiritu de la raza vasca," in *La raza y la lengua: Obras
    completas*, vol. 4, ed. Manuel Garcia Blanco (Madrid: Ecselicer, 1968), my trans-
    lation. Race in Unamuno's formulation still encompasses religion; what had
    been the Spanish empire was still heavily Catholic at the end of the nine-
    teenth and beginning of the twentieth century when he wrote. Today the
    hegemony of Hispanic Catholicism in Spanish America is being threatened
    by Protestant evangelism.
33. Jose Vasconcelos. *La raza cósmica: Mision de la raza iberoamericana* (Paris: Agencia
    Mundial de Libreria, 1925).
34. Conversations with Joanna O'Connell, whose book, *Prospero's Daughters*
    (University of Texas Press, forthcoming) elaborates this point, have helped me
    clarify and articulate it here.
35. Victoria Ocampo, "El ultimo año de Pachacutec" (1975), in Ocampo's
    Testimonios, Décima serie (Buenos Aires: Sur, 1977), 39–46, translated by Doris
    Meyer as "The last year at Pachacutec," in Doris Meyer, *Victoria Ocampo:
    Against the Wind and the Tide* (New York: Braziller, 1979), 273–77.
36. Rosario Castellanos, *El eterno femenino* (1973), (Mexico: Fondo de Cultura
    Economica, 1975), translated by Diane Marting and Betty Tyree Osiek as
    "The eternal feminine," in *A Rosario Castellanos Reader*, ed. Maureen Ahern
    (Austin: University of Texas Press, 1988). For a full discussion of Malinche in
    Mexican literature, see Cypess.
37. Cordelia Candelaria, "La Malinche, Feminist Prototype," *Frontiers* 5 (summer
    1980): 2.
38. Adelaida R. Del Castillo, "Malintzín Tenepal: A Preliminary Look into a New
    Perspective," in *Essays on La Mujer,* ed. Rosaura Sanchez and Rosa Martinez
    Cruz (Los Angeles: Chicano Studies Center, 1977).
39. Cherríe Moraga, "A Long Line of *Vendidas*," in Moraga's *Loving in the War*

Years: Lo que nunca pasó por sus labios (Boston: South End Press, 1983), 100–101.

40. Alma Villanueva, "La Chingada," in *Five Poets of Aztlán*, ed. Santiago Daydi-Tolson (Binghamton, N.Y.: Bilingual Review Press, 1985); and Margarita Cota-Cardenas, "Discurso de la Malinche (Fragment from the novel)," *Third Woman* 2, no. 1 (1984): 46–50.

41. Gloria Anzaldúa, *Borderlands/La Frontera: The New Mestiza* (San Francisco: Spinsters/Aunt Lute, 1987), 21.

42. Norma Alarcón, "*Traddutora, Traditora*: A Paradigmatic Figure of Chicano Feminism," in *The Construction of Gender and Modes of Social Division*, special issue of *Cultural Critique* 13 (fall 1989): 57–87.

43. Del Castillo, 138, 143.

44. Moraga, *Loving in the War Years*, 90–144.

45. For a historical discussion of racial definitions and theories in Cuba, Argentina, and Mexico, see essays by Aline Helg and Alan Knight in *The Idea of Race in Latin America, 1870–1940*, ed. Richard Graham (Austin: University of Texas Press, 1990).

46. Aurora Levins Morales, "Between Two Worlds," *Women's Review of Books* 7 (December 1989): 1, 3–4.

47. The absence of audible difference makes it possible for the child adopted from Spanish America into a white family to be otherwise assigned to a racial group, but assigned she will be. Cheri Register, who has written on international adoption in the United States (*Are Those Kids Yours? American Families with Children Adopted from Other Countries* [New York: Free Press, 1991]), has observed that light-skinned children who look as though they could be the parents' birth children are taken for white, Afro-Hispanic children are assumed to be African American, and *mestizo* and Indian children are taken to have been adopted from Spanish America.

48. See, for example, María Lugones, "Hispaneando y Lesbiando: On Sarah Hoagland's Lesbian Ethics," *Hypatia* 5 (fall 1990): 138–46; and Lugones, "Playfulness, 'World' Traveling, and Loving Perception," *Hypatia* 2 (summer 1987): 3–19.

49. I am grateful for my Midwestern informant, Cheri Register, for this piece of information.

50. Cristina Peri Rossi, "La influencia de Edgar A. Poe en la poesía de Raimundo Arias," in Peri Rossi's *La tarde del dinosaurio* (Barcelona: Planeta, 1976), 43–59.

51. Cristina Peri Rossi, "La ciudad," in *El museo de los esfuerzos inútiles* (Barcelona: Seix Barral, 1983), 160–77.

52. Cristina Peri Rossi, "Las estatuas, o la condicion del extranjero," in *El museo de los esfuerzos iúutiles*, 131–32.

53. Gloria Anzaldúa, *Borderlands/La frontera*.

54. Gloria Anzaldúa, "Living in the Borderlands Means You," in *Infinite Divisions: An Anthology of Chicana Literature*, ed. Tey Diana Rebolledo and Eliana S. Rivero (Tucson: University of Arizona Press, 1993), 96.

55. Cherríe Moraga, "The Breakdown of the Bicultural Mind," in *The Last*

Generation, 120.

56. Maria Lugones, "Purity, Impurity, and Separation," *Signs*, forthcoming. I am grateful to Lugones for so generously allowing me to refer to her prepublished work.

Irene Ledesma, Texas Newspapers and Chicana Workers' Activism, 1919–1974

1. *Weekly Dispatch* (San Antonio), 1 March 1935.
2. I use the term "Mexican" women to designate Chicanas prior to World War II as this was the term most commonly used then. For the postwar period, the term "Mexican American" and "Chicanas" came into use depending on regional preference, and both will be used interchangeably in the essay.
3. Joan Wallach Scott, *Gender and the Politics* of History (New York, 1988), 53–67; Elizabeth Faue, "'The Dynamo of Change': Gender and Solidarity in the American Labour Movement of the 1930s," *Gender* and History 1 (Summer 1989): 138–58; Nancy A. Hewitt, "'The Voice of Virile Labor': Militancy, Community Solidarity, and Gender Identity among Tampa's Latin Workers, 1880–1921," in *Work Engendered: Toward a New History of American Labor,* ed. Ava Baron (Ithaca, NY, 1991), 142–67.
4. On California women and a supportive union, see Vicki L. Ruiz, *Cannery Women, Cannery Lives: Mexican Women, Unionization, and the California Food Processing Industry, 1930–1950* (Albuquerque, 1987); Margaret Rose, "Traditional and Nontraditional Patterns of Female Activism in the United Farm Workers of America, 1962 to 1980," *Frontiers* 11, no. 1 (1990) and "'From the Fields to the Picket Line: Huelga Women and the Boycott,' 1965–1975," *Labor History* 31 (Summer 1990): 271–93; and Devra Weber, "Rai: Fuerte: Oral History and Mexicana Farmworkers," *Oral History Review* 17, no. 1 (1989) detail how the union's benign neglect gave Mexican-American women opportunities to be innovative. Clementina Duron, "Mexican Women and and Labor Conflict in Los Angeles: The ILGWU Dressmakers' Strike of 1933," *Aztlan* 15 (Spring 1984); Douglas Monroy, "La Costura en Los Angeles, 1933–1939: The ILGWU and the Politics of Domination," in *Mexican Women in the United States: Struggles Past and Present,* ed. Magdalena Mora and Adelaida R. Del Castillo, Chicana Studies Research Center Publications, Occasional Paper No. 2 (Los Angeles, 1980), 171–78; and Magdalena Mora, "The Tolteca Strike: Mexican Women and the Struggle for Union Representation," in *Mexican Immigrant Workers to the U. S.,* ed. Antonio Ríos-Bustamante (Los Angeles, 1981) raise questions about union behavior toward Mexican American women members. On Texas Chicanas, see Laurie Coyle, Gail Hershatter, and Emily Honig, "Women at Farah: An Unfinished Story," in *Mexican Women,* ed. Mora and Del Castillo, I 17–43; and Mario T. García, "The Chicana in American History: The Mexican Women of El Paso, 1880–1920—A Case Study," *Pacific*

Historical Review 49 (May 1980): 315–37.

5. Shawn Lay, *War, Revolution, and the Ku Klux Klan: A Study of Intolerance in a Border City* (El Paso, 1985), 29; Mario T. García, *Desert Immigrants: The Mexicans of El Paso, 1880–1920* (New Haven, 1981), 46–48, 50–51.

6. García, *Desert Immigrants*, 64, 85–88, 100–105.

7. García, "The Chicana in American History," 331–32; *El Paso City and County Labor Advocate* (hereafter *Labor Advocate*), 31 October 1919; *El Paso Herald* (hereafter *EPH*), 28 October 1919.

8. *EPH*, 28 October 1919; *Labor Advocate*, 31 October 1919; *El Paso Morning Times* (hereafter *EPMT*), 4 November 1919. For a look at El Pasoans' attitudes on Mexican immigrants in this period, see Mario T. García, "Racial Dualism in the El Paso Labor Market, 1880–1920," *Aztlan* 6, no. 2 (1975): 197–218.

9. Quotes from *Labor Advocate*, 31 October 1919. Lynn Y. Weiner, *From Working Girl to Working Mother: The Female Labor Force in the United States, 1820–1980* (Chapel Hill, 1985) includes a discussion on the way in which Progressive ideology treats Anglo working women.

10. García, "The Chicana to American History," 330; *Labor Advocate*, 7 November 1919.

11. W. H. Timmons, *El Paso: A Borderlands History* (El Paso, 1990), 205; quote from *Labor Advocate*, 31 October 1919. A study on the issue of citizenship and organized labor is Gwendolyn Mink, *Old Labor and New Immigrants in American Political Development: Union, Party, and State, 1875–1920* (Ithaca, NY, 1986).

12. *Labor Advocate*, 31 October 1919.

13. *EPMT,* 29 October 1919; *EPH,* 11 November 1919.

14. *EPH*, 11 November 1919; 29 October 1919.

15. Lay, *Ku Klux Klan*, 38–48, 54–55, 62–63.

16. First and third quotes, *EPH,* 30 and 31 October 1919; second quote, *EPMT,* 1 November 1919; fourth quote, García, "Racial Dualism," 209.

17. *EPH*, 29 October 1919; *EPMT* 30 October 1919.

18. *EPH*, 31 October 1919; *EPMT*, 17 and 18 November 1919.

19. *EPMT*, 21 November 1919; García, *Desert Immigrants*, 92.

20. *EPMT*, 17 and 18 November 1919.

21. *La Patria (*El Paso), 30 October 1919 and 1 November 1919; quote translations: "but they have not gone beyond this"; "our women are giving an example of character, enthusiasm, and racial solidarity"; "very well represented in the groups."

22. *La Patria,* 30 October 1919; quote translation: "they have behaved quite correctly."

23. *La Patria,* 30 October 1919, 3 November 1919; quote translation: "for the same reason, we should not abandon them at this time."

24. Quote from *EPMT*, 6 November 1919; *La Patria,* 3 November 1919.

25. Lay, *Ku Klux Klan*, 95–103, 155–56.

26. Richard Croxdale, "The 1938 San Antonio Pecan Sheller's Strike," in *Women in the Texas Workforce: Yesterday and Today*, ed. Richard Croxdale and Melissa

Hield (Austin, 1979); George N. Green, "The Pecan Shellers of San Antonio," unpublished paper. George Lambert Collection, University of Texas Labor Archives, Arlington, Texas (hereafter UTLA), 2–6; Harold A. Shapiro, "The Pecan Shellers of San Antonio, Texas," *Southwest Social Science* (1952): 230–32; Kenneth P. Walker, "The Pecan Shellers of San Antonio and Mechanization," *Southwestern Historical Quarterly* 69 (July 1965): 48–49; Anita Perez, interview by George Green, 9 September 1971 and 6 February 1972, Dallas, Texas, Peoples' History in Texas interviews, Oral History 19, UTLA.

27. Selden C. Menefee and Orin C. Cassmore, *The Pecan Shellers of San Antonio: The Problem of Underpaid and Unemployed Mexican Labor* (Washington, DC, 1940), 16; *San Antonio Express*, 1 and 9 August 1934; *Weekly Dispatch* (San Antonio), 22 March 1935; Texas Civil Liberties Union, "San Antonio: The Cradle and the Coffin of Texas Liberty," Austin, 1938, George Lambert Collection, UTLA, 3.

28. Quote translation: "the above mentioned leader did not take part in this move- ment spontaneously but to obey the persistent requests of the workers," *San Antonio Express,* 1, 9, and 12 February 1938; "Living History: Emma Tenayuca Tells Her Story," *Texas Observer*, October 1983, 9–10; Green, "Pecan Shellers," 7–8; Carlos Larralde. *Mexican American Movements and Leade*rs (Los Alamitos, CA, 1976), 163–64; *Daily Workers* (New York), 28 June 1938, copy from George Lambert Collection, UTLA.

29. *San Antonio Express,* 4 February 1938; *La Prensa* (San Antonio), 12 February 1938, 2 March 1938, 6 March 1938; Cordell Hull, Secretary of State, to J. W. Madden, Chairman of NLRB, 11 March 1938 and F. Castillo Najera, Ambassador, to Cordell Hull, 9 March 1938, file: [1938–1939] "Southern Pecan Shelling Company (Case No. XVI-C-239)," Formal and Informal Unfair Labor Practices and Representation Case Files, 1935–48, Records of the National Labor Relations Board, RG 25, National Archives, College Park, MD.

30. *San Antonio Express* 8–12, 15, 24–26 February 1938; letter from [Citizens Labor Aid Committee], San Antonio, to C. K. Quinn (Mayor of San Antonio), 5 March 1938, copies appear to have been sent to Maury Maverick (member of Congress), and James Allred (Governor of Texas), 5 March 1938, and a copy was attached to a letter from Mrs. Charles Britton to Frances Perkins, 11 March 1938, File: "Conciliation—Pecan Shellers," General Subject File, 1933–1945, Secretary of Labor Frances Perkins, General Records of the Department of Labor, RG 174, National Archives, College Park, MD; Green, "Pecan Shellers," 8, 9.

31. *San Antonio Express*, 2, 4, quote from 5 February 1938 and 6 and 10 February 1938; *La Prensa*, 5 February 1938.

32. *San Antonio Express*, 12 February 1938.

33. *San Antonio Express*, 1, 4. 6, 7, and 16 February 1938; Julia Kirk Blackwelder, *Women of the Depression: Caste and Culture in San Antonio, 1929–1939* (College Station, TX, 1984), 14750.

34. *San Antonio Express*, 4, 6, and 16 February 1938.

35. Quote translation: "the members of the Texas Pecan Shelling Workers Union have maintained complete order during their strike, without resorting to violence"; "a few radicals without connection to the pecan industry have tried to take part in the strike and a few were apprehended," *La Prensa*, 1, 14, and 28 February 1938.
36. Ibid., 10 and 12 February 1938.
37. *Weekly Dispatch*, 20 July 1934.
38. Ibid., 22 March 1935, 27 November 1936, 23 April 1937; quote translation: "a group of radicals who went on strike under the guidance of Emma Tenayuca Brooks and Homer Brooks."
39. *San Antonio Express*, 10 March 1938, 14 April 1938; Walker, "Pecan Shellers," 54–58; Larralde, *Mexican Americans*, 166; Green Peyton, *San Antonio, City in the Sun* (New York, 1946), 172–74.
40. Lyle Saunders, *The Spanish-Speaking Population of Texas*, Inter-American Education Occasional Papers, no. 5 (Austin, 1949), 15; Bertha Blair, Anne O. Lively, and Glen W. Trimble, *Spanish-Speaking Americans: Mexicans and Puerto Ricans in the United States* (New York, 1959), 5; *EPHP*, 9 October 1972.
41. *San Antonio Express*, 24 February 1959; *Texas Observer*, "Texas Labor 1959," 4 September 1959, 2; George Lambert, ILGWU international representative, to Harold Franzel, 17 December 1958, Collection 30: "ILGWU, Local 180, San Antonio. TX," UTLA.
42. *AFL-CIO Weekly Dispatch* (San Antonio), 16 October 1959; *Texas Observer*, "The Strike in San Antonio," 4 April 1959, 6; *Texas Observer*, "Texas Labor 1959," 2.
43. *AFL-CIO Weekly Dispatch*, 11 December 1959; flyer entitled "Una Carta Para Sus Ninos," [A Letter for Your Children], Box 1, Folder 2, Collection 30: "ILGWU, Local 180, San Antonio, TX," UTLA; flyer entitled "To All Retailers and Buyers of Children's Wear," box number unknown, George Lambert Collection, UTLA.
44. *AFL-CIO Weekly Dispatch*, 13 November 1919.
45. Ibid., 2, 9, and quote from 23 December 1960.
46. *San Antonio Express*, 25, 26, and 27 February 1959. Quote from *26* February 1959.
47. *San Antonio Express*, 14 March 1959.
48. Press release supplied by Harold Franzel, president of Tex-Son, 10 June 1959, Box 25, Folder 7, Collection 127: "George and Latane Lambert," UTLA.
49. "The Strike in San Antonio," *Texas Observer*, 4 April 1959.
50. *Texas Observer*, "Farah: The Strike that has Everything," 29 December 1972, 4.
51. Ibid., 1, 3, and 6; Bill Finger, "Victoria Sobre Farah," *Southern Exposure* (1976), 46; Coyle, Hershatter, and Honig, "Women at Farah," 126–28. *Compariera* means "sister" as in sisterhood.
52. First quote from photocopy of an advertisement for Christmas cards that Farah workers were selling, Box 1, Folder 14, Collection 93: "Justice for Farah Striker Committee," UTLA; leaflet entitled "Viva la Huelga," [long live the strike],

1973?, Box 2, Folder 7, Collection 93: "Justice for Farah Striker Committee," UTLA; second quote, handout entitled "Farah Workers on Strike," UTLA, further cataloguing information not available.

53. Janie Naranjo, interview by author. Farah striker, 6 November 1989, San Antonio, Texas, tape recording and transcription in author's possession; Coyle, Hershatter, and Honig, "Women at Farah," 117–18; Irene Ledesma, "Unlikely Sisters: Mexican American Women Strike Activity in Texas, 1919–1974," (Ph.D. diss. Ohio State Univeristy, 1992), 138–57.

54. Virginia Delgado, interview by author, 5 May 1990, El Paso, Texas, tape recording and transcription in author's possession. See also Coyle, Hershatter, and Honig, "Women at Farah," 134–35.

55. "Farah," *Texas Observer*, 1, 6–7; Rex Hardesty, "Farah: The Union Struggle in the 70's," *American Federationist* 80 (June 1973): 8; Finger, "Victoria Sobre Faith," 47.

56. Hardesty, "Farah," 7; *EPHP*, 2, 13, 16, and 17 October 1972; *El Paso Times*, 21 May 1972; quote from newsclipping, Chicano vertical file, Farah Strike pamphlet file #1, Special Collections, University of Texas-El Paso Library, El Paso, Texas; Coyle, Hershatter, and Honig, "Women at Farah," 125–27.

57. *EPHP*, 13, 16, and 17 October 1972.

58. *El Paso Times*, 21 May 1972.

59. *EPHP*, 20 and 25 February 1974; *Labor Advocate*, 22 February 1974.

60. Finger, "Victoria Sobre Faith," 48; "Farah Settles, Ending Long Strike," *Monthly Labor Review*, April 1974, 73–74; "Strike's Over," *Texas Observer*, March 1974, 12–13; Coyle, Hershatter, and Honig, "Women at Farah," 136–40.

61. Coyle, Hershatter, and Honig, "Women at Farah," 136–40.

James F. Brooks, 'This Evil Extends Especially . . . to the Feminine Sex': Negotiating Captivity in the New Mexico Borderlands

1. Jack B. Tykal, "Taos to St. Louis: The Journey of Maria Rosa Villalpando," *New Mexico Historical Review* (April 1990): 161–74.

2. Frances Swadesh (Quintana) first proposed the "nondominant frontier" concept in her "Structure of Hispanic-Indian Relations in New Mexico," in *The Survival of Spanish American Villages*, ed. Paul M. Kutsche (Colorado Springs: Colorado College Press, 1979), 53–61. For a recent synthesis of the Spanish Borderlands that reflects similar thinking, see David J. Weber, *The Spanish Frontier in North America* (New Haven: Yale University Press, 1991).

3. As used here, "borderlands political economy" indicates that despite profound and continuing cultural differences in the region, Native Americans and New Mexicans came to share some common understandings of the production and distribution of wealth, as conditioned by the social relations of power.

4. Treatments of "slavery" in New Mexico are L. R. Bailey's *The Indian Slave Trade in the Southwest* (Los Angeles: Westernlore Press, 1966), which contains

no analysis of gender differentiation or captivity among Indian groups; David M. Brugge's *Navajos in the Catholic Church Records of New Mexico, 1694–1875* (Tsaile: Navajo Community College Press, 1985), an important piece of documentary research upon which this essay relies heavily but which does not attempt a unifying analytical framework; and the recent work of Ramón Gutiérrez, *When Jesus Came, the Corn Mothers Went Away: Marriage, Sexuality, and Power in New Mexico, 1500–1846* (Stanford: Stanford University Press, 1991), whose analysis relies on an exploitation paradigm drawn from chattel slavery in the southern United States. Gutiérrez does not consider the experience of Spanish captives in Indian societies.

5. For an extended treatment of this question of the meaning of the exchange of women, see James F. Brooks (Chapel Hill: University of North Carolina Press 2002).

6. Friedrich Engels, *The Origin of the Family, Private Property, and the State* (1884; rpt., New York: Pathfinder Press, 1972); Gerda Lerner, *The Creation of Patriarchy* (New York: Oxford University Press, 1986); Claude Levi-Strauss, *The Elementary Structures of Kinship* (1949: rpt., Boston: Beacon Press, 1969); Gayle Rubin, "The Traffic in Women: Notes on the 'Political Economy' of Sex" in *Toward an Anthropology of Women*, ed. Rayna R[app] Reiter (New York: Monthly Review Press, 1975); Verena Martínez-Alier, *Marriage, Class, and Colour in Nineteenth-Century Cuba* (Cambridge: Cambridge University Press, 1974); Jane Fishburne Collier, *Marriage and Inequality in Classless Societies* (Stanford: Stanford University Press, 1988).

7. Lerner; Martínez-Alier applies this argument to nineteenth-century Cuba. Claude Meillasoux makes the case for the patrimony-to-property transition in his synthesis of indigenous/domestic African slave systems in *The Anthropology of Slavery: The Womb of Iron and Gold* (Chicago: University of Chicago Press, 1991).

8. While reiterating the ban on Indian slavery first set forth in 1542, the *Recopilación* reinforced the "just war" doctrine, whereby hostile Indians might be enslaved if taken in conflict. *Indios de rescate* (ransomed Indians), on the other hand, were "saved" from slavery among their captors and owed their redeemers loyalty and service. See Silvio Zavala, *Los Esclavos Indios en Nueva España* (Mexico City: El Colegio Nacional, 1967), for a complete treatment of these policies.

9. For theoretical and empirical cases, see the essays in Katherine Spielmann, ed., *Farmers, Hunters, and Colonists: Interaction between the Southwest and the Southern Plains* (Tucson: University of Arizona Press, 1991).

10. Report of the Reverend Father Provincial, Fray Pedro Serrano . . . to the Marquis de Cruillas . . . 1761, in *Historical Documents Relating to New Mexico, Nueva Vizcaya, and Approaches Thereto, to 1773*, trans. and ed. Charles Wilson Hackett (Washington, D.C.: Carnegie Institution of Washington, 1937), 486–87.

11. Fray Anatasio Dominguez, *The Missions of New Mexico, 1776*, ed. and trans.,

Eleanor B. Adams and Fray Angélico-Chávez (Albuquerque: University of New Mexico Press, 1956), 252. See also "Las Ferias hispano-indias del Nuevo México," in *La Espana Illustrada en el Lejano Oeste*, ed. Armando Represa (Valladolid: Junta de Castilla y Léon, Consejeria de Cultura y Bienestan Social, 1990), 119–25.

12. James S. Calhoun to Commissioner Brown, 31 Mar. 1850, in *The Official Correspondence of James S. Calhoun*, Indian Agent at Santa Fe, ed. Annie Heloise Abel (Washington, D.C.: Government Printing Office, 1915), 181–83. For the archaeology of *comanchero* sites on the Plains, see Frances Levine, "Economic Perspectives on the Comanchero Trade," in *Farmers, Hunters, and Colonists*, 155–69.

13. Because only about 75 percent of baptismal registers still exist, the actual figures are probably somewhat higher. Brugge, 2; for breakdown by tribal derivation and date, see 22–23.

14. "Analysis of the Spanish Colonial Census of 1750," Eleanor Olmsted, comp., New Mexico State Records Center, indicates a rural village population of 1,052, of whom 447 are recorded as having some Indian blood. In the "urban" areas of Santa Fe and Albuquerque, a total population of 2,757 contains only 400 individuals similarly designated. For a more detailed demographic analysis, see Brooks, chap. 2.

15. Brugge (116), estimates a sixty-to-forty female–male ratio for the Navajo captives he has studied. Working again with the Spanish Colonial Census of 1750, where individuals are designated either by proper name, or by a gendered noun (*criada/o, genízara/o, india/o*), I find that women total 153 of 282 individuals, or 54 percent. Because some bondwomen, for example, are designated simply "cinco indias criadas y ocho coyotitos" (*Spanish Archives of New Mexico* [hereafter *SANM*], New Mexico State Records Center, Santa Fe, series 1, roll 4, frame 1175), we cannot determine a precise gender breakdown. Nineteenth-century figures demonstrate continuity: Lafayette Head's 1865 census of Indian captives held in Costilla and Conejos Counties, Colorado Territory, shows women numbering 99 of 148 captives (67 percent), with children under age fifteen 96 of those 148 (65 percent) *National Archives, New Mexico Superintendency*, microcopy 234, roll 553. Microfilms in the Center for the Study of the Southwest, Fort Lewis College, Durango, Colorado. In 70, Don Augustín Flores de Vargara donated "for the sermon of the day" at the Chapel of San Miguel in Santa Fe "one Indian girl of serviceable age valued at 80 pesos." See "Certified copy of the Expenditures made by Captain Don Augustin Flores de Vargara for the Chapel of Glorious San Miguel . . . ," Crawford Buel Collection, New Mexico States Records Center, Santa Fe.

16. In 1760, a Comanche band attacked what is now Ranchos de Taos and carried fifty-seven women and children into captivity. See "Bishop Tamaron's Visitation of New Mexico, 1760," in *Historical Society of New Mexico Publications in History*, vol. 15, ed. and trans. Eleanor B. Adams (Albuquerque: National Historical Society of New Mexico, 1954), 58. See also a raid on Abiquiu in

1747, where twenty-three women and children were carried off:"An Account of Conditions in New Mexico, written by Fray Juan Sanz de Lezuan, in the year 1760," in *Historical Documents*, vol. 3, 477.

17. *"Bando* of Don Phelipe de Neve, Governor and Commander-General of the Interior Provinces of New Spain, May 8, 1784," Bexar Archives, University of Texas, Austin. For the 1830s' estimate, see Jean Luis Berlandier in *The Indians of Texas in 1830*, ed. John C. Ewers (Washington, D.C.: Smithsonian Institution Press, 1969), 119. The 1933 Comanche Ethnographic Field School in Oklahoma estimated that 70 percent of Comanche society at that time were mixed-bloods, of primarily Mexican-Comanche descent; see E. Adamson Hoebel, "The Political Organization and Law-Ways of the Comanche Indians," *Memoirs of the American Anthropological Association*, 54 (Menasha, Wis.: American Anthropological Association, 1940).

18. Dennis M. Riordan to Commissioner, 14 Aug. 1883, *Annual Report of the Commissioner of Indian Affairs for the Year 1883* (U.S. Department of the Interior, Washington, D.C.); it should be noted that here, twenty years after the Emancipation Proclamation, U.S. officials were still attempting to extinguish Indian "slavery" in New Mexico.

19. The best discussion of origins and functions of *compadrazgo* relations remains that of Sidney W. Mintz and Eric R. Wolf, "An Analysis of Ritual Co-Parenthood *(Compadrazgo),*" in *Southwest Journal of Anthropology* 6, no. 4 (1950): 341–68. In New Mexico, important new work is being done by Sandra Jaramillo Macias; see her "Bound by Family: Women and Cultural Change in Territorial Taos" (paper presented at the Carson Foundation, 30 July 1994, Taos, New Mexico), and "The Myth of High Skirts and Loose Blouses: Intercultural Marriage in the Mexican Period" (paper presented at the thirty-fifth Annual Conference of the Western History Association, 12 Oct. 1995, Denver).

20. My thinking on culturally specific structural constraints was inspired by Nancy Folbre, who in her work on the organization of social reproduction, defines "structures of constraint" as "sets of assets, rules, norms, and preferences that shape the interests and identities of individuals or social groups." In doing so, they "define the limits and rewards to individual choice." This conceptualization allows us to recognize the *simultaneity* of exploitation and agency, a key element in this essay. Nancy Folbre, *Who Pays for the Kids? Gender and the Structures of Constraint* (New York: Routledge, 1993).

21. See Fray Angélico Chávez, *Origins of New Mexico Families* (1954; rpt., Santa Fe: Museum of New Mexico Press, 1992), 49–50, for reference to Hurtado's *encomienda holdings*, including Santa Ana Pueblo.

22. "Inventory and settlement of the estate of Juana Galvana, *genízara* of Zia Pueblo, 1753," SANM 1, no. 193. I thank Frances Swadesh Quintana for suggesting Juana Hurtado as a case study in captivity and for sharing her notes with me. Her essay "They Settled by Little Bubbling Springs," *El Palacio* 84 (autumn 1978): 1949, treats the history of the Santísima Trinidad Grant at *Los*

Ojitos Hervidores.

23. SANM 2, no. 367, reel 6, frames 1010–23.

24. The journal of Don Diego de Vargas records Martín ransoming Juana at the Zuni Pueblo of Halona, along with her fourteen-year-old daughter María Naranjo, as well as a younger daughter and a son "about three years-old." This raises some confusion as to Juana's age at her capture in 1680 and suggests that at least one, and probably two, of her children were born to her during her captivity. As we will see, if true, this would have given Juana and her "Navajo" children membership in a Navajo clan and may help explain her long-term good relations with Navajos in the years to come. See J. Manuel Espinosa, trans. and ed., *First Expedition of Vargas into New Mexico,* 1692 (Albuquerque: University of New Mexico Press, 1940), 237.

25. *Archdiocesan Archives of Santa Fe* (hereafter AASF), Burials, reel 43, frame 371, New Mexico State Records; see also SANM 2, no. 406.

26. "Declaration of Fray Miguel de Menchero, Santa Barbara, May 10, 1744," in *Historical Documents*, vol. 3, 404–5.

27. Abandonment of the Pueblo for defensible mesa-top positions often preceded Pueblo-Spanish conflict. See Swadesh, "They Settled. . . ." See *SANM 2,* no. 345, for details of the incident. For a treatment in broader historical context, see Swadesh.

28. See Morris E. Opler, "The Kinship Systems of the Southern Athabascan-Speaking Tribes," *American Anthropologist,* n.s., (1936): 622–33, and "Cause and Effect in Apachean Agriculture, Division of Labor, Residence Patterns, and Girl's Puberty Rites," *American Anthropologist* 74 (1972): 1133–46; also Harold E. Driver's reply to Opler ibid., 1147–51; Jane Fishburne Collier.

29. See W. W. Hill, "Some Navaho Culture Changes during Two Centuries, with a Translation of the Early Eighteenth-Century Rabal Manuscript," in *Smithsonian Miscellaneous Collections* 100 (1939): 395–415. For Navajo kinship and marriage systems, see David F. Aberle, "Navaho," in *Matrilineal Kinship,* ed. David M. Schneider and Kathleen Gough (Berkeley: University of California Press, 1961), 96–201; and Gary Witherspoon, *Navajo Kinship and Marriage* (Chicago: University of Chicago Press, 1975).

30. For Navajo warfare, and raiding/assimilation patterns for captives and livestock, see W. W. Hill, "Navaho Warfare," *Yale University Publications in Anthropology,* no. 5 (1936): 3–19. See Arnold Van Gennep, *The Rites of Passage* (1909; rpt., Chicago: University of Chicago Press, 1960), for a treatment of the cross-cultural attributes of integration rituals.

31. Brugge, 138, citing a conversation with Bruce Yazzi, a son of Nakai Na'dis Saal. See appendix B, 175; David M. Brugge, "Story of Interpreter for Treaty of 1868. . . . ," *Navajo Times,* 21 Aug. 1968, 22B.

32. Ibid., 139. This seems an anomaly in the matrilineal reckoning of kin by Navajo clans, but given the non-kin status of an unadopted captive, it would be the only method of integrating her progeny.

33. "Agent Bowman to the Commissioner of Indian Affairs, 3 Sept. 1884," in

Annual Report of the Commissioners of Indian Affairs for the Year 1884, quoted with extensive corroborative evidence in Brugge, 142.

34. Morris E.Opler, "A Summary of Jicarilla Apache Culture," *American Anthropologist,* n.s., 38 (1936): 206, 208, 209.

35. Ibid., 213. This information, gathered by Opler in the 1930s, may reflect an intensification of social stratification following the American conquest of the 1850s.

36. Collier, 23.

37. See Adamson Hoebel, 49ff.

38. Hoebel, 51, 62. Absconding cases accounted for twenty-two of the forty-five marital disputes recorded by Hoebel.

39. See Ernest Wallace and E. Adamson Hoebel, *The Comanche: Lords of the Southern Plains* (Norman: University of Oklahoma Press, 1952), 72.

40. David E. Jones, *Sanapia: Comanche Medicine Woman* (1972; rpt., Prospect Heights, Ill.: Waveland Press, 1984). Sanapia received her medicine powers through her mother and maternal uncle, consistent with the Shoshonean levirate. They became fully developed only after she experienced menopause.

41. Stanley Noyes, *Los Comanches: The Horse People* (Albuquerque: University of New Mexico Press, 1993); Brooks, 133–35; also Dan Flores, "Bison Ecology and Bison Diplomacy: The Southern Plains from 1800–1850," *Journal of American History* 78 (September 1991): 465–85.

42. Wallace and Hoebel, 241–42.

43. Ralph Linton, "The Comanche Sun Dance," *American Anthropologist,* n.s., 37 (1935): 420–28.

44. For Loki-Mokeen's story, and others, see Maurice Boyd, "The Southern Plains: Captives and Warfare," in *Kiowa Voices: Myths, Legends, and Folktales* (Fort Worth: Texas Christian University Press, 1983), 2: 155–82.

45. Andrés Martínez' life story, see James F. Brooks, ed., *Andele: The Mexican-Kiowa Captive* (1899; rpt., Albuquerque: University of New Mexico Press, 1996).

46. Hoebel, 68.

47. Rosita Rodrigues to Don Miguel Rodrigues, 13 Jan. 1846, Bexar Archives, Barker History Center, University of Texas, Austin

48. "A Narrative of the Captivity of Mrs. Horn and Her Two Children" (St. Louis, 1839), reprinted in C. C. Rister, *Comanche Bondage* (Glendale, Calif.: Arthur H. Clarke Co., 1955), 157.

49. On the incest taboo, see Hoebel, 108. I am indebted to Tressa L. Berman for suggesting the association between captive women's low incidence of sexual abuse and the adoptive incest taboo. For similar examples among other Indian groups, see James Axtell, "The White Indians of Colonial America," *William and Mary Quarterly* 32 (January 1975): 55–88.

50. Cynthia Ann Parker, the mother of Quanah Parker, the last Comanche war chief, is the most famous example of women who remained with their captors. See Margaret Schmidt Hacker, *Cynthia Ann Parker* (El Paso: Texas Western Press, University of Texas at El Paso, 1990). Parker lived thirty-four years

among the Comanche and died "of heartbreak" shortly after her "rescue."

51. Rodrigues letter.

52. Josiah Gregg, *The Commerce of the Prairies*, ed. Milo Milton Quaife (1844; rpt., Lincoln: University of Nebraska Press, 1967), 208.

53. "*Expediente* of de Croix, June 6, 1780; Bonilla's Certification of June 15, 1780," Bexar Archives.

54. Gutiérrez, 190, 206. The *genízaros* remain the center of scholarly debate around their true status in New Mexican society, focusing on whether they constituted a caste category, defined from without, or if in time they developed as an "ethnogenetic" identity group. See Tibo Chavez, chap. 10, "The *Genízaro El Río Abajo*" (Albuquerque: Pampa Print Shop, n.d.); Fray Angelico Chavez, "*Genízaros*," in *The Handbook of North American Indians* (Washington, D.C.: Smithsonian Institution, 1980), 198–200; Robert Archibald, "Acculturation and Assimilation in Colonial New Mexico," *New Mexico Historical Review* 53 (July 1978): 205–17; Steven M. Horvath, "The *Genízaro* of Eighteenth-Century New Mexico: A Re-Examination," *Discovery* (Santa Fe: School of American Research, 1977), 25–40; Russel M. Magnaghi, "Plains Indians in New Mexico: The *Genízaro* Experience," *Great Plains Quarterly* 10 (spring 1990): 86–95.

55. See Richard White's *Middle Ground: Indians, Empires, and Republics in the Great Lakes Region*, 1640–1815 (New York: Cambridge University Press, 1991); Gregory Evans Dowd, *A Spirited Resistance: The North American Indian Struggle for Unity*, 1745–1815 (Baltimore: Johns Hopkins University Press, 1991); and Daniel H. Usner Jr., *Indians, Settlers, and Slaves in a Frontier Exchange Economy: The Lower Mississippi Valley before 1763* (Chapel Hill: University of North Carolina Press, 1992), for new, sometimes divergent, conceptualizations of these relationships. Other authors preceded White and Dowd in stressing the importance of intermarriage in patterns of accommodation, principally Sylvia Van Kirk in her *Many Tender Ties: Women in Fur Trade Society in Western Canada, 1670–1870* (Norman: University of Oklahoma Press, 1980); and Jennifer S. H. Brown in *Strangers in Blood: Fur Trade Company Families in Indian Country* (Vancouver: University of British Columbia Press, 1980).

56. Donald E. Worcester, trans., "Don Fernando de la Concha to Lieutenant Colonel Don Fernando Chacon, Advice on Governing New Mexico, 1794," *New Mexico Historical Review* 24 (1949): 236–54, quotation on 250.

57. Alfred B. Thomas, ed. and trans., "Antonio de Bonilla and the Spanish Plans for the Defense of New Mexico, 1777–1778," in Alfred B. Thomas, *New Spain and the West* (Lancaster, Penn.: Lancaster Press, 1932), 1: 196.

58. Fray Juan Augustín de Morfi, "Desórdenes que se advierten en el Nuevo Mexico, 1780," *Archivo Generale del Nacion* (Mexico City), Historia, 25: 288.

59. "Don Fernando de la Concha to Lieutenant Colonel Don Fernando Chacón," 251.

60. Marc Simmons, ed. and trans., "The Chacón Economic Report of 1803," *New Mexico Historical Review* 60 (1985): 81–83, quotations on 83, 87.

61. The economic "modernization" of New Mexico has usually been attributed

to the influence of the St. Louis-Santa Fe-Chíhuahua trade that began in 1821. For a much earlier emergence, see Ross H. Frank, "From Settler to Citizen: Economic Development and Cultural Change in Late Colonial New Mexico, 1750–1820" (Ph.D. diss., University of California, Berkeley, 1992); for this aspect in the sheep commerce, see John O. Baxter, *Las Carneradas: Sheep Trade in New Mexico*, 1700–1860 (Albuquerque: University of New Mexico Press, 1987).

62. Janet Lecompte has collected and interpreted most of the primary source material on this revolt, in *Rebellion in Río Arriba, 1837* (Albuquerque: University of New Mexico Press, 1985). Her class-conflict interpretation stressed tensions between ricos and pobres and neglects to consider the cultural issues at work.

63. Governor Manuel Armijo, "Diario del Gobierno de la Republica Mexicana," Nov. 30, 1837, translated ibid., 139.

64. For the extensiveness of the 1847 "Taos" Revolt, see U.S. Senate, 56th Congress, 1st sess., Document No. 442 (1900), *Insurrection against the Military Government in New Mexico and California, 1847 and 1848*; Michael McNierney, ed. and trans., Taos 1847: *The Revolt in Contemporary Accounts* (Boulder: Johnson Publishing Co., 1980); James W. Goodrich, "Revolt at Mora, 1847," *New Mexico Historical Review* 47 (1972): 49–60.

65. See the Spanish Colonial Census of 1750, Eleanor Olmsted comp., New Mexico State Records Center, 47, 48.

66. See Horvath.

67. Fray Miguel de Menchero claimed in 1744 that the "*genízaro* Indians ... engage in agriculture and are under obligation to go out and explore the country in pursuit of the enemy, which they are doing with great bravery and zeal." See Declaration of Menchero, in *Historical Documents*, 3: 401.

68. See "Appeal of Bentura Bustamante, Lieutenant of Genízaro Indians," *SANM* 1, no. 1229, roll 6, frames 323–35, 20 June 1780.

69. "José Manrique, draft of a Report for Nemesio Salcedo y Salcedo, Nov. 26, 1808," Pinart Collection, Bancroft Library, University of California, Berkeley.

70. Lecompte, 36–40, n. 54.

71. Gutíerrez, chap. 7–9.

72. Angelina F. Veyna, "*Hago, dispongo, y ordeno mi testamento*: Reflections of Colonial New Mexican Women" (paper presented at the Annual Meetings of the Western History Association, October 1991, Austin, Texas).

73. SANM 1, no. 344, cited in ibid.

74. "Testament of Don Santiago Roibal, 1762," fragment in New Mexico State Records Center, Santa Fe.

75. SANM 2, no. 427, roll 7, frames 1023–25.

76. Gutíerrez, 182.

77. Frances S. Quintana, *Pobladores: Hispanic Americans of the Ute Frontier* (Aztec, N.M., 1991 [originally published as *Los Primeros Pobladores: Hispanic Americans of the Ute Frontier* (South Bend: University of Notre Dame Press, 1974)], 206–10.

78. Gutíerrez, 252.

79. As early as 1714, Spanish authorities ordered "married" couples in the Rio

Grande Pueblos to establish neolocal households, rather than residing with their parents, a clear attempt to break matrilocal residence patterns and assert colonial control over the institution of marriage. See *SANM* 2, reel 4, frame 1014, as an example.

80. Swadesh, 44.

81. Marietta Morrissey, *Slave Women in the New World: Gender Stratification in the Caribbean* (Lawrence: University of Kansas Press, 1989), 13–15. See also Barbara Bush, *Slave Women in Caribbean Society, 1650–1838* (Bloomington: Indiana University Press, 1990). The ambiguous benefits of maternity to women held captive in patrilineal societies is borne out by looking at women under indigenous African systems of captivity and slavery. Among the Margi of Nigeria, for example, social integration of captive-descended children could result in the elevation of mothers, if those children achieved social prominence in trade or warfare. See James H. Vaughan, "*Mafakur*: A Limbic Institution of the Margi," in *Slavery in Africa*, ed. Suzanne Miers and Igor Kopytoff (Wisconsin: University of Wisconsin Press, 1977), 85–102.

82. Alan M. Klein, "The Political Economy of Gender: A Nineteenth-Century Plains Indian Case Study," in *The Hidden Half: Studies of Plains Indian Women*, ed. Patricia Albers and Beatrice Medicine (Lanham, Md.: University Press of America, 1983), 143–74; for a study of the bison economy, see Flores, 465–85.

83. Veyna, 9. Veyna also notes that "when tools were distributed to the settlers of Santa Cruz de la Cañada in 1712, only women were allotted *rejas*."

84. H.P. Mera, *The Slave Blanket*, General Series Bulletin No. 5 (Santa Fe: New Mexico Laboratory of Anthropology, 1938).

85. See Lansing Bloom, "Early Weaving in New Mexico," *New Mexico Historical Review* 2 (1927): 228–38; Baxter, 60. See also Suzanne Baizerman, "Textile Traditions and Tourist Art: Hispanic Weaving in New Mexico" (Ph.D. diss., University of Minnesota, St. Paul, 1987), esp. 76–79; 130–31.

86. General Campaign: Report of Governor Vélez Cachupín to Conde de Revilla Gigedo, Nov. 27, 1751," in Alfred B. Thomas, *The Plains Indians and New Mexico, 1751–1778* (Norman: University of Oklahoma Press, 1940), 74. "Juan José Lobato to Velez, August 28, 1752," ibid., 114–15.

87. "Report of Governor Vélez to Marqués de Cruillas, 1762," ibid., 152–53.

88. "Abstract of Report Offered by de Anza, as Written by Pedro Garrido y Durran, Chihuahua, December 21, 1786," in Alfred B. Thomas, *Forgotten Frontiers: A Study of the Spanish Indian Policy of Don Juan Bautista de Anza, Governor of New Mexico, 1777–1787* (Norman: University of Oklahoma Press, 1932), 296; Elizabeth A. John, *Storms Brewed in Other Men's Worlds* (Lincoln: University of Nebraska Press, 1975), 732.

89. Maria Mies, "Social Origins of the Sexual Division of Labor," in *Women: The Last Colony*, ed. Maria Mies, Veronika Bennholdt-Thomsen, Claudia van Werlhof (London: Zed Books, 1988), 67–95, 87.

90. See Gregg, 86, 208, 219.

91. The French traders Jean Chapuis and Luis Fueilli were guided to Santa Fe in

1752 by "an Indian woman of the Aa tribe, who had fled to the house of her master [in Santa Fe] four months before and was following the road to her country." See "Vélez to Revilla Gigedo, Sept. 18, 1752," in Thomas, *Plains Indians and New Mexico*, 109.

92. See SANM 1, no. 657, "Demanda puesta por Lucia Ortega contra Roque Lovato sobre una Donacion-Ano del 1769," New Mexico State Records Center.

93. See Tykal; "Report of Governor Vélez to Marqués de Cruillas," in Thomas, *The Plains Indians*, 151.Vélez had asked the Comanche leader Nimiricante of the whereabouts of the women and children seized at Ranchos de Taos in 1760, Nimiricante replied that "they might have died, or been traded to the French and Jumanos." For José Juliano's problems in San Antonio, see Salcedo to Manrique, 27 July 1809, *SANM* 2, no. 2239.

94. Author's field notes, 17 Aug. 1990.

Catherine A. Cavanaugh, 'No Place for a Woman': Engendering Western Canadian Settlement

1. Gould first applied for membership in 1987 but was turned down because she was a woman. She then took her case to the Yukon Human Rights Commission on and won. That decision was overturned by the Supreme court of the Yukon Territory. After failing to convince the Court of Appeal to reverse the lower court's decision, Gould turned to the Supreme Court of Canada. See *Gould v. Yukon Order of Pioneers*, 133 *Dominion Law Reports* (4th), 449.

2. Ibid., 460.

3. Ibid., 511.

4. Ibid., 504.

5. Gender ideology refers to that set of Euro-Canadian beliefs which underwrote social relations and institutions in the nineteenth century by "specifying difference as binary opposites that turned on sex"—what Mary Povey, *Uneven Developments The Ideological Work of Gender In Mid-Victorian England* (Chicago, 1988), describes as "the characteristic feature of the mid-Victorian symbolic economy."

6. Karen Dubinsky, *Improper Advances* (Chicago, 1993) makes a similar point for northern Ontario.

7. Sarah Carter, "Categories and Terrains of Exclusion: Constructing the 'Indian Woman' in the Early Settlement Era in Western Canada," *Great Plains Quarterly* 13 (Summer 1993) 147–61.

8. Jane Tompkins, *West of Everything The Inner Life of Westerns* (New York, 1992, 4. See also, Patricia Nelson Limerick, *The Legacy of Conquest: The Unbroken Past of the American West* (New York, 1987), and Richard Slotkin, *Regeneration Through Violence: The Mythology of the American Frontier, 1600–1860*

(Middletown, CT, 1973).

9. Richard Slotkin, *Gunfighter Nation: The Myth of the Frontier in Twentieth-Century America* (New York, 1992), 10.

10. See Ray Allen Billington, *Frederick Jackson Turner: Historian, Scholar, Teacher* (New York, 1973). For another example of the creation of this myth, see Kim Townsend, "Francis Parkman and the Male Tradition," *American Quarterly*, 38 (Spring 1986): 97–113

11. Slotkin, *Gunfighter Nation*, 29–61.

12. The antimodernist sentiments of settlement discourse coexisted with faith in the benefits of modern industrial capitalism. Indeed, it represented wilderness going as restoring individual initiative and enterprise by offering a "real life" or "authentic" experience as described T. J. Jackson Lears, *No Place of Grace Antimodernism and the Transformation of American Culture 1880–1920* (New York, 1981), especially 4–58.

13. Ralph Connor is the pseudonym of Reverend Charles W. Gordon. Connor's novels were among the most popular of the period and are reputed to have sold over five million copies. See Edward McCourt, *The Canadian West in fiction*, rev. ed. (Toronto, 1970), 24–41; J. Lee Thompson and John H. Thompson, "Ralph Connor and the Canadian Identity," *Queens Quarterly* 79 (Summer 1972), 159–70; and F. W. Watt, "Western Myth: The World of Ralph Connor," *Canadian Literature* 1 (Summer 1959), 26–36. I am grateful to Jeremy Mouat, who first urged me to read Connor's novels.

14. According to one source, *The Sky Pilot* sold thousands of copies "almost overnight" and the total sales of Gordon's books exceeded five million copies, making him one of the most popular writers of his day. See Edward A. McCourt, *The Canadian West in Fiction* (Toronto, 1970), 24–25. Other Connor novels set in western Canada are *The Prospector* (1904), *The Settler, A Tale of Saskatchewan* (Toronto, 1909) and *The Doctor: A Tale of the Rockies* (New York: 1906).

15. Connor, *The Settler*, 227

16. Ibid., 147.

17. Connor, *The Sky Pilot*, 27.

18. The antimodernist sentiments of settlement discourse coexisted with faith in the benefits of modern industrial capitalism. Indeed, it represented wilderness going as restoring individual initiative and enterprise by offering a "real life" or "authentic" experience as described T. J. Jackson Lears, *No Place of Grace: Antimodernism and the Transformation of American Culture 1880–1920* (New York, 1981), especially 4–58.

19. See Francis, *Images of the West*, 103, 125, 124, 121.

20. For a critical discussion of "gentle tamers," see Joan Jensen and Darlis Miller, "The Gentle Tamers Revisited: New Approaches to the History of Women in the American West," *Pacific Historical Review* 49 (May 1980), 173–214; Paula Petrik, "The Gentle Tamers in Transition: Women in the Trans-Mississippi West," *Feminist Studies* 11 (Fall 1985), 678–94; and Elizabeth Jameson, "Women

as Workers, Women as Civilizers: True Womanhood in the American West,"
in Susan Armitage and Elizabeth Jameson, eds., *The Women's West* (Norman,
1987), 145–64.

21. Quoted in Jeremy Mouat, *Roaring Days Rossland's Mines and the History of
British Columbia* (Vancouver: University of British Columbia Press, 1995): 112.

22. Connor, *Sky Pilot*, preface.

23. See *Land of the Lake: A Story of the Settlement and Development of the Country
West of Buffalo Lake* (Lacombe, AB, 1974), 43–44.

24. Ibid. Author's emphasis.

25. Quoted in Lewis G. Thomas, ed. *The Prairie West to 1905* (Toronto, 1975), 128.

26. On British imperialism and masculinity see Graham Dawson, "The Blond
Bedouin: Lawrence of Arabia, Imperial Adventure, and the Imagining of
English-British Masculinity," and other essays in *Manful Assertions:
Masculinities in Britain since 1800*, eds. Michael Roper and John Tosh (New
York, 1991), 113–144; J. A. Managan and James Walvin, eds., *Manliness and
Morality: Middle-Class Masculinity in Britain and America, 1800–1940* (New York,
1987). Also suggestive is Elizabeth Vibert, "'Real Men Hunt Buffalo':
Masculinity, Race and Class in British Fur Traders' Narratives," in *Gender and
History in Canada*, eds. Joy Parr and Mark Rosenfeld (Toronto, 1996), 50–67.

27. Quoted in Germaine Warkentin, ed., *Canadian Exploration Literature* (Toronto,
1993), 384–95.

28. For a critical exploration of this idea see in particular Sarah Carter, "The
Exploitation and Narration of the Captivity of Theresa Delaney and Theresa
Gowanlock, 1885," in *Making Western Canada*, Catherine Cavanaugh and
Jeremy Mouat, eds. (Toronto, 1996), 31–61, and Carroll Smith-Rosenberg,
"Captured Subjects/Savage Others: Violently Engendering the New
American," *Gender and History* 5 (Summer, 1993), 177–95.

29. Sylvia Van Kirk, *"Many Tender Ties" Women in Fur-Trade Society, 1670–1870*
(Winnipeg, 1980) does much to recover the history of Aboriginal women in
the trade, but her analysis of the role of European women falls within this
traditional interpretation. According to Van Kirk, male racism remained dormant until the arrival of European women when "the question of colour
became an issue for the first time" (p. 201). Jennifer S. H. Brown, *Strangers
In Blood* (Vancouver, 1980), also points to familial relations relatively free of
racial tensions, arguing that change occurred during the years leading up to
and immediately following the merger of the North-West and Hudson's Bay
Companies in 1821, which "were conspicuous for the rise of racial categorization and discrimination and for the economic and sexual marginality of
native born sons and daughters to the new order" (p. 205).

30. Van Kirk, *"Many Tender Ties,"* 220–230. See also her article "The Reputation
of a Lady': Sarah Ballenden and the Foss-Pelly Scandal," *Manitoba History* 11
(Spring 1986), 4–11.

31. Ballenden was the eldest daughter of chief trader Alexander Roderick
McLeod and his Indian wife. European trained and educated, her three

younger sisters resided in Canada (Quebec) following their father's death in 1840. See Brown: 183–84, 215.

32. Van Kirk, *Many Tender Ties,* 220.

33. Ibid., 221.

34. Studies of European women in colonial settings focus on Asia and Africa. See especially Jane Hunter, *The Gospel of Gentility: American Women Missionaries in Turn-of-the-Century China* (New Haven, 1984); Anne Laura Stoler, "Carnal Knowledge and Imperial Power: Gender, Race, and Morality in Colonial Asia," in *Gender at the Crossroads of Knowledge: Feminist Anthropology in the Postmodern Era*, Micaela di Leonardo (Berkeley, 1991): 51–101; and Stoler, "Rethinking Colonial Categories: European Communities and the Boundaries of Rule," in *Colonialism and Culture*, Nicholas B. Dirks (Ann Arbor, 1992): 319–52. For a thoughtful consideration of the issues raised by women and imperialism see Jane Haggis, "Gendering Colonialism or Colonising Gender?" *Women's Studies International Forum*, 13, 1/2 (1990), 105–115.

35. See Margaret Strobel, *European Women and the Second British Empire* (Bloomington, 1991).

36. Hilary Callan and Shirley Ardener, eds., *The Incorporated Wife* (London, 1984, 1–25. See also Helen Callaway, *Gender, Culture and Empire: European Women in Colonial Nigeria* (Urbana, 1987).

37. I am grateful to Sarah Carter for discussion on this point.

38. For further discussion on the ways gender constructed respectability see Erica Smith, "'Gentlemen, This is no Ordinary Trial': Sexual Narratives in the Trial of the Reverend Corbett, Red River, 1863," in Jennifer S. H. Brown & Elizabeth Vibert, eds., *Reading Beyond Words: Contexts for Native History* (Peterborough, ON, 1996), 364–80.

39. William Francis Butler, *The Great Lone Land A Tale of Travel and Adventure in the North-West of America* (Toronto, 1910): 200–201.

40. Quoted in D. J. Hall, "Clifford Sifton: Immigration and Settlement Policy," in Howard Palmer, ed., *The Settlement of the West*, (Calgary, 1977), 74.

41. Ibid.: 71.

42. Quoted in D. J. Hall, *Clifford Sifton* (Vancouver, 1985), 69.

43. *Debates*, House of Commons, Canada, cols. 9271–72, July 11, 1905. Homestead law granted heads of households, or any man over eighteen years of age, "free" access to one hundred and sixty acres of land, subject to an entry fee, residence, and improvements. In practice, this meant any man over eighteen.

44. Binnie-Clark, *Wheat and Woman* (Toronto, 1979), xxvi.

45. Ibid., 308.

46. Quoted in Hall, *Clifford Sifton*, 2: 81.

47. This policy also stipulated that an agent would be paid three dollars for every man and one dollar for every child who settled in Canada as a direct result of his efforts. See Hall, "Sifton: Immigration and Settlement Policy," 70.

48. Much has been written on the double disadvantage imposed by gender as a

system that constructs "woman" as the "Other" over and against shifting notions of "man" and "human." But see in particular Simone de Beauvoir, trans. H. M. Parshley, *The Second Sex* (1949; reprint, New York, 1953), xvii–xxv; Denis Riley, *"Am I That Name?": Feminism and the Category of Women in History* (Minneapolis, 1988), esp. 18–43; Joan Wallach Scott, *Gender and the Politics of History* (New York, 1988), 42–43.

49. Francis, *Images of the West,* 389–90.

50. Irene Parlby, "The Milestones of My Life," *The Canadian Magazine,* June, 1928, 14. Parlby arrived in the North West in 1896.

51. Eliane Leslau Silverman, *The Last Best West* (Montreal, 1984), 7.

52. *A Flannel Shirt & Liberty,* Susan Jackel, ed. (Vancouver, 1982), 100.

53. On the homestead legislation in Canada see Catherine Cavanaugh, "The Women's Movement In Alberta As Seen Through The Campaign for Dower Rights, 1909–1928," (MA thesis, University of Alberta, 1986) and "The Limitations of the Pioneering Partnership: The Alberta Campaign for Homestead Dower, 1909–25," *Canadian Historical Review,* 74 (1993), 198–225; Susan Jackel, "Introduction," Binnie-Clark, *Wheat and Woman* (Toronto: University of Toronto Press, 1979): xx-xxxi; and Margaret McCallum, "Prairie Women and the Struggle for Dower Law, 1905–1920," *Prairie Forum* 18 (Spring 1993), 19–34; and *The Matrimonial Home,* Alberta Law Reform Institute Report for Discussion No. 14, March 1995.

54. Common law dower, long established in English Canada, was abolished in the West in 1886 when the Federal government introduced the Territories Real Property Act as part of its settlement policy. As a result, married women who moved from central and eastern Canada lost the limited protection available to them in their home provinces. Similarly, women immigrants from the western United States lost the homesteading privileges available to them under the American legislation. This partly explains why the issue was raised at the time.

55. The precedent for Canadian homestead dower was American legislation which originated in the state of Texas in 1839, where it was intended to protect the home against financial misfortune. See The Manitoba Law Reform Commission, *Report On An Examination of "The Dower Act"* (Winnipeg, 1984), 160.

56. Cavanaugh, "The Women's Movement in Alberta," 67.

57. Ibid., esp. 50–52, 58–65. The bill was an important move toward a positive right of the wife in the "common estate" of the marriage. This broke with the inchoate right of dower, which remained dormant during the husband's life time and had proved a stumbling block for the courts. The bill was limited in that it established the husband as "head of the community," giving the wife what was in effect a veto over his power to encumber or dispose of community property. Nevertheless, the bill represented a break from the old common law principle of coverture, which subsumed the wife's legal personality in that of her husband. In addition to securing family property during

marriage, the bill opened the door to equal division of family assets in the event of marriage breakdown or the death of a spouse.

58. Ibid., 86.

59. Henrietta Muir Edwards, Legal Status of Canadian Women as shown by extracts from dominion and provincial laws relating to women and children (Calgary, 1908), and Legal Status of Women of Alberta as shown by extracts from dominion and provincial laws (Edmonton, University of Alberta, 1917).

60. The committee's final report did recommend establishing a provincial mediation service to assist in the event of domestic disputes and marriage break down but no action was taken.

61. Carl Frederick Betke, "The United Farmers of Alberta, 1921–1935: The Relationship Between The Agricultural Organization And The Government of Alberta" (M.A. thesis, University of Alberta, 1971), describes Brownlee as the "strong man in the party," who "exercised such amazing influence over U.F.A. votes" (p. 79). Betke's is still the most complete treatment of the Farmer's in government. He attributes UFA retreat from radical politics to Brownlee's influence as Premier and head of the party from 1925 until he resigned under a cloud of scandal in 1934.

62. Ibid., 71.

63. Ibid.

64. Cavanaugh, "The Women's Movement in Alberta," 75.

65. The married mothers' custody rights developed unevenly in statute and in case law. In Manitoba the 1922 Child Welfare Act, Statues of Manitoba c.2, s.122–147, asserted the mother's equal custody right; Saskatchewan passed similar legislation in 1919–20 as The Infants' Act, c.77, s.2., which applied to children age 14 and under; and Alberta introduced its Domestic Relations Act in 1927, s. 61 (1). Along with custody rights, the mother was also made equally liable with the father for the maintenance of the child.

66. Edmonton Bulletin, 28 October 1912: 3.

67. Western women were the first to win the vote in Canada. Manitoba passed suffrage legislation in 1916, followed by Saskatchewan, Alberta and British Columbia in 1917. Catherine Lyle Cleverdon, The Woman Suffrage Movement in Canada (Toronto, 1950) provides a detailed but dated account of the votes-for-women campaigns in Canada. See also Deborah Gorham, "Singing Up the Hill," Canadian Dimension 10 (June 1975), 26–38. For a further discussion of the effects of suffrage on women's participation in politics, see the essays in Linda Kealey and Joan Sangster, eds., Beyond the Vote: Canadian Women and Politics (Toronto, 1989). For prairie women, see Veronica Strong-Boag, "Pulling in Double Harness or Hauling a Double Load: Women, Work, Feminism on the Canadian Prairie," Journal of Canadian Studies 1 (Fall 1986), 95–106. The federal franchise was proclaimed in 1919.

68. For a further discussion of women in Alberta politics in the immediate post-suffrage era see Nancy Langford, "'All That Glitters:' The Political Apprenticeship of Alberta Women, 1916–1930" in Catherine A. Cavanaugh

and Randi R. Warne, eds., *Standing on New Ground,* (Edmonton, 1993), 71–85.

69. In Calgary Mrs. Langford and Mrs. A. Gale ran as Liberal and Independent Liberal candidates respectively; Louise McKinney and Irene Parlby ran under the UFA banner; and in Edmonton, Mrs. E. Ferris ran as a Conservative, Mary Cantin was an Independent Labour candidate, Marie Mellard, Labour Socialist, and Nellie McClung ran for the governing Liberals. See Edmonton *Bulletin,* 13 July 1921: 3. The UFA landslide victory swept the Liberals from office so that while McClung was victorious she served her term on the opposition side of the House. Parlby won her riding of Lacombe. She was re-elected twice and served in the UFA cabinet until her retirement in 1934. McKinney was defeated.

70. Edmonton, *The Morning Bulletin,* 18 July 1921, 1.

71. Calgary, *Western Standard,* 11 June 1917, 1.

72. UFA Bulletin No. 5 A (Calgary, 1918) in Violet MacNaughton Personal Papers Saskatchewan Archives Board (hereafter VMNP), G 291.7.

73. William Irvine, *The Farmers in Politics* (1920 rpt., Ottawa, 1976), 123–24.

74. Ibid., 118.

75. Irene Parlby, "Awhile Ago—And To-day," *The Canadian Magazine* (July 1928), 26.

76. Irene Parlby, "The Great Adventure," *The Grain Growers Guide* (April, 1927), 5.

77. Shielah Stier, "The Beliefs of Violet McNaughton" (MA thesis, University of Saskatchewan 1979), 92.

78. Georgina M. Taylor, "A personal tragedy shapes the future," *The Western Producer* (Saskatoon) 10 January 1991, 11.

79. Quoted in Linda Rasmussen et al, *A Harvest Yet to Reap: A History of Prairie Women* (Toronto, 1976), 170.

80. Parlby, "The Great Adventure," 5.

81. Ibid.

82. Scholars disagree on the extent to which women's reform activities reinforced existing social divisions. For example, Mariana Valverde, "'When the Mother of the Race is Free:' Race, Reproduction, and Sexuality in First-Wave Feminism," in *Gender Conflicts,* Franca Iacovetta and Mariana Valverde, eds. (Toronto, 1992), 3–26, argues that women were inevitably divided by race and class. Carol Bacchi takes a similar approach in "Race Regeneration and Social Purity: A Study of the Social Attitudes of Canada's English-Speaking Suffragists, *Historie sociale/Social History* 11 (November 1978), 460–74. Nancy M. Sheehan, "Women Helping Women: The WCTU and the Foreign Population in the West, 1905–1930," *International Journal of Women's Studies* 6 (November/December 1983), 396–411, argues that patterns varied depending upon local circumstances. For a positive interpredation of middle-class–led reform in English Canada see Christina Simmons, "'Helping the Poorer Sisters': The Women of the Joist Mission, Halifax, 1905–1945," *Acadiensis* 14 (Autumn 1984), 3–27, and Mariana Valverde, *The Age of Light, Soap, and Water:*

Moral Reform in English Canada, 1885–1925 (Toronto, 1991).

83. Nellie L. McClung, *The Stream Runs Fast* (Toronto, 1945), 175.

84. Myrtle Hayes Wright, "Mothering the Prairie," *MacLean's Magazine* 39 (1 April 1926), 22.

85. Irene Parlby, "What Business Have Women In Politics," notes for a 1928 speech, Irene Parlby's Papers, Glenbow Museum and Archives, Calgary, Alberta.

86. Parlby, "The Great Adventure," 5.

87. Nellie McClung, *In Times Like These* (Toronto, 1915), 153.

88. Stier "The Beliefs of Violet McNaughton," 115.

89. See Georgina Taylor, "Violet begins her career with the Western Producer," *The Western Producer* (Saskatoon), 31 January 1991, 12–13 and "Violet's life as a journalist," *The Western Producer* 7 February 1991, 10–11.

90. In her biography, *The Stream Runs Fast*, McClung notes that she "enjoyed" politics but felt women's efforts had left little lasting impact. Beyond this cryptic comment, she offers few details of her time in office. Her biographers, Mary Hallett & Marilyn Davis, *Firing The Heather* (Saskatoon, 1993), shed little light on McClung's silence.

91. Catherine Anne Cavanaugh, "In Search of a Useful Life: Irene Marryat Parlby, 1868–1965," (Ph.D. diss., University of Alberta, 1994).

92. The rumours were based on the UFA's emphasis on health care during the 1921 campaign and their promise to establish a minister of health. Farm women had led the debate on health care so that Parlby's appointment would have made a logical choice. Once in office, the Farmer's followed their Liberal predecessors on the question of health care, focussing on building hospitals in urban areas.

93. The issue of a salary was resolved by an order-in-council, granting ministers without portfolio an allowance of fifteen dollars "for attendance at each and every meeting of the Executive Council" in addition to the travel and living allowance available to all ministers. See "Memo: Orders in Council Re Subsistence Allowance Of Members Of Executive Council," 88.553/15, The Attorney General's Papers, Provincial Archives of Alberta, Edmonton, Alberta.

94. Irene Parlby letter to Violet McNaughton, 13 October 1921, A1 D.54, VMNP.

95. See in particular Carol Bacchi, *Liberation Deferred? The Ideas of the English-Canadian Suffragists, 1877–1918* (Toronto, 1983) and John Herd Thompson and Allen Seager, *Canada 1922–1939: Decades of Discord* (Toronto, 1985). For a reconsideration of prairie women's politics in this period see Veronica Strong-Boag, "Pulling in Double Harness or Hauling a Double Load: Women, Work and feminism on the Canadian Prairie," in *Journal of Canadian Studies* 1 (Fall 1986): 35–52.

Jean Barman, Taming Aboriginal Sexuallity: Gender, Power, and Race in British Columbia, 1850–1900

1. Earlier versions of this essay were presented at the BC Studies Conference in May 1997 and, thanks to Elizabeth Jameson and Susan Armitage, at the Western Historical Association in October 1997. I am grateful to everyone who had commented on the essay, especially to Robin Fisher at BCS, Elizabeth Jameson at WHA, and the two anonymous reviewers for BC Studies. The Social Sciences and Humanities Research Council generously funded the research from which the essay draws.

2. This statement by Bishop O'Conner was taken up forcefully in Reasons for Judgment, Vancouver Registry, no. cc9 206 17, 25 July 1996.

3. National Parole Board, Decision Registry, file 905044c, 21 March 1997.

4. The three best books for understanding Aboriginal people in British Columbia are, in my view, Robin Fisher, *Contact and ConXict: Indian-European Relations in British Columbia, 1774–1890* (Vancouver: UBC Press, 1970 and 1992); Paul Tennant, *Aboriginal Peoples and Politics: The Indian Land Question in British Columbia, 1849–1989* (Vancouver: UBC Press, 1990); and Cole Harris, *The Resettlement of British Columbia: Essays on Colonialism and Geographical Change* (Vancouver: UBC Press, 1997), each of which is driven by a male perspective as to sources, authorship, subjects, and interpretation, yet represents itself as being about Aboriginal people. Much the same observation might be made about the bulk of the ethnographic literature; a recent summary of the historiography (Wayne Suttles and Aldona Jonaitis, "History of Research in Ethnology," in Wayne Suttles, ed., Northwest Coast, vol. 7 of William C. Sturtevant, ed., *Handbook of North American Indians* [Washington, DC: Smithsonian Institution, 1990], 84–86) does not even include private life or women, much less sexuality, as topics.

5. This general point is made by, among other authors, Sandra Harding in *The Science Question in Feminism* (Milton Keynes: Open University Press, 1986); Catherine Hall in *White, Male, and Middle-Class: Explorations in Feminism and History* (New York: Routledge, 1988); and Vron Ware in *Beyond the Pale: White Women, Racism and History* (London: Verso, 1992). A handful of exceptions by Canadian scholars are principally concerned with an earlier time period, as with Karen Anderson, *Chain Her By One Foot: The Subjugation of Native Women in Seventeenth-Century New France* (New York: Routledge, 1991); Sylvia Van Kirk, *"Many Tender Ties": Women in Fur Trade Society, 1670–1870* (Norman: University of Oklahoma Press, 1980); and Ron Bourgeault, "Race, Class and Gender: Colonial Domination of Indian Women," *Socialist Studies* 5 (1989), 87–115. The two principal analyses of perceptions of Aboriginal people consider women, if at all, as extensions of their menfolk; see Robert F. Berkhofer, Jr., *The White Man's Indian: Images of the American Indian from Columbus to the Present* (New York: Vintage, 1979), and Daniel Francis, *The Imaginary Indian: The Image of the Indian in Canadian*

Culture (Vancouver: Arsenal Pulp Press, 1992).

6. Jane Katz, ed., *Messengers of the Wind: Native American Women Tell Their Life Stories* (New York: Ballentine Books, 1995), 5.

7. David Jary and Julia Jary, *Collins Dictionary of Sociology,* 2nd ed. (Glasgow: HarperCollins, 1995), 590–1. It was 1914 before the *Oxford English Dictionary* got to the letter 's.' All of its quotes were from the nineteenth century and, while the first definition of sexuality was "the quality of being sexual or having sex," the second and third were the "possession of sexual powers or capability of sexual feelings" and "recognition of or preoccupation with what is sexual." See Sir James A. H. Murray, ed., *A New English Dictionary on Historical Principles,* vol. 8 (Oxford: Clarendon Press, 1914), 582. Interest in the concept of sexuality, and more generally in regulation of the body, mushroomed with the publication of Michel Foucault's *History of Sexuality* in 1978 (Harmondsworth: Penguin, esp. vol. 1) and Peter Gay's *The Bourgeois Experience* in 1986 (Oxford: Oxford University Press, 2 vols.). Particularly helpful for interpreting Foucault is Ann Laura Stoler's *Race and the Education of Desire: Foucault's History of Sexuality and the Colonial Order of Things* (Durham: Duke University Press, 1995).

8. Gail Hawkes, *A Sociology of Sex and Sexuality* (Buckingham and Philadelphia: Open University Press, 1996), 8, 14, 42.

9. This point underlies Ronald Hyam, *Empire and Sexuality: The British Experience* (Manchester: University of Manchester Press, 1990); and Margaret Strobel, *Gender, Sex, and Empire* (Washington: American Historical Association, 1993), which critiques Hyam's contention that empire enhanced men's sexual opportunities.

10. Among the more perceptive recent examinations of aspects of this topic are Margaret Jolly and Martha MacIntyre, ed., *Family and Gender in the Pacific: Domestic Contradictions and the Colonial Impact* (Cambridge: Cambridge University Press, 1989); Strobel, *Gender, Sex, and Empire;* Robert Young, *Colonial Desire: Hybridity in Theory, Culture and Race* (London: Routledge, 1995); Stoler, *Race and the Education of Desire;* and Frederick Cooper and Ann Laura Stoler, ed., *Tensions of Empire: Colonial Cultures in a Bourgeois World* (Berkeley: University of California Press, 1997).

11. Philip Mason, *Patterns of Dominance* (London: Oxford University Press for the Institute of Race Relations, 1970), 88.

12. Ann Laura Stoler and Frederick Cooper, "Between Metropole and Colony: Rethinking a Research Agenda," in Cooper and Stoler, ed., *Tensions of Empire,* 5. Although Stoler and Cooper co-wrote this introductory essay, the insight is clearly Stoler's, since it is her research on colonial Asia that is cited.

13. As diverse examples of a similar sequence, if not necessarily interpretation, of events, see Albert L. Hurtado, *Indian Survival on the California Frontier* (New Haven: Yale University Press, 1988), 169–92; and Caroline Ralston, "Changes in the Lives of Ordinary Women in Early Post-Contact Hawaii," in Jolly and

MacIntyre, ed., *Family and Gender*, 45–82. In *Capturing Women: The Manipulation of Cultural Imagery in Canada's Prairie West* (Montreal and Kingston: McGill-Queen's University Press, 1997), Sarah Carter links the sexualization of Aboriginal women on the Canadian prairies to their participation in the 1885 uprising (esp. 8–10, 161, 183, 187, 189).

14. In *Allegories of Empire: The Figure of the Woman in the Colonial Text* (Minneapolis: University of Minnesota Press, 1993), Jenny Sharpe argues that, after rebellions in India in the 1850s, raped colonial women provided the basis for racializing Indigenous peoples as inferior.

15. The concept of wildness is examined in Sharon Tiffany and Kathleen Adams, *The Myth of the Wild Woman* (Cambridge: Schenken, 1985).

16. Patricia C. Albers, "From Illusion to Illumination: Anthropological Studies of American Indian Women," in Sandra Morgan, ed., *Gender and Anthropology: Critical Reviews for Research and Teaching* (Washington: American Anthropological Association, 1989), 132. Carol Devens appears to accept this perspective in "Separate Confrontations: Gender as a Factor in Indian Adaptation to European Colonization in New France," *American Quarterly* 38, 3 (1986), 461–80; and in her *Countering Colonization: Native American Women and Great Lakes Missions, 1630–1900* (Berkeley: University of California Press, 1992). The identification of Aboriginal women's conversion to Christianity with their desire to maintain traditional values underlies much of the special Ethnohistory issue (43, 4, Fall 1996), "Native American Women's Responses to Christianity, edited by Michael Harkin and Sergei Kan, esp. 563–66, 574–75, 6 14, 6 29–30, 655, 675–76. Others authors sidestep issues of sexuality altogether, as with most of the essays in Laura F. Klein and Lillian A. Ackerman, ed., *Women and Power in Native North America* (Norman: University of Oklahoma Press, 1995); and Nancy Shoemaker, ed., *Negotiators of Change: Historical Perspectives on Native American Women* (New York: Routledge, 1995).

17. Hall in *White, Male, and Middle-Class*, 6 1–62.

18. George W. Stocking, Jr., *Victorian Anthropology* (New York: Free Press, 1987), 199–200, 202.

19. Hawkes, *Sociology of Sex*, 14–15, 42.

20. Despite its male perspective, a good basic source, although limited to Coastal peoples, remains Suttles, ed., *Northwest Coast*.

21. Especially useful is Carol Cooper, "Native Women of the Northern Pacific Coast: An Historical Perspective, 1830–1900," *Journal of Canadian Studies* 27, 4 (Winter 1992–93), 44–75, which points out that what newcomers labeled prostitution sometimes simply continued traditional social structures wherein some persons were deprived of their autonomy as "slaves" (58) and traces the seasonal migrations of North Coast women to Victoria with their families.

22. 24 September 1860 entry, Bishop George Hills, Diary, in Anglican Church, Ecclesiastical Province of British Columbia, Archives; also letter to the

editor from C.T.W. in Victoria Gazette, 22 September 1860; and Matthew MacFie, Vancouver Island and British Columbia (London: Longman, Green, Longman, Roberts, & Green, 1865), 471.

23. Thomas Crosby, *Up and Down the North PaciWc Coast by Canoe and Mission Ship* (Toronto: Missionary Society of the Methodist Church, 1904), 17. On the relevance of missionary accounts, see Jean and John Comaroff, *Of Revelation and Revolution: Christianity, Colonialism and Consciousness in South Africa* (Chicago: University of Chicago Press, 1991).

24. This contention is supported by Chris Hanna's extensive research in the Victoria colonial press, and I thank him for sharing his findings with me.

25. "Can such things be?" *Victoria Daily Chronicle,* 16 November 1862.

26. Francis E. Herring, *In the Pathless West With Soldiers, Pioneers, Miners, and Savages* (London: T. Fisher Unwin, 1904), 173–75.

27. 21 April 1860 entry, Hills, Diary; also 12 August and 24 September 1860 and 31 January 1862 entries.

28. "The Dance Houses," *British Colonist,* 20 December 1861.

29. In *During My Time: Florence Edenshaw Davidson, a Haida Woman* (Vancouver and Seattle: Douglas & McIntyre and University of Washington Press, 1982), 44–45, Margaret Blackman links the decline to the smallpox epidemic of 1862–63, but newspaper coverage suggests that the principal cause was fewer lone men.

30. On the maritime fur trade, see Lorraine Littlefield, "Women Traders in the Maritime Fur Trade," in Bruce Alden Cox, ed., *Native People, Native Lands: Canadian Indians, Inuit and Metis* (Ottawa: Carleton University Press, 1991), 173–85; and on the land-based trade Van Kirk, *"Many Tender Ties."* Devens probes "native women as autonomous, sexual active females" in seventeenth-century New France in *Countering Colonization,* 25 and passim.

31. For a case study, see Jo-Anne Fiske, "Fishing is Women's Business: Changing Economic Roles of Carrier Women and Men," in Cox, ed., *Native People, Native Lands,* 186–98.

32. On the larger meaning of mimicry as popularized by Homi Bhabha, see his "Of Mimicry and Man: The Ambivalence of Colonial Discourse," in Cooper and Stoler, ed., *Tensions of Empire,* 152–60.

33. "A Squaw Arrests a White Man," *British Colonist,* 17 January 1862.

34. "Attempted rape," *British Colonist,* 17 August 1860.

35. Thomas Crosby, *Among the An-ko-me-nums, Or Flathead Tribes of Indians of the PaciWc Coast* (Toronto: William Briggs, 1907), 62.

36. 1 February 1862 entry, Hills, Diary.

37. Crosby, *Among the An-ko-me-nums,* 63.

38. Emily Carr, *The Heart of a Peacock* (Toronto: Irwin, 1986), 96.

39. Adele Perry admirably tackles this and related topics in "'Oh I'm just sick of the faces of men': Gender Imbalance, Race, Sexuality, and Sociability in Nineteenth-Century British Columbia," *BC Studies* 105–06 (Spring/Summer 1995), 27–43.

40. Letter of Morgan Lewis to Rev. D. R. Lewis, New Westminster, 29 October 1862, printed in Seren Cymru, 23 January 1863, quoted in Alan Conway, "Welsh Gold Miners in British Columbia During the 1860's," *Cylchgrawn Llyfrgell Genedlaethol Cymru:The National Library of Wales Journal* 10, 4 (Winter 1958), 383–84.

41. Cariboo, *The Newly Discovered Gold Fields of British Columbia* (Fairfield, Washington:Ye Galleon Press, 1975), 7–8, 19–20.

42. See Jean Barman, "What a Difference a Border Makes: Aboriginal Racial Intermixture in the Pacific Northwest," *Journal of the West,* forthcoming.

43. Carl Friesach, *Ein AusXug nach Britisch-Columbien in Jahre 1858* (Gratz: Philosophical Society, 1875), reprinted in *British Columbia Historical Quarterly* 5 (1941), 227.

44. *The West Shore,* September 1884, 275, cited in Patricia E. Roy, "The West Shore's View of British Columbia, 1884," *Journal of the West* 22, 4 (October 1984), 28.

45. For a case study, see Jean Barman, "Lost Okanagan: In Search of the First Settler Families," *Okanagan History* 60 (1996), 8–20

46. Mary Augusta Tappage, "Changes," in Jeane E. Speare, *The Days of Augusta* (Vancouver: J. J. Douglas, 1973), 71.

47. 27 May 1868 entry, Hills, Diary.

48. Francis E. Herring, "Pretty Mrs.Weldon" in her *Nan And Other Pioneer Women of the West* (London: Francis Griffiths, 1913), 122, 1 24–25.

49. The base used is the greatly diminished Aboriginal population of about 25–30,000 following the devastating small pox epidemic of the early 1860s. Another measure is the number of children resulting from the relationships, as indicated in the "Supplementary Report" to British Columbia, Department of Education, First Annual Report on the Public Schools in the Province of British Columbia, 1872, 38.

50. David R. Williams, *The Man for a New Country: Sir Matthew Baillie Begbie* (Sidney: Gray's Publishing, 1977), 106–07.

51. The age-linked, equally essentializing counterpart was, of course, an absence of sexuality.Aboriginal woman as drudge is discussed in, among other sources, Elizabeth Vibert, *Traders' Tales: Narratives of Cultural Encounters in the Columbia Plateau, 1807–1846* (Norman: University of Oklahoma Press, 1997), 127–31, 136, and 233–39.

52. In referring to men in power, I do not mean to suggest that non-Aboriginal women were completely absent from the discourse but I do contend that, at least in British Columbia, their voices were muted compared to those of men; for a brief introduction to this literature, see Strobel, *Gender, Sex, and Empire.* Myra Rutherdale, "Revisiting Colonization to Gender: Anglican Missionary Women in the Pacific Northwest and Arctic, 1860- 1945," *BC Studies* 104 (Winter 1994–95), 3–23, discusses the priorities of female missionaries but without reference to sexuality.

53. Crosby, *Among the An-ko-me-nums,* 96.

54. See, for example, private memorandum of Gilbert Malcolm Sproat, Indian Reserve Commissioner, Okanagan Lake, 27 October 1877, in dia, rg 10, vol. 3656, file 9063, C-10115.

55. Remarks enclosed with George Blenkinsop, secretary and census taker to Indian Reserve Commission, to Sproat, Douglas Lake, 20 September 1878, in dia, rg 10, vol. 3667, file 10,330.

56. Private memorandum of Sproat, 27 October 1877; and Alex C. Anderson and Archibald McKinlay, Report of the proceedings of the Joint Commission for the settlement of the Indian Reserves in the Province of British Columbia, Victoria, 2 1 March 1877, in dia, rg 10, vol. 3645, file 7936, C-10113.

57. Crosby, *Among the An-ko-me-nums,* esp. 206–32 and passim; and Crosby, *Up and Down,* passim.

58. 24 May 1866 entry, Hills, Diary.

59. Census data included with Anderson and McKinlay, Report, 21 March 1877.

60. Remarks enclosed with Blenkinsop to Sproat, 20 September 1878.

61. Such a contention is not inconsistent with Devens's view that Aboriginal men in the Great Lakes region more easily accommodated to missionaries' aspirations for them than did women; see her *Countering Colonization.*

62. Crosby, *Up and Down,* 270–71.

63. Stocking, *Victorian Anthropology,* 202.

64. Leonore Davidoff and Catherine Hall. *Family Fortunes: Men and Women of the English Middle Class, 1780–1850.* (London: Hutchinson, 1987), 322, 451.

65. Alex C. Anderson, J. P., to Sir Francis Hincks, MP for Vancouver District, Victoria, 26 August 1873, excerpted in undated memorandum of Anderson in dia, rg 10, vol. 3658, file 9404, c–10115.

66. Anderson and McKinlay, Report, 21 March 1877.

67. William Laing Meason, Indian Agent of Williams Lake Agency, to I. W. Powell, Superintendent of Indian Affairs, Lillooet, 25 March 1884, in dia, rg 10, vol. 3658, file 9404, c–10115.

68. This topic is examined in Berkhofer, Jr., *White Man's Indian,* esp. 50–6 1; Brian W. Dippie, *The Vanishing American: White Attitudes & U.S. Indian Policy* (Lawrence: University Press of Kansas, 1982), passim; Robert E. Bieder, "Scientific Attitudes Toward Indian Mixed-Bloods in Early Nineteenth Century America," *Journal of Ethnic Studies* 8 (1980), 17–30; and Robert Miles, Racism (London: Routledge, 1989).

69. R.C. Mayne, *Four Years in British Columbia and Vancouver Island* (London: John Murray, 1862), 277.

70. Anderson to John Ash, Provincial Secretary, of British Columbia, 16 April 1873, excerpted in undated memorandum of Anderson, in dia, rg 10, vol. 3658, file 9404, c–10115.

71. The fullest account of the events occurring in 1879 is by a descendent: Mel Rothenburger, *The Wild McLeans* (Victoria: Orca, 1993).

72. The sequence of events at Cache Creek School in 1877 was followed closely in the Victoria press.

73. Drawing on Stoler, Carter suggests that, on the prairies, opposition grew out of fears of mixed-race children becoming heirs; see *Capturing Women,* xvi, 14–15, 191–92.

74. The constructed nature of all Aboriginal petitions is indicated by the alacrity with which missionaries and others warned federal officials about upcoming petitions "purporting to come from the Indians," but which were in fact being organized by an opposing religious group or others not to their liking, as with Alfred Hall, Anglican missionary, to Superintendent of Indian Affairs, Alert Bay, 5 October 1889, in rg 10, vol. 38 16, file 57,045–1, c–10193.

75. Petitions of the Lillooet tribe of Indians and from Lower Fraser Indians, s.d. [summer and late fall 1885], and s.d. [summer 1885] in rg 10, vol. 3842, file 71,799, c–10148. On the Oblates' role see memo from Bishop Louis d'Herbomez, omi, to the Governor General, s.d. [1887], in same.

76. George N. Burbidge, Deputy Minister of Justice, to L. Vankoughnet, Deputy Superintendent General of Indian Affairs, Ottawa, 3 February 1886, and enclosure, in rg 10, vol. 3842, file 71,799, C–10148.

77. W.H. Lomas, Indian Agent of Cowichan Agency, to Powell, Quamichan, 20 May 1886; also draft of Vankoughnet to Powell, 13 February 1886; P. McTiernan, Indian Agent at New Westminster, to Powell, New Westminster, 9 April 1886; Meason to Powell, Little Dog Creek, 25 March 1886; J.W. Mackay, Indian Agent of Kamloops-Okanagan Agency, to Powell, Sooyoos [Osoyoos], 2 May 1886; and Powell to Superintendent of Indian Affairs, Victoria, 21 June 1886, in rg 10, vol. 3842, file 71,799, c–10148.

78. Memo from d'Herbomez, [1887]; and Hector Langevin, Minister of Public Works, to John Macdonald, Superintendent of Indian Affairs, Ottawa, 25 April 1887, in rg 10, vol. 3842, file 71,799, c–10148.

79. Petition, New Westminster, 1 September 1890, in rg 10, vol. 3842, file 71,799, c–10148.

80. Draft from Department of Indian Affairs to Deputy Minister of Justice, 17 December 1890, in rg 10, vol. 3842, file 71,799, c–10148.

81. Draft of letter from Department of Indian Affairs to A. W. Vowell, Indian Superintendent, Ottawa, 26 December 1890, in rg 10, vol. 3842, file 71,799, c–10148.

82. Meason to Vowell, Lillooet, 4 August 1890, in rg 10, vol. 3816, file 57,045–1, c–10193.

83. For the Cariboo, see Margaret Whitehead, *The Cariboo Mission: A History of the Oblates* (Victoria: Sono Nis Press, 1981).

84. Mackay to Vowell, Kamloops, 24 May 1892, in rg 10, vol. 3875, file 90,667–2, c–10193.

85. Meason to Vowell, Lillooet, 14 May 189 2, in rg 10, vol. 3875, file 90,667–2, c–10193. The incident, its impetus in Oblate policy, and its aftermath are summarized in Whitehead, *Cariboo Mission,* 96–7. At the behest of Catholic authorities, the Governor General remitted the sentences.

86. Mackay to Vowell, 24 May 1892.

87. R.H. Pidcock, Indian Agent of Kwawkwelth Agency, to Powell, Alert Bay, 3 April 1889, in dia, rg 10, vol. 3816, file 57045, c–10193.
88. Pidcock to Vowell, n.d., in rg 10, vol. 38 16, file 57,045–1, c–10193.
89. Vowell to Deputy Superintendent of Indian Affairs, Victoria, 25 March 1890, in rg 10, vol. 3816, file 57,045–1, c–10193.
90. Memorandum of Superintendent General of Indian Affairs to Privy Council of Canada, Ottawa, 20 February 1890, in dia, rg 10, vol. 3816, file 57045- 1, c–10193.
91. John S. D. Thompson, Minister of Justice, to Governor General in Council, 1890, in rg 10, vol. 3816, file 57,045–1, c–10193.
92. Henry Guillod, Indian Agent of West Coast Agency, to Vowell, Ucluelet, 22 August 1890, in rg 10, vol. 3816, file 57,045–1, c–10193.
93. Lomas to Vowell, Quamichan, 2 2 November 1890, in rg 10, vol. 3816, file 57,045–1, c–10193.
94. McTiernan to Vowell, New Westminster, 23 June 1890, in rg 10, vol. 3816, file 57,045–1, c–10193.
95. Meason to Vowell, Lillooet, 4 August 1890, in rg 10, vol. 3816, file 57,045–1, c–10193.
96. Mackay to Vowell, Kamloops, 4 July 1890, in rg 10, vol. 3816, file 57,045–1, c–10193.
97. C. Todd, Acting Indian Agent of North West Coast Agency, to Vowell, Metlakatla, 8 October 1890, in rg 10, vol. 3816, file 57,045–1, c–10193.
98. Vowell to Vankoughnet, Victoria, 25 February 189 1, in rg 10, vol. 38 16, file 57,045–1, c–10193.
99. Petition to Pidcock, Fort Rupert, 8 March 1895, in rg 10, vol. 38 16, file 57,045–1, c–10193.
100. Senator W. J. Macdonald to Minister of the Interior, Ottawa, 6 May 1895, in rg 10, vol. 3816, file 57,045–1, c–10193.
101. Deputy Superintendent General of Indian Affairs to Vowell, Ottawa, 20 May 1895, in rg 10, vol. 3816, file 57,045–1, c–10193.
102. Davidoff and Hall, *Family Fortunes,* 115.
103. Census data included with Anderson and McKinlay, Report, 21 March 1877.
104. Crosby, *Among the An-ko-me-nums,* 49–50. On the related issue of domestic hygiene, see Michael Harkin, "Engendering Discipline: Discourse and Counterdiscourse in the Methodist-Heiltsuk Dialogue," *Ethnohistory* 43, 4 (Fall 1996), 647–48.
105. Crosby, *Up and Down,* 74.
106. For example, Cornelius Bryant, Methodist missionary, to Lomas, Nanaimo, 30 January 1884; G. Donckel, Catholic missionary, to Lomas, Maple Bay, 2 February 1884; Lomas to Powell, Maple Bay, 5 February 1884; and Powell to Superintendent General of Indian Affairs, Victoria, 27 February 1884, in dia, rg 10, vol. 36 28, file 6 244–1, c–10110.
107. This point is supported by dia to Powell, 6 June 1884, in dia, rg 10, vol. 3628, file 6244–1, c–10110; and stated explicitly in E. K. DeBeck, "The Potlatch and

Section 149 of the Indian Act," Ottawa, 11 May 1921, in dia, rg 10, vol. 3628, file 6244-x, c–10110; and in C. M. Barbeau, "The Potlatch among the B.C. Indians and Section 149 of the Indian Act," 1921, in dia, rg 10, vol. 3628, file 6244-x, c–10111.

108. Confidential memo to C.M.B., 17 February 1921, in Barbeau, "The Potlatch."

109. Douglas Cole and Ira Chaikin, *An Iron Hand Upon the People: The Law Against the Potlatch on the Northwest Coast* (Vancouver and Seattle: Douglas & McIntyre and University of Washington Press, 1990), 75–83; and Douglas Cole, "The History of the Kwakiutl Potlatch," Aldona Jonaitis, ed., *Chiefly Feasts: The Enduring Kwakiutl Potlatch* (Vancouver and New York: Douglas & McIntyre and American Museum of Natural History, 1991), 150–52, discuss sexual and marriage practices of the Kwakiutl as linked to the potlatch from a perspective which, while very informative and reliable, more or less accepts at face value the critiques of men in power. In *Severing the Ties that Bind: Government Repression of Indigenous Religious Ceremonies on the Prairies* (Winnipeg: University of Manitoba Press, 1994), Katherine Pettipas essentially equates the perspective of males with the entirety of perspectives in reference both to the potlatch (90–6) and to the sundance. With a single exception noted only in passing (62), Joseph Masco does much the same in "'It Is a Strict Law That Bids Us Dance': Cosmologies, Colonialism, Death, and Ritual Authority in the Kwakwa'wakw Potlatch, 1849 to 1922," *Comparative Studies in Society and History* 37, 1 (January 1995), 41–75.

110. Empire (Toronto), received 9 February 1893, and letter from Pidcock, 16 March 1893, in Barbeau, "The Potlatch."

111. Crosby, *Up and Down,* 316.

112. G.W. DeBeck, Indian Agent of Kwawkwelth Agency, to Vowell, Alert Bay, 29 December 1902, and E. A. Bird, teacher at Gwayasdurus, to DeBeck, Alert Bay, 23 June 1902, in dia, rg 10, vol. 6816, file 486–2–5, c–8538. The meaning of "child marriage" is explored in Harkin, "Engendering Discipline," 646–47.

113. Bird to DeBeck, 23 June 1902.

114. Most recently, J. R. Miller, *Shingwauk's Vision: A History of Native Residential Schools* (Toronto: University of Toronto Press, 1996).

115. Letter from Thomas Crosby, Missionary Outlook 9 (1989), 100, cited in Bolt, *Thomas Crosby,* 64; and Crosby, *Up and Down,* 85.

116. Crosby, *Among the An-ko-me-nums,* 63.

117. Kate Hendry to sister Maggie, 26 December 1882, Kate Hendry Letterbook, British Columbia Archives, ec/h38.

118. C.J. South, Superintendent, Children's Protection Act, to Secretary, Department of Indian Affairs, Vancouver, 20 September 1905, in rg 10, vol. 3816, file 57,045–1, c–10193.

119. Bolt, *Thomas Crosby,* 64.

120. 2 October 1886 entry in Agnes Knight, Journal, 1885–87, British Columbia Archives, F7/W 15.

121. Crosby, *Up and Down,* 89, 92–3.

122. "Indian girl sold for 1,000 blankets," *World* (Vancouver), 2 January 1906
123. "Five Little Girls Sold at Alert Bay Potlatch," *World,* 4 April 1906; and "Five Indian Girls Sold, Vancouver, B.C., April 6," *Journal (Ottawa),* 9 April 1906.
124. Letter of Vowell, 16 April 1906, in Barbeau, "The Potlatch."
125. "Squaw sold for $400.00 at Alert Bay to a grizzled Chief from Queen Charlottes," *Daily News Advertiser* (Vancouver), 6 April 1907.
126. Letter of William Halliday, 9 July 1907, in Barbeau, "The Potlatch."
127. The quotes are from Emily Cummings, Corresponding Secretary, National Council of Women, to Minister of Indian Affairs, Toronto, 19 February 1910, in rg 10, vol. 38 16, file 57,045–1, c–10193, which also contains the many letters, often virtually identical in language, from the different associations.
128. DeBeck, "The Potlatch and Section 149."
129. Margaret Whitehead emphasizes this point in "'A Useful Christian Woman': First Nations' Women and Protestant Missionary Work in British Columbia," *Atlantis* 18, 1–2 (1992–93), 142–66.
130. Crosby, *Up and Down,* 92.
131. John Tate (Salaben), Gispaxloats, informant, recorded by William Beynon in 1950, in George F. MacDonald and John J. Cove, ed., *Tsimshian Narratives, collected by Marius Barbeau and William Beynon. Vol. 2: Trade and Warfare* (Ottawa: Canadian Museum of Civilization, 1987), 207.
132. A fascinating question beyond the scope of this essay, which grows out of Foucault's work on power, concerns the extent to which some Aboriginal women internalized the assertions being made about them and considered that, yes, they must be prostitutes simply because they had been so informed so many times.
133. This topic is explored in Jean Barman, "Invisible Women: Aboriginal Mothers and Mixed-Race Daughters in Rural Pioneer British Columbia," R. W. Sandwell, ed., *Negotiating Rural: Essays from British Columbia* (under review by UBC Press).
134. The 1901 manuscript census indicates persons' "colour" and mixed-race origins, making it possible to determine the character of individual households.
135. Carr, *Heart of a Peacock,* 110–1.
136. C.W. Holliday, *The Valley of Youth* (Caldwell, ID: Caxton, 1948), 155, 226.
137. DeBeck, "The Potlatch and Section 149."
138. 16, 17, and 25 June and 11 and 26 July 1966 entries in Edward Hoagland, *Notes From the Century Before: A Journal from British Columbia* (New York: Ballantine, 1969), 92, 96, 101, 141, 186, 250.

Mary Ann Irwin, 'Going About and Doing Good': The Politics of Benevolence, Welfare, and Gender in San Francisco, 1850–1880

1. Charles K. Jenness, *The Charities of San Francisco: A Directory of the Benevolent and Correctional Agencies, Together with a Digest of Those Laws Most Directly*

Affecting Their Work (San Francisco, 1894), iv. This includes sums expended by private charities and public entities (the City and County of San Francisco, which were consolidated in 1855, the State of California, and the federal government).

2. *Ibid.*

3. See, e.g., Lori D. Ginzberg, *Women and the Work of Benevolence: Morality, Politics, and Class in the Nineteenth-Century United States* (New Haven, Conn., 1990); Kathleen D. McCarthy, *Noblesse Oblige: Charity and Cultural Philanthropy in Chicago, 1849–1929* (Chicago, 1982); Suzanne Lebsock, *The Free Women of Petersburg: Status and Culture in a Southern Town, 1784–1860* (New York, 1984); Sarah Deutsch, "Learning to Talk More Like a Man: Boston Women's Class-Bridging Organizations, 1870–1940," *American Historical Review*, 90 (1992), 379–404; Anne Firor Scott, *Natural Allies: Women's Associations in American History* (Chicago, 1991); Paula Baker, *Moral Frameworks of Public Life: Gender, Politics, and the State in Rural New York, 1870–1930* (New York, 1991); Mary P. Ryan, *The Cradle of the Middle Class: The Family in Oneida County, New York, 1790–1865* (Cambridge, Eng., 1981); Karen J. Blair, *The Clubwoman as Feminist: True Womanhood Redefined, 1868–1914* (New York, 1980).

4. Seth Koven and Sonya Michel, *Mothers of a New World: Maternalist Politics and the Origins of Welfare States* (New York, 1993); Theda Skocpol, *Protecting Soldiers and Mothers: The Political Origins of Social Policy in the United States* (Cambridge, Mass., 1992); Kathryn Kish Sklar, *Florence Kelley & The Nation's Work: The Rise of Women's Political Culture, 1830–1900* (New Haven, Conn., 1995); Nancy A. Hewitt and Suzanne Lebsock, *Visible Women: New Essays on American Activism* (Chicago, 1993); Suzanne Lebsock, "Women and American Politics, 1880–1920," in Louise Tilley and Patricia Gurin, eds., *Women, Politics, and Change* (New York, 1990). Kathleen D. McCarthy acknowledges the significance of nineteenth-century benevolent women in "Parallel Power Structures: Women and the Voluntary Sphere," in McCarthy, ed., *Lady Bountiful Revisited: Women, Philanthropy, and Power* (New Brunswick, N.J., 1990). On Progressive-era reform, see also Louise C. Wade, *Graham Taylor: Pioneer for Social Justice, 1851–1938* (Chicago, 1964); Allen F. Davis, *American Heroine: The Life and Legend of Jane Addams* (New York, 1973).

5. Joan M. Jensen and Darlis A. Miller, "The Gentle Tamers Revisited: New Approaches to the History of Women in the American West," *Pacific Historical Review*, 49 (1980), 173–213; Susan H. Armitage, "Revisiting 'The Gentle Tamers Revisited': The Problems and Possibilities of Western Women's History—An Introduction," *Pacific Historical Review*, 61 (1992), 459–99. There are notable exceptions, several of which deal with San Francisco: Peggy Pascoe, *Relations of Rescue: The Search for Female Moral Authority in the American West, 1874–1939* (New York, 1990); Mary P. Ryan, *Women in Public: Between Banners and Ballots, 1825–1880* (Baltimore, 1990); Julie Roy Jeffrey, *Frontier Women: The Trans-Mississippi West, 1840–1880* (New York, 1979); Bradford F. Luckingham, "Associational Life on the Urban Frontier: San Francisco,

1848–1856" (Ph.D. dissertation, University of California, Davis, 1968).

6. See, for instance, William Issel and Robert W. Cherny, *San Francisco, 1865–1932: Politics, Power, and Urban Development* (Berkeley, 1986); Roger W. Lotchin, *San Francisco, 1846–1856: From Hamlet to City* (Urbana, Ill., 1997); Peter R. Decker, *Fortunes and Failures: White-Collar Mobility in Nineteenth-Century San Francisco* (Cambridge, Mass., 1978); Terrence J. McDonald, *The Parameters of Urban Fiscal Policy: Socioeconomic Change and Political Culture in San Francisco, 1860–1906* (Berkeley, 1986); Philip J. Ethington, "The Structures of Urban Political Life: Political Culture in San Francisco, 1850–1880" (Ph.D. dissertation, Stanford University, 1988). Ethington mentions local woman-led charities in Philip J. Ethington, *The Public City: The Political Construction of Urban Life in San Francisco, 1850–1900* (Cambridge, Eng., 1994), 331–32.

7. Ruth Shackelford, "To Shield Them from Temptation: 'Child-Saving' Institutions and the Children of the Underclass in San Francisco 1850–1910" (Ph.D. dissertation, Harvard University, 1991), 289; Mary P. Ryan, *Civic Wars: Democracy and Public Life in the American City During the Nineteenth Century* (Berkeley, 1997), 185; Issel and Cherny, *San Francisco,* 24.

8. Luckingham, "Associational Life," 28, 79, 31; Merle Stewart Jaque, "The Origins of Private Benevolence in California, 1769–1869" (Master's thesis, San Diego State College, 1966), 21–22; Mitchel Roth, "Cholera, Community, and Public Health in Gold Rush Sacramento and San Francisco," *Pacific Historical Review,* 66 (1997), 527–51.

9. Lotchin, *San Francisco,* 45–82; Decker, *Fortunes and Failures,* 34, 125, 160, 182; Shackelford, "To Shield Them from Temptation," 386; Ira B. Cross, *A History of the Labor Movement in California* (Berkeley, 1935), 68–69.

10. Hubert Howe Bancroft, *History of California* (7 vols., Berkeley, 1884–1890), 7: 352; San Francisco Benevolent Association, *Directory of the San Francisco Benevolent Association* (San Francisco, 1865), held in Bancroft Library, University of California, Berkeley; Frances Cahn and Valeska Bary, *Welfare Activities of Federal, State, and Local Governments in California, 1850–1934* (Berkeley, 1936), 199.

11. Skocpol, *Protecting Soldiers and Mothers,* 318; Shackelford, "To Shield Them from Temptation," 289; McCarthy, *Noblesse Oblige,* 54; Ryan, *Civic Wars,* 104.

12. Shackelford, "To Shield Them from Temptation," 306; Sophia Eastman to "Sister," July 18, 1850, Sophia Eastman Papers, Bancroft Library, University of California, Berkeley. San Francisco had two other medical facilities, neither of much use to the general public: The State Marine Hospital opened in 1850 and closed in 1855; it accepted non-mariners if they were wealthy enough to post bond. The U.S. Marine Hospital opened in 1854 and was abandoned in 1868; it served only seamen. Cahn and Bary, *Welfare Activities,* 139; Lotchin, *San Francisco,* 87, 185, 221; Shackelford, "To Shield Them from Temptation," 361.

13. Sam Bass Warner, Jr., *The Private City: Philadelphia in Three Periods of its Growth* (Philadelphia, 1987), 175–76; Ryan, *Civic Wars,* 163–64; Maureen A. Flanagan,

Charter Reform in Chicago (Carbondale, Ill., 1987), 35.

14. *San Francisco Bulletin*, Oct. 15, 1861, Oct. 13, 1860, in McDonald, *Parameters of Urban Fiscal Policy*, 122.

15. Social welfare services were the Alms House, City Hospital, Industrial School, and Health Department. *Ibid.*, 49.

16. *Ibid.*, 18.

17. Ryan, *Civic Wars*, 99.

18. *Ibid.*, 98–99, 104; Warner, *Private City*, 81–82.

19. Nathan Irvin Huggins, *Protestants Against Poverty: Boston's Charities, 1870–1900* (Westport, Conn., 1971); Pascoe, *Relations of Rescue*, 150–51; Scott, *Natural Allies*, 8; McCarthy, *Noblesse Oblige*, 4, 59; Wendy Kaminer, *Women Volunteering: The Pleasure, Pain, and Politics of Unpaid Work from 1830 to the Present* (Garden City, N.Y., 1984), 25–26.

20. Scott, *Natural Allies*, 8.

21. Henry G. Langley, *San Francisco directory for the year commencing April, 1876* (San Francisco, 1876), 1081.

22. Barbara Welter, "The Cult of True Womanhood, 1820–1860," *American Quarterly*, 18 (1966), 151–74. The literature on nineteenth-century female identity is extensive; Kathryn Kish Sklar, *Catharine Beecher: A Study in American Domesticity* (New York, 1973) is particularly helpful.

23. Jeffrey, *Frontier Women*, 4–13; Elisabeth Margo, *Taming the Forty-Niner* (New York, 1955).

24. According to city directories, San Franciscans created at least 103 benevolent and reform organizations between 1848 and 1879. Of these, sixty were male-led, thirty-eight female-led, four had mixed boards, and one had identical but separate boards for either sex.

25. *San Francisco Daily Alta California*, July 11, 1853, p. 2.

26. This study is limited to organizations formed by white, middle-class, Protestant women because they were the most successful in influencing state and local policy-makers. For black, Chinese, Catholic, and Jewish women in San Francisco, see, respectively, Delores Nason McBroome, *Parallel Communities: African Americans in California's East Bay, 1850–1963* (New York, 1993); Judy Yung, *Unbound Feet: A Social History of Chinese Women in San Francisco* (Berkeley, 1995); Shackelford, "To Shield Them from Temptation;" William Toll, "Gender, Ethnicity, and Jewish Settlement Work in the Urban West," in *An Inventory of Promises: Essays on American Jewish History in Honor of Moses Rischin* (Brooklyn, N.Y., 1995).

27. Cahn and Bary, *Welfare Activities*, 142. San Francisco's City Hospital treated women but not children; its first children's ward opened in the 1890s. Leontina Murphy, "Public Care of the Dependent Sick in San Francisco, 1847–1936" (Master's thesis, University of California, Berkeley, 1938), 72–74; Rickey Hendricks, "Feminism and Maternalism in Early Hospitals for Children: San Francisco and Denver, 1875–1915," *Journal of the West* 32 (1993), 61–69; Rickey Hendricks and Mark S. Foster, *For a Child's Sake: History of*

the *Children's Hospital, Denver, Colorado, 1910–1990* (Niwot, Colo., 1994); Joan E. Lynaugh, *The Community Hospitals of Kansas City, Missouri, 1870–1915* (New York, 1989); Clement A. Smith, *The Children's Hospital of Boston: They Built Better Than They Knew* (Boston, 1983).

28. Peter Decker and Philip Ethington disagree on whether San Francisco had a political "machine" during the period 1850–1880. See Decker, *Fortunes and Failures*, 127; Ethington, *Public City*, 289–90. When the state of California began allocating public funds for outdoor relief in the 1880s, observers found that officials gave significantly more aid to men of voting age and economized drastically on relief given women and children. Cahn and Bary, *Welfare Activities*, 171–72, 175.

29. Shackelford, "To Shield Them from Temptation," 290, 294, 296.

30. In their constitution and by-laws, the founders explicitly retained the authority to collect and expend funds. San Francisco Protestant Orphan Asylum (hereafter SFPOA), *Constitution and By-Laws*, 21–22, located in Bancroft Library, University of California, Berkeley.

31. Mrs. W. A. [Anna Bissell] Haight, *Some Reminiscences of the San Francisco Protestant Orphan Asylum* (San Francisco, 1900), 2, in Bancroft Library; Dolores Waldorf, "Gentleman From Vermont: Royal H. Waller," *California Historical Society Quarterly*, 22 (1943), 110–18; SFPOA, *Ninth Annual Report of the San Francisco Orphan Asylum Society* (San Francisco, 1859), 6, located in San Francisco History Room, San Francisco Public Library, San Francisco; Nellie Stow, *Tower of Strength in the City's Building: The Ninetieth Anniversary of the San Francisco Protestant Orphanage* (San Francisco, n.d.), 3–4. The records of local women's charities must be taken with a grain of salt. Especially in their annual reports (which were distributed as fund-raising tools), the women's activities were painted in the most glowing terms. The same can also be said of the other primary materials used—the annual reports of public institutions. The only other contemporary sources commenting on public and private agencies were the local newspapers, but these were not entirely objective either: Editors were as likely to castigate the administrators of public institutions for extravagance as they were unlikely to criticize the leaders of women's charities, who were often the wives of leading citizens. Despite these drawbacks, if we are to learn anything about how social welfare emerged in San Francisco, these are the best available sources.

32. Scott, *Natural Allies*, 52–53.

33. See Emanu-El Sisterhood for Personal Service, *First Annual Report, 1894–1895* (San Francisco, 1895), 7, in Emanu-El Sisterhood Papers, Judah L. Magnes Memorial Museum/The Jewish Museum of the West, Berkeley.

34. Ladies' Depository, *Annual Report of the Ladies' Depository, Constitution and Rules for the Government of the Ladies' Depository of San Francisco* (San Francisco, 1867), as well as the second and fifth annual reports (1868 and 1871, respectively) in California Historical Society, San Francisco.

35. *Ibid.*; Mary Lou Locke, "Out of the Shadows and into the Western Sun:

Working Women of the Late Nineteenth-Century Urban Far West," *Journal of Urban History*, 16 (1990), 175–204.

36. San Francisco Female Hospital (hereafter SFFH), *Report of the San Francisco Female Hospital of the State of California* (San Francisco, 1869), in California State Library, Sutro Branch, San Francisco; *Report of the San Francisco Female Hospital of the State of California* (San Francisco, 1874), 6, 9, in California Historical Society, San Francisco; Langley, *San Francisco directory for the year commencing April, 1871* (San Francisco, 1871), 883. On nineteenth-century medical philanthropy, see McCarthy, *Noblesse Oblige*, 39–42; McCarthy, "Parallel Power Structures," 17. Nineteenth-century hospitals were usually charity hospitals; those who could afford it received medical treatment at home. Morris Vogel, *The Invention of the Modern Hospital* (Chicago, 1980), 9–11, 97–106; Regina Markell Morantz-Sanchez, *Sympathy and Science: Women Physicians in American Medicine* (New York, 1985), 18–26.

37. SFFH, *Report . . . 1874*, 6–9, 11. Neither local newspapers nor surviving reports explain the opposition hinted at by Dr. Deane. My suspicion that it related to the admission of unwed mothers is based on the hospital's annual tally of illegitimate births, followed by the assertion that, without the SFFH, these infants would have "shared the fate of so many thousands of innocents murdered in their mothers' womb." SFFH leaders were, in essence, arguing that it was better to deliver the babies of "forsaken" and "erring" women than to risk the possibility of abortion. SFFH, *Report . . . 1874*, 6; Langley, *San Francisco directory . . . 1871*, 883.

38. SFFH, *Report . . . 1874*, 11–12.

39. Carol Green Wilson, *A History of the Heritage, 1853–1970* (San Francisco, 1970), 3–5; San Francisco Ladies' Protection and Relief Society (hereafter SFLP&RS), *Articles of Incorporation* (San Francisco, 1855), located in SFLP&RS Records, 1854–1969, MS 3576, in California Historical Society, San Francisco.

40. Shackelford, "To Shield Them from Temptation," 326.

41. SFLP&RS, "Minutes," May 26, 1858, Nov. 25, 1857, SFLP&RS Records, 1854–1969, MS 3576.

42. *Ibid.*, Nov. 14, 1860. According to Michael Katz, sickness was the primary reason that urban working-class families became dependent upon charity. Michael B. Katz, *Poverty and Policy in American History* (New York, 1983), 17–54.

43. SFLP&RS, *Twenty-Third and Twenty-Fourth Annual Reports of the Managers and Trustees of the San Francisco Ladies' Protection and Relief Society for the Two Years Ending September 1, 1877* (San Francisco, 1877), 6–7, SFLP&RS Records, 1854–1969, MS 3576.

44. Mary Ryan, *Civic Wars*, 248–249; Ginzberg, *Work of Benevolence*, 202; Nancy A. Hewitt, "Beyond the Search for Sisterhood: American Women's History in the 1980s," in Ellen Carol DuBois and Vicki L. Ruiz, eds., *Unequal Sisters: A Multicultural Reader in U.S. Women's History* (New York, 1990), 9–11; Christine Stansell, *City of Women: Sex and Class in New York, 1789–1860* (New York, 1990), 66.

45. Nancy Hewitt, Anne M. Boylan, and Lori Ginzberg studied the status of organized women, and found that middle- and upper-class women were more likely to join benevolent societies than "radical" organizations, such as those supporting abolition or woman suffrage. Ginzberg, *Work of Benevolence*, 6.

46. *San Francisco Daily Alta California*, July 11, 1853, p. 2.

47. Ethington, "Structures of Urban Political Life," 48–53.

48. Shackelford, "To Shield Them from Temptation," 321. The SFPOA probably lost this funding in the taxpayers' revolt of 1856; when San Francisco began publishing its *Municipal Reports* in 1860, the appropriation no longer appeared.

49. Shackelford, "To Shield Them from Temptation," 319.

50. Stow, *Tower of Strength*, 4; Haight, *Some Reminiscences*, 6–10; Shackelford, "To Shield Them from Temptation," 330, 326; Pacific Dispensary [Children's Hospital], *Second Report of the Pacific Dispensary* (San Francisco, 1878), 8, in Children's Hospital of San Francisco Records, BANC MSS 89/87c, Bancroft Library, University of California, Berkeley Ethington, *Public City*, 332.

51. Gunther Barth, *Instant Cities: Urbanization and the Rise of San Francisco and Denver* (New York, 1975), ix.

52. Stow, *Tower of Strength*, 4; Haight, *Some Reminiscences*, 8, 10–12; Luckingham, "Associational Life," 29; SFLP&RS, "Minutes," Aug. 10, 1859 SFLP&RS Records, 1854 – 1969, MS 3576; Rowena Beans, *Inasmuch . . . The One Hundred Year History of the San Francisco Ladies Protection and Relief Society, 1853–1953* (Berkeley, 1953), 3; Hospital for Children and Training School for Nurses (hereafter, Children's Hospital) *Report of the Hospital for Children and Training School for Nurses* (San Francisco, 1888), 15, 37, Children's Hospital of San Francisco Records. The "vara," a vestige of California's Spanish past, is 0.84 meters in length.

53. Luckingham, "Associational Life," 29; Haight, *Some Reminiscences*, 7.

54. Elizabeth Cady Stanton, Susan B. Anthony, and Matilda Joslyn Gage, *History of Woman Suffrage* (6 vols., New York, 1881–1922), 2: 749–68.

55. Pascoe, *Relations of Rescue*, 15–17; Linda K. Kerber "Separate Spheres, Female Worlds, Woman's Place: The Rhetoric of Women's History," *Journal of American History* 75 (1988), 9–39, 26. I found very few local women who belonged to both charitable associations and the state woman suffrage organization; the notable exception was Marietta Stow. See Donna C. Schuele, "In Her Own Way: Marietta Stow's Crusade for Probate Law Reform Within the Nineteenth-Century Woman's Rights Movement," *Yale Journal of Law and Feminism*, 7 (1995), 279–306.

56. Hendricks, "Feminism and Maternalism," 62; Dr. Adelaide Brown, "The History of the Children's Hospital in Relation to Medical Women" (typescript, n.d. [probably Sept. 1920]), Children's Hospital of San Francisco Records, BANC MSS 89/87c, 10; Joan M. Jensen and Gloria Ricci Lathrop, *California Women: A History* (San Francisco, 1987), 186.

57. Children's Hospital, *Annual Report for the Hospital for Children and Training School for Nurses* (San Francisco, 1889), 18 (emphasis in original), Children's

Hospital of San Francisco Records.

58. Kerber, "Separate Spheres," 9–39, 26; Ginzberg, *Work of Benevolence*, 68.

59. Kerber, "Separate Spheres," 9–39, 26.

60. Roth, "Cholera, Community," 534.

61. Katz, *Poverty and Policy*, 132; David J. Rothman, *The Discovery of the Asylum: Social Order and Disorder in the New Republic* (Boston, 1971), 28, 166–67, 183.

62. San Francisco Board of Supervisors, "Auditor's Report," *San Francisco Municipal Reports for the Fiscal Year 1871–1872* (San Francisco, 1872; hereafter, *Municipal Reports*). Note the city's choice of a private male-led charity to distribute outdoor relief. The *Municipal Reports* do not explain the selection, but I suspect the SFBS was chosen, in part, because the funds were to be distributed to men. For that, propriety dictated that a male-led agency would be preferable to a female-led agency. Unfortunately, I cannot determine how the funds were distributed because no SFBS organizational records survive.

63. Jenness, *Charities of San Francisco*, ii, iv. Following the 1906 earthquake, private institutions were overcrowded and the city began boarding children in private homes at taxpayer expense. When leaders realized that those funds could be used to keep children at home, the city began paying some widowed mothers to care for their own children in their own homes; these payments became the precedent for distribution of "mother's pensions" in California in 1913. San Francisco's first direct distribution of outdoor relief to adults came with the New Deal in 1933. Shackelford, "To Shield Them from Temptation," n. 69, 412; Cahn and Bary, *Welfare Activities*, 174–75.

64. Wilson, *History of the Heritage*, 23; according to its 1877 report, the SFLP&RS also gave outdoor relief in 1859, 1860, and 1869. Unfortunately, the reports from those years are not available. SFLP&RS, *Twenty-Third and Twenty-Fourth Annual Reports of the Managers and Trustees of the San Francisco Ladies' Protection and Relief Society for the Two Years Ending September 1, 1877* (San Francisco, 1877), 6–7, SFLP&RS Papers.

65. Jenness, *Charities of San Francisco*, ii, iv.

66. California Society for the Prevention of Cruelty to Children (CSPCC) records do not mention what happened to Mary Walker. CSPCC, *First Annual Report for the Year Ending December 31, 1877* (San Francisco, 1877), 16, located in Bancroft Library, University of California, Berkeley.

67. Eighteen children were placed in private, male-led facilities (thirteen were sent to St. Joseph's Youth Directory, managed by the Reverend William O. Mahoney, five to St. Vincent's Orphan Asylum, operated by the Brothers of the Order of St. Dominic). Twenty-two were placed in woman-led facilities (twelve children to the SFLP&RS Home, ten to the Home of Friendless Children). *Ibid.*, 19 Shackelford, "To Shield Them from Temptation," 312–14; Jenness, *The Charities of San Francisco*, 41.

68. CSPCC, *Third Annual Report for the Year Ending December 31, 1879* (San Francisco, 1879). The Roman Catholic Orphan Asylum and Mt. St. Joseph's Infant Asylum were managed by the Sisters of Mercy and the Sisters of

Charity, respectively. Ruth Shackelford provides an invaluable study of the charity work of Catholic women in San Francisco in "To Shield Them from Temptation," 287–428.

69. Rev. Dennis John Kavanaugh, S.J., *The Holy Family Sisters of San Francisco: A Sketch of Their First Fifty Years* (San Francisco, 1922), 27–53.

70. *Municipal Reports*, 1867–1868, p. 392.

71. SFFH, *Report . . . 1874*, 5.

72. Ginzberg, *Work of Benevolence*, 202.

73. Capt. Joseph C. Morrill, *The Industrial School Investigation, With a Glance at the Great Reformation and Its Results* (San Francisco, 1872); *San Francisco Daily Evening Bulletin*, July 2, 8–10, 13, 27, 1869.

74. *Daily Evening Bulletin*, Mar. 8, 1869, quoted in SFFH, *Report … 1874*, 5.

75. *Ibid.*

76. SFLP&RS, "Minutes," Feb. 22, 1870, SFLP&RS Records, 1854–1969, MS 3576.

77. *Ibid.*, Jan. 4, 1870.

78. *Ibid.*, Jan. 3, 1871.

79. See, e.g., employee Henry Funk's description of conditions in the City Alms House for the period 1871 to 1878, in Henry Funk, *The True Life at the Last Chance; or, Seven Years, Six Months, and Three Weeks in a Human Slaughter House* (San Francisco, 1878), held in the Bancroft Library, University of California, Berkeley.

80. Again underscoring the city's reliance on private, woman-led facilities, the Industrial School began sending female juveniles to the Sisters of Mercy Magdalene Asylum in 1869. Shackelford, "To Shield Them from Temptation," 361.

81. SFLP&RS, "Minutes," 1872–1879, SFLP&RS Records, 1854–1969, MS 3576; *Municipal Reports*, 1872–1879. Formula: The SFLP&RS provided monthly inmate figures, but public institutions only reported the number of inmates at the beginning and end of each report year. The monthly average for public institutions is the average of the beginning and ending populations. Both public and private facilities provided annual expenditures. To arrive at average cost per inmate per month for public and private institutions, I multiplied the average number of inmates per month by twelve, and divided total expenditures by this figure.

82. For the period 1872–1880, the city spent $33,000 more on Industrial School salaries ($146,056.37) than on food/provisions ($112,711.31). *Municipal Reports*, 1872–1880.

83. *Ibid.*, 1859–1880.

84. Skocpol, *Protecting Soldiers and Mothers*, 72; Warner, *Private City*, xiii, 99, 175–76, 202; Maureen A. Flanagan, *Charter Reform*, 18–20; Ryan, *Civic Wars*, 101; Michael B. Katz, *In the Shadow of the Poorhouse: A Social History of Welfare in America* (New York, 1986, 1996), 26–27; Katz, *Poverty and Policy*, 11–12; Steven Mintz, *Moralists and Modernizers: America's Pre–Civil War Reformers* (Baltimore,

1995), 85; Priscilla Ferguson Clement, *Welfare and the Poor in the Nineteenth-Century City: Philadelphia, 1800–1854* (Cranbury, N.J., 1985), 43, 59; Stephen J. Leonard and Thomas J. Noel, *Denver: Mining Camp to Metropolis* (Niwot, Colo., 1994), 68–69.

85. Lotchin, *San Francisco*, 186, 222.

86. Murphy, "Public Care," 70–72, 75; *Municipal Reports*, 1874–1875, pp. 380–81.

87. Women's Christian Association of San Francisco, *Constitution, By-Laws* (n.p., n.d.), 5, located in Bancroft Library. References to Christian thought are pervasive in the women's writings. An SFLP&RS recording secretary, for example, expressed her relief when a sick woman in the Home gave "good evidence that her heart rested in full assurance of Jesus as her Savior" before she died. SFLP&RS, *Seventh Annual Report of the San Francisco Ladies' Protection and Relief Society, December 12, 1860*, 5, SFLP&RS Records, MS Collection 3576, California Historical Society, San Francisco.

88. James T. Kloppenburg quoted in Skocpol, *Protecting Soldiers and Mothers*, 318–24.

89. California State Board of Control, "Report of the Children's Agents of the State Board of Control" (typescript, Dec. 1914), 3–4, California State Library, Sutro Branch, San Francisco; Cahn and Bary, *Welfare Activities*, 4.

90. Pascoe, *Relations of Rescue*, 188. The Associated Charities of San Francisco was formed in 1888; see Lisa Goodrich-Boyd, "Charity Redefined: Katherine [*sic*] Felton and the Associated Charities of San Francisco" (Master's thesis, San Francisco State University, 1995). On the charity organization society movement, see Katz, *Shadow of the Poorhouse*, 70, 75–78, 83–87. Like earlier women's charity organizations, settlement houses faced their own challenge of professionalization with the emergence of the Community Chest movement in the period 1910–1920. See Judith Ann Trolander, *Professionalism and Social Change: From the Settlement House Movement to Neighborhood Centers, 1886 to the Present* (New York, 1987), 21–24.

91. Millicent W. Shinn, "Poverty and Charity in San Francisco," *Overland Monthly* (1889), 535–47. On the philosophical differences between settlement houses and earlier church-based charities, see Trolander, *Professionalism and Social Change*, 7–21. On San Francisco settlements, see Ethington, *Public City*, 352–354; Toll, "Gender, Ethnicity," 294–97.

92. See, for example, Jacqueline R. Braitman, "A California Stateswoman: The Public Career of Katherine Philips Edson," *California History*, 65 (1986), 82–95; Ethington, *Public City*, 361.

93. A number of the entities described here have faded into history, but others remain. The SFPOA, that orphanage started by local church women in 1853, is still serving local families as the Edgewood Children's Center. Likewise, one and one-half centuries after it was founded, the organizational descendant of the SFLP&RS continues to house San Francisco women, now as "the Heritage," an elegant women's retirement home. One and one-quarter centuries later, the hospital started by women to serve women continues to offer

medical care as well as residency and training for doctors and nurses; now known as California Pacific Medical Center, Children's Hospital remains one of only three independent, nonprofit teaching hospitals in the state. The longevity of these institutions is perhaps the best evidence yet of the value of women's charity work to the city of San Francisco.

94. See Sandra Haarsager, *Bertha Knight Landes of Seattle: Big City Mayor* (Norman, Okla., 1994), xiii, xiv, 41, 264; Ethington, *Public City*, 208–18, 326–36.

95. Koven and Michel, *Mothers of a New World*, 2–6.

96. Paula Baker, "The Domestication of Politics: Women and American Political Society, 1780–1920," *American Historical Review*, 89 (1984), 620–47.

97. Maureen A. Flanagan, "Gender and Urban Political Reform: The City Club and the Woman's City Club of Chicago in the Progressive Era," *American Historical Review,* 95 (1990), 1032–1050; Louise Armstrong, *Of "Sluts" and "Bastards": A Feminist Decodes the Child Welfare Debate* (Monroe, Me., 1995).

Lynn M. Hudson, 'Strong Animal Passions' in the Gilded Age: Race, Sex, and a Senator on Trial

1. For the purpose of clarity, I will refer to Sarah Althea Hill as Hill or Sarah although she claimed to be Mrs. Sharon, and was eventually Mrs. Terry. Although I acknowledge the problems inherent in naming Sarah Althea Hill "Sarah" and William Sharon "Sharon" I do so intentionally to call attention to the ways they were referred to in the press.

   In one month of the 1884 *Sharon v. Sharon* trial The *New York Times*, for example, ran front page stories about it on April 8, 10, and 15. The national significance of the two cases are noted in the journal of former United States Supreme Court Justice, Stephen J. Field, *Personal Reminiscences of Early Days in California* (New York: Da Capo Press edition, 1993, originally pub. 1877).

2. Many recent studies analyze late nineteenth-century courtroom narratives and gendered discourses. See, for example, Laura Hanft Korobkin, "The Maintenance of Mutual Confidence: Sentimental Strategies at the Adultery Trial of Henry Ward Beecher," *Yale Journal of Law and the Humanities* 7:1 (1995): 1–48; Richard Wightman Fox, "Intimacy on Trial: Cultural Meanings of the Beecher-Tilton Affair" in *The Power of Culture: Critical Essays in American History*, T. J. Jackson Lears and Richard Wightman Fox, eds. (Chicago: University of Chicago Press, 1993); Anne-Louise Shapiro, "Telling Criminal Stories: The *Femme Criminelle* in Late Nineteenth-Century Paris," in *Negotiating at the Margins: The Gendered Discourses of Power and Resistance*, Sue Fisher and Kathy Davis, eds.(New Brunswick, NJ: Rutgers University Press, 1993).

3. Sharon R. Ullman has detailed this process in her study of turn-of-the-century sexual practices and discourses. See Ullman, *Sex Seen: The Emergence of Modern Sexuality in America* (Berkeley: University of California Press, 1997).

See also John D'Emilio and Estelle D. Freedmen, *Intimate Matters: A History of Sexuality in America* (New York: Harper & Row, 1988), especially chapter seven. For a rich and nuanced discussion of sexuality and prostitution in the early decades of the nineteenth century, see, Patricia Cline Cohen, *The Murder of Helen Jewett: The Life and Death of a Prostitute in Nineteenth-Century New York* (New York: Alfred P. Knopf, 1998)

4. There are striking similarities between the enracing of O. J. Simpson in the 1980s and the enracing of Pleasant in the 1880s. And while I do not have the space to discuss these in the present article, I am indebted to Ann du Cille for providing an important framework in her study of the Simpson case. Ann du Cille, "The Blacker the Juice: O. J. Simpson and the Squeeze Play of Race," in *Skin Trade* (Harvard University Press, 1996). For a concise and provocative discussion of Pleasant's history see, Lerone Bennett, "An Historical Detective Story: The Mystery of Mary Ellen Pleasant, Parts I & II" *Ebony* (April and May 1979): 90–96, 71–86.

5. Robert Kroninger, *Sarah and the Senator* (Berkeley: Howell-North Books, 1964), 25–26.

6. Pleasant reported $30,000 worth of real estate in the 1870 U.S. census. Her worth by 1884 exceeded this amount many times over. She is identified as one of the wealthiest black women in the nineteenth-century West in several studies. See, for example, William Sherman Savage, *Blacks in the West* (Westport, Conn.: Greenwood Press, 1976), 133–34; William Loren Katz, *The Black West* (Seattle: Open Hand Publishing, 1987), 138–39; Kenneth G. Goode, *California's Black Pioneers* (Santa Barbara, CA: McNally & Loftin, 1973), 65, 87–88; Joann Levy, *They Saw the Elephant: Women in the California Gold Rush* (San Francisco: Anchor Books, 1990), 210–11; Ronald Dean Miller, *Shady Ladies of the West* (Los Angeles: Westernlore Press, 1964), 64–67.

7. Mary Murphy, "The Private Lives of Public Women: Prostitution in Butte, Montana, 1878–1917," in Susan Armitage et al., eds., *The Women's West* (Norman: University of Oklahoma Press, 1987): 193–206; Marion S. Goldman, *Gold Diggers & Silver Miners: Prostitution and the Social Life on the Comstock Lode* (Ann Arbor: University of Michigan, 1981), especially chapter one. Jacqueline Baker Barnhart claimed that Pleasant "had in her colorful career in San Francisco been 'kept' by a number of men, had run or owned elegant brothels and assignation houses, and had acted as a marriage broker for some of the women who had worked for her in parlor houses." Barnhart, *The Fair But Frail: Prostitution in San Francisco, 1849–1900* (Reno: University of Nevada Press, 1986), 58. Not all accounts agree that Pleasant's boardinghouses were houses of prostitution. See, George Lane interview in Mary Ellen Pleasant Collection, San Francisco History Room/San Francisco Public Library [SFPL]. When the author and interviewer Helen Holdredge asked Lane whether they were houses of prostitution, he stated, "No. They were above anything of the sort. It was considered fashionable to be seen at her 920 Washington boardinghouse." It could also be, however, that the black

respondent felt uncomfortable discussing this aspect of Pleasant's past with a white biographer.

8. For an account of the first suit, which was dropped soon after it was filed, see, *Alta California* 17 October 1866. In the second case, against the North Beach & Mission Railroads, she initially won $500 in damages. In 1868, when the case reached the California Supreme Court on apeal, she lost. See, *John J. and Mary E. Pleasants v. NBMRR*, June 20, 1867, California State Archives, Sacramento. See, also, Lynn M. Hudson, "When 'Mammy' Becomes a Millionaire: Mary Ellen Pleasant, An African American Entrepreneur," (Ph.D. diss., Indiana University, 1996).

9. See Kroninger and Martin S. Gould, *A Cast of Hawks: A Rowdy Tale of Scandal and Power Politics in Early San Francisco* (La Jolla: Copley Books, 1985). This theory received plenty of support in the popular press during the trials and for decades since. See, for example, Zoe Battu, "Tin Types," *San Franciscan* (29 November 1929); Robert O'Brian, "Riptides," *San Francisco Chronicle* 18 and 20 February 1946.

10. Quoted in John Lawson, ed. *American State Trials* 15 (Saint Louis: F. H. Thomas Law Book Co., 1914–1936): 505.

11. *San Francisco Examiner*, 29 November 1884.

12. On the economic history of San Francisco's Gilded Age, see William Issel and Robert W. Cherny, *San Francisco: Politics, Power, and Urban Development, 1865–1932* (Berkeley: University of California Press, 1986).

13. William Ralston was the President of Bank of California responsible for the 1875 panic. When he committed suicide, William Sharon inherited his role at the Bank and his property which included the Palace Hotel. See, George D. Lyman, *Ralston's Ring: California Plunders the Comstock Lode* (New York: Charles Scribner's Sons, 1937).

14. Although this practice—of living in one state but representing another—was later outlawed, Sharon was well within his rights to do so at the time.

15. Oscar Lewis and Carroll D. Hall, *Bonanza Inn: America's First Luxery Hotel* (New York: Alfred A. Knopf, 1939, 1949 ed.): 116.

16. William Sharon Manuscripts, Bancroft Library, University of California, Berkeley.

17. Hubert Howe Bancroft and Frances Fuller Victor, *History of Nevada, 1540–1888* (Reno: University of Nevada, 1981), 204.

18. Kroninger, 18.

19. *San Francisco Chronicle*, 13 March 1884.

20. Ibid.

21. Interviews in Tennessee, #4, no date, Mary Ellen Pleasant Collection, San Francisco History Room, San Francisco Public Library [/SFPL].

22. *San Francisco Chronicle*, 11 March 1884.

23. Ibid.

24. *San Francisco Bulletin*, 4 October 1883.

25. One of the depositions was taken from Freddie Burchard who claimed to

have been engaged to Miss Hill. But Burchard, under cross-examination by Tyler, was forced to admit that he called off the relationship due to his sexual disorders resulting from venereal disease.

26. *San Francisco Chronicle,* 11 March 1884.

27. Transcript of Argument of W.H.L. Barnes, *Sharon v. Sharon* (San Francisco Superior Court, 1883), Bancroft Library, University of California, Berkeley.

28. On the iconography of slavery, and the significance of mammy, in particular, see, Deborah Gray White, *Ar'n't I A Woman: Female Slaves in the Plantation South* (New York: Norton, 1985); Hazel V. Carby, *Reconstructing Womanhood: The Emergence of the Afro-American Woman Novelist* (New York: Oxford University Press, 1987); Cheryl Thurber, "The Development of the Mammy Image and Mythology," in *Southern Women: Histories and Identities,* Virginia Bernhard, et. al., eds. (Columbia: University of Missouri Press, 1994), 87–108; Patricia A. Turner, *Ceramic Uncles & Celluloid Mammies: Black Images and Their Influence on Culture* (New York: Anchor Books, 1994).

29. I find Korobkin's argument about courtroom storytelling quite compelling: "[L]awyers inevitably, and often unconsciously, draw on the story-forms most familiar and powerful within the culture at the time . . . By suggesting that the facts of a case constitute a story much like others that they know . . . a lawyer can provide jurors with a clear moral framework to use as a guide in making credible determinations and evidentiary assessments." Korobkin, 13.

30. Kroninger, 123.

31. Transcript on Appeal, *Sharon v. Sharon* (Supreme Ct. Cal., 1885), California State Archives.

32. The original "Bridge of Sighs" connected the Doges Palace with the prison in sixteenth-century Venice; the journalists who nicknamed it this, however, were probably taking a swipe at the Senator and the traffic—and sighs—his mistresses made on the bridge.

33. Transcript of Argument of William M. Stewart, *Sharon v. Hill* (Ninth District, 1885), Bancroft Library.

34. Ibid.

35. Ibid.

36. In fact Pleasant lived at a mansion on Octavia street in San Francisco that she designed and owned. Thomas Bell and Teresa Bell moved into the house and when Thomas died in 1892, Pleasant and Teresa continued to live in the house with the Bell children until 1899. For more information on the relationship between Pleasant and the Bells, see Hudson, pp. 104–109, 160–213. See also, Teresa Bell diary, Pleasant Collection, [SFPL]; Property Deeds, Pleasant and Bell collections, California Historical Society, San Francisco.

37. On the entertainment value of Victorian courtrooms, see, Ginger S. Frost, *Promises Broken: Courtship, Class, and Gender in Victorian England* (Charlottesville, VA: University Press of Virginia, 1995), especially chapter two, "The Court as Public Theatre."

38. *San Francisco Chronicle,* 19 March 1884.

39. Ibid. Although Barnes and Tyler were the main actors in the courtroom drama, both Sharon and Hill had a team of attorneys.

40. Ibid.

41. *San Francisco Chronicle,* 15 April 1884. On that same day, another woman, Harriet T. Martin, described as "a colored woman well advanced in years," also testified. While working in the Palace Hotel in 1881, Martin said that she saw Sarah Althea hiding behind a door hoping to trap the Senator with one of his paramours. Barnes asked the witness, "Did she ever ask you about fortune-tellers?" "Yes; she asked me and offered me $20 for a love powder," stated Martin.

42. *San Francisco Chronicle,* 19 March 1884. This was one of the defenses central arguments: that Sarah had acted like a single woman throughout the period that she claimed to have been married to the Senator. See Transcript of Argument of W.H.L. Barnes, *Sharon v. Sharon* (San Francisco Superior Court, 1883), Bancroft Library.

43. On the appeal of spiritualism in the nineteenth century, see, Nell Irvin Painter, *Sojourner Truth: A Life, A Symbol* (New York: Norton, 1996). For information on voodoo in the U.S., see Lawrence Levine, *Black Culture and Black Consciousness: Afro-American Folk Thought from Slavery to Freedom* (New York: Oxford University Press, 1977); Zora Neale Hurston, *Tell My Horse* (Philadelphia: J. B. Lippincott, 1938), and *Mules and Men* (New York: Negro Universities Press, 1969). For a contemporary account of the significance of voodoo in the United States, see, Karen McCarthy Brown, *Mama Lola: A Vodou Priestess in Brooklyn* (Berkeley: University of California Press, 1991.) For an insightful analysis of the ways in which voodoo still operates as a code for the primitive in United States culture and politics, see, Kate Ramsey, "That Old Black Magic: Seeing Haiti Through the Wall of Voodoo," *Voice Literary Supplement* 27 September 1994.

44. On the exoticization of black women and their association with the primitive in the nineteenth century, see, Sander Gilman, "Black Bodies, White Bodies: Toward An Iconography of Female Sexuality in Late Nineteenth-Century Art, Medicine, and Literature," in *"Race," Writing, and Difference,* ed. Henry Louis Gates, Jr. (1986), Nell Irvin Painter "Representing Truth: Sojourner Truth's Knowing and Becoming Known," *Journal of American History* 81, no. 2 (September 1994): 461–92.

45. Transcript of Argument of W.H.L. Barnes, *Sharon v. Sharon* (San Francisco Superior Court, 1883), Bancroft Library.

46. The witnesses are respectively, Mrs. Massey, Fred Burchard or "Poor Freddy," and Nellie Brackett.

47. Gould, 217.

48. Transcript of Argument of W.H.L. Barnes, *Sharon v. Sharon* (San Francisco Superior Court, 1883), Bancroft Library.

49. The practice of baby farming—women farming out their often "illegitimate" babies to caretakers—is, of course, linked to the unavailability of effective and

safe birth control and abortion. It is not coincidental that public attention would be directed to the practice of baby farming in the Victorian era. The Comstock Law passed in 1873 and the criminalization of reproduction control continued through the end of the century. See, Janet Farrell Brodie, *Contraception and Abortion in Nineteenth-Century America* (Ithaca: Cornell University Press, 1994). On the practice of baby farming and its regulation in Great Britain, see, Carol Smart, "Disruptive Bodies and Unruly Sex: The Regulation of Reproduction and Sexuality in the Nineteenth Century," in Carol Smart, ed., *Regulating Womanhood: Historical Essays on Marriage, Motherhood, and Sexuality* (New York: Routledge, 1992). Smart notes that several important cases in Britain in the 1870s drew attention to the practice of baby-farming.

50. *San Francisco Chronicle,* 22 April 1884.
51. *San Francisco Chronicle,* 23 July 1884; for additional coverage of this episode, see, *San Francisco Call,* 23–26 July 1884.
52. Kroninger, 136.
53. *San Francisco Chronicle,* 24 July 1884.
54. *San Francisco Chronicle,* 13 August 1884.
55. *San Francisco Chronicle,* 13 August 1884.
56. Ibid.
57. Ibid.
58. *San Francisco Chronicle,* 25 March 1884.
59. Transcript of Argument of W.H.L. Barnes, *Sharon v. Sharon* (San Francisco Superior Court, 1883), Bancroft Library.
60. Transcript of Argument of William M. Stewart, *Sharon v. Hill* (Ninth District, 1885), Bancroft Library.
61. Kroninger, 145–6.
62. Kroninger, 158.
63. Ibid.
64. Ibid.
65. Kroninger, 168.
66. Kroninger, 174.
67. Quoted in Kroninger, 185.
68. Ibid.
69. The California Supreme Court ruled that Sharon and Hill were married and then reversed their decision. Kroninger, 211.
70. That David Terry and Pleasant would end up on the same side of a court battle was more than a little odd. In 1858, when Terry served as Chief Justice of the State Supreme Court, he heard California's version of the Dred Scott case, the Archy Lee case. Chief Justice Terry pardoned a slaveholder for keeping Archy Lee as a slave in California, in spite of the fact that California had outlawed slavery. Terry was probably best known for his 1859 duel against David Broderick; he resigned as Chief Justice of the State Supreme Court to fight the duel. Terry was a Democrat and vehemently pro-slavery while Broderick, then U.S. Senator, was a leader of the California anti-slavery Democrats, and

one of the state's most successful politicians. See Philip J. Ethington, *The Public City: The Political Construction of Urban Life in San Francisco, 1850–1900* (Cambridge: Cambridge University Press, 1994). Much has also been written about Terry and the Vigilance Committee; for a less scholarly but lively discussion of the subject see, Gertrude Atherton, *California: An Intimate History* (New York: Blue Ribbon Books, 1936 edition), Ch. 14, "The Vigilance Committee and David S. Terry."

71. *San Francisco Chronicle,* 14 February 1892.

72. *San Francisco Chronicle,* 10 March 1892; Sarah Terry lived at the Stockton State Hospital for the Insane for another forty-five years. She died on February 14, 1937.

73. Issel and Cherny, 124; Kroninger, 123.

74. Lloyd J. Conrich, "The Mammy Pleasant Legend," (unpublished manuscript, no date, California Historical Society), 102.

75. Ibid.

76. Michel Foucault, *Power/Knowledge* edited by Colin Gordon (New York: Random House, 1981).

77. Transcript on Appeal, *Sharon v. Sharon* (California Supreme Court, 1885), California State Archives.

78. Gould, 193.

79. Transcript on Appeal, *Sharon v. Sharon* (California Supreme Court, 1885), California State Archives.

80. Martha Hodes, "The Sexualization of Reconstruction Politics: White Women and Black Men in the South After the Civil War," *Journal of the History of Sexuality* 3:3 (1993). See, also, Robyn Wiegman, "The Anatomy of Lynching," *Journal of the History of Sexuality* 3:3 (1993).

81. Mary P. Ryan, *Women in Public: Between Banners and Ballots, 1825–1880* (Baltimore: Johns Hopkins Press, 1993).

82. Evelyn Brooks Higginbotham, *Righteous Discontent: The Women's Movement in the Black Baptist Church* (Cambridge: Harvard University Press, 1993); Paula Baker, "The Domestication of Politics: Women and American Political Society, 1780–1920," *American Historical Review* 89 (1984): 620–47; Elsa Barkley Brown, "Womanist Consciousness: Maggie Lena Walker and the Independent Order of Saint Luke," *Signs* 14: 3 (Spring 1989): 610–33; Elsa Barkley Brown, "Negotiating and Transforming the Public Sphere: African American Political Life in the Transition from Slavery to Freedom," in *The Black Public Sphere* ed. The Black Public Sphere Collective (Chicago; University of Chicago Press, 1995); Linda K. Kerber, "Separate Spheres, Female Worlds, Woman's Place: The Rhetoric of Women's History," *The Journal of American History* 75 (June 1988): 9–39.

83. See, for example, Philip J. Ethington.

84. Lawrence B. de Graff, "Race, Sex and Region: Black Women in the American West, 1850–1920," *Pacific Historical Review* 49 (May 1980):285–313.

85. Douglas Henry Daniels, *Pioneer Urbanites: A Social and Cultural History of Black*

San Francisco (Philadelphia: Temple University Press, 1980), 54–55.

86. Sander L. Gilman, "'I'm Down On Whores': Race and Gender in Victorian London," in *Anatomy of Racism*, ed. David Theo Goldberg (Minneapolis, 1990).

Laura Jane Moore, Elle Meets the President: Weaving Navajo Culture and Commerce in the Southwestern Tourist Industry

1. Kathleen L. Howard, "Weaving a Legend: Elle of Ganado Promotes the Indian Southwest," *New Mexico Historical Review* 74:2 (1999): 130–31; *McKinley County* (Gallup) *Republican*, April 30, 1903; and Albuquerque *Journal-Democrat*, May 6, 1903, 5.

2. For what little biographical information is available on Elle of Ganado see Howard, "Weaving a Legend," 127–53.

3. Barbara A. Babcock, "'A New Mexican Rebecca': Imaging Pueblo Women," *Journal of the Southwest* 32:4 (1990): 404. A large literature is available on southwestern tourism and on its relationship to the Indian art market. See, for example, Barbara A. Babcock, ed., "Inventing the Southwest," special issue, *Journal of the Southwest* 32:4 (1990); J. J. Brody, "The Creative Consumer: Survival, Revival, and Invention in Southwest Indian Arts," in *Ethnic and Tourist Arts: Cultural Expressions From the Fourth World,* ed. Nelson H. H. Graburn (Berkeley: University of California Press, 1976), 70–84; Kathleen L. Howard and Diana F. Pardue, *Inventing the Southwest: The Fred Harvey Company and Native American Art* (Flagstaff, Ariz.: Northland Publishing, The Heard Museum, 1996); Louise Lamphere, ed., "Women, Anthropology, Tourism, and the Southwest," special section, *Frontiers: A Journal of Women Studies* 12:3 (1992): 5–12; Molly H. Mullin, "Consuming the American Southwest: Culture, Art, and Difference" (Ph.D. diss., Duke University, 1993); Scott Norris, ed., *Discovered Country: Tourism and Survival in the American West* (Albuquerque, N. M.: Stone Ladder Press, 1983); Sylvia Rodriguez, "Art, Tourism, and Race Relations in Taos: Toward a Sociology of the Art Colony," *Journal of Anthropological Research* 45:1 (1989): 77–100; Edwin L. Wade, "The Ethnic Art Market in the American Southwest, 1880–1980," in *Objects and Others: Essays on Museums and Material Culture,* ed. George W. Stocking, Jr. (Madison: University of Wisconsin Press, 1985), 167–91; and Marta Weigle and Barbara A. Babcock, eds., *The Great Southwest of the Fred Harvey Company and the Santa Fe Railway* (Phoenix: The Heard Museum, 1996).

4. Scholars have usually viewed the impact of the tourist industry, and the larger market economy of which it was part, on Native American artists and their communities as highly detrimental. See, for example, Edwin L. Wade, "Straddling the Cultural Fence: The Conflict for Ethnic Artists Within Pueblo Societies," in *The Arts of the North American Indian: Native Traditions in Evolution,* ed. Edwin L. Wade (New York: Hudson Hills Press, 1986), 243–54; Tessie Naranjo, "Cultural Changes: The Effect of Foreign Systems at Santa Clara

Pueblo," in Weigle and Babcock, *The Great Southwest*, 187–96; and Kathy M'Closkey, "Marketing Multiple Myths: The Hidden History of Navajo Weaving," *Journal of the Southwest* 36:3 (1994): 185–220. Such analyses parallel and sometimes intersect with scholarship on rural women losing out as they adopt items of domestic production to an expanding national market economy, and with analyses in Native American women's history that argue that the European and Euro-American economic system disrupted indigenous gender roles to the detriment of women. For an article that combines these themes, see Terry R. Reynolds, "Women, Pottery, and Economics at Acoma Pueblo," in *New Mexico Women: Intercultural Perspectives*, ed. Joan M. Jensen and Darlis A. Miller (Albuquerque: University of New Mexico Press, 1986). In other words, the market economy has long been a villain in Native American studies. Recently, however, historians of Native American women have noted the depth and resilience of cultural systems, evidenced in particular by the fundamental maintenance of gender roles, even as Native Americans adapted to significant historical and material pressures. Other Native American historians have also examined the variety of Native responses to changing economic circumstances and the ways in which Indians brought their own economic rationales to interactions with Euro-Americans, adapting and adopting aspects of a complex, historically constructed market economy. For examples, see Theda Perdue, *Cherokee Women: Gender and Culture Change, 1700–1835* (Lincoln: University of Nebraska Press, 1998); and Arthur J. Ray, *Indians in the Fur Trade: Their Role as Trappers, Hunters, and Middlemen in the Lands Southwest of Hudson Bay, 1660–1870* (Toronto: University of Toronto Press, 1974).

5. About the Fred Harvey Company I rely particularly on two publications generated by the Heard Museum's recent exhibit on the company: Howard and Pardue, *Inventing the Southwest*; and Weigle and Babcock, eds., *The Great Southwest*. On orientalist southwestern discourse, see Weigle and Babcock, *The Great Southwest*, 6–7. On the Fred Harvey Company and the Santa Fe Railroad, see also Keith L. Bryant, *History of the Atchison, Topeka, and Santa Fe Railway* (New York: Macmillan Publishing Company, 1974); T. C. McLuhan, *Dream Tracks: The Railroad and the American Indian, 1890–1930* (New York: Harry N. Abrams, 1985); and Lesley Polling-Kempes, *The Harvey Girls: Women Who Opened the West* (New York: Paragon House, 1989).

6. Howard and Pardue, *Inventing the Southwest*, 9–15, 103. See also Kathleen L. Howard, "'A Most Remarkable Success': Herman Schweizer and the Fred Harvey Indian Department," in Weigle and Babcock, *The Great Southwest*, 87–101; Matilda McQuaid with Karen Bartlett, "Building an Image of the Southwest: Mary Colter, Fred Harvey Company Architect," in Weigle and Babcock, *The Great Southwest*, 24–35; Virginia L. Gratton, *Mary Colter: Builder Upon the Red Earth* (Flagstaff, Ariz.: Northland Press, 1980); and Marta Weigle, "Exposition and Mediation: Mary Colter, Erna Fergusson, and the Santa Fe/Harvey Popularization of the Native Southwest, 1902–1940," *Frontiers: A Journal of Women Studies* 12:3 (1992): 117–50. On using the concepts of "staged

authenticity" and "backstage" views of Indian life in analyzing Mary Colter's architecture, concepts drawn from Erving Goffman's and Dean MacCannell's work, see Weigle, "Exposition and Mediation," 120–30.

7. Leah Dilworth, *Imagining Indians in the Southwest: Persistent Visions of a Primitive Past* (Washington, D. C.: Smithsonian Institution Press, 1996), 147–48, 151.

8. Weigle and Babcock, *The Great Southwest*, 12.

9. Ruth Roessel, "Navajo Arts and Crafts," in *Handbook of North American Indians*, vol. 10, *Southwest* (Washington, D.C.: Smithsonian Institution Press, 1983), 595.

10. Interview no. 27, Hubbell Trading Post National Historic Site Oral History Collection (hereafter HTPOHC), Ganado, Arizona; and Ann Lane Hedlund, *Reflections of the Weavers' World: The Gloria F. Ross Collection of Contemporary Navajo Weaving* (Denver, Colo.: Denver Art Museum, 1992), 30. When the interviews were conducted for HTPOHC in the late 1960s and early 1970s, consent forms were not obtained for the interviews to be used in subsequent research. Kathleen Tabaha, the assistant curator at the Hubbell Trading Post National Historic Site, is in the process of contacting interviewees' family members in order to obtain such permission. In the meantime, she has asked that I not use interviewees' names.

11. Ann Lane Hedlund, "'More of a Survival Than an Art': Comparing Late Nineteenth- and Late Twentieth-Century Lifeways and Weaving," in *Woven By the Grandmothers: Nineteenth-Century Textiles from the National Museum of the American Indian*, ed. Eulalie H. Bonar (Washington: Smithsonian Institution Press, 1996), 47–48. A voluminous literature is available on Navajo weaving. In addition to those works cited above, I am relying particularly on Ellen F. Elsas and Ann Lane Hedlund, *"Well May They Be Made": Navajo Textiles from the Coleman Cooper Collection of the Birmingham Museum of Art* (Birmingham, Alabama: Birmingham Museum of Art, 1987); Ann Lane Hedlund, *Beyond the Loom: Keys to Understanding Early Southwestern Weaving* (Boulder, Colorado: Johnson Books, 1990); Ann Lane Hedlund, "Contemporary Navajo Weaving: An Ethnography of a Native Craft" (Ph.D. diss., University of Colorado at Boulder, 1983); Kate Peck Kent, *Navajo Weaving: Three Centuries of Change* (Santa Fe: School of American Research Press, 1985); Marian E. Rodee, *One Hundred Years of Navajo Rugs* (Albuquerque: University of New Mexico Press, 1995); Joe Ben Wheat, "Documentary Basis for Material Changes and Design Styles in Navajo Blanket Weaving," in *Proceedings of the Irene Emery Roundtable on Museum Textiles* (Washington, D.C.: The Textile Museum, 1976); Joe Ben Wheat, *The Gift of Spiderwoman: Southwestern Textiles, the Navajo Tradition* (Philadelphia: University Museum, University of Pennsylvania, 1984); and Roseann S. Willink and Paul G. Zolbrod, *Weaving a World: Textiles and the Navajo Way of Seeing* (Santa Fe: University of New Mexico Press, 1996).

12. Gary Witherspoon, "Navajo Social Organization," in *Handbook of North American Indians*, vol. 10, *Southwest*, 525–26; and Elsas and Hedlund, *"Well May They Be Made,"* 29–30.

13. Garrick Bailey and Roberta Glenn Bailey, in *A History of the Navajos: The*

Reservation Years (Santa Fe, N.M.: School of American Research Press, 1986), argue that even in the twentieth century, as "Navajos diversified into commercial stock raising and wage labor" they did not totally commercialize their herds but "successfully maintained high subsistence value while raising the market value of their livestock. . . . In large part rug weaving enabled them to achieve this balance" because it "gave a dimension to their herding economy that Anglo-American and Spanish-American ranchers lacked" (179–80). David Aberle contends in "Navajo Exogamic Rules and Preferred Marriages" (in *The Versatility of Kinship Essays Presented to Harry W. Basehart*, ed. Linda S. Cordell and Stephen Beckerman [New York: Academic Press, 1980]) that "traditional kinship organization is maintained because of, rather than despite, changes in the Navajo economy—that traditional kinship organization, oriented to the multiple, fluctuating resources of the traditional economy, preserves the same orientation now that the Navajos are marginal participants in the larger United States economy. Relying on multiple, fluctuating resources, which include flocks, farms, crafts, wage work, and welfare, most families have no single source of livelihood sufficient in quantity or reliability to induce them to give up the others. . . . By and large, the nuclear family provides insufficient labor power for all these activities" (123–24). On the maintenance of matrifocal kinship institutions in the midst of a dramatically changing political economy, see also Klara B. Kelley, "Navajo Political Economy before Fort Sumner," in Cordell and Beckerman, *The Versatility of Kinship*, 315, 317–18, 329. On change and persistence of Navajo women's roles and status, see Laila Shukry Hamamsy, "The Role of Women in a Changing Navaho Society," *American Anthropologist* 59:1 (1957): 101–111; Mary Shepardson, "The Status of Navajo Women"; and Christine Conte, "Ladies, Livestock, Land, and Lucre: Women's Networks and Social Status on the Western Navajo Reservation," *American Indian Quarterly* 6:1/2 (1982): 105–124; and Louise Lamphere, "Historical and Regional Variability in Navajo Women's Roles," *Journal of Anthropological Research* 45:4 (1989): 431–56.

14. Richard I. Ford, "Inter-Indian Exchange in the Southwest," in *Handbook of North American Indians*, vol. 10, *Southwest*, 721.

15. Hedlund, "'More of a Survival Than an Art,'" 54.

16. Bailey and Bailey, *A History of the Navajos*, 51.

17. Bailey and Bailey, *A History of the Navajos*, chapter 2. On the Navajo economy and trade networks, see also Klara Bonseck Kelley, "Commercial Networks in the Navajo-Hopi-Zuni Region" (Ph.D. diss., The University of New Mexico, 1977).

18. Bailey and Bailey, *A History of the Navajos*, 59–60; Kent, *Navajo Weaving*, 17–18, 83, 85–86; and Dilys Winegard, ed., *A Burst of Brilliance: Germantown, Pennsylvania and Navajo Weaving* (Philadelphia: University of Pennsylvania Press, 1994). A large and growing literature is available on trading posts in Navajo country. The story of traders and Navajo weavers has often been told as change directed by traders with weavers passively accepting white men's

suggestions. Recent scholarship has emphasized weavers' agency and analyzes trading posts as complex sites of transculteration. Three classics are Frank McNitt, *The Indian Traders* (1962, reprint, Norman: University of Oklahoma Press, 1989); William Adams, *Shonto: A Study of the Role of the Trader in a Modern Navaho Community* (Washington, D.C.: Smithsonian Institution, Bureau of American Ethnology, Bulletin 188, 1963); and Willow Roberts, *Stokes Carson: Twentieth-Century Trading on the Navajo Reservation* (Albuquerque: University of New Mexico Press, 1987). Recent studies include Martha Blue, *Indian Trader: The Life and Times of J. C. Hubbell* (Walnut, Calif.: Kiva Publishing, Inc., 2000); Laura Graves, *Thomas Varker Keam, Indian Trader* (Norman: University of Oklahoma Press, 1998); Laura Ruth Marcus, "Moving Towards Nizaad: Exploring the Dynamics of Navajo-Anglo Interaction Through Trading and Art," (Ph.D. diss., Indiana University, 1998); Nancy Peake, "Trading Post Tales: Biography of an Indian Trader on the Navajo Reservation, 1930–1980" (Ph.D. diss., University of New Mexico, 1992); and Teresa Jo Wilkins, "Producing Culture Across the Colonial Divide: Navajo Reservation Trading Posts and Weaving" (Ph.D. diss., University of Colorado at Boulder, 1999). A good recent description of the trading post economy is in Robert "Skip" Volk, "'Red Sales in the Sunset': The Rise and Fall of White Trader Dominance in the United States' Navajo Reservation and South Africa's Transkei," *American Indian Culture and Research Journal* 24:1 (2000): 69–97.

19. Marc Simmons, *Albuquerque: A Narrative History* (Albuquerque: University of New Mexico Press, 1982), 234, 275–77, 329; Bradford Luckingham, *The Urban Southwest: A Profile History of Albuquerque, El Paso, Phoenix, and Tucson* (El Paso, Texas: Western Press, 1982), 19, 35–36; and Bailey and Bailey, *A History of the Navajos*, 156, 157–58. On ways in which Navajos combined wage work with a kin-based household economy that often conflicted with their employer's expectations, see Colleen O'Neill, "Navajo Workers and White Man's Ways: Negotiating the World of Wage Labor, 1930–1970" (Ph.D. diss., Graduate School-New Brunswick, Rutgers, The State University of New Jersey, 1997); and Colleen O'Neill, "The 'Making' of the Navajo Worker: Navajo Households, the Bureau of Indian Affairs, and Off-Reservation Wage Work, 1948–1960," *New Mexico Historical Review* 74:4 (1999): 375–405.

20. The Hubbell Trading Post in Ganado is still in operation today, owned by the National Park Service as a National Historic Site. Weavers still visit the trading post's rug room to bargain with the trader in Navajo, while others demonstrate their art for tourists in the visitor's center. These weavers carry on in Elle's tradition, but much has also changed, and tourists are instructed not to photograph demonstrators without their permission.

21. Herman Schweizer to John Lorenzo Hubbell, March 13, 1903, April 29, 1903, and March 6, 1903, Fred Harvey File (hereafter FHF), Incoming Correspondence, box 36, Harvey Trading Post Collection (hereafter HTPC), Special Collections, University of Arizona.

22. Juana Sangre of Isleta Pueblo, interviewed in 1994, remembered constantly

cleaning the pots and the floors between trains. She said, "And when they tell us a train is about to be here we used to quit so they wouldn't find us [cleaning]" (quoted in Howard and Pardue, *Inventing the Southwest*, 24).

23. See, for example, Huckel to Hubbell, June 9, June 26, July 1, and July 20, 1905, FHF, HTPC. Unlike weaving, silver work continued to be an important trade item among the Diné. The heavy silver jewelry that Navajos used was inappropriate for the tourist market, so the Harvey Company encouraged some silversmiths to develop a lighter, cheaper style that they could sell in their stores. See John Adair, *The Navajo and Pueblo Silversmiths* (Norman: University of Oklahoma Press, 1944).

24. Howard and Pardue, *Inventing the Southwest*, 74, 76, 105–110.

25. Elle and Tom had no children together, which might have lessened their responsibilities back home. Still, they often brought some of Tom's grandchildren with them to Albuquerque, and Elle was frequently photographed surrounded by children. She was an ideal demonstrator because she could afford to stay away from home while still providing a matronly image (Howard, "Weaving a Legend," 132, 128).

26. Howard and Pardue, *Inventing the Southwest*, 64, 66, 68.

27. *The Great Southwest Along the Santa Fe* (Kansas City, Missouri: Fred Harvey, 1914), n.p., quoted in Marta Weigle with Kathleen L. Howard, "'To Experience the Real Grand Canyon': Santa Fe/Harvey Panopticism, 1901–1935," in Weigle and Babcock, *The Great Southwest*, 21.

28. Huckel to Hubbell, March 4, 1905; and Schweizer to Hubbell, November 17, 1904, FHF, HTPC.

29. I am touching here only lightly on the relationship between "antimodernism," the arts and crafts movement, and Indian art, a relationship that I discuss in more depth in "The Navajo Rug Trade: Gender, Art, Work, and Modernity in the American Southwest, 1870s–1930s" (Ph.D. diss., University of North Carolina at Chapel Hill, 1999). Besides those already cited, related works include T. J. Jackson Lears, *No Place of Grace: Antimodernism and the Transformation of American Culture, 1880–1920* (New York: Pantheon Books, 1981); Eileen Boris, *Art and Labor: Ruskin, Morris, and the Craftsman Ideal in America* (Philadelphia: Temple University Press, 1986); J. J. Brody, *Indian Painters and White Patrons* (Albuquerque: University of New Mexico Press, 1971); W. Jackson Rushing, *Native American Art and the New York Avant-Garde: A History of Cultural Primitivism* (Austin: University of Texas Press, 1995); Wendy Kaplan, ed., *"Art That is Life:" The Arts and Crafts Movement in America, 1875–1920* (Boston: Little, Brown and Company for Museum of Fine Arts, 1987); Miles Orvell, *The Real Thing: Imitation and Authenticity in American Culture, 1880–1940* (Chapel Hill: The University of North Carolina Press, 1989); Melanie Herzog, "Aesthetics and Meanings: The Arts and Crafts Movement and the Revival of American Indian Basketry," in *The Substance of Style: Perspectives on the American Arts and Crafts Movement*, ed. Bert Denker (Winterthur, Delaware: Henry Francis du Pont Winterthur Museum;

Hanover: University Press of New England, 1996), 69–92; Margaret D. Jacobs, "Shaping a New Way: White Women and the Movement to Promote Pueblo Indian Arts and Crafts, 1900–1935," *Journal of the Southwest* 40:2 (1998): 187–216; Molly H. Mullin, "The Patronage of Difference: Making Indian Art 'Art, Not Ethnology,'" *Cultural Anthropology* 7:4 (1992): 395–426; and Teresa J. Wilkins, "The Creation of a Usable Past," in *Diné Baa Hané Bi Naaltsoos: Collected Papers from the Seventh through Tenth Navajo Studies Conferences,* ed. June-el Piper (Window Rock, Arizona: Navajo Nation Historic Preservation Office for the Navajo Studies Conference, 1999), 203–10.

30. Switzer per Snively to Hubbell, July 9, 1903, FHF, HTPC.

31. Interview no. 20: 567 098, in Michael Joseph Francisconi, *Kinship, Capitalism, Change: The Informal Economy of the Navajo, 1868–1995* (New York: Garland Publishing, 1998), Appendix A, 220.

32. Huckel to Hubbell, October 24, 1905, FHF, HTPC.

33. See, for example, Huckel to Hubbell, April 26, 1905, and April 21, 1905, FHF, HTPC.

34. Letter from John Hudson to Grace Hudson, February 6, 1903, quoted in Howard and Pardue, *Inventing the Southwest,* 59.

35. Huckel to Hubbell, April 21 and 26, 1905; and J. Snively to Hubbell, May 6, 1905, FHF, HTPC.

36. Schweizer to Hubbell, April 29, 1905, FHF, HTPC.

37. Schweizer to Hubbell, May 31, 1905, FHF, HTPC.

38. Schweizer to Hubbell, April 6, 1905, FHF, HTPC.

39. Huckel to Hubbell, June 9, 1905, FHF, HTPC.

40. Huckel to Hubbell, June 26, 1905, and May 31, 1905, FHF, HTPC.

41. They got to the Canyon on June 25.

42. Huckel to Hubbell, July 1, 1905, FHF, HTPC.

43. Huckel to Hubbell, July 20, 1905, FHF, HTPC.

44. Schweizer to Hubbell, July 19, 1905, FHF, HTPC.

45. *Albuquerque Morning Journal,* October 3 and October 21, 1904, cited in Howard and Pardue, *Inventing the Southwest,* 61.

46. Interview with Marie Curley, Doris Duke Number 678, the American Indian History Project, Western History Center, University of Utah, September 10, 1970, copy in the HTPOHC, Ganado. Curley says that her father, Miguelito, was four, and her mother, Maria Antonio, was two, when they left Fort Sumner.

47. Gladys Reichard, *Navajo Shepherd and Weaver* (1936; reprint, Enumclaw, Wash.: MacRae Publications, 1977), *Spider Woman: A Story of Navajo Weavers and Chanters* (1934; reprint, Glorieta, N.M.: Rio Grande Press, 1968), and *Navajo Medicine Man: Sandpaintings and Legends of Miguelito* (New York: J. J. Augustin, 1939).

48. Schweizer to Hubbell, July 24, 1905, FHF, HTPC.

49. Schweizer to Hubbell, July 27, 1905, FHF, HTPC.

50. In the 1920s the Fred Harvey Company issued a series of lavishly illustrated

publications edited by J. Huckel titled "American Indians: First Families of the Southwest."

51. Schweizer to Hubbell, March 15, 1903; Huckel to Hubbell, May 23, 1905; and Schweizer to Hubbell, September 13, 1905, FHF, HTPC.

52. Interview no. 40, n.d., HTPOHC.

53. Schweizer to Hubbell, May 31, 1905, FHF, HTPC.

54. Huckel to Hubbell, March 23, 1905, FHF, HTPC.

55. Babcock, "A New Mexican Rebecca," 429. Babcock is paraphrasing Michel Foucault's discussion of "the gaze" in *Discipline and Punish: The Birth of the Prison* (New York: Pantheon Books, 1977).

56. Interview no. 7, November 15, 1971, HTPOHC.

57. *Albuquerque Journal-Democrat*, May 6, 1903.

58. Interview no. 1, January 20, 1986, Ganado oral history rug study interviews, HTPC.

Margaret D. Jacobs, The Eastmans and the Luhans: Interracial Marriage between White Women and Native American Men, 1875–1935

1. Kay Graber, ed., *Sister to the Sioux: The Memoirs of Elaine Goodale Eastman, 1885–91* (Lincoln: University of Nebraska Press, 1978), 172; Charles Eastman, *From the Deep Woods to Civilization* (1916; reprint, Lincoln: University of Nebraska Press, 1977), 124. For a firsthand account of their marriage, see the monthly journal of the Women's National Indian Association, *The Indian's Friend* 3, no. 11 (1891): 3. It is common for scholars to refer to people by their last names. However, to avoid confusion in this article that deals with couples with the same last names, I have opted to refer to all of my major subjects by their first names. I also use the terms Native American, American Indian, and Indian interchangeably, as all have become acceptable terms to refer generally to the first peoples of North America. Where possible, however, in accordance with the wishes of most Indian people, I use tribal affiliation to more accurately identify individuals.

2. Mabel Dodge Luhan, *Edge of Taos Desert: An Escape to Reality*, vol. 4 of *Intimate Memories* (1937; reprint, Albuquerque: University of New Mexico, 1997), 193.

3. Peggy Pascoe, "Race, Gender, and Intercultural Relations: The Case of Interracial Marriage," *Frontiers* 12 (1991): 5.

4. For laws and court cases, see Ian F. Haney López, *White By Law: The Legal Construction of Race* (New York: New York University Press, 1996); Byron Curti Martyn, "Racism in the United States: A History of the Anti-Miscegenation Legislation and Litigation" (Ph.D. diss., University of Southern California, 1979); David H. Fowler, *Northern Attitudes Towards Interracial Marriage: Legislation and Public Opinion in the Middle Atlantic and the States of the Old Northwest, 1780–1930* (New York: Garland Publishing, 1987); Kathleen M. Brown, *Good Wives, Nasty Wenches, and Anxious Patriarchs: Gender, Race, and*

Power in Colonial Virginia (Chapel Hill: University of North Carolina Press, 1996); Martha Hodes, *White Women, Black Men: Illicit Sex in the Nineteenth-Century South* (New Haven CT: Yale University Press, 1997); and Peggy Pascoe, "Miscegenation Law, Court Cases, and Ideologies of 'Race' in Twentieth-Century America," in *Sex, Love, Race: Crossing Boundaries in North American History*, ed. Martha Hodes (New York: New York University Press, 1999). 464–90. For social attitudes, see David Smits, "'Squaw Men,' 'Half-Breeds,' and Amalgamators: Late Nineteenth-Century Anglo-American Attitudes Toward Indian-White Race-Mixing," *American Indian Culture and Research Journal* 15, no. 3 (1991): 29–61; and Joel Williamson, *New People: Miscegenation and Mulattos in the United States* (New York: Free Press, 1980). For some studies focusing on black-white sex and intermarriage, see Hodes, *White Women, Black Men*; Williamson, *New People*; and Fowler, *Northern Attitudes*.

5. Katherine Ellinghaus is one of the few scholars to study this configuration in comparison with relationships between Aboriginal men and white women in Australia. See Katherine Ellinghaus, "Reading the Personal as Political: The Assimilationist Views of a White Woman Married to a Native American Man, 1880s–1940s," *Australasian Journal of American Studies* 18, no. 2 (1999): 23–41; and "Interracial Marriage and the Ideology of Assimilation: Hampton Institute, 1878–1923," *Virginia Magazine of History and Biography* 108, no. 3 (2000): 279–303.

6. For examples, see Noel Ignatiev, *How the Irish Became White* (New York: Routledge, 1995); Matthew Frye Jacobson, *Whiteness of a Different Color: European Immigrants and the Alchemy of Race* (Cambridge MA: Harvard University Press, 1998); David Roediger, *The Wages of Whiteness: Race and the Making of the American Working Class* (London: Verso, 1991); David Roediger, *Towards the Abolition of Whiteness: Essays on Race, Politics, and Working Class History* (London: Verso, 1994); Alexander Saxton, *The Rise and Fall of the White Republic: Class Politics and Mass Culture in Nineteenth-Century America* (London: Verso, 1990); Reginald Horsman, *Race and Manifest Destiny: The Origins of American Racial Anglo-Saxonism* (Cambridge MA: Harvard University Press, 1981); and López, *White By Law*. I have used López's concept of race as a socially and culturally "fabricated" phenomenon because it so ingeniously captures the nature of racial categorization.

7. For new studies of interracial sex and marriage, see Hodes, *Sex, Love, Race*. Other studies include Martyn, "Racism in the United States;" Fowler, *Northern Attitudes*; Brown, *Good Wives*; Hodes, *White Women, Black Men*; Williamson, *New People*; and Smits, "'Squaw Men.'"

8. George Frederickson, "Reflection on the Comparative History and Sociology of Racism," in *Racial Classification and History*, ed. E. Nathanial Gates (New York: Garland Publishing, 1997), 54.

9. For just a sampling of works in women's history and the history of sexuality that show the plasticity of gender, see John D'Emilio and Estelle Freedman,

Intimate Matters: A History of Sexuality in America (New York: Harper & Row, 1988); Gerda Lerner, *The Creation of Patriarchy* (New York: Oxford University Press, 1986); Nancy Cott, *The Bonds of Womanhood: 'Woman's Sphere' in New England, 1780–1835* (New Haven CT: Yale University Press, 1977).

10. For examples of scholarly work that offer very little gender analysis of inter-racial relationships between Europeans and Indians, see Smits, "'Squaw Men'" Gary Nash, "The Hidden History of Mestizo America," in Hodes, *Sex, Love, Race*, 10–32; Mark Alan Sigmon, "Heretics of Race: An Exploration of Indian-White Relationships in the Trans-Mississippi West, 1820–1850" (Ph.D. diss., University of California, Berkeley, 1995).

11. See Hodes, *White Women, Black Men*; Brown, *Good Wives*; and Paul Finkelman, "The Crime of Color," *Tulane Law Review* 67, no. 6 (1993): 2063–112; reprinted in E. Nathaniel Gates, ed., *Racial Classification and History* (New York: Garland Publishing, 1997), 1–50.

12. See Fowler, *Northern Attitudes*; Hodes, *White Women, Black Men*; Brown, *Good Wives*; and Finkelman, "The Crime of Color."

13. Fowler, *Northern Attitudes*, 336–439. The colonies banning Indian-white inter-marriage were Virginia, North Carolina, and New York. The territories or states banning Indian-white intermarriage were Arizona, Georgia, Idaho, Louisiana, Rhode Island, Maine, Massachusetts, Nevada, North Carolina, Oklahoma, Oregon, South Carolina, Tennessee, Virginia, and Washington. In some states mulattos were defined as children of either whites and blacks, blacks and Indians, or whites and Indians, so other colonies, states, and terri-tories that banned marriage between mulattos and whites may have had laws in effect that restricted Indian-white intermarriage as well.

14. Brian W. Dippie, *The Vanishing American: White Attitudes and U.S. Indian Policy* (Middletown CT: Wesleyan University Press, 1982), 257–58.

15. John Demos, *The Unredeemed Captive: A Family Story from Early America* (New York: Alfred A. Knopf, 1994), 98–99, 157–64, 188–98, 213–37. For more on captivity and its cultural meanings, see June Namias, *White Captives: Gender and Ethnicity on the American Frontier* (Chapel Hill: University of North Carolina Press, 1993) and James Axtell, *The Invasion Within: The Contest of Cultures in Colonial North America* (New York: Oxford University Press, 1985).

16. Demos, *The Unredeemed Captive*.

17. John Ehle, *Trail of Tears: The Rise and Fall of the Cherokee Nation* (New York: Doubleday, 1988), 188–91; and Thurman Wilkins, *Cherokee Tragedy: The Ridge Family and the Decimation of a People*, 2nd ed. (Norman: University of Oklahoma Press, 1986), 131–53.

18. See for example, William J. Scheick, *The Half-Blood: A Cultural Symbol in 19th-Century American Fiction* (Lexington: University Press of Kentucky, 1979), 4. Coeur d'Alene Indian writer Janet Campbell Hale, herself a descendant of one of these marriages, objects strenuously to this view. She correctly points out that such a viewpoint, often reiterated by historians, devalues native women by implying that no white man would willingly choose an Indian

woman as his partner or wife, and that white men in frontier regions did so only out of desperation. See Hale's *Bloodlines: Odyssey of a Native Daughter* (New York: Harper, 1994), 125–40.

19. Richard Slotkin, *Regeneration Through Violence: The Mythology of the American Frontier, 1600–1860* (Middletown CT: Wesleyan University Press, 1973), 58–65, 126.

20. Ehle, *Trail of Tears*, 189, 191–92. For discussions of *feme covert*, see Linda K. Kerber, *No Constitutional Right to Be Ladies: Women and the Obligations of Citizenship* (New York: Hill and Wang, 1998); Carol F. Karlsen, *The Devil in the Shape of a Woman: Witchcraft in Colonial New England* (New York: Vintage Books, 1987); and Brown, *Good Wives*.

21. Lydia Maria Child, *Hobomok and Other Writings on Indians*, ed. Carolyn Karcher (New Brunswick NJ: Rutgers University Press, 1986), 135–36, 137.

22. For more on the reform movement of the late nineteenth century, see Francis Paul Prucha, *American Indian Policy in Crisis: Christian Reformers and the Indian, 1865–1900* (Norman: University of Oklahoma Press, 1976), and *The Great Father: The United States Government and the American Indians*, vol. 2 (Lincoln: University of Nebraska Press, 1984); Frederick Hoxie, *A Final Promise: The Campaign to Assimilate the Indians, 1880–1920* (New York: Cambridge University Press, 1984); Margaret Jacobs, *Engendered Encounters: Feminism and Pueblo Cultures, 1879–1934* (Lincoln: University of Nebraska Press, 1999); Valerie Mathes, "Nineteenth-Century Women and Reform: The Women's National Indian Association," *American Indian Quarterly* 14, no. 1 (1990): 1–18; and Helen M. Wanken, "'Woman's Sphere' and Indian Reform: The Women's National Indian Association, 1879–1901" (Ph.D. diss., Marquette University, 1981).

23. Graber, *Sister to the Sioux*, 22.

24. Graber, *Sister to the Sioux*, 114–20; Raymond Wilson, *Ohiyesa: Charles Eastman, Santee Sioux* (Urbana: University of Illinois Press, 1983), 45–52.

25. Graber, *Sister to the Sioux*, 145–54.

26. Charles Eastman, *Indian Boyhood* (1902; reprint, New York: Dover Publications, 1971); Wilson, *Ohiyesa*, 13–20; and Marion Copeland, *Charles Alexander Eastman (Ohiyesa)* (Boise ID: Boise State University, 1978), 7–9.

27. Charles Eastman, *From the Deep Woods to Civilization*. Eastman first published this book in 1916. See also Copeland, *Charles Alexander Eastman*, 9–11; and Wilson, *Ohiyesa*, 20–62.

28. C. Eastman, *From the Deep Woods to Civilization*, 86–87, 105.

29. Graber, *Sister to the Sioux*, 155–175; C. Eastman, *From the Deep Woods to Civilization*, 92–115; Wilson, *Ohiyesa*, 62.

30. Charles Eastman, *Old Indian Days* (New York: McLure Company, 1907), 51.

31. Fowler, *Northern Attitudes Toward Inter-Marriage*, 273–81; and Steven Selden, *Inheriting Shame: The Story of Eugenics and Racism in America* (New York: Teachers College Press, 1999).

32. Gustav Spiller, "The Problem of Race Equality," in *Inter-Racial Problems: Papers from the First Universal Races Congress held in London in 1911*, ed. Gustav Spiller

(New York: Citadel Press, 1970), 38.

33. Dr. Jean Baptiste de Lacerda, "The *Metis*, or Half-Breeds, of Brazil," in Spiller, *Inter-Racial Problems*, 381.

34. Earl Finch, "The Effects of Racial Miscegenation," in Spiller, *Inter-Racial Problems*, 112.

35. Charles Eastman, "The North American Indian," in Spiller, *Inter-Racial Problems*, 375.

36. C. Eastman, *From the Deep Woods to Civilization*, 186.

37. C. Eastman, "The North American Indian," 375.

38. Wilson, *Ohiyesa*, 163.

39. Charles Eastman and Elaine Goodale Eastman, *Wigwam Evenings: Sioux Folk Tales Retold* (1909; reprint, Lincoln: University of Nebraska Press, 1990), 164.

40. Elaine Eastman to Maria Montezuma Moore, 24 February 1936, Carlos Montezuma papers (Wilmington DE: Scholarly Resources, 1984), reel 9; and Wilson, *Ohiyesa*, 163–65.

41. Peggy Pascoe, *Relations of Rescue: The Search for Female Moral Authority in the American West, 1874–1939* (New York: Oxford University Press, 1990); Barbara Epstein, *The Politics of Domesticity: Women, Evangelism, and Temperance in Nineteenth-Century America* (Middletown, CT: Wesleyan University Press, 1981); Barbara Welter, "She Hath Done What She Could: Protestant Women's Missionary Careers in the Nineteenth Century, *American Quarterly* 30, no. 5 (winter 1978): 624–38; and Jacobs, *Engendered Encounters*.

42. Elaine Eastman, "All the Days," *South Dakota Historical Review* 2 (July 1937): 178.

43. Speech of Elaine Eastman to Friends of the Indian, in *Proceedings of the 13th Annual Meeting of the Lake Mohonk Conference of Friends of the Indian* (New York: Lake Mohonk Conference, 1895), 92.

44. C. Eastman, *Old Indian Days*, 184.

45. E. Eastman, "All the Days," 182; Elaine Eastman to Mr. Winn, 7 April 1939, and Elaine Eastman to Harold G. Rugg, 19 April 1939, Charles Eastman alumni file, Dartmouth College.

46. Graber, *Sister to the Sioux*, 173.

47. E. Eastman, "All the Days," 181, 182; Graber, *Sister to the Sioux*, 174. C. Eastman, *From the Deep Woods to Civilization*, 126–95.

48. C. Eastman to Carlos Montezuma, 2 January 1911, Montezuma papers, reel 2.

49. Graber, *Sister to the Sioux*, 85.

50. C. Eastman to Mr. C. K. Ober, 26 June 1895, Montezuma papers, reel 8.

51. C. Eastman, *Soul of the Indian* (New York: Houghton Mifflin, 1911), 22, 24, 87–88.

52. C. Eastman, "The North American Indian," 369.

53. C. Eastman, *Indian Boyhood*, 20. See also Charles Eastman, *Indian Heroes and Great Chieftains* (1918; reprint, Lincoln: University of Nebraska Press, 1991), 178. For more on the "crisis" of masculinity in the late nineteenth and early

twentieth centuries and its relationship to race, see Gail Bederman, *Manliness and Civilization: A Cultural History of Gender and Race in the United States, 1880–1917* (Chicago: University of Chicago Press, 1995).

54. C. Eastman, as president of Society of American Indians, to "Friend and Fellow-Indian," 11 January 1919, Montezuma papers, reel 4; Letter from Charles Eastman to Friends of the Indians, *Proceedings of the 17th Annual Meeting of the Lake Mohonk Conference of Friends of the Indian* (New York: Lake Mohonk Conference, 1899), 66; C. Eastman, *From the Deep Woods to Civilization*, 55.

55. Jacobs, *Engendered Encounters*.

56. Mabel Dodge Luhan, *Movers and Shakers*, vol. 3 of *Intimate Memories* (1936; reprint, Albuquerque: University of New Mexico Press, 1985); and Lois Palken Rudnick, *Mabel Dodge Luhan: New Woman, New Worlds* (Albuquerque: University of New Mexico Press, 1984).

57. Luhan, *Movers and Shakers*, 532, 533–34.

58. Luhan, *Edge of Taos Desert*, 20–44, 92–271 passim.

59. Mary Austin, *Earth Horizon* (Boston: Houghton Mifflin, 1932), 340; Mary Austin to Mabel Dodge, 4 April [1923], Mary Austin to Mabel Dodge, 29 April [1923], and Stella Atwood to Mabel Sterne, 8 Jan 1923, Mabel Dodge Luhan papers, Yale Collection of American Literature, Beinecke Rare Book and Manuscript Library, Yale University, New Haven, Connecticut.

60. Rudnick, *Mabel Dodge Luhan*, 155, 251.

61. Mabel Dodge Luhan, *Lorenzo in Taos* (New York: Alfred Knopf, 1932), 235, 276–77. Lorenzo was Luhan's nickname for D. H. Lawrence, whom she invited to her home in the 1920s.

62. On Mabel's marital problems with Tony, see correspondence from Mabel Dodge Luhan to Frances G. Wickes, Frances G. Wickes papers, Library of Congress, Washington, D.C. See also Rudnick, *Mabel Dodge Luhan*, 155, 238–41. Rudnick claims Tony, on occasion, still slept with his first wife Candelaria in the 1920s, had an Anglo mistress in the 1930s in Carmel, and in the 1940s and 50s, had a Hispanic mistress. See also Ellen Kay Trimberger, "The New Woman and the New Sexuality: Conflict and Contradiction in the Writings of Mabel Dodge and Neith Boyce," in *1915, The Cultural Moment: The New Politics, the New Psychology, the New Art & the New Theatre in America*, ed. Adele Heller and Lois Rudnick (New Brunswick NJ: Rutgers University Press, 1991), 98–115.

63. Luhan, *Edge of Taos Desert*, 222.

64. Luhan, *Edge of Taos Desert*, 178, 179.

65. Mabel Dodge Luhan to John Collier, 30 November 1933, John Collier papers, microfilm edition (Sanford NC: Microfilming Corporation of America, 1980), reel 15.

66. See Jacobs, *Engendered Encounters*, 82–105; and Selden, *Inheriting Shame*.

67. Peter Iverson, *Carlos Montezuma and the Changing World of American Indians* (Albuquerque: University of New Mexico Press, 1982), 99–100.

68. Peggy Pond Church, *The House at Otowi Bridge: The Story of Edith Warner and*

Los Alamos (Albuquerque: University of New Mexico Press, 1960).

69. Carobeth Laird, *Encounter with an Angry God* (Banning CA: Malki Museum Press, 1975; reprint, Albuquerque: University of New Mexico Press, 1993).

70. Erna Fergusson, *Dancing Gods: Indian Ceremonials of New Mexico and Arizona* (New York: Alfred A. Knopf, 1931), 162–63, 246–27.

71. Gladys Brown to Maria Montezuma Moore, 29 July 1924, Montezuma papers, reel 9.

72. Mabel Dodge Luhan to Frances Wickes, "Wednesday," from St. Joseph Sanatorium, Albuquerque, Wickes papers. Mabel also mentions how her white female friends were attracted to Tony in *Edge of Taos Desert*, 102.

73. Clara True to Samuel Brosius, 16 December 1926, Indian Rights Association papers, Historical Society of Pennsylvania, Philadelphia, microfilm edition (Glen Rock NJ: Microfilming Corporation of America, 1975), reel 43.

74. Luhan, *Lorenzo in Taos*, 193. For more on primitivism and its relation to changing sexual ideals, see Jacobs, *Engendered Encounters*.

75. Mabel Dodge Luhan to Elizabeth Shepley Sergeant, 10 June [1925], Collier papers, reel 5.